A HISTORY OF
TEST CRICKET

LIAM HAUSER

A HISTORY OF
TEST CRICKET

LIAM HAUSER

The Story and Statistics of Every Test Playing Nation

NEW
HOLLAND

Contents

Introduction

Cricket has undergone many transformations since its inception — if that can be accurately traced — yet the Test match remains the ultimate battle in the sport. Limited-overs cricket, since being introduced in England during the 1960s and gradually becoming a worldwide hit, has had massive commercial appeal without being the same drawcard as Test cricket. Whilst limited overs cricket matches are decided in the space of several hours on one day and coloured uniforms are prominent, ensuring entertainment value, the Test match has been the most challenging cricket battle for any player or country: hence the word 'test'.

Tests were of varying lengths — sometimes scheduled for three, four or five days and occasionally for an unlimited number of days — before becoming a standard five-day fixture. In the age of prominent limited-overs cricket, Test matches have often been decided in four days or even less. This shows the contrast from the days of timeless Tests as, amazingly, a couple of timeless Tests were forced to be given up after several days and before a victor could be determined.

The book explores every Test series that has been played for nearly 140 years, and goes into detail about many of the prominent achievers. A statistical section is also included to show the results in each series, which gives a strong insight into how things unfolded and how each country fared in any specified time frame. The game has evolved in countless ways, with ten nations playing Test cricket (as of 2016) after ancient arch-rivals Australia and England were the only competing countries in the first 12 years. It took nearly 140 years for day–night Test cricket to be introduced, with a pink ball used instead of a traditional red ball. As the traditional form of cricket has always involved white uniforms, a red ball and playing in the daytime, the advent of day–night Test cricket has eliminated all but one of the ingredients that has characterised Test cricket. Time will tell if day–night Test cricket becomes a more common and accepted practice, and how the game will continue to evolve.

Liam Hauser

Chapter One: England

1.1 ENGLAND v AUSTRALIA

1870s–1880s

The English tour to Australia in 1876–77 featured the inaugural cricket 'Test', following four major tours by England to Australia. The 1876–77 squad was an all-professional one while neither the England, nor Australian teams, were fully representative (Australia fielded six players who were born overseas). One of the Australians, Charles Bannerman, who came from England, faced the first ball in Test cricket from Alfred Shaw and went on to score 165 before retiring hurt while none of his teammates passed 18 in a first-innings total of 245. Australia's Billy Midwinter (5–78 from 54 overs) claimed Test cricket's first instance of 5 wickets in an innings before Shaw claimed 5–38 from 34 overs in Australia's second-innings demise for 104. Needing 154, England mustered only 108 as Tom Kendall snared 7–55. England squared the two-Test series in Melbourne with a 4-wicket win, chasing a target of 121. England gained a first-innings lead of 139 after dismissing

Australia for 122, before the run chase featured some anxious moments after England lost its first 3 wickets for 9 runs.

One-off Tests were played in 1878–79 and 1880, with Australia winning by 10 wickets in Melbourne before England won by 5 wickets on the first occasion that a Test was played in England. William 'WG' Grace scored 152 in his Test debut as England tallied 420 at the Oval, and enforced th e follow-on after dismissing Australia for 149. Australian skipper Billy Murdoch bettered Grace's score by 1 run as the tourists added 140 runs for the last 2 wickets, and then had the hosts a little anxious at 31–5 when the target was just 57.

Australia won a four-Test series 2–0 on home soil in 1881–82, with the hosts winning the second Test by 5 wickets (chasing 169) and the following contest by 6 wickets (chasing 61) as George Palmer and Tom Garrett were prominent wicket-takers.

The one-off Test at the Oval in 1882 was one of the most famous Tests of all time. Australia was dismissed for 63 and 122 to set England a target of just 85, before fast bowler Fred 'The Demon' Spofforth cemented his place in cricket history. Having taken 6–48 and 7–62 in the 1878–79 Test (including Test cricket's first hat-trick and 10-wicket match haul), he claimed 7–46 in England's first innings in the 1882 Test, and then 7–44 before Harry Boyle claimed the last 2 wickets as the hosts crashed from 51–2 to 77 all out. The extraordinary nature of Test cricket was evident as one spectator died from heart failure in the late stages of the 1882 Test, while another spectator chewed through his umbrella handle. *The Sporting Times* published a mock obituary of English cricket, but England went on to win the next eight series after 'The Ashes' was born. Following England's series win in 1882–83, some Australian ladies burned a bail and sealed the ashes in an urn before presenting it to England captain Ivo Bligh.

After Australia won the first Test of 1882–83 by 9 wickets, Billy Bates was outstanding in the second Test as England recorded the first-innings victory in Test cricket. Bates scored 55 as England compiled 294 before he snared England's first ever Test hat-trick amidst match figures of 14–102 with his slow–medium pace. In the third and deciding Test in Sydney, Australia was dismissed for 83 when chasing 153 as Dick Barlow claimed 7–40. Australia technically drew the 1882–83 series after winning the fourth Test by 4 wickets, but the final Test was not considered a part of the series.

England won the three-Test series 1–0 at home in 1884, having won the second Test by an innings following standout performances from Ted Peate, AG Steel and George Ulyett. The series highlight was perhaps Murdoch becoming the first player to score a Test double century as he compiled 211 in the third Test, with teammates Percy McDonnell and 'Tup' Scott also passing 100. England gave all 11 of its players a bowl in this match, with wicketkeeper Alfred Lyttelton claiming 4 wickets as he delivered underarm lobs. Australia had a chance of drawing the series after notching 551, only for Walter Read to score 117 at number ten and help England from 181–8 to 346 to foil the tourists.

The 1884–85 series in Australia was intriguing as the tourists fielded the same XI in all five Tests. England won the first two Tests strongly before Australia won a thriller by 6 runs and then levelled the series with a crushing 8-wicket victory. The visitors bounced back with an innings win in the fifth and deciding Test, as the hosts needed 50 from Spofforth at number 11 to boost Australia's first innings to 163 before England tallied 386 and then routed its opponent again.

The decider in 1884–85 was the first of seven successive Test victories for England, which won by an innings in two of the three Tests in 1886. Arthur Shrewsbury scored 164 in the second Test before WG Grace made 170 in the third Test, having been reprieved several times. Barlow, Johnny Briggs and George Lohmann were England's main wicket-takers. Australian duo JJ Ferris and Charlie Turner took bags of wickets in several subsequent Tests, including both Tests in Sydney in 1886–87, but England won by 13 runs and 71 runs as George Lohmann captured 16 wickets at 8.56. The opening Test was remarkable in that England was dismissed for just 45 before Australia replied with 119 and later failed when chasing 111.

In the one-off Test in Sydney in early 1888, Turner claimed match figures of 12–87 from 88 overs as England managed only 113 and 137. But Australia fared even worse, mustering just 42 and 82 as Lohmann and Bobby Peel claimed 9 scalps apiece. Five months later, the Australians potentially turned a corner as they won the first Test by 61 runs after dismissing the hosts for 53 and 62, albeit on a muddy Lord's pitch following rain. But the rest of the series was disastrous for the tourists as their totals were just 80, 100, 81 and 70 as the hosts twice won by an innings, with each of the three Tests in the series being decided within two days. On a fiendishly difficult Old Trafford pitch for the third and deciding Test, England crawled to 172 in 113.1 overs before Peel took 11 wickets as the match was astonishingly over before lunch on day two. The first four batsmen failed to score in Australia's second innings as the tourists lost their first 6 wickets for 7 runs, and the 70-run total in a mere 69 minutes included a seventh-wicket partnership of 48.

1890s

England won the 1890 series 2–0, with a comfortable 7-wicket victory at Lord's followed by a tense 2-wicket triumph at the Oval. England's Frank Martin claimed 6–50 and 6–52 at the Oval before the hosts struggled to reach their 95-run target.

The Australians broke their drought as they won the opening two Tests of the 1891–92 series by margins of 54 runs and 72 runs as England sought targets of 213 and 229. England led by 24 runs on the first innings in the Melbourne Test, and seemed destined to level the series when leading by 163 runs on the first innings in the Sydney Test. In the dead rubber, Briggs captured 12 wickets as England won by an innings.

England won the next three series, with the 1894–95 Ashes in Australia proving to be one of the all-time great series. The tourists won the opening Test in Adelaide after following on. Syd Gregory scored 201 and George Giffen 161 as Australia notched 586 before falling from 130–2 to 166 all out when chasing 177, with overnight rain before the last day making a big difference. England's Archie MacLaren was dismissed from the first ball of the second Test, with the visitors crumbling for 75 before again recovering brilliantly. They compiled 475 in their second innings to set up a 94-run victory as Australia sought a target of 428.

The hosts slaughtered the tourists in the next two Tests as England made paltry totals of 124, 143, 65 and 72. Albert Trott had a sensational debut in the third Test as he made unbeaten scores of 38 and 72 at number ten and captured 0–9 and 8–43. The deciding Test was memorable even if the margin looked comprehensive. Australia scored 414 before England replied with 385 and later needed 297. The tourists were 28–2 before opener Albert Ward (93) and number four Jack Brown (140) put on a brilliant 210-run third-wicket stand to set up a 6-wicket victory.

The three-Test series in 1896 also went to a decider, following a 6-wicket win to England at Lord's and a 3-wicket win to Australia at Old Trafford. KS Ranjitsinhji scored 62 and 154 not out on debut for England in the second Test, with the Indian scoring a ton before lunch on day three after the hosts had to follow on. On a difficult pitch at the Oval, Hugh Trumble took 6–59 and 6–30 as England fell from 54–0 to 145 all out and later struggled to 84, before winning by 66 runs. Peel (2–30 and 6–23) and Jack Hearne (6–41 and 4–19) were the destroyers as Australia collapsed from 75–0 to 119 all out and later succumbed for 44, which included 16 from number 11 Tom McKibbin.

England won the opening Test of the 1897–98 series in Australia by 9 wickets but from then on the hosts dominated, with two wins by an innings followed by victories of 8 wickets and 6 wickets for a 4–1 series win as five Tests per series became the norm.

Australia regained the Ashes as the 1899 series featured four drawn Tests and just one outright result. The decisive match was the second Test at Lord's, where Clem Hill and Victor Trumper made 135 each for the tourists while Ernie Jones snared 10 wickets. The series was relatively well balanced, with Hearne claiming a hat-trick in the third Test before the final day was unfortunately washed out as England was 19–0, chasing 177. In the last two Tests, the hosts made the tourists follow on without being able to force a victory.

1900–1912

England won the first Test of the 1901–02 series by an innings and 124 runs after all of its wicket-takers were debutants, but hosts Australia won the remaining four Tests after repeatedly coming from behind. In the second Test, amazingly, 25 wickets fell on the opening day. After dismissing the Australians for 112, England was dismissed for 61 before a century to Australian Test debutant Reg Duff helped the hosts to a 229-run victory. In the last three Tests, England led on the first innings but couldn't capitalise as Australia won by 4 wickets (chasing 315), 7 wickets (chasing 118) and 32 runs (as England chased 211). The leading runscorer, Clem Hill, was dismissed for 99, 98 and 97 in successive innings while Monty Noble and Hugh Trumble were the highest wicket-takers. Noble took 11 scalps in the second Test before Trumble finished the match with a hat-trick, and then Jack Saunders snared 9 wickets on debut in the fourth Test. England's squad was under strength, and the tourists had a further setback when Sydney Barnes was injured in the third Test after capturing 19 wickets in the first two.

There were plenty of memorable moments in the 1902 series, starting with Australia being routed for 36 at Edgbaston following 7–17 from Wilfred Rhodes, before rain prevented England's victory hopes after Australia followed on. After another rain-affected draw, Australia recorded a 143-run win and then secured an unbeatable 2–0 series lead and a hold on the Ashes urn for the fourth straight series following a heart-stopping 3-run win in another one of the all-time classic Tests. Victor Trumper scored a century in the first session of the opening day before Australia finished with 299, and England replied with 262 following 128 from Stanley Jackson. Set 124 to win, the hosts were 68–1 and later 92–3 and 107–5 before stumbling. Hill took a spectacular catch before Fred Tate completed an unhappy sole Test appearance, as he was last out after dropping a vital catch in Australia's second innings. The fifth Test was another classic as England, chasing 263, was 48–5 before Gilbert Jessop scored a blazing century in just 75 minutes, having given two chances while in the twenties. George Hirst's unbeaten 58 at number eight lifted England to an unlikely 1-wicket win, with a ninth-wicket stand of 34 involving Dick Lilley, followed by an unbroken last-wicket stand of 15 with Rhodes.

The start of the 1903–04 series was just as thrilling, with Ted Arnold's first ball in Test cricket capturing Trumper's wicket before 133 from Noble helped Australia tally 285. On debut, Reg Foster made the then highest individual Test score of 287 as England amassed 577, including century stands for the last 2 wickets. Not even an unconquered 185 from Trumper could prevent England winning by 5 wickets. Fifteen wickets from Rhodes in the next Test ensured another England victory, and then Australia won the third Test by 216 runs. The hosts won the fifth and final Test by 218 runs, with Trumble taking a Test hat-trick for the second time, but not before the tourists regained the Ashes with a 157-run triumph in Sydney.

England won the 1905 series 2–0 at home, having won the first and fourth Tests comprehensively while having the better of the other three. Stanley Jackson had a sensational series with 492 runs at 70.29 and 13 wickets at 15.46. The first two Tests of the 1907–08 series in Australia could hardly have been tenser, as the hosts won by 2 wickets at Sydney after being 219–8 when chasing 274, before the visitors won by 1 wicket at Melbourne after being 243–9 when chasing 282. In the third Test, England led by 78 runs on the first innings before Hill (160) and Roger Hartigan (116) set up a 245-run win for Australia after the hosts lost their seventh second-innings wicket at 180. Following another big win to Australia in the fourth Test, England led by 144 runs on the first innings in the final Test but went on to lose by 49 runs after 166 from Trumper set up an Australian total of 422.

England won a low-scoring opening encounter by 10 wickets in 1909, only for Australia to win the next two matches by 9 wickets and 126 runs, before salvaging two draws to retain the Ashes. In the final Test, Australian opener Warren Bardsley became the first player to twice post triple figures in a Test.

Australia began the 1911–12 series with a 146-run win, but England controlled the remainder of the series and recorded four decisive victories. Sydney Barnes and Frank Foster tallied 66 wickets in the series while the only Australian bowler to take more than 12 wickets was Herbert Hordern with 32. Jack Hobbs scored 662 runs for England while Australia's leading batting aggregate was a modest 324 from Warwick Armstrong. In the fourth Test, which England won by an innings, Hobbs (178) and Rhodes (179) put on an opening stand of 323 in a total of 589 after Australia collapsed for 191.

The 1912 series was different as a triangular tournament involving England, Australia and South Africa was trialled. Wet weather proved disruptive in addition to several Australian players making themselves unavailable due to disagreements with the Australian Board of Control. Following two draws, the third and final Test involving the arch rivals resulted in a 244-run win to England after Frank Woolley starred with 10 wickets and a half-century. World War I meant that Australia had to wait more than eight years to try to regain the Ashes.

1920s

It remains a matter of conjecture as to whether Australia was so good or England so woeful, as the Australians won the first eight Ashes Tests following World War I. Warwick Armstrong, Charles Macartney, Herb Collins, Jack Gregory and Arthur Mailey were among Australia's heroes as margins were 377 runs, an innings and 91 runs, 119 runs, 8 wickets and 9 wickets in the 1920–21 series. The only decent contest in this series was the third Test as England replied to Australia's 354 with 447, and later made a fine attempt to reach the 490-run target.

The first three Tests of 1921 yielded margins of 10 wickets, 8 wickets and 219 runs, before two drawn results enabled England to avoid another 5–0 series defeat. Ted McDonald and Jack Gregory were Australia's best bowlers in this series, while Australia, surprisingly, had just one centurion (Macartney) while England had three (two to Charles 'Jack' Russell and one to Phil Mead).

The thrashings resumed on Australian soil in 1924–25 as the hosts won by 193 runs and 81 runs, before a mere 11-run victory and the retention of the Ashes was followed by England winning by an innings. Such is the uncertainty of Test cricket! Australia won the final Test by 307 runs to secure a 4–1 series win, before the first four Tests of the 1926 series were drawn as the fixtures lasted only three days each. Only 17.2 overs were possible in the first Test due to rain before the following three Tests featured nine centuries, including three to a nearly 40-year-old Macartney. In the second Test, the 43-year-old Bardsley made 193 not out. The 'timeless' final Test, which decided the Ashes winner, was notable before a ball was even bowled as England recalled 48-year-old Rhodes. Australia led by 22 runs on the first innings before losing by 289 runs as the target was 415, following centuries to England openers Hobbs and Herbert Sutcliffe.

Wally Hammond proved the main difference between the two teams in the 1928–29 series as he compiled 905 runs at an average of 113.12 in England's 4–1 triumph. The writing was on the wall in the first Test, which England won by 675 runs, after the tourists didn't enforce the follow-on when leading by 399 runs on the first innings, as the Test was timeless. An innings of 251 from Hammond helped England to an 8-wicket win in the second Test, and then he scored 200 in England's first innings of the third Test, although his team triumphed by a mere 3 wickets as the target was a challenging 332. Hammond scored a century in each innings of the fourth Test in which Australia was dismissed just 13 runs shy of a 349-run target, before Australia won the final Test by 5 wickets. Nineteen-year-old Archie Jackson appeared destined for big things as he scored 164 and 36 on debut for Australia in the fourth Test, but he died tragically from tuberculosis just four years later.

1930s

Don Bradman turned the 1930 series in Australia's favour as he accumulated 974 runs: more than double the next highest run maker. England won the first Test by 93 runs, before Australia won the next encounter by 7 wickets after Bradman's 254 enabled the Australians to top 700 in response to England's 425, which included 173 from Kumar Duleepsinhji. The third Test was drawn after Bradman scored a then-record 334 before another draw kept the series level with one Test remaining. Sutcliffe scored 161 as England made 405 before Australia compiled 695 as Bradman scored 232 and Bill Ponsford 110. England could not avoid an innings defeat as Australia won back the Ashes, before the 1932–33 series in Australia was perhaps the most controversial of all-time.

A lot has been documented about the series known as 'Bodyline', after Harold Larwood and Bill Voce repeatedly peppered the hosts with short-pitched deliveries aimed at the batsmen while the leg-side field was stacked. England captain Douglas Jardine earned the ire of the Australians for adopting this strategy, which was aimed primarily at restricting Bradman. Stan McCabe scored 187 not out as Australia tallied 360 in the first innings of the first Test. Sutcliffe (194), Hammond

(112) and Iftikhar Ali Khan (aka Nawab of Pataudi), who scored 102 on debut, set up England's 164-run lead before Larwood completed a 10-wicket match haul to set up England's 10-wicket victory. Having missed the first Test with influenza, Bradman suffered a shock first-ball duck in the second Test before scoring an undefeated 103 in Australia's second innings. Two 5-wicket hauls from leg spinner Bill O'Reilly helped the hosts level the series with a 111-run victory, before things turned nasty in Adelaide as England was on its way to a massive 338-run win. Woodfull was hit over the heart, and Bert Oldfield was struck in the head after a hook shot went awry. There were suggestions that the tour be called off early, but it lasted its duration, with England winning the last two Tests by 6 wickets and 8 wickets, as the winning runs came with a six each time. Larwood claimed 33 wickets in the series while Voce claimed 15 and Gubby Allen 21, as Allen did not adopt bodyline tactics. Bradman was Australia's highest runscorer with 396, followed by McCabe with 385, while Hammond and Sutcliffe tallied 440 for England.

The follow-up series in England in 1934 was vastly different as the home side missed Jardine, Larwood and Voce. The tourists won the first Test by 238 runs although the hosts nearly salvaged a draw, with O'Reilly capturing 11 wickets in the Test. O'Reilly finished the series with 28 wickets while fellow spinner Clarrie Grimmett captured 25. England levelled the series with an innings victory in the second Test as Hedley Verity snared 15 wickets, before two draws were followed by Australia capturing the Ashes with a 562-run victory. Bradman, who scored 304 in the fourth Test, made 244 in the final Test and added a then-record 451 runs with Ponsford, who notched 266.

The 1936–37 series had plenty of twists and turns as England recorded two massive victories before Australia came back to win three Tests in a landslide to retain the Ashes. England's Stan Worthington was dismissed with the first ball of the series before the tourists won the first Test by 322 runs, and followed up with an innings win following 231 not out from Hammond. After losing the third Test by 365 runs, England had a 42-run first-innings lead in the fourth Test before needing 392 to win and being dismissed for 243. Australia won the fifth

Test by an innings and 200 runs after three centurions set up a first-innings total of 604.

Two high-scoring draws were followed by a washout, before Australia won a low-scoring Headingley Test by 5 wickets in the 1938 Ashes. England salvaged a drawn series after recording what has remained the biggest ever victory in Test history. The margin was an innings and 579 runs, after Len Hutton scored a then-record 364 in a total of 903–7 declared. Hutton gave a stumping chance on 40, and England's other main scorers were Maurice Leyland (187) and Joe Hardstaff (169 not out). England needed to capture only 16 wickets after Australia lost Bradman and opening batsman Jack Fingleton to injury during England's innings.

1940s

After Australia was on the wrong end of the heftiest Test margin, the next Ashes Test produced Australia's biggest ever Ashes victory, after World War II meant that no Ashes cricket was played between 1938 and 1946–47. Australia won the first match of the 1946–47 series by an innings and 332 runs: the second biggest margin in Test cricket at the time and the fourth biggest as of February 2016. The result could have been so different had Bradman not survived a confident appeal for a catch when on 28. He went on to score 187, while Lindsay Hassett also scored a ton in a total of 645, before England was routed on a sticky wicket. Bradman and Sid Barnes scored 234 each in the next Test, which the hosts also won by an innings, before two draws were followed by a 5-wicket win to Australia. Incredibly, the third Test produced the first drawn Test in Australia since 1881–82.

Australia's 1948 touring team to England earned the 'Invincibles' tag after going through the tour undefeated, with Arthur Morris and Bradman the pick of the batsmen while Ray Lindwall and Bill Johnston were the pick of the bowlers in the Ashes. Margins of 8 wickets and 409 runs in the first two Tests were followed by a drawn third Test, before a 7-wicket margin was hardly a true reflection of the fourth Test at Headingley. England collapsed from 423–2 to a still competitive 496 all out, before a century from 19-year-old Neil Harvey and a few half-centuries enabled Australia to tally 458 before being set 404 in 344 minutes. Morris scored 182 and Bradman an unbeaten 173, with the duo putting on 301 for the second wicket. Lindwall snared 6–20 as England was dismissed for just 52 in the first innings of the final Test, with Australia going on to win by an innings and 149 runs. Morris scored a largely forgotten 196, after Bradman was bowled by leg spinner Eric Hollies for a second-ball duck in Bradman's final Test.

1950s

The opening Test of the 1950–51 Ashes series was bizarre as both teams declared on a rain-affected Brisbane pitch. After the hosts were dismissed for 228, the tourists stopped batting at 68–7 before Australia was 32–7 and then set England 193. England lost by 70 runs before going down by 28 runs in the second Test, and then Australia inflicted an innings defeat as Keith Miller had a superb all-round match, while mysterious leg spinner Jack Iverson continued his great series. Another big win to Australia, this time after Morris scored a double century, was followed by England achieving a face-saving 8-wicket victory to salvage a 4–1 series loss.

The first four Tests of the 1953 series were drawn, although there was some fascinating cricket. Rain hampered what could have been great Tests at Trent Bridge and Old Trafford, where Australia finished its second innings at 35–8 with a lead of 77 runs. Australia meanwhile would have won the second Test at Lord's were it not for a match-saving partnership involving Willie Watson and Trevor Bailey, who also foiled the tourists in the fourth Test. The final Test at The Oval resulted in an 8-wicket victory to England, which subsequently won the Ashes for the first time since the Bodyline series.

Australia won the first Test of the 1954–55 Ashes by an innings, but the rest of the series belonged to England as paceman Frank Tyson was Australia's arch-nemesis. The hosts led on the first innings in the second and third Tests, only to lose by 38 runs and 128 runs as they were set targets of 223 and 240. England chased 94 at Adelaide to maintain its hold on the Ashes urn, and was 18–3 before winning by 5 wickets and then having the better of a rain-affected drawn fifth Test.

Australia also took a 1–0 series lead in 1956, but this was offset as England won the third Test by an innings and 42 runs, with off spinner Jim Laker claiming match figures of 11–113 while left-arm spinner Tony Lock snared 7–81. The fourth Test at Old Trafford dominated any recollections of the 1956 Ashes after Laker captured phenomenal match figures of 19–90 (9–37 from 16.4 overs and 10–53 from 51.2 overs), while Lock managed just 1 wicket for 106 runs from 69 overs as Australia collapsed for 84 and 205. The tourists were unhappy with the pitch but there was little point arguing about it, after the hosts posted 459 batting first. Laker finished the series with 46 wickets at an average of 9.61 while Lock had 15 wickets at 22.47 as England won 2–1.

Australia led the 1958–59 Ashes 2–0 following wins by 8-wicket margins, before a draw was followed by the hosts wrapping up a 4–0 series triumph with victories by 10 wickets and 9 wickets. The first Test featured some dreadfully slow scoring, with Bailey taking 357 minutes to post a half-century before Australian opener Jim Burke scored 28 not out in 250 minutes as the hosts achieved the 147-run target. Colin McDonald topped 500 runs for Australia while captain and leg spinner Richie Benaud (31 wickets) and left-arm pacemen Alan Davidson (24 wickets) and Ian Meckiff (17 wickets) were prominent. Laker was restricted to 15 wickets in his four Tests while Lock managed only 5 scalps.

1960s

Davidson and Benaud also played vital roles in 1961, particularly in the fourth Test at Old Trafford, as both teams sought to break a 1–1 series deadlock. The visitors took the series lead with a 5-wicket win in the second Test as they chased just 69 and were in some difficulty at 19–4. The hosts squared the series with an 8-wicket triumph at Headingley before having the upper hand in the fourth Test as they led by 177 runs on the first innings. A century to opener Bill Lawry, an unbeaten 77 from Davidson and 32 from Graham McKenzie in a last-wicket stand of 98 left England needing 256. England was 150–1 before 6 wickets from Benaud led Australia to an unlikely 54-run victory. Centuries to Peter Burge and Norman O'Neill in the final Test ensured that England would not draw the series, before the subsequent series was drawn 1–1. England however would surely have won the 1962–63 Ashes had the team not dropped so many catches, as most of the matches were well fought Down Under. Either side could have won the first Test before England finished at 278–6 when chasing 378, and then a 7-wicket win to the tourists was followed by an 8-wicket win to the hosts. In the fourth Test, Harvey profited from missed chances as he scored 154 while O'Neill made 100 in a first-innings total of 393. England made 223–4 after being set 356, before Australia finished the final Test at 152–4 after being set 241 in four hours.

The 1964 Ashes featured four draws and just one outright result to give Australia the urn for the fourth straight series. Poor weather ruined the first two Tests before the visitors won by 7 wickets at Headingley after 160 from Burge set up Australia's first-innings lead of 121. Both sides topped 600 in the drawn fourth Test, with captain Bob Simpson (311) and opening partner Lawry (106) doing the bulk of Australia's scoring before Ken Barrington (256) and captain Ted Dexter (174) stood out for England. In the final Test, England fought back from a precarious position to lead by 184 runs with 6 wickets in hand when the final day was washed out.

Australia held the Ashes urn for six straight series after the 1965–66 and 1968 series were drawn 1–1. In the first Test of 1965–66, Lawry (166) and Test debutant Doug Walters (155) set up a strong Australian total before England saved the match after following on. England had the upper hand in the second Test before Australia was safe following a ton each to Burge and Walters. The tourists took the series lead with an innings win in Sydney after Bob Barber (185) and John Edrich (103) set up England's 488, only for the locals to win the next Test by an innings after openers Simpson (225) and Lawry (119) were again hard to dislodge. Bob Cowper's 307 ensured Australia would not lose the final Test of 1965–66, before Australia won the first Test of 1968 by 159 runs. Rain hampered the rest of the series, with England unlucky at having to settle for three consecutive draws before winning the final Test by 226 runs in the dying stages after a storm interrupted play on the last day. England duo Edrich (164) and Basil D'Oliveira (158) stood tall in the final Test, as did Lawry (135), but the standout was

Derek Underwood with 7–50 as Australia's second innings yielded just 125 runs.

1970s

England finally won back the Ashes in 1970–71 as this series was decided in the seventh Test after the third was washed out. Both sides topped 400 in the drawn first Test although the Test could have panned out very differently had Australian opener Keith Stackpole, who made 207, been adjudged run-out when clearly short of his ground on 18. With an innings of 171, Ian Redpath was one of four centurions in the drawn second Test before England romped to a 299-run victory in the fourth Test, and then neither side could force a victory in the next two Tests. The seventh Test in Sydney was controversial as a bumper struck Australian tailender Terry Jenner on the head before the bowler, John Snow, was grabbed by a spectator. A crowd disturbance led to a stoppage in play, before Australia went on to tally 264 in reply to England's 184. The hosts were ultimately dismissed for 160 when needing 223 to level the series, and Ray Illingworth became the first English skipper to win back the Ashes on Australian soil since Jardine in 1932–33.

A drawn series in 1972 enabled England to retain the Ashes, with the hosts winning the first and fourth Tests while the visitors won the second and fifth Tests. Following their 89-run triumph at Old Trafford, the hosts were outgunned at Lord's as swing bowler Bob Massie claimed 8–84 and 8–53 on debut to set up Australia's series-levelling 8-wicket victory. Ross Edwards' 170 not out helped Australia set England 451 in the third Test, with the hosts making 290–4. The crucial Test was at Headingley, where Underwood claimed 10 wickets as Australia made just 146 and 136 and sank to a 9-wicket loss. The tourists were unhappy with the pitch as fusarium disease had made an impact following rain in the lead-up. Australian skipper Ian Chappell and brother Greg scored a ton each at the Oval to give the tourists a decent first-innings lead before they achieved their 242-run target with 5 wickets in hand.

Six Tests were played Down Under in the 1974–75 series as lethal pacemen Jeff Thomson and Dennis Lillee tormented England while

Max Walker and off spinner Ashley Mallett were somewhat unobtrusive but also among the wickets. England was slaughtered in the first two Tests before the third was a cliffhanger as the tourists made 242 and 244 while the hosts made 241 and 238–8. Another two comprehensive victories to Australia were followed by Thomson missing the final Test with injury while Lillee exited early. England salvaged an innings win following 188 from captain Mike Denness and 146 from Keith Fletcher, before Lillee and Thomson inflicted more misery on England in the opening Test of the 1975 series as Australia won by an innings. The remaining three Tests were drawn, with honours relatively even at Lord's before vandals ruined the Headingley pitch after day four of the third Test as Australia was 220–3, needing another 225 runs. After trailing by 341 runs on the first innings in the fourth Test, England chalked up a 538-run total to avoid defeat.

The Centenary Test in Melbourne in March 1977 was a momentous occasion and, amazingly, the result was exactly the same as in the inaugural Test match. England crashed to 95 all out in response to Australia's disappointing 138, before England made a concerted bid for victory as the target was 463. Lillee's 11-wicket match haul, Derek Randall's 174 in England's second innings and Rick McCosker sustaining a broken jaw while batting in Australia's first innings were among the stand-out moments, as was Australian debutant David Hookes striking five successive fours off Tony Greig's bowling.

The formation of World Series Cricket adversely affected Australia on its 1977 tour to England, although the tourists still had Walters, Thomson, Rod Marsh and skipper Greg Chappell. The first Test was an honourable draw before England won the second Test by 9 wickets, and then took a 2–0 series lead with a 7-wicket victory. In the third Test, England was 82–5 in response to 243 before centuries to Geoff Boycott and Alan Knott turned the game around, after Boycott was crucially dropped in the slips on 20. After losing the wicket of captain Mike Brearley without a run on the board in the fourth Test, England racked up 436 following 191 from Boycott before two 4-wicket hauls from Mike Hendrick helped rout Australia for 103 and 248. In the final Test, Australia's Mick Malone excelled in his sole Test appearance as he claimed 5–63 and 1–14, and also scored 46 at number ten. Australia had the better of the final Test but still lost the series 3–0.

The absence of World Series players decimated Australia and, to a lesser extent, England in the 1978–79 series, with the tourists winning 5–1 Down Under despite Rodney Hogg capturing 41 wickets for the hosts. Australia plunged to 26–6 in the first innings of the first Test and struggled to 116 before England replied with 286. Kim Hughes and captain Graham Yallop scored a ton each as the hosts eked out a 169-run lead, but it was inadequate as the tourists won by 7 wickets. England took a 2–0 series lead with a 166-run thrashing in Perth after losing its first 2 wickets for 3 runs in the first innings. In the third Test, Australia plummeted from 247–4 to 258 all out but won by 103 runs after dismissing England for 143 and 179 as Hogg claimed 5–30 and 5–36. Having dismissed England for 152 and then gained a 142-run lead and subsequently dismissed Boycott first ball, Australia looked set to square the series in the fourth Test. But the hosts couldn't ram home the advantage as Randall scored a dour and chancy 150 before Australia collapsed for 111 when chasing 205 on the last day. England was also in strife in the fifth Test, falling to 27–5 and recovering to a still disappointing 169 before Australia fell to 24–4 and finished with a 5-run deficit. The match was wide open as England was 132–6 in its second innings, but the lower order boosted the total to 360 before Australia managed only 160 in the run chase. England won the final Test by 9 wickets after Yallop scored 121 in Australia's abysmal first innings of 198 on a great batting strip.

With the teams back to full strength, Australia won all three Tests of 1979–80 rather decisively at home, although the Ashes were not at stake. The hosts had only a small lead on the first innings in the first two Tests, but the tourists mustered only 215 when chasing 354 in Perth, before the locals chased 216 for the loss of just four wickets in Sydney. Australia had a 171-run first-innings lead in the Melbourne Test, and went on to win by 8 wickets when chasing 103. The series was largely remembered for Lillee using an aluminium bat in the first Test before he threw it away on-field amidst allegations that the bat was damaging the ball.

1980s

A one-off Test was held at Lord's in August–September 1980 to mark the Centenary of Test cricket in England, with an uninteresting draw unfolding following weather disruptions. After trailing by 180 runs on the first innings, the hosts needed 370 in 350 minutes and made 244–3 with Boycott undefeated on 128 as the match fizzled out.

The first Test of the 1981 Ashes was a low-scoring affair as the highest team total was 185, and Australia won by 4 wickets as its target was 132, after swing bowler Terry Alderman took 9 wickets on debut. The second Test was drawn, before the tourists enforced the follow-on in the third Test at Headingley. Odds of an England win were 500–1 as the hosts were 92 runs in arrears with only 3 wickets in hand. But a swashbuckling 149 not out from Ian Botham turned the tide as Graham Dilley, Chris Old and Bob Willis shared in crucial partnerships that took England to a 129-run lead. Australia, incredibly, crashed from 56–1 to 75–8 before a quick 35-run partnership unfolded, and then Willis polished off the tail to finish with 8–43 to seal a spectacular 18-run series-levelling win to England. No batsman posted a half-century at Edgbaston as another dramatic Test unfolded, with Australia needing 151 to win and crashing from 87–3 to 121 all out after Botham took 5 quick wickets and John Emburey 2. In the fifth Test, the hosts were 137–8 before 94 runs were added for the last 2 wickets, and the tourists succumbed for just 130. Another hard-hitting Botham century all but put the match beyond Australia's reach, although 123 not out from Allan Border and 114 from Yallop helped the visitors to a creditable 402 when 506 was the target. England maintained a shock 3–1 series lead as the last Test was drawn, leaving Australia wondering what might have been.

As hosts, Australia won back the Ashes with a 2–1 series victory in 1982–83 following a major setback in the drawn first Test in Perth. Alderman injured his shoulder during a pitch invasion by hooligans and was ruled out for the remainder of the series. Nonetheless, Australia won by 7 wickets when chasing 188 in Brisbane before taking a 2–0 series lead with an 8-wicket win when chasing 83 in Adelaide. South African-born left-handed opening batsman Kepler Wessels scored 162 and 46 on debut for Australia in Brisbane, before England had to follow on in Adelaide. The fourth Test in Melbourne was a classic as Australia replied to England's 284 with 287, before being 218–9 when chasing 292. Border and Thomson put on 70 runs for the last wicket and needed just 4 more when Thomson pushed forward and was caught by Geoff Miller after fellow slips fieldsman Chris Tavare fumbled the snicked ball over his shoulder. Australian opener John Dyson was fortunate not to be adjudged run-out during the first over in the fifth and final Test, before going on to make 79 in a 314-run total. England responded with 237 and had to settle for a draw after being set 460.

Player defections to South Africa caused Australia to be understrength for its 1985 tour to England. The tourists held their own for the first two-thirds of the six-match series, before losing the Ashes with hefty back-to-back losses. In the first Test at Headingley, Australia twice topped 300 but lost by 5 wickets as England chased 123, after opener Tim Robinson (175) made the most of a reprieve on 22 as the hosts gained a first-innings lead of 202. At Lord's, Border made 196 whereas England twice fell shy of 300, leaving the tourists needing 127. At 22–3 and 65–5 there were shades of Australia's 1981 failures, before Border helped his side to a 4-wicket victory. David Gower (166) and Australian duo Graeme Wood (172) and Greg Ritchie (146) excelled, as the Trent Bridge Test was always destined to be drawn. The fourth Test at Old Trafford was also drawn, although this time the Australians had to stave off defeat after starting their second innings with a 225-run deficit. In the fifth Test at Edgbaston, England led by 260 runs on the first innings following 215 from Gower, 148 from Robinson and 100 not out from Mike Gatting, who had made 160 at Old Trafford. Australia tumbled to 36–5 in response to England's 595–5 declared, but rain on the final day raised Australia's hopes of salvaging a draw to keep the series level. Play resumed, and Gower claimed a controversial catch to dismiss Wayne Phillips after the ball ricocheted off Allan Lamb's boot at silly point. England went on to win by an innings, before sealing the series with another innings win. Graham Gooch (196) and Gower (157) set up England's 464 before Richard Ellison wrecked the tourists for the second time in as many Tests as Australia made just 241 and 129.

At least one scribe reported in the lead-up to the 1986–87 Ashes that the English team couldn't bat, bowl or field. The tourists showed otherwise as they won 2–1. In the first Test, England made 456 following a slashing 138 from Botham before winning by 7 wickets after making Australia follow on. England opener Chris Broad scored three centuries in the next three Tests, with two high-scoring draws followed by an Ashes-securing innings victory to the tourists as the hosts crumbled for 141 and 194. In the final Test, Dean Jones scored 184 not out in Australia's first innings of 343 before off spinner Peter Taylor shone on debut with 6–78 and 2–76 as the Australians saved face with their first Test win in more than a year. England was dismissed 56 runs shy of its 320-run target, with leg spinner Peter Sleep bowling Emburey to seal the result with just 6 balls to spare.

The Bicentennial Test in season 1987–88 produced a high-scoring draw in Sydney, with England making 425 before Australia made 214 and then 328–2 when following on. David Boon made 184 not out in Australia's second innings after Broad made 139, although the England opener's innings was tarnished as he was fined for clobbering a stump out of the ground after he was bowled.

The Australians had plenty of critics in the lead-up to the 1989 Ashes, but the doubters were left with egg on their face as the tourists won 4–0 and would surely have won 6–0 had rain not disrupted the third and sixth Tests. Jones, Mark Taylor and Steve Waugh batted superbly while Border and Boon also showed good form, and Alderman captured 41 wickets after snaring 42 in the 1981 Ashes. A ton each to Waugh and Taylor, and two 5-wicket hauls to Alderman, set up Australia's 210-run victory in the opening Test. Nine wickets to Alderman and another ton to Waugh helped Australia to a 6-wicket triumph at Lord's, before the tourists led by 340 runs with 8 wickets in hand when the third Test ended. A maiden first-class century from England wicketkeeper Robert 'Jack' Russell couldn't prevent Australia securing the Ashes with a 9-wicket win at Old Trafford, and it was the first time since 1934 that Australia won back the Ashes on English soil. Taylor (219) and Geoff Marsh (138) put on 329 runs for the first wicket in the fifth Test, which Australia won by an innings. When the final Test ended, England was 143–5 and 260 runs shy of victory.

1990s

Following the 1989 massacre, Australia won the next seven Ashes series, with 1990–91 not much better than 1989 for England, as the hosts won the 1990–91 series 3–0. Boon was Australia's best batsman while injury-plagued left-arm paceman Bruce Reid was England's arch-nemesis, after Alderman claimed 8 wickets in the first Test. England led on the first innings in the first two Tests, only to subsequently capitulate each time, as Australia won by 10 wickets and 8 wickets when chasing targets of 157 and 197. The first Test was decided in three days, before the tourists went from 103–1 to 122–4 and then plunged from 147–4 to 150 all out in their second innings in the second Test. After 97 from Boon and 128 from all-rounder Greg Matthews helped Australia to 518 in the third Test, England fought back with centuries to Gower and slow-scoring opener Mike Atherton, before having Australia in some difficulty. Tailender Carl Rackemann scored 9 runs in 107 minutes to foil England, which briefly attempted to chase 255 runs in 28 overs before finishing at 113–4. Australian debutant Mark Waugh (138 and 23), Boon (49 and 121) and Gooch (87 and 117) shone in the fourth Test at Adelaide, where England was set 472 and made a commendable 335–5. Australia concluded the series with a 9-wicket victory at Perth as Craig McDermott snared 11 wickets after capturing 7 at Adelaide in his comeback to Test cricket, having been Australia's best bowler as a 20-year-old in the 1985 Ashes before being in and out of the team for four years.

Illness forced McDermott to miss most of the 1993 Ashes, but Australia still won 4–1. The series was most remembered for leg spinner Shane Warne's first delivery in a Test on English soil, as the ball landed well outside leg stump before turning sharply and clipping the top of off stump as the batsman on strike, Gatting, seemed clueless. The dismissal seemed to have a psychologically-damaging effect on the English batsmen for the rest of the series, with Warne capturing 34 wickets while off spinner Tim May and pacemen Merv Hughes and Paul Reiffel also took plenty of scalps.

After Mark Taylor scored 124 in Australia's modest 289 in the first Test of 1993, Warne's first wicket left England 80–2 before the hosts struggled to 210. Ian Healy's maiden Test ton helped Australia set England 512, and Gooch led the way with 133 before he was out 'handled the ball' as the hosts sank to a 179-run defeat. Taylor (111), Michael Slater (152) and Boon (164) set up Australia's 632–4 in the first innings at Lord's, and Australia's top four would have scored centuries had Mark Waugh not been dismissed for 99. Australia went on to win the second Test by an innings before struggling to save the third Test at Trent Bridge after England's Graham Thorpe scored a century on debut. In the fourth Test, Border (200 not out) and Steve Waugh (157) took Australia from 321–4 to 653–4 declared, following 107 from Boon, and the tourists subsequently won by an innings. After losing the fifth Test by 8 wickets, England won the final match by 161 runs after pace trio Devon Malcolm, Angus Fraser and Steve Watkin shone in their only Test of the series. It was England's first win against Australia in Tests since 1986–87.

England had a generally miserable tour in 1994–95: the first Ashes series since 1977 not to feature Border. Slater drove the first ball of the series to the boundary on his way to the highest individual score in the series: 176. Mark Waugh also scored a century in Australia's first innings, before Warne took 11 wickets as Australia won by 184 runs. The hosts followed up with a 295-run victory, with Boon scoring a ton before Warne claimed a hat-trick while McDermott was also among the wickets as he had a great season. England's Darren Gough impressed with bat and ball in the third Test as the tourists nearly did enough to keep the series alive. Australia only just averted the follow-on, before chasing 449 after England declared with Graeme Hick on 98 not out. Openers Taylor and Slater scored centuries before Australia lost 7–84, and then Warne and May survived the last 113 balls. Gatting scored 117 in the fourth Test before Australia's Greg Blewett made 102 not out on debut, and then an aggressive 88 from Phil DeFreitas swung the pendulum England's way. Australia crumbled for 156 to lose by 106 runs, before a series of dropped catches ruined England's hopes of forcing a drawn series. Slater scored a streaky 124 before the tourists failed to capitalise on Thorpe's 123, and then Blewett's second Test century was followed by England falling to 27–6 and eventually 123 all out to lose by 329 runs.

England won the first and sixth Tests in the 1997 series, only to lose three Tests in between. In a splendid first Test at Edgbaston, the visitors made 118 after being 54–8 before the hosts went from 50–3 to 478–8 declared following 207 from Nasser Hussain and 138 from Thorpe. Centuries to Taylor and Blewett led Australia's revival, but the loss of 9–150 left England needing 118, which was achieved for the loss of just 1 wicket. Glenn McGrath blasted out the hosts for 77 in the second Test, and then Matthew Elliott scored 112 for the tourists but rain had the final say. Conditions were tough in the third Test at Old Trafford where England's regular nemesis, Steve Waugh, scored twin centuries while Warne and McGrath shared 16 wickets in Australia's series-levelling 268-run victory. After dismissing England for 172 in the fourth Test, Australia was 50–4 when Steve Waugh departed before Elliott was crucially reprieved on 29, 63 and 132. He was eventually yorked for 199, and Ricky Ponting's 127 also set up the big total that paved the way for an innings victory. Australia sealed the series with a 264-run win at Trent Bridge, before surrendering for 104 when chasing just 124 at the Oval where McGrath, Michael Kasprowicz and England's Phil Tufnell each captured 7 wickets in an innings.

An injured Warne missed most of the 1998–99 Ashes, but his replacement Stuart MacGill was just as effective in Australia's 3–1 triumph. Steve Waugh was again Australia's batting mainstay while Slater, Healy, Mark Waugh and Justin Langer also played key roles with the bat. Poor weather helped England draw the first Test before 9 wickets to Damien Fleming helped Australia win the second Test by 7 wickets. The series was decided in the third Test which the hosts won by 205 runs, before the tourists snatched a surprising 12-run victory in Melbourne after Australia collapsed from 103–2 to 162 all out in its second innings. England had the chance to draw the series after Gough claimed a hat-trick in the final Test, but Australia won by 98 runs as England failed to reach 287 after Slater scored 123 in Australia's second-innings total of 184.

2000s

Warne and McGrath each topped 30 wickets in the 2001 Ashes series while Australia's batsmen shared the runs in a 4–1 win. A century each to Steve Waugh, Damien Martyn and Adam Gilchrist helped Australia to an innings win in the first Test, before Mark Waugh scored the only ton in the second Test, which Australia won by 8 wickets. The tourists wrapped up the series with a 7-wicket win at Trent Bridge where the highest total was 190, before the hosts won by 6 wickets when chasing 315 at Headingley as Mark Butcher made 173 not out. In the final Test, three centuries helped Australia pass 600 before the tourists won by an innings despite Mark Ramprakash scoring 133 in England's first innings of 432.

England again lost 4–1 in 2002–03 despite Michael Vaughan topping 600 runs while Andy Caddick was the equal-leading wicket-taker. Matthew Hayden (197) and Ponting (123) set up Australia's 492 in the first Test at Brisbane after Australia was sent in to bat, while England lost Simon Jones to injury. England collapsed for 325 after being 170–1, and then Hayden (103) made it back-to-back tons before Australia recorded a hefty 384-run win as England was dismissed for 79. After being fortunate not to be adjudged caught for 19 in the second Test at Adelaide, Vaughan went on to score 177 before his dismissal in the last over of day one proved decisive. England was still strongly placed at 295–4, before collapsing for 342 the following morning. Ponting made 154 as Australia topped 500 and went on to win by an innings, before the hosts also won the Perth Test by an innings. Justin Langer (250) and Hayden (102) set up a big Australian total in Melbourne before England was forced to follow on, with Vaughan scoring 145. The hosts won by 5 wickets, chasing 107, but failed in their quest for a series whitewash. Dropped catches were costly during Australia's 225-run loss in Sydney, rather than the absence of McGrath and Warne. England's 362 included 124 from Butcher, before Australia's 363 included tons to Steve Waugh and Gilchrist. Vaughan's 183 set up a 400-plus second-innings total for the tourists, before 7–94 from Caddick caused Australia's downfall.

Australia appeared destined to win a record-breaking nine successive Ashes series after winning the first Test of the 2005 series by 239 runs.

But the absence of an injured McGrath for the second and fourth Tests was one of many decisive aspects as the series unfolded. A victory for the tourists in the second Test at Edgbaston would surely have set Australia up for another series win. England had the better of most of the Edgbaston Test, although the hosts required a last-wicket partnership of 51 to boost the visitors' target to 282. Australia was 220–9 before a tense and unpredictable last-wicket partnership unfolded. With 4 runs needed, Brett Lee managed only a single from a full toss as he found a fielder in the deep, before Kasprowicz was caught-behind down the legside 2 balls later to give England a dramatic 2-run victory. England controlled the third Test, in which Vaughan and Andrew Strauss made a century each for the hosts, before 156 from Ponting guided the hosts towards safety. The last-wicket pairing of Lee and McGrath survived the final four overs to secure a draw, before the tourists were again outgunned in the fourth Test. After enforcing the follow-on, England chased a tantalising target of 129 and overcame a few frights to win by 3 wickets and grab the series lead. With the Australians needing to win the final Test to retain the Ashes, openers Hayden and Langer scored centuries in a somewhat disappointing total of 367, after Strauss scored 129 in England's 373. One of many turning points occurred when England was 93–3 in its second innings as Warne spilled a slips catch to reprieve Kevin Pietersen who was on 15. Pietersen added a further 143 runs to ensure a draw, with Australia barely starting its second innings before bad light ended play. England's long-awaited Ashes series win reinvigorated Test cricket following many years of Australian dominance. Andrew Flintoff was England's highest wicket-taker and third highest runscorer while Pietersen and Marcus Trescothick also topped 400 runs. Despite dropping a vital catch in the final Test, Warne was Australia's biggest hero as he claimed 40 wickets and kept the tourists in contention despite the hosts playing superior cricket.

The teams were largely intact for the 2006–07 series which began with England's Steve Harmison delivering a wild wide that went to second slip. Following 196 from Ponting, Australia went on to win the opening Test by 277 runs before England compiled 551–6 declared in the first innings of the second Test following 206 from Paul Collingwood and 158 from Pietersen. Ponting (142) and Michael Clarke (124) were the main contributors in Australia's reply of 513, with England ruing dropping Ponting on 35. The tourists also rued a dreadful second-innings display which left the hosts needing 168 runs, which were achieved for the loss of four wickets with 19 balls remaining in the allotted 36 overs. Australia subsequently romped to a 5–0 whitewash following winning margins of 206 runs, an innings and 99 runs, and 10 wickets. After the hosts had a small first-innings lead in the third Test, Clarke and Mike Hussey scored a century each before a whirlwind 102 not out from Gilchrist ensured England faced a virtually impossible 550-plus target. In the Melbourne Test, Australia was 84–5 in response to England's first innings of 159 before Hayden (153) and Andrew Symonds (156) massacred the bowling as Symonds scored his maiden Test ton. The Melbourne Test was over in three days before the Sydney Test went into the fourth day as McGrath, Warne and Langer retired from Test cricket on a high.

The first Test of the 2009 series was played at Cardiff in Wales, with England topping 400 before four Australians, including Test debutant Marcus North, posted centuries in a reply of 674–6 declared. Australia was just 1 wicket away from forcing an innings victory at Cardiff, before England won the second Test at Lord's by 115 runs. Strauss (161) and opening partner Alastair Cook (95) put on 196 runs before England finished with 425, and then the tourists had a disappointing first innings before Clarke (136) led an unsuccessful Australian bid for 522. Following a draw at Edgbaston, Australia levelled the series with an innings win inside three days at Headingley. The Australians needed only a draw at the Oval to retain the Ashes, but they folded for 160 in reply to 332 before England Test debutant Jonathan Trott made 119. A couple of run-outs were fatal as Australia went from 217–2 to 348 all out, to hand England a 197-run victory with more than a day to spare.

Strauss was out to the third ball of the 2010–11 series, and Peter Siddle took a hat-trick later in the day as England fell to 260 all out. Hussey (195) and Brad Haddin (136) helped the hosts to 481, only for the visitors to rack up 517–1 declared (Cook 235 not out, Trott 135 not out, Strauss 110) to guarantee a draw. England went on to win the Ashes on Australian soil for the first time since 1986–87, after winning by an innings in the second, fourth and fifth Tests. Australia lost 2 wickets without a run on the board in the first over of the second Test, and struggled to 245 before Pietersen scored 227 and Cook 148 for England. In the third Test, the hosts recovered from 69–5 to post 268 before Mitchell Johnson and Ryan Harris bowled them to a 267-run victory, while Hussey (116) excelled in Australia's second innings. In the Boxing Day Test, Australia collapsed for 98 on day one before England amassed 513 following 168 not out from Trott. In the final Test, Australia made 280 and 281, compared with England's 644, which included tons to Cook, Matt Prior and Ian Bell.

The first Test of the 2013 Ashes was fascinating as Australia was 117–9 in reply to 215 before number six Phillip Hughes (81 not out) and 19-year-old Test debutant Ashton Agar (a superb 98) took the total to 280. Agar looked set to become the first player to score a Test ton at number 11 before he pulled a catch to mid wicket. Bell (109) helped England set Australia 311, and the tourists fell from 84–0 to 231–9. Haddin (71) and James Pattinson (25 not out) put on 65 runs before Haddin was adjudged caught behind, and England maintained the upper hand thereafter. The hosts recovered from a horror start to post 361 in the first innings of the second Test, and then the visitors crashed for 128 and went on to lose by 347 runs, following 180 from England's Joe Root. Clarke (187) and Pietersen (113) shone in the third Test as a draw enabled England to retain the urn, before the hosts won the fourth Test by 74 runs after the visitors fell from 109–0 to 224 all out when chasing 299. After day four was rained off in the final Test, England was set 227 runs in 44 overs to achieve a 4–0 series win, and reached 206–5 after 40 overs when play was controversially called off due to bad light.

A change in scheduling due to the 2015 World Cup meant that an Ashes series was played Down Under only months after England won the 2013 series. The 2013–14 series was a contrast, as Australia took control, while England suffered a setback when Trott exited the tour after the first Test. The hosts were 132–6 in their first innings and went on to make 295, before the visitors lost 8–54 as they were dismissed for 136. Australia went on to win by 381 runs following a century each from David Warner and Clarke, while Mitchell Johnson had match figures of 9–103. Australia won the second Test by 218 runs before clean sweeping the series following winning margins of 150 runs, 8 wickets and 281 runs. Warner, Clarke, Haddin, Shane Watson, Steve Smith and Chris Rogers scored centuries for Australia, while Johnson claimed 37 wickets at just 13.97 each. Siddle, Harris and Nathan Lyon also bowled well for the victors.

An interesting aspect of the 2015 Ashes was that none of the Tests went into the fifth day, with the third and fourth Tests requiring only three days each. The Australians were on top early in the first Test at Cardiff as England was 43–3, but then the match changed sharply as Root was dropped behind the wicket when yet to score. He went on to make 134, and England tallied 430. Australia managed only 308 in reply after losing its first 5 wickets at 52, 129, 180, 207 and 258, and later succumbed for 242 when chasing 412. In the second Test, Steve Smith (215) and Rogers (173) set up a huge first-innings total for the tourists who went on to win by 408 runs after setting the hosts 509. The pendulum swung back England's way as 6–47 from James Anderson helped demolish Australia for 136 in the first innings of the third Test. Steven Finn took 6 scalps in Australia's second innings and, despite the lower order taking the tourists from 111–6 to 265 all out, the hosts won by 8 wickets after seeking 121. The first day of the fourth Test was astonishing as Australia crashed ignominiously for 60 in 18.3 overs following 8–15 from Stuart Broad. Root (130) was the mainstay in England's 391–9 declared, before Australia slid from 113–0 to 253 all out following 6–36 from Ben Stokes. Having lost the Ashes, Australia salvaged a 3–2 series defeat after winning the final Test by an innings, with Smith's 143 the cornerstone of a 481-run total, before England managed only 149 and 286.

England v Australia

1876–77 (A): 1–1

1878–79 (A): Australia 1–0

1880 (E): England 1–0

1881–82 (A): Australia 2–0 (2 drawn)

1882 (E): Australia 1–0

1882–83 (A): 2–2

1884 (E): England 1–0 (2 drawn)

1884–85 (A): England 3–2

1886 (E): England 3–0

1886–87 (A): England 2–0

1887–88 (A): England 1–0

1888 (E): England 2–1

1890 (E): England 2–0

1891–92 (A): Australia 2–1
1893 (E): England 1–0 (2 drawn)
1894–95 (A): England 3–2
1896 (E): England 2–1
1897–98 (A): Australia 4–1
1899 (E): Australia 1–0 (4 drawn)
1901–02 (A): Australia 4–1
1902 (E): Australia 2–1 (2 drawn)
1903–04 (A): England 3–2
1905 (E): England 2–0 (3 drawn)
1907–08 (A): Australia 4–1
1909 (E): Australia 2–1 (2 drawn)
1911–12 (A): England 4–1
1912 (E): England 1–0 (2 drawn)
1920–21 (A): Australia 5–0
1921 (E): Australia 3–0 (2 drawn)
1924–25 (A): Australia 4–1
1926 (E): England 1–0 (4 drawn)
1928–29 (A): England 4–1
1930 (E): Australia 2–1 (2 drawn)
1932–33 (A): England 4–1
1934 (E): Australia 2–1 (2 drawn)
1936–37 (A): Australia 3–2
1938 (E): 1–1 (2 drawn)
1946–47 (A): Australia 3–0 (2 drawn)
1948 (E): Australia 4–0 (1 drawn)
1950–51 (A): Australia 4–1
1953 (E): England 1–0 (4 drawn)
1954–55 (A): England 3–1 (1 drawn)
1956 (E): England 2–1 (2 drawn)
1958–59 (A): Australia 4–0 (1 drawn)
1961 (E): Australia 2–1 (2 drawn)
1962–63 (A): 1–1 (3 drawn)

1964 (E): Australia 1–0 (4 drawn)
1965–66 (A): 1–1 (3 drawn)
1968 (E): 1–1 (3 drawn)
1970–71 (A): England 2–0 (4 drawn)
1972 (E): 2–2 (1 drawn)
1974–75 (A): Australia 4–1 (1 drawn)
1975 (E): Australia 1–0 (3 drawn)
1976–77 (Centenary Test in A): Australia
1977 (E): England 3–0 (2 drawn)
1978–79 (A): England 5–1
1979–80 (A): Australia 3–0
1980 (Centenary Test in E): drawn
1981 (E): England 3–1 (2 drawn)
1982–83 (A): Australia 2–1 (2 drawn)
1985 (E): England 3–1 (2 drawn)
1986–87 (A): England 2–1 (2 drawn)
1987–88 (Bicentennial Test in A): drawn
1989 (E): Australia 4–0 (2 drawn)
1990–91 (A): Australia 3–0 (2 drawn)
1993 (E): Australia 4–1 (1 drawn)
1994–95 (A): Australia 3–1 (1 drawn)
1997 (E): Australia 3–2 (1 drawn)
1998–99 (A): Australia 3–1 (1 drawn)
2001 (E): Australia 4–1
2002–03 (A): Australia 4–1
2005 (E): England 2–1 (2 drawn)

2006–07 (A): Australia 5–0   **2013 (E):** England 3–0 (2 drawn)
2009 (E): England 2–1 (2 drawn)   **2013–14 (A):** Australia 5–0
2010–11 (A): England 3–1 (1   **2015 (E):** England 3–2
drawn)

1.2 ENGLAND v SOUTH AFRICA

South Africa hosted England in the first five series involving the two nations, with the touring team winning the first eight encounters: two in March 1889, one in March 1892, three in early 1896 and two in early 1899. Some players who represented England at varying stages, including JJ Ferris, Billy Murdoch, Sammy Woods and Albert Trott, had previously represented Australia. Frank Hearne meanwhile played for both England and South Africa.

1880s

England won the first contest by 8 wickets after dismissing the Springboks for 84 and 129 on a matting pitch in Port Elizabeth. In the second Test at Cape Town, opener Bobby Abel's 120 set up England's 292 while Gobo Ashley snared 7–95. Bernard Tancred carried his bat for 26 runs in South Africa's miserable first innings of 47 before the next innings produced an even worse total of 43. Johnny Briggs captured 7–17 and 8–11 as one of his victims was leg before wicket (lbw) while the rest were bowled.

1890s

In the one-off match in 1892, Ferris took 6–54 and 7–37 as South Africa was rolled for 97 and 83 while England's 369 included 134 not out from wicketkeeper Henry Wood at number eight. George Lohmann stole the limelight in 1896 as he achieved astonishing figures of 7–38 (all bowled), 8–7, 9–28, 3–43, 7–42 and 1–45. South Africa's totals were 93, 30 (from just 94 deliveries), 151, 134, 115 and 117, with England winning the first Test by 288 runs before twice winning by an innings. Lohmann finished the first Test with a hat-trick and dismissed the last batsman, Joseph Willoughby, for a pair of ducks after Willoughby had dismissed Lohmann for a pair.

South Africa squandered a golden chance to win both Tests in 1898–99. The hosts gained a 106-run first-innings lead before crumbling for 99 when chasing 132 in the first Test. Trott claimed 9 wickets in the match while one of 14 Test debutants, Pelham Warner, carried his bat with 132 runs in England's second innings of 237. South Africa's Jimmy Sinclair dominated the first half of the second Test as he claimed 6–26 and scored 106, with the visitors sliding from 61–1 to 92 all out before the hosts led by 85. A century from Johnny Tyldesley helped England set a target of 246, and South Africa sank from 18–0 to 35 all out (which included five byes) as Schofield Haigh took 6–11 and Trott 4–19. Nearly seven years passed before the countries next met, with England's dominance halted.

1900s

The hosts won a sensational first Test of 1905–06 by 1 wicket before going on to win the series 4–1. South Africa made just 91 in reply to 184, before chasing 284 in the opening encounter. Dave Nourse (93 not out), Gordon White (81) and wicketkeeper–captain Percy Sherwell (22 not out) were the heroes after the hosts were 105–6 and later 239–9 when Sherwell joined Nourse. South Africa won the next two Tests by 9 wickets and 243 runs, and won the final Test by an innings after England had won the fourth Test by 4 wickets. Highlights included 12 wickets from South Africa's Sibley 'Tip' Snooke in the third Test, 11 wickets from England's Colin Blythe in the fourth Test, and 62 not out from Bert Vogler at number 11 as South Africa went from 239–9 to 333 all out in the final Test.

South Africa was awarded official Test status before touring England for the first time in 1907. In the drawn first Test, England improved from 158–5 to 428 all out before South Africa's 140 included a fourth-wicket stand of 98. Sherwell's 115 helped the tourists to 185–3 in the follow-on before the third and final day was rained off. Blythe was the key as he took 8–59 and 7–40 in the rain-affected second Test, which decided the series. Aubrey Faulkner's 6–17 helped dismiss England for 76 before South Africa reached 110 after being 73–8. The Africans sought 129 after England went from 100–1 to 162 all out, but they flopped for 75 after Louis Tancred was run out without a run scored. England's Tom Hayward was dismissed with the opening delivery of the final Test, which finished with South Africa 159–5, chasing 256.

1910–World War II

The 1909–10 series was superbly fought as hosts South Africa won 3–2. The Africans won an incredible first Test by 19 runs on the back of Faulkner's scores of 78 and 123 and bowling figures of 5–120 and 3–40, as well as Vogler's 5–87 and 7–94. England went from 159–0 to 310 all out but still led by 102 runs on the first innings, before requiring 244 for victory and nearly snatching it as the last three partnerships were 70, 32 and 14. Both sides scored 199 in the second Test, with England collapsing from 94–0 before South Africa recovered from 23–3 to tally 347 in its second innings as White scored 118. The hosts led 2–0 following a 95-run victory before England won the third Test by 3 wickets after being 93–6, followed by partnerships of 95 and 33 when chasing 221. After being 2–3 in the fourth Test, England recovered to score 203 and dismiss South Africa for 207 before the home side clinched the series with a 4-wicket win after having some anxious moments when chasing 175. The tourists won the final Test by 9 wickets after the hosts followed on, following an opening stand of 221 involving Jack Hobbs and Wilfred Rhodes in England's 417.

Whilst South Africa lost twice and drew once against Australia in the weather-affected 1912 Triangular Tournament, hosts England thrashed South Africa by an innings and 62 runs, 174 runs and 10 wickets. The 1913–14 series in South Africa followed a similar pattern as England won the first two Tests by an innings, followed by a 91-run victory, a draw and a 10-wicket triumph for a 4–0 series win. Sydney Barnes wrecked the Africans in 1912 and 1913–14, starting with a 5-wicket haul as he and Frank Foster dismissed South Africa for 58 in the first innings of their opening encounter in the Triangular Tournament. Barnes had match figures of 11–110, 10–115 and 13–57 against the Africans in 1912 before following up with 10–105, 17–159, 8–128 and 14–144 in 1913–14. Had he played in the final Test, he could have captured 60 wickets in the five-Test series.

1920s

South Africa won the first Test of 1922–23 by 168 runs after trailing by 34 on the first innings and subsequently setting England 387 following South African skipper Herbie Taylor's 176. The second Test at Cape Town was marvellous as England won by 1 wicket. Following its 113 in the first innings, South Africa folded from 157–1 to 242 all out in its second innings to leave England needing 173. The sixth wicket fell at 86 before the next three fell at 154, 167 and 168. Test debutant George Macaulay, having scored 19 in England's first innings, hit the winning run after claiming a wicket with his first ball and achieving figures of 2–19 and 5–64. On debut for South Africa, Alf Hall captured 4–49 and 7–63. The third and fourth Tests were drawn, with rain disrupting the former, after England's Phil Mead came to the crease at 2–2 and scored 181. In the deciding Test, Jack Russell (140 and 111 not out) was chiefly responsible for England's totals of 281 and 241, which included a last-wicket stand of 92 to increase South Africa's target to 344. Taylor made 102 but England won the series 2–1 as the Africans were dismissed for 234.

England had beaten South Africa in four straight series after winning 3–0 at home in 1924, with two victories by an innings and 18 runs followed by a 9-wicket win and two rain-affected draws. After England batted first in the opening Test, Arthur Gilligan (6–7 and 5–83) and debutant Maurice Tate (4–12 and 4–103) dismissed the Springboks for 30 before Bob Catterall (120) set up a 390-run total in the follow-on. Another score of 120 from Catterall helped South Africa to 273 in the second Test, before England racked up 531–2 (Hobbs 211, Frank Woolley 134 not out, Herbert Sutcliffe 122, Patsy Hendren 50 not out). Hendren scored 132 in the third Test as England neared 400 and made South Africa follow on, with Tate claiming match figures of 9–106.

England looked set to win the 1927–28 series abroad after winning the first two Tests by 10 wickets and 87 runs. Sutcliffe, George Geary, Ernest Tyldesley and Wally Hammond were the main contributors in the first Test before Sutcliffe, Tyldesley, Bob Wyatt and Percy Holmes helped England overcome a first-innings deficit of 117 in the second Test to set South Africa 312. Following a drawn third Test, South Africa won by 4 wickets at Johannesburg after George Bissett and Alf Hall were the pick of the bowlers. England's first innings faltered in the final Test following 100 from Tyldesley, before 119 from Catterall helped South Africa take a 50-run lead. Bissett's 7–29 tore through the visitors for 118 to set up a series-levelling, 8-wicket victory for the Springboks.

South Africa's winless record on England soil continued in 1929 as the Springboks again had to adjust from their matting surfaces at home, to turf when abroad. The 1929 Tests contained only three days each, with time running out for either side to win the first two fixtures after the visitors led narrowly on the first innings. England had a 92-run lead in the third Test before South Africa set a 184-run target, following 129 from Tuppy Owen-Smith who combined with Sandy Bell for a last-wicket stand of 103. England was 110–5 before Woolley's unbeaten 95 set up a 5-wicket win. Tich Freeman, who claimed 10 wickets in the third Test, captured 12 in the fourth Test, which England won by an innings following 154 from Woolley and 113 from Wyatt. The Springboks gained a huge lead in the final Test, but they were foiled as Sutcliffe and Hammond made unconquered tons.

1930s

Buster Nupen claimed 11 wickets as South Africa won a brilliant opening Test of 1930–31 by 28 runs at Johannesburg, before four draws enabled the hosts to win the series. The first Test was played on grass before the last innings was crucially played on matting. South Africa's 126 included a last-wicket stand of 45 before England reached 149–4 and made just 44 more runs. Chasing 240, England was 30–3 before a 101-run fourth-wicket stand was followed by a collapse, despite the last

2 wickets adding 42 runs. South Africa almost won the second Test as England had to follow on after Bruce Mitchell, Jack Siedle and Herbie Taylor scored centuries in South Africa's 513–8 declared. The loss of day two ruined England's chances in the third Test, before the fourth Test was intriguing as the Springboks finished 37 runs, and England 3 wickets, shy of victory.

The 1935 series also yielded four draws, as South Africa again won 1–0, this time in England, as the matches were limited to three days. The Springboks followed on in the first Test before the third day was cancelled, before South Africa's first victory in England came in the form of a 157-run triumph at Lord's. The Springboks led by 30 runs on the first innings before 164 not out from Mitchell helped set a target of 309, which proved well beyond England as Xen Balaskas claimed a 9-wicket match haul. Draws followed at Headingley, Old Trafford and the Oval, with neither side able to claim superiority.

The 1938–39 series finished 1–0 in England's favour, with the sole clear-cut result in the third Test, which the tourists won by an innings. England's Eddie Paynter made 117 and 100 in the first Test before scoring 243 in the third Test, with the tourists making 469–4 declared before dismissing the hosts for 103 and 353, which included 109 from Mitchell. South Africa couldn't capitalise after leading by 134 runs on the first innings in the fourth Test, before the fifth Test at Durban was one of the most memorable all-time cricket matches. A timeless Test after the previous four Tests were limited to four days, the fifth Test contained nine days of play, two rest days and a washed out day before, incredibly, ending without a result. The hosts made 530 and then dismissed the tourists for 316 before setting a target of 696, and then Bill Edrich (219), Hammond (140) and Paul Gibb (120) inspired a potential miracle. But with England 654–5 when rain washed out the last session of the tenth scheduled day, the match was declared a draw as the tourists had to leave Durban to catch a boat for their journey home.

1940s

The 1947 series went 3–0 England's way as Denis Compton and Edrich made hundreds of runs each. Yet the Springboks dominated the first Test at Trent Bridge, with captain Alan Melville (189) and Dudley Nourse (149) setting up a 533-run total before England followed on. England's second innings of 551 left the tourists needing 227, and they made 166–1 with Melville on 104. Compton (208) and Edrich (189) set up England's 554–8 declared in the second Test, and Melville's 117 wasn't enough for South Africa to avert the follow-on. Compton took 4 wickets for the match while Edrich took 3 wickets and four catches, and the other high achiever was Doug Wright with two 5-wicket hauls in England's 10-wicket triumph. Edrich (191) and Compton (115) set up a 139-run lead for England in the third Test, and then 115 from Nourse couldn't prevent England winning by 7 wickets, as Edrich was unbeaten on 22 after claiming two 4-wicket hauls. Len Hutton (100 and 32 not out) was the standout as England won the fourth Test by 10 wickets, before the Springboks were set 451 to win the final Test. Following his 120 in South Africa's first innings, Mitchell made 189 not out as the Springboks reached 423–7 after an unbroken eighth-wicket stand of 109.

England won 2–0 in 1948–49 following nail-biting victories in the first and last Tests which went down to the wire. The tourists held some outstanding catches before seeking 128 runs in 28 overs amidst light but persistent rain in the opening Test at Durban. England struggled at 70–6 before a 45-run partnership was followed by 2 wickets falling for 1 run. The score was level with 2 balls left, before a dot ball was followed by a leg bye in desperate circumstances, to give England a 2-wicket win. Hutton combined with Cyril Washbrook for an opening stand of 359 in the second Test, but England couldn't force an outright win. In the final Test, a declaration from South Africa left England needing 172 runs in 95 minutes. The tourists were on course at 124–2 before slipping to 125–5, and later going from 152–5 to 153–7 before winning with 1 ball to spare.

1950s

South Africa entered the 1951 series without a Test victory in their past 28 Tests, spanning 16 years. The Springboks broke their drought with a 71-run victory in the first Test at Trent Bridge, only for England to come back and win the series 3–1. Both sides topped 400 at Trent Bridge, with Nourse scoring 208 despite a broken thumb before Reg Simpson and Compton made tons in England's reply. Without Nourse in South Africa's second innings, Alec Bedser ripped through the Springboks for 121 to leave England needing 186, and the hosts collapsed, as spinners Athol Rowan and Tufty Mann shared 9 wickets. Twelve wickets to Roy Tattersall helped England level the series with a 10-wicket victory, before Bedser took 12 wickets in the third Test, which England won by 9 wickets. Both teams scored more than 500 in the drawn fourth Test following 236 from South African opener Eric Rowan, before Jim Laker took 10 scalps as England won a low-scoring fifth Test by 4 wickets after trailing by 8 runs on the first innings.

The 1955 series see-sawed as hosts England won the first, second and fifth Tests while the tourists won the third and fourth Tests. England began with an innings victory after batting first and making 334, before recovering brilliantly in the second Test. Trailing by 171 runs on the first innings following 142 from South Africa's Roy McLean, England set a target of 183 before Brian Statham's 7–39 wrecked the Springboks. In the third Test, Compton made 158 in England's 284 before South Africa had three century-makers in a total of 521–8 declared, and later won by 3 wickets when chasing 145. In the fourth Test, England mustered a mere 20-run lead after dismissing South Africa for 171, before chasing 481 and losing by 224 runs, as Hugh Tayfield and Trevor Goddard took 5 wickets each. Another 5 scalps to Goddard helped rout England for 151 in the decider, only for the Springboks to collapse for 112 and later lose by 92 runs when chasing 244. Laker and fellow spinner Tony Lock were England's key bowlers, although the result could have been much different had England captain Peter May, who made an unconquered 89 in his team's second innings, not survived a confident lbw appeal on 4.

Another great series unfolded in 1956–57, with England again leading 2–0 before South Africa was this time able to secure a drawn series. The Springboks collapsed for 72 in their second innings in the first two Tests to succumb to 131-run and 312-run defeats, with Trevor Bailey the pick of England's bowlers in the first Test, before Johnny Wardle bagged a dozen wickets in the second Test. Tayfield took 8–69 in England's second innings at Durban, before South Africa finished at 142–6 when requiring 190. A sensational 17-run win to the hosts in the fourth Test at Johannesburg was the first time that the Springboks beat England on a South African turf pitch. England lost 5–45 in its first innings before pruning South Africa's first-innings lead to 89, following some useful lower-order partnerships, and then the Springboks plunged from 91–1 to 142 all out. England was 147–2 before slumping to 214 all out, with Tayfield claiming 9–113 (following 4–79 in England's first innings), while the other victim was caught by Tayfield off Goddard. The Springboks made just 164 and 134 in the final Test while England fared even worse with 110 and 130, as the Port Elizabeth pitch contained low bounce. The standout figure was 70 from Russell Endean in South Africa's first innings.

1960s

A young and not-so-experienced South African squad struggled on the 1960 tour of England as Brian Statham and Fred Trueman took plenty of wickets for England. The hosts won the first three Tests and drew the last two, as conditions were often damp. Controversy also dogged the tourists as rookie paceman Geoff Griffin was repeatedly no balled for throwing. England won the first Test by 100 runs after setting South Africa 310, and then the tourists were forced to follow on in the next two Tests. The Springboks slid to an innings defeat in the second Test before making 88 and 247 in the third Test, which England won by 8 wickets. The fourth Test was interestingly placed after play didn't start until day three, before South Africa was unable to capitalise in the fifth Test after leading by 264 runs on the first innings. Geoff Pullar (175) and captain Colin Cowdrey (155) put on an opening stand of 290 to guide the hosts to safety.

A little over four years passed before South Africa hosted the next series, and another one-sided series loomed when England won the first Test by an innings after nearing 500 and then dismissing the Springboks for 155 and 226. But the remaining Tests were drawn. The Springboks also had to follow on in the second Test, but they avoided defeat, thanks largely to Colin Bland's undefeated 144. South Africa could even have claimed a moral victory after leading on the first innings in the remaining three Tests. In the third and fifth Tests, the Springboks inched past 500 batting first but had their victory chances dented as England replied with more than 400. The Springboks finished on top in the fourth Test as England was 153–6 from 87 overs, well short of the 314-run target.

Just three Tests were played in a brilliant 1965 series, with South Africa winning the series 1–0 after winning the second Test by 94 runs. Had rain not shortened day two of the first Test, there surely would have been a result instead of a draw that left both sides wondering what might have been. England led by 58 runs on the first innings before struggling to save the match, finishing 46 runs shy of victory at 145–7 with only one batsman to come after John Edrich had retired hurt. Pollock brothers, Graeme and Peter, set up South Africa's victory at Trent Bridge, with Graeme scoring 125 and 59 in totals of 269 and 289, while Peter captured 5–53 and 5–34 as England tallied 240 and 224. After both sides barely passed 200 in their respective first innings in the third Test, England sought 399 runs and reached 308–4 when a storm cancelled the final 70 minutes. The conclusion was almost as disappointing as the one in the famous 1939 Test at Durban, and little did anyone know that England and South Africa would have to wait nearly 30 years before the countries met again in Test cricket. Such were the consequences of apartheid in South Africa.

Post-apartheid 1990s

South Africa was back in Test cricket for a little over two years when England hosted the nation that had become known as the Proteas. South Africa won the first Test of the 1994 series by a massive 356-run margin, after England was dismissed for just 180 and 99. The hosts were on top in the second Test as the visitors were 31–3, 105–5 and 199–6 in response to 477–9 declared, only for South Africa to reach 447 as the game headed towards a draw. In the third and final Test at the Oval, the Africans led by 28 runs before faltering to 175, as a fired up Devon Malcolm claimed 9–57. Thirty-five boundaries were registered as England raced to an 8-wicket win in just 35.3 overs to draw the series.

Five-match series returned to the schedule for the England versus South Africa encounters from 1995–96 to 2004–05, before two series of four Tests were followed by a three-Test series. The 1995–96 series resembled the 1930s and mid 1960s, as there was just one outright result. The first and third Tests were heavily disrupted by poor weather, and neither team could claim superiority in the second and fourth Tests. England wicketkeeper Robert 'Jack' Russell claimed 11 catches in the second Test at Johannesburg, but the hosts had the upper hand until they set the visitors 479. England skipper and opening batsman Mike Atherton batted throughout the 165 overs in 643 minutes to score 185 not out (chance at 99) and lead his team to 351–5, while Russell scored 29 not out in 274 minutes. In the decisive Test at Cape Town, South Africa won a home series against England for the first time since 1930–31 as the Proteas romped to a 10-wicket victory, after the tourists collapsed for just 153 and 157.

In 1998, the last day was washed out in the drawn first Test which was interestingly poised, before South Africa took a 1–0 lead with a 10-wicket win in the second Test at Lord's. Jonty Rhodes (117) rescued the Proteas from 46–4, with the visitors making 360 and dismissing the hosts for 110 and 264, which included 105 from Nasser Hussain. Gary Kirsten (210) and Jacques Kallis (132) helped South Africa pass 500 in the third Test, and then England succumbed for 183 before forcing a draw, as Alec Stewart's 164 and some strong resistance from other batsmen, including tailenders, helped the hosts level the score with 1 wicket to spare. England's narrow escape and South Africa's failure to secure a 2–0 series lead proved crucial as the hosts levelled the series in the fourth Test. Two 5-wicket hauls from Angus Fraser were vital, with both sides topping 300, before South Africa's demise for 208 was followed by England recording an 8-wicket victory without cruising to the 247-run target, as Atherton scored 98 not out. Atherton survived a confident appeal for caught behind and had a couple of other close shaves amidst some hostile fast bowling from Allan Donald, while Hussain was dropped behind the wicket. The decider at Headingley was a thriller, as South Africa needed 219 runs following totals of 230, 252 and 240. The Proteas looked gone at 27–5 before a sixth-wicket stand of 117 unfolded, only for Darren Gough to claim a 6-wicket haul to give England a series-winning 23-run victory.

South Africa won the first and fourth Tests of the 1999–00 series by an innings while the second and third Tests were drawn. Having taken plenty of wickets against England previously, Donald bagged 11 while Shaun Pollock took 8 in the first Test of 1999–00 as England, after losing its first 4 wickets for 2 runs, crumbled for 122 and 260, compared with South Africa's 403. Lance Klusener scored 174 at number seven for the Proteas in the second Test, before South Africa had to follow on in the third Test and subsequently avoided defeat, thanks mainly to Gary Kirsten's 275. In the fourth Test, England stumbled from 115–0 to 258 all out and later made just 126 in reply to South Africa's 421. England salvaged a 2–1 series loss with a bizarre 2-wicket win, but the Centurion Test was tarnished after it was revealed that South African captain Wessel 'Hansie' Cronje had partaken in one of many match fixing episodes that ultimately ended his career. With days two, three and four washed out, South Africa declared its first innings at 248–8 on the final day before England declared its first innings closed without a ball bowled. The Proteas did likewise in their second innings, before the tourists stumbled to victory after being on top at 228–4.

2000s

The 2003 series was fascinating as it went tit-for-tat after the first Test at Edgbaston was drawn. South African captain Graeme Smith (277) and Herschelle Gibbs (179) put on a 338-run opening stand at Edgbaston, before England opener Michael Vaughan (156) anchored a decent reply. Smith (259) again stood out in the second Test, with his team nearing 700 before England's second innings of 417 wasn't enough for the hosts to avoid an innings defeat. Tons to Mark Butcher and Hussain helped England to 445 in the third Test, and although the hosts later collapsed for 118, they won by 70 runs after the tourists never looked like achieving the 202-run target. James Kirtley took 2–80 and 6–34 on debut, although his dubious bowling action plagued his career. The Proteas were 21–4 in the fourth Test before Kirsten's 130 was the backbone of a 342-run total, and then England stuttered from 169–1 to 307 all out before losing by 191 runs after being set 401. The Proteas appeared certain of winning the series after Gibbs (183) and Kirsten (90) set up a total of 484 in the first innings of the fifth Test at the Oval. England, however, responded with 604–9 declared, following 219 from Marcus Trescothick, 124 from Graham Thorpe and 95 from Andrew Flintoff. Needing 110 to win, England triumphed by 9 wickets as Trescothick sped to 69 not out.

The two nations subsequently competed for the Basil D'Oliveira Trophy, with England winning 2–1 away from home in 2004–05 while the player of the series was South African-born England opener Andrew Strauss. His century in the first Test cancelled out Boeta Dippenaar's ton as England gained an 88-run lead before winning by 7 wickets when chasing 142. South Africa led by 193 runs on the first innings in the second Test, only for England to make a huge score and leave the Proteas needing 378. They struggled to save the Test as they finished at 290–8, before squaring the series with a 196-run victory at Cape Town. One of four century-makers in the second Test, Kallis scored another ton as South Africa made 441 and opted not to enforce the follow-on, instead setting a target of 501. Strauss (147) set up England's 411–8 declared in the fourth Test, before Gibbs (161) and some lower-order resistance helped the Proteas to a tiny lead. Following 180 from Trescothick, England won by 77 runs as South Africa's run chase yielded an inadequate 247, despite 98 from Gibbs and 67 not out from Graeme Smith. In the first innings of the final Test, the Proteas again mustered 247 before England gained a 112-run lead and did enough to protect its series lead after Kallis and AB de Villiers scored centuries in South Africa's second innings.

Ian Bell (199) and the South African-born Kevin Pietersen (152) helped England approach 600 in the first Test at Lord's in 2008. South Africa followed on before tons to top-three batsmen Smith,

Neil McKenzie and Hashim Amla secured a draw. South Africa won the second Test by 10 wickets as England barely avoided an innings defeat after AB de Villiers (174) and Ashwell Prince (149) were the cornerstone of South Africa's 522. England struggled in the third Test before Paul Collingwood (135) and Pietersen (94) helped set a target of 281. The Proteas were 93–4 but Smith (154 not out) set up a series-clinching 5-wicket win, before England saved face with a 6-wicket win at the Oval. Pietersen's 100 helped England to a 122-run lead before the hosts had few troubles when chasing 197.

The first and third Tests in the 2009–10 series were drawn, with England only just avoiding defeat in both of them. The tourists finished their second innings of the first Test at 228–9 after being set 364, with the ninth wicket having fallen with 19 deliveries remaining. In the third Test, England was set 466 and finished at 296–9 after the last-wicket pairing survived the final 17 deliveries. England led the series following an innings victory in the second Test, with the tourists having replied to South Africa's 343 with 574–9 declared, as Alastair Cook and Bell made centuries. Graeme Swann completed a 9-wicket match haul as the Proteas succumbed for 133, only for the hosts to draw the series with an innings win of their own. England never recovered after Strauss was out to the first ball of the match, with the tourists folding for 180 and 169 whereas South Africa topped 400.

The Proteas also won the opening encounter of the 2012 series by an innings, despite Cook scoring 115 in England's competitive first innings of 385, before the South Africans found themselves at 1–1. Amla (311 not out) and Kallis (182 not out) put on an unbroken third-wicket stand of 377 after Smith scored 131 in a total of 637–2 declared, before England managed only 240. The drawn second Test was evenly balanced, as 182 from South African opener Alviro Petersen was followed by 149 from Pietersen, and England later finished on 130–4 from 33 overs when needing 253 runs. England led narrowly on the first innings in the final Test before unsuccessfully chasing 346 runs to draw the series, having collapsed to 45–4 and done well to reach 294.

At Durban, in the first Test of the 2015–16 series, South Africa's Dean Elgar carried his bat as he scored 118 in a total of 214 after England tallied 303. The Proteas made only 174 in their second innings when needing 416, before the second Test was drawn after both sides topped 600. Ben Stokes (258 off 198 balls) and Jonny Bairstow (150 not out off 191 balls) put on a sixth-wicket stand of 399 for England before Amla (201) and Temba Bavuma (102 not out) were South Africa's highest contributors. At Johannesburg, the hosts surrendered the series as they crumbled for 83 in their second innings to leave the visitors a paltry target of 74. The Africans nonetheless won the final Test by 280 runs after debutant opener Stephen Cook was one of three century-makers in the first innings, followed by Kagiso Rabada taking 13 wickets.

England v South Africa

1888–89 (SA): England 2–0
1891–92 (SA): England 1–0
1895–96 (SA): England 3–0
1898–99 (SA): England 2–0
1905–06 (SA): South Africa 4–1
1907 (E): England 1–0 (2 drawn)
1909–10 (SA): South Africa 3–2
1912 (E): England 3–0
1913–14 (SA): England 4–0 (1 drawn)
1922–23 (SA): England 2–1 (2 drawn)
1924 (E): England 3–0 (2 drawn)
1927–28: (SA): 2–2 (1 drawn)
1929 (E): England 2–0 (3 drawn)
1930–31 (SA): South Africa 1–0 (4 drawn)
1935 (E): South Africa 1–0 (4 drawn)
1938–39 (SA): England 1–0 (4 drawn)
1947 (E): England 3–0 (2 drawn)
1948–49 (SA): England 2–0 (3 drawn)

1951 (E): England 3–1 (1 drawn)
1955 (E): England 3–2
1956–57 (SA): 2–2-all (1 drawn)
1960 (E): England 3–0 (2 drawn)
1964–65 (SA): England 1–0 (4 drawn)
1965 (E): South Africa 1–0 (2 drawn)
1994 (E): 1–1 (1 drawn)
1995–96 (SA): South Africa 1–0 (4 drawn)
1998 (E): England 2–1 (2 drawn)
1999–00 (SA): South Africa 2–1 (2 drawn)
2003 (E): 2-all (1 drawn)
2004–05 (SA): England 2–1 (2 drawn)
2008 (E): South Africa 2–1 (1 drawn)
2009–10 (SA): 1–1 (2 drawn)
2012 (E): South Africa 2–0 (1 drawn)
2015–16 (SA): England 2–1 (1 drawn)

1.3 ENGLAND v WEST INDIES

1920s

English teams had toured the Caribbean several times before the West Indies gained Test status, while West Indian teams had also visited England. The West Indians won a dozen matches on their tour in 1923, and had to wait another five years before playing Test cricket for the first time. England staged a three-match series, with the hosts winning by an innings each time. After Ernest Tyldesley scored 122 in England's 401 in the first Test, the West Indies reached 86–0 before falling for 177 and 166. The tourists managed only 206 after being 100–1 in the first innings of the second Test, and Tich Freeman claimed match figures of 10–93 as the West Indies made 115 in their second innings, after England tallied 351. In the third Test, the West Indies passed 100 for the loss of 1 wicket before succumbing for 238 and 129. Jack Hobbs scored 159 and was dismissed at 284–2 following an opening stand of 155 in England's 438.

1930s

The West Indians could hold their heads high as they held England to a 1–1 draw in a four-match series in the Caribbean in early 1930. Forty-year-old Patsy Hendren made scores of 80, 36 not out, 77, 205 not out, 56, 123, 61 and 55 for England, while there were plenty of other stellar figures. In the drawn first Test, opener Clifford Roach (122) scored the first Test century for the West Indies before England opener Andy Sandham notched 152, followed by 176 from George Headley at first drop in the hosts' second innings. The second Test was unpredictable before England recorded a 167-run victory. The visitors were 12–3 before reaching 208, and then the hosts needed an eighth-wicket stand of 71 to gain a 46-run lead. England led by just 6 runs when its third wicket fell, but Les Ames (105) and Hendren set up a big total before Bill Voce took 7–70 as the West Indies succumbed for 212. Roach (209 and 22), Headley (114 and 112) and 'Snuffy' Browne

(22 and 70 not out) set up West Indian totals of 471 and 290 in the third Test, with the hosts winning by 289 runs after not enforcing the follow-on when England was dismissed for 145. The final Test finished in unusual circumstances after it was intended to be played to a finish. Sandham (325) made what was then the highest individual Test score while Ames scored 149 in a ginormous total of 849. The hosts fell from 141–2 to 286 all out and later needed 836 runs to win. Headley's 223 helped them to 408–5 but, after seven days of play were followed by two washed out days, the teams agreed that the match be declared a draw.

The 1933 series in England was not unlike the 1928 series, although the tourists drew the second Test while losing the others by an innings. England went from 103–1 to 217–8 in the first innings at Lord's before an unbeaten 83 from Ames lifted the total to 296. Walter Robins (6–32) routed the tourists for 97 before they lost a wicket on the first ball in the follow-on and were dismissed for 172. In the second Test, the West Indies made 375 following 169 not out from Headley and 105 from Ivan Barrow, before England made 374. Skipper Douglas Jardine scored 127 despite 'Baron' Constantine and 'Manny' Martindale adopting bodyline tactics. Test debutant James Langridge subsequently took 7–56 as the West Indies were dismissed for 225, but there was no time for England to start a run chase. England opener Fred Bakewell scored 107 in the final Test, but the hosts needed an eighth-wicket stand of 95 to boost the total beyond 300. Charles Marriott claimed 11–96 in his Test debut as the visitors tumbled for just 100 and 195.

The West Indians recorded their maiden Test series win as they took out the 1934–35 series 2–1 at home, although the tourists won a remarkable first Test. On a wet pitch that was dangerous, but fit for play, according to the umpires at least, the West Indies struggled to 102 before England declared at 81–7. The hosts subsequently lost 6 wickets when their declaration left the visitors needing 73 runs, and England was 48–6 before winning by 4 wickets. Wally Hammond, who brought up the winning runs with a six off Martindale, made 43 and 29 not out, while Martindale claimed 3–39 and 5–22. In the second Test, the visitors did well to make 258 after being 23–5 in reply to the home side's 302, but they later went from 53–1 to 107 all out and lost by 217 runs. The third Test was rather tedious, with Eric Hollies taking

7–50 in the home side's first innings. Headley (270 not out) set up an innings win for the hosts in the fourth and deciding Test, with the West Indies passing 500 before England slipped to 26–4. The tourists rallied to score 271 thanks largely to 126 from Ames, before folding for 103 in the follow-on.

The West Indies still floundered abroad, as shown in the 1939 series which England won 1–0, as each Test was limited to three days. Headley scored 106 and 107 at Lord's but the West Indies tallied just 277 and 225, having been 147–1 in the first innings and 154–3 in their second innings. England passed 400, following 196 from Len Hutton and 120 from Denis Compton, while debutant Bill Copson's 9 scalps were also vital in England's 8-wicket triumph. Both teams struggled for runs in the drawn Test at Old Trafford, with the tourists finishing at 43–4 after being set 160. The West Indies gained a 146-run first-innings lead in the final Test following a century from 'Bam Bam' Weekes, only for Hutton (165 not out) and captain Hammond (138) to save England.

1940s

The only series involving England and the West Indies in the 1940s was in the Caribbean in early 1948, with an understrength visiting team salvaging two draws before losing 2–0. The first Test in Barbados yielded 12 debutants, with Jim Laker and Robert Christiani the pick of them as Laker claimed 7–103 and 2–95 for England while Christiani was ruled lbw for 99 in the West Indies' second innings. There were four debutants in the second Test, including England opener Billy Griffith and West Indian opener Andy Ganteaume. Griffith made 140 and 4 while Ganteaume made 112, with Ganteaume putting on an opening stand of 173 with George Carew (107), before England's second innings featured 133 from another opener, Jack Robertson. The West Indies used a different opening combination in the second innings, with the hosts making 72–3 when needing 141 in minimal time. In the remaining two Tests, the West Indies won by 7 wickets and 10 wickets after England could set targets of merely 78 and 74. In the third Test, Frank Worrell (131 not out) helped the West Indies near 300 before England was made to follow on. In the fourth Test,

England began strongly and was 129–0 before losing 10–98, followed by Everton Weekes scoring 141 in a West Indian total of 490.

1950s

The West Indies won a Test on England soil for the first time in 1950, and for good measure went on to win the series 3–1. The omens weren't good for the visitors as they lost the first Test by 202 runs after having the hosts 88–5 during day one. Hollies claimed 8 wickets while debutant Bob Berry claimed 9 as the visitors made 215 and 183. West Indian Test debutant Alf Valentine snared 11 wickets in the first Test and went on to play a major role throughout the series along with fellow rookie spinner Sonny Ramadhin. England's Roly Jenkins took 9 wickets in the second Test as the West Indies made 326 and 425–6 declared, with Allan Rae and Clyde Walcott scoring a century each. Ramadhin snared 11 wickets and Valentine 7 as England mustered just 151 and 274, despite opener Cyril Washbrook's 114 in the latter innings. After the hosts overcame a horror start to post a still sub-standard 223 in the third Test, Frank Worrell (261) and Everton Weekes (129) set up a 10-wicket win for the tourists. England nonetheless was 212–0 in its second innings and its top four batsmen tallied 332 runs, before the West Indies needed just 102. Worrell (138) and Rae (109) set up a 503-run total in the first innings of the final Test, and then Hutton's 202 not out couldn't prevent England from having to follow on, before England lost by an innings.

The West Indies looked set for a big series win at home in 1953–54 following two crushing victories, only for England to square the series with two victories by a 9-wicket margin. In the first Test, the West Indies led by 247 runs on the first innings before England fell 141 runs shy of a 457-run target. England was 130–0, 220–1 and 277–2 in the run chase before disintegrating. In the second Test, the hosts were 25–3 before making 383 thanks to 220 from Walcott, and later set a target of 495 following 166 from John Holt, who had made 94 and 1 on debut in the first Test. England fell from 258–3 to 313 all out, before its revival began in the third Test. Hutton (169) was the chief scorer in England's 435 before the West Indians had to follow on and subsequently set a small target of 73. Weekes (206), Worrell (167) and Walcott (124) helped the hosts to 681–8 declared in the fourth Test, which was headed for a draw after Peter May (135), Compton (133) and Tom Graveney (92) set up England's reply of 537. With a 2–1 series lead, the West Indies were dreadful in the final Test, as they slumped to 13–4 on their way to 139 (Trevor Bailey 7–34) before their second innings of 346, including 116 to Walcott, left England needing just 72. Hutton made 205 in England's first innings to take his series tally to 677 runs at an average of 96.71.

When the West Indies replied to England's 186 with 474 at Edgbaston in the first Test of 1957, surely nobody would have imagined that England would win the five-match series 3–0. But after Collie Smith's 161 helped the tourists to their 288-run lead, England skipper May (285 not out) and Colin Cowdrey (154) put on a then record-breaking 411-run stand, as the hosts compiled 583–4 declared. The West Indies only just escaped defeat as they finished at 72–7, before they slumped to an innings loss in the second Test. Bailey's 11 wickets restricted the tourists to 127 and 261, while Cowdrey (152) and Godfrey Evans (82) excelled with the bat for the hosts, who made 424 and benefited from numerous dropped catches after being 192–6. Graveney (258), Peter Richardson (126) and May (104) helped England pass 600 in the third Test, before the West Indies followed on despite 191 not out from opener Worrell. Collie Smith's 168 helped the visitors secure a draw, although the hosts were 64–1 from 17 overs when needing 121. England won the final two Tests by an innings after tallying 279 and 412, while the West Indies made abysmal totals of 142, 132, 89 and 86. The West Indies batted a man short in the final Test and were 68–1 in their first innings before having to follow on. Peter Loader claimed 9 victims for the victors in the fourth Test and finished the West Indies' first innings with a hat-trick, before Tony Lock snared 11–48 in the fifth Test after Graveney (164) and Richardson (107) batted well.

1960s

The 1959–60 series featured four draws, with the series decided in the second Test in Trinidad, where England won by 256 runs following crowd rioting in the first few days. Mike Smith scored 108 while Ken Barrington scored his second ton in as many Tests to set up England's 382. England batted again after dismissing the opposition for 112, before Rohan Kanhai's 110 stood out in a losing West Indian total of 244. The West Indies led on the first innings in the first, third and fourth Tests but only once dismissed England a second time. That occasion was in the third Test before the hosts finished shakily at 175–6 when requiring 230.

From 1963, England and the West Indies vied for the Wisden Trophy. There was little for the hosts to smile about in 1963 and 1966 as the tourists won both series 3–1 in England. The West Indies won the first Test of 1963 by 10 wickets after opener Conrad Hunte led the way with 182 before Lance Gibbs captured 11 wickets. The West Indies made 501–6 declared before England tallied 501 in two innings. The second Test at Lord's was a thrilling draw, after a dashing 133 from Basil Butcher left England needing 234 to win. Cowdrey sustained a broken wrist but returned to the crease — at the non-striker's end — in the last over after half-centuries to Brian Close and Barrington had England in sight of victory. David Allen defended the last two deliveries amid incredible tension to leave the hosts 6 runs, and the visitors 1 wicket, shy of victory. The third Test was interestingly balanced as England was 189–8 in its second innings and leading by 219 runs. A subsequent 89-run partnership involving debutant Phil Sharpe (85 not out) and Lock (56) was followed by a declaration, and then the West Indies plummeted to 91 all out. Fred Trueman's 7–44 gave him match figures of 12–119, but the visitors won the next Test by 221 runs before winning the fifth Test by 8 wickets. The West Indies controlled the fourth Test as they gained a 223-run lead and chose to set a monstrous target. England had a 29-run lead in the final Test before leaving their opponents a target of 253, which was achieved for the loss of just 2 wickets as Hunte made 108 not out.

In the opening Test of 1966, Hunte (135) and captain Garry Sobers (161) set up the touring team's total of 484 before Gibbs claimed 10 scalps in an innings victory. England looked set to square the series in the second Test as the West Indies led by 9 runs with 5 wickets in hand, only for Sobers and David Holford — in his second Test — to score unbeaten centuries. England opener Colin Milburn also made an undefeated ton in his second Test, with the hosts 87 runs shy of victory as they made 197–4 when rain caused an early finish. England was also soundly placed in the third Test, having gained a 90-run first-innings lead, before some poor fielding coupled with an unconquered 209 from Butcher helped the visitors set a stiff target. England's demise for 253 handed the West Indies a 139-run victory, before the tourists won the following Test by an innings, to lead the series 3–0. Sobers (174) and Seymour Nurse (137) set up a 500-run total before Sobers claimed 8 wickets as England mustered 240 and 205. The series winners seemingly eased off in the final Test, as they made 268 and 225 while England totalled 527 after being 166–7, with Graveney making 165 and John Murray 112, before the last two batsmen notched half-centuries.

England won 1–0 abroad in early 1968 before claiming the 1969 series 2–0 at home. The West Indians narrowly avoided defeat after being outplayed in the first Test of 1967–68, before a remarkable turnaround in the second Test almost enabled them to snatch a sensational victory. After enforcing the follow-on, England needed 159 to win and finished grimly at 68–8, with Basil D'Oliveira not out. The West Indies might have won had D'Oliveira not been reprieved twice, although Sobers was dropped on 7 before making 113 not out in his team's second innings. Following a dull draw in the third Test, Sobers copped plenty of flak for a declaration that left England needing 215 runs in 165 minutes to win the fourth Test. The West Indies declared their first innings at 526–7 following tons to Kanhai and Nurse, before 148 from Cowdrey was crucial in England's 404. The West Indies subsequently faced 30 overs before declaring at 92–2, and England had 53 overs to face. The target was achieved with 2 balls to spare and 7 wickets in hand following half-centuries to Geoff Boycott and Cowdrey. Sobers (152) and Kanhai (150) inspired a total of 414 in the final Test before 116 from Boycott and a ninth-wicket stand of 109 set up England's reply of 371. England's John Snow captured a 10-wicket match haul before the West Indies came achingly close to squaring the series as England finished on 206–9 after being set 308.

The West Indies had a weaker-looking team in 1969, and was thrashed by 10 wickets in the first Test at Old Trafford. Boycott (128) top-scored in England's 413 before the West Indies lost Roy Fredericks first ball and made totals of 147 and 275. England was on the ropes at 61–5 in response to the West Indies' 380 in the second Test, but centuries to debutant John Hampshire and captain Ray Illingworth helped the total to 344, which included a last-wicket stand of 83. An intriguing draw resulted as England, set 332, made 295–7 in 106 overs. The third Test was brilliant, as the highest team total was 272 from the West Indies in the final innings, but it wasn't enough to prevent England sealing a 2–0 series win with a 30-run victory. After leading by 62 runs on the first innings, England was 171–8 before partnerships of 32 and 37 proved invaluable. The West Indies were 177–2 in the run chase, but the dismissal of Sobers without scoring at 224–5 proved to be the beginning of the end for his team.

1970s

The West Indies won the first and third Tests of the 1973 series in England while the other match was drawn. In the opening encounter at the Oval, Clive Lloyd (132) and Alvin Kallicharran (80) led the way while Keith Boyce made 72 at number nine in a West Indian total of 415. Boyce subsequently claimed 11 scalps in a 158-run victory, with Test debutant Frank Hayes scoring 106 not out in England's second innings of 255. At Edgbaston, West Indian opener Roy Fredericks (150) top-scored in the second Test which yielded three totals beyond 300 and a fruitless run chase from England. At Lord's, the visitors batted the hosts out of the game as Kanhai and Sobers made 150s while Bernard Julien scored 121 in a total of 652–8 declared. England folded for 233 and 193, but drew the following Wisden Trophy series in the Caribbean less than a year later, as Sobers bade farewell to Test cricket.

The West Indies nonetheless won the first Test in Trinidad by 7 wickets after England was dismissed cheaply on day one. The West Indies made 392 before England matched this total, although Dennis Amiss (174) and Boycott (93) put on a 209-run opening stand in England's second innings before the team lost 9–64. Kallicharran made 158 in the home side's first innings, and there was major controversy as Tony Greig ran him out from the final delivery of day two as he was on 142. The stumps were broken when Kallicharran had begun walking off the field, as he believed the ball was 'dead', and the batsman was later reinstated. Several centuries were scored as three consecutive draws unfolded, with England doing well to save the second and third Tests after facing big first-innings deficits. Amiss (262 not out) rescued England in the second Test before Keith Fletcher (129 not out) did likewise in the third Test after Lawrence Rowe made 302 for the West Indies. Rain severely shortened the fourth Test, before England squared the series with a 26-run victory in Trinidad. Boycott's dour knocks of 99 and 112 were the cornerstone of England's 267 and 263, while Rowe (123) set up the West Indies for a big first-innings total, but it was confined to 305 after the score had been 224–2. Greig, who had scored two centuries earlier in the series, bowled England to victory with 8–86 and 5–70, having been threatened by local spectators in the first Test amidst the Kallicharran incident.

As captain, Greig attracted attention for the wrong reasons in the lead-up to the 1976 series in England when he said his team would make the West Indies grovel. The tourists went on to win the series 3–0 as the pacemen did plenty of damage, while Viv Richards scored lots of runs. Richards made 232 in the drawn first Test, before the West Indies finished the second Test at 241–6 when chasing 323. The tourists crashed to 26–4 in the third Test and would have made a lot less than 211 were it not for Gordon Greenidge's 134. With the series on the line, England crashed for just 71 before another ton to Greenidge and Richards set up a big total. England's demise for 126 left the West Indies triumphant by 425 runs, before the hosts squandered another potentially winnable position in the fourth Test. The tourists faltered but still tallied 450 following centuries from openers Greenidge and Fredericks, before England's 387 included 116 each from Greig and wicketkeeper Alan Knott, after the score had been 80–4. Needing 260 to level the series, England was 23–3 before recovering to 140–4 and then losing by 55 runs, despite 76 not out from Greig. In the final Test, Richards made 291 after he may have been a shade lucky not to be adjudged lbw when about 30. The West Indies amassed 687–8 declared before Amiss scored 203 in England's reply of 435. The tourists set the hosts 435 and the West Indies won by 231 runs, as Michael Holding claimed match figures of 14–149.

1980s

The 1980s was a miserable decade for England when it came to contesting the West Indies, who had series wins of 1–0, 2–0, 5–0, 5–0 and 4–0.

The 1980 series was decided in the first Test at Trent Bridge, as the visitors emerged with a 2-wicket victory, before weather disruptions hindered the remaining four Tests. There were no big scores at Trent Bridge, as it was interesting to note that England benefited from 77 sundries while conceding 33. Chasing 208, the West Indies stumbled from 109–2 to 180–7 and lost their eighth wicket at 205 before number nine Andy Roberts finished with 22 not out following his earlier score of 21 and his 8 wickets. The West Indies were in control of the second Test but England held its own thereafter, and it was a pity that poor weather sometimes spoilt what shaped up as interesting contests.

The West Indians dominated on home soil several months later in what amounted to a four-match series after the second Test was cancelled, following a deportation order against England's Robin Jackman. The first Test began late because of rain before there were further interruptions, with the hosts topping 400 and then dismissing the visitors for 178 and 169. The touring team headed to Barbados for the scheduled third Test, after refusing to play the second Test at Guyana without Jackman who, incidentally, made his Test debut at Barbados and captured 5 wickets. The hosts were 65–4 before captain Lloyd's century helped them to 265, and the tourists were rocked following day two, as assistant manager and coach Ken Barrington died from a heart attack. After England made just 122, Richards scored 182 not out as the West Indies set England 523. Graham Gooch's 116 wasn't enough to stop the West Indies winning by 298 runs. The West Indies gained a 197-run first-innings lead in the fourth Test and could have forced a win had day four not been washed out. The West Indies also had a healthy advantage in the final Test but were foiled by David

Gower (154 not out in 461 minutes), Peter Willey and Paul Downton, with the latter two lasting about three hours each.

The West Indies produced clean sweeps in 1984 and 1985–86, starting with an innings win at Edgbaston. Tailenders Eldine Baptiste (87 not out) and Holding (69) helped the total pass 600, following centuries from Larry Gomes and Richards, while Joel Garner was the main wicket-taker. England duo Graeme Fowler and Allan Lamb scored a century either side of teammate Ian Botham's 8-wicket haul in the second Test, before England declared with 1 wicket in hand and left the West Indies needing 342. Greenidge (214 not out) and Gomes (92 not out) produced a 9-wicket massacre following the run-out of Desmond Haynes for 17. Lamb (100) and Gomes (104 not out) also batted well in the third Test before England's collapse from 104–2 to 159 all out resulted in an 8-wicket win to the West Indies, who chased 128 runs. Greenidge (223) and wicketkeeper Jeff Dujon (101) set up a 500-run total in the fourth Test, which resulted in another innings defeat for England, despite another 100 from Lamb. England was on top for a short while in the final Test of 1984, before the West Indies won by 172 runs after England needed 375.

The hosts twice won by 10 wickets and once won by an innings, while the other margins were 7 wickets and 240 runs in the 1985–86 series. England failed to reach 200 in both innings in the first and third Tests, while posting a sub-200 total in each of the other matches. No English batsman scored a century, while the West Indies had two tons from Richie Richardson and one each from Haynes and Richards. Oddly, no West Indian bowler claimed 5 wickets in an innings, while Botham and teammates Richard Ellison and John Emburey did so once each.

The 1988 series began with a draw at Trent Bridge before the West Indies won the remaining Tests convincingly as Malcolm Marshall starred with 35 wickets. In the second Test, the West Indies were 54–5 and later lost 5–25 following a 130-run stand, followed by England falling from 112–2 to 165 all out. The West Indies racked up 397 and then won by 134 runs despite a century from Lamb as he and Graham Dilley (9 wickets and 28 runs) excelled in a losing cause. The hosts lost the third Test by an innings after crashing for 135 and 93, before their totals of 201 and 138 in the fourth Test led to a 10-wicket loss. England twice scraped past 200 in the fifth Test, and led on the first innings following 5 wickets from Neil Foster before the West Indies passed the 225-run target after losing just 2 wickets.

1990s

The 1990s began well for England via a 9-wicket win in Jamaica, only for the locals to recover and take the series 2–1. Angus Fraser and West Indian-born duo Gladstone Small and Devon Malcolm dismissed the West Indies for 164 and 240 in Jamaica, while Lamb (132) set up England's first-innings lead of 200. The abandonment of the second Test was followed by Malcolm claiming 10 scalps in an interestingly balanced third Test, in which England finished frustratingly at 120–5 from 33 overs when needing 151. The West Indies made 446 in their first innings in the fourth and fifth Tests, with Carlisle Best (164) standing out in the fourth Test before Haynes (167) and Greenidge (149) put on a 298-run first-wicket stand in the decider. England trailed by 88 runs in the fourth Test despite Lamb's 119, before Haynes (109) and Curtly Ambrose (8–45) set up the home team's 164-run win. In the decider, England made just 260 after being 101–1 in the first innings, before a second-innings capitulation led to an innings defeat.

England won the first and last Tests at home in the 1991 series, and needed the latter victory to square the series 2–2. In the opening encounter, the West Indies succumbed for just 173 and 162 to lose by 115 runs after England's first innings of 198 did not seem enough. Gooch's unbeaten 154 in England's second innings was pivotal, as were two 4-wicket hauls to the Caribbean-born Phil DeFreitas. Following a drawn second Test, the tourists grabbed the series lead after wins by 9 wickets and 7 wickets. Both times the West Indies gained a lead of around 100 and restricted England to modest proportions, as the hosts could set targets of only 115 and 152. England topped 400 in the final Test before left-arm spinner Phil Tufnell, in his only Test of the series, snared 6–25 as the West Indians were out for 176. Richardson made 121 as the tourists followed on, before the hosts lost 5 wickets when chasing the 143-run target.

There were highlights and lowlights as the West Indies won the 1993–94 series 3–1 at home. The visitors were 121–0 before crashing to 234 all out in the first innings of the series, and then the hosts went from 23–3 to 407 all out before winning by 8 wickets. England captain Mike Atherton appeared to lead a revival in the second Test as his 144 rescued his team from 2–2. But 167 to Brian Lara and 137 to Jimmy Adams set up an innings win for the hosts, with Atherton falling without scoring. A first-ball duck for Atherton in the final innings of the third Test precipitated the series lowlight, as Ambrose (6–24) and Walsh (3–16) routed England for 46, when the tourists needed 194 to win. England salvaged some pride with a 208-run win in the fourth Test after Alec Stewart made 118 and 143, while Fraser snared 8–75 in the West Indies' first innings. The drawn fifth Test was made memorable by Lara recording the then highest individual score in Test cricket, 375, in a total of 593–5 declared after the West Indies were 12–2. Amazingly, England was dismissed for 593 following 175 from Robin Smith and 135 from Atherton, ensuring a draw.

The 1995 series in England was also drawn 2–2, with a tit-for-tat pattern unfolding as the visitors won the first and third Tests while the hosts won the second and fourth Tests, followed by two draws. England mustered totals around 200 in a 9-wicket loss first up, before totals around 300 were the norm in the second Test, until the West Indies succumbed for 223 when chasing 296. The hosts crumbled to an innings defeat after being dismissed for 147 and 89 at Edgbaston, before recovering again as they dismissed the visitors for 216 and 314 (which included 145 from Lara) at Old Trafford, while scoring 437 in between to set up a 6-wicket triumph. Dominic Cork was a hero in England's victories as he claimed 8 wickets each time, and also snared a hat-trick and scored 56 not out in the fourth Test. A result never looked likely in the final two Tests, as there were plenty of runs.

The first Test of 1997–98 was sensationally abandoned on the first morning as the pitch was deemed too dangerous. England was 17–3 from 10.1 overs after many deliveries reared dangerously on the Jamaican pitch, and several struck the batsmen in the 56 minutes of play. A Test in Trinidad was added to the schedule and, as it turned out, the West Indies won by 3 wickets before England won by the same margin at the same venue. In the first of the Trinidad-based Tests, the hosts needed 282 runs and were in trouble at 124–5. Carl Hooper (94 not out) and David Williams (65) guided the West Indies towards victory, although the game flickered as the seventh wicket fell at 259. Fraser had match figures of 9–80 in the following Test, and England was 129–0 before stumbling to 213–7 when chasing 225. The West Indians fell from 295–3 to 352 all out in the first innings of the fourth Test, and enjoyed a chancy 70-run last-wicket stand in their second innings, whereas England collapsed for 170 and 137 to lose by 242 runs. England had the upper hand in the fifth Test but couldn't force a victory that would have levelled the series, before the hosts won the final Test by an innings to seal the series 3–1. The West Indies led by 373 runs before England fell from 295–3 to 321 all out.

2000s

England won the first four series of the 2000s as it claimed 13 wins to the West Indies' one. Incredibly, the West Indies won the 2000 series opener by an innings inside three days, before gaining a 133-run first-innings lead in the second Test at Lord's. An embarrassing West Indian second-innings total of 54 left England needing 188, and the hosts went from 95–1 to 160–8 before Cork (33 not out) secured a nervous 2-wicket win. Following a drawn third Test, England was 124–6 in reply to 172 before the hosts gained a 100-run lead and dismissed the visitors for an abysmal 61. The hosts seemingly threw away a strong position in the final Test as they went from 159–0 to 281 all out, before the visitors crumbled for 125. The West Indies ultimately needed 374 runs to square the series, but a total of 215 left England 3–1 victors.

England won 3–0 in the Caribbean in 2004, before achieving a 4–0 clean sweep in England later in the year. England won the first three Tests abroad by 10 wickets (chasing 20), 7 wickets (chasing 99) and 8 wickets (chasing 93) before winning at home by 210 runs, 256 runs, 7 wickets and 10 wickets. After both teams passed 300 in the first Test in the Caribbean, Steve Harmison's 7–12 routed the hosts for just 47. The only respite for the West Indies was in the drawn fourth Test in Antigua as Lara scored a record-breaking 400 not out while Ridley Jacobs made an undefeated 107 in a total of 751–5 declared.

The West Indies were never likely to threaten targets of 478 and 479 in the first two Tests of 2004 in England, while England's Robert Key (221 in the first Test) was one of several centurions throughout the series. In the third Test, England was 40–3 and ultimately dismissed for 330 in response to the West Indies' 395, before the visitors fell from 88–1 to 165 all out. England was 27–2 before Key (93 not out) and Andrew Flintoff (57 not out) set up an easy victory, and the hosts needed a single run to win the final Test after the West Indies made 152 and 318 in reply to England's 470.

The West Indies drew the first Test of 2007, although England had five centurions in the series opener before winning the next match by an innings and then claiming the series 3–0 following victories by 60 runs and 7 wickets. One of the centurions in the first Test, Kevin Pietersen, scored 226 in the second Test while captain Michael Vaughan made 103, before the West Indies folded for 146 and 141. Despite being on the back foot during the third Test, the West Indies made a commendable 394 in their second innings as Shivnarine Chanderpaul notched an unconquered century. Daren Ganga was out to the first ball of the final Test before Chanderpaul scored another undefeated ton, and the West Indies had the upper hand for a time before they could set a target of only 110.

The West Indies won 1–0 in 2008–09 after an innings victory was followed by four draws. Plenty of centuries were scored, with England's Andrew Strauss and West Indian Ramnaresh Sarwan particularly prominent. At Jamaica, England made 318 before the West Indies stuttered from 220–1 to 392 all out and fired out England for just 51. Jerome Taylor's 5–11 gave him match figures of 8–85 while Sulieman Benn had 8–108. The second Test at Sir Vivian Richards Stadium was abandoned after 1.4 overs due to potentially dangerous ground conditions. The old Antigua Recreation Ground was subsequently used for a makeshift third Test, with England narrowly failing to square the series. The West Indies finished at 370–9 after being set 503, with the last-wicket pairing of Daren Powell and Fidel Edwards surviving the final ten overs. The fourth Test was a run glut as England declared at 600–6 and 279–2 while the West Indies declared at 749–9, with Sarwan the pick of the centurions as he compiled 291. The hosts only just managed to maintain their series lead after scoring 544 in reply to the touring team's 546–6 declared in the final Test. Set 240 in 66 overs, the West Indies finished at 114–8.

As hosts in May 2009, England was much too strong for the West Indies as the tourists were forced to follow on in both Tests. England's Ravi Bopara scored 143 before Graham Onions (on debut), Graeme Swann and Stuart Broad were the main wicket-takers in England's 10-wicket win at Lord's. Alastair Cook made 160 at Chester-le-Street before match figures of 9–125 from James Anderson helped the hosts to an innings triumph.

As Strauss and West Indian Marlon Samuels scored strongly, England again won 2–0 in 2012, with victories of 5 wickets and 9 wickets followed by a draw. Stuart Broad claimed 11 scalps at Lord's where England controlled most of the first Test, although the hosts were 57–4 when chasing 191. In the second Test, the West Indies' second-innings total of 165 left England needing just 108. The final Test was limited to two days, and the visitors went from 283–9 to 426 all out as Tino Best scored 95 at number 11 while Denesh Ramdin worked his way to 107 not out.

The 2015 series was interesting as a 1–1 draw unfolded. In the opening encounter at Sir Vivian Richards Stadium, the West Indies were in danger of defeat at 189–6 in the final innings before finishing at 350–7 after being challenged to score 438. Joe Root's 182 not out helped England gain a first-innings lead of 165 in the second Test, before the tourists lost just 1 wicket when chasing down a 143-run target. The hosts won a low-scoring third and final Test as England made 257 and 123 while the West Indies made 189 and 194–5. Jermaine Blackwood made vital scores of 85 and 47 not out for the victors in the third Test.

England v West Indies

1928 (E): England 3–0

1929–30 (WI): 1–1 (2 drawn) 1933 (E): England 2–0 (1 drawn)

1934–35 (WI): West Indies 2–1 (1 drawn)

1939 (E): England 1–0 (2 drawn)

1947–48 (WI): West Indies 2–0 (2 drawn)

1950 (E): West Indies 3–1

1953–54 (WI): 2–2 (1 drawn)

1957 (E): England 3–0 (2 drawn)

1959–60 (WI): England 1–0 (4 drawn)

1963 (E): West Indies 3–1 (1 drawn)

1966 (E): West Indies 3–1 (1 drawn)

1967–68 (WI): England 1–0 (4 drawn)

1969 (E): England 2–0 (1 drawn)

1973 (E): West Indies 2–0 (1 drawn)

1973–74 (WI): 1–1 (3 drawn)

1976 (E): West Indies 3–0 (2 drawn)

1980 (E): West Indies 1–0 (4 drawn)

1980–81 (WI): West Indies 2–0 (2 drawn)

1984 (E): West Indies 5–0

1985–86 (WI): West Indies 5–0

1988 (E): West Indies 4–0 (1 drawn)

1989–90 (WI): West Indies 2–1 (1 drawn, 1 abandoned)

1991 (E): 2–2 (1 drawn)

1993–94 (WI): West Indies 3–1 (1 drawn)

1995 (E): 2-all (2 drawn)

1997–98 (WI): West Indies 3–1 (2 drawn)

2000 (E): England 3–1 (1 drawn)

2003–04 (WI): England 3–0 (1 drawn)

2004 (E): England 4–0

2007 (E): England 3–0 (1 drawn)

2008–09 (WI): West Indies 1–0 (4 drawn)

2009 (E): England 2–0

2012 (E): England 2–0 (1 drawn)

2015 (WI): 1–1 (1 drawn)

1.4 ENGLAND v NEW ZEALAND

Although New Zealand never beat England in the first 47 encounters spanning 48 years, there were plenty of tight series including some 0–0 results. But apart from a couple of series in the 1980s and one in the late 1990s, England has clearly had a superior record.

1930s

Strangely, the first England versus New Zealand series took place in New Zealand in early 1930 as another England team was in the Caribbean. The Kiwis faltered to 112 and 131 all out in their maiden Test in Christchurch, with Maurice Allom and Stan Nichols the pick of the bowlers as they were among six England debutants. The tourists won by 8 wickets as they needed only 63 runs to win the first Test, before the remaining Tests were drawn. Stewie Dempster made 136 and 80 not out in the second Test and shared an opening stand of 276 with debutant Jackie Mills (117) in New Zealand's first innings. After rain caused the first two days of the third Test to be abandoned, a fourth Test was arranged. England duo Ted Bowley and KS Duleepsinhji made a century each in the third Test, before England's Geoffrey Legge made 196 in the fourth Test.

A one-off Test was scheduled for Lord's in June 1931, but two more Tests were arranged after the Lord's Test was superbly contested. New Zealand made 224 before England faltered at 62–4 and 190–7, and then reached 454 following tons to Les Ames and Gubby Allen. Subsequent centuries to Dempster and 'Curly' Page, and 96 from Roger Blunt, helped New Zealand set England 240 before the hosts made 146–5. At the Oval, England declared at 416–4, following hundreds to Duleepsinhji, Herbert Sutcliffe and Wally Hammond, before winning by an innings as the Kiwis were twice dismissed just shy of 200. Sutcliffe scored another ton in the third Test, although most of the match was rained off.

Following the 'Bodyline' Ashes series in 1932–33, England drew two rain-affected Tests in New Zealand, as Hammond was the centre of attention. At Christchurch he scored 227 and then at Auckland he made a then world record individual Test score of 336 not out. Sutcliffe was dismissed from the first ball of the series, while fellow opener Eddie Paynter also made a duck, but Hammond survived an early chance to set up a total of 560–8 declared. In the second Test, England replied to New Zealand's 158 with 548–7 declared. Somewhat overlooked were a century from Ames in Christchurch, and 6–34 from Bill Bowes in Auckland.

Hammond also registered triple figures in the first Test of 1937 at Lord's, as did teammate Joe Hardstaff, and England narrowly failed to win, as the Kiwis finished at 175–8 after being set 356. The hosts nonetheless claimed the second Test by 130 runs. Len Hutton made 100 in England's first innings of 358 before Walter Hadlee top-scored with 93 in New Zealand's reply of 281. Jack Cowie completed a 10-wicket match haul for the Kiwis, before Tom Goddard took 6–29 in New Zealand's second innings of 134. Hardstaff scored 103 in the final Test, and New Zealand was dismissed twice but there wasn't enough time for England to force a victory.

1940s

Walter Hadlee scored 116 in a rain-affected drawn one-off Test at Christchurch in March 1947, before a four-match series in England during 1949 also failed to yield any outright results. Neither side could take 20 wickets in any of the Tests during the 1949 series. The tourists finished the first Test on 195–2 when needing 299, and then led on the first innings in the second Test before the hosts often had the better of the final two Tests. Among ten centuries in the series, there were two scores of 206 (one each to Hutton and New Zealand's Martin Donnelly). Another two players — England's Trevor Bailey and New Zealand's Fen Cresswell — claimed 6 wickets in an innings on debut.

1950s

After the England versus New Zealand Tests in the 1930s and 1940s comprised of only three days each, the expansion to four and, belatedly, five days, led to more outright results. New Zealand hosted two-match series in early 1951 and 1955, with England winning three of the four fixtures. The first Test in 1950–51 was a stalemate as the Kiwis passed 400 before their opponents bettered it by more than 100 runs. Wicket-takers Doug Wright and Roy Tattersall were largely responsible for England claiming the series with a 6-wicket victory at Wellington where the hosts made just 125 and 189 before the visitors needed 88 runs.

The 1954–55 series opener was remarkably similar to the previous encounter, with New Zealand again dismissed for 125 in the first innings. England's domination was halted with two washed out days, before New Zealand's second-innings demise for 132 left England requiring just 49 runs. Following an 8-wicket triumph, England clinched the series with an innings win in Auckland after the Kiwis slumped to the lowest total in Test history: 26. The visitors led by 46 runs on the first innings as they totalled 246, before the home side's second innings lasted 27 overs with a top score of 11 from opener Bert Sutcliffe, while four bowlers shared the wickets.

England won a five-match series 4–0 at home in 1958 before winning a two-match series 1–0 in New Zealand less than a year later. Conditions were wet during the 1958 series, and the Kiwis lost the first Test by 205 runs following disappointing totals of 94 and 137. The next three Tests were even worse for the tourists as they slumped to innings defeats following totals of 47, 74, 67, 129, 267 and 85. In England's innings victories, Tony Lock tallied 28 wickets, while fellow spinner Jim Laker missed the fourth Test after tallying 13 wickets in the previous two. In the third Test, England closed its first innings with a 200-run lead for the loss of just 2 wickets, as Arthur Milton and captain Peter May scored undefeated centuries. May also scored a ton in the fourth Test, in which England led by 98 runs on the first innings. Rain severely reduced the final Test, with the Kiwis leading by 33 runs with 7 wickets in hand in their second innings.

In the Christchurch Test in early 1959, Ted Dexter scored 141 in England's 374 before Lock claimed 11 wickets as New Zealand struggled to 142 and 133. Rain saved the hosts in Auckland as May's unbeaten 124 had the visitors leading by 130 runs in their unfinished first innings.

1960s

England's dominance continued with 3–0 clean sweeps in 1962–63 and 1965. England won the first two matches away from home by an innings before concluding the 1962–63 series with a 7-wicket triumph. New Zealand led by 13 runs on the first innings in the third Test before

Kiwi skipper John Reid made 100, but it was a lone hand. England easily reached the 173-run target, with Barry Knight hitting a six and two fours from successive balls to achieve the winning runs.

England won the first two Tests of 1965 by 9 wickets and 7 wickets before securing the whitewash with an innings victory. Forced to follow on in the first Test, the Kiwis made 413 but it left England with a simple target of 95, before New Zealand's second-innings total of 347 in the second Test left England needing 216. In the final Test, John Edrich (310 not out) and Ken Barrington (163) added 369 for the second wicket in a total of 546-4 declared, before the Kiwis totalled 193 and 166.

The 1965–66 series was drawn 0–all, with both sides having chances to win. The Kiwis gained a mere 5-run lead in the first Test before needing 197 runs for victory and losing 5–1 as they crawled to a woeful 48-8 from 48 overs. New Zealand also did well to draw the second Test, as England needed one more wicket while the Kiwis were just 85 runs in front. After gaining a hopeful 74-run lead in the final Test at Auckland, the hosts struggled to 129 in 102.4 overs and then seemed to lack confidence as they bowled defensively, with England making 159-4 in 75 overs.

England won 2–0 at home in 1969, with conditions proving unfavourable for the tourists. Both sides fell shy of 200 in their first innings in the opening clash at Lord's, before a John Edrich century helped set New Zealand a target of 362. Derek Underwood claimed 11 wickets in the match as England won by 230 runs, before the Trent Bridge Test was drawn after Edrich (155) and Phil Sharpe (111) dominated England's innings. Showers arguably made a huge difference at the Oval, as Underwood claimed 6–41 and 6–60 in Kiwi totals of 150 and 229, before England, needing 138, won by 8 wickets.

1970s

England also won 2–0 at home in 1973 while winning 1–0 away in 1970–71 and 1974–75. Underwood (6–12) ripped through the Kiwis for just 65 in the first innings of the first Test of 1970–71, before he claimed 6–85 in New Zealand's second innings of 254 to set up an 8-wicket victory for England. New Zealand's Bob Cunis claimed a 6-wicket haul in the second Test before Underwood claimed 5 wickets, but it was Alan Knott (101 and 96) who stymied a potential Kiwi victory bid.

The first Test of 1973 was brilliant as the Kiwis came within sight of a spectacular victory at Trent Bridge. England made 250 after sliding from 92–0 to 191–9, and then New Zealand succumbed for 97, before England went from 24–4 to 325–8 declared thanks to Tony Greig (139) and Dennis Amiss (138 not out). Chasing 479, the Kiwis were 16–2 before captain Bevan Congdon (176) and Vic Pollard (116) made the impossible become possible. New Zealand reached 402–5 but ultimately suffered a 38-run loss before failing to grasp another winnable position in the second Test at Lord's. Congdon (175), Pollard (105 not out) and Mark Burgess (105) helped the visitors to a 298-run lead before England's top-four, including Keith Fletcher (178), batted for long periods to ensure a draw. The hosts won the final Test by an innings and 1 run after Geoff Boycott made 115 in a 419-run total, which gained England a first-innings lead of 143.

Fletcher (216) and captain Mike Denness (181) helped England to 593–6 declared at Auckland in the first encounter in 1974–75. John Parker made 121 but New Zealand followed on and lost by an innings, with the match ending in worrying circumstances, as Test debutant Ewen Chatfield was hit on the temple by a Peter Lever bumper. The number 11 batsman's heart stopped beating but his life was saved as England physiotherapist Bernard Thomas raced to his aid. New Zealand's John Morrison was out to the first ball of the rain-disrupted second Test at Christchurch, where the Kiwis managed 342, before Amiss made 164 not out in England's unfinished innings of 272–2.

The first Test of 1977–78 was perhaps the most significant in New Zealand's cricket history, as the Kiwis won a remarkable Test by 72 runs at Wellington, where the Basin Reserve was engulfed by a gale-force wind. Kiwi debutant John Wright was fortunate not to be adjudged caught behind from the opening delivery, before he crawled to 55 in a painstaking total of 228, as Chris Old claimed 6 scalps. Richard Hadlee snared 4–74 in England's first innings before the tourists needed 137 to win following 5–32 from Bob Willis. Hadlee captured 6–26 while Richard Collinge had 3–35 as England was shot out for 64. It was a momentous occasion in New Zealand cricket, but a series win against England had to wait as the tourists won the second Test easily before the third Test was drawn. Ian Botham (103 and 30 not out) and Phil Edmonds (50) were damaging with bat and ball in the second Test, with Botham capturing 5–73 and 3–38, while Edmonds snared 4–38 (from 34 overs) and 2–22. Botham also held three catches while Edmonds held five. Willis claimed 4–14 as New Zealand, after trailing by 183 runs on the first innings, was out for 105 when needing 280. Geoff Howarth (122) anchored New Zealand's first innings of 315 in the third Test, before England ground out a 114-run lead following a very slow 158 from Clive Radley in his second Test. Another dour century (102) from Howarth guided the Kiwis to 382–8 to ensure a drawn series, before the follow-up series in England later in the year reverted to one-sidedness in England's favour. The margin was 7 wickets in the first and third Tests, which were spliced with an innings win to England.

New Zealand was 130–1 in the first Test before collapsing for 234, and then England lost its first 2 wickets for 7 runs before 111 from David Gower set up a 279-run total. Graham Gooch (91 not out) guided the hosts to their target of 138, before Boycott's 131 in the next Test set up a total of 429. Botham snared 9 wickets and Edmonds 6 as the Kiwis managed just 120 and 190, before Botham claimed 11 scalps in the final Test. Following 123 from Howarth, New Zealand gained a 50-run lead before Botham and Willis routed the Kiwis for just 67 to ensure another England triumph. Another five years passed before the teams next met in Test cricket.

1980s

England won the 1983 series 3–1 at home, although the second Test was memorable as New Zealand won a Test in England for the first time after 28 unsuccessful attempts since 1931. In the opening encounter, Hadlee's 6–53 restricted the hosts to 209 before Willis and Botham contained the visitors to 196, which included 84 from Hadlee. Tons to England openers Graeme Fowler and Chris Tavare and number four Allan Lamb ensured a big target, and England won by 189 runs as New Zealand mustered 270. England again made a modest start to the second Test, this time as Lance Cairns took 7–74, before the Kiwis stuttered and then recovered to post a 152-run lead. Chatfield snared 5 wickets while Gower (112 not out) shone like a beacon in England's second innings of 252. The visitors won by 5 wickets despite a 5-wicket haul from Willis, before spinner Nick Cook played a leading role in his first two Tests, as England won the third and fourth Tests by 127 runs and 165 runs. Cook claimed match figures of 8–125 and 9–150, and New Zealand was never likely to reach targets of 347 and 511. The outcome could have been far different in the third Test had Gower not been reprieved on his way to 108 in England's first innings of 326, and if New Zealand didn't lose its last 8 wickets for 44 runs in its first innings. Botham and Lamb scored a ton each in the final Test as England was in control after losing an early wicket, and opted not to enforce the follow-on.

At home several months later, the Kiwis recorded their first series win against England, 1–0, before repeating the dose in England more than two years later. In the first Test of 1983–84 in Wellington, the tourists had a 244-run first-innings lead following 164 from Derek Randall and 138 from Botham. Jeremy Coney (174 not out) and Martin Crowe (100) scored their maiden Test tons as they and Cairns (64 at number ten) guided the Kiwis to a 537-run total, which ensured safety. In the second Test at Christchurch, Hadlee (99) was the only Kiwi to pass 47 in a total of 307, before the pitch became cracked and spongy after rain caused a late start on day two. The visitors were embarrassed, as England had to follow on against New Zealand for the first time, with the tourists making just 82 and 93 and Hadlee claiming 3–16 and 5–28, while Cairns, Chatfield and Steve Boock also took wickets. England's hopes of squaring the series were dashed as New Zealand's first innings of 496–9 declared in the final Test was long and drawn out due to weather disruptions. Wright, Jeff Crowe and Ian Smith scored a century each before England overcame the first-ball dismissal of Fowler to tally 439, following 104 from Randall.

The first and third Tests of 1986 were drawn, with rain cancelling the final two days of the third Test after the Kiwis had just begun their second innings with a 101-run deficit. In the decisive Test at Trent Bridge, Hadlee (6–80) restricted England to 256 before New Zealand recovered from 144–5 to tally 413, following 110 from John Bracewell and some other solid contributions. Hadlee (4–60) and Bracewell (3–29) contained England a second time before the Kiwis lost just 2 wickets on their way to passing the 74-run target.

The 1987–88 series yielded three draws as neither side could claim superiority. In the first Test at Christchurch, the hosts trailed by 151 runs on the first innings before finishing their second innings 174 runs shy of victory at 130–4. England trio Graham Dilley, Phil DeFreitas and Paul Jarvis had fine bowling figures, as did New Zealand trio Chatfield, Danny Morrison and Martin Snedden. At Auckland, New Zealand's Mark Greatbatch scored a century in his first Test as the hosts finished their second innings leading by 328 runs with 3 wickets in hand. The Kiwis passed 500 in the third Test following hundreds to Martin Crowe and Ken Rutherford, and England was 183–2 before days four and five were washed out.

1990s

The first two Tests of the 1990 series were rain-affected draws, with England opener Mike Atherton scoring 151 at Trent Bridge before New Zealand openers Trevor Franklin (101) and Wright (98) were the top scorers at Lord's. In the final Test at Edgbaston, Gooch (154) and Atherton (82) set up England's first innings of 435 before New Zealand faltered for 249, following 6–58 from Eddie Hemmings. Atherton scored 70 as the hosts collapsed for 158 in their second innings, before Devon Malcolm completed match figures of 8–105 as New Zealand was dismissed 115 runs shy of its target.

England also won the 1994 series 1–0 at home, and won 2–0 abroad in 1991–92 and 1996–97. The opening Test of 1991–92 had a tense finish even though England won by an innings and four runs. Alec Stewart (148) top-scored as the visitors amassed 580–9 declared, before Phil Tufnell was the standout bowler with 4–100 and 7–47. The hosts had to follow on despite 99 from Dipak Patel and 61 from Chris Cairns, before Wright became the second New Zealand player dismissed for 99 in the match. The Kiwis collapsed when they looked like securing a draw, and Martin Crowe was last out when he holed out to extra cover with 11 minutes left as he sought a boundary that would have secured a draw. In the second Test, England lost its first 3 wickets with 9 runs on the board before reaching 203 as Chris Cairns snared 6–52. Chris Lewis (5–31) was the pick of England's bowlers as the Kiwis slumped from 91–2 to 142 all out, before Gooch (114) set up a handsome lead. Chasing 383, New Zealand lost its openers without scoring and sank to a 168-run defeat, before doing much better in the Wellington Test. Stewart (107) was the only batsman to pass 43 in England's 305, before the hosts gained a 127-run lead following 143 from Andrew Jones and 116 from Wright. Lamb (142) guided the tourists to safety after having a lucky escape early on the fifth day, before the match ended after England's David Lawrence snapped his kneecap when bowling.

England also began the 1994 series with an innings victory, this time as New Zealand was 90 runs shy of making England bat again. DeFreitas snared 9 wickets and scored 51 not out for the victors, while Gooch (210) and Atherton (101) were the best batsmen. New Zealand's Dion Nash performed brilliantly in the second Test as he scored 56 and snared 11 wickets, but the opposition hung on for a draw. Martin Crowe scored a superb 142 in New Zealand's 476 before England narrowly avoided the follow-on and later finished 153 runs shy of victory at 254–8, with the ninth-wicket pair surviving the last 25 minutes. Atherton scored 111 in the final Test before DeFreitas and Darren Gough were destructive with bat and ball, as England gained a first-innings lead of 231. The Kiwis avoided defeat after following on, as Crowe scored his second century of the series.

The Kiwis began the 1996–97 series promisingly with a 390-run total after Stephen Fleming scored 129, only for England to respond with 521 following 173 from Stewart and 119 from Graham Thorpe. New Zealand salvaged a draw thanks to an unbeaten last-wicket stand of 106 in a total of 248–9, with Nathan Astle making 102 not out, while batting bunny Danny Morrison scored 14 not out from 133 balls in 166 minutes. The Kiwis collapsed sharply in the second Test as they fell to 23–5 and hardly recovered in a dismal first-innings total of 124, before England tallied 383 following another ton from Thorpe. In its second innings, New Zealand lost its first wicket at 89 and its next 3 on 125 before compounding for 191, as Gough achieved match figures of 9–92.

New Zealand was well-placed to square the series after leading by 118 runs on the first innings at Christchurch, before England chased 305. Atherton led the way with 118, before England slipped from 226–3 to 231–6 but ultimately triumphed as John Crawley and Dominic Cork put on an unbroken seventh-wicket partnership.

The Kiwis also squandered a winnable position in the opening Test of the 1999 series. In reply to New Zealand's 226, England was 45–7 before reaching 126 all out following 33 from Andy Caddick at number eight and 32 not out from Alex Tudor at number nine. The Kiwis flopped to 52–8 before number ten Simon Doull (46) helped the total to 107. Starting day three needing 205 runs with 9 wickets in hand, England won by 7 wickets as Tudor, astonishingly, scored 99 not out as nightwatchman. New Zealand however was good enough to come back and win the series following victories in the second and fourth Tests, while drawing the third Test. Matthew Horne (100 and 26) and Chris Cairns (6–77 and 2–67) were the main contributors in the second Test, which the Kiwis won by 9 wickets after chasing a mere target of 58. Rain hampered New Zealand's victory bid in the third Test after 107 not out from Craig McMillan and 101 from Astle helped the Kiwis to a first-innings lead of 297. Runs were at a premium in the deciding Test at the Oval, where captain Stephen Fleming (66 not out) and number ten Daniel Vettori (51) helped New Zealand from 157–8 to 236 all out in the first innings. England collapsed for 153 following 5–31 from Cairns, who subsequently made a match-turning 80 as New Zealand improved from 39–6 to 162 all out. The hosts, nonetheless, were on course for victory at 123–2, halfway to the target, before losing 8–39 to slide to an 83-run defeat.

2000s

The 2001–02 series was drawn 1–1, with England winning at Christchurch before a draw at Wellington was followed by a Kiwi victory at Auckland. The first Test was fascinating as it came to life in the late stages after appearing lacklustre for a while. England lost 2 wickets for no runs in the first over before reaching 228 following 106 from captain Nasser Hussain. Matthew Hoggard (7–63) and

Andy Caddick (3–50) bowled out New Zealand for just 147, and then England was 106–5 before declaring at 468–6, as Thorpe was unbeaten on 200 after Andrew Flintoff made 137. Needing 550, the hosts lost by 98 runs as Caddick captured 6–122, but not before Astle gave the visitors an almighty scare. He bludgeoned 28 fours and 11 sixes in a knock of 222 from 168 balls, and was last out following a tenth-wicket partnership of 118 runs from just 65 balls. Caddick also took a 6-wicket haul at Wellington as England had the better of the contest, before New Zealand was reduced to 19–4 in the first innings of the final Test when Astle departed. The hosts struggled to 202, but then Daryl Tuffey (6–54) and debutant Andre Adams (3–44) dismissed the tourists for 160, before England was set 312 and fell for 233.

New Zealand scored adequately in the first innings of each Test in the 2004 series, but it wasn't enough to stop hosts, England, winning all three encounters. Left-handed opening batsmen excelled in the first Test at Lord's, with Mark Richardson scoring 93 and 101 for the Kiwis, while England debutant Andrew Strauss scored 112 and 83, not to mention captain Marcus Trescothick's 86 and 2 for England. The hosts were 190–0 and 239–1 before stuttering to 441 all out in reply to New Zealand's 386, and then the Kiwis were 180–1 before faltering to 336 all out. England won by 7 wickets after being 35–2, with Hussain (103 not out) and Thorpe (51 not out) putting on an unfinished stand of 139. In the next Test, England's first innings of 526 gave the hosts a 117-run lead as Trescothick (132), Geraint Jones (100), Flintoff (94) and Strauss (62) were prominent. England won by 9 wickets after needing just 45 runs, before winning the final Test by 4 wickets when chasing 284. New Zealand's first-innings total of 384 was disappointing, after openers Richardson (73) and Fleming (117) and first drop Scott Styris (108) laid the platform for a 450-plus total. England lost 2 early wickets before tallying 319, and then New Zealand managed only 218, after losing its first wicket at 94. The hosts were shakily placed at 46–3, 162–5 and 214–6 in the run chase before Thorpe (104 not out) guided them to victory.

England won 2–1 in New Zealand during March 2008 before winning 2–0 on home soil in May–June. The Kiwis won the opening Test at Hamilton after scoring 470 and 177 compared with England's 348 and

110. The visitors levelled the series as they scored 342 and 293 while the hosts scored 198 and 311 in the second Test. In the decider at Napier, England's first three batsmen tallied just 4 runs before Kevin Pietersen (129) set up a still mediocre first-innings total of 253. New Zealand was 103–1 before losing 9–65 as Ryan Sidebottom snared 7–47, and the Kiwis were challenged to score 553 following 177 from Strauss and 110 from Ian Bell. The hosts were 147–1 before a collapse left the last-wicket pair a task of adding 206 runs, and they managed 84. Having captured a 5-wicket haul in his maiden Test, Tim Southee blasted 77 not out from 40 balls as he accumulated four fours and nine sixes, including five off left-arm spinner Monty Panesar, who had claimed 6 scalps in the innings. Chris Martin scored 5 in the last-wicket stand before Sidebottom bowled him to capture his twenty-fourth wicket of the series.

The Kiwis performed creditably in a drawn first Test in England, but the tourists sank to a 6-wicket defeat at Old Trafford after losing the ascendancy. Ross Taylor made 154 not out in New Zealand's 381 before England slid from 111–1 to 202 all out, and then the Kiwis were a player short as they plunged from 85–2 to 114 all out (Panesar 6–37). The 294-run target proved relatively straightforward as the first three partnerships produced 60, 90 and 85 runs, with Strauss (106) playing the anchor role. England went on to win the final Test by an innings, incredibly, after being 86–5 in the first innings. Pietersen (115) top-scored in England's eventual 364, before New Zealand mustered 123 and 232, with James Anderson claiming 9 wickets and Sidebottom 7.

The 2012–13 series featured three draws but was far from dull, as each Test could have had a winner. After the loss of day one in the first Test at Dunedin, the hosts led by 293 runs on the first innings following 171 from debutant opener Hamish Rutherford, after another Kiwi debutant, Bruce Martin, claimed 4–43. England was assured of saving the match, following centuries to skipper Alastair Cook and opening partner Nick Compton, before Compton and number three Jonathan Trott scored tons at Wellington. The hosts had to follow on and were 49 runs in arrears with 8 wickets in hand when the last day was washed out. In the third Test at Auckland, Kiwi opener Peter Fulton scored 136 and 110 before England was set 481. The tourists looked certain to lose at 159–6 with 57.1 overs remaining, before number nine Stuart Broad lasted 137 minutes. Matt Prior's unbeaten 110 in 269 minutes was the key to avoiding defeat, while number 11 Panesar survived 5 balls after coming to the crease with 3.1 overs remaining.

In the lead-up to the 2013 Ashes, England had two convincing victories at home against the Kiwis. Southee claimed 10 wickets in the first Test before New Zealand, set 239, was skittled for 68 as Stuart Broad took 7–44. Joe Root and Alastair Cook scored a century each in the second Test while Graeme Swann's 10 wickets set up the home side's 247-run win.

The two-match series in 2015 was drawn 1–1 after some sharp pendulum swings. At Lord's, the hosts tallied 389 after being 30–4 before Kane Williamson scored 132 in New Zealand's 523, which included 67 sundries. Centuries to Alastair Cook and Ben Stokes — who scored 92 in England's first innings — helped England from 74–3 to 478 in its second innings. Needing 345, the Kiwis lost both openers without scoring and slid to a 124-run defeat, before winning the Headingley Test by 199 runs. Both sides made 350 in their first innings, with New Zealand being 2–2 and later 310–9, before England lost its first 2 wickets at 177 and 215 before being 267–8 and 318–9. The Kiwis were in early trouble again before several strong contributions led to a declaration at 454–8, and then England was on the road to defeat after falling from 47–0 to 62–4.

England v New Zealand

1929–30 (NZ): England 1–0 (3 drawn)
1931 (E): England 1–0 (2 drawn)
1932–33 (NZ): 0–0 (2 drawn)
1937 (E): England 1–0 (2 drawn)
1946–47 (NZ): 0–0 (1 drawn)
1949 (E): 0–0 (4 drawn)
1950–51 (NZ): England 1–0 (1 drawn)
1954–55 (NZ): England 2–0

1958 (E): England 4–0 (1 drawn)
1958–59 (NZ): England 1–0 (1 drawn)
1962–63 (NZ): England 3–0
1965 (E): England 3–0
1965–66 (NZ): 0–0 (3 drawn)
1969 (E): England 2–0 (1 drawn)
1970–71 (NZ): England 1–0 (1 drawn)
1973 (E): England 2–0 (1 drawn)

1974–75 (NZ): England 1–0 (1 drawn)
1977–78 (NZ): 1–1 (1 drawn)
1978 (E): England 3–0
1983 (E): England 3–1
1983–84 (NZ): New Zealand 1–0 (2 drawn)
1986 (E): New Zealand 1–0 (2 drawn)
1987–88 (NZ): 0–(3 drawn)
1990 (E): England 1–0 (2 drawn)
1991–92 (NZ): England 2–0 (1 drawn)

1994 (E): England 1–0 (2 drawn)
1996–97 (NZ): England 2–0 (1 drawn)
1999 (E): New Zealand 2–1 (1 drawn)
2001–02 (NZ): 1–1 (1 drawn)
2004 (E): England 3–0
2007–08 (NZ): England 2–1
2008 (E): England 2–0 (1 drawn)
2012–13 (NZ): 0–0 (3 drawn)
2013 (E): England 2–0
2015 (E): 1–1

1.5 ENGLAND v INDIA

1930s

India's first ten Test matches were against England, from 1932 to 1946, with the more experienced Test-playing nation winning six and drawing four. A one-off match was played at Lord's in June 1932, with the hosts in early trouble at 19–3 before reaching 259 and then dismissing the visitors for 189, after India had been 110–2. India made 187 a second time around and consequently lost by 158 runs, before hosting Test cricket for the first time in season 1933–34.

An innings of 136 from debutant Bryan Valentine turned the first Test England's way although another Test debutant — Lala Amarnath — made 118 in India's second innings, before the tourists won by 9 wickets. The hosts just managed to avoid defeat in Calcutta after being made to follow on, before their opponents inflicted a 202-run drubbing in Madras. India's Amar Singh snared 7–86 in England's first innings before England's Hedley Verity snared 7–49 and 4–104.

The first two Tests in 1936 produced the same results as the first two Tests of 1933–34, before England earned another 9-wicket victory. The touring team was disrupted when Amarnath was sent home for misconduct, but India made a decent start to the Lord's Test before crumbling for 147. Amar Singh's 6–35 helped the Indians to a shock 13-run lead before 4–17 to Verity, and Gubby Allen's second 5-wicket haul of the match, routed India for just 93. The hosts led by 368 runs on the first innings of the Old Trafford Test, following 167 from Wally Hammond and several half-centuries, before centuries to Indian openers Vijay Merchant and Mushtaq Ali steered the tourists towards safety. Hammond (217) and Stan Worthington (128) set up England's 471–8 declared in the third Test, before Allen took 7–80 when India followed on.

1940s

Alec Bedser was prominent in 1946 as he took 11 wickets in each of his first two Tests, while Dick Pollard debuted in the second Test and claimed 5–24 and 2–63. England won the first Test by 10 wickets at Lord's after Joe Hardstaff's 205 not out was 5 more runs than India's first-innings total. Chasing England's first-innings total of 294 in the second Test, India went from 124–0 to 170 all out. The tourists later hung on for a draw after the last pair survived the final 13 minutes while more than 120 runs shy of the target. The final Test was cut short by bad weather, after India had made a respectable 331 following 128 from Merchant.

1950s

Several centuries were scored as neither country could produce a result in the first three Tests of the 1951–52 series, before England won the fourth Test by 8 wickets. India managed only 121 and 157 at Kanpur, including 60 from Hemu Adhikari at number seven in the second innings, after Malcolm Hilton and Roy Tattersall were England's best bowlers. But the final Test in Madras was much different, as India beat England for the first time and thus drew the series. Vinoo Mankad claimed 12 wickets to restrict the tourists to 266 and 183, while the hosts passed 450 following centuries to Pankaj Roy and Polly Umrigar.

Several months later, a partly depleted Indian team was thrashed on England soil as the hosts won the first two Tests by 7 and 8 wickets, before an innings win was followed by a draw. The first Test was relatively even until India, astonishingly, lost its first 4 wickets without a run on the board in its second innings, and England ultimately needed 125 runs to win. England chased 77 in the second Test after Len Hutton and Godfrey Evans scored tons in England's first innings, while Mankad was brilliant in a losing cause as he claimed 5 wickets and scored 72 and 184. After another century to Hutton helped England to 347–9 declared in the third Test, Fred Trueman's 8–31 routed India for 58 before 5–27 from Bedser skittled the tourists for 82. Trueman and Bedser dismissed India for 98 in the final Test, but rain ruined England's hopes of a series whitewash.

Seven years later England produced a 5–0 whitewash as there were three innings victories while the other margins were 8 wickets and 171 runs. Peter May, Ken Barrington, Colin Cowdrey, Geoff Pullar and Mike Smith had their moments with the bat while Trueman and Statham were among more than ten bowlers to share the wickets. The most competitive Test was the fourth, as India recovered from a 282-run first-innings deficit to score 376 when chasing 548, with Umrigar (118) and debutant Abbas Ali Baig (112) leading India's unsuccessful pursuit. These were the only two centuries for Indian batsmen in the series, whereas England had four centuries during the series.

1960s

The absence of Cowdrey, Trueman and Statham could not be used as an excuse for England losing 2–0 in India in 1961–62. Neither side had the ascendancy as the first three Tests were drawn, although the tourists had to follow on in the second Test before three centuries ensured England was safe. Salim Durani was the main wicket-taker when India triumphed, taking 8 scalps in the fourth Test at Calcutta and 10 in the final Test at Madras. India won by 187 runs at Calcutta after dismissing

England for 212 and 233, before winning by 128 runs at Madras after England made 281 and 209.

All five Tests were drawn in the 1963–64 series, with England coming closest to winning the first match at Madras, as an unbroken sixth-wicket stand of 86 took the tourists to within 52 runs of their 293-run target. The only other genuine chance of an outright result was in the last Test when India followed on, but the hosts were never in trouble in their second innings. Bat dominated ball throughout the series as, 11 centuries were scored: seven for India and four for England. In the fourth Test, Hanumant Singh scored 105 on debut before Indian skipper Nawab of Pataudi made an unbeaten 203 in India's second innings.

India had a miserable tour of England in 1967 as the tourists sustained three hefty losses from as many Tests. India made 510 in its second innings of the first Test, but it wasn't enough to prevent a 6-wicket defeat. Geoff Boycott (246 not out), Basil D'Oliveira (109) and Barrington (93) set up an England total beyond 500, before Pataudi stood out for India with 64 (in a total of 164) and 148. The hosts won the second Test by an innings and 124 runs as India tallied 152 and 110, before the tourists made just 92 in their first innings of the third Test and suffered a 132-run loss after being set a 410-run target.

1970s

The 1971 series was decided in the third and final Test, which India won by 4 wickets following two draws. At Lord's, England recovered from 71–5 to post 304 before its second innings of 191 left India needing 183. A rain interruption was crucial before the tourists finished at 145–8, and then the hosts had the better of the second Test. In the decider, England improved from 175–6 to 355 all out, before gaining a 71-run lead, only to subsequently flop for 101 as Bhagwath Chandrasekhar claimed 6–38. The Indians overcame the early dismissal of Sunil Gavaskar to win a Test and series on English soil for the first time.

Tony Lewis captained England in his Test debut and led the tourists to a 6-wicket win at Delhi in the first Test of the 1972–73 series. The highest total at Delhi was 233 in India's second innings before England passed the 207-run target with Lewis on 70 and Tony Greig on 40, after

Greig made 68 not out in England's first innings of 200. Chandrasekhar took 9 wickets in the first Test, as did England seamer Geoff Arnold. In the second Test, the hosts made 210 before the remaining three totals were below 175, with Chandrasekhar and fellow spinner Bishan Bedi making the biggest impact in India's series-levelling 28-run victory. Needing 192, England was 17–4 before a 97-run fifth-wicket stand was followed by another collapse, and a last-wicket partnership of 25. Chandrasekhar, Bedi and another spinner — Erapalli Prasanna — ensured India had the better of the third Test, although the hosts had only 4 wickets in hand when they achieved their victory target of 86. The locals clung to a 2–1 series lead following two draws, with both sides topping 400 in the final Test, before India batted long enough in its second innings to thwart England.

The next six encounters were heavily one-sided, with England clean sweeping a three-Test series in 1974 before wrapping up a five-Test series with two Tests to spare in 1976–77. India may have struggled to adjust to cold and damp English conditions in 1974, as the hosts won the first Test by 113 runs before recording two innings victories. The first Test had rain interruptions, with England in control after recovering from 127–5 to 328–9 declared in its first innings, as Keith Fletcher made 123 not out. Dennis Amiss (188), captain Mike Denness (118) and Greig (106) set up England's 629 in the second Test, and then the Indians were 131–0 before the rest of the match was disastrous for them. All out for 302, they followed on and were dismissed for 42 in 17 overs as Chandrasekhar was absent, with Eknath Solkar making 18 not out while Chris Old (5–21) and Arnold (4–19) were destructive. Arnold had Gavaskar caught behind with the first ball of the third Test, and India was dismissed for 165 and 216, while England scored 459–2 declared. Opener David Lloyd scored 214 not out in his second Test while Denness (100), Amiss (79) and Fletcher (51 not out) were no passengers.

At Delhi in the first Test of 1976–77, Amiss' 179 held England's first innings together as the tourists made 381 after being 65–4. John Lever, meanwhile, had a sensational debut, scoring 53 and taking the first 6 wickets in India's first innings on his way to claiming 7–46 and 3–24 as India succumbed for 122 and 234. The hosts barely avoided an innings defeat in the second Test as the tourists won by 10 wickets, before England wrapped up only its second series win in India with a 200-run drubbing in Madras. The tourists made an unconvincing 262 but subsequently gained a 98-run lead and later dismissed the hosts for 83. India won the fourth Test by 140 runs after England twice fell shy of 200, with Chandrasekhar and Bedi doing the damage while Yajurvindra Singh held seven catches. The series concluded with an intriguing draw, as England finished 62 runs, and India 3 wickets shy, of victory.

The 1979 series was decided in the first Test at Edgbaston as England won by an innings before the remaining three matches were drawn. David Gower (200 not out) and Boycott (155) helped England pass 600 before India twice fell short of 300 at Edgbaston. The tourists made just 96 in the first innings of the second Test before rain, and a century each to Gundappa Viswanath and Dilip Vengsarkar, thwarted the hosts. Rain severely shortened the third Test before the final Test was a thriller. With the tourists chasing 438 runs after trailing by 103 on the first innings, a monumental 221 from Gavaskar had them in sight of victory. India needed 110 runs from the final 20 overs with 9 wickets in hand, and reached 366–1 before stuttering to 429–8.

1980s

Bombay hosted a Test in February 1980 to mark the Golden Jubilee in Indian cricket, but the hosts were thrashed by 10 wickets as Ian Botham had a phenomenal all-round game, while wicketkeeper Bob Taylor gloved ten catches. Botham claimed 6–58 and 7–48 as India tallied just 242 and 149, and the all-rounder hit 114, while Taylor made 43, as England progressed from 58–5 to 296 all out.

India won the first Test of 1981–82 in Bombay before hanging onto its 1–0 series lead as five draws resulted, with the series notorious for countless dubious umpiring decisions that incensed the tourists. After the hosts made just 179 in the first innings at Bombay, the visitors reached 95–1 before slumping to 166 all out as Dilip Doshi bagged 5–39 amidst some controversial umpiring. India added 70 runs for the last 2 wickets in its second innings to set England 241, before the miserable run chase included a last-wicket partnership of 27, while Kapil Dev and

Madan Lal claimed 5 wickets each. The second and third Tests fizzled out after England and then India topped 400 in their first innings. India finished the fourth Test at 170–3 after being set 306, before Viswanath (222) and Yashpal Sharma (140) helped India to 481–4 declared in the fifth Test, before this match also petered out. Rain ruined the final Test, although Botham scored an attractive 142 in England's 378–9 declared, before Kapil Dev blasted a quickfire 116 in India's 377–7.

England won the follow-up series 1–0 only a matter of months later, having won the Lord's Test by 7 wickets before the fixtures at Old Trafford and the Oval were drawn. In the first Test, the hosts were 37–3 and 166–6 before Derek Randall (126) and four lower order batsmen scored well to lift the total to 433. The Indians crashed for 128 despite Gavaskar and Kapil Dev passing 40, before 157 from Vengsarkar and 89 from Kapil Dev helped India gain an ineffective 64-run lead. Rain hampered the second Test, with Botham scoring 128 and Geoff Miller 98 in England's 425 before Sandeep Patil was on 129 as India finished at 379–8. Botham (208), Allan Lamb (107) and Randall (95) ruled out any chance of an Indian win in the third Test, although, the tourists replied to England's 594 with 410. The hosts declared in their second innings, although, the 376-run target was impossible in such a short time-frame, and the visitors made 111–3.

The 1984–85 series in India had to be revised following the assassination of Indian Prime Minister Mrs Gandhi and subsequent murder of the British Deputy High Commissioner to Western India. Botham missed the entire series as he rested at home, and England became the first visiting nation to overcome a series deficit to win a series in India. India's 8-wicket victory in the first Test broke the country's winless streak of 31 Tests, with Ravi Shastri and Syed Kirmani scoring tons, while teenager Laxman Sivaramakrishnan snared two 6-wicket hauls. Sivaramakrishnan also claimed a 6-wicket haul in the second Test, but after England's Mike Gatting scored his maiden Test ton in the first Test, the tourists levelled the series with an 8-wicket win of their own. Opener Tim Robinson scored 160 in his second Test to guide England to a 111-run lead after the Indian tail had wagged, before it flopped later on as India lost its last 6 wickets for 28 runs to leave England needing 125 runs. Kapil Dev was controversially dropped for the third Test, with Mohammad Azharuddin scoring 110 on debut while Shastri made 111, as a dull draw unfolded. Azharuddin also made a century in each of the remaining two Tests, but England won the series 2–1 after recording a 9-wicket victory and then a draw. Double centuries to Graeme Fowler and Gatting set up England's fourth Test victory, although Neil Foster's 11 scalps should not be overlooked. The Indians passed 500 in the final Test, but time was against them after their opponents batted into the last day and tallied 417.

Having lost 5–0 in the Caribbean in 1985–86, England fared little better in its next series, which was on home soil, as India came for three Tests. The hosts were 98–4 in the first Test before the fifth wicket fell at 245 as Graham Gooch departed for an important 114. England stumbled to 294 all out before Vengsarkar's unbeaten 126 helped India to a 47-run lead after the last 2 wickets added 77 precious runs. England could muster only 180 before the Indians had a couple of minor hiccups on their way to a 5-wicket win, and then racked up a series-sealing 279-run win at Headingley. England trailed by 170 runs on the first innings after being routed for 102, before Vengsarkar himself made an unconquered 102 to help India set a target of 408. In the final Test, Gatting made 183 not out after England lost its first 2 wickets for no runs. Both sides tallied 390 before India, after Chetan Sharma claimed his 10th wicket for the match, was set 236 and finished at 174–5.

1990s

A knock of 333 from Gooch highlighted the 1990 series, with England winning the first Test at Lord's by 247 runs before two draws unfolded. Thanks to Gooch, England passed 650 at Lord's before India barely averted the follow-on, and later fell for 224 when chasing a target of 472. Centuries to Allan Lamb and Robin Smith in England's first innings were largely overlooked, as were tons to Shastri and Azharuddin in India's first innings, before Gooch made 123 in England's second innings. Gooch, Smith, Lamb and Azharuddin made another century each in the second Test, as did Gooch's opening partner Mike Atherton and prodigious Indian Sachin Tendulkar. India needed 408 runs to win and was 343–6 at the end with Tendulkar unbeaten on 119. Shastri,

Kapil Dev and Gower were the centurions in the third Test, with the tourists passing 600 before the hosts had to follow on but were untroubled as they reached 477–4 declared.

The 1992–93 series in the subcontinent produced India's most comprehensive victory against England as the hosts won the first Test by 8 wickets before winning the remaining two Tests by an innings. Azharuddin's 182 comprised nearly half of India's 371 at Calcutta, before England followed on and could set a target of only 79. The tourists also followed on in Madras, and fell 22 runs shy of making the hosts bat again after Tendulkar and Navjot Sidhu scored centuries for India, before Chris Lewis scored 117 in England's second innings. Graeme Hick's best Test score of 178 helped England to 347 in the first innings of the third Test, but 224 from Vinod Kambli helped India to 591, before the tourists were dismissed for 229.

Both sides introduced several players to Test cricket in the 1996 series, with hosts England repeating a previous pattern by winning the first Test and drawing the next two. Indian totals of 214 and 219 were insufficient in the opening clash as England won by 8 wickets, chasing 121. Tendulkar and England's Nasser Hussain scored a ton each in the first Test, before England wicketkeeper Robert 'Jack' Russell and Indian debutant Sourav Ganguly registered triple figures in the second Test. Russell's 124 guided England from 107–5 to 344 all out before 131 from Ganguly, 95 from fellow debutant Rahul Dravid and 55 sundries helped India to an 85-run lead. The hosts finished the second Test 193 runs in front with a wicket in hand, before the tourists made 521 in the first innings of the third Test following 177 from Tendulkar, 136 from Ganguly and 84 from Dravid. A draw was guaranteed as 160 from Atherton and 107 (retired hurt) from Hussain paved the way for a 564-run total.

2000s

It was India's turn to win 1–0 at home when another 'win and two draws' pattern panned out in late 2001. Spinners Anil Kumble and Harbhajan Singh set up India's 10-wicket victory in the first Test, while Deep Dasgupta (100) was one of several contributors in India's 469-run total. Craig White (121) and Marcus Trescothick (99) set up England's 407 in the second Test before Tendulkar (103) was the standout in India's 291. Kumble took 10 wickets in the second Test but the hosts never looked a chance of getting near their 374-run target, before each team was dismissed once in the rain-shortened final Test.

The pattern changed in England several months later as it was a case of England win, draw, India win, and another draw to ensure the series was deadlocked. In the opening clash, Hussain's 155 was the highest score in England's 487 before a disappointing Indian innings was followed by tons to Michael Vaughan and John Crawley. India was 170–6 when chasing 568, although an unbeaten 109 to Ajit Agarkar helped the total to a respectable 397. India made 357 in the first innings of the second Test then England led by 260 following 197 from Vaughan. The tourists were 11–2 in their second innings before a ton to Dravid and nineties to Ganguly and Tendulkar ensured India was safe from defeat. Those same three batsmen made centuries in the third Test to guide India past 600, before the tourists won by an innings after enforcing the follow-on. Vaughan made 195 in the final Test as England tallied 515, but a result was virtually impossible as 217 from Dravid set up India's 508, before the last day was washed out.

The next series was also drawn, with India at home for three Tests in 2005–06. The hosts finished the Nagpur Test 108 runs shy of victory as they were 260–6, before they won the Chandigarh Test by 9 wickets, after England's second-innings demise for 181 left India needing 144. Kumble claimed 9 wickets while debutant Munaf Patel snared 7 in India's triumph, but England squared the series with a 212-run thumping at Mumbai. Andrew Strauss (128) and debutant Owais Shah (88) set up England's 400 before India fell 121 runs behind and was later bowled out for just 100.

England and India contested the Pataudi Trophy from 2007, with India winning the inaugural prize with a 1–0 series triumph following a 7-wicket victory at Trent Bridge. England came desperately close to winning the first Test, with India set 380 and finishing on 282–9 after wicketkeeper MS Dhoni (76 not out) and number 11 Shanthakumaran Sreesanth survived the last five overs, with Sreesanth facing just seven deliveries. After Kevin Pietersen scored the only ton in the first Test, his captain, Vaughan, made the only century in the second Test. But England's second innings of 355 left India a meagre target of 73, after England's first innings yielded just 198, with Zaheer Khan taking 9 wickets in the match. India virtually shut England out of the third Test with a first-innings total of 664, with Kumble making 110 not out while his ten teammates made double figures. India opted to bat again after gaining a 319-run lead, before Pietersen scored 101, as England made a creditable 369–6 from 110 overs when needing 500.

India also won 1–0 in 2008–09, with a memorable 6-wicket victory in Chennai followed by a draw at Chandigarh. Security measures were strict in the first Test following a terrorist attack only a few weeks earlier. Strauss (123) was the highest scorer in England's 316 before India tallied 241, followed by 108 each from Strauss and Paul Collingwood in England's second innings. The hosts made the 387-run target look surprisingly straightforward as Tendulkar (103 not out), Yuvraj Singh (85 not out) and openers Virender Sehwag (a hard-hitting 83) and Gautam Gambhir (66) enjoyed a run feast. In the second Test, Sehwag made a duck but Gambhir (179) and Dravid (136) set up a 453-run total before England replied with 302. Pietersen scored 144 after the first 2 wickets fell for 1 run, before Gambhir (97) and Yuvraj (86) ensured England would not win.

The Indians were simply slaughtered in 2011, with hosts England winning the first two Tests by 196 runs and 319 runs, before twice winning by an innings. India sought 458 in the first Test and 478 in the second Test, although these two fixtures unfolded very differently. Pietersen (202 not out) shone in the first innings of the opening Test as England declared at 474–8, before Dravid (103 not out) lacked support as India tallied 286. England wicketkeeper Matt Prior matched Dravid's score while Stuart Broad made 74 not out, and then Broad claimed 3 wickets while James Anderson took 5 in India's second innings. Broad was sensational in the second Test as he scored 64 and 44 at number nine and claimed 6–46 and 2–30 with the ball. Tim Bresnan meanwhile scored 11 and 90 at number eight and snared 2–48 and 5–48 with the ball. India was on top in patches, with England 124–8 in its first innings, before the total reached 221. The Indians lost a wicket first ball and were uncertainly placed at 139–4 before Dravid (117) and

Yuvraj (62) helped them to 267–4. But a collapse of 5–6 ensued, and India's lead was restricted to 67 before Ian Bell (159) stood out in a strong all-round England effort. The tourists collapsed to 55–6 on their way to a crushing defeat, and not even Sehwag's return could prevent India faring even worse in the second half of the series. Totals of 224 and 244 were dwarfed by England's 710–7 declared at Edgbaston, with Alastair Cook scoring 294 while Eoin Morgan was next best with 104. Bell (235) and Pietersen (175) led England to 591–6 declared in the final Test before India replied with 300 and 283. Dravid carried his bat for 146 runs in India's first innings, before India lost its last 7 wickets for 21 runs in its second innings.

England won 2–1 in 2012–13 and 3–1 in 2014, with India squandering a series lead both times. Cheteshwar Pujara (206 not out) and Sehwag (117) set up India's 521–8 declared in the first Test of 2012–13, and visitors, England, managed just 191 in reply before 176 from Cook and 91 from Prior ensured the hosts had to bat again. India won by 9 wickets before Gambhir hit the first delivery of the second Test to the boundary, only to be out next ball. Pujara (135) and number eight Ravi Ashwin (68) set up India's 327 before Pietersen (186) and Cook (122) helped England to an 86-run lead. Monty Panesar and fellow spinner Graeme Swann bowled brilliantly for the tourists, who won by 10 wickets after chasing 57, before the third Test panned out similarly, although it involved more runs. There were no big scores in India's 316 before England led by 207 runs following 190 from Cook. Ashwin (91 not out) delayed England, which won by 7 wickets when chasing just 41. The final Test was drawn, as the visitors declared their second innings at 352–4, with a lead of 356 following tons to Jonathan Trott and Bell.

The 2014 series began with a draw at Trent Bridge as India concluded its second innings at 391–9. India's first innings of 457 included 146 from opener Murali Vijay, 58 from number nine Bhuvneshwar Kumar and a last-wicket stand of 111 including 51 not out from number 11 Mohammed Shami. Just as remarkably, England's first innings of 496 included 154 not out from number five Joe Root, 47 from number nine Stuart Broad and a last-wicket stand of 198 including 81 from number 11 Anderson. The second Test was fairly well balanced until 7–74 from

Ishant Sharma helped India win by 95 runs as England sought 319. The rest of the series was terrible for India as England won by 266 runs and then recorded back-to-back innings victories. Bell (167) and Garry Ballance (156) helped England to 569–7 declared in the first innings at Southampton before India later needed 445 runs to win. Anderson and spinner Moeen Ali were the key bowlers in England's series-levelling win before those two, as well as Broad, were decisive in the fourth Test as India made just 152 and 161, compared with England's 367. In the final Test, the tourists flopped for just 148 (including 82 from Dhoni) and 94, while Root made 149 not out in England's 486.

England v India

1932 (E): England 1–0
1933–34 (I): England 2–0 (1 drawn)
1936 (E): England 2–0 (1 drawn)
1946 (E): England 1–0 (2 drawn)
1951–52 (I): 1–1 (3 drawn)
1952 (E): England 3–0 (1 drawn)
1959 (E): England 5–0
1961–62 (I): India 2–0 (3 drawn)
1963–64 (I): 0–0 (5 drawn)
1967 (E): England 3–0
1971 (E): India 1–0 (2 drawn)
1972–73 (I): India 2–1 (2 drawn)
1974 (E): England 3–0
1976–77 (I): England 3–1 (1 drawn)
1979 (E): England 1–0 (3 drawn)
1979–80 (I): England 1–0

1981–82 (I): India 1–0 (5 drawn)
1982 (E): England 1–0 (2 drawn)
1984–85 (I): England 2–1 (2 drawn)
1986 (E): India 2–0 (1 drawn)
1990 (E): England 1–0 (2 drawn)
1992–93 (I): India 3–0
1996 (E): England 1–0 (2 drawn)
2001–02 (I): India 1–0 (2 drawn)
2002 (E): 1–1 (2 drawn)
2005–06 (I): 1–1 (1 drawn)
2007 (E): India 1–0 (2 drawn)
2008–09 (I): India 1–0 (1 drawn)
2011 (E): England 4–0
2012–13 (I): England 2–1 (1 drawn)
2014 (E): England 3–1 (1 drawn)

1.6 ENGLAND v PAKISTAN

1950s

The first England versus Pakistan series, in 1954, came to life in the fourth and final Test, after there was little to savour beforehand. Rain prevented play until day four in the first Test at Lord's. The tourists made 87 before the hosts declared at 117–9 and then saw Pakistan finish at 121–3. England won the second Test by an innings after Pakistan was dismissed for 157 and 272, with Bob Appleyard claiming 7 wickets on debut while Denis Compton (278) and Reg Simpson (101) were the best of England's batsmen. Rain thwarted a certain England victory in Manchester, as the tourists made 90 and 25–4 in reply to 359–8 declared, following only two days of play. In the final Test at the Oval, Pakistani lower order partnerships proved vital in the context of the match. Pakistan was 77–8 before stands of 29 and 27 were followed by Fazal Mahmood (6–53) and Mahmood Hussain (4–58) dismissing England for 130. Johnny Wardle claimed 7–56 in Pakistan's second innings, but the hosts were frustrated by a ninth-wicket stand of 58 and a last-wicket stand of 24. Needing 168, England was 109–2 before folding for 143, as Fazal finished with 6–46. Another 28 years passed before Pakistan next won a Test in England and, more remarkably, it took an extra two years for Pakistan to win on home soil against England.

1960s

The first Test on Pakistani soil in 1961–62 was another great one, with England winning by 5 wickets after chasing 208. The hosts made 387–9 declared following 138 from Javed Burki and 76 from Mushtaq Mohammad, with Pakistan having collapsed from 315–3 to 337–7. England was 21–2 before Ken Barrington (139) and Mike Smith (99) set up a 380-run total, and then Pakistan struggled at 148–9 before enjoying a 52-run last-wicket partnership. The visitors were uncertainly placed at 108–5 before captain Ted Dexter and Bob Barber polished off the remaining runs. England subsequently lost a five-match series

2–0 in India, before returning to Pakistan and drawing two Tests. Hanif Mohammad scored 111 and 104 while Burki and England opener Geoff Pullar scored one century each at Dacca. Alimuddin (109) stood out in Pakistan's 253 in the third Test before Dexter (205) and Peter Parfitt (111) set up England's 507 to deny any chance of a Pakistani victory.

Pakistan was hammered 4–0 in England several months later, with the Pakistanis having only recently changed from matting to turf pitches. In the first, third, fourth and fifth Tests, Pakistan was made to follow on after England batted first and topped 400, with Parfitt and Tom Graveney often scoring heavily for the hosts. England won the first and third Tests by an innings and was foiled by rain in the fourth Test as Pakistan finished at 216–6, leading by just 7 runs with Mushtaq Mohammad on 100. England won the second Test by 9 wickets and completed the series with a 10-wicket victory at the Oval, where Colin Cowdrey (182) and Dexter (172) starred with the bat before David Larter claimed 9 wickets on debut.

Series of three Tests became regular for England and Pakistan for a while, starting in 1967. Pakistan salvaged a respectable draw at Lord's, before England recorded wins of 10 wickets and 8 wickets at Trent Bridge and the Oval. In the rain-disrupted Trent Bridge Test, Pakistan managed just 140 and 114 to leave England needing just 3 runs. At the Oval, Barrington scored his third century in the series as the hosts gained a 224-run lead before Pakistan slumped to 65–8. Asif Iqbal (146) and Intikhab Alam (51) put on a ninth-wicket stand of 190 to prevent an innings defeat, before Asif claimed 2 consolation wickets.

The 1968–69 series in Pakistan featured three draws as politically-motivated riots proved a distraction. The hosts finished the Lahore Test at 203–5 after being set 323, before England finished the Dacca Test at 33–0 after being set 168. A lively 114 not out from England's Basil D'Oliveira at Dacca was the highlight in the first two Tests, before England made 502–7 in the only innings of the Karachi Test. Opener Colin Milburn and first drop Graveney scored centuries and wicketkeeper Alan Knott was 96 not out when rioting during day three forced the Test to be cancelled.

1970s

The first two Tests of 1971 were drawn before England won the series with a 25-run victory in a superb match at Headingley. In the first Test at Edgbaston, the tourists declared at 608–7 following 274 from Zaheer Abbas, 104 not out from Asif Iqbal and 100 from Mushtaq Mohammad. England was a wicket down after 2 balls and stumbled to 148–6 before a century from Knott provided stability, but England still had to follow on. Rain on day five helped England immensely, while opener Brian Luckhurst (108 not out) was Pakistan's other obstacle in England's second innings. More than 17 hours of play were lost in the Lord's Test due to rain, before Geoff Boycott followed up his unbeaten 121 at Lord's with 112 at Headingley. England made 316 before Pakistan made 350, and then Luckhurst was out first ball before the hosts managed a 230-run lead. Pakistani opener Sadiq Mohammad made 91 in four hours but lacked support, although a 95-run fifth-wicket stand took the total to 160 and lifted the touring team's hopes.

Remarkably there were no outright results in the 1972–73, 1974 and 1977–78 series. The teams may have suffered fatigue in 1972–73, as Pakistan was at home after touring Australia and New Zealand, while England was coming off a tour of India. Student unrest again proved disruptive, although it was nowhere near as bad as four years earlier. Set 240 to win the first Test following three totals beyond 300, Pakistan had limited time and finished at 124–3. Pakistan replied to England's 487 with 569–9 declared in the second Test, and then England slid to 77–5 before losing only 1 more wicket. Majid Khan, Mushtaq Mohammad and England's Dennis Amiss departed for 99 in the third Test, with a result long out of the question when England was left a target of 259.

It was a shame that day five of the first Test in 1974 was washed out as England, after trailing by 102 runs on the first innings, was 238–6 and needed 44 more runs, while Keith Fletcher was unbeaten on 67. The last day of the Lord's Test was also washed out, with England stranded on 27–0 and needing just 60 more runs, although a couple of earlier interruptions had considerably disadvantaged Pakistan. The visitors went from 71–0 to 130–9 declared in their first innings, and 192–3 to 226 all out in their second innings as Derek Underwood claimed 5–20 and 8–51. Pakistan reached 600 in the third Test following 240 from Zaheer Abbas, but England was assured of a draw as Amiss (183) and Fletcher (122) set up a total of 545.

Pakistan had the upper hand as the first Test of 1977–78 in Lahore involved some painfully slow scoring. Mudassar Nazar took 591 minutes to score 114, compared with teammate Haroon Rasheed who scored 122 in 298 minutes, before England's 288 occupied 135.7 eight-ball overs. Pakistan was 106–3 and led by 225 when the Test ended early due to crowd trouble, before Haroon also registered triple figures in the second Test. Abdul Qadir's 6–44 reduced England to 191 all out before the tourists, set 344, reached 186–1 in 81.4 overs. Some of the tourists threatened to withdraw from the third Test in Karachi when it was revealed that the hosts might call on some World Series players, but ultimately the Pakistanis kept their side largely intact. England showed no initiative, scoring 266 in 123.1 overs and 222–5 in 89 overs while Pakistan made 281 in 95 overs, with Phil Edmonds taking 7–66. Dust-bag fights in the crowd seemed to show how attractive the cricket was.

England romped to innings wins at Edgbaston and Lord's in June 1978, with Chris Old (7–50 in Pakistan's first innings, including 4 wickets in 5 balls) a major contributor at Edgbaston as Pakistan slumped from 91–2 to 164 all out. Tons to Clive Radley and Ian Botham set up a 288-run lead, and then Pakistan reached 94 without loss before succumbing for 231. Botham made another century in the second Test as England tallied 364, after play began on day two. Pakistan made only 105 and 139, with Botham taking 8–34 in Pakistan's second innings after Bob Willis (5–47) and Edmonds (4–6) did the damage in the first innings. Rain cut short the Headingley Test, with Sadiq making 97 as Pakistan made just 201 after being 147–1, before England made 119–7.

1980s

The 1982 series produced cricket of outstanding quality as Botham and Pakistan captain Imran Khan were in brilliant all-round form. The series was level at 1–1 following two convincing results before the decider was close and hard fought. Imran took 7–52 as England made 272 in the first innings at Edgbaston, before the hosts gained a 21-

run lead. Derek Randall subsequently made 105 as an opener, but it was a last-wicket stand of 79 that was most decisive as England set a target of 313 and won by 113 runs. Mudassar was trapped by Botham without scoring with the second ball in each of Pakistan's innings, and on the latter occasion Pakistan lost another wicket without a run on the board. Mohsin Khan made 200 in Pakistan's 428–8 declared in the second Test, and then England succumbed for 227 and 276 on its way to a 10-wicket defeat. In the deciding Test at Headingley, Imran was stranded on 67 as his team made 275, before he claimed 5–49 to help Pakistan gain a 19-run lead. But the Pakistani skipper was unhappy that David Gower, who scored an invaluable 74, survived a crucial appeal on 7. Imran was also unhappy that Pakistan lost its ninth second-innings wicket controversially, as Sikander Bakht was ruled caught at short leg. Before a run was added, Imran (on 46) was caught off Botham, who claimed his ninth wicket in the match to leave the hosts a target of 219. Imran and Mudassar kept Pakistan in the hunt as England slid to 189–6 after being 103–0 and 168–1. After starting the final day at 190–6, England lost a wicket at 199 before winning by 3 wickets.

In early 1984, Pakistan finally recorded its first series win against England. An injured Imran missed the series while injury prevented Botham from playing in the second and third Tests. The opening encounter at Karachi was the only Test to feature an outright result after student disruption brought about heavy security. Five wickets to Qadir and 4 to Sarfraz Nawaz caused the tourists to collapse from 90–1 to 182 all out, before Pakistan slid from 67–0 to 138–6. A seventh-wicket stand of 75 and a 37-run last-wicket stand set up a 95-run lead, before the hosts found themselves in danger of a remarkable defeat as they fell to 40–6 when chasing just 65. A 19-run partnership took the Pakistanis to the brink of a 3-wicket victory, despite Nick Cook's 5–18, following his 6–65 in Pakistan's first innings. The second Test was a high scoring draw as injury and illness weakened the touring team, before the third Test was an eye-catching draw amidst plenty of umpiring controversies. Qadir and Sarfraz again did the bulk of the damage although England's first innings of 241 included a sixth-wicket stand of 120, before 90 from Sarfraz at number ten helped Pakistan from 181–8 to 343 all out. Gower continued his fine series as he scored

173 not out, before Pakistan was 173–0 and needed just 70 more runs. Mohsin Khan made 104 and Shoaib Mohammad 80, but a 5-wicket haul to Norman Cowans inspired a collapse of 6–26, before Pakistan reached 217–6 to draw the match and win the series.

Pakistan backed this up more than three years later with its breakthrough series win on England soil, again with a 1–0 margin, although this time in a five-match series. Rain prevented any chance of a result in the first two Tests, before Imran claimed 10 wickets in the third Test, which the visitors won by an innings after dismissing the hosts for 136 and 199. Mudassar (124) and wicketkeeper Salim Yousuf (91 not out) were largely responsible for Pakistan's 439 in the fourth Test, before England captain Mike Gatting scored 124 in a strong team display that earned the hosts an 82-run lead. The hosts sought to even the series as they needed 124 runs in 18 overs, and reached 62–3 after nine overs. Under pressure, however, England subsequently lost 3 wickets to run-outs and finished at 109–7. Javed Miandad (260), Imran (118) and Salim Malik (102) ensured the Pakistanis maintained their series lead as the tourists notched 708 at the Oval, before making the hosts follow on after Qadir captured 7–96. England appeared certain of defeat before Gatting (150 not out) and Botham (51 not out) put on an unbroken fifth-wicket stand of 176 runs in 252 minutes to save the match, with Pakistan squandering numerous chances on the final day.

Pakistan's 1–0 series win at home in late 1987 was spoilt as the tourists were angered by the umpiring. On paper, Pakistan's win in the first Test at Lahore appeared clear-cut as England mustered 175 and 130 compared with Pakistan's 392. Qadir had the tourists tied in knots as he achieved figures of 9–56 and 4–45. Qadir won seven appeals for lbw but it was obvious that at least four of them should not have been given, and a couple of other batsmen were controversially ruled caught. In the second Test at Faisalabad, England lost 8–51 to tumble to 292 all out before all hell broke loose, as Pakistan was 106–5 late on day two. Gatting and Pakistani umpire Shakoor Rana engaged in a furious and ugly slanging match, after the umpire accused the England captain of illegally waving his hand to alter a field placement as Eddie Hemmings was coming in to bowl. Shakoor refused to restart play until he received an apology from Gatting, and consequently day three was lost before the England captain complied. Weather disrupted day four, and the match fizzled out into a draw. Qadir took 30 wickets in the series after claiming 10 at Karachi, where England finished its second innings at 258–9 with a 99-run lead.

1990s

England hosted a five-match series in 1992, with the tourists winning 2–1, following a 10-wicket victory in the final Test. Both sides topped 400 in the drawn first Test, with Salim Malik (165) and Javed Miandad (153 not out) standing out for the visitors, before Alec Stewart (190) and Robin Smith (127) shone for the hosts. The second Test was a classic and involved crazy collapses, starting with England going from 123–0 to 255 all out. Pakistan slipped from 228–3 to 293 all out, followed by England losing 4–40 and later 4–1, while Stewart carried his bat with 69 runs out of 175. Pursuing 138, the tourists were 95–8 before Wasim Akram (45 not out) and Waqar Younis (20 not out) followed up their fine bowling with a match-winning 46-run partnership. Aamir Sohail's 205 helped Pakistan to 505–9 declared in the drawn third Test, before the series came alive as England won at Headingley. Pakistan made only 197 before Graham Gooch scored 135, although England plunged from 292–2 to 320 all out before winning by 6 wickets after needing 99 runs. Akram (6–67) was destructive in the first innings of the deciding Test as England crumbled for 207 after being 182–3, before Waqar's 5–52 in England's second innings was responsible for a 174-run total that left Pakistan needing just 2 runs.

Inzamam-ul-Haq starred in the first Test of 1996 as Pakistan made 340 and 352–5 declared, before winning by 164 runs after Mushtaq Ahmed and Waqar did the damage as England's run chase yielded 243 runs. Plenty of runs were scored in the second Test, as a result never looked likely, before tons to Saeed Anwar and Salim Malik helped Pakistan to a 195 run first-innings lead in the third and final Test. The tourists went on to win by 9 wickets for a 2–0 triumph.

2000s

The series in Pakistan in late 2000 yielded two draws before the tourists won the rubber with a 6-wicket victory in Karachi. Inzamam-ul-Haq (142) and Yousuf Youhana (117) rescued Pakistan from 64–3 although only 82 runs were added following their 259-run partnership. England opener Mike Atherton's 125 was followed by a last-wicket stand of 39 to trim the deficit to 17 runs, and then Pakistan capitulated for 158 before causing England the occasional fright in the run chase.

England hosted a two-Test series several months later, with the hosts recording a massive win before the tourists drew the series with a big win of their own. No batsman passed 80 in England's 391 at Lord's, before the home side won by an innings, as Darren Gough and Andy Caddick took most of the wickets. A ton from Inzamam was followed by solid contributions down the order as Pakistan made 403 at Old Trafford, before centuries from Graham Thorpe and Michael Vaughan were followed by England losing its last 5 wickets for 9 runs. Pakistan built on its 46-run lead, but England had a real chance of victory at 146–0, before collapsing to 261 all out to lose by 108 runs.

Coming off the high of its first Ashes series win for more than 18 years, England suffered a 2–0 loss on Pakistan soil in late 2005 after squandering a strong position in the first Test. The hosts initially butchered a strong position as they went from 161–1 to 274 all out, before Marcus Trescothick's 193 set up England's 418. Pakistan managed a lead of 197 following 122 from Salman Butt before the tourists slipped from 64–1 to 117–7, and then had a 49-run eighth-wicket partnership, before losing by 22 runs. Both sides passed 400 in their first innings in the second Test, and Inzamam scored two centuries before England hung on for a draw at 164–6 when needing 285 to level the series. A 101-run opening stand gave England a strong start in the third Test, before a modest total of 288 was dwarfed by Pakistan's 636–8 declared, as Mohammad Yousuf (223) and Kamran Akmal (154) dominated. England succumbed for 248 after being 205–2, with Shoaib Akhtar and Danish Kaneria the destroyers.

England won 3–0 at home less than a year later, with the fourth and final Test ending in controversy after Pakistan was well-placed to salvage a 2–1 series loss. The first Test at Lord's produced an honourable draw after centuries to Paul Collingwood, Alastair Cook and Ian Bell were followed by a double hundred to Mohammad Yousuf and a century to England captain Andrew Strauss. After reaching 90–2 in the first innings at Old Trafford, the rest of the second Test was disastrous for the Pakistanis as they folded for 119 and 222. Steve Harmison claimed 6–19 and 5–57 while Monty Panesar took 3–21 and 5–72, and the best of England's batsmen were Cook (127) and Bell (106 not out) in a total of 461–9 declared. Kevin Pietersen (135) and Bell (119) were the main contributors in England's 515 at Headingley, before Pakistan led by 23 runs following 192 from Mohammad Yousuf and 173 from Younis Khan. Strauss (116) provided the backbone of England's second innings, before Pakistan crumbled for only 155 after being challenged to score 323. In the final Test, the hosts made just 173 before reaching 298–4 in their second innings after the tourists compiled 504. But the Pakistanis refused to return to the field following a break on day four, after they had been penalised 5 runs for alleged ball tampering. The umpires awarded the Test to England on forfeit, producing the first forfeit in the 1814th contest in the history of Test cricket.

England recorded three massive victories in the 2010 series, although the series was up for grabs after Pakistan won the third Test and was briefly on top in the final Test. Despite a century each to Eoin Morgan and Matt Prior, the standout performer in the first Test was James Anderson with 5–54 and 6–17 as England won by 354 runs. Pakistan's first innings of 182 included an attacking 65 not out from Umar Gul at number nine, before the miserable second innings of 80 yielded a top score of 16 not out from Kaneria at number ten. Anderson, Stuart Broad and Steven Finn routed the visiting team for 72 at Edgbaston before Pakistan's second innings of 296, which included a recovery from 153–7 and figures of 6–65 from Graeme Swann, wasn't enough to prevent England winning by 9 wickets when chasing 118. The hosts improved from 94–7 to 233 all out at the Oval, before their second-innings collapse from 156–2 to 222 all out (Cook 110) left the tourists seeking 148, which was achieved with 4 wickets in hand. England was 47–5 and 102–7 in the fourth Test before Jonathan Trott (184) and Broad (169) put on an eighth-wicket stand of 332 in a total of 446. Swann had match figures of 9–74 as Pakistan made just 74 and 147, with Umar Akmal offering a lone hand of 79 not out in the follow-on.

The 2011–12 series was played in neutral territory, with the first and third Tests staged in Dubai while the second was in Abu Dhabi. Pakistan swept to a 3–0 whitewash with victories of 10 wickets, 72 runs and 71 runs, with the first Test decided in three days before the latter two lasted less than four days each. Saeed Ajmal claimed 10 wickets as England made 192 and 160 in the first Test, leaving Pakistan a lousy target of 15. England led by 70 runs in the second Test before flopping for an embarrassing 72 when chasing 145, as Abdur Rehman (6–25) and Ajmal (3–22) were destructive. Pakistan capitulated for 99 in the third Test before restricting England's lead to 42 and then setting a target of 324, following 157 from Azhar Ali and 127 from Younis Khan. England's top eight made double figures but no half-centuries, while Ajmal and Gul took 4 wickets apiece.

The 2015–16 series also took place in the United Arab Emirates, and Pakistan was lucky to escape with a draw at Abu Dhabi, before winning at Dubai and Sharjah. Both sides topped 500 at Abu Dhabi, with Shoaib Malik notching 245 for Pakistan before Alastair Cook made 263 for England. Pakistan's second-innings capitulation for 173 left England needing 99 runs in 19 overs, and the score was 74–4 after 11 overs when bad light forced an early finish. At Dubai, England totalled 312 when chasing 491 before gaining a 72-run first-innings lead at Sharjah. Mohammad Hafeez (151) helped Pakistan set a 284-run target, and England's quest to draw the series failed miserably, as England managed just 156.

England v Pakistan

1954 (E): 1–1 (2 drawn)
1961–62 (P): England 1–0 (2 drawn)
1962 (E): England 4–0 (1 drawn)
1967 (E): England 2–0 (1 drawn)
1968–69 (P): 0–0(3 drawn)

1971 (E): England 1–0 (2 drawn)
1972–73 (P): 0–0 (3 drawn)
1974 (E): 0–0 (3 drawn)
1977–78 (P): 0–0 (3 drawn)
1978 (E): England 2–0 (1 drawn)
1982 (E): England 2–1

1983–84 (P): Pakistan 1–0 (2 drawn)

1987 (E): Pakistan 1–0 (4 drawn)

1987–88 (P): Pakistan 1–0 (2 drawn)

1992 (E): Pakistan 2–1 (2 drawn)

1996 (E): Pakistan 2–0 (1 drawn)

2000–01 (P): England 1–0 (2 drawn)

2001 (E): 1–1

2005–06 (P): Pakistan 2–0 (1 drawn)

2006 (E): England 3–0 (1 drawn)

2010 (E): England 3–1

2011–12 (Bangladesh): Pakistan 3–0

2015–16 (UAE): Pakistan 2–0 (1 drawn)

1.7 ENGLAND v SRI LANKA

1980s

The first six Tests involving England and Sri Lanka were one-off matches between 1982 and 1998. Sri Lanka's first-ever Test was against England in Colombo during February 1982, with the hosts putting in a strong showing in patches, before losing by 7 wickets. Derek Underwood claimed 5–28 as Sri Lanka made 218, before England bettered it by only 5 runs. The home side's victory chances were rocked when John Emburey claimed 5 quick wickets, as Sri Lanka fell from 167–3 to 175 all out, and then Chris Tavare (85) set up the successful run chase.

The 1984 encounter was drawn, with Sidath Wettimuny scoring 190 in 642 minutes while Duleep Mendis (111) and Arjuna Ranatunga (84) also set up Sri Lanka's 491–7 declared. Poor weather interrupted proceedings, and Allan Lamb scored 107 in England's 370 before Sri Lanka declared at 294–7. Amal Silva's unbeaten 102 was his maiden first-class century, and skipper Mendis made a quick 94, while Ian Botham captured 6–90. England comfortably won the 1988 encounter at Lord's by 7 wickets, with Phil Newport claiming 7 wickets in his maiden Test while Robert 'Jack' Russell scored 94 in his debut.

1990s

At Lord's in 1991, the hosts struggled to 282 following a strong start, with Alec Stewart making 113 not out while Rumesh Ratnayake claimed 5–69. Phil DeFreitas captured 7–70 as Sri Lanka managed 224, and then Graham Gooch's 174 helped set the visitors 423. Sri Lanka was dismissed for 285, before winning the next three encounters.

The 1993 contest in Colombo was a good one, with the hosts making 469 in reply to 380 before Sri Lanka was 61–4 chasing 140. With unbeaten scores of 93 and 36, Hashan Tillekeratne guided the Sri Lankans to a 5-wicket triumph. John Crawley (156 not out), Graeme Hick (107) and number 11 Angus Fraser (32) helped England to 445 in the first innings of the 1998 Test at the Oval. But these contributions were overshadowed, as heroic performances from Sri Lankan trio Sanath Jayasuriya (213 and 24 not out), Aravinda de Silva (152) and Muttiah Muralitharan (bowling figures of 7–155 and 9–65, and scoring 30 at number 11) set up a 10-wicket win for Sri Lanka.

2000s

Series involving three matches took place from 2000–01 to 2011, before the following two series had just two Tests each. Marvan Atapattu (201 not out) and Aravinda de Silva (106) provided the backbone of Sri Lanka's 470–5 declared in the first Test of 2000–01 at Galle, before the hosts won by an innings. After leading by 90 runs on the first innings in the second Test, England needed 161 runs and struggled at 97–5 before partnerships of 25, 20 and 19 took England to a series-levelling 3-wicket victory. The deciding match at Colombo was a true Test, with Sri Lanka falling from 205–3 to 241 all out, before England stumbled to a mere 8-run lead as Graham Thorpe scored 113 not out. After routing Sri Lanka for just 81, England clinched the series, but not before losing 6 wickets in the small run chase.

Atapattu (185) and Mahela Jayawardene (107) helped Sri Lanka rack up 555–8 declared in the first Test of 2002, before England was forced to follow on. Centuries to Michael Vaughan and Mark Butcher amidst a strong team effort helped England to 529–5 declared to guarantee a draw. England also topped 500 in the remaining two Tests, and won by an innings in the second Test, before concluding the series with a 10-wicket triumph. Left-handers Butcher, Thorpe and Marcus Trescothick were century-makers, as was the right-handed Stewart.

The first two matches in the 2003–04 series were drawn, with Sri Lanka just 1 wicket away from victory in the first Test, as England finished 113 runs shy of a 323-run target. The Sri Lankans were also in sight of victory in the second Test, with England set 368 and finishing on 285–7, after the eighth-wicket pair of Chris Read and Gareth Batty survived the last 25 overs. Sri Lanka was convincing in the final Test at Colombo, however, with Thilan Samaraweera (142) and Mahela Jayawardene (134) helping the hosts exceed 600 in reply to England's 265, before the tourists succumbed for 148.

England looked sure to inflict a big defeat in the first Test of 2006 as Sri Lanka crumbled for 192 after 158 from Kevin Pietersen, 106 from Trescothick and other contributions enabled England to pass 550. But six half-centuries, in addition to Jayawardene's 119, helped Sri Lanka reach 537–9 to salvage a draw. Sri Lanka slumped to 141 all out in the second Test before Pietersen marginally bettered that total himself as England tallied 295. Only Michael Vandort (105) and Tillakaratne Dilshan (59) made any impression in Sri Lanka's second innings, with opener Vandort last out, before England passed the 78-run target for the loss of 4 wickets. The third Test was memorable as Sri Lanka slid from 84–1 to 139–8, before partnerships of 30 and 62 ensued. England finished 2 runs in arrears before chasing 325, and Muralitharan ensured a deadlocked series, as his 8–70 helped Sri Lanka to a 134-run victory.

The 2007–08 series was decided in the first Test at Kandy, where Sri Lanka won by 88 runs. The hosts faltered to 188 all out, despite 92 from Sangakkara and 51 from Prasanna Jayawardene, and England responded with 281 before Sangakkara (152) had better support in Sri Lanka's second innings. Also during Sri Lanka's second innings, Jayasuriya achieved the rare feat of hitting six fours in an over on his way to 78. England's second-innings total of 261 included a seventh-wicket partnership of 109 as Muralitharan completed a 9-wicket match haul. Mahela Jayawardene (195) and Vandort (138) ruined England's chances in the second Test, before the former made 213 not out in the third Test as Sri Lanka neared 500. The visitors collapsed for 81, before rain helped them escape with a draw, in addition to an Alastair Cook century.

The 2011 series also featured an outright result followed by two draws, with Sri Lanka appearing well placed after scoring 400 in the first innings of the series, following 112 to Prasanna Jayawardene. England declared 96 runs ahead following 203 from Jonathan Trott, 133 from Cook and an unbeaten 103 from Ian Bell, before Sri Lanka, incredibly, plunged to 82 all out. Both sides exceeded 400 in the second Test after Matt Prior's 126 for England was followed by 193 from Dilshan. Cook scored another ton as England never looked in danger of losing, before Sri Lanka looked like losing the final Test until Sangakkara scored 119.

Sri Lanka hosted the next series less than a year later, and slumped to 15–3 in the first four overs before Mahela Jayawardene's 180 lifted the total beyond 300. England fell shy of 200 before inducing another top order collapse, but a target of 340 proved too much as Sri Lanka won by 75 runs despite 112 from Trott. The tourists drew the series with an 8-wicket win, after a century to Mahela Jayawardene was not enough for Sri Lanka to notch a big first-innings score. Pietersen (151) was one of several strong contributors in an England total of 460 before Sri Lanka gained a small lead of 93.

England came achingly close to winning the first Test in 2014, and the drawn result had a pivotal impact on the series. Joe Root (200 not out) helped England tally 575–9 declared, after being 22–2, before centuries to Sangakkara and Angelo Mathews helped Sri Lanka to 453. Gary Ballance's unbeaten 104 helped England set a target of 390, and Sri Lanka finished on 201–9, after losing the ninth wicket from the first ball of the last over. England gained control of the second Test as opener Sam Robson's 127 laid the platform for a total of 365 in reply to Sri Lanka's 257. A knock of 160 from Mathews and a lengthy stay from Rangana Herath took Sri Lanka from 277–7 to 426–8, before more tail-end resistance increased England's target to 350. Moeen Ali made 108 not out at number seven, but England slid to a 100-run defeat after James Anderson was last out, having, incredibly, scored no runs while facing 55 deliveries in 81 minutes.

England v Sri Lanka

1981–82 (SL): England 1–0

1984 (E): 1 drawn

1988 (E): England 1–0

1991 (E): England 1–0

1992–93 (SL): Sri Lanka 1–0

1998 (E): Sri Lanka 1–0

2000–01 (SL): England 2–1

2002 (E): England 2–0 (1 drawn)

2003–04 (SL): Sri Lanka 1–0 (2 drawn)

2006 (E): 1–1 (1 drawn)

2007–08 (SL): Sri Lanka 1–0 (2 drawn)

2011 (E): England 1–0 (2 drawn)

2011–12 (SL): 1–1

2014 (E): Sri Lanka 1–0 (1 drawn)

1.8 ENGLAND v ZIMBABWE

1990s

The first Test between England and Zimbabwe was memorable, as it was the first time that a drawn Test finished with the scores level. In the Zimbabwean city of Bulawayo in December 1996, the hosts made 376 before their second-innings dismissal for 234 set the tourists a target of 205 in 37 overs. Opener Nick Knight (96) and number three Alec Stewart (73) had England on course for victory before the tourists stumbled from 154–1, and Knight was run out from the final delivery of the match to bring about the sixth wicket. Rain hampered the second Test which also finished in a draw, with England scoring 156 and 195–3, while Zimbabwe scored 215.

2000s

Zimbabwe's batting failed badly in most of its subsequent Tests against England, with the hosts winning by an innings and 209 runs at Lord's in the first Test of 2000, after the visitors were dismissed for 83 and 123.

The Zimbabwean-born Graeme Hick scored a hundred for England in this match, as did Stewart, who had also registered triple figures against Zimbabwe in the 1996–97 series. The second Test of 2000 was a rain-affected draw, with Mike Atherton scoring 136 for England, before Murray Goodwin scored 148 not out for Zimbabwe.

England also began the 2003 series with an innings win at Lord's, as Mark Butcher scored 137 in a total of 472, before Zimbabwe capitulated for 147 and 233. The hosts followed up with another innings win, this time as they recovered from 156–5 to post 416, before dismissing the visitors for 94 and 253.

England v Zimbabwe

1996–97 (Z): 0–0 (2 drawn)   **2003 (E):** England 2–0
2000 (E): England 1–0 (1 drawn)

1.9 ENGLAND v BANGLADESH

2000s

Bangladesh was no match for England in the first four series featuring the two countries, with England winning all eight encounters. England generally had the better of the first fixture, winning it by 7 wickets at Dhaka in late 2003 before the margin in the next Test was 329 runs. The 2005 series was heavily one-sided, as the host team warmed up for the Ashes with two innings victories. Opening batsman Marcus Trescothick scored 194 and 151 in England's two innings (after scoring 113 in the first Test of the 2003–04 series), and Ian Bell made unbeaten scores of 65 and 162 while Michael Vaughan (first Test) also scored a century. England's pace attack of Matthew Hoggard, Steve Harmison, Andrew Flintoff and Simon Jones shared the wickets in an ominous sign of what the Australian batsmen would soon encounter.

England won by 181 runs and 9 wickets in the 2009–10 series in Bangladesh, with off spinner Graeme Swann claiming 16 wickets. England set a virtually impossible target of 513 in the first Test after Alastair Cook (173), Paul Collingwood (145), Kevin Pietersen (99) and Bell (84) set up England's first-innings total of 599–6 declared. Bangladesh had a chance of winning the second Test after tallying 419, only for England to better it by 77 runs and then dismiss the hosts for 285. Cook (109 not out) and Pietersen (74 not out) ensured a comfortable run chase after Bell (138 in England's first innings) had again been a pain for Bangladesh.

The teams met on English soil within the next few months, and Jonathan Trott (226) set up England's 505 in the first Test before Bangladesh had to follow on. Bangladesh's second-innings total of 382 was creditable, although it could have been higher after the score had been 185–0 and 289–2, and England lost just 2 wickets when chasing 160. Bell scored 128 in England's first innings of 419 in the second Test, before Bangladesh opener Tamim Iqbal scored half of Bangladesh's first-innings total of 216. The tourists lost by an innings and 80 runs after following on, with Steven Finn taking a 5-wicket haul and finishing the series with 15 scalps.

England v Bangladesh

2003–04 (B): England 2–0
2005 (E): England 2–0
2009–10 (B): England 2–0
2010 (E): England 2–0

1.10 NOTABLE TEST PLAYERS

James Anderson

James Anderson became the first England player to register 400 Test wickets in more than 130 years of Test cricket. He claimed 5–73 against Zimbabwe at Lord's on debut in 2003, and snared a 5-wicket haul against South Africa at Trent Bridge less than three months later. But nearly four years passed before he claimed 5 wickets in a Test innings for the third time. As the ESPN *Cricinfo* staff reported in Anderson's *Cricinfo* player profile:

> For the first six years of Anderson's international career, the best way to sum up his bowling was to paraphrase Mother Goose: when he's good, he's very, very good — and when he's bad he's horrid. But when the force was with him, he was capable of irresistible spells, seemingly able to swing the ball round corners at an impressive speed.

Anderson sought to change his action in order to minimise injury possibilities, but a stress fracture kept him out of cricket for much of 2006. He had a miserable series Down Under with only 5 wickets at 82.60, before capturing 14 wickets in three Tests against India, with best figures of 5–42. Later in 2007, Anderson was expensive at Kandy, where Sanath Jayasuriya struck six fours in one over off his bowling. After not playing in the first Test against the Kiwis in 2007–08 as New Zealand won, Anderson returned in style at Wellington as he took 5–73 and 2–57 in a series-levelling win before being expensive in the decider, which England also won. As England hosted New Zealand shortly afterwards, Anderson was wayward in the first two Tests as he snared 10 wickets at 26.90 before capturing 7–43 and 2–55 at Trent Bridge, where the hosts won by an innings.

Anderson claimed 9 wickets in a Test against the West Indies in 2009, and in the 2009 Ashes he captured a 5-wicket haul at Edgbaston. Anderson had a fine year in 2010 as he took 57 Test wickets, including 5–54 and 6–17 against Pakistan at Trent Bridge. One of the keys to more consistency was the ability to bowl a good line and length, making it hard for batsmen to score off him, while he could also swing the ball. Despite not taking 5 wickets in an innings in the 2010–11 Ashes, Anderson contributed well in England's triumph with 24 scalps at 26.04 and did a lot to erase the horrors of 2006–07.

Anderson took a 5-wicket innings haul once in 2011 and once in 2012, before racing past 300 Test wickets as he claimed 7 scalps in a Lord's Test against New Zealand prior to the 2013 Ashes. Anderson claimed 5–85 and 5–73 at Trent Bridge in the first Ashes Test, but he averaged more than 40 in the next nine Tests against Australia, as England won 3–0 at home and lost 5–0 away. Anderson still managed 52 wickets from 14 Tests in 2013. Back home in 2014, Anderson took 12 wickets at 21.50 in a narrow series loss to Sri Lanka before taking 25 at 20.60 against India. Anderson's most significant contribution was at Southampton where his 5–53 and 2–24 helped England level the series before the hosts won 3–1.

In the Caribbean in 2015, Anderson became England's leading wicket-taker after Ian Botham held the record for nearly 30 years. Anderson claimed 17 wickets in the three Tests, including figures of 6–42 in the third Test, only for the West Indies to record a series-levelling victory. England also lost the Test in which Anderson reached the 400-wicket milestone: against New Zealand at Headingley, where the tourists drew the series. Anderson was restricted to three Tests in England's subsequent Ashes triumph at home, but he made his mark at Edgbaston with 6–47 before succumbing to a side injury.

As a tail-end left-handed batsman, Anderson improved after being a renowned rabbit for a while, despite lasting 54 Test innings without a duck. His maiden first-class half-century was a knock of 81 in a Test against India as he added 198 for the last wicket with Joe Root.

Anderson also made some handy contributions as a nightwatchman, and helped foil Australia in the opening Ashes Test of 2009 as he made 21 not out in 69 minutes at number ten.

James Anderson (b.1983)*

Matches: 113
Runs scored: 1032
Batting average: 10.32
100s/50s: 0/1
Top score: 81
Balls bowled: 25,185
Wickets: 433
Bowling average: 29.18
5 wickets in innings: 18
10 wickets in match: 2
Best bowling: 7–43
Catches/stumpings: 73/–
* still playing as of 2016

Ken Barrington

After scoring a duck in his first Test and then 34 and 18 in his second Test, Ken Barrington had to wait four years for another chance at the elite level. This gave him plenty of time to rework his style, and in the process he opened his stance and faced more towards the bowler. Barrington played the off-drive to good effect early in his career, but after revamping his game he played the stroke sparingly and was more of an on-side player although he played the cut shot well. Dedicated and determined, Barrington was cautious, as he often scored slowly and, as Vic Marks reported in *The Wisden Illustrated History of Cricket*, 'He sacrificed many of his shots for efficiency's sake.'

Changing his style proved worthwhile in any case, as Barrington averaged a shade below 60 following his first series. At first drop Barrington averaged 77.24, and in the following two positions he averaged 59.18 and 41.96. Remarkably, after scoring a century in his first Test appearance in the Caribbean, he did likewise in India, Pakistan and New Zealand. When he retired, he had scored at least one Test century in each Test-playing nation and English Test venue at the time. Barrington's level of success regularly mirrored England's level of success, as he was in 31 Test wins, 12 losses and 39 draws. He averaged well over 60 when England didn't lose, but only 30.50 in the dozen defeats. He was also a part-time leg spinner and a decent fielder.

Recalled for England's home series against India in 1959, Barrington batted for lengthy periods and scored well over half of his runs in boundaries, as his scores were 56, 80, 80, 87, 46 and 8. In his first Test abroad several months later, Barrington scored 128 at Bridgetown and followed up with 121 and 49 at Port-of-Spain. His form was indifferent for a short while afterwards, before he excelled in the subcontinent in 1961–62. Barrington scored 139 and 6 in a 5-wicket win over Pakistan at Lahore, and followed up with a century in each of the first three Tests in India. Following unbeaten scores of 151 and 52 at Bombay, his 172 helped save the Kanpur Test after India enforced the follow-on, and then he made 113 not out in the rain-affected Delhi Test.

After averaging more than 70 against the Australians and Kiwis in 1962–63, with two tons Down Under and one in New Zealand, it was intriguing that Barrington's nine Test centuries were overseas. In the 1964 Ashes he finally cracked triple figures in a home Test, and turned it into his highest Test score of 256, after Bill Lawry scored 311 for Australia in a high-scoring draw at Old Trafford. In his next two series, Barrington notched 508 runs at 101.60 against South Africa and 300 runs at 150 against New Zealand, with scores including 148 not out and 121 against the Springboks and 137 and 163 against the Kiwis. In another Test against South Africa, Barrington scored 49 and shared 6 wickets with Geoff Boycott before they opened the batting in a brief and pointless second innings, as the match fizzled out into a draw. Barrington was surprisingly dropped for the Test in between his 137 and 163 in New Zealand. Selectors deemed his 137 was too sluggish considering it took 437 minutes, before his follow-up 163 took 339 minutes.

In his second and final Test tour of Australia, Barrington scored 60 and 102 in an innings loss before making 115 and 32 not out, as the series remained deadlocked. Barrington was rested against the West Indies for much of the 1966 series due to the strain of playing too much cricket, before his last great series was against Pakistan in 1967. His scores were 148, 14, 109 not out, 142 and 13 not out in England's 2–0 win. In his remaining two series, Barrington notched 288 runs at 41.14 with one century in the Caribbean before scoring 75, 0, 49 and 46 not out in the 1968 Ashes. A few times in Tests he reached a century with a six, including in the 1967–68 tour of the West Indies, when he produced a straight hit off Charlie Griffith.

A heart attack ended Barrington's first-class career later in 1968, before he died from a heart attack when assistant manager of the England team during its 1980–81 tour of the West Indies.

Ken Barrington (1930–1981)

Matches: 82
Runs scored: 6806
Batting average: 58.67
100s/50s: 20/35
Top score: 256
Balls bowled: 2715
Wickets: 29
Bowling average: 44.82
5 wickets in innings: –
10 wickets in match: –
Best bowling: 3–4
Catches/stumpings: 58/–

(Sir) Alec Bedser

In *The Illustrated Encyclopedia of World Cricket*, Peter Arnold noted that Alec Bedser 'was a model bowler' who had 'a bowling action that was a marvel of economy. He took a relatively short run-up, but the swing of his massive body dragged the maximum bounce from the pitch, while allowing him to sustain life and accuracy at a fast-medium pace over long periods'. John Kay, meanwhile, reported in *Ashes to Hassett, A review of the M.C.C. tour of Australia, 1950–51* that Bedser:

> *toiled for hours without complaint, and never once looked annoyed*
> *at the missing of a catch, or at a rejected lbw appeal. A great bowler,*
> *and an example to all who aspire to cricketing fame.*

The Second World War was the main reason Bedser had to wait until he was nearly 28 to make his Test debut: against India, in 1946. He claimed 7–49 and 4–96 at Lord's on debut, and followed up with 4–41 and 7–52 at Old Trafford. Bedser found Australia a much tougher place as he claimed just 16 scalps at 54.75 in the 1946–47 Ashes which the hosts won 3–0. Yet he bowled Don Bradman for a duck in Adelaide, prompting Bradman to say the delivery was perhaps the finest ever to capture his wicket. The delivery swung in to land in line with leg stump before hitting the middle and off stumps.

Following his great debut series, Bedser had ordinary figures of 76 wickets at 39.97 in his next 23 Tests, despite having dismissed Bradman six times — usually caught on the legside. The turning point for Bedser was the 1950–51 Ashes as he was the leading wicket-taker with 30 victims at 16.07 despite Australia winning 4–1. Bedser ruined Australia's hopes of a clean sweep with two 5-wicket hauls in the final Test, which England won. Bedser also claimed 30 wickets at a low cost (17.23) in five Tests against South Africa in 1951, and took 20 wickets at 13.95 in four Tests against India the following year.

Thirty-nine scalps at 17.49 in the 1953 Ashes enabled Bedser to surpass Clarrie Grimmett's then Test record of 216 wickets, and Bedser held the record for a decade until Brian Statham passed him. Bedser claimed 7–55 and 7–44 at Trent Bridge in the opening Ashes Test of 1953, with the latter his best Test figures. Oddly, Bedser's most unproductive Test in the 1953 Ashes was the last one, which featured the only outright result in the series: a win to England. Bedser had a lot of success against Australian left-handed opener Arthur Morris, who succumbed to Bedser 18 times in 21 Tests.

After taking 10 wickets in two Tests against Pakistan in 1954, Bedser played just two more Tests. Aged 36 as England competed Down Under in 1954–55, Bedser took 1–131 in the first Test after several catches were dropped off his bowling. Bedser was omitted for the rest of the series which England won as Frank Tyson replaced Bedser as the spearhead of the bowling line-up. Bedser claimed 4 wickets in his final Test which was against South Africa at Old Trafford in July 1955, and another five years passed before he retired from county cricket.

Bedser's first-class career yielded one century from 576 innings, and his Test career yielded just one half-century. This came in the 1948 Ashes contest at Headingley where he compiled 79 at number four, after coming in as a nightwatchman.

Alec Bedser (1918–2010)

Matches: 51
Runs scored: 714
Batting average: 12.75
100s/50s: 0/1
Top score: 79
Balls bowled: 15,918
Wickets: 236
Bowling average: 24.89
5 wickets in innings: 15
10 wickets in match: 5
Best bowling: 7–44
Catches/stumpings: 26/–

(Sir) Ian Botham

Ian 'Beefy' Botham earned enormous recognition for great deeds on the cricket field, while also gaining notoriety for a number of off-field incidents. He also played soccer for Yeovil Town and Scunthorpe

United. In *Out on a Limb*, Martin Crowe described Botham as a 'daring fellow' and that 'he was probably the biggest thing the British had had since Winston Churchill.'

Botham's skill as a hard-hitting batsman and aggressive fast–medium bowler were obvious as he took 21 Tests to register 1000 runs and 100 wickets, then another 21 Tests to register 2000 runs and 200 wickets, and then another 30 Tests to register 3000 runs and 300 wickets. On five occasions he scored a ton and took a 5-wicket innings haul in the same Test, and in one Test he scored a ton and took an 8-wicket innings haul. In another Test, he made a century and claimed a 10-wicket match haul. Botham temporarily held the mantle of Test cricket's leading wicket-taker, and his fielding could also not be underestimated as he held some great slips catches.

Botham captured 5–74 on debut in the third Ashes Test of 1977, despite a wayward opening spell, with Greg Chappell his first victim as the Australian skipper uncharacteristically played a loose delivery onto the stumps. In his second Test, Botham snared 5–21 in Australia's first innings as England took an unbeatable 3–0 series lead. Botham's next opponents were New Zealand and Pakistan, and after the Kiwis beat England for the first time ever in Test cricket, Botham scored 103 and 30 not out and claimed figures of 5–73 and 3–38 in the second Test, as England squared the series. He also memorably ran out Geoff Boycott, ostensibly on purpose, as England sought quick runs in its second innings. Botham subsequently excelled as England romped to innings wins in successive home Tests against Pakistan. He scored 100 at Edgbaston, and then at Lord's he made 108 before claiming 0–17 and his best Test figures of 8–34. In the 1978–79 Ashes, Botham scored 291 runs at 29.10 and captured 23 wickets at 24.65 in England's 5–1 triumph. Australian captain Graham Yallop later suggested the series could have resulted in Australia's favour had Botham been in the Australian side. After Botham held a brilliant catch to dismiss Yallop during that series, Yallop remarked that Botham was 'worth three men in that side at times'. Following Botham's innings of 114 and match figures of 13–106 in India's Golden Jubilee Test at Bombay in 1980, England wicketkeeper Bob Taylor remarked that Botham had the energy of two men.

Yet, as Geoff Armstrong noted in *The 100 Greatest Cricketers*, Botham was much more effective from 1977 to 1982 than he was from season 1982–83 until the end of his career in 1992. He averaged 37.92 with the bat and 23.32 with the ball in his first 54 Tests before averaging 29 with the bat and 37.84 with the ball in his last 48 Tests.

A victory as Test skipper eluded Botham as he captained England in eight draws and four losses from 1980 to 1981. Admittedly, nine of those matches were against the then almighty West Indies. 'He was too much of an individual to lead a team, too undisciplined to impose authority,' Kersi Meher-Homji reported in *Cricket's Great All-Rounders*. Things went pear-shaped in the first two Tests of the 1981 Ashes as England trailed 1–0, with Botham scoring two ducks at Lord's. Botham promptly stood down as captain when the selectors were ready to reinstate Mike Brearley in any case, but then Botham produced phenomenal performances that helped England snatch two dramatic come-from-behind victories. A 6-wicket haul and a 50 were not enough to prevent England from sliding towards an innings defeat at Headingley, before he hammered 149 not out and was well supported by the tailenders. The rest, as they say, is history as Australia lost by 18 runs when needing 130, as Botham took a wicket and a catch, while Bob Willis claimed 8–43. In the next Test at Edgbaston, Botham's bowling was the catalyst for England's 29-run win as he claimed 5–1 in a 28-ball spell to dismiss Australia for 121. As the hosts gained a 3–1 series lead, Botham scored another ton and captured 5 wickets at Old Trafford, before he claimed 10 scalps in the drawn fifth Test.

Botham again had great batting figures against India in the early 1980s, and his 208 against India at the Oval in 1982 was his biggest Test score. His bowling however was patchy as he averaged in the mid 30s in some series. In the 1982–83 Ashes, Botham was remembered for taking the final wicket that gave England a 3-run victory in Melbourne, only for Australia to win back the urn.

Knee and back injuries hampered Botham at various stages in the 1980s, and the pace of his bowling gradually slowed after he gained weight. Amongst a number of escapades, Botham was handed a two-month suspension in 1986 for marijuana use. Despite the notoriety that dogged Botham, it should not be forgotten that he raised a lot of money for worthy causes, including leukemia research, as he took part in lengthy charity walks.

Botham had some cricketing highlights from 1982–83 onwards but could not produce heroic performances as consistently as he did from 1977 to 1982. In the opening Ashes Test of 1986–87 he blazed 22 runs in one over on his way to 138, but his series figures were hardly special, as he averaged a little over 30 with bat and ball. In 1987, Botham and Allan Lamb were involved in a gritty unbroken fifth partnership to save a Test against Pakistan at the Oval. In his book *Botham's Century*, Botham wrote:

> *Many observers spoke and wrote in glowing terms of the magnificent self-restraint shown by two natural-born hitters, all for the cause. The truth was that, after a skinful of curry and lager the night before, neither of us was in any fit state to do anything other than block the vindaloo out of it.*

Perhaps the biggest sign that Botham was well past his prime came in the 1989 Ashes, as the then 33-year-old was recalled as England trailed 2–0. In his three appearances, he scored just 62 runs at 15.50 and claimed 3 wickets at 80.33, as England was outplayed. Geoff Armstrong nonetheless deemed that Botham's first 54 Tests 'are the true measure of his greatness'.

Ian Botham (b.1955)

Matches: 102
Runs scored: 5200
Batting average: 33.54
100s/50s: 14/22
Top score: 208
Balls bowled: 21,815
Wickets: 383
Bowling average: 28.40
5 wickets in innings: 27
10 wickets in match: 4
Best bowling: 8–34
Catches/stumpings: 120/–

Geoff Boycott

A dogged, gritty and gutsy opening batsman who occupied the crease for long periods when well set, Geoff Boycott was renowned for scoring at a snail's pace while achieving a fine record. Many fellow England players made it clear in various publications what they thought of him. In *Botham's Century*, Ian Botham described Boycott as self-absorbed, self-motivated and hard-working, and a great player but a strange bloke. Botham considered Boycott 'was not a natural cricketer, but he made himself into a very good one'. Bob Willis wrote in his 1996 book *Six of the Best* that Boycott 'was probably the greatest manufactured talent the game has ever seen' and 'the most dependable opening batsman of his time'. As Willis remarked: 'From a technical point of view, Boycott had one of the best defensive methods there has ever been. He simply tried to eliminate any possible chance of getting out before he started to think about scoring runs.' In *Geoff Boycott A Cricketing Hero* Martyn Moxon, however, considered it 'ridiculous' that Boycott was described as a 'manufactured player'. Keith Fletcher meanwhile commented in *Ashes to Ashes*: 'It is hardly a novel observation to say that Boycott was self-centred. He would not help young batsmen in the England team, which probably came down to a fear of losing his place. To my mind, this was absolutely stupid.

In *Greatest Moments in Cricket*, RG Grant wrote that when Boycott was 37, he:

> ...had long been the most controversial figure in English cricket. Since the mid-1960s he had been without question the finest England opener, a true successor to those other great Yorkshiremen Herbert Sutcliffe and Len Hutton, with the same perfectionism, the same stubborn determination never to get out...His scoring seemed sometimes wilfully slow, a deliberate, scornful riposte to his critics. His obsession with the perfection of his own batting, it was argued, led him to neglect the interests of his team. He was accused of arrogance and egotism.

It was interesting to note that England never lost a Test featuring a Boycott century, and he reached the milestone 22 times. Boycott's maiden Test ton was in his fourth Test, which England drew before Australia won the series. Boycott averaged around 50 in his first three series: against Australia in 1964, South Africa in 1964–65 and New Zealand in 1965, before briefly losing his place amidst a disappointing series against South Africa. Boycott scored 300 runs at 42.85 without a century in the 1965–66 Ashes before his third Test century was his highest Test score, yet ironically he was dropped for the next Test. Boycott faced 555 balls in 573 minutes as he scored 246 not out against India at Headingley in the first Test of the 1967 series, having taken nearly six hours to reach 100. Boycott missed some cricket in the late 1960s and early 1970s due to injury, and in 1969 he scored two ducks in three Tests against New Zealand. But in 1967–68 and 1969 he played a vital role in England's series wins against the West Indies as he averaged 66.14 and 54, having scored a century in the first two Tests of the 1969 series. His achievements were also crucial in England's series wins against Australia in 1970–71 and Pakistan in 1971, as he scored 657 runs at 93.86 in the 1970–71 Ashes, before notching two tons in as many Tests against Pakistan. A brief form slump was followed by good scores against New Zealand and the West Indies, with Boycott's stoic double of 99 and 112 helping England win the series in the final Test of the 1973–74 series in the Caribbean. But later in 1974 he stood down from Test cricket and made himself unavailable for three years. Years later, Boycott remarked that he had lost the hunger for Test cricket, although many sources have indicated that Boycott was unhappy with the appointment of Mike Denness as England skipper. Boycott also had a number of troubles with authorities at his county, Yorkshire.

Boycott's return to Test cricket took place at Trent Bridge in the 1977 Ashes, with his 107 not out and 80 helping England to a 7-wicket triumph and 2–0 series lead. It could have been far different, however. Boycott was dropped in the slips after taking three hours to reach 20, and was chiefly responsible for the run-out of local favourite Derek Randall. In the next Test at Headingley, his home ground, Boycott not only made 191 to help England secure the Ashes, but also became the first player to reach his 100th first-class century in a Test. Boycott was easily the highest runscorer of the 1977 Ashes with 442 runs at 147.33, despite missing the first two Tests.

Boycott was appointed England captain in the final Test of a drawn series in Pakistan in 1977–78, before he led England to its first ever Test defeat against New Zealand. Boycott at least had the consolation of gaining a win as skipper when England squared the series. His returns in the 1978–79 and 1981 Ashes series were below-par, but at Lord's in the 1981 Ashes the 40-year-old Boycott played his 100th Test. Against the West Indies in 1980, Boycott often had a torrid time against a lethal pace attack but nonetheless averaged 40.89 in five Tests without a century. He didn't have a happy time in England's tour of India in 1981–82, despite passing Garry Sobers as Test cricket's highest runscorer. Boycott played in four of the six Tests before parting ways, after controversy arose during the fourth Test as he played golf following his claim that illness prevented him from fielding. Before long, he took part in a rebel tour of South Africa. His Test career over, Boycott remained a controversial figure as he played first-class cricket until 1986 and went on to become an outspoken commentator.

Geoff Boycott (b.1940)

Matches: 108
Runs scored: 8114
Batting average: 47.72
100s/50s: 22/42
Top score: 246*
Balls bowled: 944
Wickets: 7
Bowling average: 54.57
5 wickets in innings: –
10 wickets in match: –
Best bowling: 3–47
Catches/stumpings: 33/–

Denis Compton

Denis Compton was a sporting hero rather than merely a popular cricketer as he proved entertaining in cricket and soccer. Compton scored 15 goals in 54 soccer matches for Arsenal from 1936–37 to 1949–50 and collected an FA Cup winners' medal in 1950. His Test cricket career spanned nearly two decades — although World War II took a chunk out of his career — and a batting average of 50.06 did not reveal the full extent of his contributions. As David Gower reported in *David Gower's 50 Greatest Cricketers* of all time:

> Compton was as glamorous a cricketer as England have ever possessed. He played in a style that captivated the crowds, last-second sweeps blending with sumptuous cover drives, and there was a devil-may-care attitude to everything he did that meant he was not someone to take your eye off.

Peter Arnold meanwhile reported in *The Illustrated Encyclopedia of World Cricket*: 'He had the gift of communicating to the spectator all his own feelings about the bowling, whether it be confidence or concern.

This, with the fluency and apparent orthodoxy of his stroke-play, made his batting fascinating to watch.'

Only 19 years old in his Test debut against New Zealand at the Oval in August 1937, Compton scored 65 and was unluckily run-out when backing up. His next Test was his Ashes debut, in which he scored 102 at Trent Bridge, before he also helped England draw the following Test with a resilient 76 not out following rain. His second Test century was against the West Indies and, with a record of 468 runs at 52 from eight Tests, Compton lost some of, potentially, his best years in the wartime.

From 1946 to 1949, Compton scored 2664 runs at 61.95 from 28 Tests. He was one of many England players who struggled for much of the 1946–47 Ashes, but he made a brilliant double of 147 and 103 not out at Adelaide. Compton's most prolific series was against South Africa in 1947 as he scored 65, 163, 208, 115, 6, 30, 53 and 113 in England's 3–0 series win, and shared in partnerships of 370 and 228 with Bill Edrich in the second and third Tests. As England was humbled 4–0 in the 1948 Ashes, Compton was second only to Australia's Arthur Morris in the runscoring department as Compton notched 562 runs at 62.44. Compton scored 184 in an 8-wicket loss at Trent Bridge, and in a draw at Old Trafford he retired hurt early in his innings after edging a bouncer into his head, before returning to the crease and making an undefeated 145. Compton averaged around 50 against South Africa and New Zealand, but then he had a tough time after undergoing knee surgery in 1950. He scored three ducks and averaged just 7.57 in the 1950–51 Ashes, before returning to form against South Africa as he began with an innings of 112 and finished the series with 312 runs at 52. Compton averaged only in the 30s in the 1953 and 1954–55 Ashes, but had the honour of sweeping the winning runs in 1953. His two Test tons in 1954 were against the West Indies and Pakistan, with his highest Test score resulting on the latter occasion, as he took merely 287 minutes to compile 278 at Trent Bridge. Although the Pakistanis drew the series when they won the final Test, Compton scored a courageous 53 on a wet surface at the Oval.

Compton averaged 54.67 against South Africa in 1955 and scored his final Test ton as he made 158 at Old Trafford, only for the Springboks to win the match and go on to draw the series. Compton had his right kneecap removed in 1955, and played just six more Tests. He notched 94 and 35 not out in his lone appearance in the 1956 Ashes: in the final Test at the Oval. His final series contained only 242 runs at 24.20 but it was just enough to keep his average above 50.

One surprising aspect of Compton's cricket career was that he took 622 wickets in 515 first-class matches, yet bowled only occasionally in Tests. His 25 wickets, at a high cost, included innings figures of 5–70 against South Africa at Cape Town in January 1949.

Denis Compton (1918–1997)

Matches: 78
Runs scored: 5807
Batting average: 50.06
100s/50s: 17/28
Top score: 278
Balls bowled: 2710
Wickets: 25
Bowling average: 56.40
5 wickets in innings: 1
10 wickets in match: –
Best bowling: 5–70
Catches/stumpings: 49/–

Alastair Cook

Alastair Cook entered the record books numerous times, including when he became the first Englishman to score more than 22 Test centuries. A stylish, left-handed opening batsman, Cook made a triple-figure score on the first occasion he encountered India, Pakistan, the West Indies and Bangladesh in Test cricket, and he became the first player to register 1000 Test runs against six different nations. Cook was also the youngest player to register 7000, 8000 and 9000 Test runs, and he was the highest Test runscorer in the ten years leading up to May 2015. The first England cricketer to be involved in 50 Test victories,

Cook also became the first ever player to record a ton in his first five Tests as skipper. Career highlights also included holding aloft the Ashes urn on home soil in 2013 and 2015.

Cook's Test debut was at Nagpur in March 2006 when he made 60 and 104 not out in a draw, before finishing his maiden year with more than 1000 runs. He batted at number three against Pakistan, scoring 105 at Lord's and 127 at Old Trafford before the hosts won the series 3–0. His maiden Ashes series was unsuccessful as Australia won 5–0 at home, with Cook's disappointing 276 runs at 27.60, including a century at Perth. Cook also had sub-standard figures in other Ashes series, with 222 runs at 24.67 in 2009, 277 at 27.70 in 2013, 246 at 24.60 in 2013–14 and 330 at 36.67 in 2015.

In 2007 Cook again scored a Test century at Lord's and Old Trafford during a 3–0 series victory, this time against the West Indies. Later in the year, Cook failed miserably in a first Test loss to Sri Lanka before scoring 81, 62, 13 and 118 as the remaining two Tests were drawn. After failing to crack a Test ton in 2008, Cook registered two against the West Indies and one against South Africa in 2009. In England's Ashes victory, Cook's best score was 95 at Lord's. In March 2010 he scored 173 and 109 not out in successive Tests in Bangladesh, before having a lean run in home Tests against Bangladesh and Pakistan. He returned to form with 110 at the Oval, where Pakistan had its sole victory of the series. The 2010–11 Ashes was perhaps the pinnacle for Cook as his scores were 67, 235 not out, 148, 32, 13, 82 and 189, with his double ton ensuring England was safe in the first Test, before England won three of the remaining Tests by an innings. He accumulated 1287 runs in 2010 and wasn't quite as prolific in 2011, despite starting with 189 and making three further triple-figure scores, including his Test best 294 at Edgbaston, as England thrashed India.

Cook had a strong year in 2012 as he achieved 1249 Test runs, including four centuries. Having briefly deputised as captain in 2010, Cook became England's Test captain following the retirement of Andrew Strauss, after England lost 2–0 to South Africa in 2012. Cook led England to its first Test series win in India for 27 years, and notched 562 runs in the four Tests. His knocks of 41 and 176 couldn't prevent India winning the first Test by 9 wickets, before he made 122 and 18 not out in a 10-wicket victory. Cook scored 190 and 1 as his team took the series lead before he failed twice in a draw.

Cook's two Test tons in 2013 were against New Zealand, with his 116 at Dunedin helping salvage a draw, before his 130 at Headingley helped seal England's 2–0 series victory. After not making any Test tons in 2014, Cook compiled three centuries and eight half-centuries in 2015 as he amassed 1364 runs at 54.56. His 76 and 59 not out were handy in a 9-wicket win over the West Indies in the Caribbean, only for the hosts to draw the series after Cook made 105 in England's first innings at Bridgetown. England also surrendered a series lead against New Zealand, with Cook scoring 16, 162, 75 and 56 in the two-match series. Despite modest scores in England's Ashes triumph, Cook was second only to Joe Root in the England batting aggregates and averages. Cook made 263 in a high-scoring draw against Pakistan in late 2015, before making solid but not big scores as England lost 2–0 in neutral territory. Cook averaged just 23 in England's subsequent series in South Africa, but he led England to a 2–1 series win. As of February 2016, he had captained England to 19 wins, 15 losses and 11 draws.

Alastair Cook (b.1984)*

Matches: 126
Runs scored: 9964
Batting average: 46.56
100s/50s: 28/47
Top score: 294
Balls bowled: 18
Wickets: 1
Bowling average: 7.00
5 wickets in innings: –
10 wickets in match: –
Best bowling: 1–6
Catches/stumpings: 125/–
* still playing as of 2016

(Sir) Colin Cowdrey

Colin Cowdrey's batting average of 44.06 might suggest he had a commendable Test career rather than a great one, but his longevity and influence ensured he was a prominent figure in world cricket, not just English cricket. According to Ian Botham, in *Botham's Century*, Cowdrey was 'one of the greatest ambassadors world cricket has ever known'.

A gifted strokemaker with a sumptuous cover drive, Cowdrey was also a reliable slips fielder. He became the first person to play 100 cricket Tests, and he overtook Wally Hammond as the leading runscorer, after Hammond held the record for 33 years. Usually a middle-order batsman, Cowdrey opened on occasions. He matched Hammond and Geoff Boycott with 22 Test centuries, with England losing on one occasion when Cowdrey scored a Test ton, whereas England never lost when Hammond or Boycott scored a Test ton. Cowdrey not only scored a century against each Test-playing nation at the time (Australia, India, New Zealand, Pakistan, South Africa and the West Indies), but did so both home and away. Cowdrey also overtook Hammond's record of most catches by a non-wicketkeeper in Tests, and Cowdrey equalled Colin Blythe's record of six Australian tours.

Cowdrey's first Test series was the 1954–55 Ashes in which he scored 319 runs at 35.44, and his 102 in the third Test at Melbourne was a decisive contribution in the context of the series. The next best score was 30 in England's sub-standard total of 191 before England trailed by 40 runs on the first innings, but came back to win by 128 runs and lead the series 2–1, before making it 3–1. Cowdrey's first 18 Tests yielded modest figures of 1009 runs at 32.55, before England's home series against the West Indies in 1957 was the catalyst for one of Cowdrey's career highlights. After the hosts trailed by 175 runs with 7 wickets remaining in the first Test at Edgbaston, Cowdrey scored 154 as he shared a match-saving 411-run stand with Peter May who made 285 not out. Cowdrey scored 152 in the next Test which England won by an innings, before winning the series 3–0.

Cowdrey averaged beyond 50 against India in 1959 and against the West Indies in 1959–60, and skippered England in the last two Tests of each series. England cantered to a 5–0 victory against India before successive draws against the West Indies enabled England to maintain a 1–0 series lead. Cowdrey led England in eight wins, four losses and 15 draws between 1959 and 1969, but he was never the skipper in any of his visits to Australia. His first full series as captain was against South Africa in 1960, with England winning 3–0, while he had mixed results with the bat.

In the 1961 Ashes, Cowdrey's form was disappointing, apart from an innings of 93, while he and May shared the captaincy as England lost a winnable series 2–1. Ted Dexter subsequently took on the captaincy, although Cowdrey led England to an innings win over Pakistan in 1962. England accounted for Pakistan 4–0 while Cowdrey scored 409 runs at 81.80, with 159 in the first Test at Edgbaston followed by his highest Test score of 182 in the fifth Test at the Oval. After gall stones affected Cowdrey in 1962, the following year he suffered a broken wrist when facing West Indian paceman Wes Hall in a Lord's Test. Cowdrey heroically returned to the crease, albeit at the non-striker's end, with 2 balls remaining, as England hung on for a thrilling draw.

Cowdrey scored centuries in successive draws in India in 1963–64 before enjoying good form against Australia, New Zealand and South Africa in the ensuing two years. He regained the captaincy for three Tests against the West Indies in 1966, with the West Indies winning while his form was below par. Cowdrey redeemed himself as he led England to a 1–0 victory in the Caribbean in 1967–68, while he scored two centuries amidst a personal best series tally of 534 runs at 66.75. Cowdrey marked his then Test-record 100th appearance with a century against Australia at Edgbaston in 1968, before his final series as skipper was unpleasant, as riots disrupted England's 1968–69 tour of Pakistan. All three Tests were drawn, after Cowdrey scored his last Test ton in the opening encounter.

An Achilles injury set Cowdrey back in 1969, before his returns were modest in 1970 and 1971, as he became Test cricket's leading runscorer. It appeared that Cowdrey's final Test was against Pakistan in 1971, but he was recalled for the 1974–75 Ashes series Down Under, after Dennis Amiss and John Edrich were injured in the opening Test. Nearing his 42nd birthday, Cowdrey was not the oldest player in the touring party, as Fred Titmus was a month older. Cowdrey did plenty of ducking and weaving as Dennis Lillee and Jeff Thomson were in deadly form, but Cowdrey provided resistance despite managing just 165 runs at 18.33, with a highest score of 41.

Colin Cowdrey (1932–2000)

Matches: 114
Runs scored: 7624
Batting average: 44.06
100s/50s: 22/38
Top score: 182
Balls bowled: 119
Wickets: –
Bowling average: –
5 wickets in innings: –
10 wickets in match: –
Best bowling: –
Catches/stumpings: 120/–

Andrew Flintoff

Andrew Flintoff was a mercurial cricketer who had the rare ability to single-handedly change a match or series. He wasn't always as consistent as he perhaps could have been, and he also had injury problems. Averaging a little over 30 with bat and ball does not suggest Flintoff was in the top echelon of all-rounders, as he scored only five centuries and captured only three 5-wicket innings hauls in his 79 Tests. Passing 3,500 runs and 200 wickets was commendable enough in any case. Flintoff liked to attack the bowling as he was a clean striker of the ball, and with the ball in hand he could swing and cut it with devastating effect while bowling at around 145 kilometres per hour.

At times in his career, particularly early on, the man known as 'Freddie' was criticised for his lifestyle choices and for being overweight. Flintoff's first two Tests were against South Africa in 1998, with England coming from 1–0 down to win the series as Flintoff was out of form with 1 wicket for 112 runs and 17 runs at 5.67, following two ducks in the decider. After his first 21 Tests, Flintoff averaged less than 20 with the bat and more than 45 with the ball. His maiden Test ton was in his thirteenth match, which was against New Zealand at Christchurch in March 2002, before he missed the 2002–03 Ashes due to injury. Against the Proteas in 2003, Flintoff scored 142 in an innings loss before his 95 in the final Test helped England draw the series. When England toured the West Indies the following year, Flintoff finally claimed 5 wickets in an innings before he followed up with his third Test century in the next Test. As England hosted the West Indies in the same year, Flintoff blasted seven sixes at Edgbaston during his highest Test score of 167, with his father dropping one of the sixes while spectating. Flintoff also dismissed Brian Lara a few times as England romped to a 4–0 series win.

Flintoff took 68 Test scalps in 2005, with that year's Ashes series proving to be the peak of his career. His series figures of 402 runs at 40.20 and 24 wickets at 27.29 were solid, while his impact at crucial times was the key, much like Ian Botham in the 1981 Ashes. In the Edgbaston Test which England won by 2 runs to level the series, Flintoff's blazing scores of 68 and 73 were decisive; particularly the latter, which helped add 51 priceless runs for the last wicket. Flintoff also took 7 wickets at Edgbaston with some excellent bowling and, following the tense and hard-fought cricket, Flintoff consoled Lee at the end of the match in a sign of good sportsmanship. In the Trent Bridge Test, which England won to gain the series lead, Flintoff hit 102 — his final Test century — before scoring a vital 26 in a small but somewhat tricky run chase. At the Oval, where a draw was sufficient for England, Flintoff struck 72 and then took 5–78.

Flintoff also shone at crucial moments in India less than a year later as he captained the tourists to a 1–1 draw. He scored 70 and 51 and claimed 4–96 and 0–11 in a 9-wicket loss, before taking 4 wickets and twice making 50, as England squared the series. Flintoff also led England to a drawn series against Sri Lanka in 2006, although this time England squandered a 1–0 series lead. An ankle injury hampered Flintoff in 2006 and 2007, and the 2006–07 Ashes was a nightmare, as he led his country to a 5–0 defeat, while he scored 254 runs at 28.22

and took 11 wickets at 43.73. The ensuing couple of years produced mixed results for Flintoff, who continued to battle injuries, before he bowed out in a blaze of glory in the 2009 Ashes. He scored 200 runs at 33.33 and took just 8 wickets at 52.13, but again he stood out at times when it mattered most. In the second Test his 5–92 helped England to a 1–0 lead, before the hosts needed to win the final Test to regain the Ashes. Flintoff didn't impress with bat or ball, but a great piece of fielding produced the crucial run-out of Ricky Ponting in Australia's second innings as Australia gradually lost its way.

Andrew Flintoff (b.1977)

Matches: 79
Runs scored: 3845
Batting average: 31.78
100s/50s: 5/26
Top score: 167
Balls bowled: 14,951
Wickets: 226
Bowling average: 32.79
5 wickets in innings: 3
10 wickets in match: –
Best bowling: 5–58
Catches/stumpings: 52/–

(Dr) W G Grace

Although limited to 22 Tests, while his Test statistics were nothing special, Dr William Gilbert Grace was an automatic selection in this list of all-time greats due to his legacy in the sport. Some sources have even rated him as the greatest cricketer ever.

It is impossible to imagine what cricket might have been were it not for WG Grace, who was a conspicuous figure with his ample physique and long beard. He has been credited with putting cricket on the map and attracting people to the sport. His first-class record was staggering, to put it mildly, and although his figures are not 100 per cent conclusive, he played between 850 and 900 first-class matches from 1865 until at least 1908. He scored close to 55,000 runs at an average just below 40, took more than 2800 wickets at an average of about 18, and held between 850 and 900 catches. As Peter Arnold wrote in *The Illustrated Encyclopedia of World Cricket*, Grace 'dominated the world of cricket' for nearly 40 years and was reportedly the most recognised figure in England along with Prime Minister William Ewart Gladstone. Vic Marks wrote in *The Wisden Illustrated History of Cricket* that Grace 'became as celebrated as Queen Victoria herself.'

All of Grace's Tests were against Australia, although only three were in Australia. He was 32 when he made his Test debut at the Oval during 1880, in the fourth ever cricket Test, and had an outstanding match. Grace's 152 was the first-ever Test ton for England, and then he claimed 1–2 and 2–66 with the ball as the tourists had to follow-on after the hosts compiled 420. Grace scored 9 not out as England won by 5 wickets, after Billy Murdoch scored 153 not out in Australia's second innings.

Grace averaged only 28.39 with the bat in his remaining Tests, with five half-centuries and one century. His highest score was 170 which helped England to an innings win at the Oval to complete a series clean sweep in 1886, although he was dropped four times before reaching triple figures. He bowled only sparingly in Test cricket, hence claiming only 6 wickets at 28 following his debut, while his fielding was a quality factor. England won 13 and lost five of the Tests in which Grace played, with England winning the series in 1884, 1886, 1888, 1890, 1893 and 1896 while losing his sole series Down Under in 1891–92 after one-off Tests went England's way in 1880 and Australia's way in 1882. Grace was captain on 13 occasions from 1888 to 1899, with England winning eight times and losing just twice. After Allan Steel led England to defeat in the opening Test of 1888, the 40-year-old Grace took over the captaincy for the remainder of the three-Test series which England won following two innings victories. Grace was 51 when he led England at Trent Bridge in the drawn opening Test of 1899, and it turned out to be his Test farewell as he subsequently stood down, ostensibly because he felt he had become a liability in the field.

Some gamesmanship and not-so-sporting incidents have been attributed to Grace, although the authenticity of them remains doubtful. One incident that remains indisputable however was his run-out of Sammy Jones in the memorable 1882 Test which Australia won by 7 runs after dismissing England for 77. Grace broke the wicket as Jones left his crease to inspect the pitch and repair a divot; an act within the laws of the game but something that earned Pakistan's Javed Miandad plenty of criticism when he did something similar in a Test nearly a century later. Grace's actions reportedly infuriated Australian fast bowler Fred Spofforth, who promptly lived up to his nickname of 'The Demon' and inspired Australia's memorable triumph.

WG Grace (1848–1915)

Matches: 22
Runs scored: 1098
Batting average: 32.29
100s/50s: 2/5
Top score: 170
Balls bowled: 666
Wickets: 9
Bowling average: 26.22
5 wickets in innings: –
10 wickets in match: –
Best bowling: 2–12
Catches/stumpings: 39/–

Wally Hammond

Wally Hammond was Test cricket's highest runscorer from 1937 to 1970 and was known for his attractive style, as he was particularly brilliant at driving the ball through the offside. Usually a number three or four batsman, Hammond was also a fine slips fielder and useful fast–medium bowler. As was the case with Geoff Boycott, Hammond scored 22 Test centuries and was never in a losing side when he registered three figures. Hammond turned his first two Test tons into double tons, in his tenth and eleventh Tests.

Incredibly, Hammond's Test career could have been over before it even began as he was severely ill in 1925 and 1926. He recovered fully and was one of 12 Test debutants at Johannesburg in the opening Test of the England versus South Africa series in 1927–28. Hammond scored 51 and then took his best ever Test figures of 5–36 in England's 10-wicket triumph. He averaged 40.13 with the bat and had his most prolific series with the ball in his maiden series, as he captured 15 wickets. Hammond went on to establish himself as a world class batsman in the 1928–29 Ashes as he compiled 905 runs at 113.13 in England's 4–1 triumph. From the second Test to the fourth Test his scores were 251, 200, 32, 119 not out and 177, and he was the first player to score successive Test double centuries.

Hammond scored two centuries in four Tests against South Africa in 1929 before he averaged just 34 in the 1930 Ashes, as leg spinner Clarrie Grimmett dismissed him five times. In this series, Don Bradman's 974 runs eclipsed Hammond's 1928–29 series figure. Hammond averaged between 55 and 65 against South Africa and New Zealand in 1930–31 and 1931, before scoring two centuries while averaging 55 in the 1932–33 Bodyline series and also taking several handy wickets. Hammond completed the Bodyline series in style, as he sealed England's 4–1 victory with a six at Sydney. In a follow-up tour of New Zealand, Hammond scored 227 at Christchurch before compiling the then highest Test score in the second Test at Auckland. Hammond's unconquered 336 took just 318 minutes and contained 34 fours and ten sixes.

Hammond's form was disappointing in the next couple of years as he averaged in the low 20s and didn't score a half-century for 22 consecutive innings. One highlight was 43 and 29 not out to guide England to a nervous 4-wicket win on a wet and difficult Bridgetown pitch in January 1935. As was the case in the 1932–33 Ashes, Hammond struck a six to secure the result. Hammond had had some health troubles, but he showed glimpses of returning to form at home against South Africa in 1935 as he averaged 64.83 without making a century and also took 6 wickets at 24.33. Hammond scored 167, 217 and 5 not out in two home Tests against India in 1936 before scoring consistently in the next few years.

The Sydney Cricket Ground again proved a happy place for Hammond as he scored 231 not out in the second Test of the 1936–37 Ashes, after his previous Test scores in Sydney had been 251, 112, 101 and 75 not out. Hammond also claimed 12 wickets in the 1936–37 Ashes, only for England to squander a 2–0 series lead. In the first Test of the 1937 series against New Zealand, Hammond passed Jack Hobbs as Test cricket's leading runscorer during an innings of 140, before he took on the captaincy for the 1938 Ashes. He held the position until the end of his Test career in 1946–47, for a record of four wins, three losses and 13 draws.

Hammond was among several batsmen to make a massive score in the drawn Ashes series of 1938 as he scored a masterly 240 at Lord's. But the series was chiefly remembered for Len Hutton bettering Hammond's then record Test score by 28 runs at the Oval. Hammond scored 609 runs at 87 against South Africa in 1938–39, with three centuries, including 140 in the final Test, as England amassed 654–5 and needed only 42 more runs for a phenomenal victory when the Test was forced to be stopped. During the same series, Hammond took the last of his 83 Test wickets.

Hammond scored his final Test century and averaged 55.80 in a 1–0 series win against the West Indies in 1939, before being involved with the Royal Air Force. His next Test cricket experience was against India in 1946, as he notched 119 runs at 39.67 in a 1–0 series win. Hammond had an unhappy time Down Under in 1946–47 as his final Ashes series began with a landslide loss and didn't improve much as the tour progressed. Battling fibrositis, the 43-year-old Hammond scored just 168 runs at 21 with a highest score of 37, as Australia inflicted a 3–0 drubbing, and he missed the final Test of his only series defeat as skipper. His Test farewell was a one-off match in New Zealand in March 1947, with rain ensuring a draw, after Hammond scored 79 on day two.

Wally Hammond (1903–1965)

Matches: 85
Runs scored: 7249
Batting average: 58.45
100s/50s: 22/24
Top score: 336*
Balls bowled: 7969
Wickets: 83
Bowling average: 37.80
5 wickets in innings: 2
10 wickets in match: –
Best bowling: 5–36
Catches/stumpings: 110/–

(Sir) Jack Hobbs

Whilst it is hard to believe anyone will get close to Don Bradman's Test and first-class batting averages, it is also hard to imagine anyone passing Jack Hobbs' first-class aggregate and number of centuries. He accumulated 61,760 runs at 50.70 and compiled 199 centuries in 834 first-class matches from 1905 to 1934. He was the highest runscorer in Test cricket for just over 12 years from the end of 1924, and always seemed to adjust to whatever conditions and opponents he encountered. In *The Illustrated Encyclopedia of World Cricket*, Peter Arnold described Hobbs as 'a complete batsman, classical in method, calm in temperament, and supremely efficient in execution'. Known as 'The Master', Hobbs formed a tremendous opening partnership with Herbert Sutcliffe and was rated by Percy Fender as 'the greatest batsman the world has ever known', according to Hobbs' profile at *Cricinfo*.

Hobbs was introduced to Test cricket in the second match of the 1907–08 Ashes, scoring 83 and 28 in a 1-wicket triumph, before completing the series with 302 runs at 43.14 as Australia won 4–1. Hobbs was out to the first ball he faced in the 1909 Ashes, which produced 132 runs at 26.40, before he missed two Tests with a finger injury. His first away series was against South Africa in 1910, when he showed he could excel against pace and spin. He batted down the order in the third Test before reverting to opener and failing with 1 and 0 in the fourth Test, and then cracking his breakthrough Test ton in the final Test as he made 187. Hobbs also opened the bowling at times but he claimed just 1 wicket: his only ever Test scalp. Hobbs' first Ashes tour of Australia was a resounding success in 1911–12 as he scored three centuries — including another score of 187 — while amassing 662 runs at 82.75. Hobbs also had decent figures against Australia and South Africa in 1912, and didn't score a century despite coming close a couple of times against the Springboks in 1913–14. He still averaged 63.29 in that series, and his Test record stood at 2465 runs at 57.33 from 28 appearances when World War I brought a halt to international sport. After the war, a notable change in Hobbs' batting was that he played more off the back foot.

Although the 1920–21 Ashes series was a nightmare for England, Hobbs made two tons and scored 505 runs at 50.50. Hobbs played in only the third Test in the 1921 Ashes and didn't bat, having missed the first two Tests with a thigh injury, before suffering appendicitis upon his return. Illness restricted Hobbs for a couple of years before he scored 2077 runs at 67 from 21 Tests between 1924 and 1928–29.

Hobbs and Sutcliffe began their Test opening partnership in style as their first two stands were 136 and 268 runs in innings victories against the Springboks in 1924. Hobbs scored 76 and 211 in those two Tests, and finished the series with 355 runs at 71. Hobbs was prolific in the 1924–25 and 1926 Ashes, with 573 runs at 63.67 Down Under before posting 486 at 81 on home turf. In the first three Tests of the 1924–25 series, Hobbs was unfortunate that his scores of 115, 57, 154, 22, 119 and 27 were in losing causes. During his innings of 119 in the Lord's Test of 1926, Hobbs became the first person to register 4000 Test runs before he scored another century in the final Test, which England won to regain the Ashes.

Illness and injury hampered Hobbs in 1927 before he took part in the first Test series involving the West Indies: the only time Hobbs contested neither Australia nor South Africa in Tests. Hobbs missed the Lord's Test before scoring 53 at Old Trafford and 159 at the Oval, as

England won each match by an innings. Hobbs was outshone by Wally Hammond in the 1928–29 Ashes, although the 46-year-old Hobbs still averaged 50.11 with his sole century — his last in Tests — coming in the final match, which Australia won to prevent England clean sweeping the series. Injuries and health problems restricted Hobbs to one Test against South Africa in 1929, before Hobbs' last Test series was the 1930 Ashes. He started well with 78 and 74 in a victory at Trent Bridge, but he finished disappointingly with 47 and 9 at the Oval as Australia took the series. His modest series figures of 301 runs at 33.44 left him with 3636 runs at 54.27 in his 41 Tests against Australia while he had 1562 runs at 60.08 from 18 Tests against South Africa.

Jack Hobbs (1882–1963)

Matches: 61
Runs scored: 5410
Batting average: 56.94
100s/50s: 15/28
Top score: 211
Balls bowled: 376
Wickets: 1
Bowling average: 165.00
5 wickets in innings: –
10 wickets in match: –
Best bowling: 1–19
Catches/stumpings: 17/–

(Sir) Len Hutton

Len Hutton wrote himself into the record books at the age of 22 when he scored 364 as an opener for England in the final Ashes Test of 1938. It was the highest individual Test score at the time, and has remained the highest individual Test score by an England player. England's total in that Test (903–7 declared) has remained an all-time England high in Test cricket, while the margin (an innings and 579 runs) has also remained the biggest ever margin in Test cricket. Renowned cricket writer David Frith reported in *Australia versus England: A Pictorial History of Every Test Match Since 1877* that many an English schoolboy was able to recite details of this Test 'with greater ease than his multiplication tables'.

Nonetheless there were many things that typified Hutton as an all-time Test great. He was dismissed for 0 and 1 on debut against New Zealand in 1937, but an even 100 in the following Test showed it was worth persevering with him. It was in just his second series that Hutton became a Test record-breaker. In his first Ashes Test he again scored 100, before failing twice in the next Test and producing his heroics in his sixth Test appearance, as he batted for a little over 13 hours.

The suspension of cricket due to World War II was a case of bad timing for Hutton, as his record stood at 1345 runs at 67.25 from 13 Tests. As if missing Test cricket for six years wasn't bad enough, Hutton also sustained a fractured arm which, by his own admission, meant he could no longer play certain strokes the way he wanted. In any case, England still depended on him heavily in terms of runscoring. He had a strong defensive game while also being able to time the ball well. His best score was only 40 in the first three Tests of England's disappointing 1946–47 Ashes campaign, although in the second Test he hit a memorable 37 in just 24 minutes before lunch and was unluckily out hit wicket. Hutton averaged 52.13 in the series, having scored 122 in the final Test, before succumbing to tonsillitis. Hutton averaged in the 40s in successive series against South Africa, the West Indies and Australia, having scored 158 in an opening stand of 359 with Cyril Washbrook against the Africans. However, amidst Australia's dominance in the 1948 Ashes, Hutton was dropped for the third Test after appearing out of form. In the final Test of that series, England's embarrassing first innings of 52 would have been even worse were it not for 30 from Hutton.

The next four series were highly successful for Hutton, as he contested South Africa, New Zealand, the West Indies and Australia, tallying 1912 runs at 73.54 from 17 Tests. Sometimes he shone in losing causes, scoring 202 not out in an innings defeat against the West Indies before scoring 156 not out in a 274-run defeat during the 1950–51 Ashes. Hutton averaged 54 against South Africa in 1951, but also earned the dubious honour of becoming the first batsman to be given out for obstructing the field in a Test.

England broke with tradition when Hutton became captain in 1952 as the leadership was given to a professional rather than an amateur. Hutton didn't lose a series as captain, with England beating India 3–0 and Australia 1–0 before drawing the West Indies 2–2 and Pakistan 1–1, and then beating Australia 3–1 and New Zealand 2–0. Hutton led England in 23 of those Tests, winning eight and losing four. In 1953, Hutton led England to its first Ashes series win in 19 years despite losing the toss in all five Tests. In 1953–54, Hutton primarily engineered England's revival with scores of 169 and 205 in England's victories, after the West Indies won the first two Tests. The captaincy didn't seem to hinder Hutton's batting as he averaged 79.80 against India in 1952, 55.37 against Australia in 1953, and 96.71 against the West Indies in 1953–54. Yet his leadership sometimes came under criticism for negativity, and after averaging just 20.40 in his last nine Tests, he retired due to being worn out, while injury problems again arose. Hutton was knighted in 1956 before becoming a selector, journalist and broadcaster.

Len Hutton (1916–1990)

Matches: 79
Runs scored: 6971
Batting average: 56.67
100s/50s: 19/33
Top score: 364
Balls bowled: 260
Wickets: 3
Bowling average: 77.33
5 wickets in innings: –
10 wickets in match: –
Best bowling: 1–2
Catches/stumpings: 57/–

Alan Knott

Alan Knott was known among his teammates for idiosyncrasies like fidgeting, wearing a floppy hat, having his collar turned up and doing stretches between deliveries. In *Botham's Century*, Ian Botham described Knott's approach as 'unorthodox'. In *Six of the Best*, Bob Willis described Knott as 'a bit of a hypochondriac, especially on tour' as the wicketkeeper did a lot of 'strange-looking exercises' and spent a fair bit of time with the physiotherapist. In David Gower's *50 Greatest Cricketers of All Time*, Gower considered Knott 'had the silkiest of hands' and 'was a complete eccentric, but only bonkers in an endearing rather than an irritating way'.

Knott nonetheless was undeniably enthusiastic and a good influence, while having brilliant wicketkeeping skills and being a decent batsman. Knott was perhaps ahead of his time with regard to fitness and was very athletic behind the stumps, while being equally adept at keeping to spinners and pacemen. Keeping to Derek Underwood's left-arm medium-paced spinners was admirable, particularly on difficult pitches. Some of Knott's catches resulted from great dives, including a one-hander in front of first slip to dismiss Australia's Rick McCosker in 1977. This catch inspired a young teenager named Robert Charles Russell to become a wicketkeeper, with 'Jack' Russell going on to keep wicket for England in 54 Tests from 1988 to 1998.

Knott's first two Tests were on home soil against Pakistan in 1967, and he scored a duck and 28 while taking 12 catches and a stumping. Jim Parks was England's first-choice wicketkeeper for the 1967–68 tour of the Caribbean before Knott was recalled for the final two Tests. He claimed four dismissals and made crucial undefeated scores of 69 and 73 to help England win the series narrowly. His batting was disappointing against Australia in 1968 but his wicketkeeping was first-class, and in the 1968–69 tour of Pakistan he was unlucky not to score his maiden Test ton. Riots at Karachi forced an early finish to the Test as Knott was on 96 not out, before he belatedly made his first Test century in 1970–71. Knott averaged 31.71 without scoring a century — although he scored 73 as a nightwatchman in the first Test — and took 24 dismissals in England's successful Ashes campaign, before being omitted for one Test during the New Zealand tour, as Bob Taylor was chosen for his Test debut. Taylor was unlucky to play in the same era as Knott, who ultimately played 95 Tests compared with Taylor's 57.

Following Taylor's Test debut, Knott played 65 successive Tests. After regaining his place at Taylor's expense, Knott almost became the first wicketkeeper to score two hundreds in a Test as he notched 101 and 96 against New Zealand. As England was outplayed in a drawn Test against Pakistan in 1971, Knott made a worthy 116. Strong with the cut and sweep shots, Knott helped England save several Tests, including one against Pakistan in 1972–73 and another against the West Indies in 1973–74, and he also scored a stubborn 92 in a 1972 Ashes fixture.

Although England was slaughtered in the 1974–75 Ashes series amidst the pace barrage of Dennis Lillee and Jeff Thomson, Knott held his own as he scored three half-centuries and an unbeaten century. England was also well beaten by the West Indies in 1976, although Knott scored 116 in the Headingley Test. In the following fixture at the Oval, Knott scored two half-centuries amidst Michael Holding's destructive bowling, after overtaking Godfrey Evans as England's leading Test gloveman, with Knott having played 13 fewer Tests. England's 1977 Ashes triumph also had a few personal highlights for Knott, including the one-handed catch to dismiss McCosker at Headingley, and also a brilliant catch to dismiss his wicketkeeping opponent earlier in the same match. In the previous Test he made his highest Test score of 135, which was also Knott's fifth and final Test century. In the process he became the first wicketkeeper to tally 4000 Test runs.

Knott didn't play Test cricket in 1978 or 1979 due to taking part in World Series Cricket, but at least this gave Taylor a well-earned run with the gloves for England. Knott was back in the Test team when England hosted the West Indies in 1980, although he had a miserable series with the bat as he averaged just 5.16. Knott lost interest in touring, and the selectors preferred David Bairstow, Paul Downton and Taylor for the wicketkeeping role in subsequent Tests. Knott appeared in just two more Tests — the final two in the 1981 Ashes — in which he took six catches and made a vital half-century in England's second innings each time. Rod Marsh overtook Knott as Test cricket's leading gloveman during that series, and Knott graciously gave Marsh a bottle of wine and a congratulatory note. Marsh was touched by Knott's sportsmanship, which may have started a ritual as Marsh promised to give the next Test wicketkeeping record-holder a bottle of wine and a congratulatory note, and acted accordingly when Ian Healy broke Marsh's record.

Alan Knott (b.1946)

Matches: 95
Runs scored: 4389
Batting average: 32.75
100s/50s: 5/30
Top score: 135
Balls bowled: –
Wickets: –
Bowling average: –
5 wickets in innings: –
10 wickets in match: –
Best bowling: –
Catches/stumpings: 250/19

Herbert Sutcliffe

Herbert Sutcliffe was well known for his opening partnership with Jack Hobbs, as they accumulated 3249 runs in 38 opening stands, which included 15 century partnerships. Sutcliffe nonetheless was also a fine player in his own right. With a Test average slightly above 60 and an Ashes average of 66.85, Sutcliffe 'was as reliable a Test match opener as there has been' and 'was one of England's toughest cricketers', in the words of David Gower in his book *50 Greatest Cricketers of All Time*. Gower reported that Sutcliffe 'had amazing powers of concentration and tenacity' and 'was courageous, unflappable, and expert at leaving balls that did not need to be played — all good qualities in an opener'. Don Bradman reportedly said Sutcliffe 'had the best temperament of any cricketer he played with or against'.

The First World War delayed Sutcliffe's first-class debut until 1919, before he made his Test debut against South Africa in 1924 when aged 29. He made 64, and in the next Test he made 122 before scoring 83 and 29 not out in the third Test. The 1924–25 Ashes was also a big success for Sutcliffe, despite Australia's triumph, with Sutcliffe scoring four centuries and two half-centuries while compiling 734 runs at 81.56 and concluding the series with a duck. In the first Test he scored 59 and 115 in a 193-run loss before he scored 176 and 127 in an 81-run loss in the second Test. In England's first innings of the second Test he added 283 runs with Hobbs, who scored 154. In the fourth Test which England won by an innings, Sutcliffe's 143 took him past 1000 Test runs in only his twelfth innings.

One of Sutcliffe's most memorable knocks was in the 1926 Ashes, after the first four Tests were drawn. In the decider at the Oval, Sutcliffe made 161 and Hobbs 100 on a sticky wicket to set up England's 289-run triumph. Sutcliffe's only tour of South Africa was in 1927–28, and it was during this series — in his 20th Test — that his Test average finally fell below 70. He began the series strongly with 102, 41 not out, 29 and 99, but managed only 147 runs at 24.50 in the last three Tests. While averaging around 50 in the 1928–29 Ashes, the highlight for Sutcliffe was his 135 on a rain-affected Melbourne pitch in the third Test, as England chased down 332 for the loss of 7 wickets to take an unassailable 3–0 series lead. Despite five scores under 40 against South Africa in 1929, Sutcliffe also scored four centuries in the series: including 104 and 109 not out in the final Test. Sutcliffe averaged 87.20 at home against Australia in 1930, but his 161 and 54 in the final Test couldn't prevent the tourists claiming the Ashes with an innings victory. Sutcliffe's only Test against India yielded 19 and 3 in 1932, before his 194 and unbeaten single helped England win the first Test of the 1932–33 Ashes by 10 wickets. At this stage his Test average was 69.80 before it decreased as he scored no more tons. In the last four Tests of the 1932–33 Ashes, Sutcliffe averaged only 35 before scoring just 0 and 24 on New Zealand soil. Having made 117 and 109 not out when England hosted the Kiwis in 1931, Sutcliffe was caught behind with the first delivery of the series that followed the 1932–33 Ashes. He made 21 and 20 against the West Indies in 1933, having also made a few starts but no big scores against the same nation in 1928. Sutcliffe's final Ashes series yielded 304 runs at 50.67 with a top score of 69 not out in 1934, ensuring he averaged more than 50 in each of his six Ashes campaigns. Sutcliffe was lbw three times against South Africa in 1935 as he scored 61 in a draw and then 3 and 38 in a loss, before a leg injury forced his omission from the team. Aged 40, he was not recalled.

Herbert Sutcliffe (1894–1978)

Matches: 54
Runs scored: 4555
Batting average: 60.73
100s/50s: 16/23
Top score: 194
Balls bowled: –
Wickets: –
Bowling average: –
5 wickets in innings: –
10 wickets in match: –
Best bowling: –
Catches/stumpings: 23/–

Fred Trueman

When Fred Trueman became the first player to capture 300 Test wickets, it was believed that it would be difficult for anyone to match this figure. Although many players have since exceeded it, Trueman's record still has a great look about it. *Wisden* reported that Trueman was probably the best fast bowler England had produced, and in 1996 Bob Willis rated Trueman as England's best ever fast bowler. Also a fine fielder close to the bat, Trueman averaged almost one catch per Test and sometimes scored some useful runs although he never registered a Test half-century.

Known as 'Fiery Fred', Trueman would have accumulated even more Test wickets had he not missed 51 of the 118 Tests that England played between his maiden Test in 1952 and final Test in 1965. He had a lot of great qualities in a fast bowler as he could deliver outswingers, off-cutters and yorkers to devastating effect. Apart from cricket, at best he was an entertaining and interesting character with a quirky sense of humour. At worst, he got up people's noses.

Trueman's best Test figures of 8–31 were in just his third Test, and he finished that series with 29 Indian scalps at 13.31. He played only one Test in the 1953 Ashes, taking 8 wickets in the fifth and deciding match before he had little to smile about in the 1953–54 tour of the West Indies. Trueman took just 9 wickets at 46.67 from three Tests, and found himself on the outer because of his aggressive and brash conduct. He was left out of the 1954–55 Ashes before also missing several other tours within the next decade.

Trueman played two Tests in the 1956 Ashes, and missed the 1956–57 South African tour before claiming 22 wickets at 20.68 in a home series against the West Indies. He followed up with 15 victims at 17.07 against New Zealand, having formed a great bowling partnership with Brian Statham whose Test career comprised of 252 wickets from 70 appearances. Statham was Test cricket's leading wicket-taker before Trueman overtook him.

From 1959 to 1963, Trueman consistently took at least 20 wickets in each series, as England contested each Test-playing nation at the time. Trueman's best year was 1963 as he captured 62 wickets at 17.11 from 11 Tests. In the 1961 Ashes Test at Headingley, Trueman captured 5–58 and 6–30 as Statham was absent. Lord's was the scene for Trueman success on a number of occasions, including when England hosted Pakistan in 1962 and the West Indies in 1963. Trueman took 9 wickets on the former occasion and 11 on the latter occasion, and claimed 12 scalps in the 1963 Edgbaston Test, which followed the Lord's Test. The home series against the West Indies in 1963 was Trueman's best as he captured 34 wickets at 17.47, but the tourists won the series. England also lost the 1964 Ashes, with Trueman taking 4 wickets in the final Test at the Oval to take his career tally to 301. Trueman's last two Tests were against New Zealand, with England winning both on its way to a 3–0 whitewash.

Fred Trueman (1931–2006)

Matches: 67
Runs scored: 981
Batting average: 13.81
100s/50s: 0/0
Top score: 39*
Balls bowled: 15,178
Wickets: 307
Bowling average: 21.57
5 wickets in innings: 17
10 wickets in match: 3
Best bowling: 8–31
Catches/stumpings: 64/–

CHAPTER 2: AUSTRALIA

2.1 AUSTRALIA v SOUTH AFRICA

1900s–1930s

South Africa lost its first series against Australia in 1902–03, although the series was a lot more competitive than the 2–0 result suggested. On a matting pitch in Johannesburg in the first Test, the hosts scored 454 and then made the visitors follow on, but Australia batted long enough in its second innings to stymie South Africa's winning chances. The hosts also gained a first-innings lead in the second Test, this time when batting second, but then 159 not out from Warwick Armstrong helped set a decent target before the hosts collapsed for 85 to hand the visitors a 159-run win. The Africans also fell to 85 all out in the third Test, and on this occasion it meant they had to follow on. Despite South Africa's Jimmy Sinclair scoring his second century in as many Tests, as he plundered 104 runs in 80 minutes, Australia won by 10 wickets.

The 1910–11 series in Australia was predominantly one-sided as the hosts won four Tests to one while the tourists had to adjust to turf.

Australia won the first Test by an innings and followed up with an 89-run win as South Africa, paradoxically, tallied 506 and 80, compared with Australia's 348 and 327. The Africans won the third Test by 38 runs after setting a target of 378, before Australia recorded wins by 530 runs and 7 wickets. Twelve centuries were scored throughout the series, including Aubrey Faulkner's 204 for South Africa in the second Test and Victor Trumper's 214 not out for Australia in the third.

The teams met in England in 1912 as part of a Triangular Tournament, with Australia twice trouncing South Africa before the third encounter was drawn. In spite of another century from Faulkner, Australia won the first fixture by an innings after Jimmy Matthews claimed a hat-trick in both South African innings. Australia followed up with a 10-wicket win before only two innings unfolded in a shortened third Test, as South Africa made 329 and Australia 219.

Nearly ten years passed before the teams met next, with Australia having the better of two drawn Tests before winning the third by 10 wickets. Another decade passed before South Africa toured Australia, with the hosts winning a very lopsided series as they won by an innings on three occasions while the other margins were 169 runs and 10 wickets. The lowlight for South Africa was the final Test as the tourists were routed for 36 and 45 while the hosts managed 153 on a notoriously sticky pitch. An injured Don Bradman was unable to bat in the final Test, after averaging 201.50 in the first four Tests.

South Africa still couldn't beat Australia in 1935–36 despite the Springboks being on home soil, with the visitors winning by 9 wickets before a drawn result was followed by three innings victories to Australia. Clarrie Grimmett and Bill O'Reilly were in brilliant form as the spinners captured 44 and 27 wickets respectively. Jack Fingleton, Stan McCabe and Bill Brown scored heavily for the victors while the only batting of note for the vanquished was Dudley Nourse's 231 in the drawn Test.

Fourteen years passed before the teams next met, with Australia again winning 4–0 on South African soil. After the tourists recorded two comfortable victories, they were dismissed for 75 in the third Test but recovered to win by 5 wickets. The Springboks made 311 and then gained a first-innings lead of 236 but didn't enforce the follow-on and they subsequently crumbled for 99 before Australia achieved the 336-run target, as Neil Harvey scored one of his four tons of the series. Only two South Africans scored a century in the series while five Australians shared 11 centuries, with opener Jack Moroney scoring 118 and 101 not out in the drawn fourth Test.

1950s

After Australia won the opening Test of the 1952–53 series by 96 runs at Brisbane, South Africa had gone 24 Tests and 42 years without a win against Australia. This drought was broken in the second Test as the Springboks won by 82 runs, before the hosts regained the series lead with an innings victory and then had the better of a drawn Test. The final Test was perhaps the best involving the two countries up until that point. Australia batted first and plunged from 417–3 to a still formidable 520 all out, and then South Africa replied with 435 before Australia was 128–3, but the Springboks fought back and won by 6 wickets to square the series after being set 295.

Australia had much the better of the 1957–58 series in South Africa, as Ian Craig skippered Australia at the tender age of 22. The hosts began well as they tallied 470 in the first innings of the drawn first Test before the third Test was also drawn. The visitors, however, were too good otherwise as they won the second Test by an innings before winning the last two Tests by 10 wickets and 8 wickets. Richie Benaud starred with bat and ball while Alan Davidson was Australia's second best bowler as Jim Burke, Ken Mackay and Colin McDonald scored plenty of runs.

1960s

Australian left-armer Ian Meckiff was called for throwing in the first Test of the 1963–64 series, before Australia took the series lead with an 8-wicket victory in the second Test at Melbourne. A drawn series eventuated after South Africa won the fourth Test by 10 wickets, with the Springboks enjoying a third-wicket partnership of 341 involving Eddie Barlow (201) and Graeme Pollock (175). The drawn third Test was interestingly poised as the Africans finished at 326–5 when chasing 409, before they didn't have enough time to pursue a 171-run target in the final Test as they reached 76–0.

South Africa broke through for its first series win against Australia in 1966–67, following a brilliant first Test at Johannesburg. Australia was 204–1 before faltering to 325 all out in reply to South Africa's 199, and then the hosts made 620 in their second innings. Australia fell 234 runs shy of a target of 495, with South African wicketkeeper Denis Lindsay a thorn in Australia's side as he scored 69 and 182 at number seven, and claimed eight catches. Lindsay had a great series although Australia levelled the series, despite a knock of 209 from Graeme Pollock in the second Test. Bob Simpson and Keith Stackpole made tons as Australia notched 542, and South Africa managed 353 and 367 before the tourists lost 4 wickets in the successful run chase. The Springboks regained the series lead with an 8-wicket win, which was followed by a draw and a 7-wicket win to the hosts to seal a 3–1 triumph.

The South Africans had not played Test cricket for three years when they hosted the Australians in 1969–70, but the host nation won all four Tests comprehensively as the tourists were outplayed in all aspects. The margins were 170 runs, an innings and 129 runs, 307 runs and 323 runs, with Mike Procter a standout bowler while Barlow, Peter Pollock and Trevor Goddard also bowled well. Graeme Pollock and Barry Richards topped 500 runs in the series, with Pollock's 274 in the second Test a standout performance. But political factors not only stymied their Test careers, but also the prospects of South Africa taking part in Test cricket for more than 20 years.

Post-apartheid 1990s

South Africa's 1993–94 tour of Australia generated plenty of interest as it was the first time in 30 years that the nation played Test cricket Down Under. Now known as the Proteas, South Africa was captained by former Australia left-handed batsman Kepler Wessels, who joined a rare list of players to represent two countries in Test cricket.

Rain ruined the first Test, which was drawn, before South Africa won a thrilling second Test by 5 runs. The tourists were dismissed for 169 and 239 after Shane Warne captured 12 wickets, and the hosts were all but assured of victory at 51–1 before collapsing to 75–8, and then 111 all out as Fanie de Villiers was South Africa's biggest hero with 6–43 for a 10-wicket match haul. Steve Waugh returned from injury for the third and final Test, and excelled with bat and ball as Australia levelled the series with a 191-run victory. Only a matter of weeks later, the Australians toured South Africa for another three Tests.

Australia had the better of the first day before South Africa gained control of the first Test and recorded a resounding 197-run win. As he had done in Australia, Steve Waugh played a leading all-round role to help Australia level the series. The tourists cantered to a 9-wicket win, and the series remained level as the final Test turned into a bore. Australia was dismissed early on the second day, before the Proteas showed no initiative as they batted until well into the fourth day.

South Africa also hosted the next series involving the two nations, in early 1997, and the tourists recorded an innings victory in the first Test following a 385-run fifth-wicket stand involving Steve Waugh (160) and Greg Blewett (214). South Africa was destined to square the series following a poor start to the second Test. After being 95–7, the hosts were perhaps lucky not to be 95–8 before recovering to 209. The hosts seemed in an unassailable position at 87–0 after dismissing Australia for just 108, but South Africa crumbled to 168 all out before Mark Waugh scored 116 for the tourists. Australia was 258–5 before stumbling to 265–8, and then Ian Healy hit a six to seal the series before South Africa won the dead rubber by 8 wickets.

The 1997–98 series in Australia featured just one result, as the series went down to the wire. The first Test was well fought as the hosts had the upper hand for the most part but were thwarted on the final day. Warne produced some typical magic at Sydney as his 5–75 and 6–34 enabled Australia to win by an innings. South Africa racked up 517 in the third and final Test before Mark Taylor carried his bat as he scored 169 in Australia's 350. After the Proteas declared their second innings at 193–6, a series of dropped catches proved their downfall as Australia held on for a draw, finishing at 227–7. Mark Waugh scored a chancy century and survived an appeal for hit wicket with 8.3 overs remaining, as South Africa needed 4 wickets.

2000s

In seasons 2001–02, 2005–06 and 2008–09, the teams met Down Under before the Proteas hosted Australia in a follow-up series. Australia won by 246 runs, 9 wickets and 10 wickets at home in 2001–02, with South Africa never in contention when chasing 375, before the Proteas could only set minuscule targets of 10 and 53. Matthew Hayden scored a century in each Test for the victors while Justin Langer and Damien Martyn also scored a century each in the first and third Tests. The only ton for South Africa was Gary Kirsten's 153 when the Proteas followed on in the third Test, after Jacques Kallis was run out for 99 in the second Test.

Martyn (133) and Hayden (122) maintained their form in the first Test of the following series in South Africa, but the biggest star was Adam Gilchrist who scored 204 not out as Australia amassed 652–7 declared. The Proteas were smashed by an innings and 360 runs before squandering a potentially winnable position in the second Test. Following 138 not out from Gilchrist, the tourists led by 143 runs before the hosts tallied 473. Ricky Ponting (100 not out), Hayden (96) and Langer (58) set up a relatively comfortable 5-wicket win for the Australians, before the Proteas salvaged some pride with a 5-wicket victory of their own when chasing 335. Dismissed for just 167 in reply to Australia's 315, South Africa subsequently ripped through Australia surprisingly cheaply before Herschelle Gibbs (104) and Gary Kirsten (64) set up the result with a 142-run opening stand.

Unlucky to play only six Tests, Brad Hodge scored 203 not out for Australia in the opening Test of 2005–06 before South Africa hung on for a draw following a gritty unbeaten century from Jacques Rudolph. Mike Hussey (122) and Ponting (117) set up Australia's 355 in the first innings of the second Test, although a turning point came as Hussey was dropped before a last-wicket stand of 107 unfolded. Hayden (137) returned to form in Australia's second innings while Andrew Symonds hammered 72 and completed a fine all-round match as the Proteas were dismissed 185 runs shy of their 366-run target. Ashwell Prince and Kallis topped 100 each as South Africa made 451 in the third Test before gaining a 92-run lead. Bad weather was followed by the

Proteas declaring at 194–6 before Ponting, who made 120 in his team's first innings, followed up with 143 not out while Hayden made 90 as Australia cruised to an 8-wicket triumph.

Australian seamer Stuart Clark claimed 5–55 and 4–34 on debut to set up a 7-wicket victory in the first Test on South African soil, before Ponting scored 103 and 116 in the second Test, which his team won by 112 runs. Australia achieved a clean sweep after inching to a 2-wicket victory when chasing 292, with Brett Lee and Michael Kasprowicz taking their team from 275–8 to 294–8. This occurred less than a year after their last-wicket partnership at Edgbaston narrowly failed to produce a miraculous Australian Ashes victory.

The two series involving Australia and South Africa in 2008–09 produced rather decisive momentum changes, with the visiting team winning 2–1 each time. In the first Test at Perth, Australia was 15–3 before tallying 375, and then Mitchell Johnson nabbed 8–61 in South Africa's first innings. History was against the Proteas as they sought 414, considering there had been only three winning pursuits when chasing 400-plus in Test history, with 418 the highest. But two centuries and three half-centuries piloted the Africans to a memorable 6-wicket triumph.

After the Proteas were 141–6, 184–7 and 251–8 in reply to Australia's 394 in the second Test at Melbourne, JP Duminy (166) and number ten Dale Steyn (76) put on a ninth-wicket stand of 180 before Steyn took 5–67 after earlier snaring 5–87. South Africa secured the series after losing just 1 wicket when chasing 183, before Australia clinched a 103-run win in the dead rubber. South African skipper Graeme Smith bravely batted at number 11 with a broken hand, as the Proteas sought a draw after being set 376, and he was last out when Johnson bowled him as just ten deliveries remained.

Following a poor start in South Africa, the Australians scored 466 following 96 not out from Johnson and 117 from Test debutant Marcus North. South Africa managed only 220 despite 104 not out from AB de Villiers, and Johnson claimed two 4-wicket hauls as Australia won by 162 runs. In his second Test, Phillip Hughes made 115 and 160 while fellow left-handed opener Simon Katich made 108 and 30 as Australia chalked up another big win. This time the margin was 175 runs after the hosts totalled 138 and a respectable 370. AB de Villiers (163), Prince (150) and Kallis (102) massacred the series victors in the final Test as South Africa tallied 651 and won by an innings, despite Johnson scoring 123 not out in Australia's second innings of 422.

The Proteas hosted a two-match series in late 2011, and won the opening encounter in sensational circumstances before having to settle for a drawn series. Australian captain Michael Clarke (151) was largely responsible for his team's 284-run total before Shane Watson (5–17) and Ryan Harris (4–33) ripped through the hosts for just 96. In an extraordinary turn of events, Australia plunged to 21–9 and was 5 runs shy of New Zealand's Test-record low, before finishing with 47 all out (Vernon Philander 5–15, Morne Morkel 3–9 and Steyn 2–23). Luck ran with the South Africans at crucial times as Hashim Amla (112) and captain Smith (101 not out) guided the hosts to an astounding 8-wicket victory. Australia sought 310 to level the series, and made it with 2 wickets to spare, after stumbling to 19–2 and 215–6. Pat Cummins claimed 1–38 and 6–79 on debut before finishing unbeaten (on 13) along with Johnson (40).

The opening two Tests of the 2012–13 series Down Under were drawn, before South Africa romped to a 309-run win in the third and decisive Test. Centuries to Kallis and Amla enabled the Proteas to make 450 in the first Test before Australia made 565–5 declared, following 259 not out from Clarke, 136 from Ed Cowan and 100 from Hussey. South Africa was 5 wickets down when the match ended, before Australia failed to land the knockout blow in the second Test. Australia raced to a staggering 482–5 at stumps on day one, before finishing with 550, following 230 from Clarke, 119 from David Warner and 103 from Hussey. AB de Villiers and Test debutant Faf du Plessis foiled Australia on the final day as the hosts came achingly close to victory, with the visitors finishing on 248–8 after being set 430. Du Plessis survived 466 minutes and was unconquered on 110, before he also came to the rescue in the third Test. His unbeaten 78 helped South Africa recover from 75–6 to 225 before Australia tallied only 163. Amla (196) and de Villiers (169) were the main scorers as the Proteas set the hosts an impossible 632, with none of the locals making a big score, as South Africa won by 309 runs.

Batting first seemed to be the key in the 2013–14 series in South Africa, as the tourists won the first and third Tests by 281 runs and 245 runs while the hosts won the second Test by 231 runs. Shaun Marsh (148) and Steve Smith (100) put on 233 for the fifth wicket in the opening Test after Australia was 98–4, and the tourists led by 191 runs on the first innings before Warner scored 115. Set 482, South Africa was never a chance as Johnson claimed 12 wickets in the match, before the Africans recovered from 11–2 to register 423 in the second Test. Duminy (123) and de Villiers (116) excelled before the Australians, after averting the follow-on, couldn't prevent Amla scoring an unbeaten 127. An opening stand of 126 was followed by Australia losing 10–90, with opener Chris Rogers ninth out for 107 amidst a late collapse in gloomy weather on day four. Warner (135) gave the tourists a great start in the decider before Clarke (161 not out) declared, as the team was just shy of 500. Warner made 145 after Clarke declined to enforce the follow-on, and the Africans were soon 15–3 chasing 511.

Australia v South Africa

1902–03 (SA): Australia 2–0 (1 drawn)

1910–11 (A): Australia 4–1

1912 (England): Australia 2–0 (1 drawn)

1921–22 (SA): Australia 1–0 (2 drawn)

1931–32 (A): Australia 5–0

1935–36 (SA): Australia 4–0 (1 drawn)

1949–50 (SA): Australia 4–0 (1 drawn)

1952–53 (A): 2–2 (1 drawn)

1957–58 (SA): Australia 3–0 (2 drawn)

1963–64 (A): 1–1 (3 drawn)

1966–67 (SA): South Africa 3–1 (1 drawn)

1969–70 (SA): South Africa 4–0

1993–94 (A): 1–1 (1 drawn)

1993–94 (SA): 1–1 (1 drawn)

1996–97 (SA): Australia 2–1

1997–78 (A): Australia 1–0 (2 drawn)

2001–02 (A): Australia 3–0

2001–02 (SA): Australia 2–1

2005–06 (A): Australia 2–0 (1 drawn)
2005–06 (SA): Australia 3–0
2008–09 (A): South Africa 2–1
2008–09 (SA): Australia 2–1

2011–12 (SA): 1–1
2012–13 (A): South Africa 1–0 (2 drawn)
2013–14 (SA): Australia 2–1

2.2 AUSTRALIA v WEST INDIES

1930s

Australia was too strong for the West Indies at first, with the hosts winning by 10 wickets and then recording three successive innings victories in season 1930–31. Clarrie Grimmett and Bert Ironmonger were Australia's main wicket-takers with 33 and 22 scalps respectively, while the best West Indian bowler was Herman Griffith with 14 wickets. The opening encounter at Adelaide was competitive for a while, with the tourists making 296 before Alan Kippax (146) and Stan McCabe (90) scored the bulk of Australia's 376. Bill Ponsford (92 not out) and Archie Jackson (70 not out) made Australia's eventual 170-run target seem easy, before Ponsford and Don Bradman were prominent in the innings wins. Ponsford scored 183, 109 and 24 while Bradman scored 25, 223 and 152, while the tourists mustered miserable totals of 107, 90, 193, 148, 99 and 107. The West Indies nonetheless won the final Test, with Frank Martin and George Headley scoring tons. After trailing by 126 runs on the first innings, Australia fell for 220 when chasing 251, with Bradman bowled by Griffith for a duck.

1950s

Twenty-one years passed between the first and second series involving Australia and the West Indies, and the 1951–52 series Down Under was a lot more competitive than another 4–1 result suggested. Margins of

3 wickets and 7 wickets in Australia's favour were followed by a West Indian win by 6 wickets, and then Australia sneaking home by 1 wicket. The third and fourth Tests were eye-catching, with the hosts collapsing for 82 on a wet Adelaide pitch before the West Indies struggled to a mere 23-run lead and later chased down 233, as the Australians squandered their opportunities. Frank Worrell (108) set up the touring team's first innings of 272 at Melbourne, and the hosts replied with 216 before being set 260. A gutsy 102 from captain Lindsay Hassett kept them in contention, before number nine Doug Ring (32 not out) and number 11 Bill Johnston (7 not out) put on a streaky last-wicket partnership of 38 to seal Australia's series triumph. The hosts fell to 116 all out in the final Test, but the visitors made only 78 in reply and went on to lose by 202 runs.

The 1954–55 series in the Caribbean was another triumph for Australia, albeit shortly after losing the Ashes on home soil. The West Indies drew the second and fourth Tests, which featured plenty of runs, but Australia won by 9 and 8 wickets in the first and third Tests. The tourists sealed their 3–0 triumph with an innings win after declaring at 758–8, having lost their first 2 wickets for 7 runs before five batsmen scored centuries. Australia ultimately tallied 12 centuries in the series, compared with nine from the West Indians. The highest scores were 219 by West Indian stand-in captain Denis Atkinson and 204 by Australian Neil Harvey, with Atkinson and Cyril Depeiaza putting on a 347-run seventh-wicket stand in the fourth Test.

1960s

The 1960–61 series was one of the best Test series of all time as three of the five matches were nail-biting, with Richie Benaud leading Australia, while Worrell led the West Indies. The Frank Worrell Trophy was subsequently the prize on offer for Test series involving Australia and the West Indies. The first Test in Brisbane was a contender for 'greatest Test of all-time' as Test cricket's first tie resulted. There were umpteen pendulum swings before Australia lost its last 2 wickets to run-outs from the third-last and second-last deliveries of the final over. Joe Solomon earned his place in cricket folklore with a direct hit from side-on to produce the final wicket, with Ian Meckiff the dismissed batsman. Nonetheless, centuries from West Indian Garry Sobers and Australian Norman O'Neill, a magnificent all-round contribution from Australian Alan Davidson, and 9 wickets from West Indian Wes Hall, could not be overlooked. A 7-wicket win to Australia was followed by a 222-run win to the West Indies, and a drawn fourth Test was followed by Australia winning a tense deciding Test by 2 wickets as the hosts chased 258. In the drawn Test, Ken Mackay and number 11 Lindsay Kline added 66 runs in the final 110 minutes to thwart the West Indies, who appeared certain of taking a 2–1 series lead rather than ultimately being on the wrong end of this series scoreline.

The following series, in 1964–65, produced the West Indies' breakthrough series victory against Australia as the hosts won the first and third Tests handsomely while drawing the second and fourth encounters, followed by the tourists winning the final Test comfortably. Australia made big totals in the drawn Tests but the West Indies did enough with the bat to stave off the prospect of defeat. In the fourth Test, Australian openers Bill Lawry (210) and Bob Simpson (201) and first drop Bob Cowper (102) set up a total of 650–6 declared, before Seymour Nurse scored 201 as the West Indies made 573–9 declared.

The West Indians won the opening Test of the 1968–69 series Down Under with a 125-run margin, but it was their only success as their batsmen were repeatedly brought undone by Graham McKenzie, John Gleeson and Alan Connolly. Lawry (205), Ian Chappell (165) and Doug Walters (76) helped Australia to an innings victory, which levelled the series, before Lawry and Walters continued their run sprees. Walters tallied 623 runs and Lawry 348 in the last three Tests, with Walters notching 242 and 103 while Lawry notched 151 and 17 in the fifth Test. Australia took the series lead with a thumping 10-wicket win at Sydney, before the drawn fourth Test at Adelaide could easily have been won by either side. The West Indies amassed 616 after trailing by 257 on the first innings, and the Australians appeared to be cruising to victory as their first 4 wickets fell at 86, 185, 215 and 304. A few run-outs ruined Australia's chances, and the hosts battled to save the match, as they finished 21 runs shy of victory with a sole wicket in hand. With another chance to level the series, the tourists needed a mammoth

735 to win the final Test and were never a chance, despite 137 from Nurse and 113 from Sobers, with Australia winning by 382 runs.

1970s

Australia won a five-match series 2–0 in the Caribbean in 1972–73, with Australian paceman Max Walker and experienced West Indian off spinner Lance Gibbs capturing 26 wickets each. Gibbs lacked support while Jeff Hammond and Terry Jenner bowled soundly for Australia, which missed an injured Dennis Lillee for the last four Tests. The decisive Tests were the third and fourth, with the hosts batting with ten players at Trinidad, where they made 280 and 289 in a 44-run loss as top order batsman Lawrence Rowe was missing after injuring his ankle when fielding on day one. The West Indians could still have won the third Test considering they were 141–1 and 268–4 when chasing 334. Clive Lloyd scored 178 in the first innings of the fourth Test, only for the West Indies to stumble from 277–3 to 366 all out. The home side's second-innings demise for 109 left the visitors needing 135, which was achieved without the loss of a wicket.

Six decisive results occurred in the 1975–76 series in Australia, with the only success for the tourists coming in the second Test after the hosts won the first Test by 8 wickets. Following an innings defeat, Australia seized the initiative with another 8-wicket triumph, followed by victories by 7 wickets, 190 runs and 165 runs. Jeff Thomson, Dennis Lillee and Gary Gilmour were Australia's main wicket-takers while Ian Redpath and Chappell brothers Ian and Greg were prominent with the bat. Andy Roberts was the pick of the West Indian bowlers, but the only time he excelled was in the second Test when he claimed 7–54 in Australia's second innings.

The introduction of World Series Cricket ensured that Australia would be severely depleted for its 1977–78 tour to the Caribbean, and it was hardly surprising that the hosts won the first Test by an innings before romping to a 9-wicket win in the second Test. But the third Test had a different complexion, as several West Indians withdrew in protest at a couple of decisions by selectors. Maiden Test centuries to Graeme Wood and Craig Serjeant paved the way for a 3-wicket win to Australia, as its target was 359, before the hosts clinched the series with a 198-run victory in the fourth Test. Australia could have won the last Test, but a crowd disturbance caused the match to be abandoned during the final afternoon as the West Indies were 258–9, chasing 369, after Vanburn Holder was unhappy at being adjudged caught behind.

Australia hosted the West Indies and England in Test matches during the 1979–80 season, with England well beaten while the hosts were no match for the West Indians, as Australia included World Series players. An understrength West Indies team drew the first Test before a strengthened team won the remaining two Tests by 10 wickets and 408 runs, with the pace quartet of Roberts, Colin Croft, Joel Garner and Michael Holding proving formidable. Viv Richards's four scores were 140, 96, 76 and 74, while Clive Lloyd and Alvin Kallicharran made a century each in the final Test.

1980s

The 1981–82 series was eye-catching after beginning with a true battle of Test cricket on Boxing Day. Holding claimed 5–45 for the West Indies while a courageous 100 not out from Kim Hughes was responsible for Australia's total being as high as, a still lacklustre, 198. The West Indies crashed to 10–4 before gaining a mere 3-run lead, and later folded for 161 when needing 220. The West Indies had the better of the second Test but could not bowl the hosts out twice. Australian opening batsman John Dyson took an all-time classic catch in the West Indies' second innings before scoring an unbeaten century to ensure a draw. In the third and final Test, the West Indies had a first-innings lead of 151 as an undefeated century from Larry Gomes, in addition to a few solid contributions, took the West Indies to 389, after being 92–4 and 194–6. Allan Border (126), Kim Hughes (84) and Bruce Laird (78) led an Australian fightback, but the hosts lost their last 6 wickets for 24 runs to leave the tourists requiring 236 runs in 255 minutes. Lloyd (77 not out) guided the West Indies to a series-levelling 5-wicket victory following 50s from Gordon Greenidge and Richards.

Following the retirements of some key players, Australia did well to draw its first two Tests in the West Indies in 1984. In the opening

166

encounter, Rodney Hogg scored 52 at number 11 to lift the visitors from 182–9 to 279 all out, before Australia's second innings of 273–9 was adequate, after being 60–5. After initially falling for 230, the hosts finished their second innings at 250 without loss, 73 runs shy of victory, as Gordon Greenidge and Desmond Haynes made unbeaten tons. Border was Australia's main hero in the second Test at Trinidad as he scored 98 not out and 100 not out in totals of 255 and 299–9, while the West Indies compiled 468–8 declared. Terry Alderman lasted 105 minutes at number 11 in Australia's second innings to help the team save the Test, when defeat appeared certain. Australia made 429 in the first innings of the third Test, but the West Indies bettered it thanks largely to centuries from Haynes and Richie Richardson. Michael Holding and Malcolm Marshall wreaked havoc as Australia plunged to 97 all out and lost by 10 wickets. The hosts inflicted an even bigger defeat in the fourth Test — an innings and 36 runs — before inflicting another 10-wicket drubbing. Richards scored 178 and Richardson 154 in the innings victory, before Greenidge was the batting hero in the final Test. Garner however was Australia's main nemesis as he claimed 31 wickets in the series.

Being back on home soil didn't make much difference for the Australians as they began the 1984–85 series with another innings loss, this time after being skittled for 76 and then following on after the West Indies had tallied 416. Kim Hughes resigned as Australian captain after his team suffered an 8-wicket loss in the second Test before his replacement — Border — felt that the team improved a lot in the third Test, despite losing by 191 runs. Richards scored 208 in the fourth Test before Australia held on for a draw with just 2 wickets in hand, as Australia's winless streak against the West Indies stretched to 11 Tests. But this drought was broken in decisive fashion as the hosts won the final Test by an innings, as a dodgy pitch was conducive to spin. Kepler Wessels scored 173 in a total of 471–9 declared after Border riskily elected to bat, before Bob Holland claimed 10 wickets in the match.

The pace attack of Marshall, Curtly Ambrose, Courtney Walsh and Patrick Patterson was largely responsible for the West Indies winning the first three Tests of the 1988–89 series on Australian soil. With the tourists on their way to a 10-wicket victory at Brisbane, Walsh took a hat-trick across two innings before Australia's Merv Hughes did likewise at Perth, although Hughes' hat-trick, bizarrely, spanned across three overs. Hughes snared 13 wickets at Perth but it was not enough to prevent Australia losing by 169 runs, before the margin in the third Test was 285 runs. Border, somewhat surprisingly, snared 11 wickets in the Sydney Test, which his team won by 7 wickets, before the final Test was drawn after Dean Jones scored 216 in Australia's first innings.

1990s

The 1990–91 series in the Caribbean was tough and controversial in more ways than one as the West Indies won 2–1. Marshall, Ambrose, Walsh and Patterson were again the chief wicket-takers, while Richardson was the pick of the batsmen. The first and third Tests were rain-affected draws, although the Australians could have pushed for at least one win had they not let the hosts off the hook. The West Indies won the second Test by 10 wickets following centuries to Richardson and Haynes, before sealing the series with a 343-run win in the fourth Test. The tourists crashed to 134 all out after the hosts managed only 149, and then Greenidge made his highest Test score of 226 in his penultimate Test. Australia salvaged some pride with a face-saving 157-run victory in the final Test, before the West Indies again won 2–1 in 1992–93.

The 1992–93 series Down Under was perhaps the best involving Australia and the West Indies since 1960–61, with Australia coming within a hair's breadth of winning the series. In the first Test, Keith Arthurton (157 not out) helped the West Indies to a 78-run first-innings lead before David Boon (111) led Australia's second innings. Needing 231, the tourists lost 4 early wickets and narrowly escaped with a draw as they reached 133–8. In the second Test, the hosts were on top following centuries to Mark Waugh and Border before frittering away their advantage. Needing 359, the West Indies were soundly placed at 143–1 before 7 wickets from emerging leg spinner Shane Warne inspired a 139-run win for Australia. The third Test was a high scoring draw following Brian Lara's monumental 277 for the West Indies, before the West Indies levelled the series with the first 1-run victory in Test history.

The hosts sought 186 runs in a bid to win the Frank Worrell Trophy on Australia Day, and were down and out at 74–7 before partnerships of 28, 42 and 40 unfolded. On his 31st birthday, Tim May scored 42 not out after taking 5–9 the previous day, but Craig McDermott was controversially adjudged caught behind from a short-pitched Walsh delivery as Australia was poised to steal victory. The player of the series, Ambrose, captured 7–1 in 32 balls as Australia plummeted from 85–2 to 119 all out in the first innings of the final Test, which the West Indies won by an innings and 25 runs.

Australia shocked the West Indies in Barbados in the first Test of 1994–95, with the hosts losing their first 3 wickets for 6 runs and twice failing to reach 200 as they succumbed to a 10-wicket defeat. A rain-affected draw was followed by a 9-wicket win to the hosts as Ambrose took 5–45 and 4–20 in a low scoring match, before the West Indies lost a wicket with the second ball of the fourth and final Test. The hosts recovered to 103–1 but then stumbled to 265 all out, and the series was in the balance as Australia was 73–3. Steve Waugh scored 200, after surviving a crucial chance behind the wicket at 42, while twin brother Mark scored 126 as Australia won by an innings with more than a day to spare. A number of droughts were broken, as the West Indies had not lost a Test series at home since 1972–73 and not lost any Test series since 1979–80, while Australia had not won the Frank Worrell Trophy since 1975–76. Little did anyone know that Australia would keep a stranglehold on the Frank Worrell Trophy for longer than the West Indies had.

Glenn McGrath and Shane Warne took plenty of wickets for the victors in the 1994–95 series and continued to do so in 1996–97. Australia led the five-Test series 2–0 following wins by 123 and 124 runs, with Ian Healy making unbeaten scores of 161 and 45 in the first Test. Ambrose captured 5–55 and 4–17 in the Boxing Day Test which the tourists won by 6 wickets to raise their hopes of winning back the Frank Worrell Trophy, before Ambrose missed the fourth Test. Australia won by an innings as wrist-spinner Michael Bevan captured a 10-wicket match haul. The West Indies salvaged a 3–2 series loss after inflicting a 10-wicket drubbing in the final Test, with Ambrose doing plenty of damage, despite bowling nine no balls in an over at one stage.

In the wake of a 5–0 series loss to South Africa, the West Indians appeared set for another big series loss as Australia won the opening Test of the 1998–99 series by 312 runs after the hosts crashed to 51 all out. The second Test was a contrast as the West Indies, after being 34–4, made 431 following 213 from Lara, before Australia only just erased its 175-run first-innings deficit. The West Indies grabbed the series lead with a thrilling 1-wicket triumph at Barbados where Australia made 490 and had the West Indies 98–6 before the hosts fought back splendidly. Still, the hosts had only 2 wickets in hand when 60 runs shy of the 308-run target. Following 83 minutes of resistance from Ambrose at number ten, Lara (153 not out) guided the West Indies home after being dropped behind the stumps at 301–8, before Walsh survived 5 deliveries after coming to the crease at 302–9. Another blazing century from Lara in the final Test wasn't enough to prevent Australia squaring the series and retaining the Frank Worrell Trophy, as the tourists won by 176 runs.

2000s

The 2000–01 series could hardly have been more one-sided, as Ambrose had retired while the aging Walsh was well past his best. Although an injured Warne missed the series, the first two Tests were over in three days before the fourth was decided within four days. The writing was on the wall as the West Indies crashed from 53–2 to 67–9 and then 82 all out, before Australia cruised to 107–1 at stumps on day one of the series. Two innings victories to the hosts were followed by margins of 5 wickets, 352 runs and 6 wickets. The West Indies made a game of it in the third Test as Lara notched 182, before the team's disappointing second-innings total of 141 left the hosts needing 130. In the final Test, Australia needed 173 although the result could have been far different had the West Indians not slid from 147–0 to 272 all out in their first innings. Other turning points included Adam Gilchrist being dropped first ball when Australia was 289–5 before his 87 helped Australia to 452, and Michael Slater being dropped at 50–3 in the run chase before he scored 86 not out.

Australia's winning sequence over the West Indies in Test cricket stretched to nine matches as another series victory to Australia never looked in doubt during its 2003 tour to the Caribbean. Australia twice won by 9 wickets and once won by 118 runs to lead the four-match series 3–0 in 2003, before the West Indies created history in the final Test at St John's, as the hosts won by 3 wickets. Achieving the target of 418, following tons to Ramnaresh Sarwan and Shivnarine Chanderpaul, meant the West Indies recorded the highest successful run chase in Test history, after both teams were dismissed for 240 in their first innings.

Australia won all three Tests in the 2005–06 series with whopping margins of 379 runs, 9 wickets and 7 wickets. The tourists faced a target of 509 in the first Test before the hosts had little difficulty chasing targets of 78 and 182. The West Indies also failed to win a Test in the 2008, 2009–10 and 2011–12 series, with Australia winning twice and drawing once each time.

The squad from the Caribbean was very competitive at home in 2008 as the visitors set the hosts a target in each Test. The West Indies were dismissed for 191 when chasing 287, before finishing at 266–5 when chasing 372, and then tallying 387 when chasing 475. As tourists in 2009–10, the West Indies had a horror beginning as Australia won the first Test by an innings, before the second Test featured an evenly balanced draw, after the West Indies seemed content with a draw when setting Australia a target. In the third and final Test the tourists were set a target of 359 to square the series and fell 36 runs short.

The West Indies again gave Australia a decent challenge in the Caribbean in 2012, with Australia having just 3 wickets in hand when achieving a target of 192 in the first Test, before the hosts were dismissed for 294 after being set 370 to win the final Test. The subsequent series in the Caribbean in mid-2015 featured just two Tests, with the tourists winning rather easily. The hosts managed just 148 and 216 in the opening Test which Australia won by 9 wickets, after 35-year-old Adam Voges scored 130 not out for Australia in his maiden Test to set up a total of 318. The margin in the second Test was 277 runs, with Australian skipper Steve Smith scoring 199 in a total of 399 before the West Indies trailed by 179 runs on the first innings and later folded for 114, after Australia declared at 212–2.

Australia also won decisively on home soil in 2015–16, with an innings win followed by a 177-run win and a rain-affected draw. Voges (269 not out) and Shaun Marsh (182) scored heavily in the first Test before Voges, Smith, Joe Burns and Usman Khawaja scored a century each in the second Test.

Australia v West Indies

1930–31 (A): Australia 4–1

1951–52 (A): Australia 4–1

1954–55 (WI): Australia 3–0 (2 drawn)

1960–61 (A): Australia 2–1 (1 drawn, 1 tied)

1964–65 (WI): West Indies 2–1 (2 drawn)

1968–69 (A): Australia 3–1 (1 drawn)

1972–73 (WI): Australia 2–0 (3 drawn)

1975–76 (A): Australia 5–1

1977–78 (WI): West Indies 3–1 (1 drawn)

1979–80 (A): West Indies 2–0 (1 drawn)

1981–82 (A): 1–1 (1 drawn)

1983–84 (WI): West Indies 3–0 (2 drawn)

1984–85 (A): West Indies 3–1 (1 drawn)

1988–89 (A): West Indies 3–1 (1 drawn)

1990–91 (WI): West Indies 2–1 (2 drawn)

1992–93 (A): West Indies 2–1 (2 drawn)

1994–95 (WI): Australia 2–1 (1 drawn)

1996–97 (A): Australia 3–2

1998–99 (WI): 2–2

2000–01 (A): Australia 5–0

2003 (WI): Australia 3–1

2005–06 (A): Australia 3–0

2008 (WI): Australia 2–0 (1 drawn)

2009–10 (A): Australia 2–0 (1 drawn)

2011–12 (WI): Australia 2–0 (1 drawn)

2015 (WI): Australia 2–0

2015–16 (A): Australia 2–0 (1 drawn)

2.3 AUSTRALIA v NEW ZEALAND

1940s

Given the closeness in proximity, it seems surprising that Australia and New Zealand did not meet in Test cricket between 1945–46 and 1973–74. The inaugural battle involving the neighbouring countries was a one-off match in Wellington as Bill O'Reilly bade farewell to Test cricket, while Keith Miller and Ray Lindwall debuted. After the hosts chose to bat on a damp pitch, they crashed from 37–2 to 42 all out before lunch. O'Reilly claimed 5 wickets, Lindwall 1 and Ernie Toshack 4, before Australia declared at 199–8 and won inside two days as New Zealand mustered just 54, with O'Reilly taking 3–19.

1970s

Australia also won the opening Test of the 1973–74 series by an innings, before New Zealand had the better of a rain-affected draw at Sydney after the hosts managed just 162 in their first innings while the visitors twice topped 300. Australia however romped to a 2–0 series victory with another innings win, with spinners Kerry O'Keeffe and Ashley Mallett the leading wicket-takers in the series while the former also scored 85 in the third Test.

A return series in New Zealand several weeks later was very different, as Australia had to win the third and final Test to square the series. The Chappell brothers dominated the drawn first Test at Wellington, with Greg scoring 247 not out and 133, while Ian scored 145 and 121 in Australian totals of 511–6 declared and 460–8, while New Zealand amassed 484. The Chappells were contained in the second Test at Christchurch, while Kiwi opener Glenn Turner scored two centuries in New Zealand's 5-wicket win, as the hosts chased 228. Amidst plenty of failures and modest scores in the final Test, there were two standout efforts. Doug Walters made 104 not out in Australia's first innings before Ian Redpath (159 not out) carried his bat in Australia's second innings, and New Zealand managed only 158 when the target was 456.

The Kiwis hosted a two-Test series in 1976–77, and drew the first Test before the Australians won the second Test by 10 wickets, after Dennis Lillee had match figures of 11–123. The series highlight was Walters scoring 250 in the first Test before the hosts finished on 293–8 when chasing 350.

1980s

Australia wrapped up the 1980–81 series at home after winning the first two Tests by margins of 10 wickets and 8 wickets, before the final Test was drawn as New Zealand finished at 128–6 when chasing 193. The 1981–82 series in New Zealand bore some resemblance to the 1973–74 series as a draw was again followed by a 5-wicket win to the Kiwis and then the Australians squaring the series with a convincing victory. Rain destroyed the prospect of a result at Wellington, before some controversial umpiring marred the second Test at Auckland. The hosts were too good in any case, with the visitors struggling to 210 before Bruce Edgar scored 161 as the Kiwis led by 177 runs and later passed a target of 104. After Greg Chappell made 176 in Christchurch, his team won by 8 wickets, as Australia needed just 69 after making the hosts follow on.

Richard Hadlee was easily the difference between the two teams in the 1985–86 series in Australia as he captured 33 wickets in the three Tests. He snared 9–52 and 6–71 in the first Test as Australia was dismissed for 179 and 333 while Martin Crowe (188) and John Reid (108) tore the Australians apart as New Zealand reached 553–7 declared. Australian skipper Allan Border (152 not out) and fellow left-hander Greg Matthews (115) could not prevent an innings defeat, before Australia levelled the series after its spinners did well in a fluctuating Sydney Test. New Zealand's first innings of 293 included an opening stand of 79 and last-wicket stand of 124, before Australia's reply of 227 included a sixth-wicket stand of 115 and the loss of its last 4 wickets for 3 runs. The Kiwis subsequently crashed from 100–0 to 193 all out, and Australia stuttered from 132–1 to 192–5 before winning by 4 wickets. An 11-wicket haul to Hadlee was decisive in the Perth Test as Australia made 203 and 259, with the last 7 wickets falling for 64 runs in the latter innings. The Kiwis won the inaugural Trans-Tasman Trophy as they achieved their 164-run target after losing 4 wickets, before they also won the follow-up series at home.

The first two Tests were drawn, with the first Test containing just over three days of play due to rain, before Australia failed to land the knockout blow in the remaining two Tests. Border scored 140 and 114 not out in the second Test and helped his team improve from 74–5 to 364 all out in its first innings, before Martin Crowe overcame an injury setback to score 137 and rescue the Kiwis after they were 48–4. In the decisive Test, Australia slipped from 193–1 to 314 all out following a maiden Test century to opener Geoff Marsh. The Kiwis were in trouble but captain Jeremy Coney, who scored 101 not out and 98 in the first two Tests, followed up with 93 and shared in a vital ninth-wicket stand of 47 as his team tallied 258. The tourists inexplicably crashed for a miserable 103, with David Boon carrying his bat for 58 while John Bracewell nabbed 6 scalps. New Zealand overcame the early loss of Edgar to win by 8 wickets.

Australia began the 1987–88 series strongly with a 9-wicket win, before the second Test was drawn following centuries to Kiwi duo Andrew Jones (150) and Martin Crowe (137) and the Australian captain, who made 205. The final Test was tense, with the hosts chasing 247 and looking well placed at 103–2 and 209–5, before Hadlee induced a collapse. The last-wicket pair of Craig McDermott and Michael Whitney survived the final 29 deliveries to salvage a draw, although McDermott appeared lucky to not be adjudged lbw in the penultimate over.

Season 1989–90 featured one Test in Australia and another in New Zealand, with the Kiwis emerging triumphant. Boon scored 200 but Australia failed to force an outright win, after asking New Zealand to follow on in the Perth Test. Mark Greatbatch saved the Kiwis as he scored an undefeated 146 in 655 minutes at number three while Martin Snedden lasted 202 minutes in an unbroken eighth-wicket stand.

1990s

The Australians headed to Wellington after not losing any of their previous 14 Tests, but things came unstuck after they succumbed for 110 following a rain-delayed start and mustered 269 in their second innings. Off-spinning all-rounder Peter Taylor top-scored in both innings with 29 and 87 while Hadlee and Bracewell were the main wicket-takers, and Australia's lead of 177 proved too small. An unbeaten 117 from John Wright set up a 9-wicket win for the Kiwis, before he wound up his Test career in the next Trans-Tasman series in New Zealand in early 1993.

The Kiwis were thrashed by an innings in the first Test before rain prevented a result in the second Test. In the third and final Test at Auckland, Danny Morrison's 6–37 was responsible for Australia tallying just 139 before a fightback enabled the visitors to set the hosts a target of 201. A winner was hard to pick as wickets fell at 44, 65, 109, 129 and 134, before Ken Rutherford and Tony Blain helped New Zealand to a 5-wicket win to retain the Trans-Tasman Trophy.

When the teams met on Australian soil later in the year, a drawn Test first up suggested another competitive series was in store, before New Zealand faltered badly following the departure of an injured Martin Crowe. Boon, Michael Slater and Mark Waugh scored centuries in the second Test before spinners Shane Warne and Tim May decimated the visitors, who were twice dismissed for 161 to hand Australia victory by an innings and 222 runs. The final Test was not much better for the Kiwis as they lost by an innings and 96 runs following centuries to Steve Waugh and Border.

Four years passed before the next Trans-Tasman series took place, with Australia again winning 2–0 at home. New Zealand again began soundly, this time reducing the hosts to 52–4 before Australia finished with 373, as Mark Taylor (112), Paul Reiffel (77) and Ian Healy (68) contributed strongly. New Zealand made 349 before flopping to 132 all out to lose by 186 runs. Australia won the next Test by an innings after paceman Simon Cook snared 7 wickets in the first of his only two Tests. The Kiwis prevented a clean sweep as they finished the third Test 65 runs shy of victory with 1 wicket in hand as the last pair survived the final 10.4 overs.

2000s

Australia won 3–0 on New Zealand soil in early 2000, with a 62-run win followed by successive 6-wicket victories. Chris Cairns blazed 109 and 69 for New Zealand in the second Test, but 151 not out from Steve Waugh and 143 from Slater ensured Australia had the upper hand. Justin Langer (57) and Mark Waugh (44 not out) scored the bulk of the runs in Australia's second innings as the world champions chased 174. Langer was also prominent in the final Test, scoring 122 not out as Australia chased 210, while his Western Australian teammates Damien Martyn (89) and Adam Gilchrist (75 and ten catches) also played major roles.

The 2001–02 series in Australia proved intriguing despite no results occurring. Australian openers Matthew Hayden and Langer produced double-century partnerships in the first two Tests, both of which were disrupted by rain, before the third Test could have gone either way. A risky declaration from Steve Waugh almost led to New Zealand pulling off a shock victory in the first Test, with the tourists finishing 10 runs shy of victory at 274–6. In the third Test, Lou Vincent scored 104 on debut while Stephen Fleming, Nathan Astle and Adam Parore also scored centuries in a Kiwi total of 534–9 declared, before Australia finished its second innings on 381–7 when the target was 440.

Australia won the next four series 2–0, although New Zealand was left to ponder what might have been on a few occasions. In the first Test of 2004–05 Down Under, Jacob Oram's 126 not out helped New Zealand to 353 before Australia was 128–4 and 222–5 in reply. Michael Clarke (141) and Adam Gilchrist (126) swung the Test Australia's way before number nine Jason Gillespie (54 not out) and Glenn McGrath (61) put on 114 for the last wicket. New Zealand crashed to 76 all out to lose by an innings and 156 runs, but the result could have been far different had Gilchrist been given out when he appeared plumb lbw in single figures. Langer's 215 gave Australia another 500-plus total in the second Test, and the hosts won by 213 runs after opting not to enforce the follow on.

At home more than three months later, the Kiwis lost the first and third Tests by 9 wickets and were in danger of defeat in the second

Test when rain arrived, after the hosts had to follow on. New Zealand made 433 in the first innings of the first Test after Hamish Marshall scored 146, and then Australia tottered at 201–6 before Gilchrist (121) and Simon Katich (118) added 212 runs. New Zealand's subsequent demise for 131 left Australia needing 133, with Langer (72 not out) and captain Ricky Ponting (47 not out) scoring most of them. Martyn (165) and Gilchrist (162) excelled in the second Test, before Ponting (86 not out) and Langer (59 not out) ensured Australia coasted past its 164-run target in the third Test, after Ponting (105) top-scored in Australia's first innings.

Two individual batting displays helped Australia gain control of the first Test of 2008–09 at home, while Mitchell Johnson starred with the ball as he snared 4–30 and 5–39. Clarke made 98 as Australia struggled to 214 and, after New Zealand fell 58 runs behind on the first innings, Katich carried his bat for 131 in a total of 268 before New Zealand lost by 149 runs after being set 327. New Zealand made 270 and 203 in the second Test, while Clarke's 110 and Brad Haddin's 169 enabled Australia to tally 535 and win by an innings.

Clarke (168) and Marcus North (112 not out) made big scores for Australia in the first Test of the 2009–10 series in New Zealand, which had to follow on, before a total of 407 couldn't prevent Australia from winning by 10 wickets. The visitors stumbled to 231 all out in the second Test before the hosts led by just 33 despite 138 from Ross Taylor. Australia set a target of 479, which New Zealand never looked likely to achieve, with Johnson claiming 6–73 to complete a 10-wicket match haul.

The 2011–12 series began in a familiar way as Australia cantered to a 9-wicket win following a century from Clarke, before New Zealand beat Australia in a Test for the first time in more than 18 years. In a match that produced plenty of edged catches and edged boundaries, New Zealand led by 14 runs on the first innings despite tallying just 150, before setting Australia 241. Australia lost its first 2 wickets at 72 and 122 before slipping from 159–2 to 159–5 and later collapsing to 199–9. The Australians nearly stole another 2–0 series win as opener David Warner scored 123 not out in his second Test, but Doug Bracewell rattled Nathan Lyon's stumps to finish with 6–40 and leave the Kiwis victorious by 7 runs.

Lyon was at the centre of a major controversy during New Zealand's historic tour of Australia in late 2015, as the hosts were lucky to win 2–0. The Brisbane Test was lopsided as Australia won by 208 runs, before a draw at Perth was followed by a 3-wicket win to the hosts at Adelaide in the inaugural day–night Test. Joe Burns (71 and 129), Warner (163 and 116) and Usman Khawaja (174 and 9 not out) starred for the victors at Brisbane, while Kane Williamson made 140 in New Zealand's first innings. A result never looked likely at Perth where Warner (253) and Khawaja (121) were somewhat overshadowed by Kiwi duo Ross Taylor (290) and Williamson (166), before Steve Smith and Adam Voges scored a ton each in Australia's second innings. The Adelaide Test was decided in three days, with Australia chasing 187. Australia was 116–8 in reply to New Zealand's first innings of 202 before Lyon was controversially ruled not out when he appeared to have edged a catch, and this was vital as the hosts gained a 22-run first-innings lead.

Two Tests were played in New Zealand in February 2016, with Australia again winning 2–0 following a major controversy. The Australians won the first Test at Wellington by an innings but not before Voges, in single figures, was bowled by a delivery, which was called a no ball before replays showed the delivery should have been ruled legitimate. Voges went on to score 239 while Khawaja made 140 in a 562-run total. In the Christchurch Test, retiring Kiwi skipper Brendon McCullum slammed the fastest ever Test century, off 54 balls. McCullum's 145 off 79 balls set up a total of 370 before Burns (170) and Smith (138) set up a reply of 505. Australia lost just 3 wickets when chasing 201, with Burns (65), Smith (53 not out) and Khawaja (45) prominent yet again.

Australia v New Zealand

1945–46 (NZ): Australia 1–0

1973–74 (A): Australia 2–0 (1 drawn)

1973–74 (NZ): 1–1 (1 drawn)

1976–77 (NZ): Australia 1–0 (1 drawn)

1980–81 (A): Australia 2–0 (1 drawn)

1981–82 (NZ): 1–1 (1 drawn)
1985–86 (A): New Zealand 2–1
1985–86 (NZ): New Zealand 1–0 (2 drawn)
1987–88 (A): Australia 1–0 (2 drawn)
1989–90 (A): 1 drawn
1989–90 (NZ): New Zealand 1–0
1992–93 (NZ): 1–1 (1 drawn)
1993–94 (A): Australia 2–0 (1 drawn)
1997–98 (A): Australia 2–0 (1 drawn)

1999–00 (NZ): Australia 3–0
2001–02 (A): 0–0 (3 drawn)
2004–05 (A): Australia 2–0
2004–05 (NZ): Australia 2–0 (1 drawn)
2008–09 (A): Australia 2–0
2009–10 (NZ): Australia 2–0
2011–12 (A): 1–1
2015–16 (A): Australia 2–0 (1 drawn)
2015–16 (NZ): Australia 2–0

2.4 AUSTRALIA v INDIA

1940s

Australia was bound to be a tough hurdle for India to overcome when the countries first met in 1947–48, as Australia was on home soil and included the likes of Don Bradman, Arthur Morris, Lindsay Hassett, Keith Miller and Ray Lindwall. India meanwhile had only contested England in Test cricket from 1932 to 1946.

Bradman scored 185 in the first Test, which had several weather interruptions, before his declaration was followed by India collapsing for 58 and 98 to lose by an innings and 226 runs, as Ernie Toshack claimed 5–2 and 6–29. With three days washed out in the second Test, no result was possible in a low-scoring match, as India finished its second innings at 61–7, a lead of 142. Australia completed a 4–0 series win after a 233-run victory was followed by two innings victories, with Bradman the chief scorer, while other centurions included 19-year-old Neil Harvey who scored 153 in his second Test. The highlight for India was Vijay Hazare scoring 116 and 145 in the fourth Test while Vinoo Mankad also scored two centuries in the series.

1950s

With India hosting three Tests in 1956–57, Australia recorded another innings victory before India salvaged a draw and a somewhat respectable 94-run loss. Richie Benaud was the standout as his 23 wickets was nearly double the next highest wicket-takers. He claimed 11 scalps in the final Test as India twice made 136 while Australia also twice fell shy of 200.

The 1959–60 series in the subcontinent began in familiar fashion, as Australia won by an innings, before India beat Australia for the first time after the tourists declined the offer to play on a matting pitch. Off spinner Jasubhai Patel claimed 9–69 and 5–55 to dismiss Australia for 219 and 105, while Alan Davidson captured 5–31 and 7–93, as India scored 152 and 291. Only one of the final three Tests yielded a result, with Australia winning the fourth by an innings after opener Les Favell scored 101 in a total of 342.

1960s

India hosted the third consecutive series involving Australia and India when the 1964–65 series took place, and the tourists were clearly unhappy with the umpiring. Australia, nonetheless, won the first Test by 139 runs after Graham McKenzie claimed match figures of 10–91. With Australia's Norman O'Neill unable to bat, India somewhat fortuitously won the second Test by two wickets following a 93-run seventh-wicket stand and 32-run ninth-wicket stand that took the hosts past the 254-run target. The series was drawn after the final two days of the third Test were rained off.

India only played well in patches during its 1967–68 tour of Australia, with the hosts winning all four Tests. The margins were 146 runs, an innings and 4 runs, 39 runs and 144 runs. In the third Test, the tourists made a concerted effort to pursue 395 as they recovered from 61–3 to 310–5. Bob Cowper was easily Australia's leading batsman, and

Australia's bowlers shared the wickets while India's EAS Prasanna was clearly the bowler of the series.

Australia won the first Test of a sometimes ill-tempered 1969–70 series by 8 wickets, before a draw and a 7-wicket win to hosts India left the series level with two Tests to play. India's batting faltered at crucial stages as the tourists recorded wins of 10 wickets and 77 runs, with Australian off spinner Ashley Mallett the leading wicket-taker in the series, as he nabbed 28 scalps while Prasanna captured 26.

1970s

Bob Simpson came out of retirement to lead Australia against India on Australian soil in season 1977–78, as the hosts were weakened due to a number of players signing up for World Series Cricket. A great series unfolded in any case, starting with a 16-run win to Australia, as Sunil Gavaskar's 113 wasn't quite enough for India to reach its target of 341. The leading runscorer in the series, Simpson, made 176 in the second Test as Australia tallied 394 in reply to India's 402. Chasing 339, the hosts sneaked to a 2-wicket victory after nightwatchman Tony Mann scored 105. India roared back into the series with a 222-run win in Melbourne before inflicting an innings defeat in Sydney. The deciding Test in Adelaide was almost as good as the first two, with India trailing by 236 runs on the first innings before tallying a gallant 445 when the target was 493.

India recorded its first series win against Australia in late 1979 with a 2–0 result in the six-match series, as the tourists were rather inexperienced. The first two Tests were drawn and involved weather disruptions, with Allan Border and Australian captain Kim Hughes scoring centuries in the first Test before Indian duo Dilip Vengsarkar and Gundappa Viswanath did likewise in the second Test. Australian left-arm paceman Geoff Dymock claimed 12 wickets in the third Test but India won by 153 runs, after the tourists floundered with the bat on a difficult pitch. The Australians again salvaged consecutive draws, and had to follow on in the fourth Test. Some of the tourists encountered health troubles during the sixth Test while the hosts benefited from some dubious umpiring decisions, but India was much too good on a pitch that favoured spin bowling. Dilip Doshi claimed match figures of 8–103, as India won by an innings and 100 runs after declaring at 458–8.

1980s

The 1980–81 series in Australia generated plenty of attention as Greg Chappell returned as Australian skipper, while Dennis Lillee played his only series against India. Chappell scored 204 in his team's innings win in the first Test, before Kim Hughes scored 213 in the second Test. India's Sandeep Patil scored 174 in India's first innings of the second Test, but the tourists only just avoided an outright defeat as they were 8 wickets down in the second innings while a long way short of the target. India drew the series with a 59-run win in Melbourne, but not before the tourists came within a whisker of forfeiting. Viswanath made a courageous 114 before Border scored 124 as Australia gained a 182-run lead, and then India lost its first wicket at 165. India's captain, Gavaskar, was upset at being adjudged lbw, after being critical of the umpiring in the second Test, and he signalled for fellow opening batsman Chetan Chauhan to walk off with him. India's manager Wing Commander Shahid Durrani instructed Chauhan and incoming batsman Vengsarkar to play on, and India eventually set Australia a modest target of 143. But the locals fell apart on a dodgy pitch, with Kapil Dev claiming 5 wickets after Australia began day five at 24–3.

Australia was lucky to escape with three draws in the 1985–86 series on home soil as India had the upper hand each time. Australian duo David Boon and Greg Ritchie scored hundreds before Gavaskar made an unbeaten 166 in a rain-affected first Test, then Greg Matthews scored 100 not out as Australia struggled to 262 in the second Test. After his team trailed by 183 runs, Border scored 163 as he and number 11 Dave Gilbert had some luck, while the Indians lacked some initiative during a priceless last-wicket stand of 77. The tourists were unlucky, nonetheless, that rain washed out the last session as India was 59–2 and needing just 67 more runs, but captain Kapil Dev didn't blame the weather as he vented his spleen on the umpiring. Centuries to openers Gavaskar and Kris Srikkanth and first drop Mohinder Amarnath helped

India to 600–4 declared in the final Test before Australia went from 217–0 to 396 all out and narrowly avoided defeat, finishing their second innings on 119–6 after following on.

The 1986–87 series in India was also deadlocked, and this time there were no moral victors after the second and third Tests were drawn. The second Test didn't start until day four due to wet conditions, before the final Test featured just 17 wickets. The first Test nonetheless was one to savour as it produced the second tied result in Test cricket. Dean Jones scored a memorable 210 as he battled health problems in the scorching heat, while teammates Boon and Border scored 122 and 106 respectively in the total of 574–7 declared. India was in danger of having to follow on before Kapil Dev hammered 119, and Border's second declaration in the match left the hosts needing 348 on the final day. India was well placed as the first 3 wickets fell at 55, 158 and 204, and then the hosts had the odd stumble before reaching 331–6 and then stuttering to 344–9 with 8 balls remaining. Spinners Greg Matthews and Ray Bright bowled in tandem and finished with 5 wickets each, after the former also bagged 5 wickets in India's first innings. Ravi Shastri levelled the score with 3 balls remaining, before Matthews won a lbw appeal against Maninder Singh from the penultimate delivery to seal the historic result.

1990s

More than five years passed before the teams next met in Test cricket, with Australia winning a five-match series 4–0 at home. Craig McDermott had a great series as he snared 31 wickets while Merv Hughes and left-armers Bruce Reid and Michael Whitney had their moments. David Boon and Mark Taylor were Australia's best batsmen, while Shastri made the highest score of the series — 206 — in the Test that was drawn. Following big losses in the opening two Tests, the Indians had the better of the drawn Test before competing well in the fourth Test, as they scored 225 and 333 in reply to Australia's 145 and 451. Kapil Dev remained India's leading bowler but the find of the series was 18-year-old Sachin Tendulkar, who scored two classy centuries and averaged 46.

More than four years later, a one-off match in Delhi represented the start of the Border–Gavaskar Trophy for Australia versus India battles in Test cricket. Underprepared and missing an injured Warne, Australia collapsed to 182 all out as India's spinners wreaked havoc, before wicketkeeper and opening batsman Nayan Mongia converted his maiden Test century into a score of 152. India won by 7 wickets, before winning the three-Test series on home soil in early 1998.

Australia led by 71 runs on the first innings before being set 348 to win, and a few umpiring errors were costly as Australia was dismissed for 168, although India deserved to win. There could be no arguing about the result in the second Test as a strong all-round display from the hosts enabled India to win by an innings and 219 runs. Anil Kumble claimed 8 wickets and Javagal Srinath 6 wickets while Mohammad Azharuddin top-scored with 163 not out in India's 633–5 declared. Tendulkar completed another great series with 177 and 31 in the final Test, but the tourists prevented a whitewash as they replied to India's 424 with 400 before passing the 194-run target for the loss of just 2 wickets. Mark Waugh made his highest Test score of 153 not out in Australia's first innings before captain Mark Taylor scored an undefeated 102 in the run chase. But the hero was Michael Kasprowicz who snared 5–28 in India's second innings to swing the match Australia's way.

The 1999–00 series was heavily one-sided as Australia won by margins of 285 runs, 180 runs, and an innings and 141 runs. Steve Waugh and Ricky Ponting scored a century each in the first Test before Justin Langer scored 223 in the final Test, while Ponting was left not out on 141. Brett Lee had a great debut in the second Test as he snared a wicket with his fourth ball and recorded figures of 5–47 and 2–31. Tendulkar scored 116 and 52 in the second Test before VVS Laxman scored 167 in India's second innings of the third Test, but the tourists could not register a team total beyond 285.

2000s

Australia versus India series were often special following the 1999–00 series, with the 2001 series perhaps the best of them as the tourists looked certain to win a series in India for the first time since 1969–70.

Five wickets each to Glenn McGrath, Jason Gillespie and Warne, coupled with a century each to Matthew Hayden and Adam Gilchrist, set up Australia's 10-wicket win in the first Test. Despite a hat-trick to Harbhajan Singh, Australia did well enough to enforce the follow-on in the second Test. But the tourists' victory bid was foiled as Laxman (281) and Rahul Dravid (180) batted throughout the fourth day. They added 335 runs on the day, and their partnership produced 376 runs overall, before Australia needed 384. Harbhajan snared 6–73 following first-innings figures of 7–123, and India's 171-run win produced the third occasion in Test cricket that a team won after following on.

Hayden and Harbhajan were clearly the players of the series, after Hayden scored 203 and 35 in the deciding Test while Harbhajan nabbed 7–133 and 8–84. Hayden accumulated more than twice as many runs as any of his teammates while Harbhajan captured a staggering 32 wickets. Tendulkar's 126 and several solid scores from teammates enabled India to post 501 in response to Australia's 391, which featured a collapse of 7–51 that was precipitated by Steve Waugh being out, handled the ball. Chasing 155, India was on top at 101–3 when Tendulkar departed before the next 4 wickets fell at 117, 122, 135 and 135. An eighth-wicket partnership of 16 was vital before India scraped home by 2 wickets.

India staged another remarkable comeback in the second Test of 2003–04 as the series was as tight as the 1–1 scoreline suggested. The Brisbane Test was drawn following rain disruptions, before Ricky Ponting's 242 set up an Australian total of 556 in the first innings at Adelaide. The visitors plunged to 85–4 with Tendulkar out, but Dravid (233) and Laxman (148) again proved a thorn in Australia's side. They added 303 runs as India finished just 33 in arrears, before Ajit Agarkar ripped through Australia with 6–41. Needing 230, the Indians never really looked in danger as they won by 4 wickets. Australia fought back brilliantly at Melbourne as India fell from 278–1 to 366 all out, with opener Virender Sehwag having scored 195. Ponting (257) and Hayden (136) set up a 192-run lead before they were at the crease as Australia romped to a 9-wicket victory. As India needed only a draw at Sydney to retain the Border–Gavaskar Trophy, Tendulkar (241 not out) and Laxman (178) set up a total of 705–7 declared before the tourists gained a 231-run lead but opted to bat again. Set 443, Australia finished at 357–6 as Steve Waugh concluded his Test career with a score of 80.

The 2004–05 series was the first time since 1969–70 that Australia won a Test series in India. The tourists won the opening encounter by 217 runs after Michael Clarke scored 151 on debut to set up an Australian first-innings total of 474. The second Test was drawn following 13 wickets to Anil Kumble, and it was a pity that no play was possible on day five as India was 19–0 chasing 229 after Sehwag scored 155 in India's first innings. Jason Gillespie snared 9 wickets as Australia won the third Test by 342 runs to wrap up the series after Damien Martyn continued his fine form with the bat. A 3–0 result looked likely as Australia needed just 107 runs to win the final Test, but the tourists crumbled to 93 all out on a tricky pitch that suited the spinners.

Australia all but wrapped up the 2007–08 series on home soil after winning the first two Tests by 337 runs and 122 runs. The second Test was marred by dubious umpiring and allegations that Harbhajan had racially abused Andrew Symonds, who had scored a fortuitous 162 not out in Australia's 463 before India replied with 532. India later needed 333 runs and looked like salvaging a draw until Clarke bagged the last 3 wickets in 5 deliveries. The hosts fell 73 runs shy of a target of 413 in the third Test as the Indians, as had been the case in 2000–01, snapped a 16-match winning streak by Australia. The fourth Test petered out into a draw after both teams topped 500 in their first innings.

India won 2–0 on home soil in 2008–09 and 2010–11, with four Tests played on the former occasion before just two were played on the latter occasion. The first Test of the 2008–09 series finished in a draw with honours relatively even, before India won the second Test by 320 runs, after dismissing Australia for 268 and 195. Gautam Gambhir (206) and Laxman (200 not out) helped India to 613–7 declared in the third Test before Australia replied with 577, all but ensuring a draw before the hosts won the final Test by 172 runs, after the tourists unsuccessfully sought 382 to level the series.

The opening Test of 2010–11 was a cliffhanger, with India scraping home by a single wicket. Both teams topped 400, with Shane Watson topscoring for Australia in both innings with 126 and 56, before India appeared headed for defeat at 124–8 when chasing 216. Laxman and number ten Ishant Sharma added 81 before Sharma departed and, after a couple of Indians were unluckily ruled lbw, number 11 Pragyan Ojha was fortunate to survive an appeal before a run-out attempt just moments later resulted in four overthrows. Two subsequent leg byes sealed the result, and then the second Test followed a similar course to the first Test for a while, until India reached the 207-run target for the loss of just 3 wickets.

The 2011–12 series Down Under was surprisingly one-sided as the hosts won all four fixtures. The first Test was evenly balanced until India slid to 169 all out when chasing 292, before Australia won the second Test by an innings following a monumental 329 not out from Clarke. David Warner made 180 in the third Test while Ben Hilfenhaus snared 8 wickets as the hosts again won by an innings, before the margin in the final Test was 298 runs, after Ponting made 221 and 60 not out.

The 2012–13 series also featured four outright wins to the home side, although in this case it was India. The hosts were 196–4 with Tendulkar dismissed after Australia scored 380 in the first Test, before Indian captain and wicketkeeper MS Dhoni scored 224 while Virat Kohli made 107. Ravi Ashwin captured 12 wickets as India won by 8 wickets, before claiming an innings win in the second Test. Cheteshwar Pujara (204) and Murali Vijay (167) put on a second-wicket stand of 370 in India's total of 503 before Australia fell from 56–0 to 131 all out. The hosts lost four wickets when chasing 133 in the third Test, after Australia's first-innings total of 408 (with Mitchell Starc scoring 99 at number nine) was followed by India tallying 499 after openers Vijay (153) and Test debutant Shikhar Dhawan (187) put on 289. The final Test also featured a 6-wicket margin, this time as India sought 155.

Being on home soil again appeared decisive in 2014–15 as Australia won the first two Tests before having the better of two draws. Centuries to Steve Smith, Warner and Clarke helped the hosts to 517 in the first Test before the visitors made 444, after captain Kohli scored 115. Warner made another ton before Kohli (141) and Vijay (99) had India in sight of victory as the target was 364. But a 12-wicket match haul to off spinner Nathan Lyon, who admittedly conceded 286 runs, helped Australia win by 48 runs. Vijay's 144 helped India pass 400 in the second Test, but 133 from Smith and solid contributions from Australia's lower order enabled the hosts to lead by 97 runs on the first innings and later win by 4 wickets, after being set 128. Smith made 192 in the third Test as Australia made 530 before Kohli (169) and Ajinkya Rahane (147) defied the hosts. Australia finished 4 wickets shy of victory as India was 210 runs shy of the 384-run target, before India finished the final Test on 252–7 after being set 349. Smith concluded a splendid personal series with scores of 117 and 71, while Warner and Kohli scored another century each, as did Indian opener Lokesh Rahul.

Australia v India

1947–48 (A): Australia 4–0 (1 drawn)

1956–57 (I): Australia 2–0 (1 drawn)

1959–60 (I): Australia 2–1 (2 drawn)

1964–65 (I): 1–1 (1 drawn)

1967–68 (A): Australia 4–0

1969–70 (I): Australia 3–1 (1 drawn)

1977–78 (A): Australia 3–2

1979–80 (I): India 2–0 (4 drawn)

1980–81 (A): 1–1 (1 drawn)

1985–86 (A): 0–0 (3 drawn)

1986–87 (I): 0–0 (1 tied, 2 drawn)

1991–92 (A): Australia 4–0 (1 drawn)

1996–97 (I): India 1–0

1997–98 (I): India 2–1

1999–00 (A): Australia 3–0

2000–01 (I): India 2–1

2003–04 (A): 1–1 (2 drawn)

2004–05 (I): Australia 2–1 (1 drawn)

2007–08 (A): Australia 2–1 (1 drawn)

2008–09 (I): India 2–0 (2 drawn)

2010–11 (I): India 2–0

2011–12 (A): Australia 4–0

2012–13 (I): India 4–0

2014–15 (A): Australia 2–0 (2 drawn)

2.5 AUSTRALIA v PAKISTAN

1950s

The Pakistanis won by 9 wickets when they first encountered Australia in late 1956, but the match was a lot more interesting than the lopsided result suggested. The Test was played on a matting pitch at Karachi, and featured just 95 runs on the first day, without weather disruptions. Australia limped to 80 all out in 53.1 overs, and Pakistan was 15–2 at stumps, before being dismissed for 199 late on day two. Fazal Mahmood claimed 6–34 and 7–80 while Khan Mohammad had 4–43 and 3–69, and Pakistan needed just 69 runs to win. But it took the hosts 48.4 overs to reach the target, having been 6 runs shy of the target at the end of day four.

Pakistan hosted a three-Test series in late 1959, with the first Test played on matting, which was dragged over a rain-drenched grass pitch at Dacca. Pakistan was dismissed for 200 before Australia gained a 25-run lead, following 96 from Neil Harvey at first drop and an unbeaten 66 from Wally Grout at number nine. Fazal claimed 5–71 but the bowling heroes were Australian duo Richie Benaud (two 4-wicket hauls) and Ken Mackay who snared 6–42 in Pakistan's second innings, before the tourists lost only 2 wickets when chasing 110. Norman O'Neill and Lindsay Kline were Australia's best in its 7-wicket win at Lahore, with O'Neill scoring 134 before Kline captured 7–75 in Pakistan's second innings as Saeed Ahmed compiled 166. The drawn third Test at Karachi was rather tedious, with American president Dwight D Eisenhower attending the fourth day, in which Pakistan scored just 104 runs for the loss of 5 wickets.

1960s

Australia and Pakistan played out two drawn Tests in late 1964, with one in Karachi and one in Melbourne. Australian skipper Bob Simpson scored 153 and 115 in Karachi before his counterpart, Hanif

Mohammad, scored 104 and 93 in Melbourne, while Khalid Ibadulla scored 166 in the first innings in Karachi.

1970s

Australia hosted series of three Tests in 1972–73 and 1976–77, and won all three in 1972–73, although the tourists could just as easily have won the latter two. The hosts won the opening Test by an innings after centuries to Ian Chappell and Rod Marsh were followed by Ashley Mallett claiming 8–59. Pakistan required 293 runs to win the second Test after reaching 574–8 declared in its first innings, only to fold for 200 as three run-outs were costly, not to mention six batsmen reaching double figures without making a half-century. Pakistan needed only 159 to win the final Test, but Max Walker's 6–15 ensured the tourists fell 53 runs short. Bob Massie (42) and John Watkins (36) also deserved credit for a ninth-wicket partnership of 83 in Australia's second innings, as Watkins played his only Test.

Pakistan's second Test victory against Australia came a little over 20 years after Pakistan won the inaugural meeting. Pakistan fought back from a difficult position to draw the first Test of 1976–77, thanks largely to centuries from Zaheer Abbas and Asif Iqbal. Chasing 285, Australia stuttered from 201–3 to 228–6 before Gary Cosier and Rod Marsh opted not to pursue 56 runs in the final 15 overs, and they were jeered by the crowd after the hosts finished 24 runs shy of victory. Cosier scored 168 while Greg Chappell scored 121 in the second Test as Australia declared at 517–8, and Pakistan collapsed from 241–1 to 333 all out in its first innings, before crumbling for 151 in its second innings to lose by 348 runs. Imran Khan finally found his rhythm in the third Test, after being hit around in the first two Tests, and he claimed 12 wickets, while Asif's second century in the series was also decisive as Pakistan drew the series with an 8-wicket triumph.

The two-Test series Down Under in 1978–79 featured a lot of ill-feeling, starting when Asif declared that the Australian team was sub-standard. Without World Series players, Australia had just lost 5–1 to England, but the hosts began their subsequent series strongly as Pakistan was dismissed for 196. Australia's batting troubles continued, however, as Pakistan gained a 28-run lead, with Rodney Hogg unfortunately run out after leaving his crease to repair a divot. Needing 382 to win, the Australians were in the box seat at 305–3 with Allan Border having scored a century, before the hosts astonishingly crashed to 310 all out. Medium pacer Sarfraz Nawaz snared 7–1 in a staggering 33-ball spell to finish with 9–86, while the other victim was run out. In the second Test, Pakistan captain Mushtaq Mohammad's plan to make sure Pakistan drew the match backfired, as Australia won by 7 wickets. Javed Miandad scored an undefeated 129 in Pakistan's first innings, before Asif scored 134 not out in the second innings, and Australia needed 236 runs, after Sikander Bakht was controversially run out in the 'Mankad' fashion when backing up too far at the bowler's end. The final act of dubious sportsmanship occurred as Sarfraz successfully appealed for 'handled the ball', after Australian opening batsman Andrew Hilditch handed the ball to him following a wayward throw from the field.

1980s

The 1979–80 series in Pakistan featured a low-scoring match, followed by two high-scoring draws. The ball turned sharply on the Karachi pitch, which proved beneficial for Pakistan duo Iqbal Qasim and Test debutant Tauseef Ahmed, and Australia's Ray Bright. Qasim had match figures of 11–118 after taking 7–49 from 42 overs in Australia's second innings, while Tauseef had 4–64 and 3–62. Bright's match figures were 10–111 after he claimed 3 wickets in Pakistan's second innings, but the hosts won by 7 wickets as they chased just 74. The first day of the second Test was washed out before runs flowed. Greg Chappell (235) and Graham Yallop (172) were the main scorers in Australia's total of 617, while Qasim didn't take a wicket in his 56 overs. Every player in the Australian XI had a bowl, but only Geoff Dymock took a wicket as opener Taslim Arif (210 not out) and second drop Javed Miandad (106 not out) guided Pakistan to 382–2. Border capitalised on a very flat pitch in the third Test as he scored 150 not out and 153, but a result never looked likely.

After Australia tallied a disappointing 180 at Perth in the first Test of the 1981–82 series, local duo Dennis Lillee (5–18) and Terry Alderman

(4–36) skittled Pakistan for 62, after the score had been 26–8 at one stage. Australia won the Test by 286 runs, although Lillee gained some unwanted attention following an altercation with Javed Miandad. A knock of 201 from Greg Chappell and a 9-wicket match haul from Lillee enabled Australia to win the second Test by 10 wickets. Pakistan's batsmen returned to form in the final Test, as a total of 500 was enough to set up an innings win, with Imran, Sarfraz, Qasim, and Wasim Raja sharing the wickets.

Australia was completely outplayed in its 1982–83 tour of Pakistan, with the hosts twice winning by 9 wickets and once winning by an innings. Crowd violence marred the first Test, but no excuses were offered for Australia's poor showing. Pakistan owed much of its success to Abdul Qadir, who claimed 22 wickets in the series, but he was far less effective on Pakistan's 1983–84 tour of Australia.

Wayne Phillips and Yallop made hundreds before 11 wickets to Carl Rackemann set up an innings victory for the hosts in the first Test. The next three Tests were drawn, with bad weather helping Pakistan in the second Test before the tourists did well enough with the bat, but not the ball, in the following two Tests. Australia took the series 2–0 after winning the fifth Test by 10 wickets, with Lillee, Rod Marsh and Greg Chappell making their final Test appearances. Chappell scored 182 while Geoff Lawson and Lillee took a combined total of 17 wickets.

More than four years passed before the countries next met in Test cricket, and the Australians were seething at the pitch and umpiring standards, after Pakistan won the first Test at Karachi by an innings and 188 runs. The spin of Qasim and Qadir was too much for the tourists, after Javed Miandad survived many appeals during his 211. Australia drew the remaining two Tests and nearly levelled the series in the third Test, with Pakistan finishing 116 runs shy of the target after the ninth-wicket pair of Qasim and Tauseef survived the last 5.1 overs. The next two series also featured an outright win and two draws, with the home side triumphant each time.

1990s

Australia won the first Test of 1989–90 by 92 runs, but not before Pakistan put up a desperate fight. Trailing by 116 runs on the first innings before being set 429 to win in ten-and-a-half hours, the tourists were dismissed with 9.1 overs remaining, after Ijaz Ahmed, who was eighth out when brilliantly caught, scored 121 in 450 minutes. Trailing by 84 runs in the second Test, Pakistan subsequently crashed to 22–4 and then 90–5 before Imran (136) and Wasim Akram (123) put on 191 for the sixth wicket. Australia finished at 233–6 after being set 304, with Dean Jones scoring his second century of the match, before rain ruined any chance of a result in the third Test.

The opening match of the 1994–95 series in Pakistan was one that got away from Australia, which had the better of much of the match before the hosts won by 1 wicket. Inzamam-ul-Haq and Mushtaq Ahmed put on an unbroken last-wicket stand of 57 to guide the hosts past their 314-run target. An appeal for lbw was turned down during the tense last-wicket stand before the winning runs came from a missed stumping that yielded four byes. It was one of many missed chances for Australia throughout the series. After making Pakistan follow on in the second Test, Australia reprieved Salim Malik, who went on to score 237 to save the Test before becoming the third victim in Test debutant Damien Fleming's hat-trick. Another century to Malik in the final Test, which also featured centuries to teammates Moin Khan and Aamir Sohail, ensured that Pakistan maintained a 1–0 series lead.

The Pakistanis ruined their chances in the first Test of the 1995–96 series with a litany of dropped catches, and hosts Australia won by an innings after Pakistan was dismissed for 97 and 240. Shane Warne captured 7–23 and 4–54, before being unable to bowl in the second Test after suffering an injury while batting. Australia still won by 155 runs as Glenn McGrath and Paul Reiffel were the pick of the bowlers, before an 8-wicket haul to Warne in the third Test wasn't enough to prevent Pakistan winning by 74 runs, after Australia was 117–2 chasing 247. Mushtaq Ahmed claimed 9 wickets in the match while Akram and Younis also shared the wickets after Ijaz scored 137 in Pakistan's first innings.

Having not won a Test in Pakistan since 1959, Australia broke this drought with victory by an innings and 95 runs in the first Test of the 1998–99 series. Stuart MacGill captured 9 wickets in Warne's absence, while Michael Slater and Steve Waugh scored centuries, followed by scores of 98 and 82 by Darren Lehmann and Ian Healy. Both teams topped 500 in the drawn second Test, made memorable by Australian skipper Mark Taylor scoring 334 not out. He and teammate Justin Langer (116) survived lbw shouts before they had scored, and Taylor was also dropped twice before he reached 30. Saeed Anwar scored his second century in as many Tests while Ijaz continued his good record against Australia with another ton, before Taylor was dismissed for 92 in Australia's second innings. Sohail scored a century for Pakistan in the third Test, followed by a century to Mark Waugh in Australia's second innings, before another hundred to Ijaz wasn't enough for the hosts to square the series, as they finished at 262–5 after being set 419.

Australia won all three Tests in the 1999–00 series at home, although Pakistan could just as easily have won the second Test. The visitors tallied 367 before Australia racked up 575 in the first Test, with Slater and Mark Waugh posting hundreds while three teammates made 80s. Pakistan slid from 214–3 to 281 all out, following a century to Anwar, with Fleming snaring match figures of 9–124 in Australia's 10-wicket win. After Saqlain Mushtaq and Waqar Younis caused Australia to slip from 191–1 to 246 all out in the second Test, Pakistan set the hosts 369 and had them in strife at 126–5. Langer (127) and Adam Gilchrist, who scored an unbeaten 149 in his second Test, added 238 runs to set up a spectacular 4-wicket victory. In the final Test, Australian pacemen McGrath, Fleming and Michael Kasprowicz shared 19 wickets, while Langer (144) and Ricky Ponting (197) established Australia's 296-run lead. Ijaz's 115 in Pakistan's second innings wasn't enough for the tourists to avoid an innings defeat.

2000s

The 2002–03 series had a different feel as it was played in neutral territory, although the conditions were more familiar for Pakistan, as the first Test was in Colombo before the latter two were in Sharjah.

Australia led by 188 runs on the first innings in Colombo after a century to Ponting was followed by 7 wickets to Warne. Australia went from 61–0 to 127 all out as Shoaib Akhtar and Saqlain shared 9 wickets, and then Pakistan was tantalisingly placed at 91–0, 173–2 and 230–4 before losing by 41 runs. The two Tests in Sharjah were disastrous for the Pakistanis as they lost both by an innings. Warne (match figures of 8–24), McGrath, Brett Lee and Andy Bichel decimated them for 59 and 53, while Matthew Hayden scored 119 in Australia's 310 in the second Test. In the final Test, Ponting (150), Steve Waugh (103 not out) and Hayden (89) set up Australia's 444 before Pakistan twice passed 200, as Warne, McGrath and Bichel shared the wickets.

Australia won 3–0 on home soil in 2004–05 and 2009–10 before things changed away from home. Scores of 191 and 97 from Langer, coupled with 5–30 from Kasprowicz in Pakistan's first innings and 8–24 from McGrath in Pakistan's second innings, helped Australia to a 491-run win in the first Test of 2004–05. Damien Martyn (100 not out) and Ponting (98) also contributed in Australia's second innings. Australia won the remaining two Tests by 9 wickets after chasing just 126 and 62, although Pakistan was in a commanding position at times. In the second Test, the tourists were 286–3 before folding for 341, and then the hosts led by just 38 following 142 from Martyn, while Akhtar and leg spinner Danish Kaneria took 5 scalps apiece. Pakistan went from 193–1 to 304 all out in the third Test before Ponting (207) and Gilchrist (113) punished the tourists as Australia tallied 568 despite Kaneria's 7 wickets. The other leg spinners were also prominent as MacGill claimed 8 scalps and Warne 5.

Shane Watson (93 and 120 not out) was the best for Australia in its 170-run win in the first Test of 2009–10, before a seemingly miraculous 36-run victory at Sydney was clouded by match fixing allegations. Mohammad Asif's 6–41 routed Australia for 127 before Pakistan led by 206 and then had Australia 257–8. A ninth-wicket stand of 123 unfolded, and Mike Hussey made 134 not out. Several dropped catches, including a few by wicketkeeper Kamran Akmal, coupled with defensive field placings, aroused suspicions of the motives of some Pakistani players, before the tourists slid to 139 all out when needing 176, as Nathan Hauritz captured 5–53. Ponting (209) and Clarke

(166) steered the hosts towards 519–8 declared in the third Test before Salman Butt's 102 helped the tourists towards 301. Simon Katich (100) and Ponting (89) did well in Australia's second innings before Pakistan was dismissed for 206 to lose by 231 runs.

Australia and Pakistan met twice in England in July 2010 as part of the MCC Spirit of Cricket Test Series. Australia crashed from 171–2 to 253 all out in the first Test at Lord's before Watson bagged 5–40 as Pakistan succumbed for 148. Australia's tail boosted its second-innings total from 208–8 to 334 all out before Pakistan sank from 152–1 to 289 all out. The Pakistanis drew the series as they broke their drought against Australia with a 3-wicket win at Headingley. Pakistan replied to Australia's miserable 88 with 258, before Pakistan chased 180 and stumbled from 137–1 to 161–6 to cause a few heart flutters.

The 2014–15 series was also played in neutral territory, with the first Test in Dubai and the second in Abu Dhabi. Younis Khan and Sarfraz Ahmed posted tons, while other solid scores rescued the Pakistanis after their openers fell cheaply in Dubai. Despite 133 from David Warner, Australia folded for 303 in reply to 454, before another century to Younis, as well as 131 from Ahmed Shehzad enabled Pakistan to set Australia 438. Pakistan triumphed by 221 runs before winning even more comprehensively in Abu Dhabi. Younis (213), Azhar Ali (109) and captain Misbah-ul-Haq (101) starred as Pakistan compiled 570–6 declared, before batting again after gaining a 309-run lead. Misbah made an unbeaten 101 off just 57 balls while Azhar made 100 not out off 174 balls before Australia, set 603, could do no better than 246.

Australia v Pakistan

1956–57 (P): Pakistan 1–0
1959–60 (P): Australia 2–0 (1 drawn)
1964–65 (P): 0–0 (1 drawn)
1964–65 (A): 0–0 (1 drawn)
1972–73 (A): Australia 3–0
1976–77 (A): 1–1 (1 drawn)
1978–79 (A): 1–1

1979–80 (P): Pakistan 1–0 (2 drawn)
1981–82 (A): Australia 2–1
1982–83 (P): Pakistan 3–0
1983–84 (A): Australia 2–0 (3 drawn)
1988–89 (P): Pakistan 1–0 (2 drawn)

1989–90 (A): Australia 1–0 (2 drawn)

1994–95 (P): Pakistan 1–0 (2 drawn)

1995–96 (A): Australia 2–1

1998–99 (P): Australia 1–0 (2 drawn)

1999–00 (A): Australia 3–0

2002–03 (Sri Lanka, Sharjah, Sharjah): Australia 3–0

2004–05 (A): Australia 3–0

2009–10 (A): Australia 3–0

2010 (England): 1–1

2014–15 (United Arab Emirates): Pakistan 2–0

2.6 AUSTRALIA v SRI LANKA

1980s

Arjuna Ranatunga had plenty of unique achievements after playing in Sri Lanka's inaugural Test in 1981–82. He scored Sri Lanka's first half-century in Tests, captained the country for more than ten years, led Sri Lanka to World Cup glory in 1996 (with a win over Australia in the decider), and played in Sri Lanka's 100th Test. He was also part of the first Sri Lankan team to beat Australia in Tests, although he had to wait until 1999 for this.

Asgiriya Stadium in Kandy was the venue when Sri Lanka and Australia met for the first time in Tests, with Australia winning the one-off match by an innings in April 1983. David Hookes (143 not out), Kepler Wessels (141) and Graham Yallop (98) shone in Australia's 514–4 declared, before Sri Lanka managed 271 and 205. Ranatunga scored 90 and 32 while Sri Lanka had two other half-centuries: 74 from captain Duleep Mendis in the first innings, and 96 from opener Sidath Wettimuny in the second innings.

The next time the teams met was in February 1988 for another one-off Test, this time in Perth. The pattern was similar to the previous encounter as Sri Lanka followed on and was routed for 194 and 153, with Ranatunga (55 and 45) top-scoring in both innings, after Australia totalled 455.

The Sri Lankans gave a decent account of themselves in a two-Test series Down Under in late 1989, with a draw followed by a 173-run win to the hosts. The first Test never looked like yielding a result, as Australia made 367 (Tom Moody 106) and 375–6 (Mark Taylor 164) while Sri Lanka made 418. Australia nonetheless could have won had Aravinda de Silva, who scored 167, not been reprieved on 5. The second Test was superbly fought, with Australia leading by just 8 runs on the first innings before setting Sri Lanka a target of 522, following tons to Steve Waugh, Dean Jones and Mark Taylor. The visitors couldn't quite hang on for a draw after five batsmen lasted between 132 and 226 minutes each, before Sri Lanka squandered a golden opportunity to upstage Australia, as the next encounter was one for the ages.

1990s

In August 1992, Sri Lankan left-handers Asanka Gurusinha and Ranatunga scored centuries while wicketkeeper–batsman Romesh Kaluwitharana made 132 not out in his first Test to set up a total of 547–8 declared in response to Australia's 256. Sri Lanka's target of 181 could have been a lot smaller had the hosts not conceded 53 runs in no balls across Australia's two innings, and if the visitors had not had last-wicket stands of 49 and 40, as well as some other good lower order partnerships. Sri Lanka, nonetheless, was well-placed at 76–0 and 127–2, before Allan Border took a brilliant running and diving catch to account for Aravinda de Silva. The hosts lost their way against the off spin of Greg Matthews and leg spin of Shane Warne, as Australia salvaged a miraculous 16-run victory. The second and third Tests were drawn, following rain interruptions, although a result could have been possible in at least one of the Tests. The series result ultimately boiled down to the remarkable first Test at Colombo.

Sri Lanka's 1995–96 tour of Australia was marred by the no balling of Muttiah Muralitharan for throwing, but the hosts were much too strong in any case. Michael Slater (219), Mark Taylor and debutant Ricky Ponting (both 96) and one-time Test player Stuart Law (54 not out) set up a total of 617–5 declared, as Australia won the first Test by an innings. Steve Waugh tallied 362 runs in the remaining two Tests, as the hosts recorded wins by 10 wickets and 148 runs to clean sweep the series.

When pursuing a catch, a horror collision involving Waugh and teammate Jason Gillespie proved fatal to Australia's cause in late 1999. After Ricky Ponting scored 96 and Gillespie 41 in a disappointing total of 188 in the first Test at Kandy, Waugh and Gillespie were unable to bat in Australia's second innings before Sri Lanka required just 95 to win. The hosts would have been 39–4 had Mahela Jayawardene been adjudged caught, and instead the Sri Lankans lost their fourth wicket at 60, before winning by 6 wickets with Ranatunga at the crease. Sri Lanka won the series after rain affected the second and third Tests, which were drawn.

2000s

The 2003–04 series in Sri Lanka was remarkable in that the hosts led on the first innings before being beaten in each of the three Tests. Sri Lanka was set 352 on the first two occasions, having had a 161-run lead in the first Test and a 91-run lead in the second Test. Australia won the first Test by 197 runs, with Matthew Hayden, Darren Lehmann and Damien Martyn having scored centuries before leg spinners Warne and Stuart MacGill shared the wickets. Opening batsman Sanath Jayasuriya scored 131 to give Sri Lanka a chance of winning the second Test, but his departure at 218–5 was a key blow as the hosts suffered a narrow 27-run defeat. In the third Test, Australia made 401 and 375 compared with Sri Lanka's 407 and 248. Test cricket was played at Darwin and Cairns in the Australian winter of 2004, with the hosts starting uncertainly as they slumped from 72–0 to 207 all out. The tourists, however, crashed for 97 and 162 to lose by 149 runs. Hayden made 117 and 132 at Cairns and put on an opening stand of 255 with Justin Langer (162) in the first innings. Sri Lanka made 455 in reply to Australia's 517, with Marvan Atapattu (133) leading from the front. Sri Lanka's Upul Chandana bagged 10 wickets in the match, but the tourists only just escaped with a draw, as they finished at 183–8 after being set 355.

In the Australian summer of 2007–08, Australia and Sri Lanka contested the Warne–Muralitharan Trophy for the first time. Australia won the first Test by an innings and 40 runs after Michael Clarke, Mike Hussey and Phil Jaques posted centuries in a total of 551–4 declared. Jaques and Hussey scored another ton each in the second Test, as Australia again topped 500, and later set Sri Lanka 507 to level the series. Kumar Sangakkara made a brilliant 192 before he was incorrectly given out at 364–9. The last wicket fell at 410, with Brett Lee capturing 4 wickets in each of Sri Lanka's innings in the series.

Two Tests were drawn in the 2011 series in Sri Lanka, after Australia began with a 125-run victory at Galle. The hosts managed only 105 and 253 in the first Test and would have made a lot less were it not for 105 from Mahela Jayawardene and 95 from Angelo Mathews in the second innings. Off spinner Nathan Lyon dismissed Sangakkara with his first ball in Test cricket and recorded figures of 5–34 and 1–73, while Sri Lankan spinner Rangana Herath had 3–54 and 5–79. Bad weather disrupted the second Test, with Hussey (142) and debutant Shaun Marsh (141) taking Australia to a 237-run lead before Sri Lanka finished its second innings on 317–6. Hussey (118) and Marsh (81) also made the bulk of Australia's runs in the first innings of the third Test before Mathews scored an unbeaten hundred as Sri Lanka gained a handsome lead. Australia, however, followed up with 488 to guarantee a draw as Hussey (93) continued his scoring spree, while Phillip Hughes (126) and Clarke (112) also scored heavily.

Australia controlled the 2012–13 series at home, starting with a 137-run victory at Hobart, where Peter Siddle snared 9 wickets. Hussey (115 not out) again showed his liking for contesting Sri Lanka before opener Tillakaratne Dilshan scored 147 for the tourists, but nobody could make a big score when Sri Lanka chased 393. The visitors lost the second Test by an innings and 201 runs after mustering feeble totals of 156 and 103, with only 7 wickets required in Sri Lanka's second innings, as two batsmen were absent injured after Sangakkara retired hurt. Mitchell Johnson had an outstanding match as he scored 92 not out and had match figures of 6–79. In the third Test, Sri Lanka did well enough to set Australia 141 but the hosts rarely looked troubled as they recorded a 5-wicket triumph.

Australia v Sri Lanka

1982–83 (SL): Australia 1–0
1987–88 (A): Australia 1–0
1989–90 (A): Australia 1–0 (1 drawn)
1992–93 (SL): Australia 1–0 (2 drawn)
1995–96 (A): Australia 3–0

1999–00 (SL): Sri Lanka 1–0 (2 drawn)
2003–04 (SL): Australia 3–0
2004 (A): Australia 1–0 (1 drawn)
2007–08 (A): Australia 2–0
2011 (SL): Australia 1–0 (2 drawn)
2012–13 (A): Australia 3–0

2.7 AUSTRALIA v ZIMBABWE

1990s

The first time Zimbabwe encountered Australia in Test cricket was seven years after Zimbabwe gained Test status. On home turf in Harare in late 1999, Zimbabwe tallied 194 and then claimed 2 early wickets before an unbeaten 151 from Steve Waugh and 65 from number nine Damien Fleming set up a lead of 228. Zimbabwe reached 200–2 before collapsing for 232, and Australia won by 10 wickets.

2000s

Australia hosted a two-match series in late 2003, and won by an innings and 175 runs in Perth before winning the Sydney fixture by 9 wickets. The series belonged to Matthew Hayden, who achieved a then world record individual Test score of 380 in Perth, before he notched 101 not out in Sydney as Australia chased 172. Adam Gilchrist scored an unbeaten ton for Australia in the first Test before teammate Ricky Ponting scored 169 in Sydney, while Zimbabwe's Stuart Carlisle also made a century in the second Test.

Australia v Zimbabwe

1999–00 (Z): Australia 1–0   **2003–04 (A):** Australia 2–0

2.8 AUSTRALIA v BANGLADESH

2000s

Three of the first four Australia versus Bangladesh Test matches resulted in innings victories to Australia, suggesting that there was a significant gulf between the two nations in terms of cricketing strength. Yet the Bangladeshis upset Australia in a one-day match in 2005, and came achingly close to upsetting the Australians on the third occasion that the countries squared off in Tests.

Oddly, Australia hosted a two-match series in the winter of 2003, with Darwin and Cairns the venues. Bangladesh made just 97 and 178 compared with Australia's 407–7 declared in Darwin, before the tourists improved in the first innings of the Cairns Test as they were 155–1 before collapsing to 295 all out. Darren Lehmann (177), Steve Waugh (156 not out) and Martin Love (who scored 100 not out in his fifth and final Test to record his only Test ton) set up Australia's 556–4 declared in Cairns after Lehmann and Waugh also made a century each in Darwin. Stuart MacGill claimed three 5-wicket hauls in the series.

MacGill snared 8–108 in Bangladesh's first innings in the first Test of April 2006 on Bangladesh soil, but 138 from opener Shahriar Nafees and a few solid scores from teammates enabled the hosts to tally 427. Australia plunged to 93–6 before 144 from Adam Gilchrist helped the tourists reach 269, and the hosts failed to ram home the advantage as they could have set a bigger target than 307. Australia stuttered from 173–1 to 277–7 before Ricky Ponting guided his team to a 3-wicket victory with 118 not out, although not before he survived a tough but vital chance when the score was 283–7. As Australia romped to an innings and 80-run victory in the second Test, fast bowler Jason Gillespie shocked everyone with 201 not out at number three, after coming in as nightwatchman. Mike Hussey scored a comparatively forgotten 182 in Australia's 581–4 declared, while MacGill and fellow leg spinner Shane Warne shared 15 wickets in the match.

Australia v Bangladesh

2003 (A): Australia 2–0   **2005–06 (B):** Australia 2–0

2.9 AUSTRALIA v ICC WORLD XI

A series involving Australia and the International Cricket Council (ICC) World XI took place in 2005 after Australia had dominated world cricket for the past decade. Ironically, the series took place shortly after Australia lost an Ashes series to England for the first time in more than 18 years. The ICC controversially ruled that the three limited-overs fixtures and one-off Test were official contests, despite not involving one country versus another country, while the figures would be included in the records of the competing players.

Australia won the one-dayers by 93, 55 and 156 runs before winning the Sydney-based Test by 210 runs, as the World XI had three players from South Africa, two from England, two from India, one from Sri Lanka, one from New Zealand, one from Pakistan and one from the West Indies. Matthew Hayden (111 and 77) top-scored for Australia in both innings while leg spinners Stuart MacGill and Shane Warne were chiefly responsible for the World XI tallying just 190 and 144. MacGill claimed match figures of 9–82 while Warne had 6–71.

Australia v ICC World XI

2005–06 (A): Australia 1–0

2.10 NOTABLE TEST PLAYERS

Richie Benaud

Richie Benaud was well-known as a proficient commentator and analyser of cricket, but one should also not forget his standing as an Australian player and captain. Although many Test players have exceeded Benaud's runs and wickets tallies, he was the first to achieve the double of 2000 runs and 200 wickets, while also being a superb fielder in the gully. Australia did not lose any series in which Benaud was captain, as Benaud led his country to 12 wins, four losses, 11 draws and a tie.

Australia's selectors showed a lot of patience with Benaud, who scored just 309 runs at 14.05 and took 23 wickets at 37.87 with his leg spin in his first 13 Tests. He debuted against the West Indies at Sydney in January 1952, scoring 3 and 19 before taking the last wicket of the match to achieve 1–14 from 4.3 overs. Benaud made some useful contributions against South Africa in 1952–53, but he had a miserable 1953 Ashes series in England, as he took just 2 wickets and failed to reach double figures in five knocks with the bat. His form in the 1954–55 Ashes was a little better, before he followed up with a splendid tour of the Caribbean. He averaged 41 with the bat and captured 18 wickets at 27, with best figures of 4–15 in Australia's 8-wicket victory at Georgetown. Benaud's maiden Test ton was in the final match at Kingston, where he scored 121 in just 85 minutes and was one of five centuries for the tourists.

In the 1956 Ashes, Benaud shone in Australia's victory at Lord's as he scored 97, bowled economically while capturing 3 wickets, and held a brilliant catch to dismiss Colin Cowdrey. There was little else for Benaud and his teammates to savour in that series, but Australia's tour to India later that year was a big success for the leg spinner. He achieved his best Test figures of 7–72 as the tourists won by an innings at Madras, and at Calcutta he claimed 6–52 and 5–53 as the hosts were twice dismissed for 136. In South Africa in 1957–58, Benaud scored 329 runs at 54.83 and claimed 30 wickets at 21.93 as he excelled in at least one facet during each of the five Tests. He scored 122 in the first Test and 100 in the fourth Test, and claimed a 5-wicket innings haul in the last four Tests, while also claiming a 4-wicket innings haul in the second and fourth Tests.

Benaud replaced an ill Ian Craig as Australian captain for the 1958–59 Ashes, and claimed 7 wickets in the first Test which Australia won by 8 wickets. Benaud scored 132 runs at 26.40 and had his most prolific series with the ball as he snared 31 scalps at 18.84, while his team triumphed 4–0, despite England winning the toss in the first four Tests. As his team won in Pakistan and India in 1959–60, Benaud was Australia's leading bowler with 47 wickets at 20.17 from eight Tests.

Benaud and West Indian skipper Frank Worrell earned huge accolades for their leadership and style as the teams had a brilliant 1960–61 series Down Under, with Australia narrowly winning 2–1 following the historic tied Test. Benaud's series figures were modest although he scored a vital 52 in the tied Test, took 8 wickets in the Test that his team lost, and achieved a 5-wicket haul and a score of 77 in the drawn contest. A shoulder injury hampered Benaud during the 1961 Ashes in which he was well below his best, apart from one significant spell of bowling that ultimately decided the series. England was 150–1 and needed 106 more runs for a 2–1 series lead at Old Trafford when Benaud snared 6 wickets, while often bowling into the rough from around the wicket, to dismantle the hosts for 201. As hosts, Australia, drew the 1962–63 Ashes, Benaud averaged a useful 32.43 with the bat but an expensive 40.47 with the ball. Benaud's shoulder injury recurred in his last series as Australia hosted South Africa in 1963–64. He scored 43 and took 5–68 in the drawn first Test before missing the second Test with injury, and he relinquished the captaincy after Bob Simpson led Australia to victory in the second Test. Benaud was dismissed for 90 in the third Test and thus finished his career with three Test centuries, and the series was drawn after Benaud took 12 scalps at 37.42.

Richie Benaud (1930–2015)

Matches: 63
Runs scored: 2201
Batting average: 24.46
100s/50s: 3/9
Top score: 122
Balls bowled: 19,108
Wickets: 248
Bowling average: 27.03
5 wickets in innings: 16
10 wickets in match: 1
Best bowling: 7–72
Catches/stumpings: 65/–

Allan Border

Allan Border achieved many Individual Test records and was justifiably credited with helping Australia go from the doldrums to world-beaters. Border's entry to international cricket came about in 1978–79 when World Series Cricket decimated the Australian side, and he was somewhat surprisingly dropped after scoring 29, 0, 60 not out, 45 not out, 11 and 1 in his first three Tests against England. Recalled for the subsequent two-Test series against Pakistan, Border scored 20, 105, 85 and 66 not out, and was never dropped from the Test side again. His first Test tour of India in 1979–80 yielded a creditable 521 runs at 43.41 and then he floundered against the West Indies, but averaged close to 50 against England later in season 1979–80. His first tour of Pakistan reaped 395 runs in three Tests, following 150 not out and 153 in the third Test. Although he was part of batting collapses that cost Australia the Ashes in 1981, Border topped 500 runs in the series and averaged nearly 60, with the highlight his unbeaten 123 in the fifth Test. He nursed a broken finger and batted for seven hours, only for Australia to lose by 103 runs after chasing a virtually impossible target of 506.

Border averaged 67.20 against the West Indies in 1981–82, before a loss of form had him under the microscope. The left-hander redeemed himself with 62 not out against England in the fourth Test of the 1982–83 Ashes, having added 70 with number 11 Jeff Thomson, before England won by 3 tantalising runs. Consistency was an impressive part of Border's game in the ensuing years, as he regularly averaged beyond 50 in each series. His form during the 1983–84 tour of the Caribbean was notable as he scored 521 runs at 74.42, while the next best Australian batsman was Wayne Phillips with 258 runs at 25.80. Border's undefeated scores of 98 and 100 were heroic as he batted for 634 minutes in the drawn Test at Port-of-Spain. Border assumed the captaincy during the 1984–85 series against the West Indies after Kim Hughes resigned tearfully, and Border's breakthrough win as captain was in his third appearance at the helm, when Australia won by an innings to salvage a 3–1 series loss.

Lean times followed from a team point of view, as Australia underwent a rebuilding phase, and the tied Test in India was Australia's best result in 1986. Following series defeats against England and New Zealand, and a couple of drawn series against India from 1985 to 1987, Border led Australia to World Cup glory in late 1987, before savouring his first Test series win as captain when Australia held off New Zealand. During the first of two drawn Tests against the Kiwis, Border made his highest Test score of 205. Series losses against Pakistan and the West Indies took place the following season, but Border's eventual successor as Test captain, Mark Taylor, credited Border for good team spirit, even when the West Indies beat Australia repeatedly in 1988–89. Border's part-time left-arm orthodox spin was decisive in Australia's lone Test win in that series when he captured 7–46 and 4–50.

The 1989 Ashes was a major turning point in Australian cricket, with Border leading his country to a 4–0 series win. 'Captain Grumpy' became something of a prominent nickname as he showed a more ruthless attitude than in 1985, when he gained some criticism for appearing to fraternise with the Englishmen.

As Border had a strong rapport with coach Bob Simpson, Australia enjoyed many more series wins, although the West Indies remained the one major hurdle for Border. Victory was cruelly snatched from his grasp when the West Indies levelled the 1992–93 series with a 1-run win at Adelaide before Border bagged a pair of ducks at Perth in the final Test, which the tourists won by an innings.

Border, surprisingly, went four years and 36 Tests without reaching a Test century, before breaking the drought during Australia's tour of Sri Lanka in 1992. Several months later, Border overtook Sunil Gavaskar as Test cricket's leading runscorer during the first Test of a drawn series in New Zealand. In early 1994, Border retired from international cricket, after Australia achieved successive drawn series with South Africa. He had plenty of world records — since broken — to show for his hard work: most Tests (including 153 in succession), most innings, highest runscorer, most half-centuries, most catches by a fielder (as opposed to wicketkeeper), and most matches as captain. Australia won 32 times, lost 22, drew 38 and tied once with Border at the helm.

Allan Border (b.1955)

Matches: 156
Runs scored: 11,174
Batting average: 50.56
100s/50s: 27/63
Top score: 205
Balls bowled: 4009
Wickets: 39
Bowling average: 39.10
5 wickets in innings: 2
10 wickets in match: 1
Best bowling: 7–46
Catches/stumpings: 156/–

(Sir) Don Bradman

Don Bradman was remembered for scoring a duck in his final Test innings as much as he was remembered for his phenomenal record, but his final Test duck did not in any way diminish his standing in the game.

Nor should it have. Millions of words have been written about Bradman for decades, and one thing that remains scarcely believable is his record. Although players from different eras cannot be compared, while it is a matter of conjecture regarding what Bradman might have achieved had he played in a different era from what he did, he forever remains a standout figure in cricket history. He scored a century in 29 of his 80 Test innings, including 12 double centuries (including 299 not out) and two triple centuries, and his average of 99.94 is unparalleled. His average has become a frequent figure in trivia games, while it has become folklore that the outstanding batsman was bowled for a second-ball duck when he needed just 4 runs in his final Test innings to finish with a Test average of 100. His childhood habit of hitting a golf ball against a water tank with a cricket stump has also become common knowledge. Hitting the ball along the ground and being able to find the gaps consistently were things that Bradman could do like no other, with the cover drive perhaps his signature shot although hooking, pulling and cutting were also prominent.

Bradman's Test debut was inauspicious as he scored 18 and 1 while Australia lost to England by 675 runs at the start of the 1928–29 Ashes series. Bradman was relegated to twelfth man in the next Test, before he scored 79 and 112 in the third Test to cement his place in the team. The following summer he scored an unbeaten 452 for New South Wales against Queensland in the Sheffield Shield, before his scoring splurge continued during his first tour of England in 1930. He amassed 974 runs at 139.14 in five Tests, with an innings of 131 in the first Test followed by 254 in the second, 334 in the third and 232 in the fifth. His score in the third Test remained his highest in Test cricket, and Harold Larwood reportedly believed he had Bradman caught behind without scoring. Whilst spectators at any venue were treated to majestic batting from Bradman, this was never more so than at Headingley, where Bradman's Test scores were 334, 304, 103, 16, 33 and 173 not out.

After averaging 201.50 in his only series against South Africa following an innings of 299 not out, Bradman averaged a comparatively disappointing 56.57 in the infamous Bodyline Ashes series in 1932–33. In his first innings in that series, Bradman was dismissed first ball as he hooked a bumper from Bill Bowes into the stumps, and then scored a second-innings century in Australia's only win of the series. Whilst Bradman's final Test duck was well known, he was dismissed without scoring on six other occasions in Test cricket.

Once the controversial bodyline tactics disappeared following the 1932–33 series, Bradman averaged between 90 and 108.50 in the subsequent four Ashes series. He usually scored very rapidly and, incredibly, he notched more than 240 runs in a day on three occasions in Test cricket. On the first day of the 1930 Headingley Test, Bradman racked up 309 runs. He averaged 97.14 in the first Ashes series following World War II, after health issues had taken their toll. He averaged 178.75 in his only series against India before his final Ashes series, in the 'Invincibles' tour of 1948, culminated in 508 runs at 72.57.

Bradman captained Australia in his last five Test series, with Australia winning 15 Tests, losing three and drawing six. Bradman skippered his country to Ashes glory in 1936–37, 1946–47 and 1948, while Australia also regained the Ashes in 1938. Bradman's other series as captain was against India in 1947–48, when Australia won comprehensively.

Don Bradman (1908–2001)

Matches: 52
Runs scored: 6996
Batting average: 99.94
100s/50s: 29/13
Top score: 334
Balls bowled: 160
Wickets: 2
Bowling average: 36.00
5 wickets in innings: –
10 wickets in match: –
Best bowling: 1–8
Catches/stumpings: 32/–

Greg Chappell

A naturally gifted batsman, tactical captain, fine slips fielder and handy medium-pace bowler, Greg Chappell was a hugely decisive and influential figure in Australia's success in the 1970s and early 1980s. He succeeded his older brother Ian as Australian captain, after the duo, and younger brother Trevor, had had a very competitive cricketing upbringing, while former Australian Test captain Vic Richardson was their grandfather.

As Greg Chappell's career unfolded, he could play orthodox strokes all around the wicket, after he was stronger with onside strokes in the early part of his career. After scoring 108 in his maiden Test when just 22 years old, Chappell averaged just 22.50 in the remainder of the 1970–71 Ashes series. After being dropped from the team for a brief time, Chappell made plenty of runs against the Rest of the World XI in 1971–72 after a South African tour was cancelled, and was by far the leading runscorer in the 1972 Ashes. No England batsman reached 300 runs while Chappell tallied 437 at 48.56, having scored a century in both of Australia's victories in the drawn series. At the Oval he made 113 while his captain and older brother made 118, before

Greg Chappell also averaged in the high 40s in the Caribbean in early 1973. Before touring the West Indies, Chappell had a good time in a three-Test series against Pakistan as he scored one ton, averaged 60 with the bat and also claimed his only 5-wicket haul in his Test career. In early 1974, the Chappell duo scored phenomenally in a drawn Test at Wellington, as Greg notched 247 not out and 133 while Ian notched 145 and 121.

Greg Chappell scored two centuries and averaged 55.27 in Australia's successful 1974–75 Ashes campaign while battling tonsillitis, before struggling in England as he scraped together just 106 runs at 21.20 in 1975. His first series as captain was at home against the West Indies in 1975–76, and he began in style with 123 and 109 not out in an eight-wicket victory. He scored 182 not out in the fourth Test of the same series which Australia won 5–1, while the new skipper compiled 702 runs at 117, with five not outs. The 1977 Ashes tour was a disappointment as Chappell's team lost 3–0, while his own form was mixed, despite leading his team's aggregates with 371 runs at 41.22.

Following his involvement in World Series Cricket, Chappell led his country to a 2–0 loss to the West Indies, a 3–0 win over England and then a 1–0 loss to Pakistan in the same season. He registered triple figures in each series and averaged 64.53 in nine Tests, having scored 235 at Faisalabad. Season 1980–81 featured a series win against New Zealand and a knock of 204 against India, but the Indians fought back to draw the series. Chappell had his most infamous moment in 1980–81 when he instructed his younger brother to bowl an underarm delivery to deny New Zealand, which needed 6 runs from the last ball to tie a one-day international. Chappell opted to miss the 1981 Ashes due to feeling the strain from cricket and wanting to devote more time to family and business interests. He scored 201 in Australia's series-clinching victory against Pakistan at Brisbane in late 1981, but endured a form slump as he scored seven ducks in 15 international innings. Chappell returned to form in March 1982 as his 176 at Christchurch helped his team to a series-levelling victory.

Chappell led Australia to Ashes glory in 1982–83, and notched two centuries in the series. His last Test as captain was Australia's first Test encounter with Sri Lanka, with the Australians winning by an innings after Chappell scored 66. This left Chappell with 21 wins, 13 losses and 14 draws as Test captain, before his last series was against Pakistan in 1983–84 as Kim Hughes led Australia to a 2–0 win. Chappell made 150 not out in the Brisbane Test before capping off his Test career with 182 at Sydney. He subsequently had a number of other cricketing pursuits including stints as a selector, commentator and coach.

Greg Chappell (b.1948)

Matches: 87
Runs scored: 7110
Batting average: 53.86
100s/50s: 24/31
Top score: 247*
Balls bowled: 5327
Wickets: 47
Bowling average: 40.70
5 wickets in innings: 1
10 wickets in match: –
Best bowling: 5–61
Catches/stumpings: 122/–

Michael Clarke

A stylish right-handed batsman who scored a century in his maiden overseas Test and maiden home Test, Michael Clarke also scored three Test double tons and a triple ton. He also claimed 6 wickets in an innings with his part-time left-arm orthodox spin. He achieved 24 wins, 16 losses and seven draws as a Test captain while also being a World Cup winner twice, including once as skipper. Yet he never experienced Ashes glory in his four tours to England, and his career was hindered by back problems and sometimes attracting headlines for the wrong reasons.

Several of Clarke's highlights were against India, starting with his Test debut as he scored 151 at Bangalore in late 2004. Australia went on to win the match and the series: the country's first series win in India since 1969–70. In the fourth Test, Clarke took 6–9 on a spinner-friendly pitch at Mumbai before India's spinners bowled the hosts to a face-saving victory. In Clarke's first Test on home soil just weeks later, he scored 141 against New Zealand at Brisbane. But a loss of form in New Zealand and England in 2005 resulted in his omission from the team. Clarke was recalled when Australia contested Bangladesh in 2006, and later that year he scored two centuries in Australia's clean sweep against England. In 2007–08 he scored 145 not out against Sri Lanka, and against India his bowling gained more attention than his batting. Clarke made 1 and 0 in the tumultuous Sydney Test before claiming 3–5 from 11 balls to mop up the Indian tail and extend Australia's winning stretch to 16 Tests, before scoring 118 in a draw at Adelaide. Clarke became vice-captain a few months later, following Adam Gilchrist's retirement, but he missed the start of the West Indian tour before scoring a century upon returning. Clarke scored strongly against New Zealand and South Africa in 2008–09, but his reputation was blotted after Australia won the dead rubber Sydney Test as he had a stoush with Simon Katich in the dressing room. This was seen as a determining factor in Katich's Test career drawing to a close in late 2010, after Katich had averaged 45.03 in 56 Tests.

Clarke notched two centuries in a productive 2009 Ashes series, but it wasn't enough for the tourists to retain the urn. In early 2010, Clarke scored 166 at Hobart, where Australia completed a clean sweep against Pakistan, before he made 168 to help Australia beat the Kiwis in New Zealand. Along with most of his teammates, Clarke had a sub-standard 2010–11 Ashes series at home, and he led his country in the final Test as Ricky Ponting was absent. Clarke took on the captaincy full-time after Ponting stood down from the role following the 2011 World Cup, and scored one century as Australia downed Sri Lanka 1–0 in Sri Lanka. Clarke scored 151 in an Australian total of 284 in the first Test against South Africa, only for the Proteas to win by 8 wickets after Clarke's team was dismissed for an embarrassing 47 in its second innings. Clarke at least had the satisfaction of leading Australia to a series-levelling win, before Australia had to settle for a drawn series with New Zealand after Clarke scored 139 in his team's first Test victory.

Clarke began 2012 with a career-best 329 not out at Sydney and 210 at Adelaide in a series win against India. In November he scored 259 not out at Brisbane and 230 at Adelaide before South Africa later won the series 1–0. Clarke concluded the year with an innings of 106, taking his 2012 figures to 1595 runs at 106.33, as Australia romped to a 2–0 series lead against Sri Lanka before starting 2013 with another victory for a 3–0 win. Allan Border remarked in his 2015 book *Cricket as I see it*: 'Michael Clarke's greatest strength as captain of Australia is that he doesn't let the game drift. Even if Australia isn't in a dominant position in a game, he'll try to conjure something. He's got this gambler's instinct — he tries to create something to move the game forward.' Yet 2013 was a rollercoaster year for Clarke's team, and the captain was often criticised when Australia was beaten. His style and personality earned the ire of some teammates, while his captaincy brought about mixed opinions.

Australia sank to a 4–0 loss in India in early 2013, with Clarke scoring 130 in an 8-wicket defeat before making 91 in an innings loss. Clarke's team slumped to a heavy Ashes defeat abroad, with the captain scoring one century in the series, but it was only a matter of months before Clarke led Australia to a 5–0 Ashes whitewash on home soil. He scored two tons in the series Down Under before Australia became the number one ranked team in early 2014 following a 2–1 victory in South Africa, with Clarke scoring 161 not out at Cape Town. Australia lost 2–0 to Pakistan in the United Arab Emirates before Australia beat India 2–0 Down Under, with the captain making his final Test ton in a victory at Adelaide before missing the remainder of the series with a hamstring injury.

Clarke scored 74 as he led Australia to World Cup glory against New Zealand in 2015, before leading Australia to a 2–0 Test triumph in the Caribbean. But with Australia losing the Ashes in England while Clarke struggled with the bat, the captain opted to retire after the series. With the series beyond Australia's reach in Clarke's final Test, Australia won by an innings after Clarke enforced the follow-on for the only time during his captaincy tenure.

Michael Clarke (b.1981)

Matches: 115
Runs scored: 8643
Batting average: 49.10
100s/50s: 28/27
Top score: 329*
Balls bowled: 2435
Wickets: 31
Bowling average: 38.19
5 wickets in innings: 2
10 wickets in match: –
Best bowling: 6–9
Catches/stumpings: 134/–

Alan Davidson

The true testament of the left-handed Alan Davidson's ability was arguably his display in the famous tied Test during season 1960–61. His bowling figures were 5–135 (from 30 eight-ball overs) and 6–87 (from 24.6 overs), while his batting scores were 44 and 80 to take Australia to the brink of victory, only to be run out when 7 runs were needed, after he and Richie Benaud added 134 for the seventh wicket. Davidson's contribution in that match certainly compared favourably with that of an opposing left-handed batsman and bowler: Garry Sobers. The West Indian champion scored 132 and 14, and claimed 2–115 (from 32 overs) and 0–30 (from eight overs). In fact, Sobers was bowled by Davidson in the West Indies' second innings, before Davidson dismissed Sobers twice in the Sydney Test of the same series, while Sobers dismissed Davidson just once in the series. The two left-handers had some other interesting battles, with Sobers striking a massive six off Davidson in 1961–62 as Davidson played for New South Wales and Sobers for South Australia in the Sheffield Shield. The following season was Davidson's final season in first-class cricket, and in his Sheffield Shield farewell he bowled Sobers with his final delivery. Several weeks later, Davidson claimed a wicket with his final ball in Test cricket as Alan Smith was caught by Bob Simpson in a drawn match, which kept the series level and enabled Australia to retain the Ashes.

Davidson wrote the foreword for Kersi Meher-Homji's book *Cricket's Great All-Rounders* which included Davidson in the 'Top Test All-Rounders' category alongside the likes of Sobers, Hammond, Botham, Hadlee and Imran. Yet as Davidson's career figures show, bowling was clearly the stronger aspect of his game, as his highest Test score was from the tied Test, while his remaining 43 Tests yielded just four half-centuries. Meher-Homji quoted Bradman as saying that Davidson could have been a great batsman had bowling not 'taken so much of his energy'.

Davidson's maiden Test series was the 1953 Ashes in England, where he had respectable figures of 8 wickets at 26.50 and 182 runs at 22.75, with best figures of 2–22 and a top score of 76. There were attempts to convert him into a spin bowler during this tour, with history suggesting this was a crazy idea considering he became one of cricket's best fast–medium bowlers. He could move the ball either way off the pitch as he was uncannily accurate, while also being a fine fielder and fluent strokemaker.

Davidson's first eight Tests were against England, although injury restricted him to just two Tests in the 1956 Ashes. After encountering Pakistan and India once each in season 1956–57, Davidson had taken 16 wickets at 34.06 and scored 317 runs at 18.65 from 12 Tests before his bowling figures improved notably during his only series against South Africa. The retirements of Ray Lindwall, Keith Miller and Bill Johnston led to Davidson being used as a stock bowler rather than a change bowler.

In the African nation in 1957–58, Davidson had poor figures of 1–115 in the first innings of the first Test before his 6–34 in the second innings perhaps turned things around for him. In that series he snared 25 wickets at 17 and scored 127 runs at 21.17, before averaging 19 with the ball and 36 with the bat in Australia's comprehensive Ashes triumph in 1958–59. His most notable contribution in the 1958–59 Ashes came in the Melbourne Test as he captured 3 wickets in the opening over, before he also averaged fewer than 25 runs per wicket in his remaining five series and scored some handy runs. One of Davidson's performances that should not be forgotten was in a losing cause at Kanpur in 1959–60. Davidson claimed 5–31 and 7–93 as Australia sank to a 119-run defeat after leading by 67 runs on the first innings.

Success in Pakistan and India in 1959–60 was followed by 33 wickets at 18.55 and 212 runs at 30.29 against the West Indies in 1960–61, thanks largely to his figures in the tied Test. Davidson's last ten Tests were against England, with 23 wickets in 1961 and 24 in 1961–62 and a little over 150 runs in each of those two series. Davidson's most important Test innings, alongside his second-innings contribution in the tied Test, was his undefeated 77 at Old Trafford in 1961 as the series turned Australia's way. He hit 20 runs in one over, including a six over cover, and shared a priceless 98-run last-wicket stand with Graham McKenzie to increase England's target to 256, before Davidson captured 2 wickets and Benaud 6 wickets in Australia's 54-run victory.

Alan Davidson (b.1929)

Matches: 44
Runs scored: 1328
Batting average: 24.59
100s/50s: 0/5
Top score: 80
Balls bowled: 11,587
Wickets: 186
Bowling average: 20.53
5 wickets in innings: 14
10 wickets in match: 2
Best bowling: 7/93
Catches/stumpings: 42/–

Adam Gilchrist

Undoubtedly one of the finest wicketkeeper–batsmen of all time, Adam Gilchrist had a far from smooth ride to international stardom. There was disapproval from Western Australian fans in 1994–95 after Gilchrist moved from New South Wales and replaced Tim Zoehrer as Western Australia's wicketkeeper–batsman. There was disapproval from Australian fans three years later when Gilchrist replaced Ian Healy in the Australian limited-overs team. Nearly two years later, the circumstances were again far from favourable for Gilchrist as his Test debut was against Pakistan in Healy's home state, after Healy retired. There was speculation that Gilchrist would have been chosen even if Healy had not retired, and the reception for Gilchrist was mixed at first. But his blazing 81 off just 88 balls, including five fours in an over from leg spinner Mushtaq Ahmed, earned him a warm ovation. In his second Test, Gilchrist scored 149 not out as he shared a 238-run partnership with fellow Western Australian left-hander Justin Langer to lift the Australians to a 4-wicket win after they were 126–5 when chasing a 369-run target. Gilchrist also took a couple of great leaping catches against Pakistan and India in the 1999–2000 season, and when he retired eight years later he had the most Test dismissals by a wicketkeeper. There were no major blemishes in Gilchrist's wicketkeeping, although he felt retirement was imminent after he uncharacteristically dropped a few chances in the turbulent Sydney Test of 2008.

Gilchrist was in the winning side in his first 15 Tests, and he finished his career with 73 Test victories and only 11 defeats. Whilst proficient at 'keeping to the leg spin of Shane Warne and Stuart MacGill, Gilchrist took 90 catches off paceman Glenn McGrath and 81 off the faster Brett Lee. But Gilchrist's batting often gained more attention. One of the cleanest hitters in cricketing history, Gilchrist usually scored rapidly, without being reckless, as he was equally adept at finding gaps and hitting the ball over the top of the fielders. Usually coming to the crease with Australia 5 wickets down, Gilchrist was capable of changing the course of a Test. He could lift his team out of trouble or strengthen the team's position, and he was the first player to hit 100 sixes in Test cricket.

Whilst averaging in the vicinity of 30 was normal for a Test wicketkeeper, Gilchrist averaged 60.25 in his first 47 Tests, despite once scoring a king pair in India. His average in his remaining 49 Tests was a less spectacular 37.83, and admittedly he had a few bad trots. But there were still plenty of highlights. After scoring 6, 4, 4, 0, and 0 in successive innings in early 2004, Gilchrist was promoted to first drop, having scored a first innings 0 against Sri Lanka in Kandy. He returned to form with a blistering 144, but not surprisingly, he returned to his customary position down the order. Gilchrist scored 113 against Pakistan in early 2005, and followed up with 121 and 162 against New Zealand in the next two Tests.

Aside from his maiden Test ton, two classic knocks from Gilchrist that have been well-remembered were against South Africa at Johannesburg in February 2002, and against England at Perth in December 2006. At Johannesburg, Gilchrist scored a whirlwind 204 not out — his highest Test score — off just 212 balls, before hammering a largely forgotten 138 not out off 108 balls at Cape Town during the next Test. Having scored 0 in the first innings of the 2006–07 Perth Test, Gilchrist reached his century off just 57 balls in Australia's second innings after taking a mere 17 balls to go from 50 to 100.

Adam Gilchrist (b.1971)

Matches: 96
Runs scored: 5570
Batting average: 47.60
100s/50s: 17/26
Top score: 204*
Balls bowled: –
Wickets: –
Bowling average: –
5 wickets in innings: –
10 wickets in match: –
Best bowling: –
Catches/stumpings: 379/37

Matthew Hayden

There were suggestions that Matthew Hayden's Test career was over after he had played just one Test, but Hayden's doubters were made to eat humble pie as he went on to become one of the all-time great opening batsmen.

One of Hayden's captains, Steve Waugh, was quoted in Hayden's autobiography *Standing My Ground* as saying:

> *No one ever gave Haydos any free passes. He got there the hard way. The biggest accolade you can give a player is that they changed the perception of how a role should be played. Matthew took opening to a new level with his aggressive, dominating style. As a captain the greatest joy you can have is seeing a player fulfill his potential, which Haydos certainly did.*

Having begun impressively for Queensland in domestic cricket, Hayden became the first Australian to score 1000 first-class runs on a tour without playing a Test. The occasion was the 1993 Ashes, when Michael Slater beat Hayden in the challenge to be Australia's new opener alongside Mark Taylor. Hayden made his Test debut as a replacement for an ill Taylor in South Africa nearly a year later, but scored just 15 and 5, and sustained a broken thumb in the process. Hayden faced a mountainous task to regain a Test berth as Slater and Matthew Elliott were Hayden's main rivals. One of Australia's leading batsmen in the 1980s and 1990s, David Boon, no doubt echoed the thoughts of many when he remarked in his 1996 autobiography *Under the Southern Cross* with regard to Hayden, 'Quite possibly, he may never play for his country again.'

Hayden was recalled in late 1996 but he succumbed to West Indian paceman Curtly Ambrose for 5 and 0 at Melbourne. Hayden succeeded in the following Test at Adelaide as he scored a chancy 125 in Australia's innings win that clinched the Frank Worrell Trophy while Ambrose was absent with injury. In the final Test of the series, Ambrose again dismissed Hayden for a duck before Hayden carved out 47 in difficult conditions, suggesting that he had turned the corner. But a form slump in South Africa left him with just 261 runs at 21.75 from seven Tests, and this time Hayden's doubters had genuine reason to believe that his Test career was over. Twice against the West Indies and once against South Africa, Hayden was dismissed without offering a stroke.

Hayden considered Taylor, as Australian captain, did everything in his power to not let Hayden into the Australian side. But Taylor's retirement in early 1999 left a vacancy for an opening batsman, after Slater had regained a regular position. A recall for Elliott backfired, and then Greg Blewett was tried as an opener after being in and out of the side as a middle-order batsman. Blewett had some success as an opener before losing his place, and Hayden was paired with Slater seven years after they vied for one spot.

Australia's 2000–01 tour of India proved a revelation for Hayden, who tallied 549 runs at 109.80 while the next best Australian batsman was Steve Waugh with 243 runs at 48.60. Playing the sweep shot was a decisive part of Hayden's rich vein of form in the subcontinent, before he formed a special left-handed opening combination with Justin Langer in the final Test of the 2001 Ashes. Langer had also been in and out of the team in the early stages of his career, and had usually batted at number three. Hayden and Langer tallied 5655 runs from 113 innings when opening together, including six double-century stands and eight other century stands. In *The Ashes: Match of My Life*, Langer spoke about his partnership with Hayden:

> *We complement each other as batsmen, and understand each other because our careers have followed such similar paths. Batting with him in each Test is like going to Disneyland, we are like two little kids having the time of our lives.*

The first opening stand featuring Hayden and Langer produced 158 runs, and two of their next three Test partnerships topped 200 runs. Hayden finally came good in the Test arena on Australian soil as he notched 297 runs at 59.40 in three Tests against New Zealand, before tallying 429 at 107.25 in three Tests against South Africa in season 2001–02. Hayden topped 1000 runs in each calendar year from 2001 to 2005. He scored 380 against Zimbabwe at Perth in late 2003 to temporarily hold the world record individual Test score, and on two separate occasions he notched four tons in as many Tests.

Hayden crossed his chest each time he registered a Test century, with the last three occasions occurring against India in 2007–08, before he retired from Test cricket a year later following an indifferent run of form.

Matthew Hayden (b.1971)

Matches: 103
Runs scored: 8625
Batting average: 50.73
100s/50s: 30/29
Top score: 380
Balls bowled: 54
Wickets: –
Bowling average: –
5 wickets in innings: –
10 wickets in match: –
Best bowling: 0–7
Catches/stumpings: 128/–

Ian Healy

Fate seemed to be on Ian Healy's side in the early stages of his cricketing career before he endured what could be considered a raw deal in the latter stages. Healy was undeniably one of the finest ever wicketkeepers, particularly after standing behind the stumps to pacemen including Craig McDermott, Bruce Reid, Merv Hughes and Glenn McGrath, as well as record-breaking leg spinner Shane Warne. When Healy retired in late 1999, his 395 Test dismissals was a world record.

Healy was picked for Test honours after playing just six first-class matches, with Australia struggling to find a long-term wicketkeeper since Rod Marsh's retirement. Having made his first-class debut in 1986–87, Healy only received further opportunities at domestic level the following summer, after Peter Anderson broke his thumb. Anderson could have played Test cricket, but his prospects faded while Healy's meteoric rise culminated in selection for Australia's 1988 tour of Pakistan. Healy played in all three Tests, and remained a fixture in the Test team for the next decade. He was virtually thrown in at the deep end as his first Test series was promptly followed by a series against a strong West Indian line-up on Australian soil. Healy copped a couple of painful blows in the groin while batting in the Boxing Day Test, before being part of Australia's comprehensive Ashes triumph in 1989.

Some Australians deemed that Western Australia's Tim Zoehrer should have been Australia's first-choice gloveman, and although Healy averaged less than 20 with the bat in his first 23 Tests, his glovework could hardly be criticised. He took seven catches, including three classics, against Pakistan at the Adelaide Oval in January 1990, and continued to keep wicket proficiently as each series unfolded. His most notable glitch was at Karachi in 1994 when a missed stumping enabled Pakistan to clinch a 1-wicket victory that ended up deciding the series, although, it was by no means the only key moment in that series. Healy's batting improved as he became more than handy at number seven, and it was intriguing that his four first-class centuries were at Test level, while the first three of them were unconquered.

In addition to Zoehrer's fans, Healy also attracted some criticism from the likes of former Australian skipper Ian Chappell, who deemed that Healy's appealling was excessive. There were occasions that Healy's combative nature earned the ire of officials, including when he angrily threw his bat up the stairs near the dressing-room, after being wrongly given out during the third Test against South Africa at Centurion in 1996–97. Healy's encouragement to teammates could often be heard from the stump microphones, although he was also known for sledging opponents. Brian Lara was furious after Healy claimed a disputed catch during the Frank Worrell Trophy series in 1996–97 but, during the Ashes Test at Lord's in 1997, Healy was applauded for disclaiming what looked like a fair catch.

After notching his maiden Test century at Old Trafford in the 1993 Ashes, Healy's next century was against New Zealand at Zoehrer's home ground. In a disgraceful scene only a year earlier, Healy was booed and pelted with fruit by sections of the Perth crowd, as Healy represented his country in a one-day international. In 1996–97, Healy became the first Queensland-born player to score a Test century at Brisbane as he compiled his highest score of 161 not out. Another batting highlight was in the second Test of the 1996–97 series in South Africa, when Healy lifted a six over square leg to give Australia a nail-biting 2-wicket win that clinched the series.

Healy's last Test century was against England at Brisbane in late 1998, before things began to go pear-shaped within the space of a year. Nearing his thirty-fifth birthday, Healy had a sub-standard tour of the West Indies in early 1999 as he averaged just 6.62 in the drawn series, and dropped a vital catch in the dying stages of the hosts' 1-wicket win in the third Test. After taking two catches and scoring 5 in a one-off Test against Zimbabwe later in the year, Healy was in danger of losing his Test spot. The Queenslander requested to play a farewell Test in his home state at the start of the 1999–2000 season, and he would surely have reached 400 dismissals, but the selectors did not approve of the request.

Ian Healy (b.1964)

Matches: 119
Runs scored: 4356
Batting average: 27.39
100s/50s: 4/22
Top score: 161*
Balls bowled: –
Wickets: –
Bowling average: –
5 wickets in innings: –
10 wickets in match: –
Best bowling: –
Catches/stumpings: 366/29

Dennis Lillee

Dennis Lillee was an Australian icon throughout the 1970s and early 1980s as he was one of the world's finest fast bowlers. He was entertaining and had a lot of mongrel, which made him prominent in more ways than one. In *Botham's Century*, Ian Botham described Lillee as 'the complete fast bowler who could adapt to any type of wicket. DK had an aggressive temperament and was never far away from controversy. My type of player.'

Whilst full-on aggressive on the field, regardless of what level of competition he was playing, Lillee was always keen to fraternise with the opposition afterwards. Brought into the Australian side for the last two Ashes Tests of 1970–71, Lillee made an immediate impression with 5–84. He snared 8–29 in a match against the Rest of the World XI in 1971–72, before taking 31 wickets at just 17.68 each in the 1972 Ashes in England. He snared 12 scalps in three Tests at home against Pakistan in 1972–73, before a worrying back injury forced him to miss two years of cricket.

Any concerns that Lillee was a spent force were quickly dispelled as the then 25-year-old Lillee teamed with a 24-year-old Jeff Thomson to demoralise their opponents Down Under in the 1974–75 Ashes. Lillee snared 25 wickets at 23.84 while Thomson had 33 at 17.94, before the duo also proved too good for England in 1975 and the West Indies in 1975–76. Neither proficient nor a bunny with the bat, Lillee made an impact with the willow only occasionally, with his sole Test half-century coming in the 1975 Ashes, as he made 73 not out at Lord's.

Lillee continued to achieve good figures when Australia contested Pakistan and New Zealand in 1976–77, before his 6–26 and 5–139 were among many memorable aspects of the Centenary Test. After being rested from the 1977 Ashes, Lillee claimed 79 wickets in the unofficial World Series Tests before returning to traditional Test cricket in 1979–80. He had more success against England than the West Indies, as both teams toured Australia that season, and he experimented with an aluminium bat in an Ashes Test before he was forced to replace it.

The only glaringly unproductive series for Lillee in Test cricket was in Pakistan in early 1980 as he took 3 wickets at 101 on very flat pitches.

After bowling well at home against New Zealand and India in 1980–81, Lillee had great figures of 39 wickets at 22.31 in the 1981 Ashes while Western Australian teammate Terry Alderman had 42 wickets at 21.26. With Australia poised to lead the series 2–0, Lillee and Rod Marsh placed a wager at Headingley when England's victory chances were rated at 500–1, but not even winning the bet could erase their misery, as England produced a miraculous triumph that turned the series England's way.

Lillee's 85 Test wickets in 1981 included his best innings figures of 7–83 against the West Indies, and in the process he passed West Indian off spinner Lance Gibbs' then record 309 Test wickets. Lillee bowled Viv Richards with the last ball of day one to leave the tourists 10–4 in reply to 198, before he completed a 10-wicket match haul as Australia took a 1–0 series lead. Lillee was involved in an infamous altercation with Pakistan's Javed Miandad earlier that season, and was suspended from two one-day matches for deliberately kicking the Pakistani.

Lillee battled knee problems in 1982–83, and played only one Test in that season's Ashes campaign before the following season was his last in Test cricket. He claimed just 1 wicket in the first two Tests against Pakistan and may have been dropped had Carl Rackemann not become injured. Lillee nonetheless remained in the team and bowed out of Test cricket alongside Marsh and Greg Chappell. Lillee claimed two 4-wicket hauls in their final Test and took a wicket with his final ball to notch 355 Test wickets while Marsh had the exact same number of Test dismissals.

Dennis Lillee (b.1949)

Matches: 70
Runs scored: 905
Batting average: 13.71
100s/50s: 0/1
Top score: 73*
Balls bowled: 18,467
Wickets: 355
Bowling average: 23.92
5 wickets in innings: 23
10 wickets in match: 7
Best bowling: 7–83
Catches/stumpings: 23/–

Ray Lindwall

The first player to achieve the double of 1500 runs and 200 wickets in Test cricket, Ray Lindwall was influenced by Harold Larwood when watching some of the 1932–33 Ashes as an 11-year-old. Lindwall wanted to copy Larwood, but ultimately Lindwall did not gain notoriety for 'bodyline' tactics. He had plenty of admirable traits for a fast bowler, as he possessed ample pace and accuracy, and could move the ball in the air as well as move it late. His outswinger could be particularly lethal, while he was also effective at bowling bouncers and yorkers. Ninety-eight of his 228 Test wickets were bowled while another 31 were lbw. A handy lower-order batsman, Lindwall registered five half-centuries and two centuries.

A talented rugby league player, Lindwall played for St George in the 1942 and 1946 grand finals but was on the losing side both times: 11–9 to Canterbury and 13–12 to Balmain. After former Australian leg spinner Bill O'Reilly convinced Lindwall to concentrate fully on cricket, Lindwall became a feared paceman following World War II, as he and Keith Miller became a dangerous new-ball pairing. Lindwall's Test debut was in the New Zealand capital during 1946, and he claimed 1–13 and 1–16 as he twice bowled Kiwi opener Mac Anderson, who scored 4 and 1 in his only Test, as Australia won by an innings. Later that year Lindwall suffered from chickenpox in the opening Ashes encounter and then missed the second Test. He returned with a vengeance as he excelled in two draws and a victory, which sealed a 3–0 series win. At Melbourne he scored a quick 100 at number nine in Australia's second innings, and at Adelaide his first-innings figures of 4–52 included 3–0 in 4 balls to wrap up the tail. At Sydney, his 7–63 and 2–46 left him with series figures of 18 wickets at 20.39.

After taking 18 wickets at 16.89 against India in 1947–48, including his best Test figures of 7–38, Lindwall was prominent in the 1948 Ashes as he and Bill Johnston snared 27 victims each. Lindwall captured 5–70 and 3–61 at Lord's, where Australia romped to a 409-run win, and in Bradman's farewell he took 6–20 and 3–50 as England was routed for 52 and 188. Illness and a groin injury restricted Lindwall in South Africa in 1949–50, but he still claimed 12 wickets at 20.67 before, surprisingly, being dropped for the final Test.

Lindwall, Miller, Johnston and Jack Iverson had great bowling figures as Australia won the 1950–51 Ashes 4–1, before Lindwall, Miller and Johnston were also prominent against the West Indies and South Africa in the next couple of years. In the 1953 Ashes, Lindwall was easily Australia's best bowler with 26 wickets while Miller was next best with 10, but Alec Bedser stood out with 39 as England won back the urn. Lindwall claimed three 5-wicket hauls, and a virtually unplayable inswinging yorker rattled Len Hutton's stumps with the fourth ball of the fourth Test.

Injury and illness affected Lindwall at various times in the mid 1950s as he had some lean Tests without losing form for an extended period. He took 5 wickets and scored 64 not out as Australia won the opening Ashes battle in 1954–55, before the hosts lost the series, while Lindwall took 14 wickets in four Tests. In the Caribbean afterwards, Lindwall captured 6 wickets in the first Test before taking a 6-wicket innings haul in the second Test, but he claimed only 8 more wickets in the five-Test series. In the fourth Test, meanwhile, he scored his second Test century, this time at number eight.

The 1956 Ashes yielded just 7 wickets at 34 for Lindwall, before he took 1 wicket in Australia's defeat on the matting pitch at Karachi. During Australia's subsequent time in India, Lindwall skippered the tourists in the drawn second Test as Ian Johnson was sidelined with injury. After taking 7–43 in Australia's innings victory at Madras, Lindwall made 48 not out and took 2 wickets when captain at Bombay before taking 3 wickets in a win at Calcutta.

The 36-year-old Lindwall was left out of Australia's tour to South Africa in 1957–58 as selectors adopted a youth policy, but Lindwall was recalled for six more Tests. He took 7 wickets in the last two Tests of the 1958–59 Ashes while overtaking Clarrie Grimmett as Australia's leading wicket-taker. Lindwall took just 3 wickets in two Tests in Pakistan in 1959–60, before claiming 6 against India.

Ray Lindwall (1921–1996)

Matches: 61
Runs scored: 1502
Batting average: 21.15
100s/50s: 2/5
Top score: 118
Balls bowled: 13,650
Wickets: 228
Bowling average: 23.03
5 wickets in innings: 12
10 wickets in match: –
Best bowling: 7–38
Catches/stumpings: 26/–

Rod Marsh

Nicknamed 'Iron Gloves' after a number of fumbles in his Test debut, Rod Marsh was later more commonly known as 'Bacchus' as well as an all-time great wicketkeeper. Marsh did not have a lot of experience with wicketkeeping to spinners, but his wicketkeeping to fast bowlers was exemplary. At their lethal best, Dennis Lillee and Jeff Thomson tested their wicketkeeper as well as the opposing batsmen, with Marsh's reflexes, agility and gloves constantly getting a real workout. Of Marsh's 343 Test catches, 95 were off Lillee's bowling.

Marsh was known as a fighting left-handed batsman and a fierce competitor who enjoyed beer perhaps a little more than most. He was always good for team morale, as Allan Border wrote in his 1986 autobiography: 'I've never met a bloke so able to psychologically lift a side. When things were going badly, he'd divert you from your depression; when things were going well, he'd make you feel even better.' Border also remarked that 'character' was one word to sum up Marsh and that whatever Marsh didn't know about all facets of cricket 'just wasn't worth knowing'.

In his erratic maiden Test series in 1970–71, Marsh took 11 catches and three stumpings in six matches while the highlight was perhaps his 92 not out in his fourth appearance. Marsh was unlucky that captain Bill Lawry declared with 1 wicket in hand, before Marsh showed vast improvement in his second series. In England in 1972, Marsh claimed 21 catches and two stumpings in six Tests, and again came close to notching a maiden Test ton as he scored a pugnacious 91 in the first Test, which Australia lost by 89 runs, despite a desperate fightback. In the final Test of that series, Marsh made 43 not out as he and Paul Sheahan guided Australia to a series-levelling 5-wicket victory, before his next series was against Pakistan. In the first Test of a three-match series which Australia won 3–0, Marsh finally registered triple figures and, remarkably, was the first Australian wicketkeeper to make a Test century.

Marsh averaged in the high 40s with the bat in successive series against the West Indies and New Zealand in the early 1970s, with his second century coming against the Kiwis as he made his highest Test score of 132. His third and final Test century was against England, an unbeaten 110 in the Centenary Test, before he sportingly recalled England's Derek Randall, who was controversially adjudged caught behind for 161 on his way to his memorable 174. After the Centenary Test, Marsh's batting tapered off as his average in his last 49 Tests was 19.49, after being 34.31 in his first 47 Tests.

World Series Cricket kept Marsh out of the traditional Test team for a couple of years before he contested the West Indies, England and Pakistan in 1979–80. In the 1981 Ashes, Marsh overtook Alan Knott as Test cricket's leading wicketkeeper and also passed 3000 Test runs. In his final Ashes series, Marsh took 28 catches in five Tests in 1982–83 before his final series, against Pakistan the following summer, brought 21 catches in five Tests. Marsh continued to be involved in cricket, mainly at the academies in Australia and England, and he was even an England selector at one point.

Rod Marsh (b.1947)

Matches: 96
Runs scored: 3633
Batting average: 26.51
100s/50s: 3/16
Top score: 132
Balls bowled: 72
Wickets: –
Bowling average: –
5 wickets in innings: –
10 wickets in match: –
Best bowling: –
Catches/stumpings: 343/12

Glenn McGrath

As if capturing 563 Test wickets was not enormously impressive, Glenn McGrath also had the remarkable ability to recount the batsman and mode of dismissal for each wicket. Although not as terrifyingly fast as the likes of Lillee, Thomson and several West Indian quicks, McGrath was a very consistent line-and-length bowler. His unerring accuracy enabled him to regularly skittle the stumps and trap batsmen lbw, as well as find the edge of the bat for catches behind the wicket. On four occasions, McGrath snared between 62 and 68 wickets in a calendar year.

A slender-built McGrath began his international career in late 1993, aged 23, less than a year after making his domestic debut. With Craig McDermott being Australia's premier fast bowler at the time, McGrath played second fiddle, at best, in seasons 1993–94 and 1994–95, as he and several other pacemen were in and out of the team. Australia's 1994–95 tour of the Caribbean proved a watershed not only for Australian cricket but also for McGrath, who was Australia's leading wicket-taker with 17 scalps at 21.71 as McDermott and Damien Fleming were absent with injuries. Even with McDermott back in the team for one more season, 1995–96, McGrath was Australia's leading paceman with 36 wickets in six Tests. In 15 Tests from October 1996 to August 1997, McGrath captured 77 wickets at just 19.85, with best innings figures of 8–38 against England at Lord's after his first Test in England was disappointing. Whether on home soil or overseas, McGrath had the ability to adjust to the conditions and take wickets. Brett Lee, Jason Gillespie and Michael Kasprowicz were often among the other pace bowlers Australia utilised in the late 1990s and several years in the 2000s, but none of them had the same aura or consistency as McGrath.

Australian bowling line-ups were consistently formidable with McGrath and leg spinner Shane Warne, as the duo were constantly the team's leading wicket-takers. Whilst Warne was the second Australian to capture 300 Test wickets, before being the first to claim 400, 500, 600 and 700, McGrath was the third Australian to reach 300 and the second to notch the 400 and 500 milestones. For good measure, McGrath's 300th Test wicket was in the middle of a hat-trick as he dismissed West Indian trio Sherwin Campbell, Brian Lara and Jimmy Adams at Perth in late 2000. Also at Perth, McGrath recorded his best ever innings figures: 8–24 against Pakistan in season 2004–05. In the Test before he claimed his 300th wicket, McGrath claimed 6–17 from 20 overs and 4–10 from 13 overs at Brisbane as the tourists crumbled for 82 and 124. Lord's was a particularly happy place for McGrath as his Test figures at the home of cricket were 8–38 and 1–65 in 1997, 5–54 and 3–60 in 2001, and 5–53 and 4–29 in 2005.

Despite being one of the world's best ever batsmen, Lara succumbed to McGrath 15 times in Test cricket while England opener Mike Atherton was dismissed by McGrath on 19 occasions. McGrath repeatedly announced which opposition player(s) he would target, and often he backed it up with his actions. Sledging was sometimes an unsavoury part of his game, particularly in the Caribbean in 2003 when he instigated an ugly slanging match with Ramnaresh Sarwan. But McGrath's record speaks for itself, not only with regard to his number of Test wickets, but also his strike rate and average. Whilst Australia lost very few Test series during McGrath's career, it was worth noting his absence on a few occasions, even though it remains debatable as to whether or not Australia would have won had McGrath played. Two occasions were against India, which won at home in 1998 before drawing the series Down Under in 2003–04. It was certainly telling that when England won the 2005 Ashes to break Australia's run of eight successive Ashes series wins, McGrath missed the second and fourth Tests, which were the only matches which England won in that series.

A genuine number 11, McGrath's batting improved after he was dismissed first ball in his Test and one-day international debuts. After averaging 2.11 with a highest score of 9 in his first 21 Tests, McGrath increased his average to an eventual 7.37, which included 51 not outs. He hit a memorable 61 against New Zealand at Brisbane in late 2004, and slog-swept a six off experienced left-arm orthodox spinner Daniel Vettori.

Glenn McGrath (b.1970)

Matches: 124
Runs scored: 641
Batting average: 7.36
100s/50s: 0/1
Top score: 61
Balls bowled: 29,248
Wickets: 563
Bowling average: 21.64
5 wickets in innings: 29
10 wickets in match: 3
Best bowling: 8–24
Catches/stumpings: 38/–

Keith Miller

Keith Miller's cricket career was perhaps secondary to the fact that he was a fighter pilot in World War II, but the Australian still established himself as one of cricket's all-time premier all-rounders. Considered unpredictable by some teammates and opponents, Miller could hit the ball hard and bat high in the order, as well as bowl fast, vary his pace and take great catches. Miller also played Australian Rules Football for St Kilda in the Victorian Football League, although his AFL career ended shortly after he made his Test debut.

Miller was forced to wait until March 1946 to make his Test debut, when the 26-year-old scored 30 and took 2–6 in an innings win against New Zealand at Wellington. His next challenge was the 1946–47 Ashes, in which he had sensational figures of 384 runs at 76.80 and 16 wickets at 20.88. In the first Test he scored 79 and then took 7–60 and 2–17, and in the fourth Test he scored 141 not out. Against India the following year, Miller performed steadily as he averaged 37 with the bat and 24.78 with the ball, before he averaged 26.29 with bat and 23.15 with ball in the 1948 Ashes. At Trent Bridge in the first Test of the 'Invincibles' tour, Miller took 4 wickets in England's second innings as he and Bill Johnston, Ernie Toshack and Ian Johnson shouldered a heavy workload to cover for the injured Ray Lindwall. Len Hutton and Denis Compton succumbed to Miller twice each at Trent Bridge, with Hutton bowled twice and Compton bowled once before Compton was out, hit wicket, after making 184 in England's second innings.

Miller was controversially omitted from Australia's 1949–50 tour of South Africa, supposedly because he did not see eye to eye with Bradman, who was a selector. An injury to Bill Johnston enabled Miller to win back his place, and he showed what a fallacy it had been to omit him as he averaged 41 with the bat and 22.94 with the ball. Miller's best scores in the 1950–51 Ashes were 145 not out and 99 while he also took 17 scalps at 17.71. He also did well in his first series against the West Indies, as he scored one century while averaging 40.22 with the bat and 19.90 with the ball.

Miller's bowling was a little better than his batting against South Africa in 1952–53, and although he somewhat underachieved in the

1953 Ashes, his 109 at Lord's was one of his best innings. His batting was also a little below par in the 1954–55 Ashes, while he took 10 wickets in a series for the second successive time, before he starred with the bat in the Caribbean. Miller scored three centuries as he compiled 439 runs in six knocks, with his best Test score of 147 coming in the first Test at Kingston. Also at Kingston, in the final Test, Miller claimed 8 wickets and was also one of five Australians to register triple figures. Miller only once took 10 wickets in a first-class match, and this was at Lord's in the 1956 Ashes as he captured 5–72 and 5–80 in Australia's only victory of the series. Miller's Test farewell was the inaugural Pakistan versus Australia Test match on matting at Karachi, where Miller scored 21 and 11 and took 2–40 and 0–18 in a 9-wicket loss.

Keith Miller (1919–2004)

Matches: 55
Runs scored: 2958
Batting average: 36.97
100s/50s: 7/13
Top score: 147
Balls bowled: 10,461
Wickets: 170
Bowling average: 22.97
5 wickets in innings: 7
10 wickets in match: 1
Best bowling: 7–60
Catches/stumpings: 38/–

Ricky Ponting

It was prophetic that when Ricky Ponting was four years old, his grandmother gave him a shirt that contained the words 'Inside this shirt is an Australian Test cricketer'. Approaching his 21st birthday, Ponting began his Test career in fine style as he scored 96 in Australia's innings win against Sri Lanka at Perth in late 1995. He scored a streaky boundary from the first ball he faced as a difficult catch was dropped at slip, and was unfortunately denied a century when adjudged lbw to a ball that appeared certain to bounce over the stumps.

Ponting became the first player to be involved in 100 Test victories, and when he finished his career he was second only to Sachin Tendulkar on the all-time list of highest Test runscorers. Driving, pulling and cutting were among Ponting's signature strokes. But for all that Ponting achieved, he was also remembered for becoming the first Australian to lose three Ashes series as captain despite his overall captaincy figures looking good on paper: 48 wins, 16 losses and 13 draws.

Ponting took several years to cement a Test spot, as he suffered from inconsistency in the late 1990s and very early 2000s. He also had a volatile temperament at times, and had a few off-field dramas. After playing his first three Tests alongside childhood hero and fellow Tasmanian David Boon, the retirement of Boon prompted Ponting to be promoted, perhaps prematurely, from number six to number three in the batting order. Following scores of 14, 13, 88, 9, 9 and 4, Ponting was dropped. He was recalled less than a year later and instantly scored his maiden Test century at number six in the fourth Ashes Test of 1997. In late 1998 he was axed again, this time during an Ashes series Down Under, before again being recalled within a year and instantly scoring a century — his third Test ton and first in the Caribbean. It wasn't until his 45th Test innings that he made a duck, but he quickly had three successive ducks as he made a pair on his home ground before following up with 197 against Pakistan. Having scored 105 runs at 21 on Indian soil in 1998, Ponting fared even worse in India during 2001 with 0, 6, 0, 0 and 11. Instead of being dropped again, Ponting was promoted to number three for the 2001 Ashes, and he averaged just 12 in three Tests before notching 144, 72 and 62. From that point on he made the number three position his own. His fielding was also crucial as he averaged more than one catch per Test, showing great reflexes in the slips and gully region.

Ponting averaged a little over 50 in the Tests on home soil in 2001–02 and 2002–03, including centuries in two of his first three knocks in the 2002–03 Ashes. In South Africa in early 2002, an unbeaten 100 from Ponting helped Australia chase down 331 to win the series. In the

Caribbean in 2003, Ponting notched 523 runs at 130.75, having scored his first double century in Tests. Later in 2003 Ponting scored 242 and 257 (his biggest Test score) in successive Tests against India. His next Test century came a little over a year later and was also a double as he made 207 against Pakistan. Ponting notched more than 1000 Test runs in a calendar year on five occasions: 2002, 2003, 2005, 2006 and 2008. He topped 1500 runs in 2003 and 2005, and tallied 1333 in 2006. He scored five Test tons in 2002, six in 2003, none in 2004, six in 2005, seven in 2006, none in 2007, four in 2008, and only four between 2009 and 2012. In his 100th Test, Ponting led Australia to an 8-wicket win against South Africa as he scored 120 and 143 not out in January 2006.

Having been in a World Cup final loss in 1996 and World Cup final win in 1999, Ponting became Australia's limited-overs captain in 2002 and led the team to the 2003 World Cup title. Ponting became Test captain in 2004 following Steve Waugh's retirement, and Ponting's first series in charge resulted in a 3–0 win against Sri Lanka. Later that year Australia won a Test series in India for the first time since 1969–70, but Ponting missed the first three Tests with injury. The first major setback in Ponting's captaincy was the 2005 Ashes, as it was Australia's first Ashes series loss since 1986–87. Ponting was pilloried for electing to bowl in the second Test with Australia leading 1–0, yet his team lost by two tantalising runs when on the verge of taking a 2–0 series lead which would have been fiendishly tough for England to overcome. Ponting made a match-saving 156 in the third Test, before being fined for offensive conduct, after he was run out by a substitute fielder in the fourth Test.

Australia regained its winning ways, and a whitewash of the 2006–07 Ashes series was a highlight. But with Australia soon undergoing a rebuilding phase, Ponting's team lost the Ashes in 2009 and 2010–11. During season 2009–10, Ponting scored 209 against Pakistan. The last of Ponting's 41 Test centuries was a knock of 221 in 2012: his sixth Test double century and third against India. With his form having been patchy at times since 2008, and with Michael Clarke having assumed the Test captaincy in 2011, Ponting concluded his Test career after scoring just 32 runs at 6.40 in Australia's 1–0 series loss to South Africa in late 2012.

Ricky Ponting (b.1974)

Matches: 168
Runs scored: 13,378
Batting average: 51.85
100s/50s: 41/62
Top score: 257
Balls bowled: 575
Wickets: 5
Bowling average: 54.60
5 wickets in innings: –
10 wickets in match: –
Best bowling: 1–0
Catches/stumpings: 195/–

Shane Warne

Few could have imagined that Shane Warne would have such a phenomenal Test career after he captured just 1 wicket at a high cost in his first two Tests in early 1992. About three years earlier when Warne was yet to play first-class cricket, former Australian fast bowler Rodney Hogg was sacked from his position with *The Truth* newspaper for predicting that Warne would take 500 Test wickets. The reason for Hogg's sacking would not have been because someone prophetically thought that Hogg's prediction would be bettered by 208 wickets.

Whether it was sending down wrong 'uns, flippers, sliders, top spinners or regulation leg breaks, Warne was a once-in-a-lifetime cricketer, as he constantly had batsmen bewildered while it looked like he could produce a wicket at just about any given time. He also attracted plenty of notoriety as a series of off-field controversies dogged him, in addition to a 12-month drug suspension.

Warne had played just seven first-class matches when he earned his first Test cap. A double century to Ravi Shastri and a century to Sachin Tendulkar were responsible for Warne having 1–150 in his first Test, with the blond leg spinner reprieving Shastri, before Shastri was eventually caught off Warne's bowling. Warne took 0–78 in his second Test but the selectors persevered with him in Sri Lanka, where Australia was getting thrashed in the first Test after Warne had 0–107 in the first innings. But the Test surprisingly changed complexion, and Australian captain Allan Border riskily brought Warne on to bowl as the leg spinner's Test figures were 1–335, while Sri Lanka was 145–6 chasing 180. Warne claimed 3–11 as the last three batsmen were caught off his bowling, with Australia snatching a 16-run win. Warne was relegated to twelfth man for the next Test and was kept wicketless in the third Test. Warne was omitted at the start of the 1992–93 series against the West Indies, before snaring 7–52 in the last innings of the second Test to set up an Australian victory. Bowling West Indies captain Richie Richardson with a flipper was a turning point in Warne's career, and then he toured New Zealand where he took 17 wickets at 15.05 in three Tests.

Warne's first delivery in Ashes cricket, on English soil in 1993, was one of the most spectacular incidents in Test history as the ball spun viciously from outside leg stump and clipped the top of Mike Gatting's off stump. The dismissal had an immensely psychological impact on the English team, and Warne went on to take 34 wickets in the series, which Australia won 4–1. Such was the memory of the so-called 'ball of the century' that dismissed Gatting, it was almost forgotten that later in the series Warne produced another delivery that was every bit as good. In the fifth Test, Graham Gooch was bowled around his legs by another viciously turning delivery. Another of England's best batsmen, Robin Smith, was repeatedly brought undone by Warne.

Warne captured 72 Test wickets in 1993, 70 in 1994 and 52 in 1995 as many batsmen from England, South Africa, New Zealand and Pakistan succumbed too readily, with South Africa's Daryll Cullinan a prime example. After taking 15 wickets in just four Tests in 1996, Warne took 68 scalps in 1997 before notching his 300th Test wicket in January 1998 as he claimed match figures of 11–109 against South Africa. Warne's career stalled later in the year as he had a shoulder operation, and he missed most of the 1998–99 Ashes before being dropped in the Caribbean after capturing just 2 wickets in three Tests. Following speculation that Warne would retire after he excelled in Australia's 1999 World Cup triumph, he captured 49 wickets from 13 Tests in 1999–00 and overtook Dennis Lillee as Australia's leading wicket taker. A finger injury forced Warne to miss Australia's 5–0 whitewash of the West Indies in 2000–01 before an expensive series against India — virtually the only country where success for Warne was scarce — was followed by 31 wickets in the 2001 Ashes.

Having snared 58 Test scalps in 2001 and 67 in 2002, Warne was stranded on 491 Test wickets in early 2003 when he copped a 12-month suspension for using a banned diuretic. But upon his return, aged 34, he passed 500 wickets and went on to temporarily be Test cricket's leading wicket taker. Warne's 70 Test wickets in 2004 were followed by a record-breaking 96 in 2005, with his 40 scalps in the Ashes not enough to prevent England regaining the urn following eight successive series losses. Warne chose the 2006–07 Ashes series as his farewell, and he captured 23 wickets in Australia's clean sweep. He snared 7 scalps in the Melbourne Test, which featured his 700th wicket.

Warne was also a decent slips fielder and handy batsman, often at number eight. He scored 12 half-centuries and was desperately unlucky to be caught off a lofted shot when on 99 against New Zealand at Perth in late 2001, as replays showed that the bowler should have been no balled.

Another Australian leg spinner from the same era, Stuart MacGill, was a different type of bowler from Warne but was every bit as effective when chosen, usually when Warne was absent. MacGill took 208 wickets from 44 Tests, and one could only wonder what MacGill would have achieved had he not played in the same era as Warne.

Shane Warne (b.1969)

Matches: 145
Runs scored: 3154
Batting average: 17.32
100s/50s: 0/12
Top score: 99
Balls bowled: 40,704
Wickets: 708
Bowling average: 25.41
5 wickets in innings: 37
10 wickets in match: 10
Best bowling: 8–71
Catches/stumpings: 125/–

Steve Waugh

Steve Waugh was a prime example of mental toughness in Test cricket. Born just a few minutes before the arrival of twin brother Mark, Steve Waugh appeared far less gifted than Mark but the slightly older twin finished with a more impressive Test record, largely due to his steely determination.

Steve Waugh made his Test debut against India as a 20-year-old in 1985–86, and struggled as Australia was going through a lean trot. It wasn't until the 1986–87 Ashes that he showed some promise as he averaged 44.29 with the bat and snared 10 wickets. His thirteenth Test appearance featured his first victory at the elite level, while he had quite a bit of success in one-day cricket.

Waugh showed patches of brilliance against the West Indies in the 1988–89 series Down Under. He scored 90 in the first Test and bowled a few bouncers to Viv Richards, before scoring 91 in the second Test and then claiming 3–77 and 5–92 in the third Test, although the tourists won all three Tests decisively. Waugh finally came of age in the 1989 Ashes, scoring his maiden Test century in the opening Test — his 27th — as he compiled an unbeaten 177 before scoring 152 not out and

21 not out in the second Test. He finished the series with 506 runs at 126.50, but claimed only 2 wickets as back problems began to affect his bowling.

A loss of form resulted in Steve Waugh losing his place in favour of his twin brother, who scored 138 against England in his maiden Test innings in 1990–91. Steve Waugh was recalled during Australia's subsequent tour to the Caribbean but he was soon dropped again, before returning against the West Indies on Australian soil in 1992–93. Waugh scored 100 at first drop in one Test but struggled otherwise, before resurrecting his career in England as he averaged 83.20. A hamstring injury interrupted Waugh in 1993–94, but his return was crucial as he scored 164 and snared 4 wickets in a series-levelling win against the Proteas. In South Africa several weeks later, Waugh was again decisive in Australia squaring the series against the Proteas as he produced a run-out, a knock of 86 and a 5-wicket haul.

After having an iconic confrontation with Curtly Ambrose during a West Indian victory in the Caribbean in 1995, Waugh made his top Test score of 200 in the following Test as Australia belatedly won back the Frank Worrell Trophy. In the next few years, a highlight for Waugh was in the third Ashes Test of 1997. Waugh made 108 and 116 in tough conditions to help Australia level the series before going on to win it.

After replacing the retired Mark Taylor as Australian captain, Waugh fell 1 run shy of his highest Test score during the drawn 1999 series in the Caribbean. With Australia racking up 16 consecutive Test victories, Waugh was the captain in 15 of them while missing the other match, although a series victory in India eluded him, as India produced a miraculous comeback to win the 2000–01 series 2–1. Australia nonetheless won 41 and lost only 9 of 57 Tests in which Waugh was captain, after Clive Lloyd held the record for most Test wins as captain with 36.

England was again a happy place for Waugh as he averaged 107 from five innings in the 2001 Ashes, after scoring an undefeated 157 when less than fully fit in the final Test. His form tapered off to the extent that he lost his place in Australia's limited-overs team in 2002, and soon his Test spot appeared to be under scrutiny. Australia eyed a 5–0 clean sweep of the Ashes in January 2003 when he raised a century with a cover drive to the boundary from the final scheduled delivery of day two of the final Test at Sydney: Waugh's home ground. He was dismissed the following morning without adding to his score before England won to avoid a whitewash, and it was a year later that Waugh bade farewell to Test cricket. His final innings yielded 80 on his home ground as Australia made a game, but unsuccessful, attempt at chasing 449 against India, with the match and series resulting in a draw. Waugh was the most capped Test player until Sachin Tendulkar surpassed him in 2010.

Steve Waugh (b.1965)

Matches: 168
Runs scored: 10,927
Batting average: 51.06
100s/50s: 32/50
Top score: 200
Balls bowled: 7805
Wickets: 92
Bowling average: 37.44
5 wickets in innings: 3
10 wickets in match: –
Best bowling: 5–28
Catches/stumpings: 112/–
Matches: 168
Runs scored: 10,927

CHAPTER 3: SOUTH AFRICA

3.1 SOUTH AFRICA v NEW ZEALAND

1930s

The South Africans had lost 5–0 in Australia before having success in their first series against New Zealand in 1931–32. In the first Test at Christchurch, the hosts made 293 before South African openers Bruce Mitchell (113) and Jim Christy (103) put on an opening stand of 196. The visitors reached 451 and went on to win by an innings, before sealing a 2–0 series win with an 8-wicket triumph in Wellington. Giff Vivian scored 100 as New Zealand made 364 in the first innings, and then took 4–58 but South Africa led by 46 runs following an unbeaten 122 from Xen Balaskas. The Kiwis could set the Africans only 148 despite 73 from Vivian. Twenty-one years passed before the countries next met.

1950s

An innings win to South Africa in Wellington was followed by a draw in Auckland. In the first Test of 1952–53, South African opener Jackie McGlew scored an unconquered 255 while Anton Murray made 109 at number eight in a total of 524–8 declared. The hosts were twice dismissed for 172 after scoring at fewer than 1.50 runs per over in both innings, before the second Test was rather fruitless.

South Africa won a five-match series 4–0 on home soil less than a year later, although the tourists were more competitive than the result indicated. The first Test, admittedly, was lopsided, with the hosts winning by an innings, despite Kiwi captain and opener Geoff Rabone scoring 107 in New Zealand's first innings. In the second Test, New Zealand was 81–6 before reaching 187 in reply to 271, and then South Africa was 67–6 before eking out another 81 runs. The Kiwis fell from 35–0 to 100 all out to lose by 132 runs, before tallying 505 in the first innings of the drawn third Test after John Reid (135) and John Beck (run-out for 99) were the main scorers. South African duo Hugh Tayfield and Neil Adcock set up a 9-wicket win for the hosts in the fourth Test as the visitors made just 79 and 188, before the final Test was evenly balanced for the most part. Chasing 212, the hosts were 81–3 before Russell Endean (87) and John Watkins (45) turned the game South Africa's way.

1960s

The 1961–62 series in South Africa was drawn 2–2, with some great cricket played. The hosts won the first Test by 30 runs after New Zealand chased 197, with Peter Pollock (6–38 in New Zealand's second innings) and McGlew (127 not out in South Africa's first innings) making the most decisive impact for the victors. Pollock was one of seven South African Test debutants while New Zealand had five. The second Test was drawn before the Africans were on the back foot for most of the third Test, although they made a fine bid to score 408 for victory. Roy McLean (113) led the way before New Zealand prevailed by 72 runs. McGlew (120) and 'Goofy' Lawrence (match figures of 9–109) set up an innings win for South Africa in the fourth Test while Reid played a lone hand of 142 in New Zealand's second-innings total of 249. The Kiwis however squared the series with a 40-run win in a superb contest at Port Elizabeth. Paul Barton scored 109 in New Zealand's first innings of 275, and South Africa fell 85 runs behind before being set 314. The hosts struggled to 199–8 before a 60-run ninth-wicket stand unfolded and gave South Africa the chance of a miraculous escape.

The 1963–64 series in New Zealand featured patches of interesting cricket as all three Tests were drawn. The hosts finished the first Test on 138–6 after being set 268, before the visitors nearly stole victory in the second Test, which involved just three days. New Zealand tumbled to 149 and 138 all out, before South Africa finished at 42–3 from seven overs after being set 65 runs in 27 minutes. The Kiwis flopped from 247–3 to 263 all out in their first innings in the third Test before being set 309, and finishing on 191–8 after the ninth-wicket pair survived 12 minutes, before the final 13 minutes were rained off. The next time the countries met in Test cricket was in season 1994–95.

Post-apartheid 1990s

Following their return to Test cricket, South Africa remained undefeated in each series against New Zealand. The Africans won four straight series against the Kiwis on two occasions, with a drawn series in between.

South Africa came from 1–0 down to win the 1994–95 series 2–1 on home turf. After scoring 411 in the first Test, the tourists gained a strong lead and went on to win by 137 runs after setting a target of 327. New Zealand managed only 185 in the first innings of the second Test, although the Africans didn't capitalise fully as they gained a 41-run lead. The Kiwis again failed to reach 200, and the hosts lost only 2 wickets when chasing 152. The only centuries in the series were by Hansie Cronje (112) and Dave Richardson (109), as South Africa gained a decent lead in the deciding Test before winning by 7 wickets after being set just 88. Fanie de Villiers was chiefly responsible for South Africa's success as he claimed 20 wickets in the series. New Zealand hosted a one-off match in March 1995 and was well in contention after gaining a first-innings lead of 34. De Villiers again foiled the Kiwis, taking 4–42 as the hosts were dismissed for 181 to lose by 93 runs.

Four years passed before the teams next contested a Test series, with two draws followed by an 8-wicket win to South Africa. Daryll Cullinan (275 not out) and Gary Kirsten (128) starred in the first Test before Herschelle Gibbs (211 not out), Jacques Kallis (148 not out) and Kirsten (65) led South Africa to 442–1 declared in the second Test. Rain foiled the Africans on both occasions before Cullinan and Gibbs scored another ton each in the third Test in Wellington. Shaun Pollock, Steve Elworthy and Paul Adams did the bulk of the damage as the hosts managed 222 and 291.

2000s

Kallis (160) was responsible for South Africa tallying 471–9 declared in the first innings of the 2000–01 series after Boeta Dippenaar was dismissed from the second ball. The Africans won by 5 wickets after enforcing the follow-on, before winning the second Test by seven wickets. Mathew Sinclair's 150 wasn't enough for New Zealand to reach 300 in the first innings, before South Africa made 361 following 120 from Neil McKenzie and 51 from number nine Nicky Boje. South Africa's eventual target was only 86, before rain washed out most of the final Test.

The first Test in 2003–04 was a high scoring draw, as neither team dominated, before New Zealand dished out a 9-wicket drubbing in the second Test. The Africans fell from 177–0 to 296 all out, before Scott Styris (170), Chris Cairns (158) and Jacob Oram (90) helped the Kiwis tally 595. Chris Martin captured 11 wickets in the match, and Jacques Rudolph (154 not out) provided resistance before New Zealand prevailed. The third Test was delicately poised for the most part, and South Africa was 36–3 after being set 234, before captain Graeme Smith's unbeaten 125 piloted his team to a series-levelling 6-wicket triumph.

The first Test of 2005–06 had many pendulum swings, with the Kiwis recovering from 89–6 to post 327 in reply to South Africa's 276 thanks to Jacob Oram (133) and Daniel Vettori (81). The Africans recovered from 73–4 to post 299, before the Kiwis crashed to 28–6 and managed a further 92 runs. Kiwi skipper Stephen Fleming (262) and number nine James Franklin (122 not out) helped their team near 600 in the second Test, before their opponents ensured a draw with 512 following tons to Hashim Amla and Ashwell Prince. The Kiwis were 3 wickets down for 2 runs after the first seven overs in the third Test, and struggled to 119 before the Africans folded for 186 after being 99–1. South Africa later chased 217, and overcame the odd stutter to win by 4 wickets.

South Africa stumbled to 226 all out in the first innings of the first Test in 2007–08 before New Zealand fared much worse, with only 118. Kallis and Amla put on a partnership of 330 before their team won by 358 runs after New Zealand scraped together 172. The second and final Test was even more comprehensive as the Kiwis tallied 188 and 136, compared with South Africa's 383, as Kallis and Amla made another century each.

The 2011–12 series featured a draw in the first and third Tests while the second Test decided the series as the Africans won by 9 wickets. New Zealand was 137–2 chasing 401 when wet weather cancelled day five of the first Test. In the other drawn Test, the Kiwis only just averted the follow-on before finishing at 200–6 when chasing 389, with Morne Morkel having taken all 6 wickets. The decisive Test meanwhile was over in just three days. New Zealand made 185 before South Africa gained a 68-run lead and then dismissed the Kiwis for 168 as Vernon Philander bagged 6–44.

South Africa won both Tests in the 2012–13 series by an innings, with the writing on the wall after Philander (5–7), Morkel (3–14) and Steyn (2–18) decimated the tourists for 45 in the first innings at Cape Town. South Africa was 1–1 before gaining a 302-run lead and then dismissing the opposition for 275 following a collapse of 6–46. Hundreds to Amla, Faf du Plessis and Dean Elgar propelled the Africans to 525–8 declared in the final Test before New Zealand scored just 121 and 211.

South Africa v New Zealand

1931–32 (NZ): South Africa 2–0   **1952–53 (NZ):** South Africa 1–0
(1 drawn)

1953–54 (SA): South Africa 4–0 (1 drawn)
1961–62 (SA) 2–2 (1 drawn)
1963–64 (NZ) 0–0 (3 drawn)
1994–95 (SA): South Africa 2–1
1994–95 (NZ): South Africa 1–0
1998–99 (NZ): South Africa 1–0 (2 drawn)

2000–01 (SA): South Africa 2–0 (1 drawn)
2003–04 (NZ): 1–1 (1 drawn)
2005–06 (SA): South Africa 2–0 (1 drawn)
2007–08 (SA): South Africa 2–0
2011–12 (NZ): South Africa 1–0 (2 drawn)
2012–13 (SA): South Africa 2–0

3.2 SOUTH AFRICA v INDIA

1990s

After losing from a winnable position in the Caribbean in April 1992 upon returning to Test cricket, the next mission for South Africa was a four-match series at home against India in season 1992–93.

The third Test in Port Elizabeth produced the only outright result after South Africa's Jimmy Cook was dismissed from the first ball of the series. Allan Donald's 12 wickets were the most decisive aspect in the Port Elizabeth Test as India was dismissed for 212 and 215 before the hosts passed their 153-run target for the loss of just 1 wicket. Hansie Cronje's 135 was also crucial as South Africa gained a lead of 63, before Kapil Dev scored 129 after the Indians were reeling at 31–6 in their second innings. Kepler Wessels also deserved credit for anchoring the run chase as he scored 95 not out.

Some topsy-turvy results unfolded as India hosted the next series four years later. The highest team score in the first Test was 244, before Javagal Srinath's 6–21 and Anil Kumble's 3–34 inspired a 64-run win to the hosts as the tourists required 170. Andrew Hudson (146) and Gary Kirsten (102) put on an opening stand of 236 before South Africa finished with 428 in the first innings of the second Test. India was 161–7 before Mohammad Azharuddin (109) and Kumble (88) lifted the total towards 329, and then another century to Gary Kirsten was accompanied by 153 not out from Daryll Cullinan. Test debutant Lance Klusener took 8–64 as the Proteas romped to a 329-run win, but India bounced back to win the series with a 280-run victory at Kanpur. Paul Adams claimed 6 wickets as the hosts succumbed for 237, after losing their first 3 wickets at 76, 111 and 160. South Africa managed only 177 and 180, with Azharuddin ensuring the visitors had a huge target as he scored 163 not out in India's second innings.

The Africans were much too strong as they hosted a follow-up series, winning by 328 runs and 282 runs before the third Test was drawn. Match figures of 9–54 from Donald enabled the Proteas to scythe through the Indians for 100 and 66 in the first Test while Venkatesh Prasad had 10–153 for India. Gary Kirsten (103) set the platform for a big total in the second Test before Brian McMillan (103 not out) and Klusener (102 not out) took the score from 382–7 to 529–7 declared. India was 58–5 before Sachin Tendulkar and Azharuddin added 222, with Azharuddin making 115 before Hudson brilliantly ran him out. Tendulkar was last out for 169 when Adam Bacher took a sensational one-handed outfield catch, and the Indians managed only 359 as no-one other than Azharuddin and Tendulkar passed 23. The run chase was even more disappointing as VVS Laxman (35 not out) and Sourav Ganguly (30) were the only Indians to pass 16 in the miserable 144-run total while Srinath was absent ill. India's batting improved in the final Test, and the Africans narrowly avoided defeat as they were 228–8 after being set 356, with Cullinan undefeated on 122.

2000s

In the first Test of 1999–00 in Mumbai, the Proteas collapsed from 90–0 to 176 all out in reply to India's 225 before the Indians folded for 113 and went on to lose by 4 wickets. South Africa won the second and final Test by an innings, with India dismissed for 158 and 250 while the Proteas made 479.

Despite Sachin Tendulkar (155) and Virender Sehwag (105) setting up an Indian total of 379 in the first innings of the opening Test in

2001–02, the Proteas won by 9 wickets. South Africa's first-innings total of 563 included 108 from Klusener and 107 from Herschelle Gibbs, before Gibbs made 196 in the drawn second Test.

The first Test of 2004–05 was also drawn, with Proteas opener Andrew Hall scoring 163 before Sehwag scored 164 as India fell 44 runs shy of South Africa's 510–9 declared. India won the series 1–0 following an 8-wicket victory at Kolkata, with the hosts leading by 106 runs on the first innings before dismissing the visitors for 222 as Harbhajan Singh snared 7–87.

The 2006–07 series in South Africa involved many pendulum swings, with the hosts ultimately prevailing 2–1. The Proteas crashed to 84 all out in the first Test after India made 249, and it was hardly surprising that India went on to win by 123 runs. South Africa won the second Test by 174 runs after setting India 354, before the tourists lost their first 2 wickets at 153 and 202 in the decider. India tallied 414 before securing a lead of 41, and then stumbling to 169 all out. South Africa won by 5 wickets in spite of a 4-wicket haul by Zaheer Khan, before the next three series were deadlocked after they too had many ups and downs.

The first Test of 2007–08 was drawn after Sehwag's 319 was the feature, before India astonishingly plunged to 76 all out in 20 overs in the first innings of the second Test. AB de Villiers (217 not out) and Kallis (132) guided South Africa towards 500 before the Proteas won by an innings. But India drew the series with an 8-wicket triumph after South Africa's second-innings demise for 121 left the Indians a meagre target of 62.

The Proteas won the first Test of 2009–10 by an innings, only for India to return the compliment in the second and final Test at Kolkata. Hashim Amla (253 not out) and Kallis (173) rescued the Africans from 6–2 with a 340-run stand at Nagpur, with South Africa topping 500 before Steyn bagged 10 wickets. Sehwag meanwhile scored 109 in India's first innings before Tendulkar scored 100 in India's second innings. Incredibly, South Africa was 218–1 in the first innings of the second Test, before succumbing for 296 after debutant opener Alviro Petersen (100) and number three Amla (114) departed. Sehwag (165), Laxman (143 not out), MS Dhoni (132 not out) and Tendulkar (106) took India past 600 before Amla's 123 not out couldn't save the Proteas.

South Africa also won the opening Test of 2010–11 by an innings, with India making 136 and 459 while the Africans made 620–4 declared. Kallis (201 not out), Amla (140) and de Villiers (129) were harsh on India's bowlers before Tendulkar (111 not out), Dhoni (90), Gautam Gambhir (80) and Sehwag (63) gave India some hope of a miraculous escape. The second Test took on a completely different course as India made 205 and then dismissed South Africa for 131, before the Proteas made 215 in their second innings when chasing 303. The series remained even as the final Test was drawn and featured three centuries, with two to Kallis and one to Tendulkar.

The first Test of 2013–14 was also drawn, although it was arguably one of the greatest Tests of all time. At Johannesburg, India made 280 and gained a 36-run lead before setting a target of 458 after Virat Kohli made a fine double of 119 and 96, while Cheteshwar Pujara scored 153 in India's second innings. Faf du Plessis (134) and de Villiers (103) put on a 205-run partnership after South Africa was 197–4, before the run-out of du Plessis left the Africans needing 16 runs from 19 balls with 3 wickets in hand. The tail, bizarrely, chose not to go for the runs despite Steyn hitting a six, and South Africa finished on 450–7. The second and final Test turned out to be a little anticlimactic, as India fell from 198–1 to 334 all out before South Africa reached 500 and then restricted India to 223, setting up a 10-wicket win for the Proteas.

The teams started vying for the Freedom Trophy in late 2015, with India winning 3–0 at home after spinners Ravi Ashwin and Ravindra Jadeja were prominent wicket-takers. Whereas the second Test was rained off after one day, the first and third Tests were decided with two days to spare, as India won by 108 runs and 124 runs, despite tallying only 201, 200, 215 and 173. In a very tedious final Test, Ajinkya Rahane made two centuries for India before South Africa, set 481, crawled to 143 in 143.1 overs.

South Africa v India

1992–93 (SA): South Africa 1–0 (3 drawn)

1996–97 (I): India 2–1

1996–97 (SA): South Africa 2–0 (1 drawn)

1999–00 (I): South Africa 2–0

2001–02 (SA): South Africa 1–0 (1 drawn)
2004–05 (I): India 1–0 (1 drawn)
2006–07 (SA): South Africa 2–1
2007–08 (I): 1–1 (1 drawn)

2009–10 (I): 1–1
2010–11 (SA): 1–1 (1 drawn)
2013–14 (SA): South Africa 1–0 (1 drawn)
2015–16 (I): India 3–0 (1 drawn)

3.3 SOUTH AFRICA v PAKISTAN

1990s

South Africa and Pakistan didn't meet in Test cricket until January 1995, nearly three years after the African nation returned to Test cricket. A one-off match was played at Johannesburg, with the hosts winning by 324 runs after setting a target of 490. South Africa was in some difficulty at 168–5 before 72 from Jonty Rhodes, 113 from Brian McMillan and an unbeaten 66 from number ten Fanie de Villiers set up a total of 460. Pakistan tallied only half of that, with de Villiers taking 6–81 before following up with 4–27.

Pakistan hosted a three-match series nearly three years later, with two draws followed by a 53-run victory to the tourists. Both sides topped 400 in the first encounter, with Pakistan Test debutants Ali Naqvi (115 as opener) and Azhar Mahmood (128 not out at number eight) excelling while tailenders Waqar Younis (45) and Mushtaq Ahmed (59) helped the total from 231–8 to 456. The second Test featured barely two days of play, before the third Test was worthy of a decider. Opener Gary Kirsten (100 not out) and number nine Pat Symcox (81) were responsible for South Africa making a modest 239, before Pakistan led by 69. Symcox made 55 at number four as the Africans struggled to 214, and then claimed 3–8, while Shaun Pollock bagged 5–37 as Pakistan managed only 92 when chasing 146.

The teams met in another three-match series later in season 1997–98, with a rain-affected draw followed by a victory to each team. Symcox made 108 at number ten in the first Test as South Africa progressed from 166–8 to 364 all out, before Mahmood made 136 at number seven as Pakistan improved from 112–5 to 329 all out. Mahmood scored 132 in Pakistan's first-innings total of 259 in the second Test, before Saeed Anwar scored 118 in Pakistan's second-innings total of 226. Mushtaq Ahmed's 6 wickets were crucial as South Africa crashed to 133–8, before a ninth-wicket partnership of 86 threatened to steal the game from Pakistan, which belatedly won by 29 runs. From 36–3 in the first innings of the third Test, the Africans reached 293 as Waqar snared 6 wickets before de Villiers (6–23) and Allan Donald (4–47) skittled the Pakistanis for 106. Donald later took 4–27 as the Pakistanis made only 134 after being set 394.

2000s

A two-match series in 2002–03 was a mismatch as hosts South Africa won by 10 wickets before winning by an innings and 142 runs. Pakistan had to follow on in the first Test after plunging from 77–0 to 161 all out, before achieving a paltry lead of 43. Herschelle Gibbs (228) and Graeme Smith (151) put on 368 runs for the first wicket in the second Test before South Africa finished with 620–7 declared. Pakistan was dismissed for 252 and 226 despite 135 and 67 from opener Taufeeq Umar.

Pakistan beat South Africa in a Test series for the first time in late 2003 as a drawn Test followed an 8-wicket victory to the hosts. In response to 320, Pakistan made 401 as Taufeeq (111) and Test debutant Asim Kamal (99) led the way, despite South African unorthodox spinner Paul Adams snaring 7 wickets. Danish Kaneria and Shoaib Akhtar dismissed South Africa for 241 before Pakistan cruised to victory. The final Test was well fought and finished with honours even, as Pakistan was 242–6 after being set 302.

A fine series unfolded in South Africa in early 2007, as chasing a target proved a winner each time, following many pendulum swings. Ashwell Prince (138) and Gibbs (94) made decisive contributions in the first Test as South Africa gained a 104-run lead before Pakistan captured only 3 wickets, as the Africans chased 199. The hosts capitulated for

124 in the second Test, before an unbeaten 92 from Inzamam-ul-Haq helped the visitors to a 141-run advantage. South Africa eked out a 190-run lead and had Pakistan in trouble at 92–5 before Younis Khan (67 not out) and Kamran Akmal (57 not out) guided Pakistan to a 5-wicket victory. The Pakistanis made only 157 in the first innings of the decider, but remained in contention as the Africans led by just 26. Chasing 161, South Africa was 39–4 before half-centuries to Kallis and Prince set up a 5-wicket triumph.

Kallis (155 and 100 not out) played a starring role in the first Test of 2007–08, with South Africa winning by 160 runs at Karachi as the hosts sought 424. Kallis also scored a century in South Africa's second innings in the second and final Test, as did Graeme Smith. Set 457, Pakistan finished at 316–4 following 130 from Younis Khan, who had also recorded a ton in the first Test.

The two-match series in 2010–11 was played in neutral territory, in the United Arab Emirates, with several centuries recorded. The highest individual score was 278 not out by AB de Villiers, as South Africa racked up 584–9 declared in the second Test. In both Tests, Pakistan finished its second innings with 7 wickets in hand while well short of the target, although 343–3 was creditable after being set 451 in the first Test.

South Africa produced a 3–0 whitewash at home in early 2013, with a 211-run win followed by a 4-wicket win, before the final Test margin was an innings and 18 runs. The hosts made 253 in the first Test before the visitors succumbed for a dismal 49 as Dale Steyn took 6–8. He finished with match figures of 11–60. Younis Khan and Asad Shafiq made 111 each as Pakistan made 338 and then had South Africa struggling in the second Test, but the hosts recovered to score 326 before being in control for most of the run chase, after the visitors could set only 182. Test debutant Kyle Abbott was the pick of the players in the final Test with figures of 7–29 and 2–39 as Pakistan sank to totals of 156 and 235.

The 2013–14 series was played in United Arab Emirates, with Pakistan winning the first Test by 7 wickets before South Africa drew the series with an innings victory. South Africa's batting was inadequate in the first Test despite 118 from Amla in the first innings and 90 from de Villiers in the second innings, whereas Pakistan topped 400 following centuries to Khurram Manzoor and Misbah-ul-Haq. Pakistan lost 3–7 at the start of its second innings but a mere target of 40 ensured there was no panic. Collapsing for 99 in the second Test, however, put Pakistan on the back foot, before 234 from Graeme Smith and 164 from de Villiers set up a lead of 418. Pakistan recovered from 2–2 and 70–4 as Asad Shafiq (130) and Misbah-ul-Haq (88) added 197 for the fifth wicket, before Asad's eventual dismissal ended the Test as Zulfiqar Babar was absent hurt.

South Africa v Pakistan

1994–95 (SA): South Africa 1–0

1997–98 (P): South Africa 1–0 (2 drawn)

1997–98 (SA): 1–1 (1 drawn)

2002–03 (SA): South Africa 2–0

2003–04 (P): Pakistan 1–0 (1 drawn)

2006–07 (SA): South Africa 2–1

2007–08 (P): South Africa 1–0 (1 drawn)

2010–11 (Bangladesh): 0–0 (2 drawn)

2012–13 (SA): South Africa 3–0

2013–14 (Bangladesh): 1–1

3.4 SOUTH AFRICA v SRI LANKA

1990s

Sri Lanka was South Africa's third different Test opponent since the African nation's return to Test cricket, with South Africa having lost to the West Indies before beating India. The Sri Lankans looked like winning the first Test at Moratuwa in the 1993 series after setting South Africa 365. The visitors were 199–7 before finishing at 251–7, with Jonty Rhodes on 101 not out while Clive Eksteen scored 4 not out from 89 balls in 92 minutes. The second Test was completely different as Sri Lanka crumbled for 168 and 119, with Brett Schultz claiming 9 wickets. Hansie Cronje scored 122 while four teammates posted half-centuries in South Africa's 495. Only 23 wickets fell in the drawn third Test as South Africa never looked like surrendering the series lead, finishing on 159–4 with a lead of 179.

South Africa won the two-match series 2–0 at home in early 1998 as Sri Lanka was yet to be a force in Test cricket, despite winning the 1996 World Cup. The South Africans had the upper hand in the first Test after 113 from Daryll Cullinan and 92 from Shaun Pollock helped the hosts to 418. South Africa won by 70 runs after the visitors twice tallied 306 without anyone making a big score. Sri Lanka made 303 in the second Test and was well-placed to square the series after dismissing South Africa for 200, with Cullinan scoring 103. But then the visitors surrendered for 122 as Allan Donald snared 5–54, before Cronje clobbered 82, while Gary Kirsten's unbeaten 75 took South Africa to a 6-wicket win.

2000s

Sri Lanka heralded its first Test win against South Africa in 2000 with an innings victory at Galle. Mahela Jayawardene (167) and Sanath Jayasuriya (148) were responsible for a total of 522, before Cullinan scored 114 not out. There wasn't enough resistance from the rest of the South Africans as Muttiah Muralitharan's 13 wickets led to South Africa's demise for 238 and 269. The visitors were on the ropes at 34–5 in the second Test before reaching 253 following an unbeaten 118 from Lance Klusener. Sri Lanka was in a commanding position at 286–4 before the dismissal of Marvan Atapattu (120) sparked a collapse as the hosts crumbled for 308. Set 177 to seal the series, Sri Lanka lost its openers for golden ducks and soon plunged to 21–4, before looking certain winners at 130–4. In a scene resembling Sri Lanka's demise against Australia eight years earlier, the hosts snatched a 7-run defeat as Klusener and Nicky Boje did most of the damage. The dismissal of Arjuna Ranatunga for 88 was decisive as it left Sri Lanka 161–7. The series finished on even terms as Sri Lanka, set 263 in the third Test, finished on 195–4 with Jayawardene on 101.

Sri Lanka barely escaped with a draw in the opening Test of 2000–01, finishing on 149–6 after trailing by 204 runs on the first innings and later being set 345. After a day was lost due to the weather in the first Test, the remaining two Tests required only three days each as South Africa achieved two innings victories. Sri Lanka mustered just 95 and 180 in the second Test at Cape Town, followed by 119 and 252 at Centurion, while South Africa made 504 at Cape Town and 378 at Centurion.

The Africans began the 2002–03 series with another innings triumph, before sealing the series with a mere 3-wicket win at Centurion. Sri Lanka made 323 before its second-innings total of 245 left South Africa a target of 121. The first-ball dismissal of Graeme Smith was followed by the Africans tumbling to 44–5 and 73–6, before a 39-run partnership took the hosts to the brink of victory.

The first Test of 2004 was drawn, with Mahela Jayawardene scoring 237 in Sri Lanka's first innings of 486 before South Africa finished on 203–3 after being set 325. After losing Marvan Atapattu to the fourth ball of the second Test, Sri Lanka compiled 470 on the back of Kumar Sangakkara's 232. Jayasuriya bagged 5–34 with his part-time orthodox spin as South Africa succumbed for 189 before 6–29 from Chaminda Vaas helped Sri Lanka to a 313-run victory to seal a 1–0 series win.

Sri Lanka won the 2006 series 2–0 at home, with an innings win followed by a thrilling 1-wicket margin. South Africa's second-innings score of 434 couldn't compensate for a poor first-innings total of 169 at Colombo, where Jayawardene (374) and Sangakkara (287) put on a record-breaking 624-run third-wicket partnership in a total of 756–5 declared. The visitors overcame a shocking start in the second Test to tally 361 and then lead by 40, before setting a stiff target of 352. Jayasuriya hammered a quick 73 before Jayawardene's 123 kept Sri Lanka in contention. Wickets fell at 12, 94, 121, 164, 201 and 279, before Jayawardene departed at 341. Subsequent wickets at 348 and 350 left a result impossible to guess, before two singles sealed the match and series.

More than five years passed before South Africa hosted its next series involving Sri Lanka, with up-and-down results. The home side won the first Test by an innings and 81 runs, before the tourists recorded a 208-run victory. The first Test was decided with two days to spare, before the second Test finished on the penultimate day. The deciding Test also concluded on day four, with the hosts all but ensuring they wouldn't lose after making 580–4 declared in the first innings. Opener Alviro Petersen scored 109 before Jacques Kallis (224) and AB de Villiers (160 not out) batted on and on. Sri Lanka made only 239 in reply and then did just enough to make South Africa bat again, following an unbeaten 115 to Thilan Samaraweera.

Centuries to Dean Elgar and JP Duminy, and 9 wickets to Dale Steyn, were pivotal in South Africa's 153-run victory in the first Test of the 2014 series in Sri Lanka. The hosts topped 400 in the second Test following 165 from Jayawardene, and gained a lead of 139 but fell agonisingly short of levelling the series as the visitors finished on 159–8 after being set 369.

South Africa v Sri Lanka

1993–94 (SL): South Africa 1–0 (2 drawn)

1997–98 (SA): South Africa 2–0

2000 (SL): 1–1 (1 drawn)

2000–01 (SA): South Africa 2–0 (1 drawn)

2002–03 (SA): South Africa 2–0

2004 (SL): Sri Lanka 1–0 (1 drawn)

2006 (SL): Sri Lanka 2–0

2011–12 (SA): South Africa 2–1

2014 (SL): South Africa 1–0 (1 drawn)

3.5 SOUTH AFRICA v WEST INDIES

1990s

The first time that the West Indies met South Africa in Test cricket was the first time that South Africa played Test cricket after returning from exile. A one-off match was played at Barbados in April 1992, with the hosts winning a memorable encounter by 52 runs. Kepler Wessels was the sole South African with Test experience, having played 24 Tests for Australia from 1982 to 1985.

The West Indies plunged from 219–3 to 262 all out before opener Andrew Hudson scored 163 in South Africa's first innings of 345. A couple of West Indian top order batsmen had narrow escapes before a vital last wicket 62-run stand unfolded, setting the tourists a target of 201. The Africans began the final day at 122–2 before Curtly Ambrose (6–34) and Courtney Walsh (4–31) produced brilliant spells to preserve the West Indies' 57-year unbeaten record in Barbados.

The situation was far removed when the teams next met in Test cricket, in 1998–99. South Africa won all five Tests on home soil, with the West Indies copping four thrashings after starting the series with a respectable 4-wicket loss, as the hosts achieved a 164-run target. The tourists made only 121 and 141 as they lost the second Test by 178 runs, before the margin in the third Test was 9 wickets, following totals of 198 and 259 from the West Indies. Gary Kirsten was dismissed from the first ball of the fourth Test and second ball of the fifth Test, but the hosts recovered to win by 149 and 351 runs, as the tourists were set fiendishly difficult targets of 421 and 569. Extraordinarily, every member of the South African team gained man of the match honours in the final Test. Shaun Pollock claimed 29 wickets in the series, including 22 in the first three Tests, while teammates Daryll Cullinan (168) and Jacques Kallis (198 runs for once out, and 7 wickets) starred in the fourth Test. A rare highlight for the West Indies was Franklyn Rose's 7–84 in South Africa's first innings in the third Test.

2000s

The West Indians had ample incentive in future encounters with South Africa, as the teams vied for the Sir Vivian Richards Trophy from 2000–01. Following a draw at Guyana first up, the West Indies led by 56 runs on the first innings in the second Test before losing by 69 runs when seeking a 232-run target. Set 265 in the third Test, the hosts hung on by the skin of their teeth as they finished at 88–7. The Africans wrapped up the series with an 82-run win in the fourth Test, before the West Indies won the final Test by 130 runs after setting a target of 386.

Cullinan enjoyed a purple patch as he scored 103 and 73 in the second Test, followed by 134 and 82 in the third Test.

South Africa began the 2003–04 series strongly as Kallis (158) and captain Graeme Smith (132) set up a total of 561, before 202 from Brian Lara couldn't prevent the Africans leading by 151. The West Indies were all out for 188 in their second innings and thus lost by 189 runs, before facing a deficit of 394 in the second Test at Durban, as South Africa racked up 658–9 declared. Kallis (177), Herschelle Gibbs (142) and Kirsten (137) were the biggest scorers before West Indian duo Ramnaresh Sarwan (114) and Shivnarine Chanderpaul (109) excelled without being able to prevent an innings defeat. A drawn third Test in Cape Town was enough for the Africans to seal the series, although the West Indians scored a creditable 354–5 after being set 441. There were four centuries for South Africa and three for the West Indies in the third Test, before South African openers Gibbs (192) and Smith (139) put on 301 runs in the fourth Test. Kallis made 130 not out as the hosts tallied 604–6 declared, and later won by 10 wickets after Sarwan and Chris Gayle scored centuries as the tourists followed on.

Wavell Hinds (213) and Chanderpaul (203 not out) gave the hosts of the 2005 series a wonderful start, before the visitors had to follow on. South Africa nonetheless saved the match comfortably, as the West Indians were guilty of some dropped catches and negative field placings. Lara (196) scored 56.48 per cent of the home side's total in the first innings of the second Test before Graeme Smith made 148 as his team led by 51. The West Indies could set a target of only 144 despite 107 not out from Sarwan, and South Africa recorded an 8-wicket victory before winning the next Test by an innings. The West Indies would have made a lot less than 296 were it not for Lara's 176, before South Africa made 548–9 declared following 104 and 178 from openers Smith and AB de Villiers. Andre Nel claimed 10 wickets in the third Test, before the final Test was a very high-scoring draw. Smith (126) and de Villiers (114) were again hard to dislodge, as were Kallis (147) and Ashwell Prince (131), as South Africa declared 12 runs short of 600. The West Indies responded with a staggering 747 thanks to Gayle (317), Sarwan and Chanderpaul (127 each) and Dwayne Bravo (107). South Africa gave all 11 players a bowl, with record-breaking wicketkeeper Mark Boucher taking the last wicket, as Dwayne Bravo was caught by Prince.

The West Indies had high hopes of taking out the Sir Vivian Richards Trophy for the first time after winning the first Test of the 2007–08 series by 128 runs, but South Africa came back to win 2–1. The West Indians didn't enforce the follow on after leading by 213 runs in the first Test at Port Elizabeth, and their second innings was disappointing but the Africans never looked like attaining 389. The hosts limited the tourists to 243 and 262 in the second Test, which South Africa won by 7 wickets after chasing 185. The decider turned into an annihilation, as the West Indies crashed to 139 all out before losing by an innings following hundreds to Proteas trio Smith, Prince and de Villiers.

Sub-standard batting again cost the West Indians in 2010, with visitors South Africa winning the first Test by 163 runs before a draw was followed by a 7-wicket margin to seal a 2–0 result. Smith, de Villiers and Kallis scored a ton each in the drawn Test before the West Indies, surprisingly, passed South Africa's total of 543–6 declared, following 166 from Chanderpaul and 114 from Brendan Nash. No centuries were scored in South Africa's two victories, with the tourists requiring just 47 runs to win the third Test.

The Africans again won 2–0 in 2014–15 with victories in the first and third Tests. Captain Hashim Amla (208), AB de Villiers (152) and Stiaan van Zyl (101 not out) helped the hosts to 552–5 declared at Centurion, before the visitors made only 201 and 131. Rain shortened the second Test, with South African duo Dean Elgar and Faf du Plessis scoring tons before West Indian duo Kraigg Brathwaite and Marlon Samuels did likewise. In the final Test, the West Indies made 329 before the Africans replied with 421 following 148 from de Villiers. The visitors were soundly placed in their second innings at 182–3 before losing 7–33, and the hosts went on to win by 8 wickets.

South Africa v West Indies

1991–92 (WI): West Indies 1–0   **2000–01 (WI):** South Africa 2–1
1998–99 (SA): South Africa 5–0   (2 drawn)

2003–04 (SA): South Africa 3–0 (1 drawn)

2005 (WI): South Africa 2–0 (2 drawn)

2007–08 (SA): South Africa 2–1

2010 (WI): South Africa 2–0 (1 drawn)

2014–15 (SA): South Africa 2–0 (1 drawn)

3.6 SOUTH AFRICA v ZIMBABWE

1990s

Zimbabwe's inaugural Test match was played several months after South Africa was readmitted to Test cricket, but three years passed before the two African nations faced off in Test cricket for the first time. Harare Sports Club was the venue, with the hosts tallying just 170 before Andrew Hudson scored 135 in the visiting team's 346. Following an 11-wicket match haul to Allan Donald, South Africa won by 7 wickets after chasing 108, and continued to dish out thrashings thereafter.

South Africa hosted a Test before Zimbabwe did likewise in late 1999, with South Africa winning by an innings on both occasions, as Jacques Kallis and Shaun Pollock were prominent. On home soil, the Zimbabweans were embarrassed as they mustered just 102 and 141, while South Africa made 462–9 declared.

2000s

South Africa's first three batsmen (Herschelle Gibbs 147, Gary Kirsten 220 and Kallis 157 not out) set up a total of 600–3 declared in the first Test of the next all-African series, held in Zimbabwe in September 2001. Andy Flower shone like a beacon with scores of 142 and 199 not out as Zimbabwe made 286 and 391, before Boeta Dippenaar was out first ball in South Africa's 9-wicket victory. A good team effort enabled Zimbabwe to score 419–9 declared in the second Test, before an even better team showing gave South Africa a 100-run lead, with Kallis making 189 not out. The match finished in a draw after day two had been washed out.

South Africa won both Tests of the 2004–05 series by an innings, after the writing was on the wall as Zimbabwe was routed for 54 in the first innings of the opening Test. South Africa won a one-off Test by 9 wickets in Harare in August 2014, with Dale Steyn and debutant Dane Piedt capturing 8 wickets each.

South Africa v Zimbabwe

1995–96 (Z): South Africa 1–0
1999–2000 (SA/Z): South Africa 2–0

2001–02 (Z): South Africa 1–0 (1 drawn)
2004–05 (SA): South Africa 2–0
2014 (Z): South Africa 1–0

3.7 SOUTH AFRICA v BANGLADESH

2000s

The first eight Tests involving South Africa and Bangladesh resulted in seven innings victories and a 5-wicket victory to the Africans. Left-handers Graeme Smith (200) and Gary Kirsten (150) set up a total of 529–4 declared in the first meeting in East London during season 2002–03, before the visitors totalled 170 and 252. Kirsten (160), Jacques Kallis (139 not out) and Herschelle Gibbs (114) were the main contributors with the bat in the next Test, while Kallis also snared 7 wickets as South Africa won by an innings and 160 runs. When the Africans toured Bangladesh several months later, the margin in the first Test was an innings and 60 runs, before South Africa won the next Test by an innings and 18 runs. Left-arm wrist-spinner Paul Adams claimed match figures of 10–106 in the first Test while Test debutant Jacques

Rudolph (222 not out) and Boeta Dippenaar (177 not out) took South Africa from 41–2 to 470–2 declared. Robin Peterson had a fine debut in the following Test as he scored 61 at number eight and then claimed 2–22 and 3–46, with South Africa progressing from 63–4 to 330 all out before dismissing Bangladesh for 102 and 210.

After scoring a mediocre 192 in the first Test of the 2007–08 series in Mirpur, Bangladesh dismissed South Africa for 170 as Shahadat Hossain bagged 6–27. But the hosts failed to capitalise, as the visitors cruised to victory when chasing 205, before the margin in the next Test was an innings and 205 runs. Smith (232) and fellow opener Neil McKenzie (226) put on 415 for the first wicket before Smith declared at 583–7.

Smith (157) and number three Hashim Amla (112) set up a total of 441 in the opening Test of 2008–09 at Bloemfontein, before Bangladesh tallied 153 and 159. The hosts wobbled at 134–5 in reply to 250 in the second Test, before Ashwell Prince (162 not out) and Mark Boucher (117) put on 271 runs to set up victory by an innings and 48 runs.

South Africa's winning sequence ended as both Tests in the 2015 series were drawn, with rain cancelling six scheduled days of cricket. At Chittagong, where the last two days of play were washed out, the visitors were restricted to 248 before finishing their second innings at 61–0 after the hosts made 326. After one day of play in Mirpur, the hosts reached 246–8 before the rest of the match was rained off.

South Africa v Bangladesh

2002–03 (SA): South Africa 2–0
2003 (B): South Africa 2–0
2007–08 (B): South Africa 2–0
2008–09 (SA): South Africa 2–0
2015 (B): 0–0 (2 drawn)

3.8 NOTABLE TEST PLAYERS

Hashim Amla

Hashim Amla created history when he became the first African batsman to score a Test triple-century. He achieved the feat as he amassed 311 not out against England at the Oval in July 2012. Amla was also the first non-white South African to be appointed captain of the national cricket team, after Ashwell Prince was briefly a stand-in captain.

Amla had a slow start to Test cricket as he made 24 and 2 on debut in a loss to India at Kolkata in late 2004. Chosen for two Tests in South Africa's subsequent series against England, Amla failed with 1, 0, 25 and 10. After being recalled, Amla made a breakthrough 149 in a high-scoring draw against New Zealand at Cape Town in 2006. He averaged more than 50 as he scored nearly 1600 runs in his next 19 Tests, and consolidated the number three position in the batting order. Amla's second and third Test tons were also against the Kiwis in South Africa, with 176 not out and 103 in successive matches, which the hosts won. Amla notched 1012 Test runs in the calendar year of 2008, with highlights including 159 and 81 in a run-feast at Chennai, and an undefeated 104 at Lord's. He also made a ton against Bangladesh, before following up with handy rather than big scores in South Africa's series win Down Under.

Amla's 100 against England at Centurion in December 2009 was his first triple-figure score in Tests for a little over a year, before he excelled in 2010 with 1249 Test runs at 78.06. He began the year with 14 and 95 in a draw, and then 75 as the Proteas drew the series against England. With the Proteas beating India by an innings before the Indians returned the compliment, Amla's three scores were 253 not out, 114 and 123 not out. Later in the year Amla scored a century against Pakistan, and then there was another case of Amla making triple-figures in an innings victory against India, before India squared the series. South Africa also had to settle for a drawn series against Australia in late 2011 following a century from Amla in each match, with Amla's 112 helping the Proteas to a staggering come-from-behind win at Cape Town.

Amla's historic triple-century helped the Proteas to an innings win against England, before his 121 at Lord's helped South Africa to a 2–0 series victory. Later in 2012, Amla made scores of 104 and 196 in Australia. The latter innings was particularly vital as it helped South Africa win the deciding Test. Amla's two Test tons in 2013 were in victories against the Kiwis and Pakistanis, before he assumed the captaincy in 2014 after scoring a ton during a series loss to Australia. Amla's first series as captain resulted in a series victory in Sri Lanka, with Amla scoring 139 not out (in 486 minutes) and a stonewalling 25 (in 170 minutes) in the second Test as the tourists escaped with a draw. In 2014–15 Amla led the Proteas to a 2–0 win against the West Indies, with the highlight his 208 in the first Test.

Amla suffered a loss of form as he didn't score a Test ton in 2015, and he concluded a 3–0 loss to India with an uncharacteristic 25 from 244 balls as he tried in vain to salvage a draw. Amla concluded 2015 with two failures during a loss to England, before beginning 2016 with 201 as his team saved the Cape Town Test. Amla stepped down as skipper after the Cape Town Test, and he made 40 and 5 in the third Test, which England won, before Amla notched 109 and 96 in a face-saving victory.

Hashim Amla (b.1983)*

Matches: 92
Runs scored: 7358
Batting average: 51.45
100s/50s: 25/29
Top score: 311*
Balls bowled: 54
Wickets: –
Bowling average: –
5 wickets in innings: –
10 wickets in match: –
Best bowling: –
Catches/stumpings: 78/–
* still playing as of 2016

Mark Boucher

Mark Boucher had big shoes to fill as he burst onto the international scene when Dave Richardson's career neared its end. South Africa's first-choice wicketkeeper when the country was readmitted to international cricket, Richardson was unlucky not to have the opportunity to play Test cricket until he was 32. Richardson became South Africa's leading wicketkeeper with 152 dismissals from 42 Tests before his successor, who was 17 years Richardson's junior, went on to become the leading wicketkeeper in Test history.

After replacing Richardson for one Test in Pakistan in late 1997 and having little chance to contribute in a rain-affected draw, Boucher fronted up against Pakistan in South Africa a few months later and quickly showed he was a worthy successor to Richardson with gloves and bat. In the first Test at Johannesburg, Boucher scored 78 at number eight and shared a ninth-wicket stand of 195 with Pat Symcox, who made 108 at number ten. Although the Pakistanis won the second Test by 29 runs, Boucher made an admirable 52 to give the Africans a chance after they slumped to 133–8 when chasing 255. He also made

52 in the final Test, in which he also took eight catches and a stumping to help the Proteas draw the series.

Ten years after making his Test debut, Boucher became the leading gloveman in Test cricket when he passed Ian Healy's figure of 395 Test dismissals and soon became the first player to achieve 400 dismissals. Healy's successor in the Australian team, Adam Gilchrist, overtook Boucher before the South African reclaimed the record in 2008: the year that Gilchrist retired from international cricket.

Although Gilchrist's batting average was far superior to Boucher's, the South African nonetheless was a dependable batsman as he notched 35 half-centuries and five centuries. His maiden Test ton was scored at a particularly vital time against the West Indies, in the final encounter of the 1998–99 series, as it helped South Africa recover from an early collapse to post a competitive total on the way to clean sweeping the series. Boucher's second ton was later in the year when he was used as a nightwatchman against Zimbabwe at Harare. Boucher's third Test century was largely forgotten as Gary Kirsten scored 275, but the wicketkeeper's contribution was still vital as the Proteas made a huge total after being forced to follow on while protecting a series lead against England in 1999–00. More than four years passed between Boucher's third and fourth Test centuries, and then another four years passed before he notched his final Test ton. Some other knocks from Boucher deserved attention, in addition to his aforementioned contributions against Pakistan in 1997–98. Against Sri Lanka in 2000, the Africans recovered from an innings defeat to level the series with a mere 7-run victory, but not before they were reeling at 34–5 in the first innings and finished with 253, thanks partly to 60 from Boucher. Against the Sri Lankans in 2002–03, the Africans recorded an innings win before scraping to a nervous 3-wicket victory when chasing only 121. Boucher made a crucial 22 not out after coming in at 73–6.

Regularly the vice-captain while Shaun Pollock was captain, Boucher led the Proteas in four Tests and suffered defeat by an innings and 360 runs on the first occasion. It was the first Test against Australia in early 2002, when Boucher played his fiftieth Test and could only watch as Gilchrist blazed 204 not out in Australia's 652–7 declared. Australia won the series but South Africa saved face with a win in the third Test, when Boucher struck the winning runs with a six. Boucher thus achieved something that Pollock couldn't: captain the Proteas to a win against Australia.

Boucher intended to retire immediately after South Africa's tour of England in 2012, but an injury before the start of the Test series brought a slightly premature end to his career. Against Somerset, Boucher was struck in the left eye by a bail when Gemaal Hussain was bowled by leg spinner Imran Tahir. Surgery was required and AB de Villiers promptly took over as South African wicketkeeper.

Mark Boucher (b.1976)

Matches: 147
Runs scored: 5515
Batting average: 30.30
100s/50s: 5/35
Top score: 125
Balls bowled: 8
Wickets: 1
Bowling average: 6.00
5 wickets in innings: –
10 wickets in match: –
Best bowling: 1–6
Catches/stumpings: 532/23

AB de Villiers

A gifted and versatile batsman while also an adept wicketkeeper and fielder, AB de Villiers possessed a rare mix of cricketing skills. Quick on his feet, de Villiers showed an ability to play conventional and not-so-conventional strokes, while also being a fast runner between the wickets. A consistent matchwinner with a lot of quick scoring in limited-overs cricket, de Villiers paced himself well in Tests and could hardly be accused of being reckless.

De Villiers opened the batting in his Test debut, scoring 28 and 14 in a 7-wicket loss to England at Port Elizabeth in December 2004. He claimed five catches in the next Test after donning the wicketkeeping gloves, and he scored 14 and 52 not out as he batted at number seven and eight. Mark Boucher returned as wicketkeeper later in the series and, in the last Test at Centurion, de Villiers scored a fine double of 92 and 109 as the Proteas unsuccessfully sought to draw the series. In South Africa's subsequent tour of the Caribbean, de Villiers' scores included 178 and 114 as he shared two big opening partnerships with captain Graeme Smith.

Surprisingly, nearly three years passed before de Villiers notched his fourth Test century. He had a patchy time against Australia in 2005–06, and his form was mediocre for a while in 2006 and 2007 before he registered four Test tons in 2008. The first of them was an unbeaten 103 from just 109 balls in a series-clinching innings victory against the West Indies at Durban as he batted at number six. His unbeaten 217 against India at Ahmedabad was also in an innings win, before his 174 at Headingley was in a 10-wicket win. Remarkably, de Villiers avoided making a Test duck for 78 innings before being dismissed without scoring against Bangladesh in November 2008. The following month, de Villiers enjoyed South Africa's series win Down Under as he made significant contributions at Perth, where the Proteas comfortably chased 414. He held four superb catches in the slips and gully region, and made scores of 63 and 106 not out. As the Proteas lost their follow-up series to Australia, de Villiers made 104 not out in a loss before bludgeoning 163 in South Africa's face-saving win.

De Villiers' three Test centuries in 2010 included his Test-best 278 not out, scored against Pakistan at Abu Dhabi. His best score in 2011 was 99 against Sri Lanka in December, before he notched an unbeaten 160 at Cape Town where the Proteas won the third and deciding Test. He averaged 117.67 in that series. De Villiers made some other telling contributions with the bat during 2012, and also took on the wicketkeeping responsibility following Boucher's retirement. Against the Kiwis, de Villiers made a vital 83 in the only outright result during that particular series. In the third and deciding Test in Australia, his 169 helped put the match beyond the home team's reach.

De Villiers performed superbly in South Africa's clean sweep against Pakistan in early 2013 as he notched two centuries while compiling 352 runs at 88, and also held 11 catches in the opening Test. Later that year de Villiers scored 90 in a loss to Pakistan at Abu Dhabi, before he made 164 in the following Test, as the Proteas drew the series with an innings victory. The Africans subsequently beat India 1–0, with de Villiers making 103 in the drawn first Test before notching 74 in South Africa's triumph.

South Africa's 2–1 series loss to Australia in early 2014 included a century from de Villiers in the Proteas' victory at Port Elizabeth, before he made two tons in a convincing series win against the West Indies in 2014–15. With the Proteas on their way to a 3–0 loss to India in 2015–16, de Villiers made a standout 42 in two hours in a paltry 121-run total before plodding his way to 43 off 297 balls in 354 minutes during the final Test. De Villiers was given the captaincy shortly afterwards as Hashim Amla stepped down from the position during a series loss to England. De Villiers scored 36 and 0 as England clinched the series with a win at Johannesburg, before de Villiers bagged two second-ball ducks while leading the Proteas to a consolation victory at Centurion.

AB de Villiers (b.1984)*

Matches: 106
Runs scored: 8074
Batting average: 50.46
100s/50s: 21/39
Top score: 278*
Balls bowled: 204
Wickets: 2
Bowling average: 52.00
5 wickets in innings: –
10 wickets in match: –
Best bowling: 2–49
Catches/stumpings: 197/5
* still playing as of 2016

Allan Donald

Known as 'White Lightning', Allan Donald was rated the fastest white bowler in the world when South Africa resumed international cricket in the early 1990s. Donald had plenty of English county cricket experience before impressing in the 1992 World Cup and then making his Test debut, aged 25.

Donald claimed 2–67 and 4–77 in his maiden Test as South Africa lost to the West Indies at Bridgetown. Later that year, the Africans and Indians played out a four-match series which the hosts won after Donald claimed 5–55 and 7–84 to set up a 9-wicket victory at Port Elizabeth. Donald was also very impressive against India in 1996–97 as India won 2–1 at home before the Proteas won 2–0 as hosts. Donald claimed 5 or more wickets in an innings against Australia, England, India, Pakistan, Sri Lanka, the West Indies and Zimbabwe as he regularly spearheaded South Africa's attack. His best figures were 8–71 against Zimbabwe at Harare in October 1995. Donald was fortunate that South Africa had other pacemen such as Meyrick Pringle, Brian McMillan, Richard Snell, Fanie de Villiers, Craig Matthews, Shaun Pollock, Lance Klusener and the injury-prone Brett Schultz. Whilst de Villiers earned the accolades for his 6–43 which inspired South Africa to a shock 5-run win against Australia, which was rolled for 111 in the 1994 Sydney Test, Donald's 3–34 was also vital. Early on the final day, he bowled Allan Border with a splendid delivery that dislodged the off bail as the Australian captain offered no stroke.

Donald's direction and control were impressive for such a fast bowler, and there was just the odd occasion that he lost the plot. In his first encounter with England in Test cricket, Donald captured 5–74 and 2–29 in South Africa's 356-run victory at Lord's before he was hit around in the rest of the series, which ended in a 1–1 draw. Donald's career highlights nonetheless were against England, particularly in 1995–96, 1998 and 1999–00. Donald took 19 wickets in the 1995–96 series, as did England's Dominic Cork, with Donald's 7 scalps in the final Test proving decisive as South Africa took out the series with a 10-wicket win. Donald was even better in the 1998 series as he claimed 33 wickets, although England won the series 2–1. Donald was destructive for much of 1998 as he claimed 80 wickets in 14 Tests. In 1999–00 he claimed 6–53 and 5–74 in the first Test, which South Africa won easily, and he also claimed a 5-wicket haul — his last in Test cricket — in South Africa's other victory during the series.

Donald had several memorable battles with England opening batsman Mike Atherton over the years, often when Atherton captained England. Although Donald dismissed Atherton 11 times in Test cricket, the opening batsman also scored plenty of runs off Donald's bowling. Atherton was partly responsible for Donald's expensive figures in the third Test of 1994, before Donald dismissed the England skipper four times in 1995–96. But in the second Test of 1995–96, England's skipper could not be dislodged in the fourth innings as he scored 185 not out in 643 minutes to force a draw. Whilst Donald dismissed Atherton three times in the 1998 series, this was overshadowed by classic one-on-one battles at Old Trafford and Trent Bridge. At Old Trafford, Donald claimed 6–88 in England's second innings as the hosts followed on and were in danger of slipping to a 2–0 series deficit. Atherton scored 89 in 371 minutes to lead from the front before several of his teammates lasted long enough to help the hosts salvage a draw by the skin of their teeth. In the following Test, Donald took a 5-wicket haul in England's first innings before the hosts sought 247 to level the series. Donald appeared to have Atherton caught behind, off the glove, but the appeal was rejected and prompted Donald to lose his temper. As if that wasn't bad enough, the next ball was inside-edged to the boundary. Fired up like never before and coming around the wicket, Donald delivered Atherton three ferocious bouncers between 140 and 150 kilometres per hour as the tension was immense. Donald was also unlucky not to have Nasser Hussain caught behind as the snicked ball was fumbled, before England won by 8 wickets and later took out the series.

Allan Donald (b.1966)

Matches: 72
Runs scored: 652
Batting average: 10.68
100s/50s: 0/0
Top score: 37
Balls bowled: 15,519
Wickets: 330
Bowling average: 22.25
5 wickets in innings: 20
10 wickets in match: 3
Best bowling: 8–71
Catches/stumpings: 18/–

Jacques Kallis

Jacques Kallis drew comparisons with Garry Sobers when the right-handed Kallis became the second player to achieve the combination of 8000 runs, 200 wickets and 100 catches in Test cricket. Kallis ultimately played 73 more Tests than Sobers, with the South African topping 13,000 runs and holding 200 catches while falling just 8 wickets shy of the 300 milestone. Of Kallis' 45 Test centuries, only three were in fixtures that the Proteas lost. Kallis and Sobers admittedly played in vastly different eras and had completely different styles, but both players deserve to be rated among the highest calibre of Test all-rounders. Kallis' Test career spanned 18 years from December 1995, and only Sachin Tendulkar, Ricky Ponting and Steve Waugh had played more Tests than Kallis when the South African called it quits.

A fine strokeplayer on both sides of the wicket, Kallis regularly batted at number four and was a solid contributor with the ball rather than a strike bowler, despite his fast–medium pace. In his early days he bowled only part-time medium-pace, and he struggled badly with the bat, as his first seven Test scores were 1, 7, 6, 39, 0, 2 and 2. His 61 in South Africa's first ever Test in Pakistan, at Rawalpindi in October 1997, was something of a breakthrough innings. Kallis' maiden Test ton was a knock of 101 in 357 minutes to help salvage a draw against Australia in the 1997 Boxing Day Test. As the Proteas sank to an innings defeat in the following Test, Kallis resisted bravely before becoming Shane Warne's 300th Test wicket.

Kallis scored one Test century in 1998 before notching three in 1999 and two in each of 2000, 2001, 2002 and 2003. He excelled in the first week of 1999 as he scored 110 and 88 not out and took 2–34 and 5–90, as the Proteas thrashed the West Indians at Cape Town during a lopsided series. Against Sri Lanka in 2000, Kallis made a vital 87 at Kandy, where South Africa levelled the series after being annihilated at Galle. Kallis' two tons in 2001 were against Zimbabwe, before he was run out for 99 against Australia in the Boxing Day Test after wrongly being adjudged caught behind in the first innings. In a Test against Bangladesh in 2002 he claimed 2–26 and 5–21, and scored 139 not out. Kallis had 136 Test wickets to his name at the end of 2002 before claiming 115 between 2003 and 2008, and then taking just 41 at 42.87 afterwards. His best figures were 6–54 against England at Headingley in 2003, after he snared 3–38 in the first innings.

Following a lean run, Kallis had a purple patch in 2003–04 as he reeled off five centuries in five Tests. Against the West Indies he registered 158, 44, 177, 73 and two unbeaten knocks of 130, before making 92, 150 not out, 40 and 71 against New Zealand. Oddly, Kallis scored 0 and 1 in the third Test as the Proteas drew the series with the Kiwis. Kallis had another rich vein of form in 2004–05, and in the process he tallied 1288 runs at 80.50 in the calendar year of 2004. Kallis registered four centuries in the first four months of 2005, after scoring 121 and 55 in a loss to India in late 2004. It was notable that South Africa lost 2–1 to England in 2004–05, as Kallis scored a century in each of the three Tests that England didn't win. His next two tons were in draws against the West Indies while the Proteas won the other contests in the four-match series, with his unbeaten 109 in the first Test taking 411 minutes as he helped the Africans avoid defeat after following on. Also in early 2005, Kallis stood out in two innings victories against Zimbabwe with two half-centuries and 11 wickets at 9.64. In the first Test, Zimbabwe was dismissed for 54 in 31.2 overs before Kallis himself made 54 from just 25 balls.

Kallis scored two centuries during successive series losses against Australia in 2005–06 and he led the Proteas in the absence of an injured Graeme Smith in the third Test at Johannesburg, where Australia won by 2 wickets. Kallis went 18 months without a Test century before having another period of superb form as he notched five tons in four Tests from October to December 2007. Against Pakistan he made 155 and 100 not out at Karachi, and 59 and 107 not out at Lahore before scoring 29, 186 and 131 against New Zealand. He tallied 1210 runs at 86.43 in 2007 before losing form, as he averaged only 31.12 with one century in 17 Tests from January 2008 to February 2009. He again skippered South Africa when Smith missed a Test against Australia, and this time Kallis made 102 in an innings win at Cape Town in March 2009, after Australia had wrapped up a series victory.

Kallis made two Test tons in 2009 and six in 2010. His thirty-eighth Test ton was the first time he made a Test double century as he compiled 201 not out against India at Centurion, before concluding the three-match series in January 2011 with 161 and 109 not out at Cape Town. At the same venue a year later, Kallis made his highest Test score of 224 against Sri Lanka. Kallis' three other Test centuries in 2012 were away from home, before his last year of Test cricket produced just 309 runs at 25.75 in eight matches. Nonetheless he finished on a winning note as his 115 helped the Proteas beat India at Durban.

Jacques Kallis (b.1975)

Matches: 166
Runs scored: 13,289
Batting average: 55.37
100s/50s: 45/58
Top score: 224
Balls bowled: 20,232
Wickets: 292
Bowling average: 32.65
5 wickets in innings: 5
10 wickets in match: –
Best bowling: 6–54
Catches/stumpings: 200/–

Makhaya Ntini

Makhaya Ntini was charged and convicted of a serious crime in 1999 before being acquitted and becoming one of South Africa's best fast bowlers. His best calendar years were 2003, 2006 and 2008 with 59, 58 and 54 wickets respectively.

The first ethnically black player to represent South Africa in international cricket, Ntini claimed 4 wickets at 37 against Sri Lanka in his maiden Test series, which the Proteas won 2–0 at home in March 1998. Following more than a year out of the team, Ntini took his first 5-wicket innings haul against New Zealand in November 2000, as he claimed 6–66 at Bloemfontein and played a part in the team's 2–0 series win. Nearly two years passed before Ntini bagged another 5-wicket haul as he snared 5–19 against Bangladesh. In 2003 he snared 5–75 and 5–145 at Lord's as the Proteas won by an innings, only for England to later draw the series.

Ntini starred in South Africa's 3–0 win over the West Indies in 2003–04 as he captured 29 wickets at 21.38. Ntini bowled even better at Port-of-Spain in 2005 when he took 6–95 and 7–37. Ntini sometimes had good figures as South Africa lost to Australia in 2005–06, before he excelled in a 2–0 series win against New Zealand with 5–94 and 5–51 at Centurion and 5–35 in the first innings at Johannesburg. After going wicketless in an innings loss to Sri Lanka later that year, Ntini sustained a hamstring injury during the next Test and was missed badly as the Sri Lankans sneaked to a 1-wicket win to clean sweep the series.

Ntini played a vital role as South Africa beat India and Pakistan 2–1 in 2006–07, and his best innings figures in those six Tests were 6–59 in a loss to Pakistan, while he also claimed his 300th Test wicket. Against England in 2008, Ntini also excelled in a defeat amidst a 2–1 series victory as he took 5–94 at the Oval, where the hosts saved face after trailing 2–0. Ntini failed to take 5 wickets in an innings for the remainder of his Test career, which finished at the end of 2009. Ntini played his 100th Test as the Proteas contested England at Centurion, where Ntini took 2–78 and 0–41 as the hosts were just 1 wicket away from victory. Ntini returned 0–114 from 29 overs in the following Test at Durban, where the tourists won by an innings to temporarily lead the series, and Ntini was never selected for Test cricket again. He thus finished 10 wickets shy of the 400 milestone.

Makhaya Ntini (b.1977)

Matches: 101
Runs scored: 699
Batting average: 9.84
100s/50s: 0/0
Top score: 32*
Balls bowled: 20,834
Wickets: 390
Bowling average: 28.82
5 wickets in innings: 18
10 wickets in match: 4
Best bowling: 7–37
Catches/stumpings: 25/-

Graeme Pollock

South Africa's expulsion from international sport for more than 20 years robbed many players of the chance to enjoy lengthy Test careers, with Graeme Pollock perhaps rated the most highly of those affected.

Of all players to have batted at least 20 times in Tests, Pollock had the best average after Don Bradman until Australia's Adam Voges had a rich vein of form in 2015 and early 2016. Pollock was always keen to play strokes and could hit the ball hard, although he was by no means reckless, as his timing was impeccable, especially when stroking the ball through the offside. It remains a shame that Pollock's Test career was over when he was just 26 years of age. Had he played against Dennis Lillee and Jeff Thomson in their prime, as well as the likes of John Snow, Derek Underwood and some West Indian quicks, there surely would have been some fascinating battles.

Pollock made his Test debut as a teenager in South Africa's tour of Australia in 1963–64, and scored 25, 16 and 2 before rising to the occasion in the third Test with 122 and 42, and then 175 in the fourth Test. Pollock played just one Test against New Zealand in South Africa's follow-up tour, scoring 30 and 23 after missing two Tests due to injury. Pollock scored 750 runs at 53.57 in his next eight Tests which were against England, with five in South Africa and three in England. Pollock scored just 5 and 0 in his first appearance against England on home soil but he averaged 75.67 for the rest of the series, boosted by 137 and 77 not out in the final Test. Pollock's 125 against England in the second Test at Trent Bridge in 1965 was one of his finest knocks, after he came to the crease at 16–2 and saw the score deteriorate to 80–5 before South Africa finished with 269. Pollock scored 59 in the second innings, while his brother Peter excelled with 10 wickets to lead South Africa to victory.

Graeme Pollock scored heavily against Australia, with 537 runs at 76.71 in 1966–67 and 517 runs at 73.86 in 1969–70 as the Africans hosted both series. Incredibly, his 209 in the second Test of 1966–67 couldn't prevent South Africa from following on and subsequently losing by 6 wickets, as Australia levelled the series before the hosts won 3–1. In South Africa's 4–0 drubbing of Australia in 1969–70, Pollock amassed 274 in the second Test which South Africa won by an innings, before his final Test resulted in scores of 1 and 4, which lowered his Test average from 64.31.

Having represented a Rest of the World team in 1970 and scored a century at the Oval, Pollock played in 16 unofficial Tests during South Africa's exile from international sport. He retired from the international arena at the age of 42, having scored 144 against a rebel Australian team that visited the apartheid-affected nation in 1987.

Barry Richards and Mike Procter were two other South Africans who could have become Test greats had the chance come their way. Richards' only four Tests were against Australia in 1969–70 when he compiled 508 runs at 72.57. Procter also played in that series, as well as the 1966–67 series against the same country, and tallied 41 wickets at 15.02 from his seven Tests.

Graeme Pollock (b.1944)

Matches: 23
Runs scored: 2256
Batting average: 60.97
100s/50s: 7/11
Top score: 274
Balls bowled: 414
Wickets: 4
Bowling average: 51.00
5 wickets in innings: –
10 wickets in match: –
Best bowling: 2–50
Catches/stumpings: 17/0

Shaun Pollock

Shaun Pollock followed in the footsteps of a famous South African cricketing family and, unlike father Peter and uncle Graeme, did not have his career cut short by apartheid. A persistent and reliable fast–

medium bowler, Shaun Pollock was the perfect foil for the out-and-out fast Allan Donald, while also having the ability to lead the attack when necessary. His best years as a Test bowler were 1998 and 2001, with 69 and 55 wickets respectively. With a batting average beyond 30, Pollock notched two Test centuries and was effectively a bowling all-rounder.

Having captured 16 wickets at 23.56 and scored 133 runs at 26.60 against England in his maiden Test series in 1995–96, Shaun Pollock's cricket highlighted some of the best features of Peter and Graeme Pollock, according to *Wisden 1997*. His Test debut yielded 3–98 from 29 overs in a rain-shortened match in which he dismissed three of England's first five batsmen. In the final Test at Cape Town, Shaun Pollock's 5–32 in England's second innings was a pivotal factor in South Africa's series-clinching win, after Donald bagged 5 scalps in England's first innings.

A hamstring injury foiled Pollock at home against Australia in 1997 just when the Proteas needed him, after they were slaughtered in the first Test before gaining control of the second Test. Having dismissed Australian openers Mark Taylor and Matthew Hayden for the second successive time, Pollock had 2–6 from six overs but could not bowl again in the series. He was sorely missed as Australia, chasing 270, clinched the series with a 2-wicket win. Later in 1997, Pollock stood out against Pakistan with 5–37 in the final Test at Faisalabad, as the hosts crashed for 92 when needing 146 to win the series. A few months later, Pollock claimed 7–87 in Australia's first innings of the third and final Test of his first Australian tour, as South Africa needed a win to tie the series. But he was wretchedly unlucky in Australia's second innings as there were dropped catches and a couple of close shaves, including an appeal for hit wicket being rejected, as the hosts survived. Against Pakistan at Durban several weeks later, Pollock took 2–55 and 6–50 and made scores of 70 not out and 30, only for the tourists to win by 29 runs before he had a quiet match as the hosts levelled the series. In South Africa's follow-up series against Sri Lanka, Pollock scored 92 and claimed 6 wickets in a 70-run win before becoming injured in the second Test as the Africans won the series.

Pollock was prominent in South Africa's 5–0 drubbing of the West Indies in 1998–99 as he claimed 29 scalps at 16.67, including three instances of 5 wickets in an innings. He also excelled in a following tour of New Zealand as he took 13 victims at 16.62 and scored 112 runs from two knocks without being dismissed. Series wins against Zimbabwe, England and India followed, before Pollock was appointed captain under difficult circumstances in April 2000 when Hansie Cronje's international career abruptly ended amidst match-fixing allegations. Shell-shocked, the Proteas drew Sri Lanka before having series wins against New Zealand, Sri Lanka, the West Indies, Zimbabwe and India in the space of 18 months. Pollock had plenty of success with bat and ball in 2001, which included his two Test tons. After taking 6–30 against Sri Lanka at Cape Town, Pollock made 111 at Centurion as the Proteas took out the series 2–0 with back-to-back innings victories. Against the West Indies, Pollock made 106 not out and 40 at number nine in a draw, and then took 5 wickets and scored 89 unbeaten runs in a triumph, before taking 9 wickets in a loss. Against India, Pollock took 10 wickets in a victory and then claimed 5–40 and scored 55 not out in a draw.

A 3–0 loss in Australia tainted Pollock's captaincy record, and he missed the follow-up series which Australia won 2–1 on South African soil, while Donald retired. In late 2002, Pollock led his team to a 2–0 win over Sri Lanka after scoring 99 not out in the second Test, but he lost the captaincy in 2003, after the Proteas failed in the World Cup as co-hosts. This left him with a Test captaincy record of 14 wins, five losses and seven draws. Pollock's speed and wicket-taking somewhat declined, as he only twice captured 5 or more wickets in a Test innings after 2001. Both occasions were in 2003, as he claimed 6–39 against England at Trent Bridge and 6–78 against Pakistan at Faisalabad. Pollock often struggled for wickets as the Proteas lost 2–0 and 3–0 to Australia in 2005–06, and he missed one Test with a back injury before he was demoted to first change bowler shortly afterwards. Pollock had a fine series against India in 2006–07 as he helped the Proteas come from behind to beat India 2–1, but minor injuries began to hinder him. He became the first South African to capture 400 Test wickets, but he was dropped in September 2007. Recalled for the final Test of a three-match series against the West Indies in 2007–08, Pollock declared that this would be his final Test. At Durban, he took 4–35 and 1–50 as the Proteas won the series with an innings victory.

Shaun Pollock (b.1973)

Matches: 108
Runs scored: 3781
Batting average: 32.31
100s/50s: 2/16
Top score: 111
Balls bowled: 24,353
Wickets: 421
Bowling average: 23.11
5 wickets in innings: 16
10 wickets in match: 1
Best bowling: 7–87
Catches/stumpings: 72/–

Graeme Smith

Graeme Smith was effectively thrown in at the deep end as he was appointed South African captain at the age of 22 with only eight Test appearances to his name. The record holder of the most Tests as captain and most victories as captain, Smith led the Proteas to 53 wins, 29 losses and 27 draws.

The left-handed Smith debuted against Australia at Cape Town in 2002 after the tourists recorded the second biggest ever Test victory in the previous fixture. Smith made 3 and 68 as Australia wrapped up the series, before scoring 1 and 42 in a face-saving win. Smith's breakthrough century came in his third Test as he was promoted to open against Bangladesh in October 2002, and scored 200 at East London. He began 2003 with a score of 151 against Pakistan at Cape Town, before taking on the leadership after Shaun Pollock was removed as captain following the World Cup. Smith's batting was ineffective as he led South Africa to two innings wins against Bangladesh, before he made his highest Test score of 277 in the first Test against England at Edgbaston. He followed up with 259 in an innings win at Lord's, before his form faded as the series finished at 2–2.

South Africa lost to Pakistan before beating the West Indies 3–0, with Smith scoring two tons in the four-match series. Smith scored a century against New Zealand but his team could only draw the series before the Proteas lost to Sri Lanka, India and England. South Africa returned to its winning ways with a series victory against Zimbabwe in 2005 following Smith's eighth Test century, before he reached triple figures in three successive Tests against the West Indians. Smith led a World XI in October 2005, but failed with 12 and 0, as the mixed team was thrashed by Australia at Sydney. The Proteas also failed Down Under and at home against the Australians, before Smith's double of 63 and 68 helped his team to a 4-wicket win which sealed a 2–0 series triumph against the Kiwis.

Smith's 133 against Pakistan at Lahore in 2007 was his first Test ton in nearly two-and-a-half years before he had a bumper 2008, as he amassed 1656 runs at 72, with six centuries and six half-centuries. The Proteas enjoyed series victories against the West Indies, Bangladesh (twice), England and Australia, with Smith scoring at least one ton against those countries, while not scoring a ton in a drawn series against India. His highest score that year was 232 against Bangladesh, as he was involved in a record 415-run opening stand, but his biggest highlights were against England and Australia. Smith's undefeated 154 led his team to a series-clinching 5-wicket victory at Edgbaston, before he led the Proteas to a series victory in Australia. Smith's 108 at Perth helped the visitors towards a 6-wicket triumph when chasing 414, before he made 62 and 75 in the Melbourne Test, which secured the series win. Smith braved injury to try to help save the Sydney Test, only to be the last batsman dismissed in the penultimate over. Smith succumbed to injury during Australia's subsequent tour of South Africa and missed the last Test, which the Proteas won after Australia had sealed a series triumph.

Smith made no Test tons in 2009 before scoring two in January 2010 during a drawn series against England, and a further two later in the year. Smith's lone Test century in 2011 helped the Proteas to a remarkable victory against Australia after the Proteas trailed by 188 runs on the first innings. Smith's three Test tons in 2012 were followed by his final Test century in October 2013, as he made 234 against Pakistan at Dubai where the Proteas drew the series. Smith also made a clever bowling change in that Test as he brought on the rarely used Dean Elgar, who delivered two overs and broke a lengthy partnership with his first Test wicket. Smith's final series was at home in early 2014, with a dismal average of 7.50 and a highest score of just 14 in six innings, as Australia triumphed 2–1.

Graeme Smith (b.1981)

Matches: 117
Runs scored: 9265
Batting average: 48.25
100s/50s: 27/38
Top score: 277
Balls bowled: 1418
Wickets: 8
Bowling average: 110.62
5 wickets in innings: –
10 wickets in match: –
Best bowling: 2–145
Catches/stumpings: 169/–

Dale Steyn

Whilst the calibre of the world's best fast bowlers seemed to decline when the West Indies went into decline, Dale Steyn was one exception. With a rare ability to swing the ball in various ways at a high speed and to consistently be accurate, Steyn became a prominent wicket-taker and held the key to South African success along with the likes of Jacques Kallis. Steyn's ability to take wickets in all sorts of conditions ensured the Proteas won in every Test-playing country during his career.

Steyn picked up his maiden Test wicket on debut with an inswinger, which bowled England left-hander Marcus Trescothick at Port Elizabeth in December 2004. Steyn however was dropped for one Test in the series, which he finished with just 8 wickets at 52. When recalled for a home series in 2006, Steyn claimed 7 wickets in each of South Africa's two victories against the Kiwis, including 5–51 in New Zealand's second innings at Centurion, as the Proteas won by 128 runs. Steyn had decidedly mixed fortunes in a 2–0 series loss in Sri Lanka as he was hit around, and also claimed a 5-wicket innings haul. Injury disrupted Steyn when the Proteas hosted India in 2006–07, but his 6 wickets helped the Africans win the deciding Test. He was not chosen for two Tests against Pakistan before he again helped the Proteas win a decider.

Steyn was prolific in season 2007–08 as the Proteas toured Pakistan, Bangladesh and India, and hosted New Zealand and the West Indies. In Pakistan, Steyn's 5–56 helped the tourists win the first Test and ultimately the series. Against the Kiwis, Steyn took 10 scalps in each Test as two 5-wicket hauls were followed by a 4-wicket haul and a 6-wicket haul. Steyn claimed 20 scalps in three fixtures against the West Indies and then 14 scalps in two Tests against Bangladesh, before picking up 15 wickets in three Tests against India. In 2008–09, Steyn was outstanding in the Boxing Day Test, which led to a rare series loss for Australia at home, as he made a vital lower order knock of 76 and snared two 5-wicket hauls. This enabled him to chalk up 74 wickets at 20.01 from 13 Tests in 2008.

Steyn claimed his best innings figures of 7–51 against India at Nagpur in February 2010, and he completed a 10-wicket match haul in a victory before the hosts drew the series. An innings haul of 5–29 against the West Indies in Port-of-Spain during June 2010 took Steyn past 200 wickets in only his thirty-ninth Test, and he claimed 60 wickets from 11 Tests in 2010. Twenty-one wickets in three Tests against India in 2010–11 included figures of 6–50 at Durban and 5–75 at Cape Town. A 4-wicket haul and a 5-wicket haul from Steyn helped South Africa to a 2–1 win over Sri Lanka in 2011–12, and his 15 wickets in three Tests also helped the Proteas beat England 2–0.

Steyn took 51 scalps in nine Tests during 2013, having twice claimed 5 wickets in an innings and twice claimed 6 wickets in an innings. His best match was at Johannesburg where he picked up 6–8 and 5–52 against Pakistan which was dismissed for 49 and 268. Steyn clinched his 400th Test wicket when the Proteas contested Bangladesh in July

2015, and although injuries forced Steyn to miss several Tests that year, he insisted he still had plenty more overs to bowl.

Dale Steyn (b.1982)*

Matches: 82
Runs scored: 1124
Batting average: 14.22
100s/50s: –/2
Top score: 76
Balls bowled: 16,957
Wickets: 406
Bowling average: 22.53
5 wickets in innings: 25
10 wickets in match: 5
Best bowling: 7–51
Catches/stumpings: 22/–
* still playing as of 2016

CHAPTER 4: WEST INDIES

4.1 WEST INDIES v NEW ZEALAND

1950s

Sonny Ramadhin proved a decisive influence in the first two series involving the West Indies and New Zealand. He claimed 5–86 and 4–39 as the West Indies won by 5 wickets at Lancaster Park in February 1952, after leading by 51 runs on the first innings and then dismissing New Zealand for 189. Three centuries and a 99 set up a total of 546–6 declared for the West Indies in the only other fixture of the series, after the tourists were asked to bat first. The hosts were made to follow on before rain stymied the touring side's victory chances.

The West Indies won the first three Tests of the 1955–56 series in New Zealand, before the Kiwis recorded their first ever Test victory in the final match of the series. Everton Weekes starred for the victors in the first three Tests as he scored 123, 103 and 156, while Ramadhin did plenty of damage with the ball. The tourists won by an innings in the first two Tests, with the Kiwis never in the hunt in the first Test, after crashing from 36–1 to 74 all out in the first innings. In the second Test, the West Indies were 0–1 before Weekes' dismissal left them 169–6, only for captain Denis Atkinson (85), John Goddard (83 not out) and Ramadhin (33) to boost the total to 386. Alf Valentine and Collie Smith shared 9 wickets after the Kiwis had to follow on. Atkinson was the pick of the bowlers for the West Indies in the third and fourth Tests, with the former yielding a 9-wicket margin after the Kiwis again followed on and this time achieved a 12-run lead. After mustering 255 in the final Test, the Kiwis recorded a shock 190-run victory as the West Indies capitulated for 145 and 77, with Harry Cave achieving match figures of 8–43. Interestingly, Sammy Guillen kept wickets for New Zealand in the last three Tests of the 1955–56 series after being the West Indian wicketkeeper in the first series involving the two nations. Thirteen years passed before the next New Zealand versus West Indies series was played, with the Kiwis again the hosts.

1960s

The 1968–69 series was drawn 1–1 after the tourists won a fascinating first Test by 5 wickets. Bruce Taylor struck 124 at better than a run per minute at number eight to help New Zealand from 152–6 to 323 all out. West Indian opener Joey Carew made 109 while first drop Seymour Nurse made 95, but the tourists tumbled from 197–1 to 276 all out before New Zealand went from 112–0 to 235–8. Following an unbroken 62-run ninth-wicket stand, a declaration left the West Indies requiring 345. Nurse (168) and Basil Butcher (78 not out) set up the result, before the Kiwis levelled the series with a 6-wicket triumph. The tourists succumbed for 148 in their second innings before the hosts were 39–3 chasing 164, and were subsequently guided to safety as Brian Hastings made 62 not out. Nurse scored 258 as the West Indies tallied 417 in the third Test and enforced the follow-on, only for Hastings (117 not out) and several teammates to bat for lengthy periods and secure a draw.

1970s

In 1971–72 the West Indies finally hosted New Zealand, with no results in the five Tests despite some big scores. West Indian Lawrence Rowe marked his Test debut with 214 and 100 not out, and shared a second-wicket stand of 269 with Roy Fredericks (163) in the first Test. The West Indies declared at 508–4 and 218–3, and the Kiwis made 386 and 236–6, after Glenn Turner (223) carried his bat in New Zealand's first innings and was involved in a crucial sixth-wicket partnership of 220. Mark Burgess (101) starred in New Zealand's second innings. Bevan Congdon (166 not out) helped the Kiwis go from 99–6 to 348 all out in a fairly evenly balanced second Test, before 7–74 from Bruce Taylor routed the West Indies for 133 in the third Test. Tons to Congdon and Hastings in a 422-run total were followed by centuries to Charlie Davis and Garry Sobers as the West Indies reached 564–8 after being 171–5. In a rain-affected fourth Test, Turner (259) and fellow opener Terry Jarvis (182) put on 387 runs in New Zealand's 543–3 declared, after the opposition declared at 365–7, which included an undefeated 100 from Alvin Kallicharran on debut. The West Indies controlled the final Test, with Kallicharran scoring 101 in his second Test knock, but the hosts were foiled as New Zealand's eighth-wicket pair batted out the final 106 minutes.

1980s

New Zealand beat the West Indies in a series for the first time in 1979–80, although there was ample controversy over numerous umpiring decisions. The hosts won the first Test in Dunedin by 1 wicket after chasing just 104 runs. Missing Viv Richards, the West Indies were 4–3 before struggling to 140, and then the Kiwis stumbled at times but secured a 109-run lead. Richard Hadlee completed an 11-wicket match haul while Desmond Haynes scored a resolute 105 in the West Indies' second innings, before tempers flared in the run chase when Michael Holding kicked the stumps after an appeal was rejected. The West Indies however looked likely winners as the Kiwis slumped to 44–6 and 73–8, before a 27-run partnership was followed by a bye, an unsuccessful appeal for lbw, two runs off the bat and a leg bye to cap a thrilling match. Lance Cairns (6–85) caused the West Indies to slide from 190–3 to 228 all out in the Christchurch Test, before centuries to Kiwi captain Geoff Howarth and Hadlee, and 80 from Jeremy Coney, took the hosts from 53–3 to 460. As the West Indies were incensed with the match officials, Colin Croft provided a strong talking point when he knocked umpire Fred Goodall off balance while coming in to bowl. Centuries to Haynes, Rowe and Collis King saved the West Indies from defeat at Christchurch, before Bruce Edgar (127 in 432 minutes) helped New Zealand gain an 85-run lead at Auckland to thwart the tourists' victory bid.

Ewen Chatfield claimed 10 wickets for New Zealand in the first Test of the 1984–85 series, but hosts the West Indies generally had the better of the drawn contest before the second Test was also drawn. Richie Richardson (185) and several solid scores allowed the West Indies to top 500 at Guyana before 188 from Martin Crowe rescued the Kiwis, who didn't need to bat a second time. The hosts won the remaining two Tests by 10 wickets as they had mere targets of 7 and 59. The Barbados Test was dismal for the tourists as they were routed for 94 on a green pitch following a rain-delayed start. The West Indies slipped from 91–1 to 174–7, before reaching 336 thanks to Viv Richards (105), Malcolm Marshall (63) and Joel Garner (37 not out). The Kiwis had virtually no chance of levelling the series after being made to follow on in the fourth Test, although they were 223–1 (Jeff Crowe 112, Howarth 84) before losing 8–60 as an injured Coney was unable to bat.

The West Indies also won the second Test of the 1986–87 series with a 10-wicket margin, after Holding played his final Test in the first match of the series at Wellington. The West Indies looked poised for a big win at Wellington as Gordon Greenidge (78) put on an opening stand of 150 with Haynes, who went on to make 121, after New Zealand stumbled to 228. The West Indies were limited to 345 before having the Kiwis 20–2, but John Wright (138) and Martin Crowe (119) saved the home side. New Zealand failed to capitalise after choosing to bowl first on a green pitch in Auckland, with several missed chances costly, as Greenidge (213) helped the tourists pass 400 after being 14–2 and 131–4. Following on, the Kiwis squeezed out a 12-run lead and didn't quite last long enough to avoid defeat following 104 from Martin Crowe. The hosts however squared the series after Hadlee and Chatfield routed the tourists for 100, which included a 25-run last-wicket stand, in the third and final Test. The Crowe brothers and John Bracewell helped New Zealand to a 232-run lead before Martin Snedden took 5–68 and, despite being 30–5, the Kiwis were assured of victory as the target was 33.

1990s

The next New Zealand versus West Indies series was in 1994–95, just before the Australians stunned the West Indians. Following a rather uninteresting draw in Christchurch, the visitors won by an innings and 322 runs in Wellington after Brian Lara, Jimmy Adams and Junior Murray made tons. Courtney Walsh snared 7–37 and 6–18 as the hosts made just 216 and 122.

The West Indies also beat New Zealand 1–0 in 1996, with a 10-wicket win followed by a draw. West Indian opener Sherwin Campbell's 208 was 13 more than New Zealand's first-innings total, before he made all 29 of the required runs in the run chase, after the Kiwis had a last-wicket partnership of 45. Having taken 5–17 in the first innings of the first Test, Adams made 208 not out in the second Test, while teammate Robert Samuels made 125 in his second appearance. Nathan Astle scored his second century in as many Tests as New Zealand fought back, and later dismissed the West Indies, before the Kiwis finished on 130–5 after being set 296.

The two-match series in late 1999 was heavily one-sided as the Kiwis won by 9 wickets at Hamilton before winning by an innings at Wellington. Yet the West Indies seemed to be in an invincible position late on day one at Hamilton as they lost their first wicket at 276, with Campbell departing for 170 before fellow opener Adrian Griffith fell for 114 the next day. The tourists lost 10–89 before the hosts recovered from 258–6 to lead by 28 runs following a match-turning seventh-wicket stand of 116. Following his vital knock of 72, Chris Cairns snared 7–27 as the West Indies made just 97. Test debutant Mathew Sinclair made 214 as the hosts passed 500 at Wellington, before the tourists batted with ten players in each innings and mustered just 179 and 234, as Cairns again bowled superbly.

2000s

The West Indies copped another hefty loss against the Kiwis in 2002, as the visitors won the first Test in the Caribbean by 204 runs. Kiwi captain Stephen Fleming (130) was the main scorer as New Zealand made 337 after being 117–5, before the hosts crumbled for just 107 and later folded for 269 after being 133–1. Debutant Scott Styris (107 and 69 not out) played a decisive role for New Zealand in the drawn second Test, with the Kiwis finishing on 256–5, with a lead of 159, after West Indian opener Chris Gayle scored 204.

Hosts New Zealand won a three-match series 2–0 in 2006, starting with a 27-run victory at Auckland. The match was closely fought as the totals ranged from 257 to 275. With 103 not out in New Zealand's first innings, Styris again proved a bogey man for the West Indies before Brendon McCullum scored a vital 74 in New Zealand's second innings. Needing 291, the visitors were poised for victory at 148–0 before Shane Bond and Daniel Vettori ripped through the West Indies after Astle had dismissed the openers. James Franklin played a leading role with the ball in the second Test as the Kiwis won by 10 wickets. Rain denied the Kiwis a clean sweep as only 78.1 overs were bowled in the third Test, with the West Indies making 256–4.

The loss of more than two days of play also ruined the prospect of a result in the first Test of 2008–09, and the series was drawn after New Zealand finished the second Test at 220–5 when chasing 312. West Indian Jerome Taylor scored 106 in the first Test before Shivnarine Chanderpaul (126 not out and a golden duck), Gayle (34 and 197) and Kiwi opener Tim McIntosh (136 and 3) were among the stars in the second Test.

The West Indies won the 2012 series following victories by 9 wickets and 5 wickets while chasing targets of 102 and 206. In the first Test at Antigua, the Kiwis plunged from 223–2 to 351 all out in their first innings before sinking from 170–1 to 272 all out in their second innings. The hosts tallied 522 after losing their first 2 wickets at 254 and 304, with Gayle scoring 150 and Kieran Powell 134, before Gayle made 64 not out in the run chase. At Jamaica, a knock of 123 from Marlon Samuels was crucial as the hosts struggled to 209 in response to 260, before the Kiwis went from 55–0 to 154 all out. The West Indies were in trouble at 20–2 before partnerships of 74, 19, 70 and 23 followed.

New Zealand hosted three Tests in December 2013 before the West Indies hosted three in June 2014, with a draw in Dunedin followed by three successive victories for the Kiwis, a win to the West Indies and another win to the Kiwis. Ross Taylor excelled for the hosts in December 2013 as his scores were 217 not out, 16 not out, 129, 131 and 2 not out. The West Indies made 507 when following on in Dunedin, with Darren Bravo scoring 218 before New Zealand floundered at 44–4, and later finished on 79–4 from 30 overs when chasing just 112. Trent Boult was the hero in the second Test as he followed up his 38 not out at number 11 with 6–40 and 4–40 as New Zealand won by an innings after scoring 441. In the third Test, the tourists improved from 86–5 to 367 all out following centuries to Chanderpaul and wicketkeeper Denesh Ramdin. The West Indians led by 18 runs before Boult wrecked their top order, and the Kiwis lost only 2 wickets in chasing 122.

New Zealand won the first Test in mid 2014 by 186 runs after making 508–7 declared (Kane Williamson 113, James Neesham 107) and setting a target of 403 after opting not to enforce the follow-on. Kiwi off spinner Mark Craig was hit for 24 fours and eight sixes in his maiden Test but he claimed man of the match honours for snaring 4–91 and 4–97. The West Indies levelled the series with a 10-wicket victory in Trinidad after New Zealand tallied 221 and 331. The Kiwis crashed from 120–1 in their first innings, before Craig made 67 at number ten in their second innings. Kraigg Brathwaite (129) and Darren Bravo (109) set up the home side's 460, before Gayle hammered 80 from 46 balls as the West Indies raced past the 93-run target in 13.2 overs. The hosts had a good chance of winning the series 2–1 as they were 153–1 in reply to 293 in the deciding Test. The home side's lead was restricted to 24 before the tourists were 1–1, only for Williamson (161 not out) to help set a target of 308. The West Indies were 31–3 after ten overs and remained behind the eight-ball before the Kiwis clinched the series with a 53-run victory.

1951–52 (NZ): West Indies 1–0 (1 drawn)

1955–56 (NZ): West Indies 3–1

1968–69 (NZ): 1–1 (1 drawn)

1971–72 (WI): 0–0 (5 drawn)

1979–80 (NZ): New Zealand 1–0 (2 drawn)

1984–85 (WI): West Indies 2–0 (2 drawn)

1986–87 (NZ): 1–1 (1 drawn)

1994–95 (NZ): West Indies 1–0 (1 drawn)

1995–96 (WI): West Indies 1–0 (1 drawn)

1999–00 (NZ): New Zealand 2–0

2002 (WI): New Zealand 1–0 (1 drawn)

2005–06 (NZ): New Zealand 2–0 (1 drawn)

2008–09 (NZ): 0–0 (2 drawn)

2012 (WI): West Indies 2–0

2013–14 (NZ): New Zealand 2–0 (1 drawn)

2014 (WI): New Zealand 2–1

4.2 WEST INDIES v INDIA

1940s

The first two 5-match series involving the West Indies and India resulted in 1–0 wins to the West Indies, with India hosting in 1948–49 before the 1952–53 series was in the Caribbean. The Indians had to follow on in the first two Tests of 1948–49 but the West Indies couldn't bowl them out twice, before the hosts finished the third Test on 325–3 after being set 431. The tourists won the fourth Test by an innings and 193 runs after Jeff Stollmeyer (160) and Allan Rae (109) put on a 239-run opening partnership in a total of 582. The fifth Test was splendid as India sought 361 to level the series. The hosts lost wickets at 2, 9, 81, 220, 275, 285, 303 and 321 before finishing 6 agonising runs shy of the target, while the visitors needed 2 wickets.

1950s

The second Test of the 1952–53 series yielded a 142-run win to the West Indies after India required 272, before the West Indies won the 1958–59 series 3–0 after winning the second, third and fourth Tests. Fast bowlers Wes Hall and Roy Gilchrist did a lot of damage, although Gilchrist was later sent home after bowling a barrage of bumpers and beamers. The Indians secured a respectable draw in the first Test at Bombay before losing the plot at vital times in the second Test at Kanpur, as both teams made 222 in their first innings, before the tourists won by 203 runs. The tourists went from 55–0 to 88–6 before a 100-run seventh-wicket stand unfolded, and India's Subhash Gupte claimed innings figures of 9–102 before India lost its last 8 wickets for 40 runs. The West Indies subsequently lost both openers without scoring before Garry Sobers made 198, while there were strong contributions down the order, and then India made just 240, even though eight batsmen reached double figures. The West Indies won by an innings and 336 runs at Calcutta as India tallied just 124 and 154 after Rohan Kanhai (256), Sobers (106 not out) and Basil Butcher (103) set up a huge first-innings total for the visitors. Butcher (142) and Kanhai (run out for 99) were also prominent at Madras as the West Indies won by 295 runs after making 500.

1960s

After losing captain Nari Contractor to a serious head injury sustained from a fierce short-pitched delivery, India had a nightmare tour of the Caribbean in 1961–62. The hosts won all five Tests comprehensively, with Hall again taking plenty of wickets. India lost by an innings in the second and third Tests, while the other margins were 10 wickets, 7 wickets and 123 runs. In the second Test, India recovered from 89–4 to tally 395, only for Sobers, Kanhai and Easton McMorris to score tons in a West Indian reply of 631–8 declared. In the third Test, West Indian off spinner Lance Gibbs had incredible figures of 8–38 from 53.3 overs, as India made just 187 runs from 185.3 overs in its second innings, after being 158–2 at lunch on the final day when Gibbs had 0–32 from

38 overs. After the tourists had to follow on in the fourth Test, Polly Umrigar (172 not out) and Salim Durani (104) excelled but couldn't save India.

The 1966–67 series in India featured just three Tests, with the tourists winning the first two. The hosts had a horror start as they slumped to 14–3, before 121 from Chandu Borde helped India towards its eventual 296. The West Indies replied with 421 and later stumbled to 51–3 in pursuit of 192 before winning by 6 wickets. A total of 390 was enough for the West Indies to win the second Test by an innings, before both sides topped 400 in their first innings of the final Test. Chasing 322, the West Indies were in trouble at 193–7 before Sobers (74 not out) and Charlie Griffith (40 not out) added 77 runs as they batted out the final 90 minutes.

1970s

The West Indians were not as strong on home soil in early 1971 as India won a series against the West Indies for the first time. India sank to 75–5 in its first innings of the first Test, before 212 from Dilip Sardesai helped the tourists to 387. Kanhai (158 not out) helped the home side avoid defeat after being made to follow on. The second Test was the only one to feature a result, after West Indian Roy Fredericks was bowled with the first ball of the match. India gained a first-innings lead of 138 despite 9–95 from West Indian off spinner Jack Noreiga, and then the hosts slid from 150–1 to 261 all out and went on to lose by 7 wickets. The West Indies were on top in the fourth Test as India was 70–6 in reply to 501–5 declared, but the hosts were denied by Sardesai (150 in India's first innings) and Sunil Gavaskar (117 not out in India's second innings), with India finishing at 221–5 after being set 335. The final Test was superbly fought and involved some dramatic changes in fortune. Gavaskar made 124 in India's 360 before centuries to Sobers and Charlie Davis and 99 from Maurice Foster took the West Indies to 526. A monumental 220 from Gavaskar was responsible for the hosts needing 262 to square the series, and they struggled to 165–8 from 40 overs after the first-ball dismissal of Sobers left them 50–4.

A one-sided series appeared inevitable as the West Indies won the
first Test of the 1974–75 series by 267 runs before taking a 2–0 lead
with an innings victory. The West Indies tumbled from 177–0 to 289
all out in the first Test at Bangalore before India mustered 260 and
then had the visitors 75–3. Lloyd subsequently made 163 while Gordon
Greenidge scored a century on debut after falling just 7 runs shy of
triple figures in the first innings. India was never in the hunt for 386
after losing Gavaskar for a duck, and two batsmen were absent hurt.
Without Gavaskar, India made 220 and 256 in the second Test while
Viv Richards made 192 not out in his second Test to lead the West
Indies to 493. India's Sudhir Naik was dismissed with the opening
delivery of the third Test at Calcutta, before the hosts managed 233 and
restricted the West Indies to a 7-run lead following 100 from Fredericks.
Gundappa Viswanath (139) helped India set the West Indies 310, and
their demise for 224 gave India, remarkably, its first Test win against the
West Indies on Indian soil. The hosts went on to level the series as the
Madras Test was eerily similar to the Calcutta Test, with India making
190 and the West Indies 192, before the tourists crumbled for 154 to
lose by 100 runs. Gavaskar returned for the deciding Test at Bombay,
where Fredericks (104) laid the platform for a huge West Indies total
of 604–6 declared before Lloyd (242 not out) had great support from
Alvin Kallicharran (98) and Deryck Murray (91). Eknath Solkar (102),
Viswanath (95) and Gavaskar (86) couldn't prevent the West Indies
gaining a 198-run lead, before Vanburn Holder's 6–39 helped the West
Indies rout India for 202 as the hosts needed 404. Andy Roberts was
regularly the main wicket-taker for the West Indies during the series.

The 1975–76 series also began on a horror note for the Indians, who
were belted by an innings at Barbados, following a 5-wicket haul from
David Holford and subsequent centuries to Richards and Lloyd. In the
second Test at Trinidad, Richards (130) was surrounded by poor scores
as Bishan Bedi's 5 wickets dismantled the hosts for 241. Gavaskar (156)
and Brijesh Patel (115 not out) helped India gain a 161-run lead before
declaring, and only some dogged resistance from Lawrence Rowe,
Lloyd and Roberts salvaged a draw, as the hosts finished at 215–8.
The third Test also took place at Trinidad as the Georgetown venue
was unfit for play. Richards made 177 while Bhagwath Chandrasekhar

nabbed 6 scalps as the West Indies made 359 and then gained a 131-run lead. Set 403, India recorded an astonishing 6-wicket victory following 102 from Gavaskar, 112 from Viswanath and 85 from Mohinder Amarnath, who gave a crucial chance on 37. The fourth and deciding Test in Jamaica turned into a bizarre anti-climax as the hosts won by 10 wickets when chasing just 13 runs. Three touring batsmen sustained injuries against some hostile fast bowling before India declared its first innings at 306–6, and then a couple more players were injured as the West Indies gained an 85-run lead. India slumped from 97–2 to 97–5 when its second innings was declared closed as the five injured players were unable to bat.

Five of the six Tests in the 1978–79 series were drawn, with hosts, India, winning the fourth Test to clinch the series, as it turned out. The second Test at Bangalore was interestingly poised as the tourists led by 266 runs with 2 wickets remaining, but the last day was abandoned following a politically-motivated riot. After making 205 in the first Test, Gavaskar made 107 and 182 not out in the third Test, and put on an unbroken second-wicket stand of 344 with Dilip Vengsarkar (157 not out) to set the West Indies a target of 335. The tourists only just avoided defeat as they were 197–9 when poor light caused stumps to be drawn with 11 balls remaining. Batting was sub-standard in the crucial fourth Test at Madras, with Kallicharran (98) the standout in the touring side's 228 before the home side led by 27, following 124 from Viswanath. The West Indies' second-innings total of 151 included 91 from Larry Gomes before the Indians, needing 125, were 17–3 before losing wickets at 74, 82, 84 and 115 on their way to a mere 3-wicket triumph. India batted first in the last two Tests and made big totals to all but rule out the possibility of defeat, with Gavaskar, Vengsarkar and Kapil Dev scoring tons in the fifth Test before Viswanath, Amarnath and Anshuman Gaekwad did likewise in the sixth Test. Poor weather also foiled the tourists in the final Test, before West Indian opener Faoud Bacchus scored 250.

1980s

The West Indies won the 1982–83 series 2–0 at home, with a 4-wicket win in the first Test followed by two draws, a 10-wicket win and a high-scoring draw. Roberts claimed 9 wickets in the first Test, which was evenly matched and looked like being drawn following the loss of more than a day's play. But a late Indian collapse left the West Indies needing 172 runs in 26 overs, and they made it with 4 balls to spare, despite losing 4 wickets when within 45 runs of the target. The West Indies had a big lead in the second Test but couldn't force a victory, before two days of play were lost due to rain in the third Test. The tourists faltered for 209 and 277 in the fourth Test before the hosts needed a single to win the match and achieved it when wicketkeeper Syed Kirmani bowled a no ball.

India upset the West Indies by 43 runs in the 1983 World Cup final at Lord's, but the World Cup holders couldn't back this up in Test cricket, as the West Indies beat them 3–0 on Indian soil in late 1983. Having been man of the match in the World Cup decider and scored 1000 Test runs in the year, Amarnath came crashing back to earth against the West Indies as he made five ducks and a single in his six innings. The tourists won the first, third and fifth Tests while the other three Tests were drawn. The hosts made just 207 and 164 in an innings loss at Kanpur, having been 0–2, 49–6 and 90–8 in their first innings and 43–5 in their second innings. Vengsarkar (159) and Gavaskar (121) set up India's 464 in the second Test before Kapil Dev took 6–77, but the hosts couldn't do enough to win. The West Indies were 27–3 early in the third Test before struggling to 190–8 and then reaching 281, followed by India flopping from 127–0 to 241 all out. The tourists collapsed again but recovered from 74–5 to post 201 despite 9–83 from Kapil Dev. India crumbled for a dreadful 103 when chasing 242 as four pacemen shared the wickets, before the fourth Test finished with honours even. Gavaskar was out to the first ball of the fifth Test before India progressed from 63–6 to 241 all out and then reduced the opposition to 42–4, only for Lloyd (161 not out) to lead a revival. Malcolm Marshall (6–37) helped rout India for 90 as the West Indies claimed an innings win, before Gavaskar (236 not out) ensured that India would not lose the final Test.

The teams could not be separated in a four-Test series that India hosted in 1987–88. After crashing to 75 all out at Delhi, the Indians reduced the West Indies to 29–6 and 49–7 before the tourists eked out a precious 52-run lead. Vengsarkar made 102 in India's second innings but the West Indies achieved the 276-run target for the loss of 5 wickets, with Richards making an undefeated 109 after his team was uncertainly placed at 111–4. The second and third Tests were drawn, with both sides topping 500 in the latter before the hosts levelled the series with a 255-run victory at Madras. Leg spinner Narendra Hirwani claimed 8–61 and 8–75 in his maiden Test to dismiss the West Indies for 184 and 160 after India recovered from 64–3 to score 382 in its first innings, due mainly to a Kapil Dev century.

Three washed out days ensured that the first Test of the 1988–89 series in the Caribbean was drawn, after Richie Richardson scored 194 for the home side. A century to Sanjay Manjrekar helped India go from 68–4 to 321 all out in the second Test, before a ton to Greenidge was followed by the West Indies falling from 201–1 to 377 all out. Ravi Shastri's 107 in India's second innings was surrounded mostly by failures, and then an unbeaten century to Desmond Haynes set up a comfortable 8-wicket win for the hosts. India trailed by 164 runs in the first innings of the third Test after collapsing for 150, and the West Indies went on to win by 217 runs. Centuries to Richards and Richardson, coupled with a 10-wicket match haul from Courtney Walsh, helped the hosts complete the series with a 7-wicket win in Jamaica.

1990s

The West Indies salvaged a drawn series in late 1994 as Curtly Ambrose was a notable absentee. In the first Test at Bombay, half of India's first-innings total of 272 came in the sixth-wicket partnership, after a wicket fell from the second ball of the series. The West Indies lost their last 5 wickets for 13 runs to be 29 runs in arrears, before having India 11–3 and 88–5. But the Indian batsmen from five to nine tallied 270 runs before the West Indies, needing 363, fell to 2–2 and lost by 96 runs, despite a sixth-wicket partnership of 162. After honours were relatively even in a high scoring second Test, the tourists squared the series with a crushing 243-run win after Jimmy Adams scored 174 not out in a total of 443. India's first innings of 387 included a last-wicket stand of 64 before India's horror second innings of 114 included a collapse of 7–24 and a last-wicket stand of 46, after first-innings centurion Manoj Prabhakar retired hurt without scoring.

The 1996–97 series was something of a return to the 1948–49 and 1952–53 series as the West Indies won once while the other four Tests were drawn. Navjot Sidhu's 201 for India in the second Test was a highlight, before the third Test in Barbados decided the series. Shivnarine Chanderpaul made 137 not out as the West Indies improved from 193–7 to 298 all out, before a second-innings capitulation for 140 left India needing just 120. The tourists, astonishingly, never looked a chance as Ambrose, Ian Bishop and Franklyn Rose bundled them out for 81, before rain drastically reduced the amount of play in the final two Tests.

2000s

The first Test of the 2002 series was also cut short due to rain, with captain Carl Hooper (233) and Chanderpaul (140) setting up a West Indian total of 501 before Rahul Dravid made an unbeaten 144 in India's 395–7. The second Test in Trinidad was well fought as India gained a 94-run advantage before tallying 218 and winning by 37 runs, after the West Indies were well placed at 125–1. India's joy was short-lived as Shiv Sunder Das was bowled from the first ball of the third Test, which the West Indies won by 10 wickets, after dismissing India for 102 and 296. Hooper and Chanderpaul made tons for the West Indies in the third and fourth Tests, while teammate Ridley Jacobs also scored a century in the fourth Test which was a run feast at Antigua. VVS Laxman and wicketkeeper Ajay Ratra scored hundreds as India declared at 513–9 in the fourth Test, before India gave all 11 players a bowl as the West Indies made 629–9 declared. In the final Test, India was never in contention as the West Indies made 422 and led by more than 200 runs before winning by 155 runs, after setting a target of 408.

India hosted a follow-up series later in 2002, and began with an innings win at Mumbai after making 457 and then dismissing the tourists for 157 and 188. India wrapped up its first series win against the West Indies since 1978–79 with an 8-wicket triumph at Chennai, after the tourists made just 167 and 229, compared with the home team's first innings of 316. Hundreds to Chanderpaul, Wavell Hinds and Marlon Samuels helped the West Indies to a 139-run lead in the third Test before India lost Sanjay Bangar first ball, and it was left to Tendulkar (176) and Laxman (154 not out) to foil the West Indies.

The Indians won the 2006 series with a victory in the fourth Test following three draws, with the opening Test at Antigua clearly the pick. The West Indies led by 130 runs before 212 from Indian opener Wasim Jaffer put the visitors in the box seat. Set 392, the hosts only just managed to draw the match as they finished at 298–9 after the last-wicket pairing survived the final 3.1 overs. Plenty of runs were scored in the next two drawn Tests, with the loss of day four hindering India's victory charge in the second Test, after the West Indies had to follow on. In the third Test, the Indians were set the same target that they set the West Indies in the first Test, with India finishing at 298–4. The deciding Test in Jamaica was over in three days, with India recovering from 3–2 to make 200, before the West Indies crashed from 42–1 to 103 all out. Jerome Taylor had match figures of 9–95 for the hosts, who needed 269 runs, and opener Chris Gayle bagged a pair as the West Indies slid to a 49-run defeat.

Jamaica was also the venue when the teams next met, in June 2011, with India tallying 246 after being 85–6 and later losing 4–15. After trailing by 73 runs on the first innings, the West Indies were all but gone at 188–8 before reaching 262 in pursuit of 326. The second Test was well fought, with both sides suffering first innings top-order collapses before the West Indies finished at 202–7 after being set 281. The third Test was also drawn to enable India to win the series, after Ishant Sharma had a fine series with the ball.

India hosted the West Indies later in 2011, with the hosts winning the first two Tests before the third and final Test in Mumbai was a nail-biting draw. The tourists led by 95 runs on the first innings of the opening Test, before the locals won by 5 wickets as they sought 276.

Indian off spinner Ravi Ashwin impressed with 9 wickets in his Test debut. Centuries to Laxman, Dravid and MS Dhoni set up a total of 631–7 declared in the second Test, before India won by an innings, despite 136 from Darren Bravo in the West Indies' second-innings total of 463. Bravo (166) was the leading scorer as the West Indies made 590 in the final Test, and then Ashwin made 103 at number eight as India tallied 482. Ashwin again claimed a 9-wicket match haul before he was run out off the final ball of the match to leave the scores level, with 1 wicket in hand. Needing 243 runs from 64 overs for a 3–0 series win, India stuttered after being 101–1 at the 19-over mark. Nineteen runs were needed from 29 balls after the seventh wicket fell, and 4 runs were needed from 7 balls following the eighth wicket, before Ashwin clubbed the last ball to long-on and was never a chance of making the second run.

India won both Tests by an innings against the West Indies in late 2013, with each match decided in three days after the tourists batted first. Test debutant Rohit Sharma scored 177 while Ashwin scored 124 in India's 453 at Kolkata, before the hosts made 495 at Mumbai, following 113 from Cheteshwar Pujara and 111 not out from Sharma. Mohammed Shami claimed 4–71 and 5–47 on debut in the first Test before Pragyan Ojha snared 5–40 and 5–49 in the second Test.

West Indies v India

1948–49 (I): West Indies 1–0 (4 drawn)

1952–53 (WI): West Indies 1–0 (4 drawn)

1958–59 (I): West Indies 3–0 (2 drawn)

1961–62 (WI): West Indies 5–0

1966–67 (I): West Indies 2–0 (1 drawn)

1970–71 (WI): India 1–0 (4 drawn)

1974–75 (I): West Indies 3–2

1976 (WI): West Indies 2–1 (1 drawn)

1978–79 (I): India 1–0 (5 drawn)

1982–83 (WI): West Indies 2–0 (3 drawn)

1983–84 (I): West Indies 3–0 (3 drawn)

1987–88 (I): 1–1 (2 drawn)

1988–89 (WI): West Indies 3–0 (1 drawn)

1994–95 (I): 1–1 (1 drawn)

1996–97 (WI): West Indies 1–0 (4 drawn)

2002 (WI): West Indies 2–1 (2 drawn)

2002–03 (I): India 2–0 (1 drawn)

2006 (WI): India 1–0 (3 drawn)

2011 (WI): India 1–0 (2 drawn)ᵢ

2011–12 (I): India 2–0 (1 drawn)

2013–14 (I): India 2–0

4.3 WEST INDIES v PAKISTAN

1950s

Some memorable scoring took place in the first series involving the West Indies and Pakistan in early 1958, starting in the first Test at Barbados. Everton Weekes (197) and Conrad Hunte (142) set up the home side's first-innings total of 579–9 declared, before the visitors slumped to 106 all out. Following on, Pakistan guaranteed a draw with 657–8 declared after Hanif Mohammad scored 337 in a phenomenal 970-minute vigil. The hosts won the second Test by 120 runs after Pakistan, chasing 356, was soundly placed at 131–1. In the third Test, Imtiaz Ahmed made 122 in Pakistan's 328 before the West Indies made a mammoth 790–3 declared and went on to win by an innings. Hunte was run out for 260 after sharing a second-wicket stand of 446 with Garry Sobers, who amazingly turned his maiden Test century into a then world record Test score of 365 not out. In the fourth Test, Saeed Ahmed made 150 in Pakistan's 408 before the West Indies bettered it by 2 runs, following centuries to Clyde Walcott and Sobers. The hosts won by 8 wickets as Hunte and Sobers again registered triple figures and made the 317-run target seem easy. Pakistan salvaged a 3–1 series loss with an innings win after Hunte was out to the first ball of the fifth Test. Wazir Mohammad (189) was the pick of Pakistan's batsmen in the 496-run total.

Fazal Mahmood bowled splendidly on matting as Pakistan won the first Test of the 1958–59 series by 10 wickets at Karachi. Fazal had Hunte caught behind with the fourth ball of the Test and claimed 6 more wickets in the match, as the West Indies folded for 146 and 245, leaving a target of just 88. Pakistan did well to make 145 after being 22–5 in the first innings of the second Test, before 6–34 from Fazal and 3–4 from Nasim-ul-Ghani routed the West Indies for 76. The last 8 wickets fell for 20 runs as the last six batsmen didn't score, with last man Sonny Ramadhin not out. The West Indies needed 214 to level the series and lost by 41 runs as Fazal bagged 6–66, before an innings of 217 from Rohan Kanhai set up an innings win to the West Indies in the third Test.

1970s

Sixteen years after the 1958–59 series, the West Indies and Pakistan drew a two-match series 0–0 before the 1976–77 series in the Caribbean was memorable in the wake of Pakistan's breakthrough Test victory in Australia. The first Test in Barbados was a brilliant spectacle, with both sides topping 400 after the West Indies were 183–5, before Pakistan was 158–9 in its second innings. Some sloppy cricket from the West Indies enabled Wasim Raja and Wasim Bari to put on a last-wicket partnership of 133 that set the hosts 306, before the West Indies were 217–8 with more than 20 overs remaining. The hosts finished at 251–9, after the last-wicket pairing of Andy Roberts and debutant Colin Croft survived the final eight overs. Croft captured 8–29 as Pakistan made just 180 on a damp pitch in the first innings of the second Test, before a century to Roy Fredericks set up a 136-run lead for the West Indies who went on to win by 6 wickets after being set 205. The hosts led by 254 runs in the third Test before 167 from Majid Khan helped Pakistan reach 540 and salvage a draw. The tourists levelled the series with a massive 266-run win as they twice topped 300, while the hosts made just 154 and 222. Pakistani skipper Mushtaq Mohammad was damaging with bat and ball as he scored 121 and 56 and captured 5–28 and 3–69. In the deciding Test at Sabina Park, the West Indians made 280 and gained control as they dismissed Pakistan for 198 and then established a 441-run lead. The tourists were gone at 51–4, although Asif Iqbal scored a defiant 135 as the West Indies won the series 2–1 with their 140-run triumph.

1980s

Three of the four Tests in the 1980–81 series were drawn, with the West Indies winning the second Test at Faisalabad, before rain hampered the final two Tests. In the decisive contest, the visitors made 235 and could have had far less had Viv Richards (72) not been dropped on 5. Pakistan was 2–2 before hobbling to 176, and later tallied only 145, after being set 302.

When the hosts tumbled to 37–5 in the first innings of the first Test in 1986–87, a massacre looked possible. Pakistan reached 159 thanks to captain Imran Khan's 61 before the West Indies made 248, and later sought 240. Abdul Qadir nabbed 6–16 while Imran captured 4–30 as the West Indies astonishingly capitulated for 53. The West Indian pacemen seemed hell-bent on payback in the second Test at Lahore, with Malcolm Marshall, Courtney Walsh and Tony Gray combining to rout Pakistan for 131 and 77, as the tourists won by an innings and 10 runs. The third Test in Karachi was on a knife's edge as the hosts fell 1 run behind the touring team's 240, before crucially reprieving opener Desmond Haynes. He carried his bat, scoring 88 in a 211-run total before the Pakistanis hung on to draw the match and the series, as bad light induced an early finish with the score 125–7.

The 1987–88 series in the Caribbean produced cricket of the strongest calibre, with the pendulum see-sawing. Imran's 7–80 contained the hosts to 292 before 114 from Javed Miandad, and several handy scores, helped Pakistan reach 435 in the first Test. Imran and Qadir did most of the damage as the locals made just 172 in their second innings and lost by 9 wickets. Richards and Marshall returned from injury and made a decisive impact in the second Test, which went down to the very last ball. The West Indies made only 174 before Pakistan crashed to 68–7 and later gained a 20-run lead. The hosts subsequently lost wickets at 1, 55, 66 and 81, before Richards (123) and Jeff Dujon (106 not out) changed the momentum. The tourists dropped a few crucial catches, and Richards appeared lucky to survive a couple of confident appeals for lbw. Needing 372, Pakistan was shakily placed at 67–3 and 169–5, but remained in the hunt as Miandad scored 102, before the sundries count tallied 61. At 282–5 the Pakistanis were on track for a

312

series triumph, before slipping to 288–7 and 311–8. Richards won an lbw appeal with the first ball of the final over, with the total on 341, and Qadir survived the remaining five deliveries to ensure a draw. The third and final Test in Barbados was one of the best of all-time, with both sides threatening to make a big score before falling away. Pakistan made 309 and 262, while the West Indies made 306 and 268–8 to win by 2 wickets and square the series. The hosts lost wickets at 21, 78, 118, 128, 150, 159, 180 and 207 during the run chase before Dujon (29 not out) and Winston Benjamin (40 not out) emerged triumphant. The Pakistanis were unlucky that Marshall and Dujon survived appeals when the hosts were around 80 runs shy of the target.

1990s

The teams again couldn't be separated in 1990–91. Waqar Younis made the most decisive contribution in the first Test at Karachi as his 9 wickets set up an 8-wicket win for Pakistan, while Salim Malik (102), Shoaib Mohammad (86) and Imran (73 not out) also made vital contributions. Neither side reached 200 in the second Test, which the West Indies won by 7 wickets after progressing from 34–3 to 130–3. In the third Test, Carl Hooper made 134 as the West Indies managed 294 before 5-wicket hauls to Curtly Ambrose and Ian Bishop decimated Pakistan for 122. Five wickets to Wasim Akram confined the West Indies to 173, before Pakistan lost Aamir Malik first ball and later finished 104 runs shy of victory with 4 wickets in hand.

Hosts, the West Indies, wrapped up the 1992–93 series in the first two Tests before the third Test was drawn. The home side began badly with a total of 127 before Bishop and Ambrose bowled out Pakistan for 140. Haynes carried his bat for 143 runs while Brian Lara (96) also scored well, and Pakistan lost by 204 runs after being set 370. Haynes (125) was backed up by his teammates in the second Test as the West Indies made 455 and won by 10 wickets after making Pakistan follow on. Hooper (178 not out) stole the show in the final Test as the hosts totalled 438, before the match headed for an inevitable draw after Inzamam-ul-Haq made 123 in Pakistan's reply of 326.

West Indian cricket was at a decidedly different stage in 1997–98 as Pakistan inflicted two innings defeats before clean sweeping the series with a 10-wicket victory. The West Indies made 151 and 211 in the first Test at Peshawar, where Mushtaq Ahmed claimed two 5-wicket hauls for the victors. Inzamam (177) and Aamir Sohail (160) helped Pakistan to 471 in the second Test at Rawalpindi before Hooper (73 not out) stood out in the touring team's second-innings total of 139. After the West Indies faltered from 109–1 to 216 all out in the third Test, Sohail (160) and Ijaz Ahmed (151) put on 298 for the first wicket in a total of 417. Hooper scored half of the West Indian total of 212, while Saqlain Mushtaq completed a 9-wicket match haul.

2000s

The first Test of the 2000 series in the Caribbean was drawn after the fourth and fifth days were rained off. An innings of 165 from Wavell Hinds, as well as 84 not out from Test debutant Ramnaresh Sarwan, helped the hosts to a 145-run lead in the second Test. Pakistan openers Imran Nazir (131) and Mohammad Wasim (82) subsequently put on a 219-run opening stand before a declaration occurred 200 runs later, and it was no surprise that the Test was drawn. The series was decided in thrilling style at Antigua, as the hosts scraped to a 1-wicket victory in a match that bore some resemblance to the third Test in the 1987–88 series. Pakistan made 269 and 219 before the hosts, needing 216, lost wickets at 16, 31, 84, 144, 161, 169, 177, 194 and 197 before Jimmy Adams and number 11 Walsh eked out the required 19 runs in 13.1 overs.

Sharjah was the venue for a two-match series in early 2002, with Pakistan winning by 170 runs and 244 runs. Centuries to Rashid Latif and Yousuf Youhana helped Pakistan near 500 in the first Test before the West Indies made 366 and later crumbled when chasing 342 as Shoaib Akhtar and Abdul Razzaq did most of the damage. In the second Test, Younis Khan (153) and Shahid Afridi (107) set up Pakistan's 472 before the West Indies fell 208 runs in arrears and later had six batsmen lbw and three bowled in their second-innings total of 189.

Lara (130 and 48) and Shivnarine Chanderpaul (92 and 153 not out) helped the West Indies to totals of 345 and 371 in the Barbados Test of 2005. Fidel Edwards claimed 5 wickets in Pakistan's first innings before Chris Gayle replicated the feat in Pakistan's second innings, as an Afridi century couldn't prevent the hosts winning by 276 runs. But the tourists squared the series as the hosts, after making 404 in their first innings thanks to Lara's 153, plunged to 143 all out when chasing 280. Younis Khan and Inzamam made an important century each for the Pakistanis, before Danish Kaneria and Shabbir Ahmed bowled them to victory.

Mohammad Yousuf (192) and Umar Gul (5–65 and 4–99) turned the first Test of the 2006–07 series in Pakistan's favour. Pakistan gained a 279-run lead before Lara (122) and Chanderpaul (81) couldn't prevent Pakistan winning by 9 wickets. Lara (216) was well supported in the second Test at Multan as the West Indies achieved a 234-run lead, only for Pakistan to save the match as Yousuf (191) was surrounded by good contributions. In the final Test at Karachi, two centuries to Yousuf and one century from Mohammad Hafeez helped Pakistan set a huge target of 444 for the West Indies to square the series. Gayle was out second ball, and the hosts went on to win by 199 runs to claim a 2–0 series victory.

Bowlers held sway at Guyana in the first Test of the 2011 series, with the hosts winning by 40 runs after scoring 226 and 152 while the tourists tallied 160 and 178. The Pakistanis lost their first 3 wickets for 2 runs in the chase. West Indian skipper Darren Sammy (2–16 and 5–29), Ravi Rampaul (3–27 and 4–48) and debutant Devendra Bishoo (4–68 and 0–56) had fine figures, while the pick was Pakistan's Saeed Ajmal with 5–69 and 6–42. Pakistan appeared to have little hope of levelling the series after sinking to 24–3 and 74–4 in the first innings of the second Test, before a vital last-wicket 78-run stand lifted the total to 272. The West Indies also began poorly, and a 60-run ninth-wicket stand was invaluable in the 223-run total. Hundreds to Pakistani duo Taufeeq Umar and captain Misbah-ul-Haq enabled Pakistan to set a 427-run target, and then nobody passed 50 as Pakistan secured a series-levelling 196-run win.

West Indies v Pakistan

1957–58 (WI): West Indies 3–1 (1 drawn)

1958–59 (P): Pakistan 2–1

1974–75 (P): 0–0 (2 drawn)

1976–77 (WI): West Indies 2–1 (2 drawn)

1980–81 (P): West Indies 1–0 (3 drawn)

1986–87 (P): 1–1 (1 drawn)

1987–88 (WI): 1–1 (1 drawn)

1990–91 (P): 1–1 (1 drawn)

1992–93 (WI): West Indies 2–0 (1 drawn)

1997–98 (P): Pakistan 3–0

2000 (WI): West Indies 1–0 (2 drawn)

2001–02 (Sharjah): Pakistan 2–0

2005 (WI): 1–1

2006–07 (P): Pakistan 2–0 (1 drawn)

2011 (WI): 1–1

4.4 WEST INDIES v SRI LANKA

1990s

The first time the West Indies met Sri Lanka in Test cricket was in late 1993, almost 12 years after Sri Lanka played its maiden Test. Rain ruined the chance of a result at Moratuwa, as the hosts made 190 and 43–2, while the visitors made 204. A two-Test series took place in the Caribbean in 1997, with the hosts winning by 6 wickets inside three days, before the second Test was drawn. Sri Lanka led by 34 runs on the first innings in the first Test, before the West Indies pursued 187 and enjoyed a 160-run opening stand. The second Test was superbly fought, with Ravindra Pushpakumara (5–41) and Muttiah Muralitharan (3–28) dismissing the West Indies for 147 while Carl Hooper scored 81, before Hooper took 5–26 to restrict Sri Lanka's lead to 75. Brian Lara's 115 in the home side's second innings set up a run chase of 269, and the visitors were 189–3 before stuttering to 233–8 at the finish.

2000s

The West Indians went through a tough time when they next encountered Sri Lanka, which won the 2001–02 series 3–0, despite excellent form from Lara. He made 178 as the West Indies made 448 in the first innings of the first Test at Galle, only for Sri Lanka to make 590 and later win by 10 wickets, after needing just 3 runs. The hosts wrapped up the series with a 131-run win, after setting a target of 322 at Kandy, and then won by 10 wickets again, this time after needing 26 runs. In the third Test, Lara made 221 out of 390 and 130 out of 262 for the West Indies, while Sri Lanka reached 627–9 declared as Hashan Tillekeratne (204 not out) was well supported. Muralitharan claimed 24 wickets in the series while Chaminda Vaas took 26, including 14 in the third Test.

The West Indies won the 2003 series 1–0 at home as Lara shone again. He made 209 while fellow left-hander Wavell Hinds scored 113 in the drawn first Test, before Lara (80 not out) and Ramnaresh Sarwan (82) set up a 7-wicket win in the second Test, as the West Indies chased 212. Corey Collymore also played a huge part in the result, taking 7–57 as Sri Lanka was dismissed for 194 in its second innings in the second Test.

Sri Lanka recorded a 6-wicket win in the first Test of the 2005 series before registering a 240-run victory, as the West Indians again succumbed to Vaas and Muralitharan on Sri Lankan soil. Neither side reached 300 in the first Test, with the visitors leading by 58 runs before being skittled for 113, after 5 of the first 6 dismissals were lbw. The hosts were 49–3 in the run chase before partnerships of 86 and 37 sealed the result. Sri Lanka made only 150 in the first innings of the second Test following 5–25 from Daren Powell, before Vaas captured 6–22 as the West Indies fell for 148. Muralitharan's second innings 8–46 ensured that the visitors would never get near the 378-run target.

Sri Lanka finally won a Test in the Caribbean as the touring team triumphed by 121 runs at Guyana in March 2008. Two centuries and three half-centuries set up a total of 476–8 declared before the hosts narrowly avoided the follow on and couldn't threaten a 437-run target, despite reaching 156–1. The West Indians however drew the series after winning what was an evenly balanced Test for a while. Thilan Samaraweera made 125 in Sri Lanka's second innings of 268, before the West Indies were 24–2 and 73–3 chasing 253. Following scores of 80, 72 and 57, Sarwan made 102 and combined with Shivnarine Chanderpaul (86 not out) for a 157-run partnership to set up a 6-wicket victory.

Rain ruined the 2010–11 series in Sri Lanka, with all three Tests being drawn. West Indian opener Chris Gayle made 333 in a total of 580–9 declared in the first innings of the first Test at Galle, before Sri Lanka saved the match after following on. The hosts gained the upper hand in the second Test but were foiled by the weather, before the West Indies made 303–8 in the only innings of the third Test after Gayle was dismissed from the opening delivery.

With the inaugural Sobers–Tissera Trophy up for grabs in October 2015, Sri Lanka won a two-Test series at home. Dimuth Karunaratne (186) and Dinesh Chandimal (151) set up a total of 484 before 10 wickets from Rangana Herath enabled Sri Lanka to win by an innings and 6 runs at Galle. At Colombo, the hosts made only 200 and 206 but still won comfortably as the visitors tallied just 163 and 171.

West Indies v Sri Lanka

1993–94 (SL): 1 drawn
1997 (WI): West Indies 1–0 (1 drawn)
2001–02 (SL): Sri Lanka 3–0
2003 (WI): West Indies 1–0 (1 drawn)
2005 (SL): Sri Lanka 2–0
2007–08 (WI): 1–1
2010–11 (SL): 0–0 (3 drawn)
2015–16 (SL): Sri Lanka 2–0

4.5 WEST INDIES v ZIMBABWE

2000s

The first ever Test involving the West Indies and Zimbabwe was a low-scoring thriller in Trinidad in March 2000, with the Africans losing after having the upper hand for most of the time. The hosts tallied 187 before the visitors recovered from 0–2 to tally 236 thanks to an unconquered 113 from captain and wicketkeeper Andy Flower. The hosts also sank to 0–2, and the visitors later needed just 99 to win but crumbled for 63 in 47 overs, as Franklyn Rose and Curtly Ambrose did most of the damage. The tourists blew another chance in the second and final Test, with Murray Goodwin scoring 113 in Zimbabwe's total of 308 before West Indies skipper Jimmy Adams (101 not out) and Rose (69) put on a match-turning eighth-wicket partnership of 148. After trailing by 31 runs, Zimbabwe could set a target of just 72, which was passed in just 12.4 overs without the loss of a wicket.

The 2001 series marked the beginning of the West Indies and Zimbabwe vying for the Clive Lloyd Trophy. The visitors won the first Test at Harare by an innings and 176 runs, after the hosts batted first and mustered 155. Openers Chris Gayle (175) and Daren Ganga (89) put on 214 runs before captain Carl Hooper (149) helped the West Indies pass 500, followed by Zimbabwe crashing from 164–0 to 228 all out. The rot set in after opener Dion Ebrahim (71) received a dreadful lbw decision, which was followed by another three lbw verdicts, including another dubious one, but the West Indians were not to be denied. After trailing by 216 runs in the second Test, Zimbabwe finally put in a strong team display as the hosts amassed 563, including a couple of 90s, Heath Streak's unbeaten 83 and Hamilton Masakadza's century on debut, to ensure a draw.

Zimbabwe was 1 agonising wicket away from winning the first Test at Harare in the 2003–04 series. The hosts recovered from 154–5 to score 507 as the batsmen from seven to nine tallied 301 runs before the visitors, set 373, after previously making 335, finished on 207–9 after number 11 Fidel Edwards survived the last 32 minutes. Zimbabwe was also well in the hunt in the final Test, having made 377 in reply to 481 before dismissing the West Indies for 128, only for the hosts to crumble to 104 all out.

Poor batting cost Zimbabwe in both Tests in the Caribbean in early 2012–13, as only once did the visitors tally more than 175, while the hosts twice topped 300. Shane Shillingford was the standout player of the series as he claimed 9 wickets in the first Test and 10 in the second, with the West Indies winning by 9 wickets and then by an innings and 65 runs.

West Indies v Zimbabwe

1999–00 (WI): West Indies 2–0
2001 (Z): West Indies 1–0 (1 drawn)

2003–04 (Z): West Indies 1–0 (1 drawn)
2012–13 (WI): West Indies 2–0

4.6 WEST INDIES v BANGLADESH

2000s

The West Indies had the wood on Bangladesh in five of the first six series involving the two Test-playing nations, although the 2009 series was memorable from Bangladesh's perspective.

The opening encounter in the 2002–03 season was forgettable for Bangladesh after Hannan Sarkar was dismissed from the first ball of the series. The West Indies replied to Bangladesh's 139 with 536 and went on to win by an innings and 310 runs, with Jermaine Lawson achieving staggering figures of 6–3 in Bangladesh's second innings. Despite a better showing from Bangladesh in the second Test at Chittagong, the West Indies completed a 2–0 series win with a 7-wicket victory after being set 111.

The 2004 series also began with the first ball dismissal of Sarkar, as did the second Test. In the first Test in St Lucia, Bangladesh recovered to tally 416, following centuries to captain Habibul Bashar and Mohammad Rafique, before Bangladesh spilled many catches as the West Indies worked their way to 352, following a chancy 141 from Chris Gayle. Bangladesh fell to 79–6 before wicketkeeper Khaled Mashud made an unbeaten 103 and received solid lower-order support, and Bangladesh declared for the first time in Test cricket, albeit with 1 wicket in hand. Bangladesh went on to salvage a draw for only the third time in its 29 Tests until this point, after the country's twenty-eigth Test was also a draw. There was a lot of satisfaction in setting the West Indies 336 runs in 29 overs, and then Gayle (66 not out) helped the total to 113–0 before the match was called off six overs early. The second Test at Jamaica, however, belonged to the West Indies. Ramnaresh Sarwan (261 not out), Brian Lara (120) and Shivnarine Chanderpaul (101 not out) set up a first-innings lead of 275 for the hosts before they won by an innings.

Five years passed before the teams contested another series, with the West Indies fielding an inexperienced side due to pay disputes. A familiar pattern nonetheless seemed to start, as Bangladesh was all out for 238 before the West Indies made 307. But visiting team, Bangladesh, was able to set a competitive target of 277, although the Bangladeshis collapsed after being 228–1, with opener Tamim Iqbal scoring 128. The hosts were routed for 181 to lose by 95 runs, before making 237 in the first innings of the second Test. The West Indies made 209 in their second innings, setting Bangladesh 215, which was achieved for the loss of 6 wickets, after the Bangladeshis were 67–4. Having captured 8 wickets in the match, Shakib Al Hasan completed a fine personal series as he made 96 not out.

Elias Sunny starred on debut with 6–94 for Bangladesh in the first Test of 2011–12, although rain ruined the chance of a result. The West Indies won the series following a 229-run victory in the second Test, following four standout performances, which ensured Bangladesh fell well short of a 508-run target. Kirk Edwards scored 121 in the West Indies' first innings before Darren Bravo made 195 in the second innings, while Fidel Edwards and Devendra Bishoo bagged a 5-wicket haul each.

The first Test of 2012–13 in Mirpur was memorable after both teams topped 500, before the West Indies won by 77 runs. Shivnarine Chanderpaul (203 not out) and Denesh Ramdin (126 not out) put on an unbroken stand of 296, as the West Indies reached 527–4 declared after opener Kieran Powell scored 117. Bangladesh gained a shock lead of 29 following one century (108 from Naeem Islam) and four half-centuries, before Powell made another ton (110). Chasing 245, the Bangladeshis rued too many squandered starts, with Tino Best claiming 5–24 after Bangladesh's Sohag Gazi snared 9 wickets on debut. In the second Test, Bangladeshi debutant Abul Hasan scored 113 at number ten as the team went from 193–8 to 387 all out. But the Test was effectively put beyond Bangladesh's reach as Marlon Samuels (260), Chanderpaul (150 not out) and Darren Bravo (127) set up a lead of 261. Bangladesh was 82–5 before doing enough to make the West Indies bat again but a 6-wicket haul to Best, following a 6-wicket haul from Fidel Edwards, helped the West Indies to a 10-wicket win.

The West Indies also recorded a 10-wicket win in the first Test of 2014. Kraigg Brathwaite scored 212 as an opener before Bangladesh fell for 182 and 314 despite Mushfiqur Rahim scoring 116 in the second innings. A 296-run win to the West Indies wrapped up a 2–0 series result, with Chanderpaul making undefeated scores of 84 and 101 while Sulieman Benn claimed 7 wickets in each Test.

West Indies v Bangladesh

2002–03 (B): West Indies 2–0
2004 (WI): West Indies 1–0 (1 drawn)
2009 (WI): Bangladesh 2–0
2011–12 (B): West Indies 1–0 (1 drawn)
2012–13 (B): West Indies 2–0
2014 (WI): West Indies 2–0

4.7 NOTABLE TEST PLAYERS

(Sir) Curtly Ambrose

Following the retirement of Joel Garner, it took less than 12 months for the West Indies to unearth the next towering and intimidating fast bowler. The 201cm (6ft 7in) Curtly Ambrose was more interested in basketball than cricket during his teens, and whilst a number of batsmen in the late 1980s and 1990s may have preferred that he stuck with basketball, there was little doubt that Ambrose's bowling was great for world cricket. Ambrose ranked alongside Wasim Akram as the world's best fast bowler for much of the 1990s as he was quick, venomous and could generate alarming bounce, all while being very accurate. Interestingly, Ambrose played just five Tests in Pakistan, one in Sri Lanka and none in India. He was known for avoiding the media, before his autobiography was aptly titled *Time to Talk*.

Ambrose didn't generate much attention in his maiden Test series as he claimed just 7 wickets at 52.14 in three matches against Pakistan in the Caribbean. Later in 1988, when Ambrose took 22 scalps at 20.22 in England, comparisons with Garner were inevitably made. On Australian soil in 1988–89, Ambrose claimed 26 wickets in the five-Test series ,which the tourists won 3–1, and he bowled Allan Border for a duck in Border's 100th Test. Ambrose was also menacing Down Under in 1992–93 and 1996–97, particularly the former. He claimed 6–74 and 4–46 as the West Indies won the fourth Test by a single run to square the series before taking 7–25, including 7–1 in a staggering 32-ball spell, in the final Test at Perth as the tourists won by an innings. Following an ineffective start to the 1996–97 series, Ambrose snared 9 wickets in the third Test before missing the fourth, which Australia won by an innings to regain the Frank Worrell Trophy. Ambrose captured 7 wickets in the final Test, which the West Indies won easily, and delivered a 15-ball over as he seemed intent on inflicting damage, as the pitch had widening cracks.

Ambrose's best innings figures of 8–45 were on English soil in 1990, and this included five lbw verdicts after he was fortunate that a caught-behind appeal was upheld. Four years later he claimed 6–24 at Port-of-Spain as England crashed to 46 all out. Another memorable performance from Ambrose was in 1992 as South Africa played its first Test since 1970. He finished with 6–34 in South Africa's second innings as the Africans slid to a 52-run defeat when in sight of victory.

After playing with Malcolm Marshall, Courtney Walsh and Patrick Patterson early in his career, Ambrose shared the new ball with Walsh from 1994 to 2000, while other pacemen included Kenny Benjamin and Ian Bishop, whose career was interrupted by injuries. The West Indies had decidedly mixed fortunes while Ambrose often remained a prominent wicket-taker in the second half of the 1990s, and often there was too much reliance on Ambrose and Walsh. There were still some memorable times for the duo, with Ambrose bowling well in the West Indies' first tour of South Africa in 1998–99, although the hosts won all five Tests. Success against Zimbabwe and England was followed by retirement in 2000, after Ambrose became the fifth bowler to attain 400 Test wickets.

Curtly Ambrose (b.1963)

Matches: 98
Runs scored: 1439
Batting average: 12.40
100s/50s: 0/1
Top score: 53
Balls bowled: 22,103
Wickets: 405
Bowling average: 20.99
5 wickets in innings: 22
10 wickets in match: 3
Best bowling: 8–45
Catches/stumpings: 18/0

Shivnarine Chanderpaul

Topping 12,000 Test runs reflected West Indian left-hander Shivnarine Chanderpaul's ability, even if his so-called 'crab-like' style appeared unconventional. As his career progressed, his stance became more unusual, as he faced side-on to the bowler and front-on to the square leg umpire. As *Cricinfo* reported in January 2014:

> *Shivnarine Chanderpaul proves there is life beyond the coaching handbook. He never seems to play in the V, or off the front foot, but uses soft hands, canny deflections, and a whiplash pull-shot... While the cricket world was obsessed with Brian Lara's unquestionable talent, Chanderpaul has shown that there are alternate ways to be consistent and prolific in Test cricket.*

Chanderpaul made his Test debut aged 19, a year before Australia's historic 1994–95 Frank Worrell Trophy victory, which effectively began the decline of West Indian cricket. Chanderpaul endured a lot of lean times in Test cricket as he was involved in 71 losses and only 35 wins. He nevertheless became the most stable and consistent West Indian batsman, particularly after Lara retired. On several occasions Chanderpaul batted for more than 1000 minutes between dismissals in Test cricket. His number of unbeaten knocks was partly due to his own resolve, but also because he was sometimes left stranded while surrounded by unsteady batting. Eleven of his 30 Test tons were in winning causes, and nine were in losing causes.

Chanderpaul made a frustrating sequence of decent starts but not big scores during his early years, with his maiden Test ton coming in his nineteenth appearance, a little over three years after his debut. Chanderpaul's scores against England in his maiden Test series were 62, 19, 50, 77, 5 and 75 not out, and after 18 Tests he had notched 13 half-centuries, with a highest score of 82 and an average of 49.28. His breakthrough innings produced 137 unbeaten runs against India at Bridgetown, after his first four scores in the series were 52, 48, 42 and 79. His next century was nearly a year later when he scored 118 against England at Georgetown to help turn the series in the West Indians' favour. More than four years passed before he registered his third Test ton, as he was injury-prone in the meantime and earned the tag of being a hypochondriac. In late 2000, he made 62 not out in a total of 124 as the West Indies were belted by an innings in Australia, before he missed the rest of the series with a foot injury. However, his health and fitness improved immensely after a piece of floating bone was removed from his foot.

All four of Chanderpaul's Test centuries in 2002 were against India, before he reached 100 off just 69 balls in a loss to Australia the following year. In the last Test of that series, Chanderpaul battled a broken finger as he scored 104 at St John's to help the West Indies attain the highest successful Test run chase. Despite a ton against South Africa in late 2003 and another against Bangladesh in June 2004, Chanderpaul had an indifferent run of form before making unbeaten scores of 128 and 97 at Lord's, as the West Indians were on their way to a 4–0 series loss.

Chanderpaul captained the West Indies from May 2005 to April 2006 before stepping down, after feeling that the role had affected his batting. In his first Test in charge, Chanderpaul made his best Test score of 203 not out. He made another ton later in the series but South Africa won the four-match series 2–0. The West Indies subsequently drew with Pakistan 1–1, with Chanderpaul marking his first win as Test skipper with 92 and 153 not out at Bridgetown. Chanderpaul's form tapered off, however, as his team failed to win any Tests in series losses to Sri Lanka, Australia and New Zealand during his tenure. In Australia, he scored just 87 runs in six innings.

As the West Indies lost 3–0 in England during 2007, Chanderpaul starred with 446 runs at 148.67 before he tallied 442 at 147.33 at home against Australia the following year as the tourists won 2–0. Chanderpaul also excelled when Australia won 2–0 in the Caribbean in 2011–12, as he achieved 346 runs at 86.50. When he posted a century for the 26th time in Test cricket, Chanderpaul went on to equal his highest Test score as the West Indies contested Bangladesh in late 2012. It was the first time since his 17th Test ton — against South Africa in late 2007 — that a Chanderpaul Test century was in a winning cause. Chanderpaul followed up his second instance of 203 not out with a single at number 11 in the second innings and then an undefeated 150 in another win against Bangladesh. Following a ton against Zimbabwe and a ton against New Zealand in 2013, Chanderpaul made unbeaten scores of 85, 84 and 101 against Bangladesh in 2014. His last series was in the Caribbean against England in 2015 when he scored just 92 runs at 15.33, including 25 and 0 in his final Test at Bridgetown, where a West Indian triumph forced a drawn series.

Shivnarine Chanderpaul (b.1974)

Matches: 164
Runs scored: 11,867
Batting average: 51.37
100s/50s: 30/66
Top score: 203*
Balls bowled: 1740
Wickets: 9
Bowling average: 98.11
5 wickets in innings: –
10 wickets in match: –
Best bowling: 1–2
Catches/stumpings: 66/–

Joel Garner

A strong contingent of West Indian fast bowlers in the same era meant that the imposing Joel Garner was often a first change bowler for several years. Known as 'Big Bird', Garner stood about 203cm (6ft 8in) and was every bit as lethal as contemporaries including Michael Holding, Andy Roberts, Colin Croft and Malcolm Marshall. The absence of an injured Holding enabled Garner and Croft to debut against Pakistan in February 1977, with Roberts and Croft opening the bowling. Garner snared 25 wickets at 27.52 in the five-Test series, which the West Indies won 2–1 and, on the five other occasions that Garner took part in a five-Test series, he captured 19 wickets on one occasion and between 26 and 31 on the other occasions. Garner was particularly rampant in

1984 with 77 scalps in 15 Tests, after his previous best was 52 scalps in 13 Tests during 1980.

Following Roberts' departure from Test cricket in 1983, Garner often opened the bowling with Marshall while Holding was used as first change. But no matter who opened the bowling or who was first change, there was no respite for the batsmen. The West Indies lost only five of Garner's 58 Tests, while 23 were drawn.

The ability to rocket the ball down from a great height enabled Garner to extract steep bounce, while his yorkers could be murderous. Garner also claimed a lot of wickets with great line and length bowling. When Garner released the ball, 'he did so with such venomous force that it would devour anything in its path', according to Ian Botham in *Botham's Century*.

Garner's Test bowling average was statistically among the best of those to capture more than 100 wickets, let alone 200, while his first-class average was an even more miserly 18.53. Garner's consistency was notable in that he was frugal without taking big bags of wickets, evidenced by the fact that his best Test figures were 6–56, while he never took 10 wickets in a Test. The only series in which Garner clearly underachieved was in 1982–83 when he claimed 7 wickets at 43 in four Tests on Indian soil. In England in 1980, Garner had outstanding figures of 26 wickets at 14.62 before his 27 wickets against England in 1985–86 cost just 16.15 each. Garner captured 31 scalps at 18.03 against Australia in 1984, and followed up with 29 at 18.62 against England.

With bucket-like hands, Garner was a good catcher and surprisingly agile fielder, usually in the gully, while his batting could be effective. He could take a big step down the wicket and swing hard. This worked to good effect in his maiden Test innings, as he scored 43, before his highest score of 60 was made against an Australian side featuring Dennis Lillee, Rodney Hogg, Jeff Thomson and Ray Bright in the fall of 1979.

Joel Garner (b.1952)

Matches: 58
Runs scored: 672
Batting average: 12.44
100s/50s: 0/1
Top score: 60
Balls bowled: 13,169
Wickets: 259
Bowling average: 20.98
5 wickets in innings: 7
10 wickets in match: 0
Best bowling: 6–56
Catches/stumpings: 42/–

Gordon Greenidge and Desmond Haynes

Of all the opening batting pairings in Test cricket, few have had the reputation carved out by West Indian duo Gordon Greenidge and Desmond Haynes. They tallied 6482 runs in 148 innings and enjoyed four double-century stands as well as 12 other century stands, with a highest partnership of 298. As England's Bob Willis reported in *Six of the Best*: 'What made it all the more frustrating was that when they were not crashing the ball to the boundary they would often just drop it at their feet and pinch quick singles, such was their great understanding.'

Greenidge could hit the ball with bullet-like power, and he relished the chance to cut, hook, pull and drive. In his Test debut against India in 1974–75, Greenidge was run out for 93 before scoring 107 in the second innings, but was dropped the following season after a bad trot in Australia included a pair. He regained his spot in the 1976 tour of England and scored 592 runs at 65.78, including three centuries. At Old Trafford he made 134 in a total of 211 before making 101 in the second innings. Productive form against Pakistan, Australia and New Zealand followed in the second half of the 1970s, with an even 100 in the deciding Test against Pakistan in 1976–77 proving to be a standout display. The West Indies would have made far less than 280 had Greenidge not succeeded, and Pakistan's Imran Khan deemed it one of the greatest Test knocks he had seen, as Greenidge mixed defence and attack. Greenidge followed up with 82 in the second innings as the West Indies set a big target that Pakistan could not threaten.

Following a lean series against England in 1980, Greenidge's best form was perhaps between seasons 1982–83 and 1984 when he averaged 70.76 from 21 Tests, as the West Indies contested India 11 times, and Australia and England five each. His 572 runs at 81.71 against England in 1984 included scores of 214 not out and 223, with the former helping the West Indies to a 9-wicket win, after the Test had been well balanced. Greenidge passed 5000 Test runs with an average in the high 40s in 1985–86, and recorded another double ton as he notched 213 against the Kiwis on a pitch that seamed sideways in season 1986–87. Martin Crowe rated it as one of the best Test knocks he had witnessed first hand.

Greenidge's average dipped just below 45 when he finished his Test career just shy of his 40th birthday in 1991, although his penultimate Test was memorable as he scored a Test-best 226 to set up a series-clinching 343-run win against Australia. In Greenidge's last Test, coincidentally, he and Haynes were lbw to Craig McDermott in the first innings, before both openers were run out in the second innings.

Haynes had a more methodical approach than Greenidge did, although Haynes could be aggressive, particularly in one-day matches. He scored 148 in his one-day international debut in early 1978, and for a while he was the leading runscorer and century-maker in one-day internationals.

Haynes had a sound start to Test cricket as the West Indies had an innings win and a 10-wicket win in successive matches against Australia in March 1978. Haynes' scores were 61, 66 and 55 as he opened with Greenidge and had partnerships of 87, 16 and 131. Haynes scored his first Test century in early 1980 as the West Indies suffered a surprising 1-wicket loss to New Zealand in Dunedin. Haynes made painstaking, but invaluable, scores of 55 and 105 as the West Indies struggled to 140 and 212, and he was last out in both innings. Haynes' next century was in the following Test, but New Zealand won the series as the second and third Tests were drawn.

Haynes made his highest Test score of 184 during a draw at Lord's in mid-1980. In the previous Test, Haynes scored 62 in more than five hours to help the West Indies to a 2-wicket victory, as the target was 208. Haynes also scored three Test centuries in 1984, although his only Test century from 1981 to 1983 was in 1983, when he made 136 while Greenidge made 154 retired against India at St John's. A few Tests beforehand, Haynes and Greenidge were dismissed without a run on the board. When India hosted the West Indies the following season, Haynes became the fourth player to be given out for handling the ball in Test cricket.

One particularly gutsy knock from Haynes was in a draw at Karachi in late 1986, as he carried his bat for 88 runs in a 211-run total. A year later, a gritty 45 from Haynes helped the West Indies from 27–6 to 127 all out in reply to India's dismal 75 at Delhi. One of Haynes' enterprising Test knocks was against India at Bridgetown in 1989, as his undefeated 112 from 128 balls helped the hosts cruise to their 196-run target after the early loss of Greenidge.

Haynes' captaincy reign was brief, but his delaying tactics at Port-of-Spain were palpable as the West Indies were in danger of falling behind 2–0 in the 1990 series against England. A century from Haynes was decisive in the following Test as the West Indies levelled the series, before he scored 167 and Greenidge 149 in the final Test, which the hosts won by an innings following their 298-run opening stand.

Haynes had a few sub-standard tours of Australia, although he averaged more than 50 in the Test series Down Under in 1988–89 and in the follow-up series against Australia in the Caribbean in 1991. In a rare West Indian defeat against Australia in 1988–89, Haynes made 75 and 143 as he showed his improvement against spin. In the fourth Test of 1990–91, Haynes had a fiery altercation with Ian Healy after Haynes survived an appeal for caught behind. Also in 1991, as the West Indies surrendered a 2–1 series lead against England, Haynes carried his bat at Headingley as he made 75 in a 176-run total.

Amidst a disappointing tour of Australia in 1992–93, Haynes was perhaps an unsung hero as he made a great stop at short leg just before the West Indies claimed the first 1-run victory in Test cricket. Haynes returned to form as the West Indies beat Pakistan 2–0 in 1993, scoring two centuries amidst tallying 402 runs at 134 from six knocks. He carried his bat for the third time in Test cricket when he made an unbeaten 143 in a 382-run total, which set up a big West Indian victory in the opening Test at Port-of-Spain. Haynes' last series was against England in the Caribbean in 1994, with the West Indies winning 3–1, as Haynes contributed a modest 217 runs at 36.17. The West Indies Board prevented Haynes from playing in the 1994–95 Frank Worrell Trophy, which Australia won to start a lengthy period of domination in Test cricket. Haynes was ruled ineligible as there was 'a crackdown on players who did not make themselves available for the domestic season. It was a costly stipulation, and created tension in the Caribbean'. (Allan Miller 1994–95, *Allan's Australian Cricket Annual*)

Gordon Greenidge (b.1951)

Matches: 108
Runs scored: 7558
Batting average: 44.72
100s/50s: 19/34
Top score: 226
Balls bowled: 26
Wickets: –
Bowling average: –
5 wickets in innings: –
10 wickets in match: –
Best bowling: –
Catches/stumpings: 96/–

Desmond Haynes (b.1956)

Matches: 116
Runs scored: 7487
Batting average: 42.29
100s/50s: 18/39
Top score: 184
Balls bowled: 18
Wickets: 1
Bowling average: 8.00
5 wickets in innings: –
10 wickets in match: –
Best bowling: 1–2
Catches/stumpings: 65/–

George Headley

George Headley was the first great West Indian batsman and a pioneer for cricket in the Caribbean...he did a great deal to put West Indies cricket on the map and accelerate the process of black players being treated more fairly.

So wrote David Gower in 2015, many years after Headley had been dubbed the 'Black Bradman'. Headley's final Test was 24 years after his debut, yet he played only 22 Tests and joined a small list of players with an average of 60 or more. Headley had several strong attributes as he was a strong onside player as well as a fine back foot player, and often played the ball late.

Headley was among several debutants as a Test series was staged in the Caribbean for the first time in early 1930, with England the touring team. Headley made 21 and 176 on debut, before his double of 114 and 112 in the third Test was a pivotal factor in the West Indians achieving their maiden Test victory. The series remained deadlocked as Headley's 223 in the fourth and final Test took his series aggregate to 703 runs at 87.88.

Usually a number three batsman, Headley wasn't in a lot of strong West Indian teams. During Headley's sole series in Australia in 1930–31, the West Indies lost the first four Tests heavily. Headley was out to the first ball he faced in a Test on Australian soil, and his onside strokeplay hadn't developed at this stage as Clarrie Grimmett fired the ball at his leg stump and dismissed him twice in the first Test. After tallying just 27 runs in the first two Tests, Headley top-scored for the West Indies in three consecutive innings as his scores were 102 not out, 28 and 33. Bert Ironmonger dismissed Headley three times in succession before Headley's scores of 105 and 30 were in a winning cause on a rain-affected Sydney pitch in the fifth Test.

The West Indians suffered two innings losses in a three-Test series in England in 1933, although Headley's 169 not out helped draw the second Test. The next time the West Indies contested England, in early 1935, Headley enjoyed being in the first West Indies team to win a series. He made the match top score of 44 in a low-scoring first Test, which England won on a dangerous Bridgetown pitch, before scoring 25 and 93 in a series-levelling victory. Headley was the cornerstone of the West Indies winning the final Test at Kingston, as he made his best Test score of 270 not out, before his next Test experience was in England, where the hosts won 1–0 in 1939. Headley became the first batsman to score two tons in a Lord's Test, but his knocks of 106 and 107 couldn't prevent England from winning the first Test at Lord's by 8 wickets.

Having represented Jamaica and played professional English club cricket at various stages of his career, Headley played just three Tests following World War II. He became the first black player to captain the West Indies in Test cricket, but this was only for one Test. He scored 29 and 7 not out, but injured his back when fielding in the drawn first Test against England at Bridgetown in 1948. Headley contested India once in 1948–49, and when 44 years old he played his last Test against England, scoring 16 and 1. He played just one more first-class match, and finished his first-class career with a stellar average of 69.87.

George Headley (1909–1983)

Matches: 22
Runs scored: 2190
Batting average: 60.83
100s/50s: 10/5
Top score: 270*
Balls bowled: 398
Wickets: –
Bowling average: –
5 wickets in innings: –
10 wickets in match: –
Best bowling: –
Catches/stumpings: 14/–

Michael Holding

Known as 'Whispering Death', Michael Holding was poetry in motion as he had a long and graceful run-up, while many an umpire could not hear him as he approached the bowling crease. In *The Illustrated Encyclopedia of World Cricket*, Peter Arnold reported that watching Holding in his run-up could be one of the most infuriating or beautiful sights, as Holding approached the wicket 'with a feline lissomness that makes him appear to be barely touching the ground'.

To any batsman, facing Holding was frightening as he released the ball at devastating pace, and could swing it as well as generate sharp bounce. Tony Greig rated Holding as the fastest bowler he ever faced, and Imran Khan suggested Holding could bowl faster than Jeff Thomson.

Holding did not have an impressive start to Test cricket, as he and Andy Roberts shared the new ball during the West Indian tour of Australia in 1975–76. Roberts spearheaded one West Indian victory before Lillee and Thomson set up a comprehensive series win for the hosts. Holding took only 10 wickets at 61.40, before he showed on the subsequent Indian tour just how destructive he could be. He claimed

6–65 in India's first innings at Port-of-Spain, only for the tourists to come back and win by 6 wickets when chasing 403. During the final Test, which the hosts won by 10 wickets to clinch the series, several Indian batsmen were injured, as Holding's brutal bowling was one of the factors.

England's batsmen also struggled to cope with Holding in 1976 as he captured 28 wickets at 12.71 in four Tests. England openers Brian Close and John Edrich were subjected to plenty of intimidating short-pitched bowling at Old Trafford, before Holding snared 8–92 and 6–57 on a featherbed pitch at the Oval. Five of his victims were bowled and three were lbw in England's first innings before three were bowled and one lbw in the second innings.

Having taken 53 wickets in 11 Tests in 1976, Holding next played Test cricket in New Zealand nearly four years later following his involvement in World Series Cricket. Holding earned notoriety in the first Test of that series when he kicked the stumps down after an appeal was rejected, but it wasn't the only example of unsavoury conduct from the tourists who were upset with the umpiring. Holding took 20 wickets but averaged more than 30 when England hosted the West Indies in 1980.

Holding had fire in his belly for much of the return series in the Caribbean. He not only had fine figures of 17 wickets at 18.53 from four Tests, but also produced some ferocious bowling to Ian Botham and Geoff Boycott. *The Illustrated Encyclopedia of World Cricket* reported: 'One over bowled to Botham was described by Botham as the over he wanted to forget. Dropped, nearly killed, then caught behind from the one he did not see, Botham described it as one of the best overs he ever faced.' As for Holding's over to Boycott at Bridgetown, in *The 100 Greatest Cricketers* Geoff Armstrong reported: 'The pitch was hard and covered in grass, but quickly poor Boycott was jumping about as if it was on fire.' Boycott played and missed, and also prodded some brutal deliveries that reared nastily, before the sixth ball of the over sent a stump cartwheeling.

As the West Indies drew Australia in 1981–82, Holding picked up 24 wickets at 14.33 in the three Tests. He was disappointing on home soil against India in 1982–83 as he took just 12 scalps at 41.83, but in India the next season he excelled with 30 victims at 22.10. In the Ahmedabad Test, Holding made a crucial 58 at number nine to help the West Indies set a target of 242, which was well beyond India's reach as Holding snared 4–30. Although averaging less than 14 with the bat, Holding scored six Test half-centuries and struck 36 sixes on his way to notching 910 runs.

Holding had good figures in the mid-1980s as the West Indies contested England, Australia and New Zealand, with 'Whispering Death' experimenting with a shorter run-up and not always opening the bowling anymore. His Test career wound up on a somewhat unusual, as well as unsuccessful, note in early 1987, as he played in the first Test of a three-match series against New Zealand. Holding scored a duck and bowled 37 wicketless overs before succumbing to injury. Imran Khan considered that as Holding was so naturally gifted, he may not have been as fit as he could have been and that this contributed to injuries.

Michael Holding (b.1954)

Matches: 60
Runs scored: 910
Batting average: 13.78
100s/50s: 0/6
Top score: 73
Balls bowled: 12,680
Wickets: 249
Bowling average: 23.68
5 wickets in innings: 13
10 wickets in match: 2
Best bowling: 8/92
Catches/stumpings: 22/–

Rohan Kanhai

Rohan Kanhai was an important figure in West Indian cricket for many years, although he has not often been mentioned alongside other West

Indians such as those in this list of great players. A wicketkeeper and opening batsman when he began his Test career against England in May 1957, Kanhai became a very reliable batsman at first drop. Kanhai struck the ball hard and was particularly strong at cutting and hooking the ball, with his hook shots often played in an unorthodox method.

Kanhai scored just 206 runs at 22.89 without a half-century in his maiden Test series, as he batted as high as number one and as low as number seven against England in 1957. Gerry Alexander took over as wicketkeeper, and Kanhai scored three half-centuries in his first 12 Tests, before his maiden Test century turned into his highest Test score: 256 at Calcutta at the start of 1959. Kanhai was run out for 99 in the next Test, and then in a tour of Pakistan he scored 217 in the third Test to help the West Indies salvage a 2–1 series loss. Kanhai averaged 50.30 in the 1960–61 Test series Down Under, with Adelaide the place where he excelled as he scored 117 and 115. In his other three series in Australia he averaged 46.20, 37.10 and 51.14, having not made a century in the 1968–69 series. Of the 14 series Kanhai took part in between 1958 and 1973, there were just three in which he failed to reach a triple-figure score. In England in 1963 he was twice dismissed within 10 runs of a century, and in the Oval Test he hammered 77 in just 88 minutes to help set up an 8-wicket victory to seal a 3–1 series win. Kanhai scored more than 400 runs in a series on seven occasions, with his highest series aggregate being 538 runs on the 1958–59 Indian tour.

Kanhai also performed strongly in a home series against India in 1961–62 as his scores were 24, 138, 89, 139, 20, 44 and 41 as the hosts won all five Tests. Another highlight for Kanhai against India was at Kingston in the first Test of 1970–71 as his undefeated 158 helped salvage a draw after the visitors enforced the follow-on.

Kanhai succeeded Garry Sobers as West Indian captain, and led the team in three series. A 2–0 defeat in Australia in 1972–73 was followed by a 2–0 win in England and a 1–1 drawn series against England in the Caribbean, as Kanhai and Sobers finished their Test careers. Kanhai began slowly in the series in England before scoring 157 in the third and final Test, and then he struggled at home as his highest score in seven innings was just 44. His international days weren't over, as his brief limited-overs career included an innings of 55 in the first ever World

Cup final, which the West Indies won. Kanhai also became the first national coach of the West Indies cricket team, and held the position from 1992 to 1995.

Rohan Kanhai (b.1935)

Matches: 79
Runs scored: 6227
Batting average: 47.53
100s/50s: 15/28
Top score: 256
Balls bowled: 183
Wickets: –
Bowling average: –
5 wickets in innings: –
10 wickets in match: –
Best bowling: –
Catches/stumpings: 50/–

Brian Lara

Setting world records became something of a habit for Brian Lara, after he captured the attention of the cricketing world with his maiden Test century, which produced 277 runs. When he had his eye in, Lara, also known as 'The Prince', was simply unstoppable. Flashy, flamboyant, dazzling, exhilarating and graceful were descriptions that could befit him at various stages, while his backlift remained higher than the norm.

It was remarkable to think that of Lara's first seven Test tons, his lowest score was 145. His 277 was against Australia at Sydney in January 1993, and his third Test ton produced 375 at St John's as he overtook Garry Sobers' then record score of 365 not out. Several weeks later, Lara compiled the highest individual score in first-class cricket as he amassed 501 not out for Warwickshire against Durham in county cricket. Lara scored 400 not out in a Test nearly a decade later, again against England at St John's, after Australia's Matthew Hayden had scored a then Test record 380 against Zimbabwe in 2003.

During an innings of 226 against Australia at Adelaide in late 2005, Lara became the highest runscorer in Test history before Sachin Tendulkar broke the record three years later. A lesser known Test record that Lara set was hitting 28 runs (4, 6, 6, 4, 4 and 4) from one over against South Africa at Johannesburg in 2003–04: the most number of runs hit off one over in Test cricket (although Australia's George Bailey equalled the record during an Ashes Test in late 2013).

But for all his batting feats, Lara also carried a reputation for being controversial and enigmatic. In 1995–96, Lara opted out of an Australian tour in protest after being fined for being absent for a few days without permission during the recent tour of England. With the West Indians losing their reputation as world-beaters in the second half of the 1990s, Lara had some lean periods with the bat. This included the 1996–97 series against Australia, as he recorded successive scores of 2, 1, 2, 2 and 9. This was not the only time that Glenn McGrath seemed to have the wood on him. Yet at the end of his career, McGrath was quoted as saying that Lara was the best batsman he had ever played against. Likewise, the highest ever Test wicket-taker, Muttiah Muralitharan, remarked that Lara was the most dangerous batsman he had encountered.

Lara tasted victory only 32 times in his 130 Tests for the West Indies, while there were 62 losses and he was also in a losing World XI team against Australia. The early years of Lara's career coincided with the last few years of West Indian dominance, before plenty of lean times followed. Sometimes when he failed, the West Indies failed, as it appeared easy to think his team relied on him too heavily. When Australia won the deciding Test of the 1995 Frank Worrell Trophy by an innings, Lara was desperately unlucky to be ruled lbw without scoring, after Steve Waugh scored 200.

Lara had plenty of critics, as he had a largely unproductive stint as captain, but he rose to the occasion against Australia in the Caribbean in 1999. After the hosts were humiliated in the first Test, he scored 213 in the second Test before scoring a wonderful 153 not out in the third Test to lift his team to a sensational 1-wicket win. Australia subsequently drew the series, and Lara battled fitness problems at times before returning to form with a vengeance in Sri Lanka in 2001–02. His scores were 178, 40, 74, 45, 221 and 130, but Sri Lanka won all three Tests. There were other times that Lara excelled in losing causes, including occasions against South Africa, when he scored 202, 196 and 176. He also scored 153 in a 2005 match that Pakistan won by 136 runs.

Lara had another stint as captain and, following a series loss to Australia in 2003, he led the West Indies to a 1–0 series win against Sri Lanka after scoring 209 in the drawn first Test. He notched a career-best 1344 Test runs in the 2003 calendar year, after his previous best was 1222 in 1995. Lara's quadruple century came amidst a period of England dominance against the West Indies in 2004, before a sponsorship deal prompted Lara to stand down from West Indian selection in 2005. He scored 196 upon returning, but lost the captaincy before gaining the honour for the third time in 2006 and finishing with ten wins, 26 losses and 11 draws as captain. Lara bowed out from the international stage in the 2007 World Cup.

Brian Lara (b.1969)

Matches: 131
Runs scored: 11,953
Batting average: 52.89
100s/50s: 34/48
Top score: 400*
Balls bowled: 60
Wickets: –
Bowling average: –
5 wickets in innings: –
10 wickets in match: –
Best bowling: –
Catches/stumpings: 164/–

Clive Lloyd

Clive Lloyd's figures reflect a solid rather than superb career, but his greatness extended far beyond statistics. Lloyd earned a reputation as one of the best Test captains, and perhaps his greatest achievement was the way he was somehow able to unite and bring together the people of various Caribbean islands. Teams under Lloyd's captaincy not only became cohesive, but also formidable, as the West Indies became the dominant force in world cricket for about 20 years. Lloyd's Test career began in December 1966 and ended just over 18 years later, while his time as captain lasted from 1974 until his last Test. The West Indies won 36 Tests, lost 12 and drew 26 under his captaincy, and Lloyd also led the West Indies to three World Cup deciders, with victory in 1975 and 1979.

Tall and solidly built, Lloyd was easily identifiable as he had a moustache, wore thick glasses and a white sun hat. A hard-hitting left-handed batsman who also occasionally bowled right-arm medium-pace, Lloyd used a hefty bat and was not necessarily elegant, but he could club the ball hard on both sides of the wicket. He was a fine fielder in the covers before moving into the slips cordon and taking plenty of catches.

Brought into the West Indies team for its three-Test tour of India in 1966–67, Lloyd scored 82 and 78 not out on debut to play a major role in a 6-wicket victory that paved the way for the visiting team's series win. His maiden Test century was in his fourth Test as he scored 118 in a draw against England at Port-of-Spain, and he scored another ton in his sixth Test, which was also drawn before England won the series. His next challenge was Down Under, and he scored 129 in the first Test which the West Indies won, but he was a bit patchy afterwards as the tourists went down 3–1. He had a lean run as he didn't score a century for 17 successive Tests, and when playing for the Rest of the World in December 1971 he injured his back while attempting a catch.

Lloyd played three Tests Down Under in 1972–73, and scored 178 in one of them, before scoring another ton when the West Indies beat England in England. After a sub-standard home series against England in 1973–74, Lloyd succeeded Rohan Kanhai as West Indian captain, although Lloyd had a modest batting average of 38.68 from 36 Tests. In his first match as Test skipper, Lloyd scored 30 and 163 in a 267-run win over India at Bangalore, and in the last match of the series he made his best Test score of 242 not out to lead his team to a 3–2 series win. Lloyd scored three tons and averaged in the 40s in season 1975–76, as the West Indies were thumped by Australia before beating India. Lloyd's form was mediocre when he led the West Indians on their successful 1976 tour of England, before he made a vital 157 in a drawn Test against Pakistan in 1976–77.

After playing in World Series Cricket, Lloyd scored a century and led the West Indies to a series victory in Australia in 1979–80, before he had a miserable tour of New Zealand when some of his players were guilty of deplorable behaviour in a shock series loss. Success soon returned, and in Lloyd's last 32 Tests he amassed 2342 runs at 61.63 while the West Indies repeatedly accounted for England, India and Australia. Lloyd scored four centuries during a run of 11 successive Tests against India, with his undefeated 161 at Calcutta helping set up an innings win and 3–0 series lead. The West Indies lost Lloyd's final Test in which he scored 33 and 72, but not before Lloyd's team secured a comfortable series victory Down Under.

Clive Lloyd (b.1944)

Matches: 110
Runs scored: 7515
Batting average: 46.67
100s/50s: 19/39
Top score: 242*
Balls bowled: 1716
Wickets: 10
Bowling average: 62.20
5 wickets in innings: –
10 wickets in match: –
Best bowling: 2–13
Catches/stumpings: 90/–

Malcolm Marshall

Although not nearly as tall as many other great West Indian fast bowlers in the 1970s, 1980s and 1990s, Malcolm Marshall often earned higher acclaim than his contemporaries such as Joel Garner, Michael Holding and Curtly Ambrose. Marshall's bowling average and strike rate indeed made fine reading. Marshall could swing the ball both ways and deliver a great leg-cutter, and get the ball to skid while also having a dangerous bouncer, which produced a couple of nasty injuries. He didn't hesitate to go around the wicket, and he was an intelligent and thinking bowler who could suss out a batsman's weakness and exploit it. But in spite of his reputation as a fearsome bowler, Marshall was well-liked all around the cricket world, and his death from colon cancer at the age of 41 in 1999 caused a lot of grief.

Following a quiet start to his Test career, which began in India in 1978–79, Marshall had sound figures of 15 wickets at 29.07 against England in 1980 before finding himself out of the Test line-up for a couple of years. But it became clear that he was a world-class bowler as he captured 54 wickets in 11 Tests in 1983, and 73 in 13 Tests the following year. Marshall took 21 scalps at 23.57 against India in the Caribbean in early 1983, and later that year he claimed 33 victims at 18.82 on Indian soil. Marshall's figures in the first Test at Kanpur were 4–19 and 4–47, after he made his highest Test score of 92. Marshall took 4–9 from eight overs in one spell, and knocked the bat out of Sunil Gavaskar's hands.

Marshall's courage could also not be faulted, as shown at Headingley in 1984 after he fractured his thumb when fielding. At number 11 in the touring team's first innings, Marshall had his lower left arm in plaster as he batted one-handed and lasted long enough to allow Larry Gomes to press on to a century. Despite his injury, Marshall bowled his team to victory with 7–53 as he swung the ball around. A fine series in Australia in 1984–85 included two 5-wicket hauls on a lifeless pitch in Adelaide, where Marshall bowled non-stop for two hours in oppressive heat. Marshall subsequently had a brilliant series against the Kiwis as he claimed 27 wickets at 18, including 11 wickets at Bridgetown, where he also scored 63.

Marshall was repeatedly prominent as the West Indies drew with Pakistan 1–1 in late 1986 and early 1988, and he missed the first Test loss on the latter occasion. In the final Test, which the West Indies won by 2 wickets, Marshall achieved 4–79 and 5–65 as well as scores of 48 and 15. An outstanding series in England in 1988 yielded 35 wickets at 12.66, with 10 wickets at Lord's followed by 9 at Old Trafford, where his best Test figures of 7–22 included 5 scalps in an hour. After tallying 60 wickets in ten Tests in 1988, Marshall produced another standout performance against India at Port-of-Spain in April 1989 as he captured 11 wickets in a 217-run victory that secured another series win.

Despite not taking a 5-wicket haul, Marshall captured 21 wickets at 20.81 as the West Indies downed Australia 2–1 in early 1991, before his farewell series was against England. His best figures were 4–33 in a drawn series, and he played in the 1992 World Cup as the West Indies began rebuilding following the retirements of Viv Richards, Gordon Greenidge and Jeff Dujon.

Malcolm Marshall (1958–1999)

Matches: 81
Runs scored: 1810
Batting average: 18.85
100s/50s: 0/10
Top score: 92
Balls bowled: 17,584
Wickets: 376
Bowling average: 20.94
5 wickets in innings: 22
10 wickets in match: 4
Best bowling: 7–22
Catches/stumpings: 25/–

(Sir) Viv Richards

With a batting average around 50 in 121 Tests, while being a part of many all-conquering West Indian victories, Isaac Vivian Alexander Richards had a lot of success from a personal and team perspective. Yet unlike other prolific batsmen, Richards was not elegant and graceful; rather he was bold, daring and aggressive, as there often seemed to be more than a hint of recklessness about his approach. As Ian Botham remarked in *Botham's Century*: 'Viv would strike fear into the heart of opposition bowlers just from his swagger to the wicket. He played shots all around the wicket, and would set out to dominate the bowling from the moment he reached the crease.' Imran Khan meanwhile commented in *All Round View* that Richards had 'gone out against fast bowlers like Lillee and Thomson, and has not just tried to stay there but has gone for them and knocked them about as though he was playing in a school match'.

In addition to many memorable Test knocks, 'Master Blaster' Richards made some big hundreds in one-day internationals, including an unbeaten 138 which set up the West Indies' 1979 World Cup final win against England. Martin Crowe's insights into that innings were just as applicable to many other innings from Richards in both forms of the game. As Crowe commented in *Out on a Limb*:

> His body language towards the bowlers was so arrogant and commanding; he was boss and everyone knew it. He could step onto the front foot and hit the ball in any direction, especially through mid-wicket, or he would swivel off the same foot and play a kind of front foot pull or hook, totally demoralising any bowler.

Such was Richards' confidence, perhaps arrogance, that he never wore a helmet. He loved to play the hook and pull shots, and was always ready to fight fire with fire when a bowler delivered a bouncer. Some of Richards' sixes were monstrous and, as Geoff Armstrong commented in *The 100 Greatest Cricketers*, Richards had a certain aura.

Richards scored only 4 and 3 in his Test debut on Indian soil in 1974–75, before hammering 20 fours and six sixes in a brutal 192 not out in the following encounter. He averaged 50.42 in that series, and then had two disappointing Tests against Pakistan before being in the West Indian team that lost 5–1 in Australia during 1975–76. Richards averaged 38.73 in that series and scored 30, 101, 50 and 98 in heavy losses as he opened with Roy Fredericks in the last two Tests. Richards had an exceptional 1976 as he accumulated 1710 Test runs in the calendar year while usually batting at first drop. In a 2–1 series win at home against India, Richards' scores were 142, 130, 20, 177, 23 and 64. In England, Richards missed the second Test due to illness but still racked up 829 runs at 118.43, including a knock of 232 in the first Test and 291 in the last Test.

Richards had a sub-standard series against Pakistan in 1976–77, scoring just 257 runs at 28.56 without a century, before he was a prominent scorer in World Series Cricket. When back in Test cricket in 1979–80, he helped the West Indies win 2–0 on Australian soil as his scores were 140, 96, 76 and 74.

Against England and Pakistan from 1980 to 1981, Richards averaged between 60 and 85 in each series before having a disappointing tour of Australia in 1981–82. In several consecutive series from 1982–83, Richards scored one century and had good rather than great results, although there were some memorable onslaughts. In the first Test against India at Kingston in early 1983, Richards bludgeoned five fours and four sixes in his 61 from 36 balls to help the West Indies to a 4-wicket win, chasing 172. Against England at St John's in the final Test of 1985–86, as the hosts headed towards a series whitewash, Richards hammered seven fours and seven sixes in an unbeaten 110 from only 58 balls. He reached his ton from a then-record 56 deliveries.

Richards averaged a somewhat modest 41.43 in his last 39 Tests, after averaging 54.56 in his first 82 Tests, but his value to the team could not be underestimated, particularly against Pakistan in 1988. Richards missed the first Test, as did Malcolm Marshall, and Pakistan won it comfortably, before Richards made 49 and 123 in the drawn second Test, and then 67 and 39 in the third Test, which the West Indies won narrowly to draw the series.

Richards was also a fine slips fielder and part-time off spinner. He first skippered the West Indies when Clive Lloyd missed the last Test of the 1980 series against England. From 1985 until 1991, Richards led the West Indies in 50 Tests for a record of 27 wins and eight losses while, remarkably, never losing a series. He never hesitated to make life hard for opponents as he had many lethal fast bowlers at his disposal. Richards' final Test series was tough and controversial, as the 39-year-old led the West Indies to a 2–1 win against Australia in the Caribbean. Richards managed only 174 runs at 24.86, having been dismissed for 0 and 2 in his final Test which Australia won.

Viv Richards (b.1952)

Matches: 121
Runs scored: 8540
Batting average: 50.23
100s/50s: 24/45
Top score: 291
Balls bowled: 5170
Wickets: 32
Bowling average: 61.37
5 wickets in innings: –
10 wickets in match: –
Best bowling: 2–17
Catches/stumpings: 122/–

(Sir) Garfield Sobers

Having held the record for highest individual Test score and been the first player to notch 8000 Test runs, Garry Sobers excelled in every facet of the game and did everything possible to be considered the greatest cricketer of all time. He also became the first player to hit six sixes in an over in first-class cricket when he played for Nottinghamshire against Glamorgan at Swansea in English county cricket during 1968.

To say that Sobers was worth two players would not do him justice. Sobers remarked in his autobiography that for most of his international career he played for himself and for his closest friend Collie Smith.

Aged just 26, Smith died tragically after being in a car that Sobers drove when it crashed into a ten-ton cattle truck near Stone in Staffordshire at about 4.45 one morning in September 1959. Smith had looked promising in his 26 Tests as he scored 1331 runs at 31.69 and captured 48 wickets at 33.85, before his premature death temporarily left Sobers devastated and depressed. As Sobers remarked in the prologue of *Garry Sobers: My Autobiography*: 'If I was going to be a West Indian cricketer, I had to find a way to do his job and mine. It was Garfield Sobers and Collie Smith playing as one.'

A left-handed all-rounder, Sobers was versatile as he could be effective at a range of styles with bat and ball. He could attack or defend when batting and display power and elegance as he liked to go for his strokes. He batted anywhere from number two to number nine during his Test career, with five or six his usual position. He could bowl fast, medium or a mix of orthodox and unorthodox spin. Sobers' bowling average was a little on the expensive side but he wasn't used as a stock bowler for a while, and then after the retirement of Wes Hall and Charlie Griffith, Sobers bowled a lot of long spells, which might not have been preferable for him. Always keen to be in the game in some capacity, Sobers also took a lot of great catches and was equally adept at fielding close to the bat or in the outfield.

In his Test debut against England in 1953–54, a 17-year-old Sobers scored 14 not out and 26 at number nine, and snared 4–75 and 0–6 before England won by 9 wickets to draw the series. Having been promoted in the batting order, Sobers entered the 1957–58 series against Pakistan with 672 runs at 30.55 and 17 wickets at 41.06 from 14 Tests, with a highest score of 66 and best bowling figures of 4–75. Sobers claimed just 4 wickets at 94.25 in a winning series against Pakistan in 1957–58, but his batting was among the best ever seen in Test cricket, as he was usually at first drop. In the first two Tests the 21-year-old continued his then habit of making decent starts, as he twice made 52 before scoring 80, and then he finally reached three figures in his 17th Test. Amazingly, his maiden Test ton amounted to a score of 365 not out, which stood as the highest in Test cricket until 1994. Following his triple-century at Kingston, Sobers scored 125 and 109 in the next Test at Georgetown before his following series, in India, brought him another three tons to give him the unique feat of six centuries in as many Tests. He was run out for 198 on one occasion.

In Pakistan in 1958–59, Sobers was controversially ruled lbw three times as he averaged just 32 with the bat and failed to capture a wicket. Then came the Collie Smith tragedy, followed by Sobers contesting England in the Caribbean in Test cricket for the first time. His first innings in that series produced 226 at Bridgetown, before he finished the series with 709 runs at 101.29, but the tourists won the series 1–0. Sobers averaged 43 despite inconsistency with the bat during the famous tour Down Under in 1960–61, with two centuries including a sparkling 132 in the tied Test. Statistically, his best series as an all-rounder was against India in 1961–62 as he scored 424 runs at 70.67 and took 23 wickets at 20.57. In the final Test of that series he notched a ton and claimed 5 wickets in an innings. He achieved this feat twice in his career, with the second occasion coming against England at Headingley in 1966. In that 1966 series in England, Sobers claimed 20 wickets and ten catches as well as amassing 722 runs at 103.14. His scores included 174, 163 not out and 161 before he fell for a first-ball duck in the second innings of the final Test. The fifth and final time that Sobers scored three tons in a five-Test series was in 1970–71 when he averaged 74.63 against India. Against New Zealand in 1971–72, Sobers overtook Colin Cowdrey as Test cricket's leading run scorer, before injury forced the West Indian great to miss the 1972–73 series against Australia.

When he skippered the West Indies for the first time in 1964–65, Sobers became the first player to complete the double of 4000 runs and 100 wickets in Test cricket. For good measure, the West Indies went on to win the Frank Worrell Trophy. Captain of the West Indies for 39 successive Tests, Sobers led the team from the Caribbean to nine victories and ten defeats. Despite widespread criticism for his declaration against England at Port-of-Spain in 1968, Sobers could not be faulted for trying to make cricket entertaining. He also led a Rest of the World team in England and Australia in 1970 and 1971–72 respectively, with the highlight his 254 against Australia at Melbourne. Sobers was no longer West Indian skipper in his last two

Test series, which were against England in 1973 and 1973–74. He averaged 76.50 as the West Indies won 2–0 in England before the series in the Caribbean was drawn as he was disappointing with scores of 23, 57, 0, 0 and 20.

Garfield Sobers (b.1936)

Matches: 93
Runs scored: 8032
Batting average: 57.78
100s/50s: 26/30
Top score: 365*
Balls bowled: 21,599
Wickets: 235
Bowling average: 34.03
5 wickets in innings: 6
10 wickets in match: –
Best bowling: 6–73
Catches/stumpings: 109/–

(Sir) Clyde Walcott

Known as one of the 'Three Ws' along with Frank Worrell and Everton Weekes, Clyde Walcott had a career path which resembled that of Weekes in some ways. Walcott and Weekes made their Test debut at the same time and, of the 11 Test series that Walcott played in, Weekes played in ten of them.

Whilst having a batting technique that wasn't quite as orthodox as that of Worrell and Weekes, Walcott hit the ball hard as his drives and cross-batted shots raced off the bat. Walcott opened the batting and kept wickets in his Test debut, before being shuffled around in the batting order, and later relinquishing the wicketkeeping role. He averaged only 22.17 in his maiden Test series, against England in 1947–48, before having favourable results that were not quite as strong as those of Weekes in the next two series. In the first West Indies versus

India encounter, Walcott was run out for 152 before his following scores were 68, 54, 108, 43, 11 and 16. Walcott's only score of note against England in 1950 was 168 not out in the second Test, before he and several teammates struggled Down Under in 1951–52. Following his only series in Australia, Walcott was in excellent form for a few years as he accumulated 2272 runs at 78.34 in 18 Tests. Against India in 1952–53, he scored two tons and a 98 as he averaged 76.17 before he averaged 87.25 against England in 1953–54. In this drawn series Walcott tallied 698 runs after reaching triple-figures three times, before his most prolific series was against Australia in 1954–55. Although the West Indies lost 3–0 at home, Walcott compiled 827 runs at 82.70 and posted five centuries, while also becoming the first player to record two centuries in a Test on more than one occasion in the same series. Unfortunately for Walcott, his double of 155 and 110 in the final Test could not prevent an innings defeat.

Injuries and a loss of form plagued Walcott in England in 1957, before he scored 385 runs at 96.25 against Pakistan in 1957–58. He played just two more Tests, with scores of 9, 53 and 22 against England in 1959–60.

Clyde Walcott (1926–2006)

Matches: 44
Runs scored: 3798
Batting average: 56.68
100s/50s: 15/14
Top score: 220
Balls bowled: 1194
Wickets: 11
Bowling average: 37.09
5 wickets in innings: –
10 wickets in match: –
Best bowling: 3–50
Catches/stumpings: 53/11

Courtney Walsh

It is rare for Courtney Walsh to be mentioned in the same breath as other West Indian fast bowling greats such as Marshall, Garner, Holding and Ambrose. It is debatable as to whether or not Walsh was as lethal as his contemporaries, but stamina and longevity were two ways in which Walsh exceeded other West Indian pacemen. These qualities enabled Walsh to become the first player to take 500 Test wickets. Walsh bowled more than 85,000 deliveries in first-class cricket as he captured 1807 wickets, and in Tests he bowled 30,019 deliveries. His average and strike rate made good reading in a Test career that lasted from 1984 to 2001. It was also amazing to think Walsh had taken fewer than 200 Test wickets when he turned 30 in late 1992.

Admittedly when Walsh made his Test debut against Australia, he was the second change bowler, as Marshall and Garner opened before Holding came on as first change. Walsh wasn't even needed as the hosts crumbled for 76, before he took 2–43 in the second innings as the tourists romped to an innings victory, which set the tone for a 3–1 series win in which Walsh claimed 13 wickets at 33.23. For several years Walsh often bowled into the wind while Ambrose and Marshall were at the other end, and it wasn't until the 1990s that Walsh opened the bowling.

In the West Indies' 1985–86 home series against England, Walsh played only one Test as Holding, Marshall, Garner and Patrick Patterson were above him in the pecking order. Amidst some changes to the West Indian attack in the next few years, Walsh did well in some series that were drawn. He took 11 wickets at 17.73 in Pakistan in late 1986, with 3–56 and 4–21 in an innings win at Lahore. In New Zealand a few months later, Walsh's 13 wickets at 23.54 included 5–73 in the touring team's victory at Auckland. In India during 1987–88, Walsh took two 5-wicket hauls amidst a series haul of 26 scalps at 16.81. He averaged a somewhat expensive 34.33 in a convincing series victory in England, before his 17 wickets at 29.41 Down Under in 1988–89 included a hat-trick across two innings in the Brisbane Test.

The first time Walsh claimed 10 wickets in a Test was in April–May 1989 as he claimed 6–62 and 4–39 at Kingston, where the hosts wrapped up a 3–0 series victory against India. Walsh, Marshall, Ambrose and Patterson shared the wickets as the West Indies beat Australia 2–1 in early 1991 before Marshall retired from Test cricket later that year. On a memorable final day of the inaugural West Indies versus South Africa Test at Bridgetown in 1992, Walsh and Ambrose took 4 wickets each as the hosts stole a 52-run triumph.

Ian Bishop shared the new ball with Ambrose when the West Indies toured Australia in 1992–93, while Walsh took just 12 scalps at 38.92. Walsh claimed the final wicket, albeit controversially, in the Adelaide Test which the tourists won by a single run to square the series, before winning the rubber. West Indian cricket commentator Tony Cozier considered that every over Walsh bowled looked like it would be his last. Bishop's career meanwhile was plagued by back problems and, in the final Test of the 1992–93 series against Pakistan, Walsh shared the new ball with Ambrose. This began a splendid combination, with the duo sharing 421 wickets in 49 Tests. At Port-of-Spain in 1994, they needed just 19.1 overs to dismiss England for 46 when the tourists chased 194.

Walsh became West Indian captain in 1994 as Richie Richardson was rested, with Walsh's captaincy debut featuring Brian Lara's 375 in a draw with England. Walsh subsequently led the West Indies to a 1–1 draw in India and a 1–0 victory in New Zealand, with Walsh taking his best Test figures of 7–37 and following up with 6–18 in a massacre at Wellington. Richardson regained the captaincy while Walsh was the leading wicket-taker in the 1995 series when Australia beat the West Indies in a Test series for the first time since the 1970s. From then on the West Indians were not such a strong force, although Walsh was still dependable. In Pakistan's 3–0 clean sweep at home in late 1997, Walsh's figures were 5–78, 5–143, 4–74 and 0–11.

Having captured 62 Test wickets in 1995, Walsh was even better in 2000 as he captured 66 despite turning 38 that year. In March 2000 he overtook Kapil Dev as Test cricket's leading wicket-taker, and later that year his 34 wickets against England came at a cost of just 12.82 each as England won 3–1. Walsh managed just 11 wickets at 43.73 as the West Indies lost 5–0 in Australia in 2000–01, before his final Test series was at home against South Africa. Walsh was the leading wicket-taker with

25 scalps and had the satisfaction of winning his final Test, although the Africans took the series 2–1.

Walsh's batting was frequently mocked, and he registered 43 Test ducks. However he scored eight first-class half-centuries, and in at least a couple of Tests he featured in a decisive lower-order partnership. One particular occasion was in a deciding Test against Pakistan at St John's in 2000, when he made four not out off 24 balls in 72 minutes, as a last-wicket stand of 19 took the hosts to victory.

Courtney Walsh (b.1962)

Matches: 132
Runs scored: 936
Batting average: 7.54
100s/50s: 0/0
Top score: 30*
Balls bowled: 30,019
Wickets: 519
Bowling average: 24.44
5 wickets in innings: 22
10 wickets in match: 3
Best bowling: 7–37
Catches/stumpings: 29/–

(Sir) Everton Weekes

Having his batting style compared to that of Don Bradman was merely one of many things that gave Everton Weekes a strong reputation. It was also interesting to note that it took Weekes 12 innings to reach 1000 Test runs after it took Bradman 13 innings to reach the same milestone. Although Bradman's average was more than 40 runs higher than that of Weekes when the West Indian called time on his Test career, Weekes' career was very impressive, as he had only a couple of brief troughs after a patchy start. A great fielder in the covers or slips, Weekes was also the first West Indian to attain 3000 and 4000 Test runs.

One of seven West Indians to make his Test debut in the opening encounter with England at Bridgetown in 1947–48, Weekes had a frustrating time as his first five scores were 35, 25, 36, 20 and 36 while being moved around in the batting order. Then came two vicissitudes that changed his career decisively. He was dropped for the fourth Test but then gained a reprieve when an injured George Headley withdrew. Weekes gave a chance before he had scored, but he made the most of his second chance as he notched 141.

Weekes' form was phenomenal in the inaugural West Indies versus India series, as his scores were 128, 194, 162, 101, 90, 56 and 48, with his 101 the only occasion he scored a Test ton in the second innings as he achieved the feat of two centuries in a Test. He could have scored six successive Test tons had he not been run out when 10 runs shy of triple-figures at Madras, and his career average reached 88 at one stage. Averaging 56.33 in England in 1950 seemed modest by comparison, and in this series his lone century was overshadowed by Frank Worrell's 261 as the tourists took the series lead.

Weekes' Test average dropped from 74.21 to 53.59 after poor returns in Australia and New Zealand in 1951–52, before he returned to his brilliant ways in a home series against India in 1952–53 as he averaged 102.29. He made his highest Test score of 207 in the first Test at Port-of-Spain, and scored a further two tons in the series. Against England in 1953–54, Weekes fell one run shy of his highest Test score and also made a couple of 90s as he averaged 69.57. His figures of 469 runs at 58.63 in a home series against Australia in 1954–55 were boosted by successive scores of 139, 87 not out and 81 as the hosts were generally outplayed. In a 3–1 series win in New Zealand in 1955–56, Weekes produced consecutive scores of 123, 103 and 156 in massive wins before scoring 5 and 31 in a shock loss.

Weekes didn't have a happy time in the 1957 tour of England as sinus issues and a finger injury plagued him. He scored 90 in one Test, but a pair of ducks in the final Test left him with miserable series figures of 195 runs at 19.50. Weekes played only one more series and, with other batsmen including Garry Sobers and Walcott making runs in the first ever West Indies versus Pakistan series, Weekes did not miss out. He made 197 in the first Test before finishing the series with 455 runs at 65.

Everton Weekes (b.1925)

Matches: 48
Runs scored: 4455
Batting average: 58.61
100s/50s: 15/19
Top score: 207
Balls bowled: 122
Wickets: 1
Bowling average: 77.00
5 wickets in innings: −
10 wickets in match: −
Best bowling: 1−8
Catches/stumpings: 49/−

(Sir) Frank Worrell

Frank Worrell's Test career was somewhat inconsistent but, like Clive Lloyd if in a different way, Worrell had a great reputation because of his captaincy and influence. He was also 'courageous and cultured' as a batsman, in the words of David Gower. During the three series that Worrell was a Test captain, the West Indies appeared to be a more cohesive team than had been the case up until that point. Garry Sobers reported in his autobiography that Worrell was the best captain he played under:

> *He was able to motivate people and he knew the game. He was able to do things in such a diplomatic way that if you had enough sense you would understand what he was trying to put over. He was never harsh with anybody. He was flexible and would listen. One of his characteristics was that if he disagreed, he would not say so directly; instead he would often use phrases that were the opposite of what you were saying and you would eventually realise he was taking the mickey.*

Worrell's first seven Tests were against England, and in ten innings he amassed 833 runs at 104.13. At Port-of-Spain in February 1948 he made 97 and 28 not out on debut, having been caught behind with a century in sight. Worrell scored 131 not out in the next Test as the West Indies took the series lead, and he followed with five scores between 15 and 52 before compiling 261 and 138 in successive Tests as the West Indies romped to another series win.

As the West Indies were well beaten on Australian soil in 1950–51, Worrell scored a modest 337 runs at 33.70 while his bowling developed as he captured 17 wickets at 19.35. He took 6–38 in Australia's first innings at Adelaide where the tourists had their sole win of the series. In the following Test at Melbourne where Australia clinched the series with a tense 1-wicket win, Worrell scored a chancy 108 after copping a painful blow on the right hand. In a subsequent tour of New Zealand where the Kiwis and West Indians met for the first time in Test cricket, Worrell scored 71, 62 not out and 100 as the visitors won 1–0.

Worrell had a disappointing series against India in 1952–53 until he scored 237 and 23 in the final Test at Kingston as the hosts maintained a narrow series lead. Nine years passed before Worrell was in another winning Test series, as he missed West Indian series victories against New Zealand, Pakistan and India in 1955–56, 1957–58 and 1958–59 respectively. Undertaking an economics degree at Manchester University was one reason why Worrell played in only one Test series between 1955 and 1959–60. Worrell only had occasional success with the ball as he sometimes chipped in with some wickets with his left-arm seamers. Worrell had a sub-standard series against England in 1953–54, although his 167 in the drawn Test made his series figures look decent. Worrell averaged only 25.75 at home in a 3–0 loss to Australia in 1954–55, before averaging 38.89 in a 3–0 loss in England during 1957. In the drawn Test at Trent Bridge, Worrell carried his bat for 191 runs but it wasn't enough to prevent the tourists from having to follow on. In the next Test at Headingley, he achieved his best first-class bowling figures of 7–70 as the tourists sank to an innings defeat.

Worrell's ninth and final Test century was against England in 1959–60 as he again had one standout innings in an otherwise sub-standard series from a personal viewpoint. In the drawn first Test at Bridgetown,

Worrell scored 197 not out in 682 minutes and put on a fourth-wicket partnership of 399 with Sobers who scored 226 in 647 minutes. Worrell averaged only 24.60 in the remainder of the series before he was appointed captain of the West Indian team for its historic 1960–61 tour of Australia. Worrell scored 375 runs at 37.50 and took 10 wickets at 35.70 as the West Indies narrowly lost the rubber, following the Brisbane tied Test in which Worrell twice made 65. The tourists nonetheless produced an eye-catching brand of cricket which ensured Australian followers liked Worrell, and at tour's end the West Indians were treated to a ticker-tape parade.

Worrell's team went on to thrash India 5–0 in 1961–62, with Worrell scoring a duck before making 58, 77, 73 not out, 26 and 98 not out, with a century eluding him at Kingston as he ran out of partners. Worrell's Test average finished marginally below 50 after a knock of 74 not out was followed by a string of low scores in his final series, but he had the satisfaction of leading the West Indies to a 3–1 victory in England. Less than four years later, Worrell died of leukemia at the age of 42. His legacy was already assured, having been knighted in 1964, in addition to West Indies versus Australia Test series involving a trophy named after Worrell.

Frank Worrell (1924–1967)

Matches: 51
Runs scored: 3860
Batting average: 49.48
100s/50s: 9/22
Top score: 261
Balls bowled: 7141
Wickets: 69
Bowling average: 38.72
5 wickets in innings: 2
10 wickets in match: –
Best bowling: 7–70
Catches/stumpings: 43/–

CHAPTER 5: NEW ZEALAND

5.1 NEW ZEALAND v INDIA

India won its first three series against New Zealand, with the Indians on home soil in 1955–56 and 1964–65 before the Kiwis were at home in 1967–68.

1950s

Subhash Gupte was a prominent wicket-taker as India won the 1955–56 series 2–0. The first encounter was drawn, with Polly Umrigar (223), Vijay Manjrekar (118) and debutant AG Kripal Singh (100 not out) standing out for India before John Guy and Bert Sutcliffe scored a ton each for New Zealand. Vinoo Mankad's 223 set up an innings win for India in the second Test. Sutcliffe (230 not out) and John Reid (119 not out) set up New Zealand's 450–2 declared in the third Test, before Manjrekar (177) helped India guarantee a draw. The tourists were on top for a while in the fourth Test, with Reid making another century before Gulabrai Ramchand (106 not out), Pankaj Roy (100) and Manjrekar (90) turned the game around. New Zealand ultimately struggled to save the match, finishing at 75–6 after being set 235. Mankad (231) and Roy (173) put on an opening stand of 413 in the final Test, with India declaring at 537–3 before winning by an innings.

1960s

The 1964–65 series was decided in the fourth and final Test following three draws. New Zealand's Bruce Taylor scored 105 on debut while Sutcliffe (151 not out) and India's Nawab of Pataudi (153) also shone in the second Test. Taylor's 5–26 helped demolish India for 88 in the third Test, after opener Graham Dowling scored 129 in New Zealand's 297. But the hosts worked their way to a 254-run lead following 200 not out from Dilip Sardesai, 109 from Chandu Borde and 75 not out from Hanumant Singh, and India nearly stole victory as New Zealand finished on 80–8. Srinivas Venkataraghavan spun the hosts to a 7-wicket win in the final Test, claiming 8–72 and 4–80 to dismiss the visitors for 262 and 272. India led by 203 runs on the first innings following tons to Nawab of Pataudi and Sardesai, and 80s to Borde and Singh.

All four Tests in New Zealand featured an outright result in the 1967–68 series, with the hosts squandering a dominant position in the first Test. The Kiwis were 200–1 before faltering to 281–8 and then 350 all out, with Dowling scoring 143. The visitors gained a 9-run lead before losing 5 wickets in chasing 200. Dowling (239) led the Kiwis to their first Test win against India, as New Zealand levelled the series at Christchurch, having scored 502 and enforced the follow-on, before winning by 6 wickets. India regained the lead with an 8-wicket win at Wellington, with Erapalli Prasanna and Bapu Nadkarni doing the damage with the ball, while Ajit Wadekar (143) was the best of India's batsmen. Prasanna was also responsible for New Zealand's batting troubles in the final Test, while Bishan Bedi chipped in as the Kiwis flopped for 140 and 101 to hand India a 272-run win to seal a comfortable 3–1 triumph.

The first Test of 1969–70 was moved from Ahmedabad to Bombay due to riots, with the hosts making just 156, before the tourists replied with 229, and later tallied only 127 when needing 188. Prasanna and

Bedi were again the main wicket-takers, before the Kiwis struck back with a 167-run victory at Nagpur. After taking 4–66 to secure a 62-run first-innings lead for New Zealand, Hedley Howarth snared 5–34 as India crumbled for 109 in the run chase. The Kiwis would surely have won the third Test and the series had poor weather not intervened. New Zealand slumped from 106–0 to 181 all out before India made a paltry 89 after being 49–9. The hosts finished their second innings at 76–7, nearly 200 runs shy of victory.

1970s

Eleven wickets to Prasanna and 8 to Bhagwath Chandrasekhar restricted the Kiwis to modest totals in the first Test of 1975–76, while Sunil Gavaskar (116) and Surinder Amarnath (124) put on a second-wicket stand of 204 in India's 414. Following their 8-wicket win at Auckland, the Indians drew the second Test at Christchurch after trailing by 133 runs on the first innings. The hosts forced another drawn series as they won the final Test at Wellington by an innings, with Richard Hadlee taking 4–35 and 7–23 to dismantle the tourists for 220 and 81.

The Kiwis found Bedi and Chandrasekhar too hard to handle on Indian turf in 1976–77, with the hosts winning the three-match series 2–0. Bedi and Chandrasekhar also scored some handy runs, including in the first Test, after Gavaskar made 119 in the 399-run total. John Parker made 104 but New Zealand slid from 220–2 to 298 all out, and later tumbled to 141 all out when seeking 304. The Kiwis were well beaten despite some dubious umpiring, before the eighth-wicket pair of Warren Lees and David O'Sullivan saved the second Test, as the tourists finished at 193–7 after being asked to score 383. Lance Cairns (5–55) had India reeling at 3–2 early in the third Test before the hosts reached 298, and ripped through New Zealand for 140. Needing 360 to level the series, the Kiwis were never a chance as India won by 216 runs.

1980s

New Zealand finally won a series against India as a 62-run victory to the hosts was followed by two draws in 1980–81. At Wellington, Kiwi skipper Geoff Howarth (137 not out) set up his team's 375, before 5–33 from Cairns contained India to 223. An Indian win became a real possibility as the Kiwis only just reached triple figures, before India totalled 190. Rain ruined the second Test, and then the hosts had the upper hand for most of the third Test. A ninth-wicket stand of 105 helped India reach 238 before a sluggish century from John Wright formed the foundation of New Zealand's 366. Requiring 157 in 66 overs, the Kiwis contended with some light rain before the match was called off with four overs to spare as the hosts were 95–5. Invading spectators seemed more annoyed with their team's slow progress instead of being happy with the breakthrough series win against India.

More than seven years passed before the next series was staged, with two big Indian wins spliced with a sizable New Zealand victory. Navjot Sidhu (116) helped India go from 10–2 to 384–9 declared in the first Test at Bangalore, before New Zealand's disappointing totals of 189 and 164 enabled India to win by 172 runs. A first-innings total of 236 was nothing for the tourists to get excited about in Bombay, before they gained a 2-run lead and went on to win by 136 runs. Hadlee claimed 6–49 and 4–39 while John Bracewell took 6–51 in India's second innings as the hosts tallied only 145. In the decider, the Kiwis reached 254 after being 91–6, before their second-innings capitulation for 124 set up an easy 10-wicket win for the Indians.

1990s

New Zealand returned the compliment with a 10-wicket win at Christchurch in the opening Test of 1989–90, with Wright (185) the mainstay in New Zealand's 459 before India was forced to follow on. The remaining two Tests were drawn, with half of the Napier Test rained off, before Kiwi wicketkeeper Ian Smith scored a memorable 173 at number nine in Auckland. New Zealand was 131–7 before the last 3 wickets added 260 runs, and India led by 91 following 192 from captain Mohammad Azharuddin. Wright resisted for a while, and then Andrew Jones (170 not out) and Martin Crowe (113) set up New Zealand's 483–5, before India's openers put on an unfinished stand of 149.

A one-off match in March 1994 also yielded a draw, with India leading by 59 runs on the first innings before concluding its second innings at 177–3 after being set 310. The next three series contained 1–0 results, with the first Test proving crucial in 1995–96 before the second Test was the key in the 1998–99 and 1999–00 series.

Sub-standard batting from New Zealand left India a 151-run target, which was accomplished for the loss of only 2 wickets at Bangalore in October 1995. Only 71.1 overs of play were possible in the second Test, before both sides batted once in the third Test, which yielded just 177.5 overs.

The first Test of 1998–99 was abandoned, before New Zealand won a fluctuating second Test by 4 wickets at Wellington. India was 16–4 before struggling to 208 as Azharuddin played a lone hand of 103 not out, while Simon Doull claimed 7–65. New Zealand lost its seventh wicket at 208 before Dion Nash (89 not out) and Daniel Vettori (57) set up a 144-run lead. Sachin Tendulkar made 113 before New Zealand, chasing 213, was 74–5 before Craig McMillan (74 not out) and Chris Cairns (61) set up a 4-wicket win. The Kiwis lost 2 wickets without a run after five deliveries in the third Test, before recovering to 366 and subsequently facing a 50-run deficit following 190 from Rahul Dravid and 76 from number nine Javagal Srinath. Cairns (126), Nash and Vettori helped set India a virtually impossible 415, with the tourists making 249–2 following an unbroken 194-run partnership involving Dravid (103 not out) and Sourav Ganguly (101 not out).

The first Test of 1999–00 fluctuated wildly, with India all out for 83, before making 505–3 declared following two centuries and three half-centuries. Set 374, the Kiwis finished at 251–7 from 135 overs before losing the second Test by 8 wickets, after their second-innings capitulation for 155 left India needing just 82. Tendulkar (217), Ganguly (125) and Ramesh (110) helped the Indians to 583–7 declared in the third Test, but they opted not to enforce the follow-on. A New Zealand victory never looked possible, although the Kiwis made a respectable 252–2 from 95 overs after being set 424.

2000s

India's batsmen failed badly in the 2002–03 series as New Zealand won by 10 wickets in three days at Wellington, before winning a bizarre match at Hamilton by 4 wickets. Indian totals of 161 and 121 left New Zealand needing just 36 runs to win in Wellington, before the tourists succumbed for 99 and 154 in Hamilton after the first day was washed out. The Kiwis meanwhile made just 94 in their first innings, before being uncertainly placed at 136–6 on their way to their 2–0 series victory.

The 2003–04 series was much different as oodles of runs were scored in two drawn Tests. Dravid (222), Ganguly (100 not out) and New Zealand's Nathan Astle (103) scored heavily during the first Test in which New Zealand finished 98 runs, and India 4 wickets, away from victory. In the second Test, the Kiwis declared at 630–6, following centuries from the top three (Mark Richardson, Lou Vincent and Scott Styris) and number six batsman (McMillan). There was little chance of a result after Indian opener Virender Sehwag and number five VVS Laxman scored tons in a reply of 424.

New Zealand twice made 279 in the first Test of 2008–09, and lost by 10 wickets after India's first innings contained 520 runs. Tons to Jesse Ryder and Vettori helped the Kiwis recover from 60–6 in the first innings, before Tendulkar (160) received strong support. Ryder (201), Ross Taylor (151) and Brendon McCullum (115) helped New Zealand go from 23–3 to 619–9 declared in the second Test, before India was forced to follow on but had little difficulty saving the Test as Gautam Gambhir and Laxman made tons. India gained a big lead in the third Test at Wellington before Gambhir (167) helped set a 617-run target to ensure that New Zealand could not level the series; finishing at 281–8.

The 2010–11 series also went 1–0 India's way, although this time the third Test decided the series. India had three centurions (Sehwag, Dravid and Harbhajan Singh) and New Zealand two (Kane Williamson and Ryder) in the first Test, before there were three centurions in the second Test. Kiwi opener Tim McIntosh scored 102 before Harbhajan's 111 not out helped India to a 122-run lead, followed by McCullum's 225 all but ensuring another draw. The final Test at Nagpur was heavily one-sided, as New Zealand spluttered to 193 and 175, while Dravid's 191 laid the foundation for India's 566–8 declared.

India also won the first Test of the 2012 series by an innings, with Cheteshwar Pujara's 159 setting up India's 438, before New Zealand scraped together just 159 and 164, as Ravi Ashwin bagged 12–85. The Indians had to work much harder to achieve a 2–0 series win as Taylor scored 113 in New Zealand's 365 before India was 80–4 in the second Test at Bangalore. The hosts needed a century from Virat Kohli and a couple of half-centuries to reduce the deficit to 12, as Tim Southee bagged 7–64. The Kiwis extended their lead to 260 and caused two brief collapses, as India stumbled to 166–5 before winning by 5 wickets.

The two-match series in 2013–14 was decided in the first Test at Auckland, as the hosts won a topsy-turvy contest by 40 runs. McCullum (224) and Williamson (113) helped New Zealand tally 503 after being 30–3, before India fell 301 runs in arrears and promptly skittled the Kiwis for 105, after New Zealand chose to bat again. Opener Shikhar Dhawan led the run chase with 115, and India was well-placed at 222–2 before stuttering under pressure and folding for 366. The Indians looked certain to level the series after gaining a 246-run lead in the second Test, only for McCullum to score 302 and BJ Watling 124 to guide the Kiwis to safety and preserve New Zealand's series lead.

New Zealand v India

1955–56 (I): India 2–0 (3 drawn)
1964–65 (I): India 1–0 (3 drawn)
1967–68 (NZ): India 3–1
1969–70 (I): 1–1 (1 drawn)
1975–76 (NZ): 1–1 (1 drawn)
1976–77 (I): India 2–0 (1 drawn)
1980–81 (NZ): New Zealand 1–0 (2 drawn)
1988–89 (I): India 2–1
1989–90 (NZ): New Zealand 1–0 (2 drawn)
1993–94 (NZ): 1 drawn

1995–96 (I): India 1–0 (2 drawn)
1998–99 (NZ): New Zealand 1–0 (1 draw, 1 abandoned)
1999–00 (I): India 1–0 (2 drawn)
2002–03 (NZ): New Zealand 2–0
2003–04 (I): 0–0 (2 drawn)
2008–09 (NZ): India 1–0 (2 drawn)
2010–11 (I): India 1–0 (2 drawn)
2012 (I): India 2–0
2013–14 (NZ): New Zealand 1–0 (1 drawn)

5.2 NEW ZEALAND v PAKISTAN

1950s

Playing on matting seemingly proved difficult for New Zealand in its first encounter with Pakistan. At Karachi in late 1955, the tourists succumbed for 164 and 124 at fewer than 1.25 runs per over to lose by an innings and 1 run, after Zulfiqar Ahmed had amazing match figures of 11–79 from 83.5 overs. New Zealand batted better on turf at Lahore, with Noel McGregor (111) and Noel Harford (93) helping the team progress from 76–4 to 348 all out. Pakistan, incredibly, went from 111–6 to 561 all out following a seventh-wicket partnership of 308, with Imtiaz Ahmed scoring 209 and Waqar Hasan 189 before the last three batsmen tallied 86 runs. Pakistan went on to win by 4 wickets, before having the better of a drawn Test at Dacca. The first three days were cancelled, and then Khan Mohammad's 6–21 helped skittle New Zealand for 70 on a wet matting surface. Hanif Mohammad scored 103 in Pakistan's 195–6 declared, and then the Kiwis crawled to 69–6 from 90 overs.

1960s

Three draws resulted on New Zealand soil in season 1964–65. Set 259 in the first Test, the tourists were 19–5 before struggling to 140–7 as Asif Iqbal made an unbeaten 52 after taking 5–48 in New Zealand's first innings as the hosts crashed from 261–4 to 266 all out. The Kiwis finished the second Test at 166–7 after being set 220, with Pervez Sajjad's 5–42 causing New Zealand to slide from 68–0 to 102–6. An unbeaten 100 from Hanif helped set the Kiwis 314 in the final Test, with New Zealand making 223–5.

It was only a matter of weeks before Pakistan hosted a follow-up series, with Pervez's 4–42 and 4–5 setting up an innings win for the hosts in the first Test at Rawalpindi. New Zealand was dismissed for 175 and 79, while Pakistan's 318 included a last-wicket stand of 65. It was Pakistan's first Test win for six years. Hanif made 203 not out in the drawn second Test, before Pakistan won the series 2–0 following an 8-wicket victory at Karachi. Kiwi captain John Reid made 128 out of 285, before the Pakistanis led by 22 runs following 172 from Saeed Ahmed, and later knocked off the required runs comfortably thanks to 126 from Mohammad Ilyas.

The opening Test of the 1969–70 series was drawn, with Pervez taking all 5 wickets in the final innings as the Kiwis recovered from 11–3 to reach 112–5 after being set 230. The second Test at Lahore featured New Zealand's first victory against Pakistan, which crumbled for 114 and 208, before the Kiwis lost 5 wickets in chasing 82. The hosts threatened to level the series in the final Test as the Kiwis were just 84 runs in front with 2 wickets remaining in their second innings. Mark Burgess (119 not out) and Bob Cunis helped the total to 200 to force a draw, which sealed New Zealand's series win.

1970s

The first and third Tests of the 1973 series were also drawn, although this time Pakistan won the second Test. Sadiq Mohammad's 166 was the highlight of the first Test, before the crucial encounter at Dunedin featured 201 from Mushtaq Mohammad and 175 from Asif Iqbal. They added 350 runs in a total of 507–6 declared, before Mushtaq claimed 7 wickets and Intikhab Alam 11, as New Zealand totalled only 156 and 185. Both sides made 402 in their first innings in the final Test, with Pakistan enjoying a last-wicket stand of 48, before New Zealand had a staggering last-wicket stand of 151, after collapsing from 159–0 to 251–9. Richard Collinge made 68 not out at number 11 before Brian Hastings was last out for 110, and Kiwi opener Rodney Redmond scored 107 and 56 in his only Test.

Pakistan won the first two Tests of 1976–77 by 6 wickets and 10 wickets after topping 400 and enforcing the follow on. Asif Iqbal (166) and Test debutant Javed Miandad (163) put on a 281-run partnership in the first Test at Lahore, before Kiwi Test debutant Peter Petherick took a hat-trick. The tourists lost their first 3 wickets for 1 run in the follow-on before Burgess (111) and several other contributors did enough to squeeze out a 100-run lead. Centuries to Sadiq and Mushtaq set up Pakistan's 473–8 declared in the second Test, before Pakistani opening bowler Sarfraz Nawaz hit a boundary when the victory target was a single run. In the third Test, Majid Khan became the first non-Australian to score a century before lunch on the first day. Javed (206), Majid (112) and Mushtaq (107) helped Pakistan pass 560, before Warren Lees (152), Richard Hadlee (87) and Lance Cairns (52 not out) helped the Kiwis go from 104–5 to 468 all out. New Zealand drew the match after being set 388.

Without some World Series players at the start of the 1978–79 series away from home, Pakistan won the first Test by 128 runs. Javed made 81 and 160 not out, and Mushtaq had match figures of 9–119 while 129 from Bruce Edgar gave New Zealand a small first-innings lead. Following a century to Asif and New Zealand's Geoff Howarth, the Kiwis also led on the first innings in the second Test, before the match was drawn after Majid scored an undefeated ton in Pakistan's unfinished second innings. Zaheer Abbas (135) helped Pakistan gain a 105-run lead in the third Test, but New Zealand batted long enough to rule out a Pakistani victory.

1980s

Back-to-back series were held in 1984–85, with the home side winning 2–0 each time. New Zealand struggled against the spin of Iqbal Qasim and medium pace of Mudassar Nazar in the first Test at Lahore, where Pakistan won by 6 wickets. A century to John Reid was followed by a ton to Javed in the second Test, with Steve Boock's 7–87 giving New Zealand a first-innings lead, before Pakistan's spinners restricted the Kiwis to 189. Needing 227, Pakistan was 14–2 before centuries to Mudassar and Javed guided the hosts to a 7-wicket victory. New Zealand led by 98 runs in the third Test before Salim Malik and Wasim Raja helped Pakistan salvage a draw, although Pakistan's second innings contained huge controversy, as the Kiwis disputed a ruling that favoured Javed.

In the first Test of the follow-up series, day five was washed out as the Kiwis led by 273 runs with 6 wickets in hand. After making 148 in the first Test, Reid made 158 not out in the second Test, which the

Kiwis won by an innings after Pakistan managed only 169 and 183. The third Test was a classic, as the pendulum swung many times. Pakistan plunged from 241–2 to 274 all out before gaining a 54-run lead, and then enjoying an invaluable 42-run last-wicket stand to boost New Zealand's requirement to 278. The Kiwis were 23–4 before Martin Crowe (84) dominated in a 157-run partnership. Lance Cairns retired hurt as the hosts slumped to 228–8, before Jeremy Coney (111 not out) found support from number 11 Ewen Chatfield (21 not out in 104 minutes) to take New Zealand to a nerve-wracking 2-wicket triumph.

The 1988–89 series in New Zealand was drawn, with the first Test washed out before Crowe and Pakistani duo Shoaib Mohammad and Javed scored centuries in the second Test. Javed (271) and Shoaib (112) were chiefly responsible for a total of 616–5 in the third Test, before the Kiwis easily saved the match after following on.

1990s

On home soil, Pakistan achieved a clean sweep in 1990–91 as Waqar Younis was particularly prominent while fellow pacemen Wasim Akram, Aaqib Javed and Salim Jaffer also played their part. Although the Pakistanis played the better cricket, there was controversy regarding ball tampering. Shoaib made 203 not out in the first Test as the hosts won by an innings after the visitors twice failed to reach 200. Shoaib (105) helped Pakistan to a 213-run lead in the second Test despite 6–78 from Willie Watson, and then an undefeated 108 from Crowe could not prevent Pakistan winning by 9 wickets. New Zealand gained a 115-run lead in the third Test after Pakistan folded for 102, only for Shoaib (142) to foil New Zealand again. The Kiwis lost by 65 runs after being set 243, with some dodgy umpiring upsetting the Kiwis following the ball-tampering drama.

An injured Crowe missed the one-off Test at Hamilton in January 1993, with Pakistan crumbling to 12–3 and then tallying 216, before New Zealand led by just 48 following a 108-run opening stand and knock of 133 from opener Mark Greatbatch. Pakistan slumped to 39–5 before tallying 174, and subsequently won by 33 runs as Wasim and Waqar took 5 wickets each.

New Zealand led on the first innings in the first Test of 1993–94, but a dismal second-innings total of 110 left Pakistan only 138 runs to win. Following their 5-wicket victory at Auckland, the tourists clinched the series with an innings win at Wellington after Saeed Anwar, Salim Malik and Inzamam-ul-Haq made centuries. Wasim Akram claimed 20 wickets in the first two Tests and 5 in the last, but the Kiwis saved face with an impressive 5-wicket win. After trailing by 144 runs on the first innings, New Zealand achieved its 324-run target after Bryan Young and the undefeated Shane Thomson made 120 each.

In a one-off Test at Christchurch in late 1995, Pakistan plummeted from 135–0 to 208 all out before a second-innings total of 434 left New Zealand needing 357. Mushtaq Ahmed (7–56) bowled the tourists to a 161-run victory, before the 1996–97 series in Pakistan featured a win to each side as Wasim Akram was absent. New Zealand drew first blood after struggling to 155 and later scoring 311 thanks to 90s from Stephen Fleming and Chris Cairns and a vital 26 from Simon Doull in a last-wicket partnership of 48. Doull dismissed Anwar second ball and claimed 8 wickets in the match, and the 44-run margin flattered Pakistan, as Test debutant Mohammad Wasim (109 not out) tried in vain to right the sinking ship. It was New Zealand's first Test victory in Pakistan since 1969–70, but the hosts gained payback as they won by an innings at Rawalpindi, after dismissing the tourists for 249 and 168. Test newcomer Mohammad Zahid claimed 11 wickets as Waqar was missing, while Anwar (149) and Ijaz Ahmed (125) set up the 430-run total.

2000s

Mohammad Sami had a good Test debut in 2000–01 as he captured 3–70 and 5–36 while Saqlain Mushtaq claimed 4–48 and 4–24. Pakistan won the first Test by 299 runs after New Zealand was 91–0 and 105–1, before crashing from 121–2 to 131 all out. The second Test was drawn after Mathew Sinclair's 204 not out in New Zealand's 476 was offset, as Yousuf Youhana (203), Inzamam-ul-Haq (130) and Saqlain (101 not out) took Pakistan to a 95-run lead. Daryl Tuffey, Chris Martin and James Franklin bowled the Kiwis to a massive series-levelling victory at Hamilton, as Pakistan managed only 104 and 118. New Zealand's 407–4 declared included centuries from openers Mark Richardson and Matthew Bell, and 98 from Craig McMillan.

Pakistan won the 2002 series 1–0 at home after a bomb blast caused the tour to be abandoned before the second Test could start. The hosts won the first Test by an innings following a mammoth 329 from Inzamam-ul-Haq and 127 from opener Imran Nazir, as Pakistan made 643 after being 1–1. Shoaib Akhtar's 6–11 ripped through the Kiwis for just 73, before he missed New Zealand's second innings as the tourists made 246 and were beaten inside three days.

Fleming (192) and Daniel Vettori (137 not out) set up a Kiwi total of 563 in the first Test of 2003–04, but Moin Khan (137) foiled New Zealand's victory bid before the Kiwis finished their second innings at 96–8. The second Test at Wellington produced a stunning turnaround from Pakistan, which was dismissed for 196 in reply to New Zealand's 366 after the Kiwis had been 1–2. As Shoaib Akhtar completed a match haul of 11–78, the hosts slid from 95–3 to 103 all out before the visitors achieved a comfortable 7-wicket victory.

Tim McIntosh was yorked with the first ball of the 2009–10 series before the Kiwis recovered to score 429 and win by 32 runs, after their second-innings dismissal for 153 left Pakistan needing 251. A miserable total of 99 left the Kiwis 165 runs in arrears in the second Test before Pakistan won by 141 runs after setting a target of 405. Only 19 overs were bowled on the first day of the third Test, and the lost time ultimately could have made a difference. Imran Farhat carried his bat with 117 runs in Pakistan's lacklustre 223, before Vettori (134) stood out in New Zealand's 471. The Pakistanis secured a drawn match and series as they compiled 455, with the Kiwis making 90 without loss in 19 overs.

Pakistan led by 92 runs on the first innings at Hamilton in the opening Test of 2010–11, before a New Zealand collapse for 110 led to a 10-wicket win for the visitors. The second and final Test contained plenty of solid scores from both sides but only one century (110 to Vettori), and a draw was good enough for the Pakistanis as they finished 48 runs shy of victory at 226–5.

Three centuries, a 96 and an 87 helped Pakistan rack up 566–3 declared in the first Test of 2014–15 at Abu Dhabi, before Tom Latham made 103 in New Zealand's 262. After narrowly missing out on a first-innings century, Mohammad Hafeez scored 101 not out in Pakistan's 175–2 declared before New Zealand's demise for 231 left Pakistan triumphant by 248 runs. Latham also registered triple figures in the second Test, as did Ross Taylor and Pakistan's Sarfraz Ahmed, before a draw resulted as Pakistan finished on 196–5 when pursuing 261. New Zealand squared the series with an innings victory, unbelievably, after Pakistan was 285–3 in the first innings. Hafeez made 197 before Mark Craig's 7–94 restricted the total to 351. Kiwi captain and opener Brendon McCullum's 202 and Kane Williamson's 192 were accompanied by four half-centuries as New Zealand gained a whopping 339-run lead. Craig added another 3 wickets to his tally as Pakistan folded for 259 despite 137 from Asad Shafiq.

New Zealand v Pakistan

1955–56 (P): Pakistan 2–0 (1 drawn)

1964–65 (NZ): 0–0 (3 drawn)

1964–65 (P): Pakistan 2–0 (1 drawn)

1969–70 (P): New Zealand 1–0 (2 drawn)

1973 (NZ): Pakistan 1–0 (2 drawn)

1976–77 (P): Pakistan 2–0 (1 drawn)

1978–79 (NZ): Pakistan 1–0 (2 drawn)

1984–85 (P): Pakistan 2–0 (1 drawn)

1984–85 (NZ): New Zealand 2–0 (1 drawn)

1988–89 (NZ): 0–0 (2 drawn)

1990–91 (P): Pakistan 3–0

1992–93 (NZ): Pakistan 1–0

1993–94 (NZ): Pakistan 2–1

1995–96 (NZ): Pakistan 1–0

1996–97 (P): 1–1

2000–01 (NZ): 1–1 (1 drawn)

2002 (P): Pakistan 1–0 (1 abandoned)

2003–04 (NZ): Pakistan 1–0 (1 drawn)

2009–10 (NZ): 1–1 (1 drawn)

2010–11 (NZ): Pakistan 1–0 (1 drawn)

2014–15 (UAE): 1–1 (1 drawn)

5.3 NEW ZEALAND v SRI LANKA

1980s

New Zealand was Sri Lanka's fourth different opponent in Test cricket when the teams met for the first time in early 1983, just over a year after the Sri Lankans played their inaugural Test. New Zealand won both encounters in the first series involving the two nations, although the Kiwis were in trouble at 171–7 during the first Test at Christchurch before reaching 344. Sidath Wettimuny carried his bat as he scored 63 in a sub-standard Sri Lankan total of 144, and the visitors were 25 runs shy of making the hosts bat again when the game ended late on day three. Sri Lanka led by 39 runs on the first innings in the second Test following a 5-wicket haul to Vinothen John, but New Zealand cruised to a 6-wicket win after dismissing Sri Lanka for just 93.

John also took a 5-wicket haul in the first Test of 1983–84 in Kandy, after play began on the afternoon of day two. Sri Lanka trailed by 61 runs on the first innings following a last-wicket stand of 60, and later lost by 165 runs after falling to 18–6 and then 97 all out, as Steve Boock and Richard Hadlee shared 9 wickets, while Arjuna Ranatunga made 51. Neither side reached 200 in its first innings in the second Test, before Roy Dias (108) and Wettimuny (65) set up a reasonable second-innings total for Sri Lanka. The Kiwis needed 266 runs in just over a day and, strangely, opted to block their way to a draw as they crawled to 123–4. New Zealand won the final Test by an innings as Hadlee bagged two 5-wicket hauls and Ewen Chatfield one 5-wicket haul, while John Reid scored 180 in New Zealand's slowly accumulated total of 459.

The 1986–87 series in Sri Lanka featured no outright results after the second and third Tests were cancelled following a bomb explosion. The first Test was a dull draw, with Brendon Kuruppu scoring 201 not out in Sri Lanka's 397, before Jeff Crowe and Richard Hadlee scored unbeaten tons as the Kiwis improved from 160–5 to 406–5 when the match ended.

1990s

The three-match series in New Zealand in early 1991 was also drawn 0–0, although there was some genuine Test cricket. Aravinda de Silva compiled 267 as Sri Lanka made 497 in response to New Zealand's disappointing 174 in the first Test at Wellington. Martin Crowe and Andrew Jones (186) subsequently put on a then record-breaking partnership that took the Kiwis from 148–2 to 615–3 and ensured a draw. The final twist in the contest was Crowe (on 299) being caught by diving wicketkeeper Hashan Tillekeratne in the final over with New Zealand finishing on 671–4. Jones (122 and 100 not out) and Sri Lanka's Asanka Gurusinha (119 and 102) were the standout batsmen in the second Test, while John Wright scored 101 in New Zealand's second innings. Sri Lanka finished on 344–6 after being challenged to score 418, before another evenly-poised draw took place. De Silva was the only century-maker in the final Test, before New Zealand scored 261–5 in 99 overs after being set 383.

In 1992–93 a bomb again disturbed a Kiwi cricket tour of Sri Lanka. Although the New Zealanders continued the tour this time, the team was below full strength after several players returned home. Rain helped the Kiwis draw the first Test at Moratuwa after Sri Lankan opener Roshan Mahanama top scored with 153. In the second Test, Sri Lanka beat New Zealand for the first time in Tests, as the hosts triumphed by 9 wickets. Mahanama (109), Tillekeratne (93) and Ranatunga (76) contributed strongly in a 394-run total, before the Kiwis crashed from 57–0 to 102 all out, and then made 361 when following on, after Crowe scored 107.

Sri Lanka hardly looked like winners when slumping to 88–6 and then 183 all out in the first Test of 1994–95 in Napier, before the hosts fared even worse as they fell for 109. New Zealand's second innings of 185 was hardly better, as the Kiwis needed 427, with the Sri Lankans enjoying their first Test win away from home. A subsequent draw enabled Sri Lanka to win a series away from home for the first time, although New Zealand had a chance of levelling the series after leading by 74 runs on the first innings. The Kiwis were foiled as Gurusinha (127), Tillekeratne (108) and Ranatunga (90) batted for lengthy periods.

A year after winning the 1996 World Cup, Sri Lanka looked anything but a champion side in the long form of the game, as New Zealand produced two thrashings. Kiwi opener Bryan Young's 267 not out in the first Test at Dunedin led to a total of 586–7 declared, before Sri Lanka was dismissed for 222 and 328. The Kiwis made only 222 in the second Test but they gained a 52-run lead before setting the Sri Lankans 326 and dismissing them for 205.

The Kiwis showed their ability to win away from home as they took the first match of the 1998 series by 167 runs at Colombo. Stephen Fleming (174 not out) and Craig McMillan (142) played leading roles as New Zealand set a target of 465, while off spinner Paul Wiseman claimed 7 wickets on debut. The series swung decisively in the second Test at Galle, where the tourists mustered only 193 and 114, while Mahela Jayawardene's 167 set up Sri Lanka's 323. Kumar Dharmasena bagged 6 scalps in New Zealand's first innings while Niroshan Bandaratilleke claimed 9 wickets in the match. The hosts made just 206 in the first innings of the deciding Test, before gaining a somewhat surprising 13-run lead. From 36–4, the Sri Lankans reached 282 following a last-wicket stand of 71 and then recorded a resounding 164-run win as Muttiah Muralitharan (5–30) and Bandaratilleke (4–52) wreaked havoc. It was nearly five years later that the teams next met in Test cricket.

2000s

Two draws resulted in 2003. Fleming's undefeated 274 helped his team to 515–7 declared in the first Test, before the home side went from 134–4 to 483 all out, following 144 from Tillekeratne. There was no play on day one of the second Test, before Sri Lanka finished its second innings at 72–1 from 30 overs after being set 191. The first match in the 2004–05 series was also drawn, with plenty of runs scored. A double century to Lou Vincent, 7 wickets from Chris Martin and 6 from Nathan Astle helped New Zealand to an innings victory in Wellington to win the series.

A low-scoring opening Test of 2006–07 was over in three days, with the Kiwis ahead by 52 runs on the first innings before an unbeaten ton from Kumar Sangakkara could not give Sri Lanka a big enough lead.

New Zealand won by 5 wickets, chasing 119, only for Sri Lanka to square the series with a 217-run victory at Wellington. Sangakkara (156 not out) made well over half of Sri Lanka's first-innings total of 268, before Lasith Malinga and Muralitharan ripped through New Zealand for 130. Chamara Silva (152 not out) helped the Sri Lankans set a target beyond 500, which never looked achievable as Muralitharan claimed 6–87.

After losing a wicket to the third ball of the 2009 series, Sri Lanka posted 452 following strong scores from Thilan Samaraweera (159), Jayawardene (114) and Tillakaratne Dilshan (92). Sri Lanka later set a target of 413 following 123 not out from Dilshan, and New Zealand managed just 210. Samaraweera and Jayawardene also starred in the second Test, with Sri Lanka making 416 in its first innings, before New Zealand fell 97 runs shy of a 494-run target after Daniel Vettori made 140 at number eight.

The first Test in the 2012–13 series was strange, with the Kiwis having a 90-run fourth-wicket partnership in a total of 221 before hosts Sri Lanka had a 156-run sixth-wicket partnership in a total of 247. Eight New Zealand batsmen made double figures but none passed 20 in a dismal total of 118, before Sri Lanka won by 10 wickets. The Kiwis were 14–2 early in the second Test, before centuries to Kane Williamson and skipper Ross Taylor set up a 412-run total. New Zealand gained control and levelled the series with a 167-run victory after Sri Lanka lost Tharanga Paranavitana first ball when pursuing 363.

New Zealand won the first Test of the 2014–15 series by 8 wickets, before Sri Lanka must have wondered how a seemingly certain series-levelling victory slipped away. Kiwi captain Brendon McCullum scored 195 at Christchurch, before Sri Lanka's miserable 138 was followed by 407 after opener Dimuth Karunaratne scored 152. New Zealand made only 221 in its first innings at Wellington, before 203 from Sangakkara ensured Sri Lanka gained a decent lead. But unbeaten knocks from Williamson (242) and BJ Watling (142) took the Kiwis from 159–5 to 524–5 declared, and Sri Lanka could tally only 196, after being asked to score 390.

New Zealand also won 2–0 on home soil in late 2015, as the margins were 122 runs and 5 wickets. Kiwi opener Martin Guptill made 156 in the first innings at Dunedin, where the hosts gained control as they earned a 137-run first-innings lead and set a target of 405. At Hamilton, the tourists had a first-innings lead of 55 but then collapsed for 133, and Williamson (108 not out) set up a successful run chase.

New Zealand v Sri Lanka

1982–83 (NZ): New Zealand 2–0
1983–84 (SL): New Zealand 2–0 (1 drawn)
1986–87 (SL): 1 draw (2 abandoned)
1990–91 (NZ): 0–0 (3 drawn)
1992–93 (SL): Sri Lanka 1–0 (1 drawn)
1994–95 (NZ): Sri Lanka 1–0 (1 drawn)

1996–97 (NZ): New Zealand 2–0
1998 (SL): Sri Lanka 2–1
2003 (SL): 0-all (2 drawn)
2004–05 (NZ): New Zealand 1–0 (1 drawn)
2006–07 (NZ): 1–1
2009 (SL): Sri Lanka 2–0
2012–13 (SL): 1–1
2014–15 (NZ): New Zealand 2–0
2015–16 (NZ): New Zealand 2–0

5.4 NEW ZEALAND v ZIMBABWE

1990s

Following a respectable draw with India in Zimbabwe's inaugural Test in late 1992, the African nation promptly hosted New Zealand in a two-Test series. Zimbabwe salvaged another draw first up, finishing at 197–1 after being set 329. Kevin Arnott became Zimbabwe's second centurion in Test cricket as he made 101 not out in Zimbabwe's second innings following two declarations from New Zealand. The hosts were in contention for a while in the second Test, before collapsing for 137 when chasing 315, as Dipak Patel nabbed 6–50.

The next two series were drawn 0–0, with neither side able to land the knockout blow as victory was up for grabs. In New Zealand during

January 1996, Zimbabwe finished the first Test at 208–6 after being set 257, before finishing the subsequent Test at 246–4 after being set 367.

In Zimbabwe during September 1997, New Zealand finished the first Test at 304–8 when pursuing 403, before finishing the following fixture on 275–8 after being set 286. Grant Flower made 104 and 151 for Zimbabwe in the first Test, before Guy Whittall made 203 not out in the second Test, after being reprieved on 5.

The Kiwis proved vastly superior as they hosted the Zimbabweans in February 1998, with New Zealand winning by 10 wickets before recording an innings victory. Zimbabwean totals of 180 and 250 were insufficient in the first Test as Craig McMillan's 139 inspired New Zealand to a total of 411. The second Test followed a similar pattern, with the visitors totalling 170 and 277, while 157 from Matthew Horne and 114 from Nathan Astle set up New Zealand's total of 460.

2000s

On home soil in September 2000, the Zimbabweans scored at barely 2 runs per over as they tallied 350, before a century from Horne enabled New Zealand to score 338 as Paul Strang took 8–109. The hosts faded as 5–31 from Chris Cairns and 3–54 from Paul Wiseman, who earlier captured 5–90, routed Zimbabwe for 119. Strang completed a 10-wicket match haul but it couldn't stop New Zealand soaring to a 7-wicket triumph. Cairns (124) was among the biggest scorers in the second Test as the Kiwis tallied 465, before dismissing the Zimbabweans for 166 and then having them 48–4 in the follow on. Despite an undefeated 188 from Whittall and some lengthy resistance from Andy Flower and Heath Streak, New Zealand won by 8 wickets, after needing 72 for victory. The Kiwis were at home as the teams played a Boxing Day Test in 2000, with McMillan (142) and Astle (141) setting up a total of 487–7 declared. Another two declarations left the Zimbabweans needing 301, before finishing at 60–2.

The 2005 series in Zimbabwe could not have been more one-sided, as the visitors won both matches by an innings. After being 113–5, the Kiwis declared at 452–9 following hundreds to Brendon McCullum and Daniel Vettori, who subsequently claimed 2–1 and 4–28 as Zimbabwe flopped for 59 and 99. Zimbabwe managed 231 in the second Test, before New Zealand more than doubled it following 128 from Astle. Shane Bond completed a 10-wicket match haul as Zimbabwe fell 46 runs shy of making New Zealand bat again.

Zimbabwe hosted a one-off Test in late 2011, before New Zealand did the same in early 2012, with the Kiwis winning a close contest before inflicting a massacre. Kiwi opener Martin Guptill's knock of 109 was followed by several decent scores in a total of 426, before Zimbabwe fell from 284–5 to 313 all out. Set a stiff target of 366, Zimbabwe was 265–3 before Brendan Taylor departed for 117, and New Zealand went on to win by 34 runs, as Doug Bracewell bagged a 5-wicket haul on debut, while Vettori again played a vital role. Ross Taylor and BJ Watling scored a ton each in the following encounter as New Zealand neared 500, before Zimbabwe made only 51 and 143, as Chris Martin bagged 8 wickets.

New Zealand v Zimbabwe

1992–93 (Z): New Zealand 1–0 (1 drawn)

1995–96 (NZ): 0–0 (2 drawn)

1997–98 (Z): 0–0 (2 drawn)

1997–98 (NZ): New Zealand 2–0

2000–01 (Z): New Zealand 2–0

2000–01 (NZ): 1 drawn

2005 (Z): New Zealand 2–0

2011–12 (Z): New Zealand 1–0

2011–12 (NZ): New Zealand 1–0

5.5 NEW ZEALAND v BANGLADESH

2000s

New Zealand recorded innings victories in its first four Test encounters with Bangladesh, and won the first three series 2–0 before a couple of 1–0 results were followed by a drawn series.

The Kiwis struggled at 51–4 in the first innings of their opening encounter at Hamilton in late 2001, before reaching 365–9 declared following centuries to Mark Richardson and Craig McMillan. Daniel Vettori claimed 20 wickets in the 2004–05 series, while Bangladesh's Mohammad Rafique deserved credit for taking 6–122 from 59.1 overs in the first Test. Kiwi skipper Stephen Fleming scored 202 in the second Test of 2004–05, before Matthew Bell and Jacob Oram registered a ton each in the first Test of 2007–08. Bangladesh was able to make New Zealand bat a second time in this match, with the Kiwis winning by 9 wickets, as they needed just 35 runs. New Zealand won the following Test by an innings before the 2008–09 series was much more competitive.

Shakib Al Hasan nabbed 7–36 as the Kiwis tallied just 171 in response to the home side's 245, before Al Hasan hit 71 as Bangladesh set a target of 317. New Zealand triumphed by 3 wickets as several batsmen contributed well, including Vettori, who scored 55 not out and 76 and took 9 wickets in the match. Vettori also did well in the final match but rain prevented a result.

A one-off Test involving the two countries took place at Hamilton in February 2010, with Bangladesh a lot more competitive than its 121-run defeat suggested. New Zealand was 158–5 before declaring at 553–7, after Martin Guptill (189) and Brendon McCullum (185) enjoyed a sixth-wicket partnership of 339. Mahmudullah (115) top-scored in Bangladesh's first innings of 408 before Shakib Al Hasan scored 100 in the team's second innings of 282.

The 2013–14 series was well fought without producing a result, and the Bangladeshis could have claimed they had turned a corner, despite remaining winless against New Zealand. Centuries to Kane Williamson and BJ Watling helped the Kiwis to 469 in the first Test, before the Bangladeshis impressively led by 32 runs, after losing a wicket first ball. Mominul Haque made 181 at number four before Sohag Gazi remained unbeaten on 101 after coming in at number eight. Gazi claimed a hat-trick before Bangladesh finished on 173–3, after being set 256. In the second Test, New Zealand topped 400 following 116 from Corey Anderson, after Bangladesh made 282, before Haque was not out on 126 as Bangladesh finished the match on 269–3.

New Zealand v Bangladesh

2001–02 (NZ): New Zealand 2–0   **2008–09 (B):** New Zealand 1–0
2004–05 (B): New Zealand 2–0   (1 drawn)
2007–08 (NZ): New Zealand 2–0   **2009–10 (NZ):** New Zealand 1–0
                                                        2013–14 (B): 0–0 (2 drawn)

5.6 NOTABLE TEST PLAYERS

Martin Crowe

Martin Crowe could hardly have had a more inauspicious start to Test cricket as his first four scores were 9, 2, 0 and 9 against Australian teams featuring Dennis Lillee, Jeff Thomson and Bruce Yardley in 1981–82. But in 1986, the then Australian captain Allan Border anticipated that Crowe would become the world's premier batsman. Border's prediction had plenty of merit. Crowe was the player of the 1992 World Cup after scoring 456 runs at 114, only for the Kiwis to lose in the semi-finals.

Had he played in some stronger Test teams, Crowe could have had an even better record than his eventual 5444 runs at 45.36. After debuting at 19, Crowe had modest figures against England and Sri Lanka in the next couple of years, although he notched his maiden century in his eighth Test: against England at Wellington in 1983–84. In early 1985, Crowe (84) featured in a 157-run sixth-wicket stand with Jeremy Coney to help the Kiwis to a 2-wicket win and 2–0 series victory against Pakistan in New Zealand. The same year was a personal triumph for Crowe as, remarkably, he was twice dismissed for 188. The first occasion was against a strong West Indian team at Georgetown after Richie Richardson scored 185 for the hosts. The Kiwis drew the Test before the West Indies won the third and final Test to claim the series 1–0. New Zealand's Ken Rutherford had a horror debut series, not unlike Crowe's introduction to Test cricket, while Crowe admittedly also had a miserable series, apart from his one big score. The second time Crowe made 188 was against Australia at Brisbane, where the Kiwis won by an innings and subsequently beat Australia in a Test series for the first time.

The Kiwis backed this up with a series win against Australia on New Zealand soil, with Crowe's most important innings coming in the second drawn Test, as he retired hurt after being hit on the chin, before returning and making 137. It was one of the most courageous innings Australia's captain had seen; Border reported in his 1986 autobiography *An Autobiography*, 'You couldn't possibly overrate it. It was a gem.'

After scoring a ton at Lord's in 1986, Crowe was prominent against the West Indies in 1987, this time scoring 119 to help draw the first Test, before his 104 in the second Test couldn't prevent defeat after the Kiwis followed on. Crowe had the satisfaction of being not out in the final Test at Christchurch as the hosts squared the series. Crowe had health issues for a while in the 1980s, and at one stage he did not play cricket for several months.

Good results against Australia and England were followed by scores of 174, 0, 78 and 9 not out in a 0-0 drawn series with Pakistan in the late 1980s, before a century enabled him to average more than 50 in a three-match series against India in 1989–90. Crowe scored an unbeaten century during a 3–0 loss to Pakistan in late 1990, before he had a career highlight in the subsequent 0–0 drawn series with Sri Lanka. In the opening Test at Wellington, New Zealand trailed by 323 runs on the first innings before registering 671-4 in its second innings. Crowe and Andrew Jones put on 467 runs for the third wicket, at that stage the highest ever partnership in Test cricket. Crowe, agonisingly, departed one run shy of 300 in the final over, before Brendon McCullum became the first New Zealand player to score a Test triple ton 23 years later.

Crowe had more than his share of critics, especially when captaining his country. His captaincy record didn't look too good on paper: two wins, seven losses and seven draws. Yet he averaged 54.30 when captain, compared with 42.77 when non-captain. A major problem for

Crowe for several years in the 1990s was an ongoing knee injury, and this ultimately brought his career to a somewhat premature end.

Crowe rated his fifteenth and sixteenth Test centuries as his best two. The 15th was on New Zealand's tour of Sri Lanka in late 1992. The Kiwis fielded a depleted squad and drew the first Test before Sri Lanka beat New Zealand in a Test for the first time. Crowe was bowled for a duck before his team followed on in Colombo, and although his team lost by 9 wickets, Crowe was thrilled with his second innings score of 107, after he battled a hamstring strain.

Crowe's departure from the 1993–94 tour of Australia proved a severe setback for the tourists. He played in the drawn first Test before returning home for knee surgery, while the Kiwis lost the second and third Tests by an innings. Crowe toured England in 1994, and scored 142 in the drawn Lord's Test and 115 in the drawn Old Trafford Test after England won the first Test at Trent Bridge by an innings. He rated his 142 as his best ever Test innings, before his 115 turned out to be his final Test ton. Mediocre scores against South Africa in 1994–95 were followed by scores of 11, 24 and 15 against India in late 1995, and this proved to be the end of his Test career.

Martin Crowe (1962–2016)

Matches: 77
Runs scored: 5444
Batting average: 45.36
100s/50s: 17/18
Top score: 299
Balls bowled:1377
Wickets: 14
Bowling average: 48.28
5 wickets in innings: –
10 wickets in match: –
Best bowling: 2–25
Catches/stumpings: 71/–

Stephen Fleming

Stephen Fleming did not have the reputation of Richard Hadlee or Martin Crowe, but he was one of New Zealand's most respected players. Fleming became New Zealand's highest run scorer in Tests and limited-overs internationals, and was also the country's most experienced captain, after leading the Kiwis to 28 victories, 27 defeats and 25 draws in Tests. Fleming's batting average was nothing brilliant, as he scored only nine centuries in his 111 Tests, having been dismissed between 70 and 99 many times. Fielding nonetheless was one of Fleming's biggest assets as he held 171 catches, mainly in the slips cordon.

An elegant, left-handed batsman who was strong at driving, cutting and leg-side shots, Fleming fell just 8 runs shy of a debut Test century against India at Hamilton in March 1994. More than two years later, Fleming was stranded on 92 not out at Lahore as the Kiwis were on their way to their first Test win in Pakistan since 1969–70. Fleming had to wait until his twenty-third Test to crack his maiden ton, as he notched 129 against England at Auckland in January 1997. Two Tests later he replaced Lee Germon as captain, as Fleming was several weeks shy of his twenty-fourth birthday. New Zealand had the chance to draw the series as England needed 305, but the tourists won by 4 wickets to clinch a 2–0 victory. Fleming's first tour of Australia began brightly with a knock of 91, but the rest of the series was a horror as a duck was followed by 10 and 4 and a pair of ducks in a 2–0 loss.

Fleming's second Test century was in his thirty-fifth appearance, as he scored 78 and 174 not out in a resounding win at Colombo, only for Sri Lanka to come back and win the series. A career highlight was in 1999 when Fleming led his team to a come-from-behind 2–1 series victory in England. The following year, Fleming became New Zealand's most successful skipper when the country beat Zimbabwe, as it was the twelfth time the Kiwis won a Test under his captaincy.

The drawn series in Australia in late 2001 proved an interesting time for Fleming, who avoided scrutiny for choosing to bowl in the first two Tests. Australia's openers put on more than 200 runs in the first innings in both Tests, although a convincing lbw appeal was controversially denied in the first over of the opening Test. In the third Test of the series — Fleming's 63rd Test — he scored his third Test ton and first against Australia. Fleming's fourth Test century inspired the Kiwis to a series win in the Caribbean in 2002, before his two Test tons the following year were in drawn matches. He scored a career-best 274 not out and then 69 not out against Sri Lanka at Colombo, and made 192 against Pakistan at Hamilton.

After scoring 117 as an opener in a loss to England at Trent Bridge in 2004, Fleming turned his last two Test tons into double centuries. He made 202 as he led the Kiwis to a comprehensive win over Bangladesh in late 2004, and compiled 262 in a draw at Cape Town in April–May 2006, before South Africa won the series. In Fleming's last series, the Kiwis surrendered a 1–0 lead at home as England won 2–1, with the Kiwi skipper scoring 297 runs at 49.50 to lift his overall aggregate beyond 7000 runs and average just above 40.

Stephen Fleming (b.1973)

Matches: 111
Runs scored: 7172
Batting average: 40.06
100s/50s: 9/46
Top score: 274*
Balls bowled: –
Wickets: –
Bowling average: –
5 wickets in innings: –
10 wickets in match: –
Best bowling: –
Catches/stumpings: 171/–

(Sir) Richard Hadlee

The name 'Hadlee' was synonymous with New Zealand cricket after Walter captained the Kiwis before two of Walter's sons, Richard and Dayle, also represented New Zealand. As it turned out, Dayle's and

Walter's careers were largely overshadowed, as Richard became arguably the country's best ever cricketer. New Zealand was starved of success when Hadlee began his international career and, whilst he helped the team achieve some memorable victories, the Kiwis often relied rather heavily on him.

A right-arm fast bowler and left-handed batsman, Richard 'Paddles' Hadlee was a bowling all-rounder who became the first player to achieve 400 Test wickets. He could swing and cut the ball as he was particularly dangerous with the new ball, and he consistently bowled an immaculate line and length, while rarely bowling a bumper. Hadlee shortened his run-up in the 1980s as he became more of a fast–medium bowler, but he proved to be as dangerous as ever even when well into his.

Hadlee's first couple of years in Test cricket were nothing special, as he could not maintain a regular berth in the team. He perhaps tried to bowl too fast, as he often bowled too short, and his first three Tests yielded just 3 wickets at 119.67 and 65 runs at 16.25. He claimed 4–33 and 2–16 against Australia in his fourth Test, which was on Australian soil in 1973–74, before taking 1–102 from 28 overs in the following Test. With the Kiwis subsequently hosting Australia for three Tests, Hadlee missed the first one but then claimed 3–59 and 4–71 as New Zealand enjoyed its first Test win against its neighbouring rival.

In 1975–76, Hadlee helped the Kiwis draw a home series with an innings victory against India at Wellington, where he snared 4–35 and 7–23. In season 1976–77 Hadlee was not at his best against Pakistan, India and Australia, as he snared 29 wickets at 42.72 while scoring 417 runs at 29.78 in eight Tests. His batting included a double of 44 and 81 not out in a 10-wicket loss to Australia at Auckland. At Wellington, however, Hadlee had another career highlight when the Kiwis played there in 1977–78, as he inspired New Zealand to its first ever victory against England. Hadlee claimed 4–74 in England's first innings before the tourists, chasing 137, were shot out for 64, as Hadlee took 6–26. From then on, Hadlee had much more consistent results with the ball, while his batting form remained variable.

Hadlee played vital roles with bat and ball when the Kiwis upset the West Indies 1–0 in 1979–80, starting with match figures of 11–102 and scores of 51 and 17 in New Zealand's tense 1-wicket triumph at

Dunedin. In the following Test, Hadlee was one of several centurions as his 103 was his maiden Test ton. His only other Test ton was against Sri Lanka in April 1987, as he made 151 not out in a draw at Colombo.

Hadlee, nonetheless, had some other batting highlights, including hitting a six for the winning runs against Australia in 1981–82..In 1983 when the Kiwis won a Test on England soil for the first time, Hadlee scored 75 but surprisingly didn't take a wicket. He was worn out after this series, and sought help from a motivation expert to help him get back on track. In season 1983–84, when New Zealand beat England at Christchurch, Hadlee scored 99 and claimed match figures of 8–44.

Hadlee peaked with 64 Test wickets in 1985, and was chiefly responsible for New Zealand beating Australia in successive series in 1985–86. He claimed 33 wickets in three Tests Down Under and 16 in three Tests at home. At Brisbane, Hadlee claimed his best innings figures of 9–52 and caught the other victim off Vaughan Brown, before scoring 54 and then taking 6–71 in an innings victory. His 11 wickets in the third Test set up New Zealand's first series win against Australia, and in the Boxing Day Test two years later Hadlee claimed 10 wickets in a Test for the eighth time as the Kiwis narrowly failed to draw the series. This left Hadlee on 373 Test wickets: level with Ian Botham. Hadlee became Test cricket's leading wicket-taker during New Zealand's 1988–89 tour of India, after missing most of New Zealand's previous series against England with injury.

Occasionally, Hadlee was at the centre of friction. One such instance was in 1986–87 when the touring West Indies led the Kiwis 1–0 with one match remaining in a three-Test series. Hadlee angered captain Jeremy Coney and coach Glenn Turner for publicly criticising the team's lack of professionalism in the second Test. After feeling inclined to withdraw from the third Test due to falling out with Coney, Hadlee snared 6–50 and 3–101 to help New Zealand draw the series. Amazingly, there was no communication between Hadlee and Coney, even when Coney took three fine catches off Hadlee's bowling.

Hadlee took his ninth and final haul of 10 wickets in a Test during New Zealand's 1988–89 tour of India, before retiring in 1990 after a three-Test series in England. In between two drawn Tests, Hadlee was knighted and then earned man-of-the match honours for scoring 86 and taking 4 wickets in the Lord's Test. His final Test ended in defeat at Edgbaston, but he had the satisfaction of claiming 8 wickets, including an innings haul of 5–53, which contained wickets with his fourth-last and last deliveries.

Richard Hadlee (b.1951)

Matches: 86
Runs scored: 3124
Batting average: 27.16
100s/50s: 2/15
Top score: 151*
Balls bowled: 21,918
Wickets: 431
Bowling average: 22.29
5 wickets in innings: 36
10 wickets in match: 9
Best bowling: 9–52
Catches/stumpings: 39/–

Daniel Vettori

Daniel Vettori was thrown in at the deep end when selected for Test cricket just after his eighteenth birthday in early 1997, as he had only two first-class matches under his belt. Nearly 18 years later he was New Zealand's most experienced Test and limited overs cricketer. Vettori, who wore prescription spectacles when playing, was chosen primarily as a left-arm orthodox spinner but developed into an all-rounder. Despite not turning the ball as much as other frontline spinners, Vettori's drift, guile, and variety ensured batsmen had to be watchful every time they faced him.

England won by an innings in Vettori's maiden Test, but the debutant acquitted himself well with two not outs at number 11 and figures of 2–98 from 34.3 overs. He was more impressive in the next Test, which England also won, as he scored 25 and 29 not out at number nine and had economical figures of 1–13 from 12 overs and 4–97 from 57 overs. As the Kiwis followed up with a home series win against Sri Lanka, Vettori shone in the second Test with match figures of 9–130 from 53.2 overs.

Later in 1997, Vettori bettered his then highest first-class score of 29 not out as he made a vital 90 at number nine in a draw against Zimbabwe. Yet it wasn't until his forty-seventh Test that he reached 1000 runs, before he posted his first Test century in his forty-ninth appearance. In his first tour of Australia in late 1997, Vettori was tidy, if not penetrative, as he claimed 6 wickets in three Tests. He took 6 wickets in an innings against Sri Lanka in 1998, before doing likewise against India in 1999, but the Kiwis lost both times. Vettori nevertheless played a key role in a memorable series victory against England in 1999, as he scored 51 at number ten before taking 5 wickets in the final Test.

Vettori's best Test figures were against Australia as he claimed 5–62 and 7–87 at Auckland in 2000, and in the process he passed 100 wickets in his twenty-ninth Test. Vettori claimed 5 wickets in one innings and 6 wickets in another innings during the drawn series Down Under in late 2001, but he had an unproductive time in the next couple of years, as he claimed just 16 wickets in nine Tests at one stage. His breakthrough century was an unbeaten 137 against Pakistan at Hamilton in late 2003, but ten months passed before he made a bowling contribution of note. As the Kiwis demolished Bangladesh in two Tests, Vettori claimed three 6-wicket hauls following a 2-wicket haul, but he again had the misfortune of taking a 5-wicket haul during two losses to Australia. His second Test century was in a win over Zimbabwe in 2005, and he also took 2–1 and 4–28 in that match. The following year, Vettori took 3–53 and 7–130 in a heavy loss to Sri Lanka before 2008 was a fine year for him, as he captured 5 wickets in an innings on four occasions and 6 wickets in another innings. Two of his 5-wicket hauls were in a 2–0 series loss in England, before his next two hauls were in a 1–0 series win against Bangladesh. His 6–56 was in a draw with the West Indies.

Vettori captained his country in 32 Tests from November 2007 but the Kiwis won only six of them and lost 16, with four of the victories against Bangladesh. Vettori captured his 300th Test wicket when the Kiwis toured Sri Lanka in 2009, but the all-rounder had more success with the bat that year, after taking 54 scalps in 2008. He notched a century against India, Sri Lanka and Pakistan, only for New Zealand to lose on the first two occasions. Against Pakistan, Vettori scored 99 in a Test win before scoring 134 in the third Test of the series, which was drawn to ensure the series remained deadlocked.

Vettori's sixth and final Test ton was his third against Pakistan, and it occurred in a draw at Wellington in 2011, before the tourists won the series. Vettori's last Test was against Pakistan at Sharjah in November 2014 as New Zealand salvaged a drawn series with an innings victory.

Daniel Vettori (b.1979)

Matches: 113
Runs scored: 4531
Batting average: 30.00
100s/50s: 6/23
Top score: 140
Balls bowled: 28,814
Wickets: 362
Bowling average: 34.36
5 wickets in innings: 20
10 wickets in match: 3
Best bowling: 7–87
Catches/stumpings: 58/–

CHAPTER 6: INDIA

6.1 INDIA v PAKISTAN

1950s

India hosted the first series involving arch-rivals India and Pakistan, with the hosts winning the first Test of the 1952–53 series in Delhi by an innings and 70 runs. India reached 372 following a last-wicket stand of 109, with Hemu Adhikari scoring 81 not out at number eight while Ghulam Ahmed scored 50 at number 11. With nine Test debutants, Pakistan mustered only 150 and 152 as Vinoo Mankad captured 8–52 from 47 overs before following up with 5–79 from 24.2 overs.

The Pakistanis hit back as they won the second Test at Lucknow by an innings and 43 runs, with India scoring 106 and 182 while missing Mankad. Fazal Mahmood showed his liking for bowling on matting pitches as he snared 5–52 and 7–42, while Pakistani opener Nazar Mohammad was another hero, as he carried his bat while scoring 124. Mankad had a fine all-round game as India won the third Test at Bombay by 10 wickets, while Vijay Hazare and Polly Umrigar scored centuries for India in its first-innings total of 387–4 declared. The final two Tests were drawn, with the fourth featuring just two days of play, and little did anyone know how long it would take for another India–Pakistan Test to feature a winner.

The five-Test series in Pakistan in 1954–55 featured five draws, as did the 1960–61 series in India, as the arch-enemies seemed more intent not to lose rather than take a chance that could produce an outright result.

1960s

Of the ten drawn Tests from 1954–55 to 1960–61, the final encounter of 1960–61 was one that could have featured a clear-cut result. India led by 177 runs on the first innings and enforced the follow-on, before dismissing Pakistan for 250. Pakistan's second innings, however, yielded a 38-run last-wicket stand that used up precious time before India's second innings comprised of just two overs that cost 16 runs.

War involving the two countries prevented the nations contesting another Test series until 1978–79.

1970s

Pakistan won a three-Test series 2–0 on home soil in 1978–79, after a high-scoring draw was followed by Pakistani triumphs by 8 wickets, after being set targets of 126 and 164. Several centuries were scored, with Pakistan's Zaheer Abbas among the stars as he scored 235 not out in the second Test and finished the series with 583 runs at an average of 194.33.

The 1979–80 series in India also began with a high scoring draw, although rain ruined the prospect of a result. The second Test was a superbly fought draw as the hosts finished on 364–6 after being set 390, before India enjoyed its first victory against Pakistan for 27 years, as Pakistan fell well short of a 322-run target at Bombay. Rain on the final day of the fourth Test helped India maintain its series lead, before Sunil Gavaskar scored a vital 166 in the fifth Test. With Kapil Dev subsequently capturing 7–56, India won by 10 wickets after requiring just 76 runs, and maintained a 2–0 series lead as the final Test was drawn.

1980s

Zaheer returned to form with 215 in the first Test of 1982–83, but the match was drawn before the hosts won the second Test at Karachi by an innings following another big score from Zaheer. He made 186 before 8–60 from Imran Khan routed the Indians. Zaheer and Imran were also among Pakistan's heroes in the third Test as the hosts won by 10 wickets, after Zaheer was one of four century-makers in Pakistan's first innings. Pakistan tallied 581–3 declared in the fourth Test following a 451-run third-wicket partnership involving Mudassar Nazar (231) and Javed Miandad (280 not out), and Pakistan's bowlers subsequently forced an innings win. Rain destroyed the chance of a result in the fifth Test before the sixth Test was also drawn, with day four disrupted by rioting students. Zaheer, Mudassar and Javed averaged more than 100 with the bat while Imran captured 40 wickets.

The 1983–84 and 1984–85 series were almost a case of returning to the days of 1954–55 and 1960–61, as there were no results. The three-match series in India in 1983–84 was marred by ill-feeling and disagreements, with Javed and Zaheer in the thick of it. The following series in Pakistan featured two high-scoring draws, with Pakistan unable to dismiss India a second time when a Pakistani victory beckoned in the first Test.

The first four Tests of the 1986–87 series in India were also drawn, with Indian captain Kapil Dev blaming his counterpart, Imran, for negative cricket while Pakistan's captain deemed that the hosts produced pitches that were not conducive to exciting cricket. But the fifth and final Test at Bangalore was an all-time classic as Pakistan won a series in India for the first time. Pakistan managed just 116 before India gained a small lead of 29 and was later set a target of 221. Sunil Gavaskar made a resilient 96 but India was dismissed for 204, with 35 of the 40 wickets falling to spinners.

The 1989–90 four-match series in Pakistan failed to yield any outright results although the first, second and fourth Tests were quite competitive compared with the third Test, which featured a run glut. Sanjay Manjrekar scored 218 in India's total of 509, before Pakistan made 699–5, with Shoaib Mohammad (203 not out), Javed Miandad

(145) and Aamir Malik (113) the main scorers. Another nine years passed before India and Pakistan met in another Test series due to turmoil involving the two countries, but the two-match series was worth waiting for as there was some world-class cricket.

1990s

Pakistan won a memorable first Test at Chennai by just 12 runs, and perhaps the highlight was the parochial Indian crowd giving the victors a standing ovation at the end. India led by 16 runs on the first innings before a slashing 141 from Shahid Afridi enabled the visitors to set the hosts 271. India was 82–5 before a masterful 136 from Sachin Tendulkar took the locals to 254–6, only for Tendulkar's demise to spark a lower order collapse. Anil Kumble claimed 6 wickets in Pakistan's first innings before Venkatesh Prasad did likewise in Pakistan's second innings. Saqlain Mushtaq claimed two 5-wicket hauls for Pakistan in both Tests, but Kumble was the superstar in the second Test, as India drew the series. Kumble took 4–75 as Pakistan fell 80 runs shy of India's first-innings total of 252, and subsequently became only the second bowler (after Jim Laker was the first) to capture 10 wickets in a Test innings. Kumble claimed 10–74 as Pakistan was dismissed for 207 after being set 420.

The teams met again on Indian soil in early 1999 for the first match of the Asian Test Championship, with Pakistan winning by 46 runs. Pakistan recovered from 26–6 to tally 185 in its first innings as wicketkeeper Moin Khan scored 70, and went from 262–3 to 316 all out in its second innings as opener Saeed Anwar scored 188 not out. India was well-placed in the run chase at 108 without loss before losing 10–124.

2000s

The four series from 2003–04 to 2007–08 featured some sharp pendulum swings, with success shared. India won the first and third Tests of the 2003–04 series by an innings, while hosts Pakistan won the second Test by 9 wickets. Virender Sehwag (309) and Tendulkar

(194 not out) added 336 runs for the third wicket as India chalked up 675–5 declared in the first Test, before Pakistan managed 407 and 216. Pakistan's 489 in the second Test secured a 202-run lead before the hosts had to chase just 40, followed by India dismissing its arch-rival for 224 and 245 in the final Test. Sehwag was dismissed with the first ball of India's innings before Rahul Dravid scored 270 while three teammates scored half-centuries in a total of 600.

Sehwag scored 173 as India gained a first-innings lead of 204 in the first Test of the 2004–05 series, before Pakistan recovered from 10–3 to secure a draw as several batsmen including wicketkeeper Kamran Akmal (109) took the total towards 500. The second Test was intriguing as India stumbled from 278–2 to 407 all out, before Pakistan slid from 281–2 to 393 all out (Younis Khan 147, Yousuf Youhana 104). Dravid (135) was the mainstay as India set Pakistan 422, and Kumble's 7–63 ensured the Pakistanis mustered only 226. The visitors drew the series with a 168-run victory at Bangalore, after Younis Khan (267) and Inzamam-ul-Haq (184) put on a third-wicket stand of 324 in a total of 570. Sehwag's 201 couldn't prevent Pakistan leading by 121 runs, before India managed only 214 after being set 383.

The first two Tests of the 2005–06 series were drawn, although there were plenty of batting highlights. Mohammad Yousuf was stumped for 173 before Younis Khan was run out for 199, followed by centuries to Shahid Afridi and Kamran Akmal, as Pakistan tallied 679–7 declared in the first Test. Following a few disrupted days, India finished at 410–1 shortly after the dismissal of Sehwag for 254 while Dravid remained unbeaten on 128. Pakistan made 588 in the second Test following centuries to Inzamam and Afridi, followed by India making 603 as tons from Dravid and MS Dhoni were accompanied by 90 each from VVS Laxman and Irfan Pathan. Younis Khan (194) and Mohammad Yousuf (126) kept the runs flowing as Pakistan reached 490–8 declared.

In the final Test at Karachi, Pathan claimed a hat-trick in the first over without a run on the board before the hosts crumbled to 39–6 and later reached 245, thanks largely to Akmal's 113. India struggled to 238 before Pakistan's first seven batsmen scored between 53 and 139 runs each in a total of 599–7 declared. Yuvraj Singh made 122 in India's second innings but Pakistan romped to victory by 341 runs.

Batting was not so strong as India won the 2007–08 series at home after a 6-wicket triumph was followed by two draws. Neither side reached 300 in the first Test before India had just a couple of anxious moments in pursuit of 203, and then run gluts returned in the remaining two Tests. India scored 616–5 declared (Wasim Jaffer 202, Laxman 112 not out, Sourav Ganguly 102) and 184–4 declared while Pakistan tallied 456 (Misbah-ul-Haq 161 not out, Akmal 119) and 214–4 (Younis Khan 107 not out) in the second Test. In the final Test, India was 61–4 before Ganguly (239), Yuvraj (169) and Pathan (102) set up a total of 626 while Test debutant Yasir Arafat unobtrusively claimed 5 wickets. Misbah-ul-Haq was Pakistan's only century-maker while there were 76 sundries in the total of 537, before Ganguly fell 9 runs shy of another century. India nearly stole an unlikely victory, having taken 7 wickets as Pakistan faced 36 overs.

India v Pakistan

1952–53 (I): India 2–1 (2 drawn)
1954–55 (P): 0–0 (5 drawn)
1960–61 (I): 0–0 (5 drawn)
1978–79 (P): Pakistan 2–0 (1 drawn)
1979–80 (I): India 2–0 (4 drawn)
1982–83 (P): Pakistan 3–0 (3 drawn)
1983–84 (I): 0–0 (3 drawn)
1984–85 (P): 0–(2 drawn)
1986–87 (I): Pakistan 1–0 (4 drawn)

1989–90 (P): 0–0 (4 drawn)
1998–99 (I): 1–1
1998–99 (I): Pakistan (Asian Test Championship)
2003–04 (P): India 2–1
2004–05 (I): 1–1 (1 drawn)
2005–06 (P): Pakistan 1–0 (2 drawn)
2007–08 (I): India 1–0 (2 drawn)

6.2 INDIA v SRI LANKA

1980s

Sri Lanka's first Test against India took place on Indian soil in September 1982, seven months after Sri Lanka was defeated in its first ever Test against England. The two Asian nations had a well-fought draw in their first encounter, with Duleep Mendis twice scoring 105 for Sri Lanka which tallied 346 and 394 before setting the hosts 175 in limited time, after Sunil Gavaskar and Sandeep Patil scored centuries in India's big first-innings total. Ashantha de Mel bagged 5 wickets as Sri Lanka nearly snatched victory, with India pursuing the target for a while before finishing at 135–7 from 28 overs.

Sri Lanka won a series for the first time as India was defeated 1–0 in a three-match series on Sri Lankan soil in August–September 1985. The hosts generally had the better of a drawn first Test before winning the second Test by 149 runs after 111 from Amal Silva was followed by a 9-wicket match haul to Rumesh Ratnayake. Following an unbeaten innings of 116 from India's Mohinder Amarnath, the third Test was fascinating as Sri Lanka, set 377, was 34–3 before recovering to 250–3 thanks to 106 from Roy Dias and 124 from Mendis. The hosts slipped to 267–7 but progressed to 307–7 to secure a draw and series victory.

India was much too strong on home soil in season 1986–87 after the first Test was a high-scoring draw, with Mohammad Azharuddin scoring 199, Gavaskar 176 and Kapil Dev 163 for the hosts. India won the remaining two Tests by an innings, with Dilip Vengsarkar scoring two big centuries, while Maninder Singh and Shivlal Yadav were the main wicket-takers in the second Test.

1990s

A one-off Test in late 1990 also resulted in an innings win to the Indians at home, despite the hosts notching a modest 288 batting first. Asanka Gurusinha made an undefeated 52 at first drop in Sri Lanka's appalling first innings of 82 while Venkatapathy Raju claimed 6–12.

Sri Lanka hosted three Tests in the second half of 1993 before India hosted three Tests several months later, with Sri Lanka sometimes competitive at home before being comprehensively outplayed away. After only 12 overs of play were possible in the first Test in Sri Lanka, the hosts were dismissed halfway to a target of 472 in the second Test, before a drawn third Test ensured an Indian series win. On Indian soil, the hosts won all three matches by an innings. In the first Test, India made 511 before Sri Lanka collapsed from 120–0 to 218 all out and then fell from 100–1 to 174 all out, with Anil Kumble taking 11 wickets. Raju picked up 11 wickets in the third Test after Sri Lanka's highest total in the series, 231, was scored in the second Test.

A two-match series was drawn 0–0 in 1997, as was a three-match series in 1997–98. It would be an understatement to say the opening Test of 1997 in Colombo was a run glut. Sachin Tendulkar (143), Azharuddin (126) and Navjot Sidhu (111) were chiefly responsible for India making 537–8 declared, before Sri Lanka racked up a phenomenal 952–6 declared. Sanath Jayasuriya (340) and Roshan Mahanama (225) put on a staggering second-wicket partnership of 576 before 615–1 became 615–3 as the duo departed. Aravinda de Silva (126), Arjuna Ranatunga (86) and Test debutant Mahela Jayawardene (66) kept the runs flowing, while Indian debutant Nilesh Kulkarni had 1–195 from 70 overs after capturing the first wicket of the innings. De Silva scored two tons in the second Test and put on a 218-run partnership with Jayasuriya (199) in Sri Lanka's second innings, and India was set 373 after earlier making 375 (Tendulkar 139, Sourav Ganguly 147). India finished on 281–5, with Azharuddin not out on 108.

Ganguly scored two tons and a 99 in the 1997–98 series while Sidhu and Tendulkar made one century each. De Silva and Marvan Atapattu registered a century each for Sri Lanka while Atapattu fell 2 runs shy of another triple-figure score. The Sri Lankans hung on by the skin of their teeth as they were 166–7 at the end of the third Test after being set 333.

Centuries were again prominent as the teams met at Colombo in the Asian Test Championship in early 1999, with Sadagoppan Ramesh (143) and Rahul Dravid (107) the main contributors in India's 518–7 declared. Mahela Jayawardene (242) scored almost exactly half of Sri Lanka's total, and another draw resulted after Tendulkar made a ton in India's second innings.

2000s

The 2001 series in Sri Lanka had a different feel as there were three comprehensive results, with Muttiah Muralitharan the chief wicket-taker for Sri Lanka. The hosts won the first Test by 10 wickets after the visitors made just 187 and 180, before the visitors won the second Test by 7 wickets after being set 264. The deciding Test turned out to be somewhat anticlimactic, as the Sri Lankans won by an innings, after their total of 610–6 declared included four centurions.

The Indians hosted the next series more than four years later, and recorded two big wins after a rain-disrupted opening Test was drawn. The first three days of the series were washed out, and the scoreboard from the first Test quirkily resembled a limited-overs scoreboard, as Sri Lanka finished at 168–4, after India made 167. In the second Test, the hosts led by 60 runs on the first innings and went on to win by 188 runs after setting a target of 436. The Sri Lankans appeared to have a good chance of levelling the series after reducing the Indians to 97–5 in the first innings of the third Test, but 104 from VVS Laxman and several solid contributions down the order helped India to 398. Sri Lanka narrowly avoided the follow-on, before sparking a collapse, only for the Indian tail to wag again. Sri Lanka needed 509 runs, and managed only 249.

Results were up-and-down in the three series from 2008 to 2010 as one team would inflict a thrashing before the other team returned the compliment. Four century-makers enabled Sri Lanka to declare at 600–6 in the first Test of 2008 at Colombo, before India collapsed for 223 and 138. In the second Test, India flopped from 167–0 to 329 all out, as opener Virender Sehwag made 201 not out, and then gained a 37-run lead before setting Sri Lanka 307. Harbhajan Singh took 10 wickets in the match as India squared the series with a 170-run victory, before faltering to 249 all out in the final Test. A century to Kumar

Sangakkara helped Sri Lanka to a 147-run lead, before the hosts won by 8 wickets, after requiring 122 runs.

The first Test of 2009–10 at Ahmedabad was a high scoring draw after several centuries were recorded, with Mahela Jayawardene's 275 the peak. The second Test began with India's first three batsmen making hundreds (Gautam Gambhir 167, Sehwag 131 and Dravid 144) in a total of 642. Sri Lanka lost a wicket first ball and slid to an innings defeat, and also lost the final Test by an innings, despite tallying 393 batting first. Sehwag made 293 as India lost its first 2 wickets at 221 and 458 before topping 700 and then dismissing Sri Lanka for 309, despite 137 from Sangakkara.

Sri Lanka hosted India several months after the completion of the 2009–10 series, and the hosts began brilliantly as Tharanga Paranavitana (111) and Sangakkara (103) laid the platform for a total of 520–8 declared. India made only 276 after Sehwag scored 109, before losing by 10 wickets, after squeezing out an ineffective 94-run lead. In the second Test, Paranavitana (100) and Jayawardene (174) were partly overshadowed as Sangakkara scored 219 in Sri Lanka's 642–4 declared. Tendulkar (203), debutant Suresh Raina (120) and Sehwag (99) shone as India compiled 707 and ensured a drawn result. Sri Lanka missed Muralitharan for the second and third Tests, but appeared to secure a series victory with a total of 425 in the first innings of the final Test, following an undefeated century from Thilan Samaraweera. India led by 11 runs before Sri Lanka plunged to 125–8 and recovered to 267 after Samaraweera (83) and Ajantha Mendis (78) put on 118 for the ninth wicket. Sehwag was out for a duck before India fell to 62–4. Tendulkar posted a half-century before departing at 171–5 as Suraj Randiv claimed his fifth wicket of the innings and ninth in the Test. A superb contest concluded as Laxman (103 not out) and Raina (41 not out) put on an unbroken partnership to level the series with a 5-wicket win.

Sri Lanka produced a brilliant fightback to lead the 2015 series, only for India to eventually win 2–1. At Galle, Ravi Ashwin's 6–46 contained the hosts to 183 before the visitors were 28–2 and later 255–2, before succumbing for 375 following tons to Shikhar Dhawan and skipper Virat Kohli. Sri Lanka quickly lost its first 3 wickets for 5 runs, only for wicketkeeper Dinesh Chandimal to make 162 not out to guide the hosts to 367. Rangana Herath captured 7–48 as India slid to a 63-run loss, before winning the next two Tests by 278 runs and 117 runs. At Colombo, India was 12–2 before 108 from opener Lokesh Rahul laid the platform for a 393-run total. After being 241–3 in reply, Sri Lanka made only 306 following 102 from captain Angelo Mathews. Following 126 from India's Ajinkya Rahane, Sri Lanka was never in the hunt for 413, as Ashwin claimed 5–42. In the decider, India began poorly before Cheteshwar Pujara carried his bat for 145 runs in a total of 312. Sri Lanka crashed to 47–6 and managed another 154 runs, and then India was 3 down for 7 runs before making 274. Chasing 386, the hosts were 2–2 and later progressed from 107–5 to 242–5 as Mathews scored a hundred before the final 5 wickets fell quickly.

India v Sri Lanka

1982–83 (I): 0-all (1 drawn)
1985–86 (SL): Sri Lanka 1–0 (2 drawn)
1986–87 (I): India 2–0 (1 drawn)
1990–91 (I): India 1–0
1993 (SL): India 1–0 (2 drawn)
1993–94 (I): India 3–0
1997 (SL): 0–0 (2 drawn)
1997–98 (I): 0–0 (3 drawn)

1998–99 (SL): 1 drawn (Asian Test Championship)
2001 (SL): Sri Lanka 2–1
2005–06 (I): India 2–0 (1 drawn)
2008 (SL): Sri Lanka 2–1
2009–10 (I): India 2–0 (1 drawn)
2010 (SL): 1–1 (1 drawn)
2015 (SL): India 2–1

6.3 INDIA v ZIMBABWE

1990s

Zimbabwe became the first Test nation since Australia (in the first ever Test) not to lose its debut Test, as Zimbabwe's inaugural Test produced a draw with India in Harare in late 1992. On a lifeless pitch, the hosts amassed 456 following 121 from David Houghton, before India struggled to 307 as Sanjay Manjrekar scored a sluggish 104. Forty-five-year-old John Traicos, who played four Tests for South Africa in 1970, claimed 5–86 from 50 overs including the wicket of Sachin Tendulkar for a duck. Zimbabwe finished the match at 146–4, before another one-off Test involving Zimbabwe and India was held on Indian soil several months later. The hosts declared at 536–7 after Vinod Kambli scored 227, and the spin duo of Anil Kumble and Maninder Singh dismissed the visitors for 322 and 201 despite a fine double of 115 and 62 not out from Andy Flower, whose brother Grant scored 96 in Zimbabwe's first innings.

Zimbabwe's breakthrough win against India in late 1998 was the African nation's second Test victory in its thirty-first Test. India led by 59 runs following a knock of 118 from Rahul Dravid in the one-off Test in Harare, before falling 62 runs short of the 235-run target after the openers failed to score.

2000s

Andy Flower (183 not out), Dravid (200 not out) and Tendulkar (122) posted big scores in the first Test of the 2000–01 series in India before Grant Flower registered a pair while fellow opener Gavin Rennie also fell without scoring. Following 9 wickets in the match to Javagal Srinath, India overcame two early setbacks to comfortably reach the target of 190. India made Zimbabwe follow on in the second Test after the hosts made 609–6 declared, with Tendulkar (201 not out), Dravid (162) and Shiv Sunder Das (110) leading the way. But the African nation made 503–6 to deny India victory as Andy Flower (232 not out) could not be removed while Alistair Campbell (102) also foiled the home side.

India won by 8 wickets when the teams met at Bulawayo in mid 2001, but the hosts drew the series after winning the second Test by 4 wickets. India won the first Test of the 2001–02 series at Nagpur by an innings as Kumble snared 9 wickets while Tendulkar, Das and Sanjay Bangar posted triple figures. Zimbabwe was more competitive in the second Test but India won by 4 wickets after pursuing 122. Prolific wicket-taking from Irfan Pathan swung the 2005 series dramatically in India's favour as the touring team won the first Test by an innings and 90 runs before recording a 10-wicket victory to secure a 2–0 triumph.

India v Zimbabwe

1992–93 (Z): 1 drawn	**2001 (Z):** 1–1
1992–93 (I): India 1–0	**2001–02 (I):** India 2–0
1998–99 (Z): Zimbabwe 1–0	**2005 (Z):** India 2–0
2000–01 (I): India 1–0 (1 drawn)	

6.4 INDIA v BANGLADESH

2000s

Bangladesh's first ever Test was a one-off match against India at Dhaka in late 2000, and things looked promising for the hosts for a while. They tallied exactly 400 following 145 from Aminul Islam, before India was 236–6. But the visitors recovered to gain a 29-run lead before the hosts managed just 91 in their second innings, setting up a 9-wicket win for India as Sunil Joshi excelled with 92 runs and 8 wickets.

The Indians won both matches of the 2004–05 series by an innings as Bangladesh was reduced to totals of 184, 202, 333 and 124. Irfan Pathan snared 11 wickets in the first Test while Sachin Tendulkar scored 248 not out and shared in a last-wicket stand of 133 with Zaheer Khan (75). Rahul Dravid and Gautam Gambhir made hundreds in the second Test as India again topped 500 before an undefeated 158 from Mohammad Ashraful couldn't prevent Bangladesh from having to follow on.

Mashrafe Mortaza dismissed Wasim Jaffer with the first ball of the 2007 series in Bangladesh, but India recovered to post 387 before the match finished with honours even, as the hosts were 104–2 after being set 250. The second Test was heavily one-sided as India's first four batsmen made centuries: Dinesh Karthik (129), Jaffer (138 retired ill), Dravid (129) and Tendulkar (122 not out). Bangladesh lost a wicket first ball in reply to India's 610–3 declared, and the hosts were dismissed for 118 and 253.

The opening Test of the 2009–10 series was well fought for the first couple of days before visitors India gained control. India led by 1 run on the first innings, before Bangladesh wicketkeeper Mushfiqur Rahim made 101 as his team finished 114 runs shy of the 415-run target. Dravid scored 111 in the second Test while Tendulkar registered his second century of the series as India gained a lead of 311. Bangladesh opener Tamim Iqbal scored 151 but the hosts only just managed to avoid an innings defeat following a 7-wicket haul from Zaheer Khan, and the visitors scored the required two runs from byes.

A one-off Test was played at Fatullah in June 2015, with India having the better of a rain-affected draw. Openers Shikhar Dhawan (173) and Murali Vijay (150) set up India's 462–6 declared before Bangladesh made 256 and finished at 23–0 when following on.

India v Bangladesh

2000–01 (B): India 1–0   **2009–10 (B):** India 2–0
2004–05 (B): India 2–0   **2015 (B):** 1 drawn
2007 (B): India 1–0 (1 drawn)

6.5 NOTABLE TEST PLAYERS

Rahul Dravid

One of India's most dependable batsmen, Rahul Dravid averaged more than 51 in home Tests and a touch above 53 away from home, and scored the bulk of his 13,288 runs in the vital number three position. Dravid became the first player to face 30,000 deliveries in Test cricket, and was involved in many century partnerships. Among the most capped Test players, Dravid was renowned as a defensive batsman, although his strokeplay developed as his career progressed. A fine fielder, Dravid captained India in 25 Tests from 2003 to 2007, achieving eight wins, six losses and 11 draws.

Batting at number seven in his Test debut against England at Lord's in June 1996, Dravid was just 5 runs shy of 100 when he edged a catch behind. In his second Test he was caught behind for 84 before being promoted to number five in the second innings and scoring 8. Dravid batted in various positions as India contested the Proteas at home and away in 1996–97, and he averaged just 29.17 in a 2–1 win at home before averaging 55.40 in a 2–0 loss in South Africa. Dravid batted two hours for 27 not out as India capitulated for 66 when needing 395 at Durban, before he was promoted at Cape Town and failed twice. At number three in Johannesburg, Dravid cracked his maiden ton as he made 148 before following up with 81 in India's second innings. India also lost a series to the West Indies despite Dravid making 360 runs at 72.

Having scored 15 half-centuries and just one century in his first 22 Tests, Dravid made his second century in a rare loss to Zimbabwe at Harare in late 1998. Although a little over two years passed before India finally won a Test that involved a Dravid century, it wasn't until July 2011 that India lost another Test in which Dravid made a triple-figure score. His third and fourth tons were against New Zealand at Hamilton as he began 1999 with 190 and 103 not out, but his form fell away sharply. Dravid had an abysmal tour of Australia in 1999–00 as he averaged just 15.50 in a 3–0 loss. Dravid's form slump ended as he scored 200 not out, 70 not out and 162 in a series win against Zimbabwe in late 2000, before he played a memorable role in India's come-from-behind victory against Australia at Calcutta in early 2001. After being lowered to number six, Dravid scored 180 and shared a series-turning 376-run stand with VVS Laxman as India triumphed after following on.

Dravid's form dipped again, before five centuries in 2002 enabled Dravid to have his most prolific calendar year as he collected 1357 runs at 59. He batted at number five when he made 144 not out in a draw against the West Indies in Guyana, before returning to number three in the next Test. During a drawn series in England, Dravid scored 602 runs at 100.33 after notching three centuries, including 217 at the Oval. He scored another hundred against the West Indies in 2002, enabling him to record a century in four consecutive Test innings. Dravid's two tons in 2003 were doubles, as he made 222 in a draw against the Kiwis at Ahmedabad before notching 233 against Australia at Adelaide as Dravid and Laxman inspired another memorable Indian victory.

Against Pakistan in 2004, Dravid was run out without facing a ball in India's second innings at Lahore, before making his biggest Test score in the decider at Rawalpindi, where India won by an innings. Dravid's 270 lasted 740 minutes, before his next ton was against Bangladesh. Dravid's two tons in 2005 were in the same match as he notched 110 and 135 against Pakistan at Kolkata, where the hosts won before the visitors drew the series. His run of 94 successive Test appearances ended in 2005 when he missed a Test against Sri Lanka because of gastroenteritis. While captaining India and opening the batting against Pakistan in early 2006, Dravid scored centuries in two successive drawn Tests. He shared a 410-run partnership with Virender Sehwag in the first Test before failing miserably in the third and deciding match, which Pakistan won. Dravid scored 496 runs at 82.67 in a 1–0 win against the West Indies, before his three Test centuries in 2006 were followed by one in 2007 and two in 2008. Unproductive form in 2008 suggested his career could soon conclude, before he scored two tons in 2009 in successive Tests in November, as he made 177 and 144 against Sri Lanka. Three centuries in 2010, including 191 in a deciding Test win against New Zealand at Nagpur, were followed by a great year in 2011, as he notched five centuries before playing his last Test in January 2012. As India was repeatedly thrashed in England, Dravid compiled 461 runs at 76.83, including three triple-figure scores. He had better fortune against the West Indies, scoring one ton in the Caribbean and another in India, as India won both series, before being thrashed in Australia as Dravid scored 194 runs at 24.25.

Rahul Dravid (b.1973)

Matches: 164
Runs scored: 13,288
Batting average: 52.31
100s/50s: 36/63
Top score: 270
Balls bowled: 120
Wickets: 1
Bowling average: 39.00
5 wickets in innings: –
10 wickets in match: –
Best bowling: 1–18
Catches/stumpings: 210/0

Sunil Gavaskar

Peter Arnold reported in *The Illustrated Encyclopedia of World Cricket* that India's Sunil Gavaskar was 'a model opening batsman' who was 'as near free from error as possible in defence', and could handle fast and slow bowling. Arnold also described Gavaskar as having 'limitless patience'. Indeed it was interesting to note that the Indian maestro could score quickly while exhibiting exquisite strokeplay, and at other times be dour and slow. Perhaps it depended on the situation of the game or the mood he was in at the time. Either way, he was adept off the front foot and back foot, and he timed the ball well and found gaps instead of trying to hit the ball hard. Gavaskar was also a fine slips fielder.

At barely 165cm (5ft 5in) tall, Gavaskar showed that being diminutive wasn't detrimental when it came to facing fast bowlers of various heights and styles. Whether contesting Australia, the West Indies, Pakistan or England, Gavaskar encountered many pacemen of the highest class in the 1970s and 1980s. In *Botham's Century*, Ian Botham rated Gavaskar as the best opening batsman he had bowled to. According to Botham, Gavaskar 'had just about the perfect frame for dealing with quick and slow bowlers alike', while other attributes Botham mentioned included 'a fantastic eye and wonderful balance', and immense courage and determination. Botham remarked that the Indian opener's powers of concentration were such that 'when he dug himself in it was like trying to remove a tower block'.

It was remarkable that 13 of Gavaskar's 34 Test centuries were against the West Indies. The first West Indian pace attack was by no means the most dangerous that he faced, but Gavaskar showed in his first-ever Test series that he was destined for big things. As a 21-year-old in the Caribbean in 1971 his scores were 65, 67 not out, 116, 64 not out, 1, 117 not out, 124 and 220. His 220 helped India maintain its series lead, and the innings was all the more commendable considering he battled toothache. Gavaskar was disappointing in his next 11 Tests, all against England, as he averaged just 27.86 with one century. He regained form abroad in 1975–76 as he averaged 66.50 against New Zealand and 55.71 against the West Indies. In Port-of-Spain, he excelled in successive Tests as he scored 156 during the drawn second Test and then 102 as the tourists squared the series when they passed a 403-run target for the loss of just 4 wickets.

Gavaskar's figures were solid rather than superb in his next three series, and during the first three Tests against Australia in 1977–78 he had an uncanny habit of failing in the first innings and scoring a century in the second innings. From 1978–79 to 1979–80 he was perhaps at his peak as he scored 2748 runs at 68.70 from 26 Tests. On home soil against the West Indies in 1978–79, in his first series as captain, Gavaskar scored 205, 73, a golden duck, 107, 182 not out, 4, 1, 120 and 40 as India won 1–0. In 1979 Gavaskar scored 221 against England at the Oval where India heroically made 429–8 when needing 438 to square the series.

Gavaskar captained India at various stages from the late 1970s to mid 1980s, and was at the centre of a major controversy when skipper in 1980–81. He struggled on Australian and New Zealand soil that season, and in the Melbourne Test he asked his opener partner Chetan Chauhan to leave the field with him when the Indian captain was unhappy at being adjudged lbw following other decisions that upset the tourists. India ultimately fought back brilliantly to steal a 59-run victory and draw the series.

Gavaskar notched 500 runs in six Tests against England in 1981–82 with a top score of 172, before making 155 in India's maiden Test clash with Sri Lanka. As India was well beaten by Pakistan in 1982–83, Gavaskar averaged a creditable 48.22 and carried his bat at Faisalabad, where he scored 127 in a total of 286. He averaged just 30 following one decent score of 147 not out against the West Indies in 1982–83, before averaging 66 on Pakistani soil and 50.50 against the West Indies in 1983–84. Gavaskar's 1310 runs in the calendar year of 1983 were second only to his 1555 runs in 1978. In the third Test at Ahmedabad in 1983–84 he overtook Geoff Boycott as Test cricket's leading runmaker, and in the sixth Test he made his highest Test score. After being relegated to number four, Gavaskar came to the crease with India 2 wickets down without a run scored, before he compiled 236 not out. It was his thirtieth Test ton, and his next three were against Australia, before his last was against Sri Lanka.

The tied Test involving India and Australia in 1986 was Gavaskar's 100th successive Test, and his 90 gave India a strong chance of reaching the 348-run target. In his last Test innings, his dogged 96 was in vain as India sought 221 and lost by 16 runs, as Pakistan won a series on Indian turf for the first time. Gavaskar's last two series as captain were in 1984–85, when he averaged 40 against Pakistan and a dismal 17.50 against England. Gavaskar led India to nine wins, eight losses and 30 draws, with Gavaskar and Kapil Dev alternating as captain. Gavaskar angered the Calcutta crowd in 1984–85 when he delayed a declaration against England following the controversial sacking of Kapil for one Test, and remarked that he would never play in the city again. In 1987, Gavaskar honoured his word as he made himself unavailable for the

Calcutta Test against Pakistan, thus ending his run of successive Test appearances at 106, before his farewell was at Bangalore.

Sunil Gavaskar (b.1949)

Matches: 125
Runs scored: 10,122
Batting average: 51.12
100s/50s: 34/45
Top score: 236*
Balls bowled: 380
Wickets: 1
Bowling average: 206.00
5 wickets in innings: 0
10 wickets in match: 0
Best bowling: 1–34
Catches/stumpings: 108/–

Kapil Dev

For many years Kapil Dev was considered India's greatest cricketer, and few would argue that Sachin Tendulkar has since held that mantle. Hardly surprising, but not necessarily fair either, considering Kapil became the first (and as of early 2016, the only) cricketer to achieve the double of 5000 runs and 400 wickets. He was Test cricket's leading wicket-taker for six years from March 1994. Kapil's personal achievements in the 1983 World Cup have been well documented elsewhere, with the man himself leading India to the unexpected title of world champions in limited-overs cricket. He also took 75 Test wickets during 1983.

As Ian Botham remarked in *Botham's Century*, Kapil 'was the first Indian cricketer to experience the Bollywood treatment. From the moment the "Haryana Hurricane" started to brew up his storm, his approach was pure box-office, and how the Indian fans idolized (sic) him for it.' Yet his profile and influence compared with that of another

Indian hero — Sunil Gavaskar — may have made it hard for Indian selectors to decide who should be captain. They had more than one stint each, with India winning four Tests, losing seven, tying one and drawing 22 under Kapil's leadership.

Kapil was primarily a bowler in his early years, but as his career progressed he was just as likely to be a matchwinner with the bat. He was by no means an orthodox batsman as he often played cross-batted shots and liked to hit the ball hard, with some monstrous sixes to show for it. As a fast–medium bowler, Kapil had a fine outswinger and had the unenviable task of bowling on docile pitches at home, while for several years being the only class paceman in the Indian team. Regarding Kapil's bowling, Kersi Meher-Homji reported in *Cricket's Great All-Rounders*, 'To be a fast bowler and an Indian sounds like an oxymoron but Kapil succeeded on lifeless Indian pitches with dedication and natural talent...Kapil swung the ball like a boomerang and his snake-like break-back struck with the speed of a cobra.' Regarding Kapil's batting, Meher-Homji reported, 'To expect Kapil to bat defensively is equivalent to asking a Formula One driver to keep to a speed limit of 80 kmh (kilometres per hour).'

In his Test debut at Faisalabad in October 1978, Kapil bowled a bouncer to experienced Pakistani opener Sadiq Mohammad who wasn't wearing a helmet. Sadiq promptly replaced his cap with a helmet and saved himself serious injury as, sure enough, Kapil bowled another bouncer, which this time struck the helmet, before Sadiq became Kapil's first victim. Kapil took only 7 wickets at 60.86 in his maiden Test series, while scoring 159 runs at 31.80. His second series was against the West Indies, and at Madras his 7 wickets and second-innings score of 26 not out helped India to a 3-wicket win before his maiden Test ton at Delhi helped the hosts maintain their series lead.

Kapil bowled soundly in England in 1979, and claimed all 5 wickets when England compiled 633–5 in the first Test. His batting, however, was dismal, and in the final Test he perished to a slog when more composure was needed as India sought 438 to draw the series and fell frustratingly short. Kapil had good figures with bat and ball in series wins at home against Australia and Pakistan in 1979–80, with a

413

standout match against Pakistan at Madras, where he scored 84 and took 4–90 and 7–56.

Having captured 74 wickets in 18 Tests in 1979, Kapil had another bad trot with the bat in 1980–81 but he braved injury to bowl India to a series-levelling victory in Australia. At home against England in 1981–82 and then in England in 1982, Kapil was somewhat expensive with the ball while his batting was dangerous. He recorded his second Test century when he made 116 off just 98 balls in the final Test of 1981–82 at Kanpur to again help India keep a series lead intact. Although England subsequently won the first Test by 7 wickets at home, Kapil had a sensational match as he took 5–125, then scored 41 (off 69 balls) and 89 (off 55 balls), and took 3–43. His next two innings produced 65 and 97 at better than a run per ball, before he had mixed success in Pakistan in 1982–83 as his innings figures included 5–102 (28.5 overs), 7–220 (38.4 overs) and 8–85 (30.5 overs).

Kapil averaged 42.33 with the bat and 24.94 with the ball in his first series as captain, although the West Indies won 2–0 in the Caribbean. Kapil's third Test century helped draw the Port-of-Spain Test before he made 98 in a draw at St John's. His best Test innings figures of 9–83 couldn't save India against the West Indies in the Ahmedabad Test of 1983–84, and he lost the captaincy following the 3–0 series loss. In 1984–85 he was dropped for one Test against England for supposedly reckless batting, after clubbing a six and being out next ball at Delhi, where India frittered away its series lead.

With Kapil back at the helm, India lost a series in Sri Lanka before India had the better of a 0–0- drawn series Down Under. Kapil was scathing of Australia's umpires after rain denied India what appeared a certain victory at Melbourne. Kapil finally won a Test series as captain when India beat England in 1986 before India had another drawn series with Australia. Kapil surprisingly failed to take a wicket in the three-Test series, but his fourth Test century helped India out of trouble in its first innings of the tied Test. After making his highest Test score of 163 against Sri Lanka in late 1986, Kapil took his 300th Test wicket the following month. But his pace declined, after years of carrying the Indian attack had taken their toll. Kapil captained India for the last time in 1987.

Kapil took a 5-wicket haul and a 6-wicket haul against the West Indies in 1989, but his 400th Test wicket came five years after he achieved the 300 milestone. In the meantime he still made some vital batting contributions. Against the West Indies in 1987–88, his century was a key factor as India drew the series in the final Test although Narendra Hirwani was the main hero with 16 wickets on debut. In the 1990 Lord's Test that was known for Graham Gooch's 333, Kapil struck off spinner Eddie Hemmings for four consecutive sixes as India needed 24 runs to avert the follow-on with 1 wicket in hand. Kapil's seventh Test ton came later in that series, before his eighth and final Test century could not prevent South Africa winning by 9 wickets at Port Elizabeth in late 1992.

Kapil overtook Richard Hadlee as Test cricket's leading wicket-taker during a series whitewash against Sri Lanka in early 1994, and he retired the following month after India drew with New Zealand in a one-off Test. Kapil and Hadlee were the only players to take 400 Test wickets at the time of Kapil's retirement.

Kapil Dev (b.1959)

Matches: 131
Runs scored: 5248
Batting average: 31.05
100s/50s: 8/27
Top score: 163
Balls bowled: 27,740
Wickets: 434
Bowling average: 29.64
5 wickets in innings: 23
10 wickets in match: 2
Best bowling: 9–83
Catches/stumpings: 64/–

Anil Kumble

Anil Kumble did not gain as much recognition as fellow spinners Muttiah Muralitharan and Shane Warne, but sitting third on the all-time Test wicket-taking list showed Kumble had a superb career. Kumble also holds the distinction of taking 10 wickets in a Test innings, after England's Jim Laker was the only other player to achieve this milestone. Kumble bowled at a reasonably quick pace for a leg spinner and did not turn the ball as much as many other spinners did, but his accuracy meant batsmen had to play at the ball far more often than not. Kumble had the most number of lbw dismissals in Test cricket, and also held 35 catches off his own bowling.

Kumble had respectable figures of 3–105 from 43 overs and 0–65 from 17 overs in his Test debut at Old Trafford in 1990, as England amassed 519 and 320–4 declared in a drawn match. His next Test experience was in the inaugural India versus South Africa Test series in season 1992–93, when he claimed 18 wickets in four Tests and conceded fewer than 2 runs per over. In South Africa's second innings in the drawn second Test at Johannesburg, Kumble bowled five batsmen on his way to capturing 6–53 from 44 overs. Kumble subsequently snared 21 wickets in three Tests against England, and he reached the 50-wicket milestone in his tenth Test, before taking another 11 Tests to reach 100 wickets. It wasn't until his fourteenth Test that he captured a 10-wicket match haul, as he claimed 4–69 and 7–59 in an innings victory against Sri Lanka.

Kumble's 10-wicket innings haul was against Pakistan at Delhi in February 1999, after the Pakistanis won a memorable first Test at Chennai by 12 runs despite Kumble's 6–70 in Pakistan's first innings. Kumble subsequently took 4–75 in Pakistan's first innings at Delhi before the visitors needed 420 runs. India won by 212 runs as Kumble had three lbw appeals upheld, bowled two batsmen and had five caught while conceding 74 runs in 26.3 overs, with number 11 Waqar Younis the only Pakistani not to be dismissed by Kumble in either innings.

In late 1999, Kumble was prominent in India's 1–0 series win against New Zealand as he claimed 10 wickets in the only Test that featured an outright result. He toured Australia for the first time shortly afterwards and found it hard as he captured just 5 wickets at 90 while India was thrashed 3–0, after he had previously captured 32 wickets at 17.22 against Australia in four Tests on Indian soil. Injury forced Kumble to miss India's memorable series win against Australia in the subcontinent in 2001, before he finally came good on Australian soil in 2003–04. He captured 24 wickets in the four-match series which was drawn 1–1, with innings analyses including 5–154 from 43 overs, 6–176 from 51 overs, and 8–141 from 46.5 overs.

Although India lost a series at home against Australia in late 2004 — the first time this had happened since 1969–70 — Kumble had fine figures. After achieving the 400-wicket milestone in the first Test, he took 7–48 and 6–133 in the second Test before claiming 6 wickets in the fourth Test as India salvaged a 2–1 series loss. All up, Kumble took 74 wickets in the calendar year.

On his way to passing 500 Test wickets, Kumble had a thoroughly successful time from late 2005 to mid 2006 as India beat Sri Lanka, drew England and beat the West Indies. He claimed 20 wickets at 18.70 against Sri Lanka, and captured 9 wickets when India beat England at Chandigarh. With India winning a series in the Caribbean for the first time in 35 years, Kumble scored 45 in India's first innings of 200 before capturing 6–78 to dismiss the hosts for 219 when they sought 269.

A useful late-order batsman, Kumble scored his only Test ton in his 118th Test when he made 110 not out against England at the Oval. He captained his country in 14 Tests, with India gaining three wins and five losses. Kumble enjoyed a 1–0 win against Pakistan in 2007–08 before a 2–1 series loss Down Under was overshadowed by ill-feeling between the two teams. Kumble claimed his 600th Test wicket during the controversial tour of Australia, before retiring from international cricket in late 2008 after India hosted Australia. Kumble led India to two draws in that series and missed the other two Tests when MS Dhoni led India to two victories. Kumble didn't take a wicket in his 51 overs in the first Test before claiming 3 scalps in 47.3 overs in what turned out to be his farewell Test, as he injured a finger and was forced to withdraw from the fourth Test.

Anil Kumble (b.1970)

Matches: 132
Runs scored: 2506
Batting average: 17.77
100s/50s: 1/5
Top score: 110*
Balls bowled: 40,850
Wickets: 619
Bowling average: 29.65
5 wickets in innings: 35
10 wickets in match: 8
Best bowling: 10–74
Catches/stumpings: 60/–

Virender Sehwag

Virender Sehwag 'changed perceptions as to what was possible from an opening batsman in Test cricket', as David Gower reported in *David Gower's 50 Greatest Cricketers of All Time*. Amidst an array of attacking strokes and a liking for hitting the ball in the air, Sehwag was particularly strong with the cut shot as he scored a lot of his runs in boundaries. It was remarkable that the Indian had a strike rate of 83.10 runs per 100 balls in his 170 innings as an opener in Tests, while averaging around 50. It was worth noting that Sehwag's average was around 40 runs better in India's first innings than second innings, and only once did he post triple figures in India's second innings. Unlike other batsmen with attacking instincts, Sehwag was not necessarily prone to surrendering his wicket when in dangerous form. Fourteen of Sehwag's 23 tons were scores in excess of 150 while he sometimes scored at quicker than a run per ball, and he joined a small group of players to score two Test triple centuries.

Sehwag didn't make his Test debut until November 2001, after making his one-day international debut in April 1999. Batting at six, Sehwag marked his maiden Test with 105 and 31 while Sachin Tendulkar also scored a ton, but South Africa won by 9 wickets at Bloemfontein. In the following Test, Sehwag earned a one-match suspension for excessive appealling before returning when India hosted England and Zimbabwe. In the first Test during India's tour of England in 2002, Sehwag was promoted to open, as there was no room for him in the middle order. He scored 84 and 27 as Indian fell to a hefty loss, before making 106 and three failures in the drawn series. Later that year as India beat the West Indies, Sehwag's 147 in the opening Test was the first time he reached a triple-figure score in a home Test.

Sehwag's first six Test tons were against six different nations, and he was particularly destructive when on song between December 2003 and July 2008 as his 11 Test tons in this period were scores between 150 and 319. Sehwag fell 5 runs shy of 200 against Australia at Melbourne in December 2003, before his sixth Test century turned into a mammoth 309 against Pakistan at Multan in March 2004. Against Pakistan a year later, Sehwag made 173 and 36 in a draw and then 81 and 15 in a win, before his 201 and 38 at Bangalore couldn't prevent India's arch-rival drawing the series. The Lahore Test in January 2006 was drawn after Sehwag scored 254, as were the next three Tests that featured a big Sehwag innings. His peak was against the Proteas at Chennai in March 2008 when he scored 319, after taking just 278 balls to reach his triple ton. Yet he had the occasional bad trot throughout his career, and none of his Test tons were against Bangladesh or Zimbabwe. In 2007, Sehwag was temporarily dropped as he was out of form. In August 2011, he scored two first-ball ducks in a landslide loss to England at Edgbaston.

In the second half of 2008, Sehwag carried his bat for 201 runs as India totalled 329 against Sri Lanka at Galle, with India winning the match to level the series, before the hosts won the decider. Although not making a century against England in late 2008, Sehwag blasted 11 fours and 4 sixes in a knock of 83 to set up a successful run chase, as the target was 387. Sehwag's next two Test tons were in a 2–0 series win against Sri Lanka, with 131 at Kanpur followed by Sehwag falling just 7 runs shy of notching a third Test triple century when he scooped a caught-and-bowled to Muttiah Muralitharan at Mumbai.

In February 2010, Sehwag scored 109 in an innings defeat against South Africa at Nagpur, before his 165 helped the hosts to a series-levelling innings victory at Kolkata. Sehwag made a further three Test centuries in 2010, with two scores of 109 in a drawn series against Sri Lanka, followed by 173 in a draw against New Zealand, before India won the series. Sehwag notched 1422 Test runs in 2010, after notching 1462 in 2008. Sehwag's final Test ton was in a victory in November 2012, but England won the series.

A useful part-time off spinner, Sehwag once claimed 5 wickets in a Test innings, as he snared 5–104 against Australia at Delhi in late 2008.

Virender Sehwag (b.1978)

Matches: 104
Runs scored: 8586
Batting average: 49.34
100s/50s: 23/32
Top score: 319
Balls bowled: 3731
Wickets: 40
Bowling average: 47.35
5 wickets in innings: 1
10 wickets in match: –
Best bowling: 5–104
Catches/stumpings: 91/–

Harbhajan Singh

Controversy never seemed far away from Indian off spinner Harbhajan Singh, but playing more than 100 Tests and topping 400 wickets revealed his talent, not to mention dismissing Ricky Ponting ten times in Tests. The legality of Harbhajan's bowling action came under scrutiny at first and, whilst that issue faded into obscurity, he repeatedly came under fire for unsavoury conduct and also lost his place in the team several times. Anil Kumble was repeatedly chosen as a sole specialist spinner, particularly when India played away from home.

Harbhajan returned 2–112 and 0–24 in his Test debut against Australia at Bangalore in 1998, as the tourists won after the hosts had already secured the series. Harbhajan appeared intermittently in the next three years, before India's historic home series against Australia in 2001 proved a turning point. In Kumble's absence, Harbhajan claimed 32 wickets at 17.03 in India's 2–1 triumph, while none of his teammates achieved more than 3 scalps. Harbhajan was the only bowler to dismiss Ponting, who tallied 17 runs and registered three ducks. In the second Test, which India won after following on, Harbhajan claimed 7–123 and 6–73. He was lucky to snare a hat-trick in the first innings considering one of his victims was adjudged lbw after the ball pitched well outside leg stump and clipped an inside edge before hitting the pad. In the deciding Test, Harbhajan's figures were 7–133 and 8–84 before he hit the winning runs.

Harbhajan lost form and his place in the side, although he still captured 60 wickets from 12 Tests in 2001. Harbhajan earned a suspended one-match ban for dissent and excessive appealing during the South African tour, before he took two 5-wicket innings hauls in India's home series win against England during December. Harbhajan subsequently captured 63 scalps in 2002. His 12 wickets in two Tests against Zimbabwe included 6–62 at Delhi, and he again had the thrill of scoring the winning runs. Harbhajan was in and out of the team during a series loss in the Caribbean but he shone at home against the West Indies with 20 wickets at 16.75 in a series victory, with best figures of 7–48 at Mumbai.

Harbhajan had an unhappy 2003 as he sustained a finger injury and struggled for form, including during tours of Australia and New Zealand, before he was sidelined for five months following surgery. He nabbed 11 wickets in a home Test in late 2004, only for Australia to win the match and the series, before Harbhajan took 5–29 in the final Test as India achieved a face-saving victory. Several weeks later, Harbhajan bowled India to a series win against the Proteas as he claimed 7–87 in South Africa's second innings.

It wasn't until late 2007 that Harbhajan regained a regular Test berth, although he occasionally produced good figures. He claimed a 5-wicket haul, a 6-wicket haul and a 7-wicket haul in 2005, before patchy form in 2006 and 2007 included a rare highlight abroad, with 5–13 from 27 balls in a series win against the West Indies. In his first series in Pakistan in early 2006, Harbhajan conceded 355 runs without taking a wicket in two Tests. Harbhajan's wickets came at a high cost during India's 2007–08 tour of Australia, and he was at the centre of a major conflict during the Sydney Test as he was suspended for racial abuse, before the ban was quashed after the charge was downgraded following an appeal. Harbhajan claimed 19 wickets at 26.11 in a drawn series against the Proteas in 2008, and for the second time he claimed 63 Test wickets in a calendar year. He reached the 300-milestone during a series win over Australia in India, and then Kumble's retirement allowed India to field a different leg spinner: Amit Mishra.

Harbhajan captured 6–63 in a victory on New Zealand soil in 2009, and he achieved only two further instances of 5 or more wickets in a Test innings. He snared 5–59 against South Africa in February 2010, and 7–120 against the same country nearly a year later. A useful lower-order batsman, Harbhajan scored his two Test tons at number eight in successive drawn matches against the Kiwis in November 2010 as he notched 115 at Ahmedabad and 111 not out at Hyderabad. In an Indian win at Kingston in June 2011, Harbhajan made a vital 70 before being sidelined with injury in England, and he found himself on the outer for a while. He was dropped after taking 3 wickets in a win against Australia in early 2013, and he also claimed 3 scalps in his last Test, against Bangladesh in June 2015.

Harbhajan Singh (b.1980)

Matches: 103
Runs scored: 2224
Batting average: 18.22
100s/50s: 2/9
Top score: 115
Balls bowled: 28,580
Wickets: 417
Bowling average: 32.46
5 wickets in innings: 25
10 wickets in match: 5
Best bowling: 8–84
Catches/stumpings: 42/–

Sachin Tendulkar

Whilst players from different eras cannot be compared, Sachin Tendulkar deserves to be considered one of the classiest batsmen of all-time. His longevity was also prominent, as he became the only cricketer (as of 2016) to play 200 Tests. A Test debutant at just 16 years of age, the 165cm (5ft 5in) Tendulkar became the leading runscorer in Tests and one-day internationals. He tallied nearly 16,000 Test runs and more than 18,000 one-day internationals runs, while also chipping in with some handy wickets. Tendulkar was elegant, as he made scoring runs look effortless, and had the ability to caress the ball, time it or hit it hard in virtually any direction. The Indian public developed enormous, and perhaps unrealistic, expectations of Tendulkar, but rarely did he cause disappointment. When he failed, one simply had to remember that he was human and could not succeed every time.

Tendulkar scored two half-centuries while achieving 215 runs at 35.83 against Pakistan in his maiden Test series in 1989–90, before fulfilling his ability on an England tour in 1990. He struggled in the first Test, which England won, before making 68 and 119 not out at Old Trafford, as his maiden Test ton helped India to 343–6, after being set

408. Although India was trounced 4–0 in Australia a little over a year later, the 18-year-old Tendulkar captured every onlooker's attention with two sparkling centuries. It was quickly apparent that he was destined to score a gigantic number of runs for many years to come, and that his was the most prized wicket for any opponent. Somewhat paradoxically, he wasn't often a genuine matchwinner in Test cricket, as only 20 of his 51 Test tons were in victories, while 11 were when he was on the losing side. He scored a Test double century on six occasions, with the first one in his seventy-first Test, after his first 20 Test tons were scores between 104 and 179. In 2010, Tendulkar became the first player to score 200 in a one-day international.

It was interesting to note that ten of Tendulkar's first 13 Test centuries were scored away from home, before he finished with 22 centuries at home and 29 abroad, as he played 12 more away Tests than home Tests. He was involved in 72 wins, 56 losses and 72 draws, while his captaincy record was four wins, nine losses and 12 draws.

Having not recorded a Test century in 1995, after scoring eight before then, Tendulkar reached triple figures 23 times in Tests from the start of 1996 until the end of 2002, while his time as captain began in 1996 and ended in 2000. After scoring 79 and 117 against the West Indies in 2002, he uncharacteristically had successive scores of 0, 0, 8 and 0, yet he notched 1392 Test runs that year. Tendulkar didn't score a Test ton in 2003, as he had another bad trot, and in one innings in Australia he made a duck as he was adjudged lbw when it was clear that the ball would have bounced over the stumps. He had also copped a couple of rough decisions Down Under in December 1999, including when he was adjudged lbw after ducking into a bouncer and being hit on the shoulder, also without scoring.

Tendulkar began 2004 in style with 241 not out against Australia at Sydney, and his next two tons were unbeaten, as he made 194 against Pakistan at Multan and his best first-class score of 248, against Bangladesh at Dhaka. A tennis elbow injury set him back, before Tendulkar had his longest spell without a Test century as he went for 17 innings between December 2005 and May 2007 without achieving the figure. Tendulkar battled a shoulder injury during that time, and at one stage he was even jeered by his home crowd after a failure against England at Wankhede.

Three of Tendulkar's four Test tons in 2008 were against Australia, and in October of that year he overtook Brian Lara as Test cricket's leading runscorer. Tendulkar had his most prolific calendar year in 2010, as he achieved 1562 Test runs at 78.10, following seven centuries: two against Bangladesh, three against South Africa, and a double against Sri Lanka and Australia. He began 2011 with 146 against the Proteas: his last Test century. Twenty-four years after his Test debut, Tendulkar bowed out of Test cricket after scoring 10 and 74 in innings victories, as India won a home series 2–0 against the West Indies.

Sachin Tendulkar (b.1973)

Matches: 200
Runs scored: 15,921
Batting average: 53.78
100s/50s: 51/68
Top score: 248*
Balls bowled: 4240
Wickets: 46
Bowling average: 54.17
5 wickets in innings: –
10 wickets in match: –
Best bowling: 3–10
Catches/stumpings: 115/–

CHAPTER 7: PAKISTAN

7.1 PAKISTAN v SRI LANKA

1980s

The first two series involving Pakistan and Sri Lanka resulted in 2–0 series wins to the Pakistanis on home soil, although the Sri Lankans sometimes put in a decent challenge. Pakistan, it should be noted, was depleted in the first two Tests of the opening series following a falling-out involving several players and the Board.

Pakistan was 126–6 in its first innings when the teams met at Karachi in early 1982, before recovering to post 396. Haroon Rasheed scored 153 while lower order duo Tahir Naqqash and Rashid Khan made half centuries on debut. Sri Lanka totalled 344 before 19-year-old Pakistani Salim Malik, also on debut, made 100 not out as Pakistan set a target of 354 and won by 204 runs. Sri Lanka had the better of a drawn Test in Faisalabad, with opener Sidath Wettimuny making 157 and Roy Dias and Ranjan Madugalle topping 90, as the visitors compiled 454, before Pakistan finished its second innings at 186–7, after being set 339. Were it not for some contentious umpiring decisions, the Sri Lankans may well have won. The return of Imran Khan made a huge difference for Pakistan in the final Test as he snared 8–58 and 6–58. Sri Lanka tallied just 240 and 158 despite a century to Dias in the first innings. Pakistan reached 500–7 declared following centuries to Mohsin Khan and Zaheer Abbas.

Pakistan appeared more dominant against Sri Lanka in late 1985, after the first Test was a high-scoring draw. Pakistan replied to Sri Lanka's 479 with 555–3, as Qasim Umar (206) and Javed Miandad (203 not out) put on 397 for the third wicket. A match haul of 9–95 from Imran enabled Pakistan to win the second Test by 8 wickets, despite Ravi Ratnayeke capturing 8–83, as the hosts tumbled from 181–2 to 259 all out in their first innings. Pakistan concluded the series with a 10-wicket win, before touring Sri Lanka within the next few months and encountering a lot of unpleasantness.

The Sri Lankans were unhappy with the umpiring in Pakistan, before the Pakistanis were adamant that the umpiring in Sri Lanka was biased in favour of the home side. Pakistan nonetheless won the first Test at Kandy by an innings and 20 runs as the hosts managed only 109 and 101. Off spinner Tauseef Ahmed claimed 3–32 and 6–45, and at one stage the match was halted for about half an hour as the umpires and Sri Lankan batsmen left the field after the Pakistanis made unsavoury remarks when Arjuna Ranatunga survived one of many appeals. In the second Test at Colombo, the tourists were thrashed by 8 wickets, after struggling to acclimatise to the heat. Kosala Kuruppuarachchi claimed a wicket with his third delivery in Test cricket and snared 5–44, as Pakistan made 132, and the touring team's second innings was only a little better, as Ravi Ratnayeke captured 5–37, before the hosts easily achieved the paltry target of 32. Sri Lanka was 18–2 and 83–3 after trailing by 37 runs on the first innings in the third Test, before 19-year-old Asanka Gurusinha (116 not out) and 21-year-old Ranatunga (135 not out) put on an unbroken 240-run partnership to salvage a draw. Rain prevented a few hours of play on day four before Pakistan rued several missed chances on the final day, with Ranatunga reprieved five times before he reached 30.

1990s

Two rain-affected draws were followed by a worthy decider, which hosts, Pakistan, won by 3 wickets in season 1991–92. Sri Lanka was well-placed at 81–0 and 130–2, before slumping to 240 all out, and Pakistan was 102–0 before losing 10–119. Needing 185 to win, Pakistan was 60–4 and later lost wickets at 149, 156 and 179 as Sri Lanka fought bravely.

The Sri Lankans were outclassed on home soil in 1994, with the Pakistanis winning the first and third Tests with huge margins, while the second Test was washed out. The visitors twice topped 300 in the first Test while the hosts made 226 and 181 to lose by 301 runs. In the final Test, Waqar Younis (6–34) and Wasim Akram (4–32) routed Sri Lanka for 71 before an unbeaten 100 from Inzamam-ul-Haq helped Pakistan to a 286-run lead. Another 5 wickets to Waqar set up an innings win, before the Pakistanis also won the first Test of the 1995–96 series by an innings. But the Sri Lankans fought back brilliantly in the second Test to claim the nation's first win on Pakistani turf. Another rout looked likely as Sri Lanka plunged to 33–4, before 115 from Hashan Tillekeratne helped the total to 223. Pakistan led by 110 runs before Sri Lanka capitalised on the absence of injured duo Wasim and Waqar, with the latter missing the entire match. Chasing 252, Pakistan stumbled to 209 all out and went on to lose the series, as Wasim and Waqar were sidelined for the deciding Test. Sri Lanka, nonetheless, struggled to 232 before gaining a small lead and then setting 357. Moin Khan made 117 not out and shared in a last-wicket partnership of 65, but the rest of the batting was dismal, as Pakistan made 212 after being 15–5.

The 1997 series was drawn 0–0, with the first Test finishing after Sri Lanka declared its second innings at 423–8, to set a target of 376. The second Test featured an honourable draw as Pakistan was 285–5 after being set 426. Pakistan bizarrely lost its first wicket without a run on the board in all three Pakistan innings in the 1997 series, before this trend continued in its first innings of the next encounter with Sri Lanka.

The teams met twice in the Asian Test Championship in 1999, with Wasim Akram claiming a hat-trick in both encounters. A draw occurred at Lahore before Pakistan won the final by an innings and 175 runs at a neutral venue, in Dhaka. Sri Lanka made 231 and 188, while Ijaz Ahmed (211) and Inzamam-ul-Haq (200 not out) helped Pakistan to 594 as Upul Chandana claimed 6–179 on debut for Sri Lanka.

2000s

A fluctuating series unfolded in early 2000, starting with Pakistan coming close to pulling off an unexpected victory at Rawalpindi. The hosts made 182 before facing a deficit of 171, and then Pakistan went from 236–8 to 390 all out following 107 from Younis Khan and 79 from Wasim Akram. Chasing 220, Sri Lanka went from 116–3 to 177–8 before winning by 2 wickets thanks to wicketkeeper Romesh Kaluwitharana and the experienced Ranatunga, who returned to the crease after retiring hurt at 146–5. The highest total in the second Test was just 268, and Sri Lanka won by 57 runs as Muttiah Muralitharan had match figures of 10–148. The third Test was interestingly poised for a while, before the Pakistanis progressed from 159–5 to 421 all out in their second innings, and went on to win by 222 runs.

Just a few months later, Pakistan won the return series 2–0 in Sri Lankan territory. Sri Lanka's second-innings collapse to 123 all out in the first Test left Pakistan a mere 131-run target, but the visitors stumbled from 51–1 to 66–4 and 89–5 before winning by 5 wickets. In the second Test which included a hat-trick from Pakistan's Abdul Razzaq, Sri Lanka made just 181 and 256, while Pakistan had four centurions in a total of 600–8 declared. The rain-disrupted final Test featured just 155.4 overs, with the hosts working their way to 467–5, after Marvan Atapattu (207 not out) and captain Sanath Jayasuriya (188) put on 335 for the first wicket.

The Sri Lankans avenged their abysmal showing from the 1999 Asian Test Championship as they won the final of the 2002 Championship by 8 wickets at Lahore. Sri Lanka lost Atapattu first ball after Pakistan made 234, before Kumar Sangakkara scored 230 in a total of 528. Pakistan squeezed out an ineffective lead of 31 following 99 from Inzamam-ul-Haq, 70 from Shahid Afridi and 54 sundries.

Sri Lanka lost its first 3 wickets for 9 runs in the first Test of 2004–05 at Faisalabad, before 100 from Thilan Samaraweera helped the total to a still modest 243. Pakistan led by just 21 runs before Atapattu bagged a pair, only for Jayasuriya to change the game as he scored 253 to set up a 201-run win for the visitors. Muralitharan missed the series, which finished on level terms as Pakistan won by 6 wickets at Karachi. Centuries to Younis Khan and Inzamam-ul-Haq helped Pakistan to a 270-run lead, before centuries to Jayasuriya and Sangakkara ensured Pakistan had to chase 137. At 57–4 the hosts were in trouble, before Shoaib Malik and Razzaq knocked off the required runs.

The first Test of 2005–06 was drawn, after both sides failed to pass 185 in their first innings, before Pakistan finished the match on 337–4 after being set 458. Sri Lanka scored 279 (Mohammad Asif 6–44) and then dismissed Pakistan for 170 (Muralitharan 5–39) in the second Test at Kandy, only for Asif (5–27) and Razzaq (4–20) to subsequently rip through Sri Lanka for 73. The match was decided in three days as the visitors lost only 2 wickets in the run chase. The 2008–09 series in Pakistan featured loads of runs and was drawn 0–0 after a scary conclusion. Mahela Jayawardene (240) and Samaraweera (231) helped Sri Lanka to 644–7 declared in the first Test, only for Younis Khan (313) and Kamran Akmal (158 not out) to help Pakistan to 765–6 declared. Samaraweera (214), Tillakaratne Dilshan (145) and Sangakkara (104) set up Sri Lanka's 606 in the second Test at Lahore. Pakistan was 110–1 when the Test was abandoned due to a terrorist attack against the Sri Lankans as they headed to the venue for day three.

Missing Muralitharan as Sri Lanka hosted Pakistan later in 2009, the Sri Lankans won by margins of 50 runs and 7 wickets before the third Test was drawn. The first Test was evenly balanced until the visitors slipped from 36–0 to 39–2 and crashed from 71–2 to 117 all out in their second innings. The Pakistanis plunged to 90 all out in the second Test, before opener and debutant Fawad Alam scored 168 in a second-innings total of 320, which left Sri Lanka needing 171 runs. Sri Lanka's Nuwan Kulasekara claimed 4–21 and 4–37. Needing 492 to clean sweep the series, Sri Lanka finished on 391–4.

The 2011–12 series was played in Bangladesh, with Pakistan winning the second Test by 9 wickets while the other two Tests were drawn. Opener Taufeeq Umar (236) put Pakistan in an impregnable position in the first Test, only for Sangakkara (211) to save Sri Lanka. Totals of 239 and 257 were inadequate for Sri Lanka in the second Test, as Saeed Ajmal claimed 8 wickets for Pakistan, which made 403 in its first innings.

Sri Lanka hosted Pakistan for three Tests in mid 2012, with the hosts always in control of the first Test after Sangakkara (199 not out) and Dilshan (101) set up a first-innings total of 472. After the Sri Lankans won the first Test by 209 runs, two draws followed. The Pakistanis topped 500 in the second Test thanks to Mohammad Hafeez (196) and Azhar Ali (157), before Sangakkara (192) and Dilshan (121) thwarted them again. Sangakkara also ensured the Sri Lankans were safe in the third Test as they reached 195–4 from 62 overs after being set 270.

In the first Test of the 2013–14 series in Bangladesh, Sri Lankan skipper Angelo Mathews was chiefly responsible for his team salvaging a draw. He made 91 out of 204 and an unbeaten 157 in a second-innings total of 480–5 declared, before Pakistan could not achieve a target of 302. Sri Lanka won the second Test by 9 wickets, having gained a 223-run lead, before Pakistan eked out a 136-run lead, after being 19–3. Sri Lanka recovered from 166–5 to post 428–9 declared in the third Test, and Pakistan faltered from 114–0 to 341 all out following 147 from opener Ahmed Shehzad. Sri Lanka's wayward second innings left the Pakistanis needing 302 runs to square the series and they achieved this with a 5-wicket victory, as Azhar Ali (103) and captain Misbah-ul-Haq (68 not out) played the major roles.

In the first Test of 2014, it was again a case of the team batting first going on to lose after topping 400. Younis Khan's 177 was the cornerstone of Pakistan's 451, before 221 from Sangakkara and 91 from Mathews set up Sri Lanka's 82-run lead. A 6-wicket haul to Rangana Herath set up a 7-wicket win for the Sri Lankans, who needed just 99 runs, before Herath captured 14 wickets in the second Test. This contest was on an even keel until Pakistan, chasing 271, flopped to 165 all out to lose the series 2–0.

The three-Test series in Sri Lanka during 2015 was brilliantly fought as there were countless pendulum swings. In the first innings of the opening Test, the hosts stuttered from 142–1 to 300 all out before the visitors recovered from 96–5 and 302–8 to tally 417. Pakistan cruised to a 10-wicket win after Yasir Shah's 7–76 helped dismiss Sri Lanka for 206. In the second Test, Tharindu Kaushal took 5–42 as Pakistan fell from 51–1 to 138 all out, before Shah's 6–96 couldn't prevent Sri Lanka gaining a 177-run lead. Azhar Ali made 117 but Pakistan's lead of 152 was insufficient as Sri Lanka won by 7 wickets, before the visitors returned the compliment in a memorable decider at the Pallekele International Cricket Stadium. Dimuth Karunaratne made 130 in Sri Lanka's 278 as Shah took 5–78, before Pakistan made 215, followed by Mathews scoring 122, after coming to the crease at 35–3. Needing 377 to win the series, Pakistan was 13–2 before a 242-run third-wicket partnership was followed by an unbroken 127-run fourth-wicket stand. Opener Shan Masood made 125, and Younis Khan was left unbeaten on 171, while captain Misbah-ul-Haq (59 not out) brought up the winning runs with a six.

Pakistan v Sri Lanka

1981–82 (P): Pakistan 2–0 (1 drawn)

1985–86 (P): Pakistan 2–0 (1 drawn)

1985–86 (SL): 1–1 (1 drawn)

1991–92 (P): Pakistan 1–0 (2 drawn)

1994 (SL): Pakistan 2–0 (1 abandoned)

1995–96 (P): Sri Lanka 2–1

1996–97 (SL): 0–0 (2 drawn)

1998–99 (P and Bangladesh): 1 drawn, 1 Pakistan win (Asian Test Championship)

1999–00 (P): Sri Lanka 2–1

2000 (SL): Pakistan 2–0 (1 drawn)

2001–02 (P): Sri Lanka 1–0 (Asian Test Championship)

2004–05 (P): 1–1

2005–06 (SL): Pakistan 1–0 (1 drawn)

2008–09 (P): 0–0 (2 drawn)

2009 (SL): Sri Lanka 2–0 (1 drawn)

2011–12 (Bangladesh): Pakistan 1–0 (2 drawn)

2012 (SL): Sri Lanka 1–0 (2 drawn)

2013–14 (Bangladesh): 1–1 (1 drawn)

2014 (SL): Sri Lanka 2–0

2015 (SL): Pakistan 2–1

7.2 PAKISTAN v ZIMBABWE

1990s

Pakistan was one of just two countries to lose to Zimbabwe in Test cricket before Bangladesh gained Test status. Pakistan had the better of most of the encounters with Zimbabwe until 2015–16, but some of Zimbabwe's most memorable moments in Test cricket occurred against Pakistan.

Waqar Younis bagged 13 wickets in Wasim Akram's absence, as Pakistan won the first meeting by 131 runs in Karachi in 1993–94. The Zimbabweans were poised to level the series in the second Test at Rawalpindi and achieve their maiden Test victory as they were 135–1 when chasing 240, only for Akram and Younis to rip through the visitors for 187. Rain hampered Zimbabwe's victory hopes in the third Test, after the visitors responded to Pakistan's 147 with 230.

Zimbabwe's maiden Test victory was at Pakistan's expense as the Zimbabweans won the first Test of 1994–95 by an innings and 64 runs in Harare. The hosts lost their first 2 wickets for 9 runs before Grant Flower (201 not out), Andy Flower (156) and Guy Whittall (113 not out) set up a mammoth total of 544–4 declared. Heath Streak took 6–90 and 3–15 as Pakistan folded for 322 and 158, before the visitors struck back in the second Test. Pakistan won by 8 wickets after Zimbabwe twice failed to reach 175, before the deciding Test could have gone either way. The Africans led by 12 runs on the first innings before chasing 239, and losing wickets regularly as Pakistan won by 99 runs.

Centuries to Grant Flower and number eight Paul Strang helped Zimbabwe to 375 in the first Test of 1996–97 at Sheikhupura Stadium, before Pakistan was 237–7. Pakistan, incredibly, reached 553 after Wasim Akram scored 257 not out and shared a 313-run eighth-wicket stand with Saqlain Mushtaq (79). Zimbabwe escaped with a draw, before Pakistan clinched the series with a 10-wicket win, after Akram claimed 10 wickets as Zimbabwe made just 133 and 200.

Pakistan also won the 1997–98 series 1–0, although Zimbabwe could just as easily have won both Tests. After Grant Flower carried his bat, scoring 156, Zimbabwe led by 65 runs before setting Pakistan 368, after Murray Goodwin (166 not out) and Andy Flower (100 not out) took Zimbabwe from 25–4 to 302–4 declared. Pakistan was 258–6 when the first Test concluded before Zimbabwe gained the upper hand during the second Test. From 187–8 in reply to Zimbabwe's 277, Pakistan rallied as Mohammad Wasim (192) and Mushtaq Ahmed (57) added 147 runs for the ninth wicket. After Zimbabwe tallied 268, Pakistan lost wickets at 14, 59, 77, 105, 138, 162 and 186 as the Africans remained an outside chance of victory.

The 1998–99 series in Pakistan was historic, as Zimbabwe won a Test series for the first time, albeit in bizarre circumstances. The visitors won the opening Test by 7 wickets as they chased 162, after dismissing the hosts for 103. Neil Johnson made an important 107 as Zimbabwe struggled in reply to Pakistan's 296, before gaining control. Poor weather was decisive in the following two fixtures, with Zimbabwe 48–0 in its second innings and trailing by 94 runs when the second Test ended, before the third Test was, peculiarly, abandoned due to fog.

2000s

Pakistan convincingly won the 2002–03 series away from home, with margins of 119 runs and 10 wickets. The Zimbabweans weren't disgraced as they were never likely to achieve a target of 430 in the first Test, before the Pakistanis dominated the second Test, as Yousuf Youhana scored 159 after Zimbabwe made 178.

Zimbabwean opener Tino Mawoyo scored 163 not out, as Zimbabwe topped 400 in the one-off Test at Bulawayo in September 2011, only for Pakistan to better it after Mohammad Hafeez made 119. A Zimbabwean collapse left the Pakistanis a mere 88-run target, which was accomplished for the loss of 3 wickets.

Pakistan maintained its dominance with a 221-run victory at Harare in 2013, albeit after the hosts had surrendered control. Zimbabwe made 327 after Pakistan struggled to 249, and then the visitors were 23–3, before an unconquered 200 from Younis Khan lifted the total beyond 400. Mawoyo was dismissed from the second delivery of the second Test, before Zimbabwe tallied 294 and restricted Pakistan to

230, after the visitors had been 182–3. Chasing 264, Pakistan faltered as Tendai Chatara's 5-wicket haul inspired a 24-run win for Zimbabwe to square the series.

Pakistan v Zimbabwe

1993–94 (P): Pakistan 2–0 (1 drawn)

1994–95 (Z): Pakistan 2–1

1996–97 (P): Pakistan 1–0 (1 drawn)

1997–98 (Z): Pakistan 1–0 (1 drawn)

1998–99 (P): Zimbabwe 1–0 (1 drawn, 1 abandoned)

2002–03 (Z): Pakistan 2–0

2011 (Z): Pakistan 1–0

2013 (Z): 1–1

7.3 PAKISTAN v BANGLADESH

Bangladesh upset Pakistan in a 1999 World Cup match, but the Test arena proved a much different scenario, as Pakistan won the first eight contests. Bangladesh could just as easily have won one of them, but the other seven battles were comprehensive, as four of them yielded innings victories to Pakistan.

2000s

In its fourth ever Test, Bangladesh tallied just 134 and 148 as Danish Kaneria bagged 12 wickets, while five Pakistanis scored between 101 and 110 in a total of 546–3 declared. This Test was played at Multan Cricket Stadium as part of the 2001–02 Asian Test Championship, before two Tests were played in Bangladesh in January 2002. Pakistan won both in three days, with the hosts totalling 160 and 152 in the first Test, before twice making 148 in the second Test. The Pakistanis made 490–9 declared and 465–9 declared in their innings wins, with Kaneria taking 9 wickets in the first Test before Yousuf Youhana scored 204 not out in the second Test.

Bangladesh was more competitive away from home in 2003 as Pakistan won by 7 wickets, 9 wickets and 1 wicket. Yasir Hameed scored 170 in Pakistan's first innings before following up with 105 as the hosts chased 217 in the first Test, while Habibul Bashar impressed for Bangladesh with 71 and 108. Javed Omar (119), Bashar (97) and Mohammad Ashraful (77) helped the tourists to 310–2 in the first innings of the second Test, before Bangladesh folded for 361 and 96, with fast bowler Shoaib Akhtar achieving match figures of 10–80. Mohammad Hafeez made an undefeated 102, as Pakistan easily passed the target of 163, before the final Test was one that slipped from Bangladesh's grasp. After scoring 281 and then dismissing Pakistan for 175, as Mohammad Rafique and Khaled Mahmud shared 9 wickets, Bangladesh set the hosts 261. Pakistan was 164–7, 205–8 and 257–9 but Bangladesh couldn't land the knockout blow as Inzamam-ul-Haq scored 138 not out and received solid support from the lower order.

Pakistan won the first Test of the 2011–12 series in Bangladesh by an innings and 184 runs, with Younis Khan scoring 200 not out, while Mohammad Hafeez and Asad Shafiq also passed 100 in a total of 594–5 declared. Shakib Al Hasan (144) and Shahriar Nafees (97) set up a total of 338 for Bangladesh in the first innings of the second Test, before Pakistan replied with 470. Pakistan passed the target of 103 for the loss of just 3 wickets, with captain Misbah-ul-Haq striking a six for the winning runs.

Bangladesh salvaged a respectable draw at Khulna in 2015, before Pakistan won the two-match series with a 328-run victory at Mirpur. In the first Test, Hafeez made 224 as Pakistan racked up 628 in reply to Bangladesh's 332. Bangladesh openers Tamim Iqbal (206) and Imrul Kayes (150) subsequently put on 312 for the first wicket to ensure the hosts were safe, before the team finished at 555–6. Azhar Ali (226), Younis Khan (148) and Asad Shafiq (107) led the Pakistanis to 557–8 declared in the second Test, and they later set the Bangladeshis 550 rather than enforce the follow-on.

Pakistan v Bangladesh

2001 (P): Pakistan (Asian Test Championship)
2001–02 (B): Pakistan 2–0

2003 (P): Pakistan 3–0
2011–12 (B): Pakistan 2–0
2015 (B): Pakistan 1–0 (1 drawn)

7.4 NOTABLE TEST PLAYERS

Imran Khan

Imran Khan was one of cricket's premier all-rounders, while also very durable, as he represented Pakistan between 1971 and 1992 despite some injury troubles. Pakistan achieved 14 wins, 8 losses and 26 draws under his captaincy from 1982 to 1992, and he pulled the pin after leading Pakistan to World Cup glory in 1992, aged 39. In *Cricket's Great All-Rounders*, Kersi Meher-Homji described Imran as, 'a natural leader of men, perhaps autocratic at times — especially in selecting players he wanted. A talented but undisciplined Pakistan team needed a strong man at the helm and Imran was just that.'

Imran's first-class debut could hardly have been less satisfactory, after the 16-year-old was chosen as an opening batsman and opening bowler. Imran's cousin captained the team while the chairman of selectors was Imran's uncle, and the teenager ducked out to take a nap as rain delayed the start of the match. Imran had to be replaced as an opening batsman due to the game starting before his belated return to the venue, but his bowling came a long way in the next two years and earned him a Test cap against England in 1971. He was run out for 5 before delivering 28 wicketless overs, having failed to capitalise on conditions suited for swing bowling, after he began with four swinging full-tosses.

Staying in England and playing for Worcestershire benefited Imran immensely, as did being a scholar at Oxford University. His second Test appearance came three years after his debut, and his three appearances in England in 1974 produced an average of just 18.40 with the bat and only 5 wickets at 51.50. Imran returned to his home country and played for Pakistan International Airways, before earning a regular Test berth. In New Zealand in 1976–77 he was banned from bowling in one Test after delivering too many short-pitched balls, before his form improved during tours of Australia and the West Indies as his pace increased. Imran claimed 12 wickets in the third Test at Sydney as Pakistan drew Australia 1–1. Imran played World Series Cricket before a rib injury hampered him during Pakistan's unsuccessful tour of India in 1979–80, although he still claimed 19 wickets at 19.21.

Imran's maiden Test century was in his thirtieth Test when he scored 123 against the West Indies at Lahore in 1980–81. In the next few years, Imran really came into his own as a top-class bowler. As Pakistan lost 2–1 Down Under in 1981–82, Imran stood out with 16 wickets at 19.50. Turmoil among Pakistani cricket forced Imran to miss the country's first two encounters with Sri Lanka before he claimed 14–116 in the final Test, including his best Test innings figures of 8–58. In 1982 he captured 62 wickets at a miserly 13.29 in nine Tests. Imran's first series as captain yielded a 2–1 loss which included Pakistan's first Test victory in England for 28 years, and Imran was the player of the series after scoring 212 runs at 53 and taking 21 wickets at 18.53. In a 3–0 clean sweep against Australia in Pakistan, Imran took 13 wickets at 13.15 and scored 64 runs for once out. His performances in a 3–0 series win against India in 1982–83 were heroic as he scored 247 runs at 61.75 and captured 40 wickets at just 13.95 with best figures of 8–60. In the Faisalabad Test, he scored his second Test century and also captured 11 wickets. A stress fracture in his shin, however, stymied his career for a couple of years. He played two Tests as a specialist batsman against Australia in 1983–84 before his next Tests were against Sri Lanka in 1985–86, as he took 32 wickets in six appearances: three in Pakistan and three in Sri Lanka.

Having missed Pakistan's first Test series win against England in 1983–84, Imran led his country to a drawn series against world champions the West Indies in late 1986, and captured 18 wickets at 11.06 in the three Tests. The following year, Imran led Pakistan to its first series win on Indian soil, followed by a series win in England. His batting was a lot better than his bowling in India, before his all-round contribution was strong in England. Imran declared his retirement after Pakistan bowed out of the 1987 World Cup with a semi-final loss to eventual champions Australia, but he was enticed to play on.

With Imran capturing 23 wickets at 18.09, Pakistan drew the West Indies 1–1 in the Caribbean in 1988, although the tourists could just as easily have won all three Tests rather than only the first one. Imran didn't play on home soil against Australia in late 1988, before he led his country Down Under in 1989–90. The Pakistanis lost 1–0 but it was the first time in almost five years that they lost a Test series. Imran's pace had slowed although he could still deliver an impressive inswinger, while his batting was perhaps better than it had ever been. He averaged more than 80 in a period from early 1989 to early 1990, and made his highest Test score of 136 against Australia at Adelaide after lasting a little over eight hours. Imran led his country to another drawn series with the West Indies, before he had a triumphant farewell to Test cricket as Pakistan beat Sri Lanka by 3 wickets to win a series 1–0.

Imran Khan (b.1952)

Matches: 88
Runs scored: 3807
Batting average: 37.69
100s/50s: 6/18
Top score: 136
Balls bowled: 19,458
Wickets: 362
Bowling average: 22.81
5 wickets in innings: 23
10 wickets in match: 6
Best bowling: 8–58
Catches/stumpings: 28/–

Inzamam-ul-Haq

Inzamam-ul-Haq burst onto the international scene in the 1992 World Cup as he blasted 60 off 37 balls to help Pakistan upset New Zealand in a semi-final, before he made an invaluable 42 off 35 balls in the decider, which Pakistan won against England. It was little surprise that Inzamam also succeeded at Test level, even if his running between the wickets brought about too many run-outs to remember.

Inzamam made his Test debut in England ten weeks after the 1992 World Cup decider, and he was dropped after four Tests due to averaging 13.20 with a highest score of 26. But he was back in the side within six months, and scored a vital 75 in a one-off Test against New Zealand in early 1993. Pakistan was 39–5 in its second innings, still 9 runs in arrears before Inzamam helped set a target of 127, which the Kiwis failed to achieve. His maiden Test century was during a series loss in the Caribbean in 1993, before his second century was against New Zealand during a Pakistani innings win that clinched a series victory. Later in 1994, Inzamam's 58 not out helped Pakistan to a 1-wicket win against Australia at Karachi.

Many times Inzamam rescued his team from difficult situations; always the sign of a player with high acclaim. Pakistan came from 1–0 down to beat Zimbabwe 2–1 in early 1995, and surely would have lost the decider were it not for Inzamam's knocks of 101 and 83. Inzamam's batting was also decisive as Pakistan won 2–0 in England in 1996, before his 177 against the West Indies in the second Test of 1997–98 helped the Pakistanis clinch the series. An Inzamam innings of 135 rescued Pakistan in the first Test of the 2000 series against the West Indians, who ultimately sneaked to a 1–0 series win. Inzamam's 142 helped Pakistan draw the 2000–01 series with England, and his 138 not out against Bangladesh in September 2003 helped Pakistan to a 3–0 series win with a 1-wicket victory in the final Test.

In three-match series against Sri Lanka in late 2004, and against India in early 2005, Inzamam scored a ton in the third Test each time, as Pakistan won to square each series. His 184 against India was a memorable way to mark his 100th Test, while teammate Younis Khan scored 267. Also in 2005, a crucial century from Inzamam helped

Pakistan draw the West Indies 1–1 before he scored two tons in a draw against England which lost the other two Tests in the series. Inzamam's 25 Test hundreds included a double-ton and a triple-ton, both in innings victories. His 200 not out was against Sri Lanka in the 1998–99 Test Championship final, and his 329 was against New Zealand in the only match of the 2002 series, before a bomb cancelled the tour.

Solidly built, Inzamam had quick footwork and could play powerful cross-batted shots as well as flick the ball off his pads with skill. He captained Pakistan in 31 Tests from 2003 to 2007, achieving 11 wins, 11 losses and nine draws. Unfortunately his record was tarnished by the infamous incident at the Oval in 2006 when the touring team refused to take the field for a prolonged period following ball-tampering allegations. Pakistan was well-placed to salvage a 2–1 series loss before the result became 3–0, as Inzamam became the first captain to forfeit a Test. Inzamam's team was cleared of ball tampering but the captain was banned from four one-day internationals for bringing the game into disrepute. His captaincy reign ended after Pakistan exited the 2007 World Cup with a surprise loss to Ireland, before he retired from international cricket later that year. At the time Inzamam was Pakistan's highest runscorer in one-day cricket and second highest runscorer in Tests, just 3 runs behind Javed Miandad.

Inzamam-ul-Haq (b.1970)

Matches: 120
Runs scored: 8830
Batting average: 49.60
100s/50s: 25/46
Top score: 329
Balls bowled: 9
Wickets: –
Bowling average: –
5 wickets in innings: –
10 wickets in match: –
Best bowling: 0–8
Catches/stumpings: 81/–

Javed Miandad

Javed Miandad's Test career was off to a flying start as he scored 163 and 25 not out on debut, 25 in his second Test and then 206 and 85 in his third Test. Pakistan won the home series 2–0 against New Zealand in late 1976 as Javed was only 19 years old. He also took 8 wickets in his maiden Test series, although he claimed just 9 scalps in his remaining 121 Tests. Having made his one-day international debut in 1975, Javed played his last international in 1996, having taken part in the first six World Cup tournaments. He had intermittent stints as captain, with Pakistan winning 14 Tests, losing 6 and drawing 14 under his leadership.

Javed's career figures and longevity were impressive, yet he gained a lot of attention for irking teammates and opponents. Following his great debut series, Javed averaged just 29.60 in Australia in 1976–77, and also took 5 wickets. He was hard to dismiss on home soil against England in 1977–78 and against India in 1978–79, with 262 runs at 131 in five innings on the former occasion and 357 runs at 178.50 in five innings on the latter occasion including two centuries. He floundered during Pakistan's 1978 series loss in England, but excelled in New Zealand as he scored 81 and 160 not out in a win at Christchurch. Javed also scored a century on Australian soil in early 1979, only for Pakistan to lose the Test after winning the first one. The Australians were incensed that Javed ran out Rodney Hogg as the batsman left his crease to inspect the pitch during the first Test, and this set the stage for an unpleasant series.

Javed was appointed captain following a series defeat in India, and he led Pakistan to a 1–0 win against Australia while also scoring one century. In Australia in late 1981, Pakistan's skipper was in the spotlight for a skirmish with Dennis Lillee as Pakistan was on its way to a couple of hefty defeats. Javed did not earn the respect of his teammates, and he was replaced as captain following Pakistan's 2–0 win against Sri Lanka in 1982. Javed averaged 35.60 in a close series loss to England, before returning to form with 138 as Pakistan completed a 3–0 rout of Australia in Pakistan. During Pakistan's 3–0 win at home against India in 1982–83, Javed made his best Test score of 280 not out in the Hyderabad fixture as he put on 451 runs with Mudassar Nazar. Another highlight at Hyderabad for Javed came in 1984–85 when he scored 104 and 103 not out to help the hosts to a 2–0 series victory against the Kiwis. But the Pakistanis lost the follow-up series 2–0 in New Zealand with Javed as captain and unable to make a big score.

In 1985–86, Javed scored 203 not out in the drawn first Test against Sri Lanka at Faisalabad as he and Qasim Umar put on 397 runs. Pakistan won the series 1–0 under Javed's leadership before drawing the next series 1–1 in Sri Lanka, after Imran regained the captaincy. Javed nearly came to blows with the Sri Lankans as he was upset with an lbw verdict against him during Pakistan's defeat at Colombo, and then he sought to get even with a spectator who threw a stone at him.

Javed was in vintage form in the late 1980s as he compiled three double-centuries on his way to 1424 runs at 89 in 12 Tests. His 260 against England in the fifth Test of 1987 ensured Pakistan would protect its series lead, and his 211 in late 1988 led to a Pakistan series win at home against Australia, although he was controversially reprieved several times. In his only two innings in a drawn series in New Zealand in early 1989, Javed made 118 and 271. Javed also made two important tons in the 1988 series in the Caribbean, with the first one resulting in a win before the second one threatened to produce a Pakistani series win.

Javed made 145 in a draw with India in December 1989, but he scored only one more Test ton in his remaining four years of Test cricket. Although his results were modest against New Zealand in late 1990, he led the Pakistanis to a 3–0 whitewash as Imran was missing. Following his important runmaking in Pakistan's 1992 World Cup triumph, Javed captained his country to a 2–1 win in England, having scored 153 not out in the drawn first Test. Javed also led Pakistan to victory in a one-off Test in New Zealand in January 1993, with the skipper making a crucial 92 in his team's first innings of 216. Wasim Akram led Pakistan during Javed's final Test series, which Pakistan won 2–0 against Zimbabwe, after Javed scored 31 in the drawn third Test.

Javed Miandad (b.1957)

Matches: 124
Runs scored: 8832
Batting average: 52.57
100s/50s: 23/43
Top score: 280*
Balls bowled: 1470
Wickets: 17
Bowling average: 40.11
5 wickets in innings: –
10 wickets in match: –
Best bowling: 3–74
Catches/stumpings: 93/1

Mohammad Yousuf

Mohammad Yousuf was named Yousuf Youhana before changing from Christianity to Muslim, and he was one of the most stylish batsmen in international cricket. He averaged less than 30 against Australia, South Africa and Sri Lanka, yet still finished with an overall average above 50. He also skippered Pakistan in nine Tests.

Yousuf made just 5 and 1 on debut against South Africa in early 1998, with Pakistan winning at Durban before Yousuf was omitted for the final Test in which the hosts drew the series. In Zimbabwe, Yousuf scored 60, 64, 9 and 52 in a 1–0 series win before Zimbabwe won 1–0 on Pakistani soil later that year as Yousuf scored 75, 14 and 120 not out — his maiden Test ton. Yousuf didn't score any Test tons in 1999, although he came close in his first Test on Australian soil, as he made 95 and 75 before failing in the remaining two Tests as Pakistan was hammered 3–0. Yousuf notched four Test centuries in 2000, with two in the Caribbean and two against England in Pakistan, but the Pakistanis lost both series 1–0. The first of Yousuf's two Test tons in 2001 was a score of 203 against the Kiwis at Christchurch in a drawn match and drawn series. Yousuf finally made a century in a winning cause as he scored 102 not out against Bangladesh in the Asian Test Championship. His next Test ton was also in a big win against Bangladesh, as his undefeated 204 helped the Pakistanis to a 2–0 series victory in 2002. Yousuf's two other Test tons in 2002 were in victories, against the West Indies and Zimbabwe.

Yousuf went almost 18 months without making a Test century before his eleventh, twelfth and thirteenth tons could not prevent Pakistan from losing. Yousuf finished 2003 on a strong note as his knocks of 60 and 88 not out contributed to an astonishing come-from-behind victory in the New Zealand capital, after he captained Pakistan to a win against South Africa in October. Pakistan's first Test in 2004 was a disaster, as India inflicted an innings defeat at Multan, despite Yousuf scoring 35 and 112. Yousuf took on the captaincy later in 2004 as Pakistan trailed Australia 1–0 Down Under, and he could not prevent the hosts cantering to a 3–0 whitewash, despite scoring 111 at Melbourne. Yousuf's remaining six Tests at the helm were in 2009–10.

Yousuf's two Test tons in 2005 included his highest Test score of 223, with Pakistan winning the home series against England. Yousuf had a record-breaking 2006 as he compiled nine centuries amidst 1788 runs at 99.33 in the calendar year. His scores against India were 173, 65, 126, a golden duck and 97 before he made 17 and 14 not out against Sri Lanka. Against England, Yousuf made 202, 48, 38, 15, 192, 8 and 128, before his scores against the West Indians were 192, 56, 191, 102 and 124. Pakistan won three of those series, with England the exception.

Issues involving the Indian Cricket League affected Yousuf's international career for a couple of years, and he did not play any Tests in 2008. At Galle in July 2009, Yousuf marked his return to the scene with his twenty-fourth and last Test century, only for Sri Lanka to win the match and the series. Yousuf subsequently led his team to a drawn series in New Zealand and a 3–0 defeat in Australia, with the Pakistanis surrendering an inevitable victory in the second Test Down Under. Following an inquiry, the Pakistan Cricket Board (PCB) banned Yousuf from playing international cricket. The reason was not fully clear, although various reports indicated that ill-discipline and being a supposed bad influence were the problems. He declared his retirement from international cricket in March 2010, but the PCB asked him to come out of retirement during Pakistan's 2010 tour of England. Yousuf returned for the third Test and made 56 and 33 in a Pakistani victory after England won the first two Tests. The fourth Test was Yousuf's last, in which he scored 0 and 10 in an innings loss.

Mohammad Yousuf (b.1974)

Matches: 90
Runs scored: 7530
Batting average: 52.29
100s/50s: 24/33
Top score: 223
Balls bowled: 6
Wickets: –
Bowling average: –
5 wickets in innings: –
10 wickets in match: –
Best bowling: 0–3
Catches/stumpings: 65/–

Wasim Akram and Waqar Younis

Whilst Australian duo Dennis Lillee and Jeff Thomson were known as a lethal pair and various West Indian fast bowlers had strong combinations, it was hard to think of a duo that was as destructive as Pakistanis Wasim Akram and Waqar Younis. Both were introduced to Test cricket as teens, although Wasim's debut was in early 1985 before Waqar debuted nearly five years later. In the 61 Tests they played together, Wasim took 282 wickets at 21.33 while Waqar claimed 277 at 22.90. In his other 43 Tests, Wasim took 132 wickets at 28.50 while Waqar, when not playing with Wasim, took 96 wickets at 25.47 from 26 Tests. Perhaps their most destructive time as a bowling pair was at Kandy in August 1994, when Waqar took 6–34 and Wasim 4–32, as the hosts crumbled for 71 in 28.2 overs without any bowling changes. When Sri Lanka beat

Pakistan in a Test series for the first time just over a year later, it was telling that Wasim and Waqar had succumbed to injury.

Waqar's strike rate was an outstanding 43.50 compared with Wasim's 54.65 while Wasim was on the winning side 41 times to Waqar's 39. They were also among many Pakistanis who were handed the captaincy at various stages, with Wasim at the helm for 25 Tests and Waqar for 17 after Waqar first became captain aged just 22. Pakistan won 12 Tests and drew eight under Wasim, and won ten and lost seven under Waqar.

Wasim was arguably the world's best bowler for much of the 1990s, and he has been rated by some commentators as indisputably the greatest ever left-arm fast bowler. Wasim's heroics in Pakistan's 1992 World Cup victory have been well documented elsewhere, and he was the first player to take 400 wickets in Tests and one-day internationals. He could vary his pace, swing and cut the ball both ways, deliver unplayable yorkers, bowl a great line and length, and sometimes seemed more effective with an old ball than a new one. Allan Miller wrote in his 2000 cricket annual: 'You could apply a hundred adjectives to Wasim Akram's persona and still come up short. Enduring, resilient, reliable, admirable, talented, powerful, determined, resourceful, penetrative, dynamic...But he is not superman.' Peter Roebuck reported in *The Sydney Morning Herald*:

> In Akram's hands a ball does not so much talk as sing. With a flick of the wrist and an arm that flashes past his ears like a thought through a child's brain he pushes the ball across the batsman and makes it dip back wickedly late, or bends it early where upon it changes direction after landing.

Wasim was at the centre of ball-tampering and match-fixing allegations at various stages of his career and also had run-ins with Pakistani cricket authorities. As Ian Botham remarked in *Botham's Century*, 'controversy was never more than a couple of steps behind' Wasim, and that 'someone, somewhere always had a bad word to say about Wasim'. Wasim nevertheless always seemed to overcome adversity. Despite being chosen as a bowler, Wasim could be considered a bowling all-rounder, as he had a top score of 257 not out, although his left-handed batting was sometimes spoilt by his tendency to attempt big shots a little too often. He burst onto the international cricket scene as an 18-year-old and, after taking 2–105 in a heavy defeat on debut, he claimed 5–56 and 5–72 in his second Test, as Pakistan slid to a 2-wicket loss in New Zealand.

Wasim was sometimes overshadowed by Imran Khan and spinners such as Abdul Qadir in the 1980s, although Wasim had his moments in the spotlight. As the Pakistanis thrashed the West Indians in a 1986 Test, Wasim claimed 6–91 and scored 66. A groin injury restricted Wasim towards the end of the decade, but in 1989–90 he had a marvellous tour of Australia. In a 92-run loss at Melbourne he claimed 6–62 and 5–98 which took him to 105 wickets from 30 Tests, before his performance in a draw at Adelaide was his most cherished memory in Test cricket. His driving through the offside was superb as he scored 52 and 123, and he also captured 5–100 and 1–29.

Wasim claimed 4–61 and 5–28 against the West Indies at Lahore in late 1990, with his last 4 wickets coming in 5 balls while a dropped catch prevented him from taking a hat-trick. Pakistan drew that series but lost 2–0 to the West Indies under Wasim's captaincy a couple of years later, although Pakistan had substantial success in the early 1990s in addition to World Cup glory. Wasim was vital in Pakistan's Test victories against Sri Lanka, England, New Zealand, Zimbabwe and Australia. As the Pakistanis romped to an insurmountable 2–0 series lead over the Kiwis in 1994, Wasim snared 9 wickets in one Test and 11 in the other.

Wasim's highest score came at number eight against Zimbabwe at Sheikhupura Stadium in October 1996, and included 22 fours and 12 sixes. The match was drawn, but he bowled Pakistan to victory in the second Test with 6–48 and 4–58. Wasim captured 240 wickets at 20.05 in 48 Tests from the start of 1990 until the end of 1997 and, although he took a more modest 80 wickets at 28.96 from 1998 onwards, there were still some career highlights. Wasim skippered the Pakistanis as they won the inaugural Asian Test Championship, which also involved Wasim's two Test hat-tricks. Both were against Sri Lanka, with the latter one in the final. Several weeks earlier, Wasim led Pakistan in its memorable 1–1 draw with India, but later that year his own form was sub-standard as he led his country to a 3–0 loss Down Under. The following year Wasim took 11 wickets in a 1-wicket loss to the West Indies and was again a thorn in Sri Lanka's side. Wasim scored 78 and 20 not out and took a 5-wicket haul in a 5-wicket win over Sri Lanka, and then notched his third and final Test ton in the following Test, which Pakistan won by an innings.

Yorkers and reverse swing were among Waqar's specialties, although he could also adopt short-pitched tactics. Waqar was a huge hit early in his one-day international career in late 1989, around the time of his eighteenth birthday, although there was often conjecture and confusion about his age. In his Test debut, which was also in late 1989, Waqar and Wasim took the new ball and claimed 4 wickets apiece in India's first innings of a draw at Karachi. Waqar's figures were disappointing in Pakistan's subsequent tour of Australia, although there was a glimmer in the Adelaide Test in which Wasim excelled. Sheer pace enabled Waqar to bowl Allan Border for 13 and have him caught behind for 8.

During the same eight-year period in which Wasim captured 240 wickets at 20.05 from 48 Tests, Waqar captured 232 wickets at 21.23 from 46 Tests. One of Waqar's best series was against New Zealand in 1990–91, as he snared 29 wickets in three Tests with innings figures including 7–86, 7–76 and 5–54, although the umpires seemed to overlook ball tampering. A back injury forced Waqar to miss the 1992 World Cup, before he and Wasim inspired a Test series win in England. In a 2-wicket win at Lord's, they shared 13 wickets before putting on an unbroken ninth-wicket stand of 46 to clinch the result. In the final Test at the Oval, they shared 15 wickets to set up a 10-wicket victory that decided the series.

Waqar snared six 5-wicket hauls in 1993, starting with 5–22, as he and Wasim, who snared 5–45, routed the Kiwis for 93 when they needed 127 to win a one-off Test. Waqar's figures against Zimbabwe that year were 7–91, 6–44, 5–88, 4–50 and 5–100. Waqar claimed two 6-wicket hauls and a 5-wicket haul in 1994, before another back injury put his career on hold as he had 190 wickets from 33 Tests at a miserly average of 19.16. Waqar was a little patchy thereafter as he achieved only two more 6-wicket hauls and one 5-wicket haul, as his last 54 Tests yielded a still creditable 183 wickets at 28.13.

In spite of Wasim's and Waqar's brilliant partnership, there was friction and squabbling which sometimes brought about problems for the team, as well as themselves. Perhaps there was rivalry which brought out the best and worst in them. Waqar didn't play for his country during a period in 2000 when Wasim was captain, before Waqar later became captain. Also in 2000, Waqar was fined and suspended for ball tampering. With Waqar at the helm, the Pakistanis won six successive Tests in 2001–02 as they beat England to draw a series 1–1 before defeating Bangladesh 3–0 and the West Indies 2–0. But 2002 had low points for the Waqar-led Pakistan, which lost 3–0 to Australia before losing 2–0 to South Africa in 2002–03. Waqar's stints as bowling coach and head coach of Pakistan also had mixed fortunes, but his and Wasim's achievements on the field for their country should always be held in high regard, despite the controversies.

Wasim Akram (b.1966)

Matches: 104
Runs scored: 2898
Batting average: 22.64
100s/50s: 3/7
Top score: 257*
Balls bowled: 22,627
Wickets: 414
Bowling average: 23.62
5 wickets in innings: 25
10 wickets in match: 5
Best bowling: 7–119
Catches/stumpings: 44/–

Waqar Younis (b.1971)

Matches: 87
Runs scored: 1010
Batting average: 10.20
100s/50s: 0/0
Top score: 45
Balls bowled: 16,224
Wickets: 373
Bowling average: 23.56
5 wickets in innings: 22
10 wickets in match: 5
Best bowling: 7–76
Catches/stumpings: 18/–

Younis Khan

There was a lot that showed what a fine batsman Younis Khan was, besides becoming the first Pakistani to register 9000 Test runs. He scored more Test centuries than half-centuries, he posted a triple-figure score against every other Test-playing nation, and made several of his tons after the age of 35. A strong player against spin with the ability to score a lot of runs on the legside, Younis was a strong driver but also an lbw candidate at times, and was sometimes dismissed when not offering a stroke.

Younis scored 12 and 107 in his maiden Test, only for Sri Lanka to win the match and the series. Pakistan however won a follow-up series in Sri Lanka, with Younis making 116 in an innings triumph at Galle. His one Test ton in 2001 was in New Zealand, and in 2002 he made 119 against Bangladesh at Chittagong, before his knocks of 153 and 71 at Sharjah helped Pakistan beat the West Indies 2–0. Pakistan's failure in the 2003 World Cup prompted several team changes, and Younis briefly retained his spot before losing it as his form was below par.

Recalled when Pakistan trailed Sri Lanka 1–0 in late 2004, Younis helped level the series with his 124 at Karachi. In 2005 he also helped

Pakistan salvage deadlocked series results against India and the West Indies. The Pakistanis had lost their first 2 wickets for 7 runs at Bangalore before Younis made 267 and 84 not out in a 168-run win, after he scored 147 and a second-ball duck in a 195-run loss at Kolkata. Younis skippered Pakistan in the first Test in the Caribbean, and scored 31 and 0 in 276-run defeat at Barbados. Inzamam-ul-Haq regained the leadership at Jamaica where Younis scored 106 and 43 in a 136-run triumph.

Pakistan's home series against India in early 2006 was an enormously successful if somewhat frustrating time for Younis. He was run out for 199 at Lahore, brilliantly caught for 83 and then lbw for 194 at Faisalabad, with both matches drawn. Younis captained the team to a big victory in the decider at Karachi as Inzamam was unavailable, with Younis making a golden duck and 77 as he was twice adjudged lbw. During Pakistan's 3–0 series loss in England, Younis was run out for 173 at Headingley, where the hosts won by 167 runs. Two of Younis' centuries in 2007 were against South Africa while the other was against India, with Pakistan losing both series. With India leading 1–0, Younis replaced Shoaib Malik as skipper for the second and third Tests, and made 43, 107 not out, 80 and 0 in two draws.

After rejecting the offer to captain Pakistan on a permanent basis in 2006 and 2007, Younis finally accepted the honour in 2009. A two-match series against Sri Lanka was drawn 0–0, with Younis' only innings producing his best Test score as he amassed 313 at Karachi. Later that year the Sri Lankans won 2–0 at home as Younis failed to fire, and he stepped down from the captaincy amidst infighting, match-fixing allegations and issues with the PCB. In March 2010 the PCB banned Younis from playing for Pakistan, although the ban was lifted after three months. His next Test was against South Africa in November 2010, when his 35 and 131 not out helped Pakistan to a draw. His next Test ton was a year later as his 122 at Sharjah helped the Pakistanis protect their series lead against Sri Lanka. The following month, Younis made 200 not out and 49 in innings victories against Bangladesh.

One Test ton in 2012 and two in 2013, including 200 against Zimbabwe at Harare, were followed by a vintage 2014 calendar year in which Younis compiled 1213 runs at 71.35. He began the year with 136 against Sri Lanka in a series that was ultimately drawn, and in August he made 177 in a 2–0 loss to the Sri Lankans. Younis had much better fortune against Australia in neutral territory as he rattled off 106, 103 not out, 213 and 46 in a 2–0 triumph. He followed up with 100 not out against New Zealand before tapering off with 28, 72, 44, 5 and 0 in a drawn series. Each of his three centuries in 2015 was in a series win, with the highlight his unbeaten 171, which helped Pakistan pass a 377-run target for the loss of just three wickets against Sri Lanka at the Pallekele International Cricket Stadium.

Younis Khan (b.1977)*

Matches: 104
Runs scored: 9116
Batting average: 53.94
100s/50s: 31/30
Top score: 313
Balls bowled: 804
Wickets: 9
Bowling average: 54.56
5 wickets in innings: –
10 wickets in match: –
Best bowling: 2–23
Catches/stumpings: 110/–
* still playing as of 2016

CHAPTER 8: SRI LANKA

8.1 SRI LANKA v ZIMBABWE

1990s

A drawn series involving Sri Lanka and Zimbabwe in 1994–95 was followed by Sri Lankan dominance, with record-breaking wicket-taker Muttiah Muralitharan particularly prominent. He wasn't so convincing in the 1994–95 series, which yielded three draws, as Zimbabwe's David Houghton scored 266 in the second Test at Bulawayo and 142 in the third at Harare. Sri Lanka's Sanjeeva Ranatunga also scored two centuries in the series, which was disrupted by rain, with Zimbabwe coming the closest to notching a victory, after Sri Lanka was forced to follow on in the second Test.

On home turf in September 1996, Sri Lanka won the first Test by an innings before cantering to a 10-wicket victory as Muralitharan snared 7 wickets in each Test. The hosts lost their first 2 wickets for 4 runs before tallying 349, and the visitors fell for 145 and 127 after never recovering from the first-ball dismissal of Grant Flower in their first innings. Zimbabwe batted first in the second Test and made 141 before its second innings of 235 left Sri Lanka a target of just 27.

Muralitharan snared 12 wickets in the first Test of 1997–98 while Marvan Atapattu scored 223 in Sri Lanka's 8-wicket victory in Kandy. Zimbabwe could have won the second Test after leading on the first innings and later having Sri Lanka 10–2 and 137–5 when chasing 326. Unbeaten scores of 143 and 87 from Aravinda de Silva and Arjuna Ranatunga took Sri Lanka to a 5-wicket triumph, although the Zimbabweans were upset with a number of contentious decisions that favoured Sri Lanka's batsmen.

In 1999–00, Sri Lanka won 1–0 while there were two draws. Rain prevented visitors, Sri Lanka from achieving a likely victory in the first Test at Bulawayo after 6–60 from Pramodya Wickremasinghe was followed by 216 not out from Atapattu. Nuwan Zoysa took a hat-trick in the second over of the second Test as Zimbabwe fell to 0–3, and Sri Lanka gained a big lead as Tillakaratne Dilshan scored 163 not out in just his second Test before the visitors lost four wickets in chasing 35.

2000s

Sri Lanka won all three Tests in 2001–02 and both in 2004 as these two series were heavily one-sided, with Sri Lanka winning by an innings four times. Sri Lanka topped 500 in the first two Tests of 2001–02 and had little trouble dismissing Zimbabwe for sub-250 scores. In the third Test, the African nation managed just 79 after being set 395. Muralitharan snared 9–51 in Zimbabwe's first innings in the second Test, before finishing the 2001–02 series with 30 wickets.

The 2004 series was hardly Test cricket as hosts Zimbabwe lost by an innings and 240 runs, before the margin in the second Test was 14 runs heavier. Opening duo Atapattu (170) and Sanath Jayasuriya (157) were the best batsmen in the first Test as Sri Lanka made 541, before Atapattu (249), Kumar Sangakkara (270) and Mahela Jayawardene (100 not out) set up a total of 713–3 in the second Test. Muralitharan claimed 14 wickets in the series as Zimbabwe's highest total was 231.

Sri Lanka v Zimbabwe

1994–95 (Z): 0–0 (3 drawn)   **1999–00 (Z):** Sri Lanka 1–0 (2
1996 (SL): Sri Lanka 2–0   drawn)
1997–98 (SL): Sri Lanka 2–0   **2001–02 (SL):** Sri Lanka 3–0
                                        2004 (Z): Sri Lanka 2–0

8.2 SRI LANKA v BANGLADESH

2000s

The Sri Lankans often needed to bat only once as they won 14 of the first 16 encounters with Bangladesh. The first meeting was decided in three days at Colombo in September 2001 as part of the Asian Test Championship, with Sri Lanka winning by an innings after dismissing Bangladesh for 90 and 328. Muttiah Muralitharan claimed 5–13 and 5–98, while Test debutant Mohammad Ashraful scored a commendable 114 in Bangladesh's second innings. Marvan Atapattu (201 retired) and Mahela Jayawardene (150 retired) were the main scorers as the hosts racked up 555–5 declared in just 103.3 overs.

Muralitharan again bagged two 5-wicket hauls as Sri Lanka also won the first Test of the 2002 series by an innings in Colombo, within three days. Aravinda de Silva (206) and Sanath Jayasuriya (145) were Sri Lanka's biggest runmakers in the first Test, before de Silva and Muralitharan didn't play in the second Test, which the hosts won by 288 runs after setting a target of 473.

The 2005 series in Colombo produced two innings wins to the hosts, again with just three days needed each time. Bangladesh was soundly placed in the first Test at 155–2 before crashing to 188 all out and later flopping for 86. In the second Test, Sri Lanka was in strife at 48–4 before Tillakaratne Dilshan (168 off just 179 balls) and Thilan Samaraweera (138) shared a fifth-wicket stand of 280.

In early 2006, Bangladesh hosted two Tests and made each of them go well into the fourth day, as Sri Lanka won by margins of 8 wickets and 10 wickets. Mohammad Ashraful (136) helped the hosts to a creditable 319 in the first Test, before Sri Lanka was a wicket down after three deliveries. The visitors gained a mere 19-run lead before a target of 163 proved simple. In the second Test, the tourists were 43–4 in reply to 234, before opener Upul Thangara's 165 comprised of 52.21 per cent of Sri Lanka's total. Shahadat Hossain claimed 5–86 in Sri Lanka's first innings before Tharanga (71 not out) was again the main scorer, this time as the Sri Lankans chased 120.

The series in mid-2007 was hardly a contest, as hosts Sri Lanka won all three fixtures by an innings. Among several centuries by Sri Lankans, the star was Kumar Sangakkara with unbeaten scores of 200 and 222 following his first Test score of 6. With Muralitharan the major wicket-taker, Bangladesh crumbled for first-innings totals of 89, 62 and 131 while second-innings totals were better: 254, 299 and 176. Ashraful made a courageous 129 not out in the second Test.

The first Test of the 2008–09 series was very competitive, despite the 107-run margin suggesting a comfortable win for visitors, Sri Lanka. The tourists made 293 and 405–6 declared to set a practically impossible target of 521, and the Bangladeshis were virtually gone at 180–5. Ashraful (101), Shakib Al Hasan (96) and Mushfiqur Rahim (61) boosted the total to 413, with a sixth-wicket stand of 112 followed by a seventh-wicket stand of 111. In the second Test, Bangladesh fell 466 runs shy of a target of 624 after Dilshan (162 and 143) rescued Sri Lanka from 75–4 in the first innings and took 4–10 late in the match.

With Muralitharan retired, the first Test of 2012–13 in Galle was a run glut as Sri Lanka made 570–4 declared and 335–4 declared while Bangladesh made 638 and 70–1. Sangakkara made two tons while Dilshan, Lahiru Thirimanne and Dinesh Chandimal made one each for Sri Lanka, while Bangladesh's heroes were Rahim (200) and Ashraful (190). In the second Test, centuries to Sangakkara and Chandimal gave Sri Lanka a 106-run lead before the hosts won by 7 wickets after being set 160.

The opening Test of 2013–14 in Mirpur yielded an innings win to the visitors, after Mahela Jayawardene (203 not out), Kaushal Silva

(139) and Kithuruwan Vithanage (103 not out) set up a total of 730–6 declared. Sangakkara (319 and 105) stole the show in the second Test as Sri Lanka compiled 587 and 305–4 declared, but the result was an honourable draw. After losing a wicket without a run on the board, Bangladesh had Imrul Kayes (115) and Shamsur Rahman (106) to thank for a first-innings total of 426. Set 467, Bangladesh finished on a creditable 271–3 with Mominul Haque unbeaten on 100, after Chandimal was on the same score when Sri Lanka declared.

Sri Lanka v Bangladesh

2001 (SL): Sri Lanka 1–0 (Asian Test Championship)
2002 (SL): Sri Lanka 2–0
2005 (SL): Sri Lanka 2–0
2005–06 (B): Sri Lanka 2–0
2007 (SL): Sri Lanka 3–0

2008–09 (B): Sri Lanka 2–0
2012–13 (SL): Sri Lanka 1–0 (1 drawn)
2013–14 (B): Sri Lanka 1–0 (1 drawn)

8.3 NOTABLE TEST PLAYERS

Aravinda de Silva

Aravinda de Silva experienced many highs and lows as he represented Sri Lanka from 1984 to 2003. His Test record reflected a solid rather than outstanding career, although one should remember that Sri Lanka was not among the leading teams. With de Silva as captain, Sri Lanka drew two Tests and lost four.

With one leg a little shorter than the other, de Silva had an unusual stance. He chopped his bat towards his feet, a little like a woodchopper, but there was little doubt that his style worked for him, even if he didn't always make big scores as often as he may have liked. In the 1989–90 edition of *Allan's Australian Cricket Annual,* author Allan Miller remarked that de Silva was a brilliant strokemaker 'whose special ability with the bat is exceeded only by his ambitious disposition'. Six years later, in the 1996 version of the Annual, Miller commented that de Silva 'always had a reputation as a kamikaze batsman...Aravinda can play the most memorable innings or seemingly throw it away just at the moment his team needs him'.

De Silva's career highlight was probably the 1996 World Cup final when he took 3–42 with his part-time off spin and scored 107 not out in Sri Lanka's 7-wicket victory against Australia. De Silva's Test career had plenty of highlights in any case. He scored 20 centuries, with his first two coming on Pakistani soil in late 1985. Intriguingly, only two of de Silva's first 15 Test tons were part of Sri Lankan victories, before his last five centuries were in winning causes.

There was a gap of more than four years between his second and third Test hundreds, and as it turned out his eighth Test ton was the first that occurred in a Sri Lankan victory. Having failed miserably, as Sri Lanka was hammered in its first Test in Australia in February 1988, de Silva followed up with scores of 167 (which included a vital reprieve on 5), 75 and 72 in a 1–0 series loss Down Under less than two years later. In early 1990 de Silva scored 267 against New Zealand at Wellington, but opponent Martin Crowe bettered it by 32 runs, as the hosts drew the match and subsequently the series. De Silva scored one century amidst two thrashings that Sri Lanka copped against Pakistan in 1994, before missing the first Test of the 1995–96 series as Pakistan again won easily. His return in the second Test was decisive, as Sri Lanka won in Pakistan for the first time. De Silva scored a duck before his 105 helped Sri Lanka overcome a 110-run deficit and level the series, and later win it.

De Silva's Test average hovered in the mid 30s in 1996 before he amassed 1220 runs in 1997, including seven centuries. He scored 23, 168, 138 not out and 103 not out against Pakistan, and then 126, 146 and 120 against India as both series were drawn 0–0. In another 0–0 drawn series with India later in 1997, de Silva scored 33, 110 not out, 66 and 18 before his two Test tons in 1998 included 152 at the Oval as Sri Lanka thrashed England by 10 wickets in a one-off Test.

A knock of 112 from de Silva in a 2-wicket win was pivotal in Sri Lanka's series triumph against Pakistan in early 2000 before de Silva's 106 a year later was in an innings victory, only for England to come back and win the series. De Silva bade farewell to Test cricket in a 2-match series against Bangladesh in 2002, scoring 206 and taking a wicket with his last delivery in an innings win before missing the second Test which Sri Lanka also won by an innings. His farewell to international cricket was in the 2003 World Cup, with Sri Lanka eliminated during the semi-finals.

Aravinda de Silva (b.1965)

Matches: 93
Runs scored: 6361
Batting average: 42.98
100s/50s: 20/22
Top score: 267
Balls bowled: 2595
Wickets: 29
Bowling average: 41.65
5 wickets in innings: –
10 wickets in match: –
Best bowling: 3–30
Catches/stumpings: 43/–

Sanath Jayasuriya

Sanath Jayasuriya was partly credited with changing limited-overs cricket as he and Romesh Kaluwitharana pioneered a strategy of opening batsmen taking the initiative from the outset rather than merely trying to survive the opening 10–15 overs. The left-handed Jayasuriya's career had a number of ups and downs, but in the second half of his career he had become one of the most dangerous batsmen in Tests and one-day internationals. In *Cricket's Great All-Rounders*, Kersi Meher-Homji described Jayasuriya as 'dizzily dangerous' and one of the 'most uncompromising hitters of the ball'.

Jayasuriya's explosive batting was a key factor in Sri Lanka's successful 1996 World Cup campaign, but at that stage his record made disappointing reading. He had averaged just 22.60 from 108 one-day internationals while he had played 17 Tests and scored 771 runs at 35.04, with his maiden century coming in his seventeenth Test as Sri Lanka sank to a 3–0 series defeat in Australia.

Jayasuriya's Test career had a much more credible look as he accumulated 1271 runs in 1997, with three centuries in drawn matches. He scored 113 against Pakistan before his third Test ton was the highest Test score by a Sri Lankan at that stage, as he notched 340 against India. In the very next Test, he scored 32 and 199, with his first-innings score comprising of eight boundaries. More than a year passed before he next posted triple figures in a Test, when he scored 213 in a victory against England at the Oval. Jayasuriya didn't score a Test hundred in 1999, before he made 188 and 148 against Pakistan and South Africa in 2000. Jayasuriya's last four Test centuries were in 2004, including a knock of 253 against Pakistan. He played his last Test in late 2007 but continued playing in the limited-overs arena for another three-and-a-half years.

Jayasuriya achieved 18 wins and 12 losses as he captained Sri Lanka in 38 Tests from 1999 to 2002, and he became the first player from his country to play 100 Tests. He had a strong record in his 17 Tests against Pakistan, averaging 51.38, while his highest score boosted his record against India to 938 runs at 67. He averaged in the 30s against Australia, England, South Africa and the West Indies: modest figures maybe. Perhaps it was out of character for Jayasuriya not to score a Test century after 2004, although he had a couple of memorable encounters with fast bowlers. In 2006 he took the attack to South Africa's Dale Steyn, and in Jayasuriya's last Test series he struck six fours in an over off England's James Anderson.

As a bowler, Jayasuriya was more than handy with his left-arm orthodox spinners as he captured 98 Test wickets, including two 5-wicket hauls. In one-day internationals he had a unique record in that he topped 13,000 runs and took more than 300 wickets in 445 appearances.

Sanath Jayasuriya (b.1969)

Matches: 110
Runs scored: 6973
Batting average: 40.07
100s/50s: 14/31
Top score: 340
Balls bowled: 8188
Wickets: 98
Bowling average: 34.34
5 wickets in innings: 2
10 wickets in match: –
Best bowling: 5–34
Catches/stumpings: 78/–

Mahela Jayawardene

Playing Test cricket for 17 years enabled Mahela Jayawardene to become one of Sri Lanka's highest achievers, while being the eighth most capped Test player (as of February 2016). A gifted strokemaker on the front and back foot, Jayawardene recorded the highest individual Test score for a right-hander when he compiled 374 against South Africa in 2006. Sixteen of his 34 Test centuries were scores of 150 or more, and he was involved in record-breaking partnerships of 624 (for any wicket), 437 (fourth wicket) and 351 (sixth wicket). Jayawardene was also a fine fielder, as 77 of his 205 catches were off record-breaker Muttiah Muralitharan's bowling.

Jayawardene accumulated ten fours in an unobtrusive 66 against India on debut in the memorable Colombo run glut in 1997. Against New Zealand the following year, Jayawardene made two 50s in a hefty loss before helping Sri Lanka level the series. He made 167 in a 323-run total which was enough to set up an innings victory on a difficult Galle pitch, before Sri Lanka went on to win the series. Jayawardene turned his second Test century into a score of 242 against India in early 1999 before his third ton was another score of 167, this time in a win against South Africa in 2000.

Jayawardene scored at least one Test century in each year from 1998 to 2014 with the exception of 2013, and he reached the three-figure milestone against every opposing country. The Australians and Pakistanis seemingly troubled him the most, as he averaged in the low 30s against them while averaging between 44 and 76.40 against the other nations. His two centuries at Kandy in 2001 were in losses — one to England and one to India — before his other two centuries in 2001 were in victories — against India and Bangladesh in Colombo. Jayawardene's first eight Test centuries were on home soil before he made 107 in a draw at Lord's in May 2002. Sri Lanka lost that series, but late the following year Jayawardene made 134 at Colombo in an innings victory which resulted in a series triumph against England.

Jayawardene scored 237 against South Africa at Galle in August 2004, before his highest score was made against the same nation at Colombo nearly two years later. When Marvan Atapattu was injured in 2006, Jayawardene assumed the captaincy and enjoyed a 2–0 win against Bangladesh and a 1–1 draw with England, both away from home. In the first Test against England, Jayawardene's 119 helped save the match. Jayawardene subsequently led his country to a 2–0 win over South Africa, with his 374 occurring in the first Test as he shared Test cricket's biggest partnership with Kumar Sangakkara. The previous highest score by a Sri Lankan was 340 from Sanath Jayasuriya in Jayawardene's Test debut. In the second Test against South Africa in 2006, Jayawardene's 123 helped his team towards a thrilling 1-wicket victory. In 2007, Jayawardene scored two centuries while leading his team to a 3–0 win against Bangladesh. Later that year he scored 104 in a losing cause Down Under, and then made 195 and 213 not out in successive draws against England to help Sri Lanka win the series 1–0.

Following three Test tons in 2008, Jayawardene relinquished the captaincy after a 0–0 series against Pakistan in early 2009. He scored 240 at Karachi and 30 at Lahore where a terrorist attack forced the series to be called off. Jayawardene made 275 against India at Ahmedabad later that year, and 174 against the same country the following year. When contesting South Africa in December 2011, Jayawardene became the first Sri Lankan to record 10,000 Test runs. Following the 2–1 series loss, he was reinstated as captain after Tillakaratne Dilshan resigned. Jayawardene promptly scored 180 and 5 in a win at Galle, before his 105 and 64 could not prevent England drawing the series. The Sri Lankans held on to beat Pakistan 1–0, but they surrendered a 1–0 lead against New Zealand in another series that finished level. A horror 3–0 loss in Australia was followed by Jayawardene missing a 1–0 win against Bangladesh, and stepping down from the captaincy again. His captaincy record was identical to that of Jayasuriya: 18 wins, 12 losses and eight draws.

Jayawardene's score of 129 helped Sri Lanka win a Test against Pakistan in January 2014, but again the Sri Lankans were forced to settle for a drawn series. Sri Lanka followed up with a 1–0 win against Bangladesh, with Jayawardene scoring 203 not out at Dhaka. After Sri Lanka won 1–0 against England in June 2014, Jayawardene's last Test ton was in a draw, which enabled South Africa to win a two-match series in July 2014. The following month, Jayawardene finished his Test career with a 2–0 win against Pakistan as his scores were 59, 26, 4 and 54, leaving his Test average marginally below 50.

Mahela Jayawardene (b.1977)

Matches: 149
Runs scored: 11,814
Batting average: 49.84
100s/50s: 34/50
Top score: 374
Balls bowled: 589
Wickets: 6
Bowling average: 51.67
5 wickets in innings: –
10 wickets in match: –
Best bowling: 2–32
Catches/stumpings: 205/–

Muttiah Muralitharan

Being Test cricket's all-time leading wicket-taker with 800 scalps was a phenomenal achievement for Sri Lankan off spinner Muttiah Muralitharan, as he averaged 6.015 wickets per Test. Yet few if any cricketers polarised opinion to the extent that he did. Muralitharan's unusual bowling action ensured his career was plagued with controversy, as many observers considered him a blatant chucker who should have been forced out of cricket, while other observers were in awe of what he could do with a cricket ball. Considering Muralitharan was born with a deformity that prevented him from fully straightening his arm, it remains a matter of opinion as to whether or not he gained an unfair advantage. In any case, it was hard to deny that he was immensely talented, tenacious, resilient and durable, and that he overcame a lot of adversity. Muralitharan did not appear to allow any controversy to set him back or get the better of him.

Muralitharan's wristy action prompted Australian captain Allan Border to think he was a leg spinner when Muralitharan began his Test career as a 20-year-old on home soil in 1992. Muralitharan achieved decent figures in the next few years but Australia was the place that dogged him the most. Muralitharan was called for throwing in Test and limited-overs cricket in 1995–96 before being called again in a limited-overs game Down Under three years later. Despite taking 10 wickets at an expensive 51.40 as Sri Lanka was thrashed by Australia in 1995–96, Muralitharan already became Sri Lanka's highest Test wicket-taker at the time with 81 scalps at 33.89 in 23 Tests. His future was in doubt nonetheless, particularly since the careers of Australian Ian Meckiff and South African Geoff Griffin had ended after they had been called for throwing between 30 and 40 years earlier.

Muralitharan however continued playing international cricket following examinations and analyses by biomechanics. The International Cricket Council (ICC) cleared his action in 1996 and 1999, but his 'doosra' generated plenty of debate in 2004. An off spinner's wrong 'un that spun from leg to off, the 'doosra' looked decidedly more suspect than Muralitharan's other deliveries, including top spinners and regulation off breaks. Muralitharan was revealed to flex his arm at 14 degrees for the 'doosra' — nine degrees beyond the legal limit — but the ICC controversially changed the regulations for all bowlers in 2005. A limit of 15 degrees was allowed following revelations that most bowlers flexed their arm to some extent. With Muralitharan having long become an established part of the game, there was little point arguing his merits or otherwise. England was one of a few countries that had qualms about Muralitharan, yet as Ian Botham remarked in *Botham's Century* with regard to Muralitharan being called for throwing:

> *I have always disregarded that so-called controversy as a frivolous sideshow conducted by umpires trying to make a name for themselves, and those who seized upon it (including England, at one stage, I'm sorry to say) were only doing so to create a smokescreen for their own batsmen's deficiencies.*

Muralitharan was Sri Lanka's strike bowler for many years: a rare thing to say about a spinner. Shane Warne, by comparison, was repeatedly accompanied by a number of fine pacemen. Muralitharan first became Test cricket's leading wicket-taker when he passed Courtney Walsh's record in May 2004, before Warne overtook Muralitharan, who subsequently surpassed the Australian leg spinner in December 2007. Muralitharan reached the 800 milestone as he claimed a wicket with his final delivery in Test cricket in July 2010.

Another unique achievement for Muralitharan was claiming at least one 10-wicket match haul against every opposing Test nation. He also claimed 10 wickets in a Test on 22 occasions: 12 more than Warne. Muralitharan was on the winning team in 54 out of 132 Tests that he played for Sri Lanka, while his other Test was for the ICC World XI, which lost to Australia in October 2005. Incredibly, he averaged 8.11 wickets per Test when on the winning side. Muralitharan reportedly said his career highlight was in a one-off Test at the Oval in 1998, when he claimed 7–155 from 59.3 overs and 9–65 from 54.2 overs in Sri Lanka's 10-wicket victory against England. He claimed 68 Test wickets in 1998 and exceeded this figure in three other calendar years, with 75 wickets in 2000, 80 in 2001 and 90 in 2006. Muralitharan's highlights are too many to mention, and his figures speak for themselves.

Muttiah Muralitharan (b.1972)

Matches: 133
Runs scored: 1256
Batting average: 11.67
100s/50s: 0/1
Top score: 67
Balls bowled: 44,039
Wickets: 800
Bowling average: 22.72
5 wickets in innings: 67
10 wickets in match: 22
Best bowling: 9–51
Catches/stumpings: 72/–

Kumar Sangakkara

An elegant and versatile left-handed batsman, Kumar Sangakkara was a class act in more ways than one. As if scoring 12,400 Test runs at 57.40 wasn't impressive enough, more than 5000 of them were scored away from home while 11,679 of them were scored in the number three position. It was also telling that Sangakkara averaged around 40 when he played as a wicketkeeper–batsman in 48 Tests from 2000 to 2008, while accumulating runs at a much higher average as non-wicketkeeper. A very methodical cricketer who repeatedly thrived under adversity, Sangakkara was equally adept at playing off the front foot and back foot with attractive strokes on both sides of the wicket.

Sangakkara's 38 Test centuries included a triple ton, ten double tons, and eight scores between 150 and 199. Sangakkara enjoyed batting with Mahela Jayawardene in particular, with the duo accumulating 6554 runs when batting together including a record 624-run stand. Jayawardene told Sri Lankan cricket writer Andrew Fidel Fernando on *Cricinfo*:

> *There were quite a lot of times when he bailed me out and bailed a lot of other guys out by seeing the tough bowlers out. It's a crucial*

position that he batted in for almost 15 years...We do put bowling
attacks under pressure together and feed off each other. Because of that
we've probably scored more runs. We understand each other's roles,
and because of that we've probably scored more runs together, having
batted together for a long period of time.

Sri Lanka had five wins, three losses and seven draws under Sangakkara's leadership from 2009 to 2011, as he was an aggressive captain. He was willing to try things rather than let a game drift, although he had issues with some people, including administrators. Jayawardene sensed Sangakkara would have been a better leader if he was given more freedom to do things the way he wanted. Although statistics suggest his batting was less effective when he was burdened with the wicketkeeping responsibility, Sangakkara averaged 69.60 when captain.

After a mediocre start to his Test career against South Africa in July 2000, Sangakkara posted his maiden Test ton in August 2001. He had come close on two occasions beforehand, having been dismissed for 98 in an innings defeat against South Africa at Centurion, and 95 in a close loss to England at Kandy. His 105 not out against India at Galle was followed by two other Test tons in 2001: 140 against the West Indies at Galle and 128 against Zimbabwe at Colombo. Sangakkara turned his fourth, fifth and sixth Test tons into monstrous scores as he made 230 against Pakistan in 2002, 270 against Zimbabwe in 2004 and 232 against South Africa in 2004. His 230 was in the Asian Test Championship final, which Sri Lanka won at Lahore, after Sangakkara arrived at the crease following the loss of a wicket to the first ball of the innings.

Sangakkara was also prolific in 2006 as he scored 1242 Test runs that year. The Sinhalese Sports Club Ground at Colombo was a productive place for him as he made 185 against Pakistan and 287 against South Africa as he put on 624 runs with Jayawardene. Sangakkara made 100 not out in a 170-run total as Sri Lanka lost at Christchurch, before he scored an unconquered 156 in a 268-run total at Wellington, where Sri Lanka drew the series. From July to early December 2007, Sangakkara made 200 not out and 222 not out against Bangladesh, followed by 57 and 192 against Australia, and 92 and 152 against England. He was desperately unlucky not to reach 200 against Australia as he copped a dreadful decision, and the umpire apologised to him afterwards. Having made four Test tons in 2006 and in 2007, Sangakkara did likewise in 2009 following just one in 2008. His best scores in 2010 were 103 and 219 against India and 150 against the West Indies, before his four Test tons in 2011 included his first in England. Against Pakistan in late 2011, Sangakkara's scores were 2, 211, 78, 30, 144 and 51 as Sri Lanka slid to a 1–0 defeat. Against the same nation several months later, the series result was reversed after Sangakkara scored 199 not out, 1, 192, 24 not out, 0 and 74 not out.

Sangakkara scored three tons against Bangladesh in March 2013 before his next two tons were also against Bangladesh. These were in a draw at Chittagong in February 2014, as the 36-year-old made a career-best 319 in the first innings and followed up with 105. An innings of 147 against England at Lord's and 221 against Pakistan at Galle helped Sangakkara towards an eventual 1493 runs in the calendar year. Sangakkara started 2015 with 203 and 5, only for the Kiwis to romp to a 2–0 series win at home. Sangakkara played his final Test in August 2015 as Sri Lanka squandered a 1–0 series lead against India.

Kumar Sangakkara (b.1977)

Matches: 134
Runs scored: 12,400
Batting average: 57.40
100s/50s: 38/52
Top score: 319
Balls bowled: 84
Wickets: 0
Bowling average: –
5 wickets in innings: –
10 wickets in match: –
Best bowling: –
Catches/stumpings: 182/20

Chaminda Vaas

The impact which Chaminda Vaas had on the Sri Lankan bowling attack for many years could not be overlooked, even though the team relied heavily on Muttiah Muralitharan. Sri Lankan bowlers captured 1968 wickets in the 132 Tests that Muralitharan played for his country, with the record-breaking off spinner claiming 795 of them, while Vaas was next with 309, with nobody else even achieving 100 wickets.

Far from being lethally fast despite being lively, the left-handed Vaas constantly took the new ball and had a fine inswinger and off-cutter. Vaas played 41 more Tests than Dennis Lillee but had the same number of wickets, although Vaas' record could have been much different if Sri Lanka had more pacemen of a similar calibre.

Vaas' Test debut was a horror as he went wicketless and scored 0 and 4 in an innings loss to Pakistan at Kandy in August 1994. Several months later he excelled in New Zealand as he took two 5-wicket hauls and made handy 30s in a 241-run victory, then followed up with 51 and 6–87 in a draw. Vaas had a happy time in Pakistan in September 1995 as he claimed 5–99 in an innings loss before taking two 4-wicket hauls and making some handy runs in Sri Lanka's come-from-behind series win.

Vaas was not so prolific in the late 1990s and was sometimes out of the team, before he had a magnificent home series against the West Indies in late 2001. He took 6 wickets in each of the first two Tests before claiming 7–120 and 7–71 at Colombo as the hosts sealed a 3–0 clean sweep. After taking 58 Test scalps in 2001, Vaas again had some mediocre returns before he snared 6–29 to help Sri Lanka to a series win over South Africa in 2004. At Wellington the following year, Vaas deserved credit for taking 6–108 as the Kiwis racked up 522–9 declared before inflicting an innings defeat.

Vaas had some memorable moments in 2005, as he took 13 wickets at 5.54 in a 2–0 victory against the West Indies before claiming his 300th wicket when Sri Lanka lost to India. He was also chiefly responsible for a Sri Lankan victory in Guyana during 2008, as he scored 54 not out and snared 3–48 and 5–61, only for the West Indies to draw the series in the ensuing Test. Vaas' sole century came about in his ninety-seventh

Test, as he made 100 not out against Bangladesh at Colombo. Vaas' Test career fizzled out in 2009, as he missed the first two Tests in which Sri Lanka beat Pakistan, before he took 1–43 and 0–47 in the drawn third Test, which turned out to be his final Test.

Chaminda Vaas (b.1974)

Matches: 111
Runs scored: 3089
Batting average: 24.32
100s/50s: 1/13
Top score: 100*
Balls bowled: 23,438
Wickets: 355
Bowling average: 29.58
5 wickets in innings: 12
10 wickets in match: 2
Best bowling: 7–71
Catches/stumpings: 31/–

CHAPTER 9: ZIMBABWE and BANGLADESH

9.1 ZIMBABWE v BANGLADESH

2000s

Tests involving Zimbabwe and Bangladesh generated ample interest for those two nations as success for both Test teams was rare. After Bangladesh's maiden Test yielded a 9-wicket loss to India, Bangladesh's next two Tests were staged in Zimbabwe in April 2001. Andy Blignaut took 5 wickets as Bangladesh scored 257, before Zimbabwe gained a 200-run lead following a century from Guy Whittall and half-centuries to Heath Streak and Flower brothers, Andy and Grant. Bangladesh lost by an innings and 32 runs but Javed Omar enhanced his reputation as he carried his bat with 85 not out, following 62 in the first innings. In the second Test, Zimbabwe led by 167 runs before winning by 8 wickets after Bangladesh set a target of 100.

Bangladesh hosted Zimbabwe later in 2001, with the hosts sliding to 107 all out in the first Test before the visitors replied with 431. This was Bangladesh's sixth ever Test, and the first time that the Bangladeshis avoided defeat, admittedly as rain saved them, before Zimbabwe claimed the series with an 8-wicket victory at Chittagong Stadium. Hundreds to Craig Wishart, Andy Flower and Trevor Gripper helped Zimbabwe pass 500 before Bangladesh fell 291 runs in arrears despite a century to Habibul Bashar. Bangladesh was 195–1 when following on before falling to 301 all out, with Grant Flower taking 8 wickets in the match.

More than two years passed before the so-called 'minnows' next met in Test cricket, with hosts Zimbabwe winning the first Test by 183 runs before rain prevented a result in the second Test as Zimbabwe finished at 210–2 in reply to Bangladesh's 168. Nearly a year later, Bangladesh beat Zimbabwe in Test cricket for the first time. Bangladesh tallied 488 despite no centurions, and Zimbabwe recovered from 86–5 to score 312 before falling for just 154 when chasing 381. In the second Test, Zimbabwean captain and wicketkeeper Tatenda Taibu completed a great series as he scored 153 out of 286 in his team's second innings. Chasing 374, Bangladesh finished at 285–5 after opener Nafees Iqbal made 121, while the hero for the series victor was Enamul Haque jnr who claimed 6 wickets in the first Test and 12 in the second.

August 2011 was the next time that the teams met in Test cricket, with Zimbabwe winning a one-off match by 130 runs at Harare following a century each to Hamilton Masakadza and captain Brendan Taylor. The 2013 series in Zimbabwe featured many complexion changes, and perhaps it was fitting that the series was deadlocked. Taylor's 171 rescued Zimbabwe, before Bangladesh trailed by 255 runs after crashing from 102–1 to 134 all out. Taylor (102 not out) excelled again as Zimbabwe opted not to enforce the follow on, while Robiul Islam claimed 9 wickets in the match for Bangladesh. Zimbabwe won by 335 runs after setting a target of 483, before Bangladesh scored 391 in the first innings of the second Test and gained a first-innings lead of 109 as Robiul Islam bagged 5 wickets. Bangladesh slipped to 18–3 before declaring at 291–9, and only Masakadza (111 not out) made any impression for the Zimbabweans, as they lost by 143 runs.

Given the nature of the first six series involving Zimbabwe and Bangladesh, it seemed somewhat surprising that a 3–0 clean sweep resulted in late 2014. The first Test at Mirpur was superbly fought before Bangladesh recorded a tense 3-wicket victory. Shakib Al Hasan took 6–59 as Zimbabwe scored 240, before Tinashe Panyangara claimed 5–59 as Bangladesh gained a mere 14-run lead. Taijul Islam snared a wonderful 8–39 to rout Zimbabwe for 114, before Bangladesh lost 3 wickets without a run on the board. A couple of crucial catches were spilled before the fourth wicket fell at 46, and the hosts stuttered to 82–7, before Taijul Islam scored 15 in an unbroken 19-run partnership. In the second Test, Bangladesh made 433 following centuries to Tamim Iqbal and Al Hasan, before tons to Masakadza and wicketkeeper Regis Chakabva couldn't prevent Bangladesh gaining a 65-run advantage. The hosts went on to win by 162 runs, before claiming a 186-run triumph in the final Test. Imrul Kayes (130) and Tamim Iqbal (109) put on an opening stand of 224 in Bangladesh's first innings of 503, before Mominul Haque made 131 not out in Bangladesh's second innings.

Zimbabwe v Bangladesh

2000–01 (Z): Zimbabwe 2–0

2001–02 (B): Zimbabwe 1–0 (1 drawn)

2003–04 (Z): Zimbabwe 1–0 (1 drawn)

2004–05 (B): Bangladesh 1–0 (1 drawn)

2011 (Z): Zimbabwe 1–0

2013 (Z): 1–1

2014–15 (B): Bangladesh 3–0

9.2 NOTABLE TEST PLAYERS

Andy Flower and Heath Streak (Zimbabwe)

As Zimbabwe often struggled to make an impact in Test cricket, Andy Flower was a standout batsman while Heath Streak was a standout bowler. Few would argue that these two were the most prominent Zimbabwean cricketers, but political and racial issues led to their Zimbabwean cricketing careers ending earlier than they might have.

Born in South Africa, Flower kept wickets in 55 of his 63 Tests and was the captain on 20 occasions. He was in a victorious team only seven times. Flower savoured Zimbabwe's first ever Test win, as it was also his only victory as Test captain. He marked the occasion with 156, while his brother Grant made 201 not out against Pakistan in early 1995, after the African nation had drawn six and lost four of its ten Tests up until that point. Andy Flower made a first-ball duck and unbeaten scores of 17 and 60 in Zimbabwe's first-ever series win, against Pakistan in 1998–99 as Alistair Campbell was captain.

After scoring a century against Sri Lanka in his one-day international debut in 1992, Flower recorded his maiden Test century on Indian soil just over a year later. Another highlight on Indian soil was in late 2000 as he notched 550 runs from four innings, having scored 183 not out at Delhi and followed up with his Test-best 232 not out at Nagpur. Flower compiled more than 1400 runs and averaged in excess of 100 between November 2000 and the following November. He scored 142 and 199 not out against South Africa at Harare in September 2001, but the Proteas won by 9 wickets after Zimbabwe had to follow on. Indeed there were several times that Flower's brilliance could not prevent the other team from winning. This began in Zimbabwe's fourth Test when he made 115 and 62 not out in an innings loss to India. His 183 not out in late 2000 was in a loss, although his 232 not out was enough to salvage a draw. In Colombo in January 1998, Flower made 105 not out before Sri Lanka won by 5 wickets when chasing 326. At Harare in November 1999, Flower's 129 did little more than make Zimbabwe's defeat against Sri Lanka a little more respectable than it otherwise would have been.

The 2003 World Cup proved to be the beginning of the end for Flower in Zimbabwean cricket, after he and teammate Henry Olonga wore black armbands in protest against Robert Mugabe's regime. Subsequently retiring from Zimbabwean cricket, Flower went on to play in England and Australia, before becoming assistant coach and then team director and then head coach of England. Flower was the head coach for five years, and relished England's Ashes series wins in 2009, 2010–11 and 2013 before Australia won the 2013–14 Ashes 5–0.

Streak meanwhile captained Zimbabwe in four Test victories, with two series wins against Bangladesh and a 1–1 drawn series with India. Having made his Test debut against Pakistan in late 1993 at the age of 19, Streak went wicketless in his first Test before capturing 3–58 and 5–56 in his second Test. In Zimbabwe's drawn series against Sri Lanka the following season, Streak was the leading wicket-taker with 13 scalps. Later that season, when Zimbabwe achieved its maiden Test win, Streak captured 9 wickets in the match. Although the African nation went on to lose the series 2–1, Streak was the leading bowler with 22 wickets at 13.54. A pace bowler with the ability to move the ball off the seam, Streak claimed his best figures of 6–73 in a 10-wicket loss to India at Harare in 2005. It turned out to be his last Test, with Streak having encountered trouble amidst the turmoil that engulfed Zimbabwean cricket. Streak's batting had improved to the extent that he could have been considered a bowling all-rounder. He fell just shy of 2000 Test runs, with his one century coming in a draw against the West Indies at Harare in November 2003, as he compiled 127 not out at number eight.

Andy Flower (b.1968)

Matches: 63
Runs scored: 4794
Batting average: 51.54
100s/50s: 12/27
Top score: 232*
Balls bowled: 3
Wickets: –
Bowling average: –
5 wickets in innings: –
10 wickets in match: –
Best bowling: –
Catches/stumpings: 151/9

Heath Streak (b.1974)

Matches: 65
Runs scored: 1990
Batting average: 22.35
100s/50s: 1/11
Top score: 127*
Balls bowled: 13,559
Wickets: 216
Bowling average: 28.14
5 wickets in innings: 7
10 wickets in match: –
Best bowling: 6–73
Catches/stumpings: 17/–

Shakib Al Hasan (Bangladesh)

Shakib Al Hasan established himself as Bangladesh's premier cricketer as he averaged nearly 40 with the bat and snared 147 wickets in 42 Tests. A consistent and accurate left-arm orthodox spinner and gifted left-handed batsman, Shakib was ranked by the International Cricket Council (ICC) as the world's top Test all-rounder in 2011.

After making his one-day international debut in 2006 and playing in the 2007 World Cup, Shakib made his Test debut against India in May 2007. He made modest scores in the two-Test series which India won 1–0, and didn't take his first Test wicket until his fourth Test, when Bangladesh contested New Zealand at Wellington in January 2008. Shakib also made little impact against South Africa in early 2008, but later that year he produced a brilliant performance against the Kiwis at Chittagong. He claimed 7–36 and then hit 71 before taking a further two scalps, only for New Zealand to win by 3 wickets. Shakib followed up with a 5-wicket haul and a 6-wicket haul against South Africa, only for the Proteas to win both Tests by an innings. Shakib was also on the losing side after taking a 5-wicket haul and scoring 96 in a Test against Sri Lanka.

After being appointed Bangladesh's vice-captain in mid 2009, the 22-year-old Shakib assumed the captaincy during the first Test against the West Indies at St Vincent when Mashrafe Mortaza suffered a knee injury. Shakib promptly led Bangladesh to its first overseas Test victory and second ever Test win, and then as official captain he sparked the country's first series triumph with a 2–0 clean sweep, following 8 wickets and a knock of 96 not out at Grenada. In a one-off Test against New Zealand in early 2010, Shakib notched his maiden Test ton but his scores of 87 and 100 couldn't prevent a Kiwi victory. As Bangladesh slumped to two 2–0 series losses to England in the same year, Shakib snared a couple of 4-wicket hauls and a 5-wicket haul, and fell 4 runs shy of another century. He stepped down from the captaincy after feeling the pressure of the role in addition to being an all-rounder, leaving his record at one win and eight defeats at the helm.

Against the West Indies in late 2011, Shakib was again impressive in a series loss as he scored 168 runs in three innings and captured 10 wickets. In Bangladesh's next series, Shakib scored 144 in a total of 338 and then took 6–82 in a Pakistani total of 470, before Pakistan completed a 2–0 series win. A year later, Shakib became Bangladesh's leading Test wicket-taker after passing Mohammad Rafique's figure of 100 wickets. In a home Test against Zimbabwe in late 2014, Shakib helped secure a series win following scores of 137 and 6, and figures of 5–80 and 5–44. In the process, Shakib joined a special group of players to score a century and take 10 wickets in a Test.

Despite his fine record in a struggling side, Shakib found himself at the centre of a number of unsavoury incidents. In July 2014 he was banned from playing cricket for six months for a supposed attitude problem, according to the Bangladesh Cricket Board.

Shakib Al Hasan (b.1987)*

Matches: 42
Runs scored: 2823
Batting average: 39.76
100s/50s: 3/19
Top score: 144
Balls bowled: 9782
Wickets: 147
Bowling average: 33.31
5 wickets in innings: 14
10 wickets in match: 1
Best bowling: 7–36
Catches/stumpings: 19/–
* still playing as of 2016

Chapter 10

TEST RECORDS

Results summary

		Mat	Won	Lost	Tied	Draw	W/L	%W
Australia	1877–2016	788	372	208	2	206	1.78	47.20
Bangladesh	2000–2015	93	7	71	0	15	0.09	7.52
England	1877–2016	969	346	282	0	341	1.22	35.70
ICC World XI	2005–2005	1	0	1	0	0	0.00	0.00
India	1932–2015	495	127	157	1	210	0.80	25.65
New Zealand	1930–2016	408	83	165	0	160	0.50	20.34
Pakistan	1952–2015	395	126	111	0	158	1.13	31.89
South Africa	1889–2016	400	145	134	0	121	1.08	36.25
Sri Lanka	1982–2015	245	75	90	0	80	0.83	30.61
West Indies	1928–2016	513	164	177	1	171	0.92	31.96
Zimbabwe	1992–2014	97	11	60	0	26	0.18	11.34

Results summary (by opposition)

			Mat	Won	Lost	Tied	Draw	W/L	%W
Australia	v Bangladesh	2003–2006	4	4	0	0	0	–	100
	v England	1877–2015	341	140	108	0	93	1.29	41.05
	v ICC World XI	2005–2005	1	1	0	0	0	–	100
	v India	1947–2015	90	40	24	1	25	1.66	44.44
	v New Zealand	1946–2016	57	31	8	0	18	3.87	54.38
	v Pakistan	1956–2014	59	28	14	0	17	2.00	47.45
	v South Africa	1902–2014	91	50	21	0	20	2.38	54.94
	v Sri Lanka	1983–2013	26	17	1	0	8	17.00	65.38
	v West Indies	1930–2016	116	58	32	1	25	1.81	50.00
	v Zimbabwe	1999–2003	3	3	0	0	0	–	100
Bangladesh	v Australia	2003–2006	4	0	4	0	0	0.00	0.00
	v England	2003–2010	8	0	8	0	0	0.00	0.00
	v India	2000–2015	8	0	6	0	2	0.00	0.00
	v New Zealand	2001–2013	11	0	8	0	3	0.00	0.00
	v Pakistan	2001–2015	10	0	9	0	1	0.00	0.00
	v South Africa	2002–2015	10	0	8	0	2	0.00	0.00
	v Sri Lanka	2001–2014	16	0	14	0	2	0.00	0.00
	v West Indies	2002–2014	12	2	8	0	2	0.25	16.66
	v Zimbabwe	2001–2014	14	5	6	0	3	0.83	35.71
England	v Australia	1877–2015	341	108	140	0	93	0.77	31.67
	v Bangladesh	2003–2010	8	8	0	0	0	–	100
	v India	1932–2014	112	43	21	0	48	2.04	38.39
	v New Zealand	1930–2015	101	48	9	0	44	5.33	47.52
	v Pakistan	1954–2015	77	22	18	0	37	1.22	28.57
	v South Africa	1889–2016	145	58	32	0	55	1.81	40.00
	v Sri Lanka	1982–2014	28	10	8	0	10	1.25	35.71
	v West Indies	1928–2015	151	46	54	0	51	0.85	30.46
	v Zimbabwe	1996–2003	6	3	0	0	3	–	50.00
**	v Australia	2005–2005	1	0	1	0	0	0.00	0.00
India	v Australia	1947–2015	90	24	40	1	25	0.60	26.66
	v Bangladesh	2000–2015	8	6	0	0	2	–	75.00
	v England	1932–2014	112	21	43	0	48	0.48	18.75
	v New Zealand	1955–2014	54	18	10	0	26	1.80	33.33
	v Pakistan	1952–2007	59	9	12	0	38	0.75	15.25
	v South Africa	1992–2015	33	10	13	0	10	0.76	30.30
	v Sri Lanka	1982–2015	38	16	7	0	15	2.28	42.10
	v West Indies	1948–2013	90	16	30	0	44	0.53	17.77
	v Zimbabwe	1992–2005	11	7	2	0	2	3.50	63.63

			Mat	Won	Lost	Tied	Draw	W/L	%W
New Zealand	v Australia	1946–2016	57	8	31	0	18	0.25	14.03
	v Bangladesh	2001–2013	11	8	0	0	3	–	72.72
	v England	1930–2015	101	9	48	0	44	0.18	8.91
	v India	1955–2014	54	10	18	0	26	0.55	18.51
	v Pakistan	1955–2014	53	8	24	0	21	0.33	15.09
	v South Africa	1932–2013	40	4	23	0	13	0.17	10.00
	v Sri Lanka	1983–2015	32	14	8	0	10	1.75	43.75
	v West Indies	1952–2014	45	13	13	0	19	1.00	28.88
	v Zimbabwe	1992–2012	15	9	0	0	6	–	60.00
Pakistan	v Australia	1956–2014	59	14	28	0	17	0.50	23.72
	v Bangladesh	2001–2015	10	9	0	0	1	–	90.00
	v England	1954–2015	77	18	22	0	37	0.81	23.37
	v India	1952–2007	59	12	9	0	38	1.33	20.33
	v New Zealand	1955–2014	53	24	8	0	21	3.00	45.28
	v South Africa	1995–2013	23	4	12	0	7	0.33	17.39
	v Sri Lanka	1982–2015	51	19	14	0	18	1.35	37.25
	v West Indies	1958–2011	46	16	15	0	15	1.06	34.78
	v Zimbabwe	1993–2013	17	10	3	0	4	3.33	58.82
South Africa	v Australia	1902–2014	91	21	50	0	20	0.42	23.07
	v Bangladesh	2002–2015	10	8	0	0	2	–	80.00
	v England	1889–2016	145	32	58	0	55	0.55	22.06
	v India	1992–2015	33	13	10	0	10	1.30	39.39
	v New Zealand	1932–2013	40	23	4	0	13	5.75	57.50
	v Pakistan	1995–2013	23	12	4	0	7	3.00	52.17
	v Sri Lanka	1993–2014	22	11	5	0	6	2.20	50.00
	v West Indies	1992–2015	28	18	3	0	7	6.00	64.28
	v Zimbabwe	1995–2014	8	7	0	0	1	–	87.50
Sri Lanka	v Australia	1983–2013	26	1	17	0	8	0.05	3.84
	v Bangladesh	2001–2014	16	14	0	0	2	–	87.50
	v England	1982–2014	28	8	10	0	10	0.80	28.57
	v India	1982–2015	38	7	16	0	15	0.43	18.42
	v New Zealand	1983–2015	32	8	14	0	10	0.57	25.00
	v Pakistan	1982–2015	51	14	19	0	18	0.73	27.45
	v South Africa	1993–2014	22	5	11	0	6	0.45	22.72
	v West Indies	1993–2015	17	8	3	0	6	2.66	47.05
	v Zimbabwe	1994–2004	15	10	0	0	5	–	66.66

		Mat	Won	Lost	Tied	Draw	W/L	%W
West Indies	v Australia	1930–2016	116	32	58	1	25	0.55	27.58
	v Bangladesh	2002–2014	12	8	2	0	2	4.00	66.66
	v England	1928–2015	151	54	46	0	51	1.17	35.76
	v India	1948–2013	90	30	16	0	44	1.87	33.33
	v New Zealand	1952–2014	45	13	13	0	19	1.00	28.88
	v Pakistan	1958–2011	46	15	16	0	15	0.93	32.60
	v South Africa	1992–2015	28	3	18	0	7	0.16	10.71
	v Sri Lanka	1993–2015	17	3	8	0	6	0.37	17.64
	v Zimbabwe	2000–2013	8	6	0	0	2	–	75.00
Zimbabwe	v Australia	1999–2003	3	0	3	0	0	0.00	0.00
	v Bangladesh	2001–2014	14	6	5	0	3	1.20	42.85
	v England	1996–2003	6	0	3	0	3	0.00	0.00
	v India	1992–2005	11	2	7	0	2	0.28	18.18
	v New Zealand	1992–2012	15	0	9	0	6	0.00	0.00
	v Pakistan	1993–2013	17	3	10	0	4	0.30	17.64
	v South Africa	1995–2014	8	0	7	0	1	0.00	0.00
	v Sri Lanka	1994–2004	15	0	10	0	5	0.00	0.00
	v West Indies	2000–2013	8	0	6	0	2	0.00	0.00

** ICC World XI

TEST RECORDS

Leading runscorers

		Mat	Inns	NO	Runs	HS	Ave	100	50	0
SR Tendulkar (India)	1989–2013	200	329	33	15921	248*	53.78	51	68	14
RT Ponting (Aus)	1995–2012	168	287	29	13378	257	51.85	41	62	17
JH Kallis (ICC/SA)	1995–2013	166	280	40	13289	224	55.37	45	58	16
R Dravid (ICC/India)	1996–2012	164	286	32	13288	270	52.31	36	63	8
KC Sangakkara (SL)	2000–2015	134	233	17	12400	319	57.40	38	52	11
BC Lara (ICC/WI)	1990–2006	131	232	6	11953	400*	52.88	34	48	17
S Chanderpaul (WI)	1994–2015	164	280	49	11867	203*	51.37	30	66	15
DPMD Jayawardene (SL)	1997–2014	149	252	15	11814	374	49.84	34	50	15
AR Border (Aus)	1978–1994	156	265	44	11174	205	50.56	27	63	11

		Mat	Inns	NO	Runs	HS	Ave	100	50	0
SR Waugh (Aus)	1985–2004	168	260	46	10927	200	51.06	32	50	22
SM Gavaskar (India)	1971–1987	125	214	16	10122	236*	51.12	34	45	12
AN Cook (Eng)	2006–2016	126	226	12	9964	294	46.56	28	47	8
GC Smith (ICC/SA)	2002–2014	117	205	13	9265	277	48.25	27	38	11
Younis Khan (Pak)	2000–2015	104	186	17	9116	313	53.94	31	30	16
GA Gooch (Eng)	1975–1995	118	215	6	8900	333	42.58	20	46	13
Javed Miandad (Pak)	1976–1993	124	189	21	8832	280*	52.57	23	43	6
Inzamam–ul–Haq (ICC/Pak)	1992–2007	120	200	22	8830	329	49.60	25	46	15
VVS Laxman (India)	1996–2012	134	225	34	8781	281	45.97	17	56	14
MJ Clarke (Aus)	2004–2015	115	198	22	8643	329*	49.10	28	27	9
ML Hayden (Aus)	1994–2009	103	184	14	8625	380	50.73	30	29	14

The leading runscorers for the other teams are:

		Mat	Inns	NO	Runs	HS	Ave	100	50	0
SP Fleming (NZ)	1994–2008	111	189	10	7172	274*	40.06	9	46	16
A Flower (Zim)	1992–2002	63	112	19	4794	232*	51.54	12	27	5
Tamim Iqbal (Bang)	2008–2015	42	80	1	3118	206	39.46	7	18	6

Highest batting averages (minimum 20 innings)

		Mat	Inns	NO	Runs	HS	Ave	100	50	0
DG Bradman (Aus)	1928–1948	52	80	10	6996	334	99.94	29	13	7
AC Voges (Aus)	2015–2016	15	21	7	1337	269*	95.50	5	4	1
RG Pollock (SA)	1963–1970	23	41	4	2256	274	60.97	7	11	1
GA Headley (WI)	1930–1954	22	40	4	2190	270*	60.83	10	5	2
H Sutcliffe (Eng)	1924–1935	54	84	9	4555	194	60.73	16	23	2
SPD Smith (Aus)	2010–2016	41	75	11	3852	215	60.18	14	16	3
E Paynter (Eng)	1931–1939	20	31	5	1540	243	59.23	4	7	3
KF Barrington (Eng)	1955–1968	82	131	15	6806	256	58.67	20	35	5
ED Weekes (WI)	1948–1958	48	81	5	4455	207	58.61	15	19	6
WR Hammond (Eng)	1927–1947	85	140	16	7249	336*	58.45	22	24	4

Highest individual scores

BC Lara	400*	West Indies v England	St John's	10 Apr 2004
ML Hayden	380	Australia v Zimbabwe	Perth	9 Oct 2003
BC Lara	375	West Indies v England	St John's	16 Apr 1994
DPMD Jayawardene	374	Sri Lanka v South Africa	Colombo (SSC)	27 Jul 2006
GS Sobers	365*	West Indies v Pakistan	Kingston	26 Feb 1958
L Hutton	364	England v Australia	The Oval	20 Aug 1938
ST Jayasuriya	340	Sri Lanka v India	Colombo (RPS)	2 Aug 1997
Hanif Mohammad	337	Pakistan v West Indies	Bridgetown	17 Jan 1958
WR Hammond	336*	England v New Zealand	Auckland	31 Mar 1933
MA Taylor	334*	Australia v Pakistan	Peshawar	15 Oct 1998
DG Bradman	334	Australia v England	Leeds	11 Jul 1930
GA Gooch	333	England v India	Lord's	26 Jul 1990
CH Gayle	333	West Indies v Sri Lanka	Galle	15 Nov 2010
MJ Clarke	329*	Australia v India	Sydney	3 Jan 2012
Inzamam–ul–Haq	329	Pakistan v New Zealand	Lahore	1 May 2002
A Sandham	325	England v West Indies	Kingston	3 Apr 1930
V Sehwag	319	India v South Africa	Chennai	26 Mar 2008
KC Sangakkara	319	Sri Lanka v Bangladesh	Chittagong	4 Feb 2014
CH Gayle	317	West Indies v South Africa	St John's	29 Apr 2005
Younis Khan	313	Pakistan v Sri Lanka	Karachi	21 Feb 2009

The highest individual scores for the other teams are:

HM Amla	311*	South Africa v England	The Oval	19 Jul 2012
BB McCullum	302	New Zealand v India	Wellington	14 Feb 2014
DL Houghton	266	Zimbabwe v Sri Lanka	Bulawayo	20 Oct 1994
Tamim Iqbal	206	Bangladesh v Pakistan	Khulna	28 Apr 2015

Most runs by an individual in a match

	1st	2nd	Runs			
GA Gooch	333	123	456	England v India	Lord's	26 Jul 1990
MA Taylor	334*	92	426	Australia v Pakistan	Peshawar	15 Oct 1998
KC Sangakkara	319	105	424	Sri Lanka v Bangladesh	Chittagong	4 Feb 2014
BC Lara	400*	–	400	West Indies v England	St John's	10 Apr 2004
GS Chappell	247*	133	380	Australia v New Zealand	Wellington	1 Mar 1974

	1st	2nd	Runs			
ML Hayden	380	–	380	Australia v Zimbabwe	Perth	9 Oct 2003
A Sandham	325	50	375	England v West Indies	Kingston	3 Apr 1930
BC Lara	375	–	375	West Indies v England	St John's	16 Apr 1994
DPMD Jayawardene	374	–	374	Sri Lanka v South Africa	Colombo (SSC)	27 Jul 2006
GS Sobers	365*	–	365	West Indies v Pakistan	Kingston	26 Feb 1958

Highest partnerships

		Wkt			
KC Sangakkara, DPMD Jayawardene	624	3rd	Sri Lanka v South Africa	Colombo (SSC)	27 Jul 2006
ST Jayasuriya, RS Mahanama	576	2nd	Sri Lanka v India	Colombo (RPS)	2 Aug 1997
AH Jones, MD Crowe	467	3rd	New Zealand v Sri Lanka	Wellington	31 Jan 1991
WH Ponsford, DG Bradman	451	2nd	Australia v England	The Oval	18 Aug 1934
Mudassar Nazar, Javed Miandad	451	3rd	Pakistan v India	Hyderabad (Sind)	14 Jan 1983
AC Voges, SE Marsh	449	4th	Australia v West Indies	Hobart	10 Dec 2015
CC Hunte, GS Sobers	446	2nd	West Indies v Pakistan	Kingston	26 Feb 1958
MS Atapattu, KC Sangakkara	438	2nd	Sri Lanka v Zimbabwe	Bulawayo	14 May 2004
DPMD Jayawardene, TT Samaraweera	437	4th	Sri Lanka v Pakistan	Karachi	21 Feb 2009
JA Rudolph, HH Dippenaar	429*	3rd	South Africa v Bangladesh	Chittagong	24 Apr 2003
ND McKenzie, GC Smith	415	1st	South Africa v Bangladesh	Chittagong	29 Feb 2008
MH Mankad, P Roy	413	1st	India v New Zealand	Chennai	6 Jan 1956
PBH May, MC Cowdrey	411	4th	England v West Indies	Birmingham	30 May 1957
V Sehwag, R Dravid	410	1st	India v Pakistan	Lahore	13 Jan 2006
SG Barnes, DG Bradman	405	5th	Australia v England	Sydney	13 Dec 1946

Leading wicket–takers

		Mat	Inns	Balls	Runs
M Muralitharan (ICC/SL)	1992–2010	133	230	44039	18180
SK Warne (Aus)	1992–2007	145	273	40705	17995
A Kumble (India)	1990–2008	132	236	40850	18355
GD McGrath (Aus)	1993–2007	124	243	29248	12186
CA Walsh (WI)	1984–2001	132	242	30019	12688
N Kapil Dev (India)	1978–1994	131	227	27740	12867
JM Anderson (Eng)	2003–2016	113	212	25185	12638
Sir RJ Hadlee (NZ)	1973–1990	86	150	21918	9611
SM Pollock (SA)	1995–2008	108	202	24353	9733
Harbhajan Singh (India)	1998–2015	103	190	28580	13537
Wasim Akram (Pak)	1985–2002	104	181	22627	9779
DW Steyn (SA)	2004–2015	82	152	16956	9150
CEL Ambrose (WI)	1988–2000	98	179	22103	8501
M Ntini (SA)	1998–2009	101	190	20834	11242
IT Botham (Eng)	1977–1992	102	168	21815	10878
MD Marshall (WI)	1978–1991	81	151	17584	7876
Waqar Younis (Pak)	1989–2003	87	154	16224	8788
Imran Khan (Pak)	1971–1992	88	142	19458	8258
DL Vettori (ICC/NZ)	1997–2014	113	187	28814	12441
DK Lillee (Aus)	1971–1984	70	132	18467	8493
WPUJC Vaas (SL)	1994–2009	111	194	23438	10501

The leading wicket–takers for the other teams are:

		Mat	Inns	Balls	Runs
HH Streak (Zim)	1993–2005	65	102	13559	6079
Shakib Al Hasan (Bang)	2007–2015	42	68	1630.2	4897

Best bowling averages (minimum 20 wickets)

		Mat	Balls	Runs
GA Lohmann (Eng)	1886–1896	18	3830	1205
JJ Ferris (Aus/Eng)	1887–1892	9	2302	775
W Barnes (Eng)	1880–1890	21	2289	793
W Bates (Eng)	1881–1887	15	2364	821

Wkts	BBI	BBM	Ave	Econ	SR	5	10
800	9/51	16/220	22.72	2.47	55.0	67	22
708	8/71	12/128	25.41	2.65	57.4	37	10
619	10/74	14/149	29.65	2.69	65.9	35	8
563	8/24	10/27	21.64	2.49	51.9	29	3
519	7/37	13/55	24.44	2.53	57.8	22	3
434	9/83	11/146	29.64	2.78	63.9	23	2
433	7/43	11/71	29.18	3.01	58.1	18	2
431	9/52	15/123	22.29	2.63	50.8	36	9
421	7/87	10/147	23.11	2.39	57.8	16	1
417	8/84	15/217	32.46	2.84	68.5	25	5
414	7/119	11/110	23.62	2.59	54.6	25	5
406	7/51	11/60	22.53	3.23	41.7	25	5
405	8/45	11/84	20.99	2.30	54.5	22	3
390	7/37	13/132	28.82	3.23	53.4	18	4
383	8/34	13/106	28.40	2.99	56.9	27	4
376	7/22	11/89	20.94	2.68	46.7	22	4
373	7/76	13/135	23.56	3.25	43.4	22	5
362	8/58	14/116	22.81	2.54	53.7	23	6
362	7/87	12/149	34.36	2.59	79.5	20	3
355	7/83	11/123	23.92	2.75	52.0	23	7
355	7/71	14/191	29.58	2.68	66.0	12	2

Wkts	BBI	BBM	Ave	Econ	SR	5	10
216	6/73	9/72	28.14	2.69	62.7	7	0
147	7/36	10/124	33.31	3.00	66.5	14	1

Wkts	BBI	BBM	Ave	Econ	SR	5	10
112	9/28	15/45	10.75	1.88	34.1	9	5
61	7/37	13/91	12.70	2.01	37.7	6	1
51	6/28	9/81	15.54	2.07	44.8	3	0
50	7/28	14/102	16.42	2.08	47.2	4	1

		Mat	Balls	Runs
SF Barnes (Eng)	1901–1914	27	7873	3106
CTB Turner (Aus)	1887–1895	17	5179	1670
R Peel (Eng)	1884–1896	20	5216	1715
J Briggs (Eng)	1884–1899	33	5332	2095
H Ironmonger (Aus)	1928–1933	14	4695	1330
FR Spofforth (Aus)	1877–1887	18	4185	1731
FH Tyson (Eng)	1954–1959	17	3452	1411
C Blythe (Eng)	1901–1910	19	4546	1863
JH Wardle (Eng)	1948–1957	28	6597	2080
G Ulyett (Eng)	1877–1890	25	2627	1020
AK Davidson (Aus)	1953–1963	44	11587	3819
FR Foster (Eng)	1911–1912	11	2447	926
K Higgs (Eng)	1965–1968	15	4112	1473
MD Marshall (WI)	1978–1991	81	17584	7876
J Garner (WI)	1977–1987	58	13169	5433
CEL Ambrose (WI)	1988–2000	98	22103	8501

Highest partnerships for each wicket

1st	415	ND McKenzie, GC Smith	South Africa v Bangladesh	Chittagong	29 Feb 2008
2nd	576	ST Jayasuriya, RS Mahanama	Sri Lanka v India	Colombo (RPS)	2 Aug 1997
3rd	624	KC Sangakkara, DPMD Jayawardene	Sri Lanka v South Africa	Colombo (SSC)	27 Jul 2006
4th	449	AC Voges, SE Marsh	Australia v West Indies	Hobart	10 Dec 2015
5th	405	SG Barnes, DG Bradman	Australia v England	Sydney	13 Dec 1946
6th	399	BA Stokes, JM Bairstow	England v South Africa	Cape Town	2 Jan 2016
7th	347	DS Atkinson, CC Depeiaza	West Indies v Australia	Bridgetown	14 May 1955
8th	332	IJL Trott, SCJ Broad	England v Pakistan	Lord's	26 Aug 2010
9th	195	MV Boucher, PL Symcox	South Africa v Pakistan	Johannesburg	14 Feb 1998
10th	198	JE Root, JM Anderson	England v India	Nottingham	9 Jul 2014

Wkts	BBI	BBM	Ave	Econ	SR	5	10
189	9/103	17/159	16.43	2.36	41.6	24	7
101	7/43	12/87	16.53	1.93	51.2	11	2
101	7/31	11/68	16.98	1.97	51.6	5	1
118	8/11	15/28	17.75	2.35	45.1	9	4
74	7/23	11/24	17.97	1.69	63.4	4	2
94	7/44	14/90	18.41	2.48	44.5	7	4
76	7/27	10/130	18.56	2.45	45.4	4	1
100	8/59	15/99	18.63	2.45	45.4	9	4
102	7/36	12/89	20.39	1.89	64.6	5	1
50	7/36	7/57	20.40	2.32	52.5	1	0
186	7/93	12/124	20.53	1.97	62.2	14	2
45	6/91	8/70	20.57	2.27	54.3	4	0
71	6/91	8/119	20.74	2.14	57.9	2	0
376	7/22	11/89	20.94	2.68	46.7	22	4
259	6/56	9/108	20.97	2.47	50.8	7	0
405	8/45	11/84	20.99	2.30	54.5	22	3

Best bowling figures in an innings

	Overs	Mdns	Runs	Wkts			
JC Laker	51.2	23	53	10	England v Australia	Manchester	26 Jul 1956
A Kumble	26.3	9	74	10	India v Pakistan	Delhi	4 Feb 1999
GA Lohmann	14.2x5	6	28	9	England v South Africa	Johannesburg	2 Mar 1896
JC Laker	16.4	4	37	9	England v Australia	Manchester	26 Jul 1956
M Muralitharan	40.0	19	51	9	Sri Lanka v Zimbabwe	Kandy	4 Jan 2002
RJ Hadlee	23.4	4	52	9	New Zealand v Australia	Brisbane	8 Nov 1985
Abdul Qadir	37.0	13	56	9	Pakistan v England	Lahore	25 Nov 1987
DE Malcolm	16.3	2	57	9	England v South Africa	The Oval	18 Aug 1994
M Muralitharan	54.2	27	65	9	Sri Lanka v England	The Oval	27 Aug 1998
JM Patel	35.5	16	69	9	India v Australia	Kanpur	19 Dec 1959
N Kapil Dev	30.3	6	83	9	India v West Indies	Ahmedabad	12 Nov 1983
Sarfraz Nawaz	35.4x8	7	86	9	Pakistan v Australia	Melbourne	10 Mar 1979
JM Noreiga	49.4	16	95	9	West Indies v India	Port of Spain	6 Mar 1971
SP Gupte	34.3	11	102	9	India v West Indies	Kanpur	12 Dec 1958
SF Barnes	38.4	7	103	9	England v South Africa	Johannesburg	26 Dec 1913
HJ Tayfield	37.0x8	11	113	9	South Africa v England	Johannesburg	15 Feb 1957
AA Mailey	47.0	8	121	9	Australia v England	Melbourne	11 Feb 1921
HMRKB Herath	33.1	3	127	9	Sri Lanka v Pakistan	Colombo (SSC)	14 Aug 2014
GA Lohmann	9.4x5	5	7	8	England v South Africa	Port Elizabeth	13 Feb 1896
J Briggs	14.2x4	5	11	8	England v South Africa	Cape Town	25 Mar 1889

Best bowling figures in a match

	Overs	Mdns	Runs	Wkts			
JC Laker	68.0	27	90	19	England v Australia	Manchester	26 Jul 1956
SF Barnes	65.3	16	159	17	England v South Africa	Johannesburg	26 Dec 1913
ND Hirwani	33.5	6	136	16	India v West Indies	Chennai	11 Jan 1988
RAL Massie	60.1	16	137	16	Australia v England	Lord's	22 Jun 1972
M Muralitharan	113.5	41	220	16	Sri Lanka v England	The Oval	27 Aug 1998
J Briggs	33.3x4	16	28	15	England v South Africa	Cape Town	25 Mar 1889
GA Lohmann	25.3x5	11	45	15	England v South Africa	Port Elizabeth	13 Feb 1896
C Blythe	38.3	10	99	15	England v South Africa	Leeds	29 Jul 1907
H Verity	58.3	23	104	15	England v Australia	Lord's	22 Jun 1934
RJ Hadlee	52.3	13	123	15	New Zealand v Australia	Brisbane	8 Nov 1985
W Rhodes	30.2	3	124	15	England v Australia	Melbourne	1 Jan 1904
Harbhajan Singh	80.1	26	217	15	India v Australia	Chennai	18 Mar 2001

Most dismissals by a wicketkeeper

		Mat	Inns	Dis	Ct	St	Max Dis Inns
MV Boucher (ICC/SA)	1997–2012	147	281	555	532	23	6 (6ct 0st)
AC Gilchrist (Aus)	1999–2008	96	191	416	379	37	5 (5ct 0st)
IA Healy (Aus)	1988–1999	119	224	395	366	29	6 (6ct 0st)
RW Marsh (Aus)	1970–1984	96	182	355	343	12	6 (6ct 0st)
MS Dhoni (India)	2005–2014	90	166	294	256	38	6 (6ct 0st)
BJ Haddin (Aus)	2008–2015	66	128	270	262	8	6 (6ct 0st)
PJL Dujon (WI)	1981–1991	81	150	270	265	5	5 (5ct 0st)
APE Knott (Eng)	1967–1981	95	174	269	250	19	5 (4ct 1st)
MJ Prior (Eng)	2007–2014	79	146	256	243	13	6 (6ct 0st)
AJ Stewart (Eng)	1990–2003	133	141	241	227	14	6 (6ct 0st)
Wasim Bari (Pak)	1967–1984	81	146	228	201	27	7 (7ct 0st)
RD Jacobs (WI)	1998–2004	65	122	219	207	12	7 (7ct 0st)

		Mat	Inns	Dis	Ct	St	Max Dis Inns
TG Evans (Eng)	1946–1959	91	175	219	173	46	4 (4ct 0st)
D Ramdin (WI)	2005–2016	74	131	217	205	12	5 (5ct 0st)
Kamran Akmal (Pak)	2002–2010	53	99	206	184	22	5 (5ct 0st)
AC Parore (NZ)	1990–2002	78	121	201	194	7	5 (5ct 0st)

Most dismissals in an innings

	Dis	Ct	St	Inns			
Wasim Bari	7	7	0	1	Pakistan v New Zealand	Auckland	23 Feb 1979
RW Taylor	7	7	0	1	England v India	Mumbai	15 Feb 1980
IDS Smith	7	7	0	2	New Zealand v Sri Lanka	Hamilton	22 Feb 1991
RD Jacobs	7	7	0	1	West Indies v Australia	Melbourne	26 Dec 2000

Most dismissals in a match

	Dis	Ct	St			
RC Russell	11	11	0	England v South Africa	Johannesburg	30 Nov 1995
AB de Villiers	11	11	0	South Africa v Pakistan	Johannesburg	1 Feb 2013
RW Taylor	10	10	0	England v India	Mumbai	15 Feb 1980
AC Gilchrist	10	10	0	Australia v New Zealand	Hamilton	31 Mar 2000

Most catches (fielders)

	Mat	Ct
R Dravid (ICC/India)	164	210
DPMD Jayawardene (SL)	149	205
JH Kallis (ICC/SA)	166	200
RT Ponting (Aus)	168	196
ME Waugh (Aus)	128	181
SP Fleming (NZ)	111	171
GC Smith (ICC/SA)	117	169
BC Lara (ICC/WI)	131	164
MA Taylor (Aus)	104	157
AR Border (Aus)	156	156
VVS Laxman (India)	134	135

	Mat	Ct
MJ Clarke (Aus)	115	134
ML Hayden (Aus)	103	128
AN Cook (Eng)	126	125
SK Warne (Aus)	145	125
GS Chappell (Aus)	87	122
IVA Richards (WI)	121	122
AJ Strauss (Eng)	100	121
IT Botham (Eng)	102	120
MC Cowdrey (Eng)	114	120

Most catches in an innings

VY Richardson	5	Australia v South Africa	Durban	28 Feb 1936
Yajurvindra Singh	5	India v England	Bangalore	28 Jan 1977
M Azharuddin	5	India v Pakistan	Karachi	15 Nov 1989
K Srikkanth	5	India v Australia	Perth	1 Feb 1992
SP Fleming	5	New Zealand v Zimbabwe	Harare	18 Sep 1997
GC Smith	5	South Africa v Australia	Perth	30 Nov 2012
DJG Sammy	5	West Indies v India	Mumbai	14 Nov 2013
DM Bravo	5	West Indies v Bangladesh	Kingstown	5 Sep 2014
AM Rahane	5	India v Sri Lanka	Galle	12 Aug 2015
J Blackwood	5	West Indies v Sri Lanka	Colombo (PSS)	22 Oct 2015

Most catches in a match

AM Rahane	8	India v Sri Lanka	Galle	12 Aug 2015
GS Chappell	7	Australia v England	Perth	13 Dec 1974
Yajurvindra Singh	7	India v England	Bangalore	28 Jan 1977
HP Tillekeratne	7	Sri Lanka v New Zealand	Colombo (SSC)	6 Dec 1992
SP Fleming	7	New Zealand v Zimbabwe	Harare	18 Sep 1997
ML Hayden	7	Australia v Sri Lanka	Galle	8 Mar 2004

Most matches

SR Tendulkar (India)	200

RT Ponting (Aus)		168
SR Waugh (Aus)		168
JH Kallis (ICC/SA)		166
S Chanderpaul (WI)		164
R Dravid (ICC/India)		164
AR Border (Aus)		156
DPMD Jayawardene (SL)		149
MV Boucher (ICC/SA)		147
SK Warne (Aus)		145
VVS Laxman (India)		134
KC Sangakkara (SL)		134
M Muralitharan (ICC/SL)		133
AJ Stewart (Eng)		133
A Kumble (India)		132
CA Walsh (WI)		132
N Kapil Dev (India)		131
BC Lara (ICC/WI)		131
ME Waugh (Aus)		128
AN Cook (Eng)		126

Most matches as captain

		Mat	Won	Lost	Tied	Draw
GC Smith (ICC/SA)	2003–2014	109	53	29	0	27
AR Border (Aus)	1984–1994	93	32	22	1	38
SP Fleming (NZ)	1997–2006	80	28	27	0	25
RT Ponting (Aus)	2004–2010	77	48	16	0	13
CH Lloyd (WI)	1974–1985	74	36	12	0	26
MS Dhoni (India)	2008–2014	60	27	18	0	15
SR Waugh (Aus)	1999–2004	57	41	9	0	7
A Ranatunga (SL)	1989–1999	56	12	19	0	25
MA Atherton (Eng)	1993–2001	54	13	21	0	20
WJ Cronje (SA)	1994–2000	53	27	11	0	15
MP Vaughan (Eng)	2003–2008	51	26	11	0	14
IVA Richards (WI)	1980–1991	50	27	8	0	15
AJ Strauss (Eng)	2006–2012	50	24	11	0	15

Most matches as an umpire

		Matches
SA Bucknor (WI)	1989–2009	128
RE Koertzen (SA)	1992–2010	108
Aleem Dar (Pak)	2003–2016	101
DJ Harper (Aus)	1998–2011	95
DR Shepherd (Eng)	1985–2005	92
BF Bowden (NZ)	2000–2015	84
DB Hair (Aus)	1992–2008	78
SJA Taufel (Aus)	2000–2012	74
S Venkataraghavan (India)	1993–2004	73
HD Bird (Eng)	1973–1996	66
SJ Davis (Aus)	1997–2015	57

Largest victories (by an innings)

England	inns & 579 runs	v Australia	The Oval	20 Aug 1938
Australia	inns & 360 runs	v South Africa	Johannesburg	22 Feb 2002
West Indies	inns & 336 runs	v India	Kolkata	31 Dec 1958
Australia	inns & 332 runs	v England	Brisbane	29 Nov 1946
Pakistan	inns & 324 runs	v New Zealand	Lahore	1 May 2002
West Indies	inns & 322 runs	v New Zealand	Wellington	10 Feb 1995
West Indies	inns & 310 runs	v Bangladesh	Dhaka	8 Dec 2002
New Zealand	inns & 301 runs	v Zimbabwe	Napier	26 Jan 2012
New Zealand	inns & 294 runs	v Zimbabwe	Harare	7 Aug 2005
England	inns & 285 runs	v India	Lord's	20 Jun 1974

Largest victories (by runs)

England	675 runs	v Australia	Brisbane	30 Nov 1928
Australia	562 runs	v England	The Oval	18 Aug 1934
Australia	530 runs	v South Africa	Melbourne	17 Feb 1911
Australia	491 runs	v Pakistan	Perth	16 Dec 2004
Sri Lanka	465 runs	v Bangladesh	Chittagong	3 Jan 2009
West Indies	425 runs	v England	Manchester	8 Jul 1976
Australia	409 runs	v England	Lord's	24 Jun 1948
West Indies	408 runs	v Australia	Adelaide	26 Jan 1980

| Australia | 405 runs | v England | Lord's | 16 Jul 2015 |
| Australia | 384 runs | v England | Brisbane | 7 Nov 2002 |

Smallest victories (by runs)

West Indies	1 run	v Australia	Adelaide	23 Jan 1993
England	2 runs	v Australia	Birmingham	4 Aug 2005
Australia	3 runs	v England	Manchester	24 Jul 1902
England	3 runs	v Australia	Melbourne	26 Dec 1982
South Africa	5 runs	v Australia	Sydney	2 Jan 1994
Australia	6 runs	v England	Sydney	20 Feb 1885
Australia	7 runs	v England	The Oval	28 Aug 1882
South Africa	7 runs	v Sri Lanka	Kandy	30 Jul 2000
New Zealand	7 runs	v Australia	Hobart	9 Dec 2011
England	10 runs	v Australia	Sydney	14 Dec 1894

Smallest victories (by wickets)

England	1 wicket	v Australia	The Oval	11 Aug 1902
South Africa	1 wicket	v England	Johannesburg	2 Jan 1906
England	1 wicket	v Australia	Melbourne	1 Jan 1908
England	1 wicket	v South Africa	Cape Town	1 Jan 1923
Australia	1 wicket	v West Indies	Melbourne	31 Dec 1951
New Zealand	1 wicket	v West Indies	Dunedin	8 Feb 1980
Pakistan	1 wicket	v Australia	Karachi	28 Sep 1994
West Indies	1 wicket	v Australia	Bridgetown	26 Mar 1999
West Indies	1 wicket	v Pakistan	St John's	25 May 2000
Pakistan	1 wicket	v Bangladesh	Multan	3 Sep 2003
Sri Lanka	1 wicket	v South Africa	Colombo (PSS)	4 Aug 2006
India	1 wicket	v Australia	Mohali	1 Oct 2010
England	2 wickets	v Australia	The Oval	11 Aug 1890
Australia	2 wickets	v England	Sydney	13 Dec 1907
England	2 wickets	v South Africa	Durban	16 Dec 1948
Australia	2 wickets	v West Indies	Melbourne	10 Feb 1961
India	2 wickets	v Australia	Mumbai (BS)	10 Oct 1964
Australia	2 wickets	v India	Perth	16 Dec 1977
West Indies	2 wickets	v England	Nottingham	5 Jun 1980
New Zealand	2 wickets	v Pakistan	Dunedin	9 Feb 1985
West Indies	2 wickets	v Pakistan	Bridgetown	22 Apr 1988

Pakistan	2 wickets	v England	Lord's	18 Jun 1992
Australia	2 wickets	v South Africa	Port Elizabeth	14 Mar 1997
England	2 wickets	v South Africa	Centurion	14 Jan 2000
Sri Lanka	2 wickets	v Pakistan	Rawalpindi	26 Feb 2000
England	2 wickets	v West Indies	Lord's	29 Jun 2000
India	2 wickets	v Australia	Chennai	18 Mar 2001
Australia	2 wickets	v South Africa	Johannesburg	31 Mar 2006
Australia	2 wickets	v South Africa	Johannesburg	17 Nov 2011

Highest team totals

Sri Lanka	952/6d	v India	Colombo (RPS)	2 Aug 1997
England	903/7d	v Australia	The Oval	20 Aug 1938
England	849	v West Indies	Kingston	3 Apr 1930
West Indies	790/3d	v Pakistan	Kingston	26 Feb 1958
Pakistan	765/6d	v Sri Lanka	Karachi	21 Feb 2009
Sri Lanka	760/7d	v India	Ahmedabad	16 Nov 2009
Australia	758/8d	v West Indies	Kingston	11 Jun 1955
Sri Lanka	756/5d	v South Africa	Colombo (SSC)	27 Jul 2006
West Indies	751/5d	v England	St John's	10 Apr 2004
West Indies	749/9d	v England	Bridgetown	26 Feb 2009

The highest totals for the other teams are:

India	726/9d	v Sri Lanka	Mumbai (BS)	2 Dec 2009
South Africa	682/6d	v England	Lord's	31 Jul 2003
New Zealand	690	v Pakistan	Sharjah	26 Nov 2014
Zimbabwe	563/9d	v West Indies	Harare	27 Jul 2001
Banglades	638	v Sri Lanka	Galle	8 Mar 2013

Lowest team totals

New Zealand	26	v England	Auckland	25 Mar 1955
South Africa	30	v England	Port Elizabeth	13 Feb 1896
South Africa	30	v England	Birmingham	14 Jun 1924
South Africa	35	v England	Cape Town	1 Apr 1899

South Africa	36	v Australia	Melbourne	12 Feb 1932
Australia	36	v England	Birmingham	29 May 1902
New Zealand	42	v Australia	Wellington	29 Mar 1946
Australia	42	v England	Sydney	10 Feb 1888
India	42	v England	Lord's	20 Jun 1974
South Africa	43	v England	Cape Town	25 Mar 1889
Australia	44	v England	The Oval	10 Aug 1896
South Africa	45	v Australia	Melbourne	12 Feb 1932
England	45	v Australia	Sydney	28 Jan 1887
New Zealand	45	v South Africa	Cape Town	2 Jan 2013
England	46	v West Indies	Port of Spain	25 Mar 1994
New Zealand	47	v England	Lord's	19 Jun 1958
South Africa	47	v England	Cape Town	25 Mar 1889
West Indies	47	v England	Kingston	11 Mar 2004
Australia	47	v South Africa	Cape Town	9 Nov 2011
Pakistan	49	v South Africa	Johannesburg	1 Feb 2013

The lowest totals for the other teams are:

Zimbabwe	51	v New Zealand	Napier	26 Jan 2012
Bangladesh	62	v Sri Lanka	Colombo (PSS)	3 Jul 2007
Sri Lanka	71	v Pakistan	Kandy	26 Aug 1994

BIBLIOGRAPHY

BOOKS

Armstrong, Geoff (2009) *The 100 Greatest Cricketers*, New Holland Publishers (Australia) Pty Ltd, Sydney.

Arnold, Peter (1987) *The Illustrated Encyclopedia of World Cricket*, Golden Press, Sydney.

Austin, David and co. (1997) *200 Seasons of Australian Cricket*, Pan Macmillan Australia, Sydney (NSW).

Baldwin, Mark (2005) *The Ashes' Strangest Moments*, Robson Books, London.

Boon, David (1996) *Under the Southern Cross*, HarperCollins Publishers Pty Ltd, Sydney.

Border, Allan (1990) *An Autobiography*, Mandarin Australia, Melbourne (Victoria).

Border, Allan (1993) *Beyond 10,000*, Swan Publishing, Nedlands (Western Australia).

Border, Allan (2014) *Cricket As I See It*, Allen & Unwin, Crows Nest.

Botham, Ian (2001) *Botham's Century*, Collins Willow, London.

Chappell Greg (1981) *Unders and Overs*, Swan Publishing, Byron Bay (NSW).

Crowe, Martin (1995) *Out on a Limb*, Reed Publishing, Auckland.

Dawson, Graham and Wat, Charlie (1996) *Test Cricket Lists*, The Five Mile Press Pty Ltd, Noble Park.

Dawson, Marc (1997) *Balls, Bats, Stumps and Stats*, ABC Books, Sydney.

Dawson, Marc (2009) *1000 Memorable Ashes Moments*, HarperCollins Publishers, Sydney (NSW).

Fletcher, Keith and Tennant, Ivo (2005) *Ashes to Ashes*, Headline Book Publishing, London.

Frith, David (1993) *Australia Versus England: A Pictorial History of Every Test Match Since 1877*, Richard Smart Publishing, Sydney (NSW).

Gilchrist, Adam (2008) *True Colours*, Pan Macmillan Australia, Sydney (NSW).

Giller, Norman (1989) *The World's Greatest Cricket Matches*, Octopus Books, London.

Gower, David (2015) *David Gower's 50 Greatest Cricketers of All Time*, Icon Books Ltd, London.

Grant, RG (1991) *Greatest Moments in Cricket*, Bison Books Ltd, London.

Hauser, Liam (2013) *A Century of Cricket Tests*, New Holland Publishers (Australia) Pty Ltd, Sydney.

Hayden, Matthew (2010) *Standing My Ground*, Penguin Group (Australia), Camberwell.

Imran Khan (1988) *All Round View*, Chatto and Windus, London.

Marks, Vic (1988) *The Wisden Illustrated History of Cricket*, Angus and Robertson Publishers, North Ryde (NSW).

Marsh, Rod (1982) *The Gloves of Irony*, Lansdowne Press, Sydney (NSW).

Meher-Homji, Kersi (2008) *Cricket's Great All-Rounders*, New Holland Publishers (Australia) Pty Ltd, Sydney.

Miller, Allan *Allan's Australian Cricket Annual*: 1987–88, 1988–89, 1989–90, 1990–91, 1991–92, 1992–93, 1993–94, 1994–95, 1996, 1997, 1998, 1999, 2000, 2001, self-published.

Pilger, Sam and Wightman, Rob (2013) *The Ashes Match of My Life*, Pitch Publishing, Durrington.

Ponting, Ricky and Staples, Peter (1998), *Punter: Ricky Ponting*. Pan Macmillan Australia Pty Limited, Sydney.

Rippon, Anton (1982) *Classic Moments of the Ashes*, Moorland Publishing, Derbyshire.
Sobers, Garry (2002) *My Autobiography*, Headline Book Publishing, London.
Taylor, Mark (1995) *Taylor Made*, Pan Macmillan Australia, Sydney.
Taylor, Mark (1997) *A Captain's Year*, Pan Macmillan Australia, Sydney.
Various authors, Hook, Jeff (illustrator) *Ashes Battles and Bellylaughs*, (1990) Swan Publishing, Byron Bay (NSW).
Ward, Andrew (1994) *Cricket's Strangest Matches*, Robson Books, London.
Willis, Bob (1996) *Six of the Best*, Hodder and Stoughton Ltd, London.
Yallop, Graham (1979) *Lambs to the Slaughter*, Outback Press, Collingwood (Victoria).

NEWSPAPERS
Courier-Mail
Daily Telegraph
Herald Sun
New Zealand Herald
Sydney Morning Herald

INTERNET
Cricinfo
Cricket.com.au
Wikipedia
www.wellpitched.com/2013/11/wasim-akram-vs-waqar-younis-statistical.html?m=1

First published in 2016 by New Holland Publishers Pty Ltd
London • Sydney • Auckland

The Chandlery Unit 704 50 Westminster Bridge Road London SE1 7QY
United Kingdom
1/66 Gibbes Street Chatswood NSW 2067 Australia
5/39 Woodside Ave Northcote, Auckland 0627 New Zealand

www.newhollandpublishers.com

ISBN 9781742577579

Managing Director: Fiona Schultz
Publisher: Alan Whiticker
Project Editor: Liz Hardy
Designer: Thomas Partridge
Cover Design: Andrew Quinlan
Production Director: James Mills-Hicks
Printer: Toppan Leefung Printing Ltd
10 9 8 7 6 5 4 3 2 1

Keep up with New Holland Publishers on Facebook
www.facebook.com/NewHollandPublishers

UK: £16.99